A HISTORY OF
RUSSIAN THOUGHT
FROM THE ENLIGHTENMENT
TO MARXISM

———

A HISTORY
OF RUSSIAN
THOUGHT
FROM THE
ENLIGHTENMENT
TO MARXISM

ANDRZEJ WALICKI

TRANSLATED FROM THE POLISH BY
HILDA ANDREWS-RUSIECKA

STANFORD UNIVERSITY PRESS
STANFORD, CALIFORNIA 1979

A History of Russian Thought:
From the Enlightenment to Marxism
was originally published in Polish in 1973 under the title
Rosyjska filozofia i myśl społeczna od oświecenia do marksizmu

Stanford University Press
Stanford, California

© 1979 by the Board of Trustees of the
Leland Stanford Junior University

Printed in the United States of America
LC 78-66181
ISBN 0-8047-1026-0

CONTENTS

PREFACE

TO THE ENGLISH TRANSLATION

The present book has been written in Poland, as the final result of about twenty years of my studies of Russian intellectual history.[1] To a certain extent it is a product not only of my individual efforts but also of the vivid exchange of ideas among Polish historians of philosophical and social thought, as well as among Polish historians of Russian literature. My interest in Russian thought originated from the awareness, shared by many people in my country, that a sympathetic understanding of Russian culture is of vital importance for the Poles. There is a Polish tradition behind this book to which I am greatly indebted. Despite the widespread notion of an alleged Polish hostility toward everything Russian, even in partitioned Poland there were scholars and writers who fully appreciated, and sometimes even admired, the great traditions of the Russian intelligentsia, and who conceived of their task as creating intellectual bridges between Russia and Poland or, more ambitiously, between Russia and the West. Suffice it to mention that one of the first histories of the Russian revolutionary movement (and the best before the First World War) was written by a Polish Marxist, Ludwik Kulczycki;[2] that the first historical novel extolling the heroes of the "People's Will" and the whole intellectual tradition of Russian Populism was written by the most influential Polish philosopher and literary critic of the beginning of our century, Stanisław Brzozowski;[3] and finally that a Polish Catholic philosopher, Marian Ździechowski, was one of the first men in Europe (along with the Czech

1. Its Polish title is *Rosyjska filozofia i myśl społeczna od Oświecenia do marksizmu* (Warsaw, 1973).

2. See L. Kulczycki, *Rewolucja rosyjska* (2 vols.; Lvov, 1909). A German translation, *Geschichte der russischen Revolution*, was published in Gotha in 1910. A Russian translation, made from a specially prepared version of the author's manuscript, appeared under the title *Istoriia russkogo revolutsionnogo dvizheniia* in St. Petersburg in 1908.

3. The title of the novel (published in 1908) is *Płomienie*, which means "The Flames." Brzozowski was fascinated by Russian culture and devoted many pages to it in his books. Among other things he wrote a splendid essay on Herzen.

ix

philosopher and statesman T. G. Masaryk) to recognize fully the importance of Russian religious philosophy. The first two of the authors just mentioned exerted a strong influence on my imagination and thinking when, in changed historical circumstances, I started my own research in the field of the history of Russian ideas.

Having said this, I am glad to add that this book is also a product of my frequent visits to Great Britain and the United States. What it owes to my contacts with British and American scholars is very difficult to define, but without these contacts it would quite certainly have been different from what it is. In a Preface to the English translation this fact should, I feel, be duly acknowledged.

Soon after publishing my first book[4] I received a Ford scholarship for one year's study in the United Kingdom and the United States. My first stop was Oxford, where I met Sir Isaiah Berlin, who showed a genuine interest in my ideas and greatly encouraged me to undertake the ambitious plan of writing a comprehensive monograph on the Slavophile-Westernizer controversy in nineteenth-century Russia. Soon afterwards I came to the United States and found myself among young but already prominent American specialists in Russian intellectual history (R. Pipes, J. H. Billington, M. Malia, N. V. Riasanovsky, G. L. Kline, and others) who devoted much time to talking with me and who shared my feeling of the importance of our common field of study. Russian intellectual history was by then becoming (in 1960) a fashionable subject in the United States, for reasons that were obvious: as in Poland, this growing interest was above all an expression of the increasing awareness among American intellectuals that a deeper knowledge and understanding of Soviet Russia was of vital importance for their country, and that one of the keys to such an understanding was to be found in the study of the intellectual biography of the Russian nation. Like my American colleagues, I had the privilege of discussing my ideas with the eminent representatives of the old generation of scholars who had come to the United States from Russia: Roman Jakobson, Alexander Gerschenkron, Pitirim Sorokin, Father George Florovsky, and Boris Nikolaevsky. At the University of California, Berkeley, I was given the opportunity to deliver my first lecture in English.[5]

4. A. Walicki, *Osobowość a historia. Studia z dziejów literatury i myśli rosyjskiej* [*Personality and History: Studies in the History of Russian Literature and Thought*] (Warsaw, 1959).

5. It was published in *California Slavic Studies*, no. 2 (1963), under the title "Personality and Society in the Ideology of Russian Slavophiles. A Study in the Sociology of Knowledge."

It was, at the same time, the first outline of my interpretation of Russian Slavophilism that I developed later in my book *The Slavophile Controversy*.[6]

In later years I found most fruitful two visiting fellowships in All Souls College, Oxford (1966–67 and autumn 1973), which enabled me to broaden my contacts with British scholars, and a visiting professorship at Stanford in the winter and spring terms of 1976. In the 1966–67 academic year I participated in Sir Isaiah Berlin's seminar on Russian intellectual history and wrote my book on Russian Populism.[7] My stay at Stanford, as the visiting Kratter Professor of History, increased the number of my American friends (in this connection I would like to mention, above all, Professor Terence Emmons) and gave me the precious opportunity to acquire a teaching experience with American students. As a result of this experience I came to the conclusion that the present book could be used in the United States and other English-speaking countries as a handbook of Russin intellectual history.

At this point, perhaps, a certain reservation should be made. Since I am a historian of philosophy (although my approach to philosophy is more historical than purely philosophical), this book puts more emphasis on philosophical problems than most American books on Russian intellectual history do. However, philosophy —along with theological, political, economic, and other ideas—is treated in it not as an autonomous academic discipline but as a part of the general history of those currents of thought that shaped the minds of thinking Russians from the epoch of the Enlightenment to the turn of our century. It seems to me that the philosophical aspects of Russian intellectual history are, relatively, the most neglected by American historians (probably because most of them lack special philosophical training).[8] Very often American students have

6. This book appeared in Polish under the title *W kręgu konserwatywnej utopii. Struktura i przemiany rosyjskiego słowianofilstwa* (Warsaw, 1964). The emphasis of the Polish title was preserved in the Italian translation *Una Utopia Conservatrice* (Turin, 1973). It appeared in English as *The Slavophile Controversy: History of a Conservative Utopia in Nineteenth Century Russian Thought* (Oxford, 1975). The English translation then, as in the present book, was by Hilda Andrews-Rusiecka.

7. *The Controversy over Capitalism. Studies in the Social Philosophy of the Russian Populists* (Oxford, 1969). The first version of this book was written and published in Polish, as an introduction to an anthology of Russian Populist writings (*Filozofia społeczna narodnictwa rosyjskiego*, ed. by A. Walicki [2 vols.; Warsaw, 1965]).

8. An important exception to this rule is the contributions to the study of Russian intellectual history made by the professional philosopher George L. Kline. It is interesting also to note that the most valuable American anthology of Russian thinkers, widely used by students of Russian history, bears the title *Russian Philosophy*. See

to use the old classic book of Masaryk (which, though no doubt very valuable, is out of date and written from a very special philosophical point of view),[9] or they have to draw their knowledge of Russian philosophy from the very one-sided books written by Russian Orthodox philosophers in exile, which is even worse.[10] Under these circumstances, it is my hope that the philosophical parts of my book will be useful not only to the small number of American and other scholars specializing in Russian philosophy as such, but also to the more numerous category of readers interested in Russian intellectual history broadly conceived.

The present edition of the book is essentially the same as the Polish original. The only significant class of changes has been made in the notes, where in order to make the book more up-to-date and to increase its didactic value to English-speaking readers I felt it desirable to include more bibliographical references to important recent books published in English. This was a difficult decision in that the bulk of the literature on the subject is naturally written in Russian. In taking it I was guided by the same reasons I set forth in the short summary of the book published in *The Russian Review*: the vast Russian and Soviet secondary literature, I wrote there, "is known by the specialists, and nonspecialists can easily find bibliographical information in the books published in English."[11]

Andrzej Walicki
August 1978

Russian Philosophy, ed. by J. M. Edie, J. P. Scanlan, and M. B. Zeldin, with the collaboration of George L. Kline (3 vols.; Chicago, 1956).

9. T. G. Masaryk, *The Spirit of Russia* (2 vols.; London and New York, 1955). First published in German in 1913.

10. Two examples are N. O. Lossky, *History of Russian Philosophy* (London, 1952); and V. V. Zenkovsky, *A History of Russian Philosophy*, trans. by G. L. Kline (2 vols.; London, 1953). The second of these books is valuable as a study of religious currents in Russian thought, but both give a very distorted picture of nonreligious trends in Russian philosophy.

11. A. Walicki, "Russian Social Thought: An Introduction to the Intellectual History of Nineteenth Century Russia," *The Russian Review*, 36, no. 1 (Jan. 1977), p. 2n.

PREFACE

TO THE ORIGINAL EDITION

Some readers who take up this history of Russian thought may wonder why philosophy is treated in it in such close association with social thought, and perhaps also why the author chose to start his account in 1760 and end it at the close of the nineteenth century.

To deal with the first point: there are clearly both advantages and disadvantages to writing a history of the philosophy of one particular country. Theoretical philosophy, for instance, could hardly be forced into a national framework unless at a given period it happened to represent a separate chapter in world philosophy. On the other hand, the historian who is primarily interested in the "world views" expressed in philosophical theories—in their historical determinants and social functions, will prefer to treat his subject against its national background, in order to show the links between ideas and their concrete political and cultural context. Such an approach, however, would necessarily imply a shift of emphasis from purely theoretical philosophy to the philosophical foundations of different currents of political and social thought.

In the case of Russia there are several other good arguments in favor of including social thought in a history of philosophy. To begin with, philosophy made a comparatively late appearance in Russia and did not find it easy to become established as a separate academic discipline. This was partly a result of the exceptionally difficult political situation, which prevented the development of speculative thought at the strictly controlled universities. A certain improvement in this respect only became noticeable in the latter half of the nineteenth century. Another factor that militated against the emergence of philosophy as an autonomous discipline was the special position of the intelligentsia in nineteenth-century Russia. The painful awareness of political oppression, backwardness, and urgent social problems waiting to be solved distracted attention from issues not immediately related to social practice. Philosophical reflection, therefore, was bound to be concerned with ethical, historical-philosophical, political, and frequently religious issues, to the partial neglect of traditional problems of ontology and episte-mology. In Populist circles, the most influential section of the intel-ligentsia during the second half of the nineteenth century, working on "pure philosophy" was considered immoral, a betrayal of the sacred cause of the people.

The features just described have made writing a history of Rus-sian philosophy from a narrowly professional point of view a par-ticularly thankless task. Proof of this are books on the subject pub-lished by Radlov, Shpet, and Jakovenko before and after the First World War.[1] By concentrating on academic philosophers and mak-ing use of formalistic criteria to define philosophy, these authors give an impoverished picture of the history of Russian ideas and in the final analysis deny them all originality. This conclusion can be refuted by the authors' own arguments, but there is no doubt that in a restricted view of the subject, the originality of Russian philoso-phy is not easy to define whereas its dependence on Western Eu-ropean thought is obvious. Its striking originality can only be perceived when we examine it within the context of Russian intel-lectual history, i.e. from the point of view of the issues that were closest to the hearts of educated Russians, and felt by them to be most relevant to the future of their country. This is especially true of the nineteenth century: here we have a most unusual cross-fertilization of ideas and influences; the rapid modernization of a great nation compressed into a short span of time; the curious coexistence of ar-chaic and modern elements in the social structure and in ways of thinking; the rapid influx of outside influences and resistance to them; the impact on the intellectual elite of the social realities and ideas of Western Europe on the one hand, and their constant redis-covery of their own native traditions and social realities on the other. All these factors help to make the history of Russian ideas in the nineteenth century more interesting and more dramatic than the intellectual history of many more advanced nations with far richer philosophical traditions. To this must be added the uncom-promising ideological commitment of the Russian intelligentsia, their passionate search for ethical ideals, and their acute under-standing of the "accursed problems" with which they were faced.

This is not to suggest that philosophical problems should only be studied as part of a sociopolitical tradition. The following chap-ters only deal with those aspects of Russian social thought that have

1. E. L. Radlov, *Ocherk istorii russkoi filosofii* (St. Petersburg, 1912); G. Shpet, *Ocherk razvitiia filosofi v Rossii* (Petrograd, 1922); B. Jakovenko, *Dějiny ruské filosofie* (Prague, 1939).

important philosophical implications. Concrete political programs are not discussed unless such discussion is required for an understanding of the development of social philosophy. Philosophical theories are considered from the point of view of their social significance and historical importance; but philosophers who stood apart from the mainstream of Russian thought and had little influence are also dealt with. After all, one of the author's aims in writing this study was to provide a useful work of reference; it was necessary to make a selection, but the inclusion or omission of individual thinkers was influenced primarily by purely philosophical criteria.[2]

The choice of dates, on the other hand, was determined by historical rather than philosophical criteria. The nineteenth century in Russia—an age that saw the superb flowering of literature and culture—had a number of distinctive features that allow us to treat it as a structural whole. This was the age that saw the emergence of the intelligentsia—in the specifically Russian meaning of the term as a body of educated people who felt responsible for their country's future—a group not unanimous in its views but united by the common ethos of struggle against reaction. Used in this sense, "intelligentsia" was an ethical category (or even a political category, when the standpoint of the intelligentsia was identified with opposition to the government).[3] The questions Russians were asking themselves at this time were all concerned with their national iden-

2. It should be noted that the book does not discuss the history of logic in Russia, or the philosophy of science.

3. Here a very characteristic example is the neo-Populist history of Russian social thought by Ivanov-Ruzumnik, *Istoriia russkoi obshchestvennoi mysli* (St. Petersburg, 1907), which interprets Russian history as the struggle between two abstract principles: nonconformist "ethical individualism" (culminating in personal sacrifice for the common good), and the philistine egoism—or acceptance of reality—of the bourgeoisie. In Razumnik's view "intelligentsia" is an ethical category *par excellence;* only someone who is an "individualist" and opposed to the bourgeoisie can be called a member of the intelligentsia.

Ivanov-Razumik's work is a panegyric to the Russian intelligentsia and mythologizes its role. In the nineteenth century this tone would have been out of the question, for the Russian intelligentsia was at that time inclined to be self-critical. Only in the twentieth century, when its role as leader of the struggle against reaction was over, could it indulge in such far-reaching self-glorification.

It seems worthwhile to note that another classical case of the intelligentsia as a social stratum defined by its value system was presented by Poland. Contrary to popular opinion, the term "intelligentsia" (in Polish "inteligencja") was coined not in the 1860's in Russia but in the 1840's in Poland. A useful analysis of the similarities and differences between the Polish and Russian intelligentsias is contained in A. Gella, "The Life and Death of the Old Polish Intelligentsia," *Slavic Review*, 30, no. 1 (Mar. 1971).

tity: "Who are we?" "Where do we come from and where are we going?" "What is the contribution we can make to humanity?" "What can we do in order to carry out the mission entrusted to us?" In trying to find answers to these problems, thinking Russians took advantage of the special "privilege of backwardness," which enabled them to look at their own situation from the perspective of the more advanced countries, and to make use of those countries' theoretical perceptions. Tracing the reception of ideas, therefore, is not just a matter of academic interest—it is important as part of the endeavor to establish the intellectual context in which Russian thought became formed and that stimulated its rapid development.

Thinkers of the second half of the eighteenth century have been included because the issues they wrote about foreshadow those discussed in the nineteenth century. The problem of Russia's future development—which was to have such an important place in Russian philosophy—first began to exercise men's minds during the reign of Catherine II, which also saw the gradual breakup of the alliance between the elites of power and intellect. The educated elite established its independence both from the main body of the nobility and from the tsarist autocracy that, by initiating the process of Westernization, had been responsible for its emergence. As Miliukov pointed out, the uninterrupted tradition of *critical* social thought in Russia had its roots in the age of Catherine.[4]

Some readers may wonder why this study ends in 1900 rather than in 1917. The decision not to go beyond the closing years of the nineteenth century was made for a number of reasons. The early twentieth century—the last stage in the crisis of absolutism—saw the emergence of strong political groupings. Russian Marxism in Russia was no longer just a movement of the intelligentsia but gained supporters in the labor movement, leading to the establishment of a well organized political party at the second Social Democratic convention in 1903. After the 1905 Revolution, political parties began to function openly. At the same time there was a crisis within a section of the intelligentsia that came to a head in 1909 with the publication of *Vekhi* (*Signposts*). In this work a number of prominent intellectuals attacked nineteenth-century radical traditions and insisted that the only mission of the intelligentsia should be the creation of cultural values. At the other pole of the Russian politi-

4. P. N. Miliukov, *Ocherki po istorii russkoi kultury* (St. Petersburg, 1901), vol. 3, pp. 248–50. See also Marc Raeff, *Origins of the Russian Intelligentsia: The Eighteenth-Century Nobility* (New York, 1966); and Nicholas V. Riasanovsky, *A Parting of Ways: Government and the Educated Public in Russia, 1801–1855* (Oxford, 1976).

cal spectrum, the strategy and tactics of the day-to-day struggle began to seem more important than philosophical reflections on Russia's history and her future. At the same time, academic philosophy developed along professional lines and concentrated on previously neglected ontological and epistemological problems.

This does not mean that the beginning of the twentieth century saw a radical break in the continuity of Russian thought. On the contrary, nineteenth-century polemics—including the controversies over the relationship between Russia and Europe and over the role of the intelligentsia—were continued both in a philosophical and in a political context. Nevertheless, in view of the growing professionalism of philosophy and the closer connection between political thought and action, it is doubtful whether any purpose would be served by discussing early-twentieth-century philosophy and social thought in this book.

The present study is the outcome of eighteen years of research into Russian philosophy and intellectual history. Inevitably, therefore, it is based on other books and articles by the author published in Poland and abroad.[5]

Finally, I would like to express my hope that this account of the history of Russian thought will prove of interest not only to the specialist but also to the general reader who wishes to know more about the background to one of the great modern European literatures.

A. W.

5. See especially three books of mine: *Osobowość a historia. Studia z dziejów literatury i myśli rosyjkiej* [*Personality and History: Studies in the History of Russian Literature and Thought*] (Warsaw, 1959): *The Slavophile Controversy: History of a Conservative Utopia in Nineteenth-Century Russian Thought* (Oxford, 1975; first published in Polish in 1964); and *The Controversy over Capitalism. Studies in the Social Philosophy of the Russian Populists* (Oxford, 1969).

A HISTORY OF
RUSSIAN THOUGHT
FROM THE ENLIGHTENMENT
TO MARXISM

———

CHAPTER 1

TRENDS IN ENLIGHTENMENT
THOUGHT

Conditions for the emergence of Enlightenment thought in Russia evolved gradually over several decades. Although this process was initiated by the reforms of Peter the Great and the forcible Westernization of Russia, historians nevertheless agree that the Enlightenment proper did not commence until the second half of the eighteenth century, or the first years of the reign of Catherine II (1762–96).

Peter's reforms had as their chief aim the fastest and most efficient military and technical modernization of the Russian state. As Plekhanov pointed out, the prominent leaders of the first half of the eighteenth century looked at the Enlightenment "from the point of view of its immediate practical benefits."[1] It did not occur to them that the political and social system might require thorough reform. They had a deep-seated belief in the "Mosaic rod" of autocracy, in its civilizing mission that would awaken the nation and lead it forward toward enlightenment and progress. Even Mikhail Lomonosov (1711–65), the great Russian scientist, poet, literary theorist, and founder of Moscow University, still shared this conviction.

Catherine's reign, however, saw the emergence of something like an independent public opinion that differed from the views held in enlightened court circles. The time appeared to be ripe for taking stock of the social and moral effects of Westernization and its future prospects. A greater sensitivity to moral issues now led to a more critical view of reality and a wider recognition of current evils. Once the process of reflection had begun, men started to look for the origins of these evils in the formerly unquestioned principles on which the social system and the authority of the government were founded. Thus there emerged the beginnings of a modern political

1. G. Plekhanov, *Istoriia russkoi obshchestvennoi mysli*, in *Sochineniia* (2d ed.; Moscow-Petrograd, 1920–27), vol. 22, p. 307.

opposition, which naturally dampened the "enlightened" autocracy's enthusiasm for reform. The resulting repressions in their turn brought about a growing dissonance between the authorities and the country's intellectual elite.

An important role in this process was played by French Enlightenment philosophy, which burst on Russia during the reign of Catherine II. The Russian Enlightenment in fact came to maturity in an atmosphere conditioned by French Enlightenment thought, with its critical attitude toward unreflectively accepted traditions and social institutions; as we shall see, even the most convinced enemies of Enlightenment were not uninfluenced by this atmosphere.

CATHERINE II AND ENLIGHTENMENT PHILOSOPHY

To begin with, the empress herself encouraged the influx of French thought. What is more, she even attempted to use French Enlightenment philosophy as a tool in her own home and foreign policies.[2] She hoped to stimulate an intellectual movement that she would be able to steer from above, retaining the initiative in her own hands. Catherine has been called one of the "Philosophic Monarchs," although this is perhaps too flattering a description of her. Voltaire wrote in a letter to d'Alembert that "pupils such as our beautiful Catho bring little credit to philosophy." Nevertheless, Catherine should not be overlooked in an account of the history of Russian philosophy. One might even say that her role was vital, not because of her own contribution but because all the more prominent Russian thinkers of her time had to pay attention to her ideas and carried on open or camouflaged discussion with her.

What appealed to Catherine's ambitious nature was the vision of an "enlightened monarch" who would use his authority to change the hitherto "irrational" course of history. She was urged on by a boundless desire for fame and a wish to astonish the world; at the same time she appeared to have a greater chance than other rulers to make her vision come true. She was a foreigner (a member of the ruling house of the petty German principality of Anhalt-Zerbst) and thus was not held back by any prejudices in favor of or against her new home. Formally, at least, she had absolute power; moreover, she was in command of a country where ancient traditions that might have proved an obstacle to the rational will of an enlightened

2. This is discussed in detail in **P. N. Miliukov**, *Ocherki po istorii russkoi kultury* (St. Petersburg, 1901), vol. 3. See also G. Makogonenko, *Novikov i russkoe prosveshchenie XVII veka* (Moscow-Leningrad [henceforth "M-L"], 1951), chap. 4.

ruler had been overturned or undermined by the violent reforms of Peter the Great. Diderot laid special stress on this latter circumstance. In his memorial to Catherine entitled *Essai historique sur la Police* he declared that it was impossible to reform existing legislation in France because it was too strongly bound up with traditional property relations, whereas in Russia "Your Imperial Highness is fortunate in being able to undertake everything and fortunate in desiring only good." Diderot saw the Russia of Peter the Great as an emerging society unhampered by ancient petrified traditions and therefore particularly pliant material to the creative will of a wise legislator. "How happy is the nation where nothing has as yet been done!"[3]

On coming to power, Catherine entered into a lively correspondence with the French encyclopedists (Voltaire, Diderot, and M. Grimm). She referred to herself as their pupil and promised to realize their aims. In view of the difficulties the *Encyclopédie* was facing in France, she even offered to have further volumes published in Russia. This found an enthusiastic response in the "Philosophers' Republic." In a letter to Diderot, Voltaire wrote: "What astonishing times we live in! France persecutes philosophy and the Scythians offer it their protection." Catherine tried to give the impression that she was essentially a republican and was aiming at the gradual abolition of despotism. She even tried to get in touch with so radical a thinker as Rousseau and invited him to Russia. Rousseau accepted neither the invitation nor the offer of a hundred thousand rubles, which he called an attempt by the "Russian tyrant" to defile his name in the eyes of posterity. Other Enlightenment philosophers, however, were suitably impressed by Catherine's gestures. Writing to Voltaire, Diderot said she combined "the soul of Brutus with the charm of Cleopatra," and in a letter to Catherine herself he declared: "Mighty Empress, I prostrate myself at your feet, I stretch out my hands toward You; I should like to speak to you, but my heart is convulsed, my head swims, my thoughts are confused, I am moved like a child."

As a further step in her campaign to gain the reputation of an "enlightened monarch," Catherine undertook to introduce important legislative changes. In 1767 she convened a Legislative Commission

3. Quoted in Plekhanov, *Istoriia russkoi . . . mysli*, p. 144. Plekhanov quoted D. Fonvizin (see below) as writing: "If they began to live earlier here, then we at least—in commencing our lives—can choose any form we wish, and avoid those inconveniences and evils which have taken root here. *Nous commençons et ils finissent.*" The idea of the "privilege of backwardness" was later taken up by Chaadaev, as well as by Herzen, Chernyshevsky, and the Populists.

to codify new laws and herself drew up the *Instructions* to the Commission making liberal use of formulations borrowed from the writings of Montesquieu and Beccaria. She affirmed her belief in the Enlightenment theory of natural law and promised to turn Russia into a law-abiding state that would respect the natural rights of all men. "God forbid," she declared, "that after the completion of these legislative measures, there should be even one nation in the world ruled more justly than Russia and therefore more prosperous. If that were so the intention of our legislation would not have been realized; I would not wish to live to see this misfortune."

Doubt is cast on the sincerity of this sweeping declaration by one significant fact: a luxury edition of the *Instructions* was published in several languages for foreign readers, but inside Russia Catherine prohibited its wider dissemination.

The Legislative Commission consisted of 564 representatives of various estates, including over 100 delegates representing the state peasants. Yet the serfs, who made up over half the peasantry, were not represented. Their fate had been decided even before the Commission was set up. Soon after coming to the throne, Catherine had traveled widely throughout Russia and had received over 500 desperate petitions from peasants. The result was that in 1765 a law was passed forbidding peasants to make complaints against their masters. The gentry, on the other hand, were granted the right to punish their serfs by exiling them to Siberia.

In Pushkin's words, Catherine's Commission was only the "indecorous performance of a farce." Its deliberations turned into a collective hymn of praise to the empress. Several delegates, however, dared to put forward ideas that went beyond the proposals in the *Instructions*: Y. Kozelsky made a bitter attack on the privileged position of the hereditary nobility; the merchants demanded an extension of their rights; and G. S. Korobin, as well as a representative of the state peasants, I. Chuprov, went so far as to plead for the mitigation of serfdom by "reasonable and humane" legislation. Debates began to get out of control, and it is hardly surprising that Catherine used the outbreak of war with Turkey (in 1768) as a pretext for disbanding the Commission, which was not subsequently recalled.

There is also another side to this episode. The failure of the experiment with the Commission marked the defeat not only of the hypocritical despot but also of the "enlightened monarch." The public's attitude to the elections must have given rise to melancholy reflections: most of the electorate obviously thought of representative functions as a burden that everyone would try to avoid. There were instances of the most unpopular men being elected, and such delegates complained comically that they had been chosen "to spite them." The deliberations of the Commission and the detailed instructions the electors furnished to their delegates gave Catherine insights into the unvarnished reality of Russian life. No doubt they convinced her that it was by no means easy to ensure the happiness of mankind, that powerful particular interests stood on guard over the status quo, and that attempts to enact the humane precepts of Enlightenment philosophy were a highly fallible way of gaining popularity in a society where even the proposal to abolish torture in criminal investigations aroused intense opposition.

Catherine's flirtation with the French *philosophes* was not an easy relationship either; in fact only Grimm became something like an agent of the Russian empress. Diderot, d'Alembert, and Voltaire (who at the time of the Commission had even compared her to Solon and Lycurgus) soon became disillusioned with their self-styled disciple. It is true that they continued to praise her, but only in order to retain at least some influence over her. That Catherine was not deceived by this stratagem is shown by one of her letters to Grimm, where she writes that "these men often said one thing and meant quite another." Her own attitude to the encyclopedists also became increasingly equivocal. Despite Diderot's insistent reminders and her own solemn assurances, the new revised edition of the *Encyclopédie* did not make an appearance in Russia. In 1773 Diderot himself visited Russia. His notes of the long conversations he had with Catherine during his five-month stay in St. Petersburg make fascinating reading.[4]

St. Petersburg made a depressing impression on Diderot: in this city of huge palaces and government buildings everything bore witness to the unlimited powers of autocracy; there were hardly any ordinary streets, no signs of any active, independent public life. "A long tradition of repression," he noted, "has resulted in a general atmosphere of reticence and distrust, a recollection of terror in the mind, as it were, that is in complete contrast to the noble openness characteristic of the free and self-confident mentality of the Frenchman or Englishman." Asking "Why is Russia governed worse than France?" Diderot answered: "Because individual freedom is reduced to zero here, the authority of one's superiors is still too great and the natural rights of man are as yet too restricted." He tried to persuade Catherine that there was just as much danger in

4. Published by J. M. Tourneux in *Diderot et Catherine II* (Paris, 1899).

a "just and enlightened despotism," since it encouraged the nation to fall into a "sweet but mortal sleep." "After three rulers such as Elizabeth, the English would have been subjugated painlessly for many years," Diderot told the empress, who made an equivocal answer expressing agreement.

Asked by Diderot if there were any legal ordinances governing the relationship between the gentry and their peasants, Catherine could only reply that legal guarantees were unnecessary since "every farmer looks after the cow that provides him with milk."

Diderot took pains to remind Catherine of her promise to recall the Legislative Commission, and even urged her to transform it into a permanent representative body. "Does that mean that you advise me to set up a parliament on the English model?," she asked him. He replied: "I believe it would come into being tomorrow if your Highness could bring it about with one wave of a sorcerer's wand." He tried to impress on her the manifold benefits associated with an institution of this kind: "Even if it only gives the illusion of liberty," he suggested, "it will nevertheless exert an influence on the national character. The nation either must be free, which is to be preferred of course, or at least must believe itself to be free, for such a belief can have valuable results."

On his way home from Russia, Diderot reread Catherine's *Instructions* and wrote down his comments. He suggested, for instance, that if Catherine wished to avoid being a despot she ought to make a formal renunciation of her absolute powers. Then again he noted that the people have the right to remove a monarch who has transgressed the law and even to punish him by death. Catherine only received these comments after their author's death, and it is hardly surprising that she was not enraptured by them. In a letter to Grimm she dismissed them as "mere babble that shows neither knowledge of the subject nor discretion, nor insight."

Later Catherine tried to discredit Diderot by presenting him as a naive and unpractical dreamer. She was fond of repeating her reply to his projects: "You, as a philosopher, work on paper, which will bear everything; whereas I, poor empress, work on human skin, which is far more sensitive." There was a good deal of truth in what she said, although in this particular instance it was clearly not so much Diderot's plans that were naive (he was ready to make necessary changes) as his faith in Catherine's good intentions.

It should be added that Diderot's stay in Russia coincided with the Pugachev rising, and therefore came at a highly inopportune moment. The Pugachev rebellion (1773–74) was a peasant uprising led by a Don Cossack who claimed to be the surviving tsar, Peter III, and promised the peasants "land, meadows, and woods," as well as "beards"—in other words, a return to the old traditions of pre-Petrine Russia. The rebellion attracted widespread support: it was joined by metalworkers from the Urals as well as members of the Bashkir tribes, and became the greatest peasant war in Russian history, posing a serious threat to the empire.

After suppressing the rebellion, Catherine entered the second phase of what she herself called her "legislative mania." She now rejected the theory of natural rights and chose as her mentor the conservative English jurist William Blackstone in preference to Montesquieu and Beccaria. In her new legislation a sober, matter-of-fact tone replaced the former liberal phraseology; the chief aim of the legislation was clearly to strengthen the position of the gentry through the establishment of self-governing bodies subordinated to the tsarist bureaucracy. Catherine now referred to her famous *Instructions* as "idle chatter" and summed up her efforts during the early part of her reign as follows: "My ambitions were not in themselves bad, but perhaps I took too much upon myself, being convinced that men might become rational, just, and happy."

Equally significantly, Catherine now turned away from the Francophile enthusiasm and shallow Voltairianism of the aristocratic salons to the primitive nationalism characteristic of the petty provincial nobility. She justified the partitioning of Poland and her Balkan policies with theories that anticipated Pan-Slavism, began to take an interest in old traditions, and steeped herself in Russian history. One of her cherished projects was to show that the names of mountains and rivers in France and Scotland were of Slavic derivation, that the Merovingian dynasty could be traced back to Slavic origins, and that even the name Ludovic [Lud+dvig] was Slavic in origin. In a book with the characteristic title *Antidotum* (1770), a polemic against the Prince de Chappe's malicious comments on Russia, she set out to prove that Russia was a prosperous country surpassing Western Europe in its observance of legality and in the living standards of its people.

The French Revolution was the final blow. At first Catherine ascribed it solely to the tactical blunders of Louis XVI: in a conversation she told Prince Khrapovitsky that in the French king's place "I should have invited the ambitious LaFayette to join me and would have turned him into my defender. Take note of how I acted here after coming to the throne."

This admission throws a good deal of light on Catherine's tactics, including her flirtation with the *philosophes*. Subsequent events, however, made it clear that there were situations too serious for the application of such tactical skills. The execution of the king of France left her "stunned as by a hammer-blow" and brought about her final parting of the ways with the encyclopedists. She had their busts removed from the Hermitage one by one, until only that of Voltaire was left. Finally, he, too, was banished to the palace cellar.

At the same time Catherine dealt summarily with the progressive thinkers of the Russian Enlightenment: Radishchev was exiled to Siberia in 1790 and Novikov was imprisoned without trial in the Schlüsselburg Fortress in 1792.

THE EMERGENCE OF RUSSIAN ENLIGHTENMENT PHILOSOPHY

Quite apart from Catherine's real attitude to the ideas of the Age of Reason, the atmosphere of the early part of her reign favored the widespread influx of French Enlightenment thought into Russia and a more active interest in philosophy in general. This helped to reduce the influence of Wolffianism (which in the 1750's had come to dominate the University of Moscow, the Academy of Sciences in St. Petersburg, and even Russian theological academies),[5] and led to the emergence in Russia of a genuine Enlightenment philosophy, practiced by professional philosophers and emancipated from the influence of religion.[6]

A characteristic figure in this trend was YAKOV KOZELSKY (d. after 1793).[7] Kozelsky, who was born about 1728 in the Ukraine and educated at the Academy of Sciences in St. Petersburg, in 1768 published his *Philosophic Proposals*, the first systematic exposition of philosophical ideas by a Russian author. The book still bears traces of Wolffian thought (for instance in the schematic arrangement of the material and in the emphasis on definitions rather than analysis), but there is a striking attempt to shake off this influence. The popular textbooks of logic, metaphysics, and moral philosophy written by Wolff's disciple Baumeister are subjected to strict critical analysis, and their pedantry and formalist concentration on meaningless problems are held up to ridicule. Kozelsky himself adopted a deist

5. See V. Y. Kogan, *Prosvetitel XVIII veka Y. P. Kozelsky* (M, 1958), pp. 101–2.

6. The chief works of the thinkers discussed here—Kozelsky, Anichkov, and Desnitsky—have been reprinted in *Izbrannye proizvedeniia russkikh myslitelei vtoroi poloviny XVIII veka* (M, 1952), vol. 1, with an Introduction by I. Y. Shchipanov.

7. He should be distinguished from his brother and namesake, a delegate to the Legislative Commission.

position and made no attempt to construct a system of "natural theology." He defended the autonomy of philosophy and opposed the teleological tendencies and utilization of philosophy to vindicate divine providence and theological dogma that were characteristic of Wolffian apologetics. He also criticized Wolffian idealism and rejected the conception of the soul as a totally autonomous spiritual monad. On the problem of the relationship between body and soul he was closer to materialism (although he did not state this plainly), and on the question of immortality he significantly did not comment at all. To the authority of the Wolffian school Kozelsky opposed that of Voltaire, Helvetius, Montesquieu, and Rousseau; in moral philosophy he also referred to Shaftesbury, whom he had read in French translation. His interest in and wide reading of French philosophy is shown by the fact that two years after the *Philosophic Proposals* appeared he published his own translation of the articles on philosophy and (in a separate edition) on moral philosophy included in Diderot's *Encyclopédie*.

Kozelsky defined philosophy as a science that investigates the causes of "natural," "logical," and "moral" truths. It could be divided into theoretical philosophy, which includes logic (or in other words a general theory of knowledge) and metaphysics (ontology and psychology), and practical philosophy, which includes jurisprudence (ethics and legal science) and politics. In epistemology Kozelsky supported a moderate sensationalism—he cited Helvetius but opposed the reduction of concepts to sense perceptions. Ontology he defined as a science of things, with a "thing" being everything that is "possible"; the inner essence of things, however, was unknowable (a thesis that was intended to protect philosophy from the dangers of scholasticism). In psychology—the science that deals with beings endowed with will and reason—Kozelsky based himself on Helvetius's *De l'esprit*, but in order to avoid an open conflict with the Church he toned down its main arguments and combined them, somewhat eclectically, with certain Wolffian ideas.

For Kozelsky, practical philosophy was of primary importance. Although his exposition was largely theoretical, he had a very practical aim: he hoped that the humanitarian principles expounded in his book would have some effect on the work of the Legislative Commission. His acceptance of the theory of natural law led him to condemn depotism; though he supported enlightened absolutism, he suggested that from a theoretical point of view the most perfect system was republicanism. The ignorance of the common people was regrettable, he wrote, but before they could acquire "polish" it would be necessary to improve their lot. He admired Rousseau as the greatest exponent of "practical philosophy" and shared his idealization of the state of nature; however, he recognized (as Rousseau did himself) that this primary state had been irretrievably lost and that at present every effort must be made to take advantage of the positive sides of the social state. He condemned luxury and extreme inequality, defended the dignity of manual work, and even spoke up for the ideal of an eight-hour working day. In his ethics Kozelsky followed Shaftesbury rather than Helvetius and valued virtue higher than reason and moral training higher than intellectual education. He proposed that men's conduct should be regulated by virtue rather than by enlightened self-interest, since virtue engenders solidarity and mutual aid. In cases of misfortune, he even suggested that the needy should be assured the help of society as a whole. Politics, too, should be founded on ethical principles; Kozelsky defined it as the science concerned with the realization of just aims by the most effective and just means. Though accepting the need for defense, he condemned wars of conquest (including colonial conquests) and argued that the defensive capacity of a state depended not only on the strength of its armies, but also —and even chiefly—on its internal relations.

Twenty years after the *Philosophic Proposals*, Kozelsky published a philosophical dialogue entitled *Reflections of Two Hindus, Kalan and Ibrahim, on Human Cognition* (1788). This dialogue, which was intended to be the first part of a larger work, contained philosophical meditations on natural history that on many points came close to a materialist approach.

An important contribution to the raising of the standard of philosophical discussion in Russia was made by DMITRY ANICHKOV (1733–88), a philosopher and mathematician, and a professor at Moscow University. His works include the *Discourse on the Principles and Origins of the Natural Cult of Deities* (1769), *Concerning the Properties of Human Cognition* (1770), the Latin essay *Annotationes in Logicam et Metaphysicam* (1782), and *On Different Ways of Explaining the Close Connection Between Soul and Body* (1783).

The earliest of these works is without doubt the most original and also most typical of Enlightenment thought. In it Anichkov ascribed the origins of religion to terror of natural phenomena, to "hallucinations" or the play of the imagination, and to "admiration" or the cult of heroes—that is, the ignorant masses' adoration of individuals of exceptional physical strength, dexterity, and talent.

Discussing the transformation of religion into an organized cult, Anichkov stressed that the material interests of the priests and theocratic rulers forced upon them a policy of conscious duplicity. His main sources were *De rerum natura* by Lucretius and eighteenth-century travelers' tales with accounts of the beliefs of primitive peoples. The views he put forward in the *Discourse* in theory concerned only pagan religions, but they nevertheless aroused bitter opposition in clerical and conservative academic circles. The Synod ordered almost the entire edition to be publicly burned, and only a few copies survived. Some time later Anichkov was permitted to publish a new edition of the *Discourse*, but only after introducing a number of emendations. He also had to change the title in order to leave no doubt that his work only concerned the religions of "unenlightened peoples."

In his essay on cognition, in which he examined the theory of innate ideas, Anichkov supported the view that there was nothing in the mind that had not previously been in the senses. At the same time he followed Kozelsky in opposing the extremes of sensationalism and suggested that cognition consisted of three stages—sense perception, the arrangement of sense impressions into concepts, and thinking with the help of these concepts. In listing the sources of errors, he described approvingly Bacon's theory of idols and expressed support for the Cartesian principle of methodical doubt. In a separate essay dealing with obstacles to cognition (published in 1774), he expounded, among other things, characteristic Enlightenment views on the role of nurture and the environment in intellectual development, drawing special attention to the harmful effects of contact with the superstitious masses.

In his essay on the relationship between soul and body, Anichkov discussed materialist, idealist, and dualist theories; among the proponents of the last-named he distinguished the occasionalists, who believed in a Leibnizian "pre-established harmony," and the Peripatetics. He preferred the latter's views because they assumed a soul acting upon the body rather than a parallelism of two entirely independent series of phenomena. The moral argument was decisive: he rejected the dualism of body and soul on which the systems of Leibniz and Malebranche were based because it undermined the foundations of morality by implying that the soul bore no responsibility for the sins of the flesh, which it was powerless to prevent.

A theory of the origins of religion resembling that of Anichkov was put forward by SEMYON DESNITSKY (d. 1789) in his succinct *Le-*

gal Discourses on Holy Matters (1772). In it he traced religion back to terror, ignorance, and anthropomorphism, although he naturally made an exception for Christianity. Desnitsky, who was the first theoretical jurist in Russia, and who published an annotated translation of the first three volumes of Blackstone's *Commentaries on the Laws of England,* was probably the most outstanding and perhaps also the most original Enlightenment thinker of his generation. He came from a merchant family in the Ukraine and was educated at the University of Moscow and then in Glasgow, where he studied under Adam Smith. After returning to Russia in 1767, he succeeded to the chair of jurisprudence at Moscow University. The most important formative influence in his intellectual development was undoubtedly his stay in Scotland, which led him to view Britain rather than France as the home of philosophy. In his work *On the Direct and Simplest Method of Teaching Jurisprudence* (1768), he referred to Hobbes, Sidney, Locke, Berkeley, Mandeville, Bolingbroke, Harrington, Hutcheson, and, above all, the great Scottish scholars David Hume and Adam Smith. It is tempting to add the name of Adam Ferguson to this list, for it seems likely that his influence was responsible for the most characteristic and valuable aspect of Desnitsky's social philosophy, namely his ability to perceive social phenomena as part of a historical, evolutionary process.

Using Pufendorf as an example, Desnitsky criticized the traditional, abstract theory of natural law and suggested that instead of being preoccupied with "imaginary conditions of the human race," one might more appropriately study the historical genesis and evolution of ownership, property, and inheritance. He developed this line of thought in his *Juridical Discourse on the Views of Various Nations Concerning Property and Various Forms of Social Relationships* (1781). In this work he distinguished four stages of social evolution based on economic criteria: the hunting, pastoral, agricultural, and (highest in the evolutionary scale) commercial stages. Each of these stages, Desnitsky wrote, is associated with a specific form of ownership; private property only emerges during the agricultural stage, and ownership in the full meaning of the word (i.e. the right to dispose freely of a given thing and to take it away from anyone who has taken illegal possession of it) does not develop fully until the commercial stage, when it replaces other forms of ownership. Laws and forms of government depend on the social relationships obtaining in a given community and on the forms of ownership appropriate to them.

Desnitsky believed that the evolution of the family was subject to similar laws. In his *Juridical Discourses on the Principles and Origins of Marriage* (1775), he argued that sexual relationships were closely related to the phases of social evolution: in the hunting stage there were no institutionalized forms of marriage; in the pastoral stage there emerged polygamy; in the agricultural stage patriarchal monogamy rose to prominence; and in the commercial stage (though the principle of monogamy still survived) conditions were now ripe for the granting of equal rights to women, a step that Desnitsky warmly supported.

Desnitsky's views on the origins of the authority of the state are also worth examining. He avoided the concept of the "social contract" and regarded the state as a product of historical development arising out of men's natural inequality.[8] For primitive people physical strength was of primary importance, and their leaders were therefore chosen from among those who excelled in this respect. At later historical stages intellectual inequality took on growing significance, so that cunning, intelligence, and foresight came to be in greater demand. During the commercial phase wealth became the decisive factor, and it was this that now determined the influence of the ruling elite and access to it. Desnitsky thought that this was responsible for certain negative features of the social system in the commercial phase, and in his annotations to Blackstone stressed that the millionaire lobby had a harmful influence on the English government and judiciary.[9] Nevertheless, he was confident that the commercial stage represented an evolutionary peak, since no one contributed more than the merchant class to the power, wealth, and unity of the State, and to the victory of centralizing over decentralizing tendencies.

This brief survey makes it clear that Desnitsky's social philosophy was essentially bourgeois in character. This became even more apparent when he attempted to give it practical application. In 1768, in connection with the setting up of the Legislative Commission, Desnitsky presented Catherine with a draft plan entitled *A Letter Concerning the Establishment of the Legislature, Judiciary, and Executive Authorities in the Russian Empire.* His plan proposed that a permanent representative body known as the Senate should be elected every five years; formally this body was to have only advisory capacity, but there is no doubt that Desnitsky wanted to ensure some form of control and restriction of absolutism. The Sen-

8. See S. V. Utechin, *Russian Political Thought. A Concise History* (New York and London, 1964), p. 55.

9. See *Izbrannye proizvedeniia*, vol. 1, pp. 290–91.

ate was to consist of from 600 to 800 persons elected not only by nobles (including the poor, landless gentry) but also by merchants, artisans, clergy, and university teachers. If this plan had been implemented, delegates of the middle classes and the *raznochintsy*[10] would have played a prominent if not leading role in the representative body.

Desnitsky's plan also called for the reorganization of fiscal policy, the administration, and the judiciary (among other things by the introduction of open trials). He also touched on the peasant question, but confined himself to putting forward various timid suggestions such as that the sale of peasants without land should be prohibited and that families should not be split up against their will merely in order to provide domestic servants for the manor.

The names of Kozelsky, Anichkov, and Desnitsky were soon forgotten and have only been rediscovered by Soviet scholars. On the whole this neglect has been unjust: they were not, perhaps, outstanding intellects or great literary talents, but in the Russia of their time they were nevertheless pioneers, men who stood for the introduction of new and forward-looking philosophical and social ideas.

NIKOLAI NOVIKOV AND FREEMASONRY

In keeping with the spirit of the Age of Reason, which was fond of using popular literary forms to propagate its ideas, the chief representative of humanitarian ideas in eighteenth-century Russia was not a professional philosopher or university teacher, but the writer and satirist NIKOLAI NOVIKOV (1744–1818).

Novikov's family belonged to the impoverished provincial gentry. He attended a secondary school attached to Moscow University but for some reason was not able to complete his studies. All his life he regretted various gaps in his education, especially his poor knowledge of foreign languages. In 1767 and 1768 he was one of the secretaries of the Legislative Commission: he kept the minutes of the special committee set up to consider "members of the middle estate" and at times also those of the chief Commission. This work allowed him to gain wide insight into the social problems of the time, especially as they affected the "middle estate" and even the peasants. It seems likely that this experience influenced his entire future activity. After the Commission had been disbanded, Novikov threw himself with great energy into the publication of satirical journals—

10. The term *raznochinets* was applied to educated men of varying social origins who had to support themselves by their own work. It is worth noting that this term was already used by Desnitsky.

not only as publisher, but also as editor and main contributor.[11]

The first Russian satirical journal, *All Sorts of Everything (Vsia-kaia vsiachina)*, was published on the initiative of Catherine herself. By this gesture she wished to show that in spite of disbanding the Commission she had no intention of giving up her enlightened liberalism. The journal was officially published by the empress's private secretary, Kozitsky, but it was well known in literary circles that the real editor was Catherine herself. In the first number she set out to encourage men of letters in Russia to follow her example. This was intended to stimulate social initiatives that could be exploited in support of the policies of the government. Her encouragement met with considerable success—rather more, probably, than was to her taste. Soon there emerged a prolific crop of satirical journals. Catherine's journal tried to play the role of a "grandmother" who would hold the others on leading strings and make sure that criticism did not exceed certain well-defined bounds, but this task proved by no means easy.

The most interesting and boldest of the ungrateful "grandsons" was Novikov's *Drone (Truten')*, which appeared as a weekly in 1769–70. Right from the first number Novikov disputed Catherine's advice that satire should be "cheerful and good-natured, that the satirist should not forget the injunction to love his fellowmen, and that criticism of reality was permissible only if attention was also drawn to its positive aspects." To the threats that appeared on the pages of *All Sorts* he reacted with witty reminders to Catherine of the rules of the literary game she had herself laid down, including several malicious allusions to the empress herself. This sharp (though only indirect) criticism of Catherine the editor alternated in the *Drone* with panegyrics to Catherine the empress. For some time these tactics enabled Novikov to continue his pointed social satire and relentless attacks on *All Sorts*. Finally Catherine had heard enough and resolved to have recourse to administrative measures. First she imposed strict censorship, and later she decided to close satirical journals down altogether. *All Sorts* itself ceased to appear, and not long afterwards the *Drone* informed its readers that it must take its leave of them, though not of its own volition.

Novikov was given another chance in 1772, when Catherine's comedy *Oh, Our Times!*, ridiculing the conservative aristocratic opposition, was performed in St. Petersburg. Novikov knew how to flatter Catherine's vanity, and by claiming the patronage not only

11. Novikov's satirical writings are discussed in detail in D. Blagoy, *Istoriia russkoi literatury XVIII veka* (M, 1946).

of the empress but also of the author of the new comedy he was granted permission to publish another periodical, *The Artist* (*Zhivopisets*).

The chief targets of Novikov's satire were bad and foolish landowners: men boastful of their noble birth but cruel toward their peasants and of no use to society. The most remarkable of his satirical pieces is the *Fragment of a Journey to . . .* , printed in one of the early numbers of *The Artist*. This contains a striking description of a "ruined village," the "abode of weeping," groaning under the yoke of a "cruel tyrant." No other condemnation of serfdom published in Russia before Radishchev was as emphatic as this. It is not surprising, therefore, that many scholars later ascribed the authorship of the *Fragment* to the young Radishchev.

The main difference between the *Fragment of a Journey to . . .* and the *Journey from St. Petersburg to Moscow* is that Radishchev's peasants are shown to be capable of protest and even rebellion, whereas Novikov's are cowed and humble. There was nothing in Novikov's appeal to the public conscience that could be construed as an attack on the nobility as a class, but nevertheless the *Fragment* aroused the utmost indignation in influential circles and *The Artist* ceased to appear in July 1773, after only a year.

What sort of social vision did Novikov have in mind when he was writing his searching criticism of Russian conditions? His ideal model was clearly a patriarchal monarchy raised above all particular interests and uniting all estates in harmonious activity for the common good. In this system the nobility would not own the peasants or rule over them, but would be responsible for mediating between the peasantry and the supreme authorities. In fulfilling their supervisory functions, Novikov suggested, the nobility ought to act in a "paternal" manner, looking after their peasants and lending a helping hand in times of floods, fires, bad harvests, or other natural disasters. Although he was aware how far removed his patriarchal idyll was from Russian reality, he retained his faith in this idealized vision of a good landlord who would be a father to his peasants, and a good tsar who would be a father to the whole nation.[12]

This patriarchal utopia had little in common with the bourgeois ideologies of the Age of Reason, which advocated replacing personal dependence by relations based on impersonal, rational legislation. Novikov believed that national wealth was founded on agriculture, and he disliked capitalist tendencies. Though he felt respect and

12. See Makogonenko, *Novikov*, pp. 202–5.

even sympathy for the merchant class, he could not see the need for industrial capital and detested all financial machinations. If we take a closer look at his social ideal, we find that it is an idealized picture of certain aspects of the social relationships prevailing in pre-Petrine Russia.

The main readership of Novikov's periodicals was to be found among the minor gentry and the middle and merchant classes. There are good grounds, in fact, for calling him the Russian ideologist of the "third estate." It must be remembered, however, that this third estate in Russia was not a revolutionary force capable of overthrowing the feudal system.

A characteristic element in the ideology of the "Russian third estate" was its Francophobia, directed chiefly against the aristocracy and wealthy nobility, who were increasingly given to uncritical imitation of everything French. Although he was not extreme in his condemnation. Novikov shared this dislike and in the *Drone* also attacked the prevalent contempt for the vernacular, the uncritical pursuit of the latest Paris fashions, and other defects of the "young aristocratic hogs" drilled in the French manner.

As was mentioned earlier, Catherine too became interested in upholding national traditions after the fiasco of her contacts with the encyclopedists. Novikov, who enjoyed enormous popularity, looked like a potential ally in this campaign. Hence Catherine subsidized his *Ancient Russian Library*, a serial publication in which he published various texts of historical interest. Taking advantage of Catherine's support, Novikov made another attempt in 1774 (his last) to publish a satirical journal. The symbolic title of this periodical—*Bag-wig (Koshelek)*—referred to the silk bag holding the back hair in the wigs worn by fashionable men of the day, and was in itself an indication that the journal would fight the cult for foreign fashions.

Novikov gave vent to his Francophobia in a satire on a certain Chevalier de Mensonge (*mensonge*="lie"), who was a master of the art of hairdressing in France but in Russia made a career as a teacher of aristocratic offspring, in whom he inculcated hatred of their native land. His opponent is a likable German who defends the Russians and contrasts those true jewels "the great and ancient Russian virtues" with the synthetic glitter of French gallantry. This is how the German concludes the discussion:

Ah, if only some human force could give back to the Russians their former morals that have been destroyed by the introduction of bag-wigs; then they would become a model to the rest of humanity. It seems to me that earlier, wise Russian tsars foresaw, as it were, that as a result of the introduction of the arts and sciences into Russia the Russian people's greatest treasure, their morals, would disappear forever; that is why they preferred their subjects to be ignorant of many things but to remain virtuous and faithful to God, the tsar, and the motherland.[13]

This would seem to close the argument, but Novikov apparently had some doubts and in the next number of his journal published a letter purporting to be from an "unknown" defender of the French, who had this to say to the lover of ancient Russian virtues:

Why don't you stop spoiling paper to no avail? Today's young people are lively, witty, flighty, and irreverent and scoff at your ancient love of the motherland. You ought to have been born long ago, in the days when the Russian tsars smeared their hair with honey on their wedding-day and the following morning visited the bathhouse with their brides and ate a meal there; in the days when the whole of learning was contained in the pages of the church calendar; when mead and wine were drunk by the jugful; when young men were married to brides they did not know; when a long beard was synonymous with all virtues; when people were burnt at the stake or, by a peculiar kind of piety, buried alive for a deviation in their way of making the sign of the cross.[14]

Novikov promised his readers an answer to this defense of French manners. In the second part of the letter he tried to make his "correspondent" look ridiculous by putting into his mouth various exaggerations—that Russians could not be considered human, for instance, unless they learned to dance and greet each other in the French manner. Nevertheless, it seemed that he was unable to find new arguments in defense of "ancient Russian virtues," and the readers of the *Bag-wig* waited in vain for the promised reply.[15]

During the years he was engaged in editing these satirical journals, Novikov was, in his own words, "halfway between religion and Voltairianism." One might add that he was also torn between patriotic feelings, which in the circumstances of his day meant traditionalism, and the progressive but cosmopolitan ideas of the Enlightenment, in whose name he criticized Russian reality. In 1774, when he was editing the *Bag-wig*, he experienced a serious crisis that was deepened by the shock of the recent Pugachev rebellion. The solution to this crisis for Novikov was provided by the Masonic movement, which he joined in 1775. Perhaps it would be more correct to say that he was received into a lodge rather than that he joined it,

13. N. I. Novikov, *Izbrannye sochineniia* (M-L, 1951), p. 85.
14. *Ibid.*, pp. 86–87.
15. See Plekhanov, *Istoriia russkoi ... mysli*, p. 307.

for his sponsors were willing even to do without the official initiation ceremony in order not to discourage their new recruit.[16]

In the eighteenth century the Masonic movement was a most powerful and influential set of secret or (depending on the circumstances) semisecret societies transcending national boundaries. The ideology of Freemasonry has never been clearly formulated; of course any unequivocal statement would not have been in keeping with the conspiratorial nature of the movement and its esoteric doctrines. Different systems and even different individual lodge members could represent the most varied social and political beliefs, from radical liberalism to out-and-out reaction. What was common to all Masons was a belief in the universal brotherhood of man, in the goal of moral self-perfection and the coming golden age. This belief was not, however, linked to any systematic program of political action.

Basically, Freemasonry was a specific secularized form of religious life, the product of the disintegration of feudal society and the authority of the Church, as well as of the total or partial loss of faith in traditional religious beliefs. For men who, like Novikov, stood halfway between traditional religious faith and rationalism, Freemasonry became a surrogate for religion while the Masonic lodges, with their hierarchic order and elaborate cult, became a kind of surrogate for the Church.

In relation to traditional religion, Freemasonry had a dual function: on the one hand, it could draw people away from the official Church and, by rationalizing religious experience, could contribute to the gradual secularization of their world view; on the other hand, it could attract people back to religion and draw them away from the secular and rationalistic philosophy of the Enlightenment. The first function was fulfilled most effectively by the rationalistic and deistic wing of the movement, which set the authority of reason against that of the Church and stood for tolerance and the freedom of the individual. The deistic variety of Freemasonry flourished above all in England, where it had links with the liberal movement, and in France, where it was often in alliance with the encyclopedists. The second function was most often fulfilled by the mystical trend, although this too could represent a modernization of religious faith, since the model of belief it put forward was fundamentally antiecclesiastical and postulated a far-reaching internalization of faith founded on the soul's immediate contact with God.

Mystical Freemasonry had its adherents mainly in the economi-

16. See Makogonenko, *Novikov*, pp. 299–300.

cally backward states of Germany, although Germany also gave birth to the Illuminati, an extreme rationalist branch of Freemasonry that did not shrink from political action. Masonic mysticism drew its inspiration largely from the writings of Jakob Boehme and Saint-Martin, which had been translated into Russian. Saint-Martin, especially, enjoyed great popularity in Russia, particularly among the "Martinists," with whom Novikov was connected (the term "Martinist," however, derived not from the name Saint-Martin but from that of his teacher, the Portuguese mystic Martines Pasqually).

The first Masonic lodges appeared in Russia in the middle of the eighteenth century, during the reign of the Empress Elizabeth. From the memoirs of the eminent Freemason I. P. Elagin it seems clear, however, that these early lodges were more like social clubs for polite society and offered little in the way of intellectual or spiritual stimulus. The movement became prominent only in the reign of Catherine II, who showed herself hostile to Freemasonry. It counted among its members some of the most prominent representatives of the ancient nobility, including the Panin brothers and Prince Shcherbatov (leaders of the aristocratic opposition), and such eminent writers as Sumarokov, Kheraskov, and Karamzin. Even Radishchev belonged to the "Urania" lodge. The majority of Freemasons came from the nobility, but non-noble members of the intelligentsia or even servants could also occasionally be found as members.

Masonic lodges began to multiply rapidly in the second half of the 1770's, after the Pugachev rising. At this time the more enlightened younger members of the nobility were faced by a disturbing dilemma: the peasant uprising represented a terrible warning and an inducement to abandon their enlightened liberal ideas; but at the same time they could not contemplate a return to the previous matter-of-course acceptance of the exploitation of the peasantry by the upper classes. What remained was flight into the realm of individualistic self-perfection, the "inner life of the soul," or, in other words, the Masonic lodge. This was the climate that also gave rise to Russian sentimentalism and other preromantic trends.

Unlike much of Western European Freemasonry, the Masonic movement in Russia played a negligible role in the process of secularization. From the time of Peter the Great, Orthodoxy had almost entirely lost its hold on the educated elite, and the heads of state (with the possible exception of the Empress Elizabeth) gave it very little respect. In these circumstances Freemasonry was primarily a reaction against the "Voltairianism" of enlightened society. Hence the Moscow Metropolitan Platon was favorably inclined toward the movement in spite of Catherine's undoubted hostility.

One of the most eminent Freemasons of the day, IVAN LOPUKHIN (1756–1816), had been a warm adherent of the encyclopedists in his youth. He was so impressed by Holbach's *System of Nature* that he translated the last chapter, entitled "The Code of Nature," which recapitulates the earlier argument. Lopukhin was delighted with his translation and toyed with the idea of distributing it to a wider circle. But, as he tells us, as soon as the first copy was ready he was overcome by disquiet and pangs of conscience; he was unable to fall asleep until he had consigned his impious manuscript to the fire, and only regained his peace of mind when he had written a special essay on the "abuses of reason." Since he could not, however, go back to the traditional Orthodox faith, he found consolation in Masonic mysticism.[17]

A usual consequence of interest in mysticism was the gradual abandonment of interest in social and political reform. Lopukhin was a man of warm humanitarian impulses widely known for his philanthropy, but at the same time he was a decided opponent of radical social change. In a work entitled *Outpourings of a Heart Revering the Benefits of Autocracy and Full of Misgivings When It Sees the Pernicious Fantasies of Equality and Liberty Run Riot* (1794) he put forward a theory justifying social inequality as one of the laws of nature: nature herself, he declared, exemplifies the principle of differentiation and hierarchy; if there were no inequalities, the world would lose its diversity, harmony, and beauty.

Another outstanding Freemason was the *raznochinets* SEMYON GAMALEIA (1743–1822), a close friend and collaborator of Novikov. He had the reputation of being a saintly man who despised material benefits; on being offered the gift of 300 peasant "souls" in return for government service in Belorussia, he is said to have refused on the grounds that he found it difficult to cope with one soul—his own. According to another anecdote he was attacked by bandits, gave up his watch and money without offering resistance, and on returning home prayed that the stolen property might not be put to misuse. Another time he was robbed by one of his own servants. When the servant was caught Gamaleia made him a present of the stolen money and told him to "go with God."[18]

17. See Miliukov, *Ocherki*, vol. 3, p. 162.
18. See Plekhanov, *Istoriia russkoi . . . mysli*, p. 279.

These anecdotes show that Gamaleia subscribed both in theory and in practice to the Tolstoyan principle of nonviolent resistance to evil. This emphasis on individual morality—the conviction that evil could only be overcome by perfection of the self and moral rebirth—was very characteristic of the ideology of Russian Freemasonry and led Miliukov to call it the "Tolstoyism" of the eighteenth century.[19] Although this comparison rightly draws attention to one particular aspect of Masonic beliefs, it is nevertheless misleading in that it ignores the fact that even the evangelical ethics professed by Gamaleia were far removed from the social radicalism that was so characteristic of Tolstoy.

From a purely philosophical point of view, the most interesting individual among Russian Freemasons was a Russified German from Transylvania, JOHANN GEORG SCHWARZ (1751–84). Schwarz came to Russia as a tutor, and in 1779 was appointed professor at Moscow University. Shortly afterwards he met Novikov, with whom he founded the Scholarly Society of Friends. In the early 1780's the two men published two periodicals: the *Moscow Press (Moskovskoe Izdanie)* and the *Evening Glow (Vecherniaia Zaria)*.

Apart from his two special qualities of enthusiasm and idealism, Schwarz also had a considerable talent for teaching. He used his entire fortune, which he had worked hard to acquire, to found a "pedagogical seminar" attached to Moscow University where he trained future teachers by means of a critical study of Spinoza, Rousseau, and the French materialists. With his students' help he also set up a "translation seminar" where the works of Western European philosophers, mystics, and moral philosophers were translated into Russian. When a quarrel with the university authorities forced him to hand in his resignation, he continued to lecture in his own home. He played an important part in the history of Russian Freemasonry not only as an ideologist but also as an organizer, for he established a Russian branch of the Order of Rosicrucians, with whom he had come into contact during a journey to Germany in 1781. The Moscow Rosicrucians formed a conspiratorial elite within the main body of Russian Freemasonry.

Schwarz was not only a mystic and theosophist—and an ardent disciple of Jakob Boehme—but also an enthusiastic believer in the "occult sciences." He practiced alchemy and believed that it was possible to gain magical insight into the secrets of nature and be granted a vision of its true uncorrupted face as it was before the

19. See Miliukov, *Ocherki*, vol. 3, p. 345.

Fall of man. To some extent he may be said to have prepared the way in Russia for the Schellingian philosophy of nature.[20]

Schwarz expounded his ideas in articles in the *Evening Glow*.[21] His philosophy was primarily concerned with the nature of man. Schwarz distinguished between the body, the spirit, and the soul, the last being in his view a product of the chemical fusion of the corporeal and spiritual elements. He believed that animals, too, have souls and that man is an intermediate link in the chain of beings connecting the world of animals and the world of pure spirits. The body is governed by the senses, the soul by the intellect, and the spirit by "reason." The intellect—or in other words the faculty that the Enlightenment philosophers called "reason"—can only function by means of the senses, whereas true reason is capable of transcendental cognition, can comprehend divine truths that are beyond the grasp of ordinary experience. True knowledge is synonymous with morality. With the attainment of absolute knowledge man will also attain absolute morality; he will be reborn, "rise after the fall," and this will usher in a new golden age.

Let us now return to the views and activities of Novikov, who after Schwarz's premature death became the leading figure among Moscow Rosicrucians. For Novikov the Masonic movement represented a compromise between rationalism and religious faith and not, therefore, a complete renunciation of his previous beliefs. Unlike Schwarz, Novikov was not interested in the occult and was only to a minor degree affected by mysticism; in short, he largely represented the rationalistic trend in Freemasonry.

In 1777 Novikov brought out the first Russian philosophical and moralistic journal, the *Morning Light* (*Utrennii Svet*). Unlike the later *Evening Glow*, which was published by Novikov but in reality edited by Schwarz, the *Morning Light* was entirely the work of Novikov. One of the most significant articles published in this journal was his essay "On the Dignity of Man in His Relations to God and the World." [22] By implication this was an attack on the popular mystical view of man as a fallen creature who in the sight of God was a mere speck of dust, a "rotten and putrid vessel of original sin." In its place Novikov proposed a truly Renaissance vision of man as the "lord of the universe." Man as well as the smallest

20. See V. V. Zenkovsky, *A History of Russian Philosophy*, trans. George L. Kline (2 vols.; London, 1953), vol. 1, pp. 97–98.

21. Discussed in Miliukov, *Ocherki*, vol. 3, pp. 360–63.

22. See Novikov, *Izbrannye sochineniia*, pp. 387–93.

grub, he argued, were created by God out of dust, but man alone was created in the likeness of God and endowed with reason; his nature alone contains an element of the divine. Man is therefore a connecting link between the world of matter and the world of the spirit. The nature of humanity is contradictory: man is a worm and at the same time divine; a slave and at the same time a ruler. He must be humble toward the Creator but has the right to be proud as the proper representative of God on earth.[23]

Several practical conclusions could be drawn from this theory. Novikov praised human reason for its divine attributes, and suggested, for instance, that the conquest of the world by reason was the most appropriate tribute that could be paid to God. Moreover, since human nature was divine, it followed that every human being deserved respect, irrespective of his origins or social status. In the name of human dignity, he also called for active participation in work for the common welfare. Man is in himself both end and means, he wrote in the conclusion to the article: an end, since no one is entitled to treat another man as a means, and a means, since every individual ought to devote himself to work for the common good. Whoever regards his own person as an end in itself, he concluded, is nothing better than a parasite, a useless drone.

Novikov was not an original thinker, but then his important place in the history of Russian ideas does not depend on originality. Essentially he was a great popularizer. He may be called a central figure of his age largely because he represented aspects of all the leading (often mutually contradictory) intellectual trends of the day: both Enlightenment universalism and the defense of traditionally conceived national values; both rationalism and religious reaction against rationalism. First and foremost, however, he was an untiring reformer, a man who by his own life proved that there could be no going back to the period when the dissemination of education was the monopoly of autocracy.

The Masonic movement in Russia had a wealthy and influential

23. This same idea—that man is an intermediate link in the chain of being, both a worm and divine—is to be found in Derzhavin's famous "Ode to God." Makogonenko (*Novikov*, pp. 334–35) concludes from this that Derzhavin was influenced by Novikov and calls Novikov's philosophy of man a "generalization of the historical path of the Russian nation." It is worth noting, therefore, that Novikov took up what was then a generally accepted interpretation of the "great chain of being." He could have come across it in the *Night Thoughts* of the English poet Edward Young, which he certainly knew well. One of the poems in this cycle ("Man") also conceives of man as halfway between nothingness and divinity, someone who combines the nature of the worm with the nature of God.

membership and was at that time the only powerful organization independent of the government. It is hardly surprising that Novikov thought it could play a role in bringing about social reforms. As early as 1777 he used the revenues from sales of the *Morning Light* to open two schools in St. Petersburg for children of the middle classes. In the capital, however, under the eyes of the empress herself, his plans had little hope of success. In 1779 he therefore moved to Moscow, where he leased the university press and became active in the field of education. In 1784 he took advantage of the decree permitting the setting up of private printing presses to found his famous Typographical Company (using the capital of wealthy Freemasons from the Scholarly Society of Friends). His publishing activities were on a scale unprecedented in Russia. He was not only editor but also distributor, seeing to it that his books reached the most distant parts of the empire, including Siberia. Thanks to Novikov the middle class—and some peasants, too—gained access to the new ideas reaching Russia. Some 28 percent of all books published in 1781–90 (749 out of 2,585) were printed by his press.[24] Of these only a relatively small number were devoted to orthodox Masonic ideas, occultism, or mysticism. Indeed, Novikov was reluctant to publish works of this kind and was often accused by Schwarz of a lack of proper enthusiasm for Masonic matters. There was even an open quarrel with his wealthy Rosicrucian backers, who threatened to withdraw their capital. Most of his publications were historical or educational works (including the first Russian reader for children), and his list of leading authors and scholars included Milton, Shakespeare, Young, Lessing, Klopstock, Fielding, Sterne, Corneille, Racine, Bacon, Locke, Mendelssohn, Rousseau, and even Voltaire and Diderot. There was also a separate, carefully edited series of selected works of Russian writers. During these busy years Novikov still found the energy to undertake other activities. After the bad harvest of 1787 he used his great organizational talents to arrange help on a large scale for the starving peasants.

Novikov's activities could hardly meet with Catherine's approval. She was uneasy about educational and civic operations undertaken on such a scale and without her supervision. In her battle with her former opponent she made skillful use of his association with the Rosicrucians in order to discredit him in the eyes of the public as an obscurantist mystic, while she herself assumed the mantle of defender of the rational ideals of the Enlightenment. In the 1780's she initiated an all-out campaign against Freemasonry and herself wrote

24. See Makogonenko, *Novikov*, p. 507.

comedies ridiculing the movement (*The Siberian Shaman, The Swindler,* etc.). She also issued an anonymous brochure with the significant title *Secrets of a Preposterous Society* and tried to persuade the Metropolitan Platon to accuse Novikov of heresy. These measures were dictated not only by dislike of Novikov's zeal, but also by the fear that the Masonic lodges were engaged in a plot to overthrow her and replace her with the heir to the throne, the Crown Prince Paul.

The French Revolution persuaded Catherine that it was time to apply more drastic sanctions. In 1792 she had Novikov arrested and condemned without trial to fifteen years' imprisonment in the Schlüsselburg Fortress. The Typographical Company was dissolved, and many books and periodicals printed there were burned. Novikov was released four years later, during the reign of the Emperor Paul. In poor health and reduced circumstances, he now more than ever looked for comfort to religious mysticism. Together with Gamaleia he spent the last years of his life in preparing a vast anthology of theosophical, magical, and cabalistic writings.

In the first quarter of the nineteenth century Freemasonry experienced a short-lived revival. Its sudden decline was largely due to the accession to the throne of the Emperor Nicholas I, who would not tolerate any secret or semisecret societies, and who regarded the Freemasons with particular abhorrence.

THE ARISTOCRATIC OPPOSITION

Although Catherine's domestic and foreign policies undoubtedly served the best interests of the nobility, the most outspoken aristocratic opposition to absolutism came to a climax in her reign. At times this opposition claimed to be rooted in the ancient boyar traditions of the pre-Petrine age—the traditions of the Land Assemblies and the Boyar Duma—but basically it was the product of Westernization. What its leaders wanted in principle was to replace autocracy by a monarchical system of the Western European type. Their ideas stemmed from the political philosophy of Montesquieu, with its emphasis on the importance of uninterrupted historical continuity, and their outlook is well summed up in his phrase "no monarch no nobility, no nobility no monarch, but there may be a despotic prince."[25]

The ideological representative of the extreme right wing of the

---

25. Montesquieu, *The Spirit of Laws,* trans. by Thomas Nugent (n.d.), vol. 2, p. 14.

opposition was Prince MIKHAIL SHCHERBATOV (1733–90). During the meetings of the Legislative Commission he had shown himself to be an excellent orator and an ardent defender of the traditional rights of the ancient nobility, which felt its very existence threatened by Peter's Table of Ranks.[26] Only the monarch should have the right to confer nobility, Shcherbatov argued. Ennoblement as an automatic privilege attached to a given military or bureaucratic rank led to careerism and servility and transformed the monarchy into a despotic bureaucracy. Shcherbatov also opposed all concessions to the peasantry (e.g., legal limitations of serfdom) or to the merchants (e.g., the establishment of merchant manufactories)—opposed anything, in fact, that might help to undermine the traditional privileges of the aristocracy and hereditary nobility, who were, to him, the mainstay of honor and liberty, the only section of society capable of maintaining its independence without recourse to servility or flattery. In his unpublished articles Shcherbatov stated openly that the political system in Russia was not monarchy but despotism, the worst form of government, or rather misgovernment, "a tyranny where there are no laws but the crazy whims of the despot."

As a historian (he was the author of a seven-volume *History of Russia* up to the year 1610), Shcherbatov propounded the view that despotism was not a form of government native to Russia. The former Russian princes and tsars had shared their power with the boyars, and the alliance of tsar and boyars, which was strictly adhered to by both sides, was the main factor in the uninterrupted growth of Russian strength. In order to reconcile this conception with the despotic but politically successful reign of Ivan the Terrible, Shcherbatov was forced to divide Ivan's reign into two periods. The first period was beneficial to Russia, for the tsar still restrained his passions and took the advice of his Boyar Duma; in the second period he became a bloody tyrant, murdered his advisers, and brought ruin upon his country.

The reign of Peter the Great presented Shcherbatov with even greater difficulties. In spite of his brutal treatment of the boyars and his introduction of the Table of Ranks, Peter had consolidated and greatly increased Russia's strength. Shcherbatov did not deny this, but set out to show that these were merely superficial successes for which too high a price had been paid. He developed these ideas

26. The Table of Ranks introduced in 1722 established a hierarchy of 14 civil ranks and their military counterparts. Noble rank (for life or hereditary) was automatically linked to a certain grade in the civil or military service.

in an interesting essay entitled *A Discourse on the Corruption of Morals in Russia*. This essay could not possibly have passed the censor and was clearly not written for publication. It only became available when Herzen published it abroad in 1858.

As his starting point for the *Discourse* Shcherbatov took the contradiction inherent in the notion of progress obtained at the cost of moral retrogression. In order to prove his thesis he drew an idealized picture of primitive tribal life and contrasted its simplicity with the temptations of civilization. He even praised the primitive egalitarianism of such tribal societies (including the communal ownership of property), although he pointed out that it could not possibly survive, since the advance of civilization implied social differentiation.

In many respects Shcherbatov's ideas differed widely from the popular Enlightenment stereotype. Tribal life as he saw it was not a carefree existence in a "state of nature"—on the contrary, its most noteworthy feature was strong social cohesion, and it was this rather than "natural freedom" that he contrasted with the inner laxity, egoism, and moral anarchy typical of the state of civilization. Primitive tribes, he argued, had no conception of "voluptuousness" (*slastoliubie*)—that is, the unrestrained urge to satisfy all sensual appetites, the constant proliferation of sophisticated and artificially induced needs that go hand in hand with unhealthy ambition and the desire to impress others. The originality of these views lies in the fact that Shcherbatov placed this precivilized state in the comparatively recent past rather than in remote prehistoric times, so that the antithesis of primitive tribes and civilized nations in his interpretation largely coincides with the antithesis of pre- and post-Petrine Russia.

In olden times, Shcherbatov pointed out, life in Russia was simple and untouched by excessive luxury. The upbringing of children was completely subordinated to religion, and although this encouraged some irrational and superstitious beliefs, it also inculcated a healthy fear of "God's law." Noble status was not attached to rank in government service but, on the contrary, rank was decided by the prestige and traditions of the noble family. This principle favored the flowering of civic virtues, for it restrained the personal ambitions of individuals, subordinating them to the interests of family and estate.

Shcherbatov's assertion that Peter's reforms introduced a formerly unknown "voluptuousness" into Russian life has some authority, for he personally knew many people who still remembered Peter's reign. In many respects, therefore, his *Discourse* has the weight of a historical document and gives us an insight into how much Peter's reforms did for the emancipation of the individual from the domination of tradition and religious ritual. Ruthless absolutist power, state centralization, and bureaucratic regimentation were far less of a burden on the individual than the rigorous discipline of religious ceremonies, continual fasts, and traditional conventions idealized by Shcherbatov. The "voluptuousness" of the *Discourse* is nothing other than individualism, whose first primitive stirrings are sometimes repellent as well as naive, as Shcherbatov's long list of examples of demoralization, careerism, and profligacy (largely taken from the life of the court and the newly created court aristocracy) bears witness.

Shcherbatov drew special attention to the individualization of personal relations and to the consequent changes in the attitude to women. In Peter's reign it became customary for the bride and bridegroom to meet before the wedding, joint "assemblies" were organized for men and women, and more attention was paid to personal appearance. "Passionate love, unknown in earlier primitive conditions, began to hold sway over sensitive hearts."[27] The only hairdresser in Moscow was besieged by her clients—for feast days some of them came to her three days in advance and had to sleep sitting upright for three nights in order not to spoil their coiffure. Dandies of both capitals vied with each other in extravagance and fashionable dress. Peter, Shcherbatov admitted, had no great love of luxury himself, but he encouraged excess in others in order to stimulate industry, handicrafts, and trade.

Another cause of the corruption of morals was the bureaucratic hierarchy established by Peter, which encouraged personal ambition and placed government officials above the nobility. "Is it possible," Shcherbatov asked, "for people who from early youth tremble at the stick in the hands of their superiors to preserve virtue and strength of character?"[28] The brutal suddenness of the reforms had been injurious to the nation's morals: Peter had waged too radical a war on superstition; Shcherbatov compared him to an inexperienced gardener who prunes his trees too far. "There was less superstition, but also less faith; the former servile fear of hell disappeared, but so did love of God and His holy laws."[29]

27. See M. Shcherbatov, *O provrezhdenii nravov v Rossii, s predislovien Iskandera* (London, 1858), p. 17.
28. *Ibid.*, p. 28.
29. *Ibid.*, p. 29.

In his criticism of the Petrine reforms and his unusually acute and comprehensive treatment of the issue of "ancient and modern Russia," Shcherbatov was to some extent a precursor of the Slavophiles, as Herzen was to point out. It is significant that Shcherbatov, like the Slavophiles, was strongly critical of the transfer of the capital from the old boyar stronghold of Moscow to the newly built St. Petersburg, which personified the supremacy of bureaucratic absolutism.

The analogy between Shcherbatov and Slavophilism is, however, largely superficial and even unreliable. In his *Discourse* there is no antithesis between Russia and Europe; and his views on juridical questions, social systems, and the significance of political rights clearly derived from Western European (especially Enlightenment) sources and were therefore far removed from the romanticism of the Slavophiles and their idealization of the common people. His faith in the role of the aristocracy was equally "occidental"; the Slavophiles, as we shall see later, viewed "aristocratism" as a negative phenomenon that was fortunately quite alien to the "truly Christian" principles of ancient Russia.

An interesting light is cast on Shcherbatov's political ideals by his utopian tale *Journey to the Land of Ophir* (1784). In the apt description of a contemporary scholar, this presents an idealized version of the "orderly police state."[30] This work would not have been to the taste of either the Slavophiles or Montesquieu, from whose writings Shcherbatov drew arguments in support of his critique of despotism.

The population of Ophir is divided into hermetically sealed-off free estates and serfs, whom the author quite simply calls "slaves." The daily life of every inhabitant is subject to the most detailed control, and excessive luxury or the relaxation of morals is severely punished. Strict regulations lay down what clothes a citizen of each class may wear, how large a house he may live in, how many servants he may have, what utensils he may use, and even what gratuities he may dispense. In his ideal state the opponent of bureaucracy and despotism carried the despotic and bureaucratic regimentation of life to extremes. To Shcherbatov himself there was no contradiction in this, since he did not consider the strict control of morals to be inconsistent with political liberty. In the state of Ophir there were, after all, such guarantees against despotism as "fundamental rights," representation of the estates, the abolition of the household guard,

30. M. Raeff, "State and Nobility in the Ideology of M. M. Shcherbatov," *The American Slavic and East European Review* (Oct. 1960), p. 374.

and so on. One of the important guarantees of liberty was to be the law forbidding peasants to lay complaint against their masters to the sovereign. In Shcherbatov's eyes the right to petition the emperor was only likely to reinforce the uncouth peasantry's belief in the "good tsar," whereas rulers, made aware of the people's support, might become presumptuous and turn into despots.

Some of the features of Shcherbatov's utopia can be traced to his Freemasonry and the Masonic cult of formalism, hierarchy, and outward distinctions. This influence is most obvious in the sections devoted to education and religion. Education in Ophir is free and compulsory for every citizen, although its extent differs for every estate. Religion is reduced to a rationalistic cult of the supreme being, and there is no separate priesthood that gains a livelihood from religious practices. Sacraments, offerings, and all mysteries are discarded, prayers are short and few, and communal prayers resemble Masonic ritual. Atheism, however, is forbidden, and attendance at church is compulsory, on pain of punishment.

The Masonic provenance of certain elements of the utopia does not account for it altogether. The best key to an understanding of Shcherbatov's tale is probably to be found in his views on "ancient and modern Russia." Attention has been drawn to the fact that the detailed bureaucratic system of the state of Ophir reflects certain features of post-Petrine Russia.[31] However, a comparison between Ophir and the picture of pre-Petrine Russia drawn in the *Discourse* would seem to offer an even more fruitful approach. In both cases private life is governed by strict regulations and norms—in one by legal decrees, and in the other by hallowed traditions and religion. In both cases the division into estates and the hermetic isolation of those estates—especially the isolation of the nobility—are guarantees of social cohesion and the flowering of civic virtues. Finally, in both cases strict morals and moderate requirements prevent the spread of the insidious "voluptuousness." It is important to note that his examination of the differences between ancient and modern Russia had convinced Shcherbatov that strict control and regimentation of morals should not be confused with despotism. Ancient Russia, he claimed, had not on the whole been a despotic society, largely because it had remained faithful to a traditional way of life that set out appropriate spheres of activity for everyone—including the tsar—and thus precluded arbitrary rule. In modern Russia, on the other hand, despotism had spawned "the corruption of morals that was to become its most faithful ally."

31. *Ibid.*, p. 375.

Shcherbatov was without a doubt the most interesting figure in the aristocratic opposition, but he was a theorist rather than an active politician. The men who were generally acknowledged to be the leaders of the opposition (with supporters in the diplomatic corps and the army) were the Panin brothers—Count NIKITA PANIN (1718–83), for many years Russian ambassador to Sweden and during Catherine's reign the first councillor to the Foreign Affairs Commission and tutor to the heir to the throne, the Crown Prince Paul, and PETR PANIN (1721–89). Toward the end of his life, Nikita Panin employed as his private secretary DENIS FONVIZIN (1744–92), the outstanding satirist and playwright of the second half of the eighteenth century, author of the comedies *The Brigadier* (*Brigadir*) and *The Minor* (*Nedorosl*).

The Panin brothers' program was far more liberal than Shcherbatov's and more obviously modeled on modern constitutional theories. Though it aimed at extending the political privileges of the gentry, it also envisaged some limitation of serfdom and the granting of certain legal rights to the peasantry. Nikita Panin took part in the coup that brought Catherine to the throne. At the beginning of her reign he presented her with a plan for the limitation of her sovereignty by specific laws and for an extension of the role of the Senate (a representative body of the nobility). Despite her promises, Catherine did not put this plan into effect, preferring instead to rely on the support of the middle and small gentry, who feared a government takeover by the aristocratic oligarchy.

The Panin brothers did not, however, give up their plans. They engaged in a plot to put the crown prince on the throne in place of his mother. But Catherine quickly found out about their intentions and was able to forestall the scheme. The plotters were magnanimously forgiven, and indeed the only sanction applied was that Nikita Panin ceased to be the crown prince's tutor. The Pugachev rebellion, which broke out shortly afterwards, made the disagreements between Catherine and the aristocratic opposition seem trivial. General Petr Panin was to play a leading role in the suppression of the peasant revolt.

After Nikita Panin's death, a interesting document was found among his papers that is known under the title *A Discourse on the Disappearance in Russia of All Forms of Government and Likewise on the Unstable Position of the Empire and Sovereigns Arising Therefrom*. This was Panin's political testament, intended for his former pupil, Crown Prince Paul, who—as is well known—realized not one iota of the hopes placed in him. The *Discourse* was given literary polish by Fonvizin.

Panin's *Discourse* is undoubtedly one of the most penetrating documents of eighteenth-century Russian political thought. It contains a bold demand for constitutional reforms and a warning that rebellion will break out if these are denied. There is a graphic description of the disappearance of all forms of social bonds in the despotic state, "that giant upheld only by chains." "Where the arbitrary rule of one man is the highest law," Panin warns, "there can be no lasting or unifying bonds; there is a state, but no fatherland; there are subjects, but no citizens; there is no body politic whose members are linked to each other by a network of duties and privileges."

The warning contained in the title of the *Discourse* is justified by the author's description of a "certain state that is unlike any other": a state that may soon be brought to the abyss by its peasants, "whose human faces are the only thing that distinguishes them from cattle" (an allusion to the Pugachev uprising); a state where the throne is dependent on a "band of rioters" (i.e. on the royal guard that was responsible for palace revolutions). In this state men are owned by men, almost everyone is both tyrant and victim; it is "a state where the most venerable of the estates, motivated by honor alone, exists in name only, and the right to call himself a member is sold to every scoundrel who plunders his native land; where nobility—the only goal of noble souls, the just reward for services rendered to one's country by one's ancestors from time immemorial—is obscured by backstairs patronage. . . . A state that is not despotic, for the nation has never confided itself to the sovereign's arbitrary rule . . . , nor a monarchy, for it has not been granted fundamental legislation, nor aristocratic, for its supreme authority is a soulless machine set in motion by the arbitrary will of the sovereign. Nor can you speak of democracy in a country where the common people, steeped in abysmal ignorance, drag without complaint the cruel yoke of slavery."[32]

The constitution envisaged by the *Discourse* was intended to protect the inviolability of freedom and property. The most obvious guardian of these constitutional freedoms was clearly that estate whose material and social status ensured its complete independence from the reigning sovereign—i.e. the wealthy aristocracy.

The *Discourse* could only be published in Russia after the 1905

32. See D. I. Fonvizin, *Sobranie sochinenii* (M-L, 1956), vol. 2, pp. 255, 258, 266.

Revolution (although Herzen published it in London in 1861). It was not, however, entirely unknown in Russia before that time. A copy even fell into the hands of Catherine, who made the ironic comment: "Dear me! Now even Monsieur Fonvizin wants to teach me how to govern."

The *Discourse* had a considerable influence on the political evolution of the Decembrists. It was known in the Northern Union thanks to General M. A. Fonvizin, a relative of Denis Fonvizin and a member of the Decembrist movement. Nikita Muraviev rewrote it as a political pamphlet, adapting it to the reign of Alexander I.

For the sake of accuracy it should be pointed out that Denis Fonvizin's ideas differed to some extent from Panin's, and that the aristocratic bias of the latter's constitutionalism was in fact alien to the former. Fonvizin's own views were closer to those of the provincial gentry. This is shown, for instance, by the nationalistic note in his letters to General Petr Panin written from France and Germany in 1777–78; the aristocracy, to which the Panins belonged, tended rather to be cosmopolitan in their outlook. Fonvizin was far more critical of Western Europe than the Panins and made a distinction between legal and "actual" freedom; in spite of his freedom in the eyes of the law, the French peasant, Fonvizin wrote, has no "actual freedom" and is worse off than the peasant in Russia. Observations of this kind show that Fonvizin was capable of some insight but also tended (as Plekhanov pointed out)[33] to confuse patriotism with the defense of native backwardness, which led him to the reassuring thought that serfdom was not in fact such a great evil.

After Count Nikita Panin's death, Fonvizin experienced an ideological crisis and not only gave up writing satires but also renounced his former independent views on politics and religion. In this his intellectual biography resembles that of Gogol.

33. See Plekhanov, *Istoriia russkoi . . . mysli*, pp. 73–85.

CHAPTER 2

THE CULMINATION OF THE ENLIGHTENMENT IN RUSSIA: ALEKSANDR RADISHCHEV

Historians who use the term "Enlightenment" have in mind either a specific period in the history of philosophy and social thought—the Age of Reason as a whole—or a particular ideology associated with this period. In the latter, more narrow sense, the term describes an ideology that stood for a rationalistic universalism, that was antifeudal and freethinking by definition, and that set out to liberate the individual from the confines of the feudal estates by using arguments based on "reason" and "human nature," which were thought to be common to all men and therefore superior to privileges and superstitions sanctified by custom. It is clear that if we accept this particular narrow definition of the term we must distinguish between degrees of "Enlightenment," and that not all thinkers belonging to the Age of Reason were "enlightened" in the sense of the structural model outlined above. Shcherbatov, for instance, as a defender of feudalism, was certainly a less "enlightened" thinker than Novikov, who was himself far from being an ideal representative of the age. Without a doubt the Enlightenment thinker par excellence was ALEKSANDR RADISHCHEV, the most radical and consistent representative of the Age of Reason in Russia.[1]

RADISHCHEV'S LIFE

The author of *A Journey from St. Petersburg to Moscow* was born in 1749 on the family estate in the village of Verkhneye Ablazovo (in Moscow according to other accounts), the son of a prosperous landowner. His parents were both educated and humane people, in contrast to the neighboring gentry. A certain Zubov, for instance, a

1. Two monographs in English on the philosophical ideas of Radishchev are Jesse V. Clardy, *The Philosophical Ideas of A. Radishchev* (New York, 1964); and Allen McConnel, *A Russian Philosophe, Alexander Radishchev* (The Hague, 1964).

nearby landowner, was a sadist who kept his peasants chained up in a special prison and forced them to eat from a trough like cattle. The peasants on the Radishchev estate valued the good treatment they received at the hands of their landlord and during the Pugachev rebellion hid some members of the family in the forest. Radishchev's younger brothers and sisters were taken into the villagers' own homes after having their faces smeared with soot to make them look more like peasant children.

The young Aleksandr was educated in the Corp des Pages in St. Petersburg. He graduated with distinction, and together with other pages was sent by Catherine to study law at the University of Leipzig. While in Leipzig he also studied the works of Leibniz and Wolff, as well as French Enlightenment philosophy; he was especially interested in Helvetius, Rousseau, and Mably. At this time he became deeply attached to two of his fellow-students: Fedor Ushakov and Aleksei Kutuzov. Some years later he wrote a very sympathetic biographical sketch of Ushakov after his premature death, and to Kutuzov he dedicated the *Journey from St. Petersburg to Moscow*.

In his *Life of Fedor Ushakov* (1789), Radishchev relates a dramatic incident from their student years. The Russian students were sent to Leipzig in the care of a steward, a Major Bokum, who appropriated the funds intended for their upkeep but at the same time insisted on supervising their lives in petty detail and treated them with the utmost brutality, even to the extent of using corporal punishment. His victims appealed to Ushakov, as the eldest of the students and the one who enjoyed the greatest authority, and determined to defend themselves. At one point there was an open revolt: a student who had been slapped in the face challenged Bokum to a duel and, on being refused, returned the insult. Bokum was forced to run away and ask for help from the local military authorities, who put the rebels under house arrest. The affair was smoothed over by the Russian Consul in Dresden, who by and large settled it in the students' favor. For the young Radishchev this personal experience of collective protest against a "tyrant" was an event of enormous significance that was to play its part in the formation of his world view.

After his return to Russia, Radishchev was introduced to Novikov and in 1773 produced his first published work: a translation, with introduction and notes, of Mably's *Observations sur l'histoire de la Grèce*. He also entered government service, first as clerk to the Senate and later as military prosecutor on the General Staff in St. Petersburg. In 1775 he asked for his discharge in protest against the cruelty with which the last survivors of Pugachev's defeated rebel army were being treated. A year later he returned to government service in the Department of Commerce, which was then headed by Count Aleksandr Vorontsov, an educated man of liberal views who recognized Radishchev's unusual qualities and took a personal interest in his career. Radishchev, for his part, devoted himself to his new profession with enthusiasm and used every opportunity to study economic developments in Russia.

After the publication of his translation of Mably, Radishchev wrote a number of original works, including an "Ode to Liberty" and a *Letter to a Friend Living in Tobolsk* (1782), but for various reasons he decided against publishing them. In 1789 he produced the remarkable *Conversation on What It Means to Be a Son of the Fatherland*, which was printed anonymously in the periodical *The Storyteller* (*Beseduiushchii Grazhdanin*). A year later he published the *Journey from St. Petersburg to Moscow*, one of the most outstanding literary fruits of the European Enlightenment. This work was so outspoken that, although by some strange oversight it secured the stamp of approval of the St. Petersburg police, no printer was willing to accept responsibility for its publication. Radishchev was therefore forced to print the work on a press he had bought himself.

The appearance of the book caused a sensation, even though Radishchev had decided to sell only a tiny part of the whole edition. Fantastic sums were paid for even a short-term loan of the *Journey*. Catherine, too, found occasion to read it and called the author "a rebel worse than Pugachev." As soon as she discovered the true identity of the author (the *Journey* was published anonymously), Radishchev was immediately placed under arrest and imprisoned in the Peter and Paul Fortress. The investigation was entrusted to the same Sheshkovsky who had interrogated Pugachev, and whom Pushkin later christened Catherine's "household executioner." Radishchev was only saved from physical torture by the jewels of his deceased wife's sister, Elizaveta Rubanovskaia, who married him and followed him into exile (as the wives of the Decembrists were to do later). Radishchev was condemned to death by beheading, but the empress graciously commuted the sentence to banishment for ten years to Ilimsk in eastern Siberia. While he was in prison Radishchev had known moments of weakness, but after sentence was passed he regained his peace of mind, supported by feelings of duty accomplished and readiness to accept responsibility for his actions. In a poem written on the way to his place of exile he movingly reaffirms his commitment to the path he had chosen:

You ask who I am and where I am going?
I am as I was and shall be forever:
Neither beast, nor log, nor slave—but a man!

Radishchev's banishment in Siberia was made bearable by the influence of his former chief and faithful friend Vorontsov. He was allowed to have books and to study geology, geography, and history. Only a few days after his arrival in Ilimsk he started on his next work, a philosophic essay *On Man, His Mortality and Immortality* (published in 1809). His other writings at this time include the *Concise Statement on the Annexation of Siberia* and the *Letters on Chinese Trade*, an economic study prepared at the request of Count Vorontsov.

After Catherine's death the new emperor, Paul I, permitted Radishchev to return to European Russia and live on his estate under police supervision. When Alexander I succeeded to the throne after Paul's assassination, Vorontsov, who was one of the young emperor's liberal advisers, persuaded him to grant Radishchev a complete amnesty. In September 1801 Radishchev returned to St. Petersburg, and shortly afterwards he was appointed a member of the commission working on a revision of the laws. He threw himself into his new task with unabated enthusiasm, but all his proposals were rejected as too radical. Pushkin relates that the chairman of the commission, Count Zavadovsky, was astonished "at the youthfulness of his grey hairs" and said to him: "Eh, Aleksandr Nikolaevich, so you really want to talk the same old nonsense? Didn't you have enough of Siberia?"

On September 11, 1802, Radishchev committed suicide. There are grounds for assuming that this act was not the result of a temporary fit of depression. Suicide had never been far from his thoughts. In the *Journey from St. Petersburg to Moscow* he wrote: "If outrageous fortune hurl upon you all its slings and arrows, if there is no refuge left on earth for your virtue, if, driven to extremes, you find no sanctuary from oppression, then remember that you are a man, call to mind your greatness and seize the crown of bliss which they are trying to take from you. Die."[2]

A similar thought is to be found in the essay *On Man*, where he wrote: "Torment, sickness, banishment—everything has its limits beyond which temporal authority means nothing. No sooner has the vital spirit left the wracked and wounded body than the might

2. A. N. Radishchev, *A Journey from St. Petersburg to Moscow*, trans. by Leo Wiener, ed. by Roderick Page Thaler (Cambridge, Mass., 1958), p. 123.

of tyrants is seen to be vain, their power vanishes, their strength crumbles, their fury is ineffective, their cruelty foiled, their pride absurd. When the unhappy mortal man ends his days, so does the tormentors' spite come to an end, while their barbarity arouses only derision."

In the light of these quotations, Radishchev's suicide appears to have been a considered act of political defiance. This seems to be confirmed by a piece of paper found among his documents after his death, on which he had written the words "Posterity will avenge me."

RADISHCHEV'S SOCIAL PHILOSOPHY

The outlook of the leading figures of the Enlightenment, or more accurately of the Enlightenment's radical wing, was well summed up by Engels in the phrase "juridical world view."[3] Helvetius wrote *"la législation fait tout,"* thus expressing the conviction that society was mainly shaped by law and that social ties depended—or at least ought to depend—on specific juridical relations. According to this view, society itself and the authority of the ruler are derived from the "social contract," the agreement whereby the individual relinquishes part of his innate freedom for the sake of his own safety and the universal good. However this contract was understood (and it was hardly ever taken literally), it was undoubtedly an idealistic conception that reversed the real relationship between society and legislation. It was, moreover, an abstract approach that set up the conscious and rational decisions of the individual as the guiding principle of society and attempted to reduce the complicated network of social relationships to a simple mechanism of rationalized, contractual bonds.[4] On the other hand, it was also a truly revolutionary conception that was directed not only against arbitrary and despotic government but also against all forms of traditionalism. The argument that society was founded on reason and self-interest could of course be used to sanction rebellion against any forms of social relations that could not prove their rationality or utility.

Not all aspects of the "juridical world view" were represented equally clearly in Radishchev's work. Like other radical Enlightenment thinkers (Rousseau, and Kozelsky in Russia) Radishchev tended to reject the extreme rationalization of morals. In his dis-

3. K. Marx and F. Engels, *Sochineniia* (M, 1937), vol. 16, p. 296.
4. See B. Baczko, *Filozofia francuskiego Oświecenia* [*The Philosophy of the French Enlightenment*] (Warsaw, 1961), pp. 51–52.

sertation on legislation, for instance, he emphasized that the main-stay of collective morality was custom, and in the "Ode to Liberty" he even called the law an "unfeeling deity." Nevertheless, in his social philosophy he made use of such basic categories of the juridical world view as "natural law" and the "social contract" and drew political conclusions from them.

Radishchev thought of the original presocial state of mankind as a form of isolated existence in which men were not subject to any hierarchical pressures. Human imperfections, however, made it impossible for this state to continue; men formed nations and thus entered the social state. Radishchev had a wholly rationalist and nominalist view of the nation as "a collection of citizens"[5] rather than a supra-individual whole endowed with a "collective soul." A nation, as he put it, is a "collection of individuals," a political society composed of men who "have come together in order to safeguard their own interests and security by their collective efforts; it is a society submitting to authority. Since all men, however, are by nature free, and no one has the right to deprive them of this freedom, the setting up of a society always assumes real or tacit agreement."[6] As this quotation shows, "nation" for Radishchev was a juridico-political concept indistinguishable from society, which in its turn was inseparably bound up with state organization. Radishchev even attempted to make a legal definition of "fatherland" as a set of people linked together by mutually binding laws and civic duties. The essay *On What It Means to Be a Son of the Fatherland* is an excellent illustration of this. Only a man who enjoys civic rights can be a son of his fatherland, Radishchev argues. Peasants cannot claim this privilege since they bear "the yoke of serfdom"; they are not "members of the state," or even people, but "machines driven by their tormentors, lifeless corpses, draft oxen." In order to be a son of the fatherland it is not enough, however, to possess civic rights; it is equally important to show civic virtue by doing one's best to fulfill one's duties. Men who are without nobility or honor, who make no contribution to the general good, and who do not respect prevailing laws cannot therefore claim to be sons of the fatherland.

In keeping with current thinking, Radishchev distinguished between natural law and civil law, the first being an unwritten, innate right, an inalienable attribute of humanity, the second being a writ-

5. A. N. Radishchev, *Opyt o zakonodavstve*, in *Izbrannye sochineniia* (M-L, 1949), p. 619.

6. A. N. Radishchev, *Polnoe sobranie sochinenii* (M-L, 1938–52), vol. 1, p. 188.

ten code that only comes into being after the establishment of the social contract. The worst political system is despotism, since in it the arbitrary will of the ruler is placed above the law. Even in his first work—the notes to his translation of Mably's *Observations sur l'histoire de la Grèce*—Radishchev gives the following definition of autocracy: "Autocracy is the system most repugnant to human nature. ... If we relinquish part of our rights and our inborn sovereignty in favor of an all-embracing law, it is in order that it might be used to our advantage; to this end we conclude a tacit agreement with society. If this is infringed, then we too are released from our obligations. The injustice of the sovereign gives the people, who are his judges, the same or an even greater right over him than the law gives him to judge criminals. The sovereign is the first citizen of the people's commonwealth."[7] A poetic illustration of these words is to be found in the "Ode to Liberty," which contains a sublime defense of tyrannicide.

In the *Journey from St. Petersburg to Moscow*, a nobleman tells his sons who are about to enter government service: "The law, however bad it is, is the bond that holds society together."[8] In keeping with this assumption, Radishchev regarded legality—i.e. respect for civil law by all, including the sovereign—as the basic requirement for the proper functioning of society. But it is not enough to replace arbitrary rule by the rule of law; civil law cannot be contrary to natural law and must be founded on the agreement of the entire nation. Where natural law conflicted with civil law, Radishchev gave priority to the former. In the *Journey* he wrote:

Every man is born into the world equal to all others. All have the same bodily parts, all have reason and will. Consequently, apart from his relation to society, man is a being that depends on no one in his actions. But he puts limits to his own freedom of action, he agrees not to follow his own will in everything, he subjects himself to the commands of his equals; in a word, he becomes a citizen. For what reason does he control his passions? Why does he set up a governing authority over himself? Why, though free to see fulfillment of his will, does he confine himself within the bounds of obedience? For his own advantage, reason will say; for his own advantage, inner feeling will say; for his own advantage, wise legislation will say. Consequently, wherever being a citizen is not to his advantage, he is not a citizen. ... If the law is unable or unwilling to protect him, or if its power cannot furnish him immediate aid in the face of clear and present danger, then the citizen has recourse to the natural law of self-defense, self-preservation, and well-being. . . . No

7. Quoted in Blagoy, *Istoriia russkoi literatury XVIII veka* (M, 1951), p. 539.
8. Radishchev, *Journey*, p. 120.

matter in what estate heaven may have decreed a citizen's birth, he is and will always remain a man; and so long as he is a man, the law of nature, as an abundant wellspring of goodness, will never run dry in him, and whosoever dares wound him in his natural and inviolable right is a criminal.[9]

This quotation comes from the chapter headed "Zaitsevo," in which Radishchev tells the story of a cruel landowner (the assessor) who was killed by his peasants. The narrator comments as follows on this incident: " . . . the peasants who killed the beastly assessor are not guilty before the law. On rational grounds my heart finds them not guilty and the death of the assessor, although violent, is just."[10]

Among the natural and inviolable rights of man Radishchev included freedom of conscience and total freedom of speech, which is dealt with in the *Journey* in the chapter entitled "Torzhok." Censorship, Radishchev suggested, sprang from the same source as the Inquisition and was thought up by priests, who "have always been the inventors of fetters with which they have at various times burdened the human mind, . . . [and] clipped its wings lest it should soar aloft to greatness and freedom."[11] Truth and virtue have no need of censorship, for they are capable of undertaking their own defense. Freedom of thought is only terifying to a ruler whose "rapacity makes him break the law" and betray the general good, whom flattery has deprived of the power to distinguish between good and evil. "In the province of truth, in the kingdom of thought and spirit, no earthly power can or should pass judgment."[12] Censorship had been appointed nursemaid to reason and imagination, "but where there are nurses, there are babies and leading strings that often lead to crooked legs; where there are guardians, there are minors and immature minds unable to take care of themselves. If there are always to be nurses and guardians, then the child will walk with leading strings for a long time and will grow up to be a cripple."[13] Radishchev's conclusion was explicit: "Let anyone print anything that enters his head. If anyone finds himself insulted in print, let him get his redress at law."[14]

Radishchev's ideal political system was a republic. He disagreed sharply with Rousseau's view that republics are only feasible in small countries and that large states must inevitably be governed by a monarch. He was inclined to idealize ancient Rome and, like the

9. *Ibid.*, pp. 102–3.
10. *Ibid.*, p. 103.
11. *Ibid.*, p. 172.

12. *Ibid.*, p. 103.
13. *Ibid.*, p. 165.
14. *Ibid.*, p. 167.

Decembrists, the "merchant republics" of Novgorod and Pskov. "It is known from the *Chronicles*," he wrote in the *Journey*, "that Novgorod had a popular government. They had princes, but these had little power. All the power of government was vested in the civil and military officials (*posadniki* and *tysiatskie*). The people in its assembly, the *veche*, was the real sovereign."[15] This was proof that Russians possessed an innate love of liberty and that only brute force had brought absolutism to power. Because of his dislike of absolutism, Radishchev was also critical of Peter the Great (although he appreciated his greatness and fully approved of his reforms). In the *Letter to a Friend Living in Tobolsk* he says that Peter would have deserved greater praise if he had established safeguards for individual liberty. Not that there had ever been a monarch who had voluntarily restricted his authority, he could not help adding.

Radishchev's criticism of Peter has nothing in common, of course, with Shcherbatov's earlier attack. Far from idealizing ancient boyar freedom, Radishchev makes it clear that he fully approves of Peter's measures against the hereditary nobility, whom he refers to as "superannuated and fallen into contempt."[16] At the beginning of the *Journey*, he holds up to ridicule a defender of the ancient nobility who complains that through the Table of Ranks Peter "opened the way for everyone to obtain a noble title, and, so to speak, trampled the old nobility into the mud."[17] Radishchev advises him to sell his genealogical tables to peddlers as wrapping paper and concludes that "boasting of one's ancient lineage" is an evil fortunately almost eradicated in Russia.

The two countries Radishchev approved of most warmly were England and the United States, both of which he praised for assuring their citizens the widest range of civil rights and political freedoms. This preference even led him to make the unusual suggestion that the first foreign language taught to children should be not French but English, since English shows "the elasticity of the spirit of freedom."[18] In his defense of freedom of speech there are echoes of Milton, and in the "Ode to Liberty" we find praise of the English Revolution. Like Raynal, he was severe in his condemnation of slavery, but this did not dampen his enthusiasm for the American Revolution and the American Constitution. George Washington was one of his great heroes.

Radishchev's attitude toward the French Revolution, on the other

15. *Ibid.*, p. 83.
16. *Ibid.*, p. 144.

17. *Ibid.*, p. 45.
18. *Ibid.*, p. 115.

hand, was somewhat ambivalent. He approved of its aims, but in the *Journey* expressed regret that "the National Assembly, proceeding just as autocratically as the King before it," had violated the principle of freedom of speech."[19]

Radishchev's philosophy of history is well summed up in the aphorism "This is the law of nature: from tyranny, freedom is born, from freedom, slavery. . . ."[20] This formulation shows the influence of the cyclical theory of history and the characteristic identification of the laws of history with the laws of an essentially unchanging Nature. Throughout Radishchev's work we find evidence of this typically eighteenth-century belief in the immutable laws of nature, in an abstract Human Nature, an abstract Reason, and an abstract Virtue. Although attempts have been made to discover elements of historicism in his world view, these do not seem convincing. Radishchev boldly pitted an idealized Reason and Virtue against real history; his moral absolutism permitted no historical justification for stupidity or crime, no understanding of historical relativity. This lack of historical perspective was of course closely bound up with the revolutionary boldness of his ideas, as tended to be the rule in the eighteenth century. Liberal conservatives such as Montesquieu might have a sense of historical relativity, but there was no trace of it in the ideology of the Jacobins. Radishchev condemned Robespierre for his use of terror, but shared with the Jacobins something that postrevolutionary conservative thinkers were to call "intellectual terrorism"—an uncompromising adherence to principle and unbending negation.

RADISHCHEV'S VIEWS ON ETHICS AND EDUCATION

Radishchev's conception of society might be called nominalism or sociological individualism; he saw society not as a supraindividual, organic, and ordered whole but as a collection of individuals whose welfare was its greatest concern. Some of his statements seem almost to anticipate Chernyshevsky's belief that national wealth cannot be considered apart from the welfare of the common people. In the *Journey* he wrote: "What good does it do the country if every year a few thousand more bushels of grain are grown, when those who produce it are valued on a par with the ox whose job it is to break the heavy furrow? Or do we think our citizens happy because our granaries are full and their stomachs empty?"[21]

19. *Ibid.*, p. 186.   21. *Ibid.*, p. 159.
20. *Ibid.*, p. 200.

Such "sociological individualism" (which was in fact one of the characteristic features of Enlightenment thought) was not inevitably accompanied by individualism in the sphere of ethics or education. Quite the contrary: it often went hand in hand with a heroic belief in an abstract "Virtue" and a sense of man's social commitment. Radishchev was one of the Enlightenment thinkers who put special stress on this aspect.

It is particularly interesting, in this context, to examine Radishchev's criticism of the educational views in Rousseau's *Emile*. In his autobiographical *Journal of a Single Week*, Radishchev criticizes Rousseau's notion that man is by nature a recluse and prizes nothing so much as complete independence of other people. The *Journal* is an account of the sufferings of loneliness: the hero tries to follow Rousseau's advice to seek consolation "within himself" but concludes that the advice is bad, that consolation and oblivion must be sought among men, and that loneliness is not joy, but "ruin, death, and inferno." Although the *Journal* is a product of sentimentalism, it is also critical of exaggerated sensibility. Radishchev rejects the excesses of self-analysis, the individualistic apotheosis of loneliness, and the "poetry of the tomb," though he accepts the sentimental cult of friendship and the ideal of the "tender heart" sympathetic to the sufferings of humanity—in a word, the social aspect of the cult of sentimentality.

Eighteenth-century historical idealism assumed that the world was ruled by ideas and that its future thus depended largely on the type of education provided for the younger generation. In keeping with these assumptions, educational problems have an important place in Radishchev's work.

In the *Journey from St. Petersburg to Moscow*, Radishchev sets out his educational views in a farewell speech made by a nobleman from Kresttsy to his two sons. Following Rousseau, he recommends simplicity, avoidance of luxury, physical labor in the household and on the land, and disdain for "high society." He recommends moderation in the passions, but, like Helvetius, opposes their repression; for though "excess in passion is destructive, absence of passion is moral death."[22] "The highest end of human action," he insists, is virtue; virtue, however, has a social as well as a personal aspect, and since social virtue is often associated with vanity and ambition, a truly virtuous man is one in whom both aspects are fused. It is interesting to note that the nobleman's advice makes no mention of religion. Radishchev's ethic is the secular ideal of the autonomous

22. *Ibid.*, p. 118.

individual motivated by virtue, personally responsible for his actions, and ready to die rather than capitulate.

It should be stressed that this ethic was not one-sidedly rationalistic. In contrast to the mechanical materialists of the Enlightenment—philosophers such as Helvetius, Holbach, or La Mettrie—Radishchev did not base his moral philosophy on rational self-interest and calculated advantage. In fact, he appealed to unselfish motives and accepted the existence of an inner voice of conscience, an autonomous moral element inseparable from man's humanity. In the *Journey* he wrote: "Oh if man would but look into his soul more frequently, and confess his deeds to his implacable judge, his conscience! Transformed by its thunderous voice into an immovable pillar, he would no longer dare to commit secret crimes; destruction and devastation would become rare. . . . "[23]

It is clear, therefore, that the abstract rationalism which was the dominant feature of Radishchev's views on society and history became modified in his views on ethics. In his conception of man he allowed a place to the heart as well as the head. He was in fact closer to Rousseau than to the encyclopedists: no doubt that is why he was at one time attracted to the Masonic movement,[24] and why his writings reveal many of the features we normally associate with sentimentalism.

RADICAL REFORM OR REVOLUTION?

Radishchev was perhaps most original in his treatment of Russia's foremost social problem—the condition of the peasants—which is the main theme of the *Journey from St. Petersburg to Moscow.* That is why the book seemed to represent such a serious threat to Catherine II, for whom the Pugachev rebellion was still a vivid memory.

Radishchev called the peasants "dead to the law." In a series of unbearably moving scenes of peasant life he drew a gloomy picture of what it meant to be a serf. His burning indignation reaches its climax in his bitter indictment of the gentry:

Ravening beasts, insatiable leeches, what do we leave for the peasants? What we cannot take from them, the air. We frequently take from them not only the gifts of the earth, bread and water, but also the very light.

23. *Ibid.*, p. 221.
24. We know very little about Radishchev's links with the Masonic movement except that he attended the "Urania" lodge, which included atheists among its members, and that he was hostile to Masonic mysticism.

The law forbids us to take their life—that is, to take it suddenly. But there are so many ways to take it from them by degrees! On one side there is almost unlimited power; on the other, helpless impotence. For the landlord is to the peasant at once legislator, judge, executor of his own judgment, and, if he so desires, a plaintiff against whom the defendant dare say nothing. It is the lot of one cast into fetters, of one thrown into a dismal dungeon: the lot of the ox under the yoke.[25]

In the *Journey* Radishchev describes two possible variants of a solution to the peasant question. The first is a reformist solution presented in the chapter called "Khotilov." In a bundle of papers left behind by another, earlier traveler, Radishchev finds drafts of laws referring to the gradual abolition of serfdom. According to these drafts the first thing to be abolished would be "domestic serfdom"—i.e. the sale of peasants without dwelling or land, frequently on their own, into domestic service. Instead, a peasant who was taken into the landlord's house as a servant or artisan would at once become free. Another law would ensure the legal protection of the peasants and their property by allowing them to own the plots they cultivated for their own maintenance. Landlords would no longer have unlimited jurisdiction over their serfs, who would enjoy the right to be judged by their peers, that is in courts in which manorial peasants would also be chosen to serve. These preliminary measures were to be followed by the complete abolition of serfdom.

As this summary of his views shows, Radishchev's plans (in contrast to nineteenth-century land reform proposals) envisaged the granting of land to peasants even before the abolition of serfdom. He was, of course, equally opposed to the extortion of labor dues and urged—on humanitarian as well as economic grounds—that they be replaced by rents.

Radishchev was not convinced that this solution had any real hope of success. Freedom, he wrote, is to be expected not from the counsels of the great landed proprietors, but rather "from the heavy burden of slavery itself."[26] After outlining the proposals for gradual reforms, he relates the story of a certain "famous landowner" who owed his successes to his cruel exploitation of his peasants, and concludes by calling on the peasants to revenge themselves on their landlord: "Destroy the tools of his agriculture, burn his barns, silos, and granaries, and scatter their ashes over the fields where he practiced his tortures."[27] The time might come, he even suggested, when a

25. Radishchev, *Journey*, pp. 220–21.   27. *Ibid.*, p. 160.
26. *Ibid.*, p. 191.

victorious peasant uprising would lead to the emergence of a new intellectual elite from among the masses to replace the old elite destroyed during the revolution: "Oh, if the slaves weighted down with fetters, raging in their despair, would, with the iron that bars their freedom, crush our heads, the heads of their inhuman masters, and redden their fields with our blood! What would the country lose by that? Soon great men would arise from among them, to take the place of the murdered generations; but they would be of another mind and without the right to oppress others. This is no dream; my vision penetrates the dense curtain of time that veils the future from our eyes. I look through the space of a whole century."[28]

Some scholars feel that there is a contradiction between the proposals in the *Journey* for a reformist solution to the peasant problem and Radishchev's expectation and indeed moral justification of revolution. Makogonenko, for instance, suggests that the plans outlined in the "Khotilov" chapter do not have the support of the author but are only one of the illusions of which the narrator is cured in later chapters.[29] Although in recent years this point of view has found many energetic supporters,[30] it does not seem entirely convincing. There is perhaps more to be said for the standpoint adopted by another outstanding authority on eighteenth-century Russian literature, Dmitry Blagoy, who, while allowing that Radishchev was skeptical about the chances of reform, nevertheless does not present him as an absolutely consistent and unswerving revolutionary. A careful reading of the *Journey* shows that its author expected and justified revolution, but certainly would have preferred to avoid bloodshed; that he foresaw a victorious revolution *in the future*, but knowing that there was no immediate hope of a successful uprising, wished to ease the peasants' suffering right away. Radishchev perhaps doubted whether the ruling elite was capable of undertaking the necessary reforms, but at the same time he realized that no one else could do so. The *Journey* was therefore conceived as an appeal to the sovereign and to the nobility, an appeal rendered more urgent by its description of the threat of a popular rebellion. The appearance of the book coincided with the French Revolution, and this made the threat even more real. The literary form chosen by Radishchev was very convenient, since it enabled him to present specific issues from various points of view

28. *Ibid.*, p. 209.

29. See G. Makogonenko, *Radishchev. Ocherk zhizni i tvorchestva* (M, 1949).

30. See Y. F. Karakin and E. G. Plimak, *Zapretnaia mysl' obretaet svobodu. 175 let bor'by vokrug ideinogo naslediia Radishcheva* (M, 1966.)

without necessarily expressing his own standpoint. It should also be stressed that the plans outlined in "Khotilov" were extremely radical for those years—far more radical than the reforms suggested by the Decembrists, and more generous than the land reform of 1861, which did not grant the peasants all the land they had cultivated for themselves as serfs.

On social issues Radishchev was also more radical than the encyclopedists. This can be seen most clearly in his attitude to the common people, whom the encyclopedists—ideological representatives of a wealthy and enlightened middle class—regarded with distaste, fear, and even contempt (some of Voltaire's comments are particularly revealing in this respect). On the other hand, there is a clear dividing line between Radishchev and the extreme radical wing of the French Enlightenment represented by the utopian communists—Morelly and Mably. The absence of radical utopian motifs in Radishchev's writings are largely the result of his concentration on the peasant issue. His outlook expressed the interests and hopes of the peasants and other small producers who were anxious to ensure the just and more widespread distribution of private property rather than its abolition.

That Radishchev only expressed peasant hopes and aspirations indirectly is, of course, self-evident. In view of his social background he might be called the first Russian gentry revolutionary. His rupture with his own class was so radical, however (far more so than in the case of the Decembrists, the classic representatives of gentry revolutionism), that one should really abandon the word "gentry" and simply call him Russia's first revolutionary intellectual. He was a wonderful example of the process described by Herzen, by which a "universalist education" uprooted thinking Russians from their "immoral soil" and turned them into opponents of official Russia.[31] In some respects his ideas anticipated the views of the revolutionary democrats of the 1860's.

Radishchev's tragedy was that he stood alone. In his days the feudal system in Russia was still firmly established and circumstances were not favorable to the emergence of an organized radical movement. The Jacobin Terror and Napoleon's imperial ambitions disappointed his early hopes in the French Revolution. It is understandable, therefore, that on his return from banishment, when Paul was succeeded by Alexander I—who had been brought up on the ideas of the Enlightenment—Radishchev was ready to put his trust once again in an enlightened monarchy. In his fine poem "The

31. See A. Herzen, *Sobranie sochinenii* (30 vols.; M, 1954–65), vol. 2, p. 155.

Eighteenth Century," he compared the bygone age to a raging river swollen with blood: "Happiness, virtue, and freedom were engulfed in the waters' depths." The age was not without its achievements, however. Two Russian rulers—Peter and Catherine—stood like two unyielding rocks amid the bloody waters and already reflected the rays of the future dawn. Yet Radishchev's optimism rested on very fragile foundations. Unwilling to face new disappointments, he committed suicide a year after his return to St. Petersburg.

THE TREATISE ON IMMORTALITY

The treatise *On Man, His Mortality and Immortality* stands apart in Radishchev's work. This essay, which was written in Siberia, undoubtedly represents the highest achievement of Russian Enlightenment thought in the sphere of pure philosophical speculation. Its conclusion states that the human soul is immortal, and that since its goal is self-perfection it will continue to perfect itself even after the death of the body.

Radishchev reaches this conclusion by a very involved argument. Pushkin aptly observed that "although Radishchev revolts against materialism, the disciple of Helvetius is still visible. He much prefers to expound arguments in favor of absolute atheism than to refute them."[32]

The essay *On Man* consists of four parts. In the first two the author—mainly following Holbach—puts forward the argument against immortality. In his ontology he takes as his starting point the basic thesis of materialism, which he formulates as follows: "Things exist independently of our knowledge of them—they exist in their own right."[33] In his epistemology he takes the sensationalist position that there is nothing in the mind that was not previously in the senses. From these premises he demonstrates that man is a wholly mortal being.

In the third part of his essay Radishchev attempts to refute this conclusion without, however, abandoning his ontological or epistemological premises. He does this by differentiating between the concepts "soul" and "spirit" with the help of the hylozoist thesis that every particle of matter is animated to a greater or lesser degree. According to this argument nothing in nature perishes;

---

32. From Pushkin's article "Aleksandr Radishchev." Perhaps it would be more accurate to say that Radishchev's arguments in favor of atheism were more convincing, rather than more enthusiastic.

33. Radishchev, *Izbrannye sochineniia*, p. 423.

it merely disintegrates into small particles. After death man's physical remains fuse with matter while his spiritual element fuses with the spirit of the universe that animates all of nature. This cannot be called individual immortality; man's individual soul is mortal and only the spirit—the spiritual element in its universal embodiment—has eternal life.

This conclusion did not, however, satisfy Radishchev, who understood man's craving for individual immortality. In order to prove its possibility, he made use of Moses Mendelssohn's essay *Phaedon, or the Immortality of the Soul* and works by Leibniz and Bonnet. The human soul is a simple substance, Radishchev's argument runs, and cannot therefore disintegrate or be deprived of its individual existence; its goal is unceasing self-perfection, so that its existence after physical death is more perfect than temporal existence, just as the life of a butterfly is more perfect than that of a caterpillar or chrysalis. Since the instrument of the soul's perfection is the body, in its life after death the soul will also be endowed with some kind of corporeal existence, superior to human existence. This idea, which in Radishchev's essay is barely touched upon, is related to Bonnet's conception of immortality as a form of progressive reincarnation—an unceasing upward progress through a series of different incarnations—and his hypothesis that in the "great chain of being" there must be reasoning beings more perfect than man.

Radishchev makes it clear that these are only conjectures, a matter of faith rather than knowledge. He proclaims his belief in the immortality of the soul and the continued process of perfection after death because they seem to him to be essential prerequisites of morality; nevertheless, he admits that these are beliefs for which no adequate theoretical arguments can be deduced.

This line of argument was very characteristic of the moral philosophy of the Enlightenment. Nikolai Novikov justified his belief in immortality in similar terms. There is also a certain analogy between Radishchev's treatise and the philosophy of Kant. Kant recognized the existence of God and immortality of the soul as "postulates of practical reason"; in other words, he recognized them because (like Radishchev) he regarded them as a guarantee of morality.

In eighteenth-century Russia, where philosophy was still in its infancy, the essay *On Man* was something unique. In it Radishchev displayed his great talent and erudition: he utilized the arguments of nearly all leading French and German eighteenth-century thinkers and showed his knowledge of classical Greek philosophy. His systematic exposition of arguments both for and against immortality enabled him to show the controversial nature of the problem. In spite of this, however, the work did not exert any influence on the evolution of Russian thought—the heirs to Radishchev's democratic and libertarian ideas were not concerned with the problem of immortality, whereas religious philosophers did not seek inspiration in the works of Enlightenment thinkers.

CHAPTER 3

GENTRY CONSERVATIVES
AND GENTRY REVOLUTIONARIES

The reign of Alexander I (1801–25) was essentially a period of transition. On the one hand it ushered in the new nineteenth century, but on the other it represented a continuation and even culmination of eighteenth-century intellectual trends. This dual nature of the age is expressed above all in its political ideas, especially in the conservatism of Karamzin and the revolutionary ideas of the Decembrists. Karamzin's backward-looking conservatism, with its idealization of the reign of Catherine, nevertheless also contained the germs of a new nineteenth-century conservatism. The Decembrist movement was the first revolutionary organization in Russia, but at the same time represented a continuation of the eighteenth-century aristocratic opposition. For all their disparity, the two trends had something in common: both Karamzin's conservatism and the revolutionary ideas of the Decembrists expressed the intellectual ferment and political ambitions of the educated Westernized gentry, which had been stimulated by the Napoleonic Wars and the new emperor's liberal gestures and promises of reform.

NIKOLAI KARAMZIN

NIKOLAI KARAMZIN (1766–1826) was Russia's official government historian during the reign of Alexander. In his literary work he was the most typical representative of Russian sentimentalism, a trend with which Radishchev, too, had been associated. Unlike the latter, however, the young Karamzin was less interested in civic virtue or social reform than in the ideal of moral self-perfection. As a young man he rejected "the world's clamor" in favor of solitary meditation and "sweet melancholy, the passion of tender souls." This pose of sentimental egocentricity dominates the *Letters from a Russian Traveler*, in which Karamzin describes his travels in Europe in the years 1789–90. It is instructive to compare the *Letters* with Radishchev's *Journey from St. Petersburg to Moscow*, also an account of travels. "I looked about me," Radishchev wrote, "and my soul was wounded by suffering humanity."[1] Karamzin, on the other hand, was completely uninterested in social problems (although the French Revolution broke out during his stay in Europe). The *Letters* are only a "lyrical pamphlet," he writes, an account of sub-jective impressions: "They are a mirror of my soul during the last eighteen months. Twenty years from now (if I should live that long) they will still be a delight to me—even if only to me. I shall peruse them and I shall see what kind of person I was, what I thought and what I dreamed. And between ourselves, what is more interesting to man than his own self?"[2]

Outside events, however, forced Karamzin to think in social and political categories. The beginning of the French Revolution might have awakened some vague idealistic sympathies in him, but the second phase—the guillotining of the king and the Jacobin Terror —filled him with horror. "The Revolution clarified our ideas," was how he himself described the profound change that took place in his system of values. He abandoned his sentimental and rather ab-stract humanitarianism in favor of an ardent defense of autocracy as the only permanent mainstay of the old order. Where formerly he had believed in Europe, he now criticized it as a hotbed of revolu-tion, chaos, and disintegration, and praised Russia as the very an-tithesis—a country with a settled social order, enlightened absolutist government, and unshaken Christian beliefs.

Karamzin was strengthened in his conservative nationalism by Russia's reverses in the Napoleonic Wars and by Tsar Alexander's early liberalism, particularly the intended juridical and administra-tive reforms that Mikhail Speransky was then planning at the em-peror's behest. The conservative opposition was indignant that the plans for the reorganization of the state were modeled on the Code Napoléon, sponsored by and named after the man who was not only Russia's enemy, but also a usurper and heir to the French Revolution. In 1811, when Speransky's influence was at its height, Karamzin gave expression to this widespread mood of dissatisfaction in his *Memoir on Ancient and Modern Russia*, in which he set out in detail his reflections on Russian history and some bold and search-ing criticism of the government's policies. The leitmotivs of the

1. A. N. Radishchev, *A Journey from St. Petersburg to Moscow*, trans. by Leo Wiener, ed. by Roderick Page Thaler (Cambridge, Mass., 1958), p. 5.
2. N. M. Karamzin, *Letters of a Russian Traveler*, trans. by Florence Jonas (New York, 1957), p. 340.

Memoir are belief in the salutary force of autocracy and an extreme notion of historical continuity—so extreme that it rejects all legislation that does not spring from national traditions but is based on foreign theoretical premises or models. In what was no doubt an exaggerated fear that Alexander was aiming to impose constitutional limitations on autocracy, Karamzin addressed him as follows:

If Alexander, inspired by generous hatred for the abuses of autocracy, should lift a pen and prescribe himself laws other than those of God and his conscience, then the true virtuous citizen of Russia would presume to stop his hand to say: "Sire! You exceed the limits of your authority. Russia, taught by long disasters, vested before the holy altar the power of autocracy in your ancestor, asking him that he rule her supremely, indivisibly. This covenant is the foundation of your authority, you have no other; you may do everything, but you may not limit your authority by law."[3]

In order to understand this strange standpoint, one must realize that Karamzin thought of autocracy as undivided rather than unlimited power. The tsar's authority was absolute in affairs of state, but did not extend to the private sphere, which was outside the realm of politics. If we accept this scheme, we realize why from Karamzin's point of view the freedom of the individual (this was, of course, understood to refer only to members of the gentry) was infinitely greater under autocracy than under the Jacobins' "sovereignty of the people." It was consistent with his early sentimentalism—when he had prized isolation and apolitical freedom in a quiet rural setting—that he should now fear above all the "tyranny of popular rule" and regard the monarchy as a "sheet anchor."

Even in the political sphere, however, Karamzin felt that the sovereign should avoid arbitrary rule. While his authority was not limited by any written laws or constitution, it was limited by an unwritten historical tradition that was laid down in custom and moral convictions. A monarch who did not take account of this tradition—and a strong part of it was the triple alliance between autocracy, nobility, and Orthodox Church—was in danger of becoming a despot. In the name of these notions Karamzin inveighed against the "hydra of aristocracy"—the nobility's attempts to limit absolutism by legal restrictions—but also against the policies of those tsars who had ruled against the wishes and interests of the nobility. He called Ivan the Terrible a tyrant worse than Caligula or Nero, but argued that this

3. R. Pipes, *Karamzin's Memoir on Ancient and Modern Russia* (Cambridge, Mass., 1959), p. 139.

did not absolve Kurbsky from the charge of treason.[4] Peter the Great, too, Karamzin considered a despotic ruler; he gave him credit for his modernization of Russia, but considered his methods a brutal infringement of national traditions and an illegal incursion of political authority into the private sphere.

It should be added that Karamzin defended absolutism not as the ideal political system but merely as a historical necessity arising out of human imperfections. It is interesting, therefore, to see what he thought of the folkmoots or *veche* (whose role in Kievan Russia he greatly emphasized), and also of the ancient Russian "merchant republics" of Novgorod and Pskov. In his tale *Marfa, or the Subjugation of Novgorod* (1803), he seems to side with the victorious principle of autocracy, but he also praises the "republican virtues" of the citizens of Novgorod. The downfall of their "exuberant freedom" is painted in a spirit of elegiac melancholy. There are similar descriptions of the struggle of autocracy with old Russian "republican" institutions in the *Memoir* and in the twelve-volume *History of the Russian State*. In a letter written toward the end of his life Karamzin even stated that "at heart he had remained a republican."

The fundamental concepts underlying Karamzin's conservatism—the belief in historical continuity and the separation of politics (the legitimate sphere of absolutist rule) from private life—fulfilled a dual function. On the one hand, they represented an attempt (albeit timid and partial) to protect the individual against the arbitrary interference of authority; on the other, they were a determined protest against any move to change the status quo (which was favorable to the gentry) by even the most minor reforms. In particular Karamzin stressed historical continuity as a powerful argument against any limitation of serfdom. Through Karamzin, the Russian gentry renounced their struggle for political rights but in return demanded guarantees that their social position would continue to be stable and indeed strengthened.

In justice to Karamzin, it must be said that he represented an enlightened conservatism far removed from the reactionary anti-Western obscurantism of such men as Arakcheev, Magnitsky, and Runich, whose influence on the government's educational policies was to become more and more disastrous during the last years of

4. Prince Andrei Kurbsky, the commander of the Muscovite army against the Livonian Order, fled to Poland when he heard of the bloody persecution of the boyars by Ivan the Terrible. In his remarkable correspondence with the Tsar, he eloquently defended the rights of the boyars and justified his flight to Poland by the ancient right of the nobility to refuse to serve an unjust monarch.

his life. Nor can there be any comparison between his nationalist sentiments and the chauvinistic xenophobia that filled the columns of S. N. Glinka's *Russian Messenger (Russkii Vestnik)*. Karamzin's "loyal submission" was far from servile, and his bold and even bitter criticism of the tsar in the *Memoir* prevented it from being published for many years. His sentimental "republicanism" did not stop him from praising autocracy as the "Palladium of Russia," but he was still unorthodox enough to be denounced by an overzealous informer as a man whose works were full of "Jacobin poison" and should be burned.

A comparison between Karamzin and the Decembrists makes it clear how widely divergent were the views of these two representatives of the Russian gentry. Whereas Karamzin opposed the emperor's projected reforms because he thought them too far-reaching, the Decembrist movement emerged because of doubt about the sincerity of these plans and gained ground as the government's policies became increasingly reactionary. And yet the Decembrists eagerly read the ninth volume of Karamzin's *History* and were delighted by his criticism of Ivan the Terrible. The earlier volumes, too, provided them with much interesting information on the "republican traditions" of Russian history, even if Karamzin's judgments did not often agree with theirs. Pushkin, who had many contacts with the Decembrists, wrote that the *History* was an absolute revelation: "You would have said that Karamzin discovered ancient Russia as Columbus discovered America."

THE DECEMBRISTS

A discussion of the history of the Decembrist movement, named after the ill-fated uprising that took place in December 1825, lies outside the scope of this book.[5] In the present context we shall only deal with the mature ideology of the Decembrists in the years immediately preceding the revolt, without going more deeply into the genesis or evolution of their theories. In those last years, the idea of an armed revolt against the tsar began to gain ground among the members of the movement. They were encouraged by the example of military rebellions in Spain and Naples (1820), the revolution in the kingdom of Piedmont (1821), the Greek uprising (1821), and also the mutiny in the Semenovsky guard regiment in 1820. The Union of Welfare, founded in 1818 as the successor to the Union

5. The main books on the Decembrists in English are A. G. Mazour, *The First Russian Revolution, 1825* (2d ed., Stanford, Calif., 1961), and M. Raeff, *The Decembrist Movement* (Englewood Cliffs, N.J., 1966).

of Salvation founded two years earlier, was unsuited to the new aims of the movement. It therefore became desirable to dissolve it in order to shed uncertain or unreliable members and to form a new organization. In 1821 the Union of Welfare was succeeded by two secret societies consisting largely of army officers, which remained in close touch with each other. These were the Northern Society in St. Petersburg and the Southern Society in Tulchin, the headquarters of the Second Army in the Ukraine. The membership of the Northern Society represented a wide range of political views, but was on the whole far less radical than the Southern Society grouped around Colonel Pavel Pestel. For the sake of clarity, therefore, it will be more convenient to discuss the views of each of these groups separately.

The Northern Society

In the ideology of the Northern Society especially there were certain elements reminiscent of the views of the aristocratic opposition of the reign of Catherine II. Many of the members in this branch of the Decembrist movement were descendants of once powerful and now impoverished boyar families, some even tracing their descent from the legendary Prince Rurik (Prince Sergei Trubetskoi, Prince Evgeny Obolensky, and Prince Aleksandr Odoevsky). Nikita Muraviev claimed that the movement was rooted in the traditions of Novgorod and Pskov, of the twelfth-century Boyar Duma, of the constitutional demands presented to Anne by the Moscow nobles in 1730, and of the constitutional plans of the Panin brothers and the eighteenth-century aristocratic opposition. The poet Kondraty Ryleev painted an idealized portrait of Prince Andrei Kurbsky (the leader of the boyar revolt against Ivan the Terrible) and even devoted one of his "Elegies" to him (modeled on the "Historical Songs" of the Polish poet Julian Niemcewicz). In his evidence before the Investigating Commission after the suppression of the revolt, Petr Kakhovsky stated that the movement was primarily a response to the high-handedness of the bureaucracy, the lack of respect for ancient gentry freedom, and the favoritism shown to foreigners. Another Northern Decembrist, the writer and literary critic Aleksandr Bestuzhev (who later continued to publish his works under the pseudonym "Marlinsky"), wrote that his aim was "monarchy tempered by aristocracy." These and similar facts explain Pushkin's view, expressed in the 1830's, that the Decembrist revolt had been the last episode in the age-old struggle between autocracy and boyars.

There is little doubt that memories of ancient "liberties" and dislike of the bureaucracy, whose social status was a reward for servility and careerism, heped to fan the Decembrists' hatred of tsarist despotism. This does not mean that they were only motivated by egoistic class interests (the view held by M. N. Pokrovsky and the so-called "vulgar-sociological" school of Soviet historiography). Even those Decembrists who went furthest in idealizing ancient liberties had no wish to revive the past; their plans to overthrow despotism were to benefit the whole nation, not only the nobiity, and gave an important place to the abolition of serfdom. If the political program of the Decembrists had been put into effect, it would have created a base for the rapid development of capitalism, which not only would have taken away the nobility's political privileges but also would have undermined its economic position. Although its gentry origins made for certain obvious limitations, Decembrist ideology was essentially an example of modern liberalism. Moreover, insofar as it postulated the overthrow of autocracy—the main pillar of the old order—it was also a revolutionary ideology. Altogether it was a phenomenon familiar from Polish history: a revolutionary antifeudal ideology whose main exponents were members of a privileged class—"the best sons of the gentry," or "gentry revolutionaries," as Lenin called them.

The reconciliation of disparate elements was made easier by the fact that the Decembrists used the term "republic" loosely, without appearing to be fully aware that there were essential differences between, for instance, the Roman republic, the Polish gentry republic, the old Russian city states, and modern bourgeois republics. The theorists of the Northern Society made no distinction between criticism of absolutism from the standpoint of the gentry and similar criticism from a bourgeois point of view. Hence they saw no difficulty in reconciling liberal notions taken largely from the works of Bentham, Benjamin Constant, and Adam Smith with an idealization of former feudal liberties and a belief in the role of the aristocracy as a "curb on despotism." The theoretical premise here was the "juridical world view" of the Enlightenment, according to which legal and political forms determined the revolution of society.

The most important document reflecting the views of the Northern Society was the draft constitution prepared by Nikita Muraviev. Muraviev's draft abolished serfdom in all its forms but made no mention of any land grants. On the contrary, it stated clearly that all land would remain in the possession of the gentry; it was only in the face of pressure from the more radical members of the Society that an amendment was introduced permitting peasants to own their homestead and two desentines (about five acres) of arable land. In view of the backward state of agriculture in Russia at the time, such a tiny holding was quite inadequate to support a family. It will be seen from this that Muraviev was anxious to ensure the continued economic dependence of the peasantry on their masters even after the abolition of serfdom. One of the paragraphs in the constitution (removed in the final draft) even stated that future legislation would decide the amount of indemnity for loss of labor a peasant would have to pay his landlord if he wished to leave his village.

Another feature of Muraviev's constitution was the high level at which property qualifications for citizenship were fixed. Only men who owned real estate worth at least 500 silver rubles or other property worth twice that sum were allowed to use the title "citizen." Similar qualifications governing recruitment to the civil service were fixed on a rising scale: the highest offices were to be open only to men with estates worth at least 60,000 silver rubles! In a later version of the draft Muraviev lowered this barrier and conferred the title "citizen" on all inhabitants of the Russian state. Even this version, however, granted full voting rights only to landowners and capitalists and deprived a considerable proportion of the population of an active part in politics. The only office open to "anyone without exception or distinction" was that of head of a commune.

Muraviev modeled his plan for a political system on the United States. The future Russia was to be a federation of fourteen states, each of which was to have its own capital. For example, there was to be a Volkhov state, whose capital would be in "the city of St. Peter," a Charnov state wtih its capital in Kiev, and a Ukrainian state with its capital in Kharkov (the state boundaries did not coincide with ethnic boundaries). The Kingdom of Poland (within ethnic boundaries) was to remain within the federation, but was to have a greater measure of independence than the other states. Each state was to have a two-chamber parliament, which would enjoy independence in economic, administrative, and cultural matters but would not have legislative powers. The supreme authority in the federation as a whole was to be vested in a Popular Assembly (*Narodnoe Veche*) made up of a Supreme Duma and a House of Representatives. The tsar would be no more than the federation's leading official. In order to avoid the pernicious influence of court cliques, persons in the imperial service were to be temporarily deprived of political rights. Moreover, there was even a clause forbidding the emperor to travel abroad, so that he might not give heed to the evil promptings of foreigners.

The most progressive feature of Muraviev's constitution was its stand on civil liberties. There was to be complete freedom of worship, assembly, and speech; censorship was to be abolished; and there was to be no state interference in research, art, or teaching. On social issues, however, and especially on the peasant issue, Muraviev's plan revealed the limitations of the gentry mentality all too clearly. The conviction that the peasants ought to be overjoyed merely at the abolition of serfdom was shared by many Decembrists. Yakushkin, for instance, could not conceal his exasperation at his peasants' demand for land when he offered to free them. When they were told that the land would remain the property of the landlord, their answer was: "Then things had better stay as they are. We belong to the master, but the land belongs to us."

Muraviev's constitution played a significant role in helping to crystallize the views of his fellow members, but it cannot be considered an official expression of the standpoint of the entire Northern Society. In any case, it was agreed that the final choice of constitution was to be left to the legislative assembly convened after the overthrow of the government. Apart from the trend represented by Muraviev, there was a more radical faction whose aim was not a constitutional monarchy but a republic. The leading representative of this trend was the poet Ryleev, a friend of the Polish poet Adam Mickiewicz.

Nikolai Turgenev

Among those who were close to the Northern Society, a separate stand was taken by NIKOLAI TURGENEV (1789–1871), a member of the former Union of Welfare and son of the Freemason Ivan Turgenev, one of Novikov's close collaborators. During the Decembrist uprising Turgenev was out of the country. Condemned to death in absentia, he remained abroad.

Unlike Muraviev and the Decembrists proper (i.e. those who were members of secret societies and had decided on armed rebellion), Turgenev was a reformer rather than a revolutionary. He, too, wished to transform Russia into a country enjoying civil liberties and the rule of law, but he was suspicious of the political ambitions of the gentry. Indeed, he believed that of the two evils, absolutism was preferable to aristocratic oligarchy, and that only a strong central government would be able to tackle land reform. Unlike Muraviev, he was also against the imposition of property qualifications; to regard wealth or property as a guarantee of patriotism or love of liberty was, he maintained, an insult to humanity. Nevertheless, in his proposals on the vexed issue of land reform Turgenev went no further than Muraviev. In a book entitled *An Essay on a Theory of Taxation* (1818), he suggested that peasants should be freed without land grants but should be allowed the right to purchase land. From his personal diary it seems that he was in favor of partial land grants but feared that to introduce legislation of this kind would only strengthen the gentry's opposition to what he considered to be the essential reform, namely the abolition of serfdom and the changeover to free hired labor. Turgenev, interestingly enough, was particularly emphatic about the need to dissolve the village commune, which he considered to be the main obstacle in the way of agricultural modernization. Muraviev, too, was an opponent of the commune, although he did not explain his dislike by any economic arguments.

The Southern Society

In the Southern Society of Decembrists the dominant figure was Colonel PAVEL PESTEL (1793–1826). His views are set out in his draft for a constitution, entitled *Russian Justice*. This detailed description of the future political system to be introduced in Russia was a document to which the Southern Society attached great importance. Unlike the leaders of the Northern Society, Pestel maintained that the question of a constitution should not be left to a future assembly but should be decided in advance, and that after the success of the military coup an Interim Government should be established with dictatorial powers.

The most interesting parts of *Russian Justice* are the sections dealing with land reform. Pestel backed up his arguments with a critical analysis of two theories concerning land tenure: the first considers land to be a gift of nature and therefore communal property; the second considers it to be the property of those who cultivate it. Pestel felt that both these theories contained particles of truth, and he therefore attempted to reconcile them in his own program, which was based on two assumptions: that every man has a natural right to exist and thus to a piece of land large enough to allow him to make a basic living; and that only those who create surplus wealth have a right to enjoy it. After the overthrow of tsarism, therefore, Pestel proposed to divide land into two equal sectors: the first would be public property (or, more accurately, the property of the communes); the second would be in private hands. The first would be used to ensure everyone a minimum living, whereas the second would be used to create surplus wealth. Every citizen was entitled to ask his commune for an allotment large enough to support a family; if the commune had more land available, he would even be able to demand several such allotments. The other sector would remain in private hands. Pestel felt that his program ensured every individual a form of social welfare in the shape of a communal land allotment but also left scope for unlimited initiative and the opportunity of making a fortune in the private sector.

Pestel believed that his program had every chance of success since land ownership in Russia had traditionally been both communal and private. Here he obviously had in mind the Russian village commune; it should be emphasized, however, that Pestel's commune differed essentially from the feudal *obshchina* in that it did not restrict its members' movement or personal freedom and did not impose collective responsibility for individual members' tax liabilities.

The idea that the village commune contained the seeds of Russia's future social system was to have an astonishing career in the history of Russian ideas. To a certain extent Pestel was a precursor of this conception, but it is worth noting that he did not associate the commune with any socialist tendencies (although Herzen thought otherwise). He was convinced of the importance of large-scale capitalist ownership, and his economic ideas were strongly influenced by Adam Smith.

Pestel's constitution abolished the feudal estates, including the nobility. His attitude toward the latter was, however, marked by a certain ambiguity: he was reluctant to damage their position and even argued that it was important to preserve certain privileges for the most deserving citizens. Unlike the members of the Northern Society, Pestel had no sympathy for the ancient aristocracy; any sense of fellowship he might have had would have been with the civil service nobility who owed their social status to government service rather than to birth. This comes out clearly in his *Russian Justice*, where decisions on social issues are largely entrusted to government officials. In the new Russia all independent unions, societies, and associations were to be forbidden by law, and private persons were not even to be permitted to found schools or charitable bodies.

Although Pestel's land reform proposals were more radical than the plans of the Northern Society, they, too, showed a tendency to compromise with the large landowners. Estates were to be divided into three categories: landlords owning more than 10,000 desentines (about 25,000 acres) were to give up half their land without compensation; those owning from 5,000 to 10,000 desentines were to receive partial compensation for half their land; owners of smaller estates were to give up half their land but were entitled to full compensation or a grant of an equivalent amount of land in a less populated region. This reform was to ensure the setting up of a pool of land in every commune (mainly for the benefit of the peasants) consisting of half the entire acreage. After the conclusion of the land reform there was to be no upper limit to the size of private estates. Serfdom was to be abolished at once, but labor obligations (corvée) were to be retained for a transitional period lasting from ten to fifteen years.

Unlike Muraviev, Pestel was firmly opposed to the imposition of property qualifications. He favored the existence of men of wealth as an advantage to the state but opposed any connection between political privileges and wealth; a financial aristocracy, he thought, was more harmful than an aristocracy of birth. Russia was to be a republic where the suffrage was to be granted to all male citizens over the age of twenty. Legislative powers were to be vested in a single-chamber popular assembly and executive powers in a five-member State Duma elected by the popular assembly for a five-year term. Juridical and supervisory functions were to be entrusted to a Supreme Council composed of 120 elected life members.

Pestel's constitution also differed from Muraviev's in its views on civil liberties and the structure of government. *Russian Justice* envisaged freedom of worship and movement, inviolability of the home, and freedom of the press (authors of articles were to be responsible only to the courts), but forbade the setting up of any societies or associations and entrusted the conduct of government and civic affairs to the bureaucracy. Pestel favored a strong central government and thought that Muraviev's federalism was too reminiscent of medieval Russia's division into appanage states, which he felt had laid the country open to the Tartar invasions. He even went so far as to oppose the granting of autonomy to the peoples making up the Russian empire, since he felt they should become assimilated into one great Russian nation. The only exception he made was in favor of Poland, as a country with a tradition of statehood capable of forming a strong and separate government. In secret negotiations with the Polish Patriotic Society, Pestel promised the Poles national independence provided they were willing to enter into a close alliance with Russia and introduce a similar social system. The revived

Polish state was to include almost the whole of Belorussia, Volhynia, and the western Ukraine.

It is worth looking at Pestel's proposals for a solution to the Jewish question. Jews who were not willing to become assimilated were to be helped to acquire territory in the Near East to form their own state. "If all Russian and Polish Jews," Pestel wrote, "come together in one place, there will be more than two million of them. If a large body of people like that set out to look for a fatherland, they will conquer all obstacles with ease." [6]

The ease with which Pestel himself decided the future of more than a dozen nations, among them nations with such rich and ancient cultural traditions as the Georgians, was not so much the result of his chauvinism as of his abstract rationalism, the tendency to look at nations from a bureaucratic-etatist point of view. For the author of *Russian Justice* the only rational bond between fellow men was a bond based on juridical premises. Taking advantage of the ambiguity in meaning of the Russian word *obshchestvo* (corresponding to the different meanings of the English "society"), Pestel maintained that "society" was simply an association of citizens "for the attainment of a definite goal." [7] His definition of a nation was an "association of all those members of one and the same state who form a society of citizens in order to ensure the realizable well-being of each and all." [8] This utilitarian definition makes no distinction between a "nation" and the population of a given state, thus ignoring internal linguistic or cultural divisions. If the foundations of society rest on an act of association for the sake of achieving a certain goal, then this society can be dissolved and a new association formed on different and superior principles thought up by revolutionaries. Pestel's views were influenced by the "Jacobin" conviction that societies can be planned and that such plans can be put into effect through decrees issued by a central authority.

The Society of United Slavs

Apart from the Southern Society of Decembrists, another organization, the Society of United Slavs, founded in 1823 by the Borisov brothers and the Polish revolutionary Julian Lubliński, was active in the Ukraine at this time. In the autumn of 1825, on the eve of the Decembrist revolt, this organization joined the Southern So-

6. Quoted from M. V. Nechkina, *Dvizhenie dekabristov* (M, 1955), vol. 2, p. 86.
7. *Izbrannye sotsial'no-politicheskie i filosofskie proizvedeniia dekabristov* (M, 1951), vol. 2, p. 75.
8. *Ibid.*, p. 80.

ciety as a separate section—the Slavic Board. In contrast to the "true" Decembrists, the "Slavs" were mainly lower-ranking officers from the impoverished petty gentry. Their principal aim was the formation of a democratic, republican federation of Slavic peoples (but including also Hungary, Moldavia, and Wallachia), which was to extend from the Black Sea to the White Sea and from the Baltic to the Adriatic. Unlike the Decembrists, the "Slavs" were not afraid to agitate for their program among the army rank and file. Although their program of social reforms was vague, it was more democratic than that of either of the Decembrist societies; moreover, the "Slavs" were in favor of a popular revolution based on mass support rather than a military revolt.

The leading ideologists of the Decembrist movement were not uninterested in the concept of "Slavdom," but this interest was mainly in relation to the foreign policy to be adopted by the future Russia. The notion of a Slavic federation based on equal rights was an original contribution made by the Society of United Slavs and had rather a cool reception. Mikhail Bestuzhev-Riumin and Sergei Muraviev-Apostol tried to persuade their colleagues of the Slavic Board that their ideas would distract attention from the immediate aims of the movement, and that "one must give more thought to one's countrymen than to foreigners." It is no coincidence that the "Slav" program originated in the border area—the meeting place of Poland, Russia, and the Ukraine—and that one of its originators was a Pole. It may even be argued convincingly that the "Slav idea" came to Russia from Poland, where interest in "Slavdom" was at that time very widespread.[9]

The Decembrist Philosophy of Russian History

The idealization of "ancient Russian liberties," which was so characteristic of the Decembrists, showed itself also in their liking for archaisms and historical reminiscences. Decembrist documents are full of such old terms as *duma, sobor* (council), *uprava* (governing body), *veche* (folkmoot), and *boyar*. For the capital, of course, the Decembrists preferred Moscow or Nizhni Novgorod to traditionless St. Petersburg. Even Pestel was affected by this trend: he named his draft constitution after the earliest surviving Russian legal document.

Finding not only theoretical arguments but also historical parallels to lend support to one's own ideological position was common practice at the beginning of the nineteenth century. For Russia, as

9. This is discussed in G. Luciani, *La Société des Slaves Unis* (Paris, 1963).

for Germany, the war against Napoleon played a special role in this process. In the personal biographies of most of the Decembrists the campaign of 1812 represented a turning point. Jakushkin called it an event that "woke the Russian nation." The patriotic war stimulated widespread interest in Russian history and in the "distinctive" quality or "native principle" (*samobytnost'*) of the Russian nation. From this interest emerged the Decembrist interpretation of Russian history, worked out largely by members of the Northern Society and conceived as an antithesis to Karamzin's theory of the beneficial role of autocracy.

An innate Russian characteristic, the Decembrists maintained—one that later developments had blunted but not destroyed—was a deep-rooted love of liberty. Autocracy had been unknown in Kievan Russia: the powers of the princes had been strictly circumscribed there and decisions on important affairs of state were taken by the popular assemblies. The Decembrists were especially ardent admirers of the republican city-states of Novgorod and Pskov. This enthusiasm was of some practical significance, since they were convinced that the "spirit of liberty" that had once imbued their forebears was still alive; let us but strike the bell, and the people of Novgorod, who have remained unchanged throughout the centuries, will assemble by the bell tower, Ryleev declared. Kakhovsky described the peasant communes with their self-governing *mir* as "tiny republics," a living survival of ancient Russian liberty.[10] In keeping with this conception, the Decembrists thought of themselves as *restoring* liberty and bringing back a form of government that had sound historical precedents.

These arguments remind us of the fact that the word "revolution" meant originally a "restoration." This archaic meaning of the term was still alive in the world view of the gentry revolutionaries in Poland and in Russia. It is worth adding, however, that there were also some direct links between the ideas of the Russian and Polish revolutionaries. One of the men who influenced the Decembrists' view of the past, for instance, was the Polish historian Joachim Lelewel, whose review of Karamzin's *History* (published in the periodical *Northern Archive*) aroused considerable and understandable interest within the movement.[11] The victory of autocracy in the sixteenth century was presented by the Decembrists as a victory of

---

10. See S. S. Volk, *Istoricheskie vzgliady dekabristov* (M-L, 1958), p. 303.

11. The Decembrists were also greatly interested in the research into ancient Slav traditions undertaken by I. Rakowiecki and Zorian Dołęga-Chodakowski (see Volk, *Istoricheskie*, pp. 314–18).

Tartar political principles, alien to the Russian spirit. Their greatest distaste was for Ivan the Terrible; by contrast, Kurbsky was considered a national hero. They also tended to idealize the first two Romanovs, mainly because they had been elected by the Land Assembly and therefore took some heed of boyar advice. Both the Boyar Duma and the Land Assembly were thought to contain the seeds of representative government.

Even this brief account of the Decembrists' interpretation of history reveals very clearly the influence of the ideas of the old hereditary nobility. The Decembrists identified with the boyars in their conflict with autocracy and used every opportunity to underline the common interests of the boyars and the nation as a whole. They even maintained that the old boyar nobility had been part of the people and that serfdom had been introduced against the boyars' will in order to reward the new military and official caste for their faithful service to the tsars.

The role of Peter the Great presented the Decembrists with a considerable difficulty. On the one hand he seemed to be a bloody tyrant—another Ivan the Terrible—but on the other he was the creator of the modern Westernized state. When Turgenev called Peter a tyrant, Bestuzhev replied "I love this tyrant passionately." [12] Ryleev praised Peter, but in his poem "Voinarovsky" painted an idealized portrait of Mazepa, the Cossack hetman who had fought Peter in defense of an independent Ukraine and ancient Cossack liberties. Peter was criticized for his lack of respect for national traditions, but there was general agreement that his reforms had been essential. For the sake of this historical necessity Peter was partly forgiven his despotism, but his successors were treated more harshly. The constitutional demands of 1730, for instance, had the Decembrists' full sympathy.

This divergence of judgment as far as Peter was concerned has a ready sociological explanation. The Decembrists were descendants of the hereditary nobility humiliated by Peter, but at the same time represented its Westernized elite, which owed its very existence to the Petrine reforms. They were against despotism, but as Russian patriots were aware of the benefits brought by Peter's reign to the Russian state. Although grateful to Peter for bringing them closer to Europe, they detested the despotic system he had strengthened because they felt themselves to be Europeans and thought of autocracy as the main obstacle to further Westernization.

12. *Ibid.*, p. 413.

The Decembrists' Place
in the History of Russian Thought

The Decembrist uprising proved a failure in almost every respect. The regiments whose conspiring officers led them to the Senate Square in St. Petersburg on December 14, 1825, did not know what they were fighting for, and it is hardly surprising that they dispersed after the first few canister shots. Colonel Sergei Trubetskoi, who had been elected military dictator, deserted the cause at the last moment and failed to make an appearance. Many of the rebels joined the uprising in a mood of defeatism, merely in order to demonstrate a desperate, forlorn heroism that would be an example to future generations. The St. Petersburg contingent did not act with sufficient energy and were too afraid of a mass uprising to take advantage of the sympathy shown by the populations of the capital. In the south, too, the revolt was unsuccessful, despite the undoubted heroism shown by Bestuzhev-Riumin and Muraviev-Apostol. And yet this unsuccessful enterprise was to acquire a legendary aura not altogether undeserved. Before the Decembrist revolt, Russia had known only boyar conspiracies or uncontrolled, primitive Jacqueries. This was the first time that an educated elite with its own considered program of social change had taken up arms against Russian autocracy. The gallows from which the five leaders were to hang (Pestel, Muraviev-Apostol, Bestuzhev-Riumin, Kakhovsky, and Ryleev) made a horrifying impression on Herzen, who was to be a living link between the traditions of the gentry revolutionaries and the radicals of the 1860's. The "best sons of the gentry" initiated the Russian revolutionary movement, and their work, Lenin stressed, was not in vain.

Despite this element of continuity, it must be said that the Decembrist ideology found no continuators in later Russian revolutionary thought. No radical movement in Russia was to put forward a liberal or even liberal-cum-aristocratic conception of freedom or to support economic liberalism. It is true that two Russian political émigrés, Ivan Golovin (1816–90) and Nikolai Sazonov (1815–62), harked back to the Decembrists, but they were not part of an organized movement and their ideas—which emphasized republican principles—had no influence on Russian revolutionary thought.[13] Herzen, too, considered himself an heir to the Decembrists, but his doctrine of "Russian socialism" gave rise to an entirely different

13. Their views are treated at length (on the basis of little-known sources) in W. Śliwowska, *W kręgu poprzedników Hercena* (Wroclaw, 1971).

social and political tradition. In Russia liberalism became an openly antirevolutionary force, and the revolutionary movement was dominated by various versions of socialist ideas; these were usually accompanied by dislike and suspicion of republican traditions, which were largely dismissed as "bourgeois."[14] That is why Lenin wrote at the beginning of the twentieth century of the importance of creating a revolutionary republican tradition in Russia; there was no such tradition in Russia, he pointed out, "if we leave out of account the long-forgotten republican ideas of the Decembrists."[15]

14. This was especially characteristic of the Populists. See Chapter 12 below.
15. V. I. Lenin, *Collected Works* (Eng-lang. ed.; M, 1960–66), vol. 6, p. 122n.

CHAPTER 4

ANTI-ENLIGHTENMENT TRENDS IN THE EARLY NINETEENTH CENTURY

The Decembrists' plans for political reforms were imbued with the spirit of eighteenth-century rationalism. Their philosophy of history and views on literature also showed the influence of the Romantic Movement, but it was rare to find among them any awareness that the values of the Enlightenment and romanticism were often incompatible. Many Decembrists (for example W. Küchelbecker) were decidedly in favor of the classical style and held that classical poetry was better able to express the ancient spirit of "republican virtues."

Despite his distinctive position, Karamzin, too, was closely influenced by the intellectual tendencies of the Enlightenment. His arguments on the importance of historical continuity were largely borrowed from Montesquieu (although he categorically opposed his theory of the division of powers). Karamzin respected religion as one of the pillars supporting the social order, but called religious mysticism "nonsensology."

The present chapter deals with those trends in Russian intellectual history that showed an extreme reaction against Enlightenment philosophy—a retreat from eighteenth-century rationalism toward either mystical religiosity or an idealistic metaphysics tinged with mysticism.

MYSTICISM

Mysticism during the reign of Alexander I was a direct heir to the mystical trend within Russian Freemasonry, represented at the end of the eighteenth century by Schwarz and the Rosicrucians. The persecution of Freemasons by Catherine and Paul did not succeed in halting the growth of this trend, and original works as well as translations of the works of foreign mystics appeared in increasing numbers.

One of the main reasons for the outburst of mysticism during Alexander's reign was the Napoleonic Wars. Napoleon's defeat was interpreted as proof that Russia had been entrusted with a holy mission, that she had been chosen by Providence to oppose the Antichrist and bring about a rebirth of Christianity. The French emperor's downfall was compared to the overthrow of the White Horseman of the Apocalypse, and seen as an example of the impermanence of temporal glory and the insignificance of human strength compared to the will of God. This was also an argument against "the conceit of human reason," and therefore *ipso facto* against the claims made by Enlightenment philosophers that the kingdom of God could be established on earth without divine inspiration.

The tone of this movement was set by Alexander himself. During the latter half of his reign the tsar, who had been educated by the Swiss liberal rationalist La Harpe, came under the influence of the Baroness de Krüdener and collaborated with her on a book with the significant title *A Cloud over the Holy Place, or Something That Proud Philosophy Dares not even Dream of.* Alexander asked the advice of the Baroness when he drafted the text for the Holy Alliance, which was signed in September 1815 by the king of Prussia and the Austrian emperor. This text referred to the allied states as members of "one Christian nation" and called the three monarchs the temporal representatives of Providence. It should be pointed out that Alexander sincerely believed in this imaginary Christian commonwealth and for its sake was even prepared to risk Russia's national interest. The two other monarchs signed the Holy Alliance from purely political motives. The Austrian emperor and his powerful minister, Prince Metternich, even thought that the phraseology of the treaty showed that its author's mind was unhinged.

The Holy Alliance has been aptly described as an alliance of international feudal reaction. Russian mysticism during the reign of Alexander cannot, however, be dismissed as uniformly reactionary. Apart from reactionary (often utterly obscurantist) trends, there were genuine attempts to sublimate religious experience. Many disciples of mysticism were sharply critical not only of eighteenth-century rationalism but also of the official Orthodox Church, and this led to efforts to found an extra-ecclesiastical "inner religiosity" that would appeal directly to feelings and intuitions. There was much sympathy for the Protestant sects, especially for the Quakers, who taught that a mystical "natural light" burning in the soul of every Christian believer showed the way to salvation without the mediation of the clergy. The activities of the British Bible Society in St. Petersburg also attracted much attention.

The most eminent figure among the Russian mystics at this time was ALEKSANDR LABZIN (1766–1825). At Moscow University he had been one of the favorite students of the Rosicrucian Schwarz, and under his influence joined the Masonic movement. In 1806 he founded a periodical, *The Messenger of Zion* (*Sionsky Vestnik*), which was almost at once suppressed at the insistence of the Church hierarchy. However, in 1817, a year after the Director General of the Holy Synod A. Golitsyn, himself a mystic, took over the Ministry of Education, the journal was allowed to appear. In the years 1817–18 *The Messenger of Zion* was extremely influential—so much so that even Orthodox bishops became infected by its ideas. The Archbishop Photius, a bitter enemy of heterodox mysticism, called Labzin a "man-idol" worshiped by the Synod and the St. Petersburg Theological Academy. This was a gross exaggeration, of course; the majority of the clergy were understandably hostile to Labzin, and the Synod favored his ideas not so much from conviction as from a desire to curry favor with the emperor and Prince Golitsyn.

The Messenger of Zion preached the notion of "inner Christianity" and the need for a moral awakening. It promised its readers that once they were morally reborn and vitalized by faith, they would gain suprarational powers of cognition and be able to penetrate the mysteries of nature, finding in them a key to a superior revelation beyond the reach of the Church.

Labzin's religion was thus a nondenominational and antiecclesiastical Christianity. Men's hearts, he maintained, had been imbued with belief in Christ on the first day of creation; primitive pagan peoples were therefore closer to true Christianity than nations that had been baptized but were blinded by the false values of civilization. The official Church was only an assembly of lower-category Christians, and the Bible a "silent mentor who gives symbolic indications to the living teacher residing in the heart." All dogmas, according to Labzin, were merely human inventions: Jesus had not desired men to think alike, but only to act justly. His words "Come unto me all ye that labor and are heavy laden" showed that he did not mean to set up any intermediate hierarchy between the believers and God.

When Tsar Alexander began to come under the influence of the Archbishop Photius, Labzin's fate was sealed. His periodical was once again suppressed, and as soon as the first occasion presented itself he was condemned to banishment, from which he did not return.

One of the interesting figures in Russian mysticism was MIKHAIL SPERANSKY (1772–1839), who was mentioned earlier in connection with Karamzin.[1] Speransky was banished in 1812 for his alleged support of Napoleon, but the ideas of this legislative reformer who was educated at the Theological Academy and was a friend of the Freemason Lopukhin reveal an interesting and rather curious mixture of mysticism and eighteenth-century juridical rationalism. While studying the Code Napoléon, Speransky also read the works of Jakob Boehme, Saint-Martin, Madame Guyon, and the Greek Church Fathers. His government reforms were inspired by the vision of a truly Christian social order. He believed that the introduction in Russia of the principles of representation, the rule of law, and fiscal accountability would be in accordance with the injunctions of the Gospels, which he treated as containing the solution to all political problems. In exile Speransky became an even more fanatical mystic and a bitter opponent of the Church. Official Church doctrine, he wrote, is an "entirely false system of Christianity."

After Nicholas I came to the throne, mystical trends soon received short shrift. The most important step in this respect was the closing of the Masonic lodges, which had been the core of the movement. They had been forbidden as early as 1822, but in the atmosphere of fear that prevailed after the failure of the Decembrist revolt any underground continuation was out of the question. Hidden mystical tendencies continued to exist, however, and can be traced in the ideas of Chaadaev and the romantic Wisdom-lovers, as well as in the young Bakunin and the Slavophiles.

THE WISDOM-LOVERS AND RUSSIAN SCHELLINGIANISM

Apart from mysticism, the most important expression of reaction against eighteenth-century rationalism was philosophical romanticism, largely represented by the secret Society of Wisdom-lovers founded in 1823. In principle this society had only five members (V. F. Odoevsky, D. V. Venevitinov, N. M. Rozhalin, and the later Slavophiles I. V. Kireevsky and A. I. Koshelev), but thanks to its close contacts with the literary society of S. E. Raich, which was allowed to function openly, its influence was considerable. The Wisdom-lovers propagated their ideas in the almanac *Mnemosyne*,

1. See M. Raeff, *Michael Speransky: Statesman of Imperial Russia* (2d rev. ed., The Hague, 1969).

published from 1824 to 1825. For the word "philosophy" they substituted the mystical Masonic term *lyubomudrie* (love of wisdom) in
order to establish their independence from the French *philosophes*.
"To this day everyone imagines a philosopher to resemble one of
those eighteenth-century French rattles," wrote Odoevsky, the society's chairman, in *Mnemosyne*; "I wonder whether there are many
people who are capable of understanding the enormous difference
between a truly divine philosophy and that of some Voltaire or Helvetius?" This "truly divine" philosophy the young Wisdom-lovers
sought in Germany: "Land of ancient Teutons! Land of noble ideas.
It is to you I turn my worshipful gaze," was how Odoevsky expressed
their feelings.[2]

Interest in German idealist philosophy represented a turning
away from the political interests that were so typical of the Decembrists and their associates. The latter could not accept the Wisdom-
lovers' habit of looking at the world from the heights of the Absolute, which encouraged them to despise earthbound "empiricism"
and to shut their eyes to the burning social and political issues of
the day. The correspondence of the two Odoevsky cousins casts an
interesting light on these differences. The elder cousin, Aleksandr,
who was a Decembrist, accused the younger of "Idolatry," of losing
himself in abstractions; the younger, Vladimir, accused the elder of
a lack of understanding of the higher concerns of the spirit.

As A. Koyré has aptly pointed out,[3] the differences between the
Wisdom-lovers and the Decembrists reflected a gap not only between
generations (the Wisdom-lovers belonged to a younger generation
for whom the patriotic war of 1812 had not been the greatest formative influence), but also between the two Russian capitals. The philosophy of the Wisdom-lovers evolved in Moscow, whereas the main
center of the Decembrists was St. Petersburg. "For God's sake," the
Decembrist Küchelbecker wrote to Vladimir Odoevsky, "tear your-
self away from the rotten, stinking atmosphere of Moscow." Semi-
patriarchal Moscow, with its old noble families, was the capital of
ancient Muscovy and the center of Russian religious life; it was also
the main stronghold of conservatism, mysticism, and resistance to
rationalist, revolutionary, and even liberal thought. In the eighteenth century it had been the chief center of the Rosicrucians, the
mystical wing of Freemasonry, and in the nineteenth it was to give

2. See P. N. Sakulin, *Iz istorii russkogo idealizma. Kniaz' V. F. Odoevsky* (M, 1913),
vol. 1, pp. 138, 139.
3. See. A. Koyré, *La Philosophie et le problème national en Russie au début du
XIX siècle* (Paris, 1929), p. 43.

birth to the Slavophile movement. St. Petersburg, on the other hand, was a town without a past and at that time the only modern city in Russia; it was the cradle of the *raznochintsy*, the uprooted intelligentsia, and the main center of liberal, democratic, and socialist thought.

To begin with, the young Wisdom-lovers were primarily interested in Schelling's philosophy of nature and philosophy of art. They saw the world as a living work of art, and art as an organic unity of unconscious and conscious creation. The inspired artist, they felt, did not imitate reality but created anew according to divine principles of creation; he therefore truly deserved to be called a divine being. Art, moreover, was closely related to philosophy; one of the tools of philosophy was in fact artistic intuition. It is no wonder that with such beliefs the young Wisdom-lovers were implacably hostile to all manifestations of classicism and all "imitations of French models."

The Wisdom-lovers' nature philosophy was influenced by two Russian Schellingians—D. M. VELLANSKY (1774–1847), a student of Schelling and Professor of Natural History at the St. Petersburg Academy of Medicine and Surgery,[4] and M. G. PAVLOV (1793–1840), a professor at the University of Moscow and a contributor to *Mnemosyne*. Unlike their two mentors, the Wisdom-lovers had no scientific training, so that their ideas on nature easily took flight into the realm of fancy. Following Schelling, they were opposed to atomistic and mechanistic physics and saw everything in terms of polarity: nature was a living, spiritual whole containing within it the creativity, movement, and struggle of opposites, both attraction and repulsion; at the same time, nature was only the outer garment of the spirit, and all its manifestations therefore had a secret symbolic meaning. The key to an understanding of these symbols and thus to the interpretation and mastery of nature was to be found in speculative philosophy. In his semiautobiographical *Russian Nights*. Odoevsky described the period of his youth as follows: "My youth was spent at a time when metaphysics was as much in the air as the political sciences are now. We believed in the possibility of an absolute theory that would allow us to create (we used the term 'construct') all the phenomena of nature, just as today we believe in the possibility of a social order that would satisfy all human needs."[5]

4. In 1834 Vellansky translated into Russian and published the work of the Polish follower of Schelling Jozef Goluchowski, *Die Philosophie in ihren Verhältnissen zum Leben ganzer Völker und einzelner Menschen* (1822).

5. V. F. Odoevsky, *Russkie Nochi* (M, 1913), p. 8.

Another important ingredient of the Wisdom-lovers' world view was romantic nationalism. Many articles in *Mnemosyne* called for a truly national and "distinctive" culture. This seemed to coincide with the literary program of the Decembrists, which was why Küchelbecker contributed articles to *Mnemosyne*. The ideological basis for this collaboration was, however, very slender. According to the rationalistic Enlightenment view (which had a considerable influence on the Decembrists), the nation was above all a "body politic" shaped by legislation and an "aggregation of citizens." The Wisdom-lovers, on the other hand, conceived the nation as a whole transcending its individual parts, a unique collective individuality evolving historically by its own "distinctive" principles. Potentially, this interpretation could lead to an idealization of irrational elements in national existence, and to a condemnation of all "mechanical changes" or revolutions that might interrupt historical continuity. The conviction that history had destined every nation to have its own separate mission was likely to clash with the rationalistic universalism that was one of the main (though not always consciously formulated) premises of Decembrist thought.

The failure of the Decembrist revolt and the conspirators' fate had a profound effect on the Wisdom-lovers. In the interests of safety their society was at once disbanded, but members continued to meet informally. In the latter half of the 1820's they were still a relatively homogeneous group and published their work in the *Moscow Herald (Moskovsky Vestnik)*, a periodical edited by the historian M. Pogodin. Their main interest shifted away from the philosophy of nature to the philosophy of history, and the issue that now engaged their attention was the position of Russia vis-à-vis Western Europe—especially the problems caused by contacts between the two and by the tension between the purely national element and the Western values transplanted by Peter the Great. This issue was discussed in a short but interesting article, "On the State of Enlightenment in Russia" (1826), by Dmitri Venevitinov, a poet and philosopher. The author's central thesis was that Russian culture lacked a distinctive "native principle." The only way to let Russia find her true nature, he suggested, was to isolate her from Europe and demonstrate to her an overall view of the evolution of the human spirit grounded in firm philosophical principles; only then would she discover her own place and separate historical mission.

In the 1830's the president of the Society of Wisdom-lovers, VLADIMIR ODOEVSKY (1803–69), perhaps the most talented representative of the conservative trend in Russian romanticism, became well known as a writer. In 1844 he published his *Russian Nights*. This interesting book, which consists of conversations between friends interspersed with various tales, has something of the value of a historical document since (in the author's own words) it gives "a reasonably accurate picture of the intellectual activity of young Muscovites in the 1820's and 1830's."[6]

Like Schelling himself, Odoevsky turned increasingly toward theosophy and a religious philosophy of history, and devoted more time to reading the works of mystics and theosophers such as Boehme, Pordage, Saint-Martin, and Baader. One of the vital philosophical issues that now engaged his attention was the problem of original sin. Man, in Odoevsky's view had once been a free spirit; his present dependence on nature was the outcome of the Fall, and the flesh should therefore be called a disease of the spirit. Regeneration was possible, however, through love and art—mankind's aesthetic evolution had shown that humanity was capable of regaining its lost integrality and spiritual harmony. Art must, however, be permeated by religion; when divorced from religion it is a "self-centered force." The same was true of science, which could bring about the nation's spiritual death if divorced from religion and poetry.

The force capable of integrating a nation and turning it into a living whole, according to Odoevsky, was something he called "instinct."[7] This instinct was of course not a biological concept but a powerful irrational force—something akin to the "divine spark" that the mystics said had survived in man after the Fall and made possible his future regeneration. Primitive peoples possessed enormous reserves of such instinctive powers, but these had become weakened by the advance of civilization, especially by the rationalism of Roman civilization. Although Christianity had initiated a new age of instinct, at a higher stage than before, the wellspring of these powers was once more drying up. This was the effect of rationalism and excessive analysis, which had given rise to materialism and modern industrialization. It should be noted that the attack on capitalism (closely associated with the critique of rationalism) characteristic of early nineteenth-century conservative romanticism here made its first appearance in Russian thought.

True philosophy, in contrast to the rationalism and empiricism of the Enlightenment, is based directly on instinct, Odoevsky de-

6. *Ibid.*, p. 21.
7. See Sakulin, *Iz istorii russkogo idealizma*, pp. 469–80.

clared. Cognition that is capable of perceiving its object synthetically as a living whole is not possible without "innate ideas" springing directly from the instinct. Fortunately art, which retains part of the primitive energy lost under the impact of rationalism, can help to strengthen the weakened instincts. Poetic intuition never errs, and "the poetic impulse is the soul's most precious power." Poetry should permeate not only knowledge but also the living social tissue of mankind; like religion, it is a powerful instinctive force integrating society; where the advance of science has led to the disappearance of religion and poetry, society has become a degenerate organism. Instinct is a creative principle, an organic force without which all human endeavor—whether art, science, or legislation—is lifeless. Without instinct there are no living social bonds; rationalism is only capable of creating a "mechanical and lifeless" society.

An important aspect of Odoevsky's theory was his conviction that the wealth of instinctive powers lost by the inhabitants of Western Europe had been preserved in Russia—a young country still living in its "heroic age." Thanks to Peter's reforms the Russians had assimilated European achievements, had gained the experience of old men without ceasing to be children. That was why Russia had now been entrusted with a lofty mission, that of breathing new life into Europe's old, fossilized culture. It is worth adding that Odoevsky's German mentors shared some of these ideas. In 1842, when Odoevsky was in Berlin, Schelling told him that Russia "was destined for something great";[8] and toward the end of his life the German philosopher Franz von Baader sent a memoir to Count Uvarov, the Minister of Education, with the significant title "The Mission of the Russian Church in View of the Decline of Christianity in the West."[9]

In Odoevsky's conception, Russia and Western Europe were not two opposing poles of an antithesis; Russia's mission was to save European civilization rather than to replace it with a new and radically different culture. In some respects he anticipated Slavophile criticism of Europe, but his hope that Russia would absorb and breathe new life into all that was best in European civilization was shared by Stankevitch, Belinsky, and the young Herzen.

In his views on society, Odoevsky was (in the 1830's and 1840's) a typical representative of conservative romanticism, with its critical attitudes toward capitalist industrial development and liberal ideas.

8. *Ibid.*, p. 386.
9. See E. Susini, *Lettres inédites de Franz von Baader* (Paris, 1942), pp. 456–61.

He dismissed bourgeois society as a mechanism lacking the poetic element, an agglomeration of individuals motivated by self-interest and not held together by any moral bonds. Russia's semifeudal system seemed to him incomparably superior to the bourgeois state, although he conceded that it was capable of improvement: the landowning gentry, for instance, as guardians of the people would do well to take a special moral and scientific examination. Nonetheless, Odoevsky considered this latter notion so daring that he did not expect it to be implemented until the beginning of the twentieth century.

The ideas of the Wisdom-lovers and their continuation in Odoevsky's later work were an important transitional stage in Russian intellectual history. On the one hand, by popularizing German philosophy in Russia—particularly Schelling—the Wisdom-lovers prepared the ground for the reception of Hegelianism. On the other hand (and perhaps chiefly), they were the immediate precursors of the Slavophiles (the living links between *lyubomudrie* and Slavophilism were Koshelev and Kireevsky). The future ideologists of official Russian conservatism—the historian M. Pogodin and the literary critic S. Shevyrev—were also associated with the Wisdom-lovers. Finally, the ideas that the Wisdom-lovers had first discussed were to give rise to Chaadaev's *Philosophical Letters*.

CHAPTER 5

PETR CHAADAEV

PETR CHAADAEV (1794–1856), a nephew of Prince Mikhail Shcherbatov and a friend of Pushkin, was associated in his youth with the Decembrist movement. The young Pushkin had good grounds for considering him to be one of the outstanding liberals of the 1820's, and his well-known verse "To Chaadaev" (1818) ends with the following lines:

> Comrade, believe: joy's star will leap
> Upon our sight, a radiant token;
> Russia will rouse from her long sleep;
> And where autocracy lies, broken,
> Our names shall yet be graven deep.[1]

By an ironic twist of fate, the man to whom these optimistic lines were addressed was later to conceive a profoundly pessimistic view of Russia.

Early in 1821, at their Moscow congress, the Decembrists decided to initiate Chaadaev into their secret society. The invitation came too late, however: at that very time Chaadaev was about to give up his promising army career (for reasons that have never been clarified), withdraw from salon society, and steep himself in the works of religious writers. Shortly afterwards he went abroad (in 1823) and became confirmed in his leanings toward Roman Catholicism, which at that time exerted a considerable influence on the Russian aristocracy. On his return to Russia in 1826 he withdrew for several years into almost complete seclusion and devoted himself entirely to the philosophical formulation of his new world view. The fruits of this period are the eight *Philosophical Letters* (written in French from 1828 to 1831), of which only the first—devoted to Russia—was published during its author's lifetime (in 1836) in the journal *Tele-*

---

1. Quoted from *The Poems, Prose and Plays of Alexander Pushkin* (New York, 1936). The most comprehensive monograph on Chaadaev in English is Raymond T. McNally, *Chaadayev and His Friends* (Tallahassee, Fla., 1971).

scope (*Teleskop*).[2] After completing the *Letters*, Chaadaev returned to Moscow society and soon became one of the most sought-after guests in the city's literary salons. It was in discussions—more often perhaps arguments—with him that the later views of both Western-izers and Slavophiles began to take shape.

CHAADAEV'S METAPHYSICS AND PHILOSOPHY OF HISTORY

Chaadaev's *Philosophical Letters* are a work of rich texture and intellectual depth, firmly rooted in the European intellectual tra-dition as well as in contemporary thought. Some of their leitmotivs can be traced back to Neoplatonism, which survived in European and Russian religious philosophy and also in certain aspects of Her-metism and Masonic theosophy. Neoplatonic ideas also reached Chaadaev through Schelling (with whom he corresponded for some years after meeting him personally in 1825). It is worth noting that Chaadaev had also read Kant and even Hegel, something of a rarity in Russia of the 1820's. The major influence on him, however, was that of the French Catholic philosophers, especially de Maistre (who was ambassador in Russia from 1803 to 1817 and called one of his important works *Les Soirées de Saint-Petersbourg*), de Bonald, Bal-lanche, Chateaubriand, and Lamennais in his theocratic period.

In contrast to the philosophers of the Enlightenment, Chaadaev held that the aspiration to individual freedom is not natural to man. His true inclination is to subordinate himself, being is hierarchical in structure and the natural order is based on *dependence*. Human actions are directed from outside by a force transcending the in-dividual, and the power of man's reason is in direct proportion to his obedience, submissiveness, and docility. The individual is noth-ing without society; his consciousness and knowledge flow from a social, supraindividual source. The mind of the individual is an-chored in the universal mind and draws its nourishment from it. An element of this universal mind (something like divine revelation) is still deeply embedded in human consciousness. Individual rea-son in isolation is something artificial, the reason of man after the Fall; therefore, men who proclaim the autonomy of their limited

2. Three *Letters* were published for the first time abroad by the Jesuit priest Father I. S. Gagarin (*Oeuvres choisies de Pierre Tschaadaïef*) and were reprinted by Gershenzon in 1913 with a Russian translation. The remaining *Letters* were found in 1935 by D. Shahovskoi and published in *Literaturnoe nasledstvo*, nos. 22–24 (1935). This edition unfortunately published the letters in their Russian translation only.

reason, who seek to reach by themselves for the apple from the tree of knowledge, are guilty of a repetition of original sin. Chaadaev suggested that Kant's *Critique of Pure Reason* showed the impotence of the isolated individual's reason—what Kant called "pure reason" was in fact only individual reason claiming autonomy for itself and for that very reason unable to solve its antinomies or comprehend the highest truths. This type of subjective reason separates man from the universe and makes true understanding impossible. Such understanding can only be attained through collective knowledge, through participation in a collective consciousness that transcends individual minds; this superior consciousness derives from God, who is the supreme principle of the oneness of the universe.

On this assumption it was a logical step to deny the moral autonomy of the individual. For Chaadaev moral law, like truth, was not something autonomous, as Kant suggested, but a force outside us. Only the great, divinely inspired heroes of history can both act spontaneously and also conform to the precepts of a higher morality; ordinary human beings, whose actions are not guided by "mysterious stimuli," must submit to the strict discipline of inherited traditions. Chaadaev, it should be noted, considered that psychology must recognize the heredity of ideas, the existence of a historical memory transmitted from generation to generation; he was bitterly opposed to what he called "empirical" psychology, which he accused of reducing the human psyche to a mechanical plaything of fortuitous associations.

To underpin this argument, Chaadaev evolved a metaphysical conception of a hierarchy of states of being. The Great All about which he wrote in the *Letters* has a hierarchical structure consisting of four grades. At the summit of the hierarchy is God. Next, his emanation is the universal mind that Chaadaev identified with the *social sphere*, i.e. the collective consciousness preserved in tradition. Considerably below this comes the empirical individual consciousness—the consciousness of individuals who have lost their grasp on the wholeness of being. The lowest (fourth) grade is nature prior to man. In this way God is neither identified with the universe, as in pantheism, nor separated from it, as in traditional theism.

Chaadaev's conception of the "social sphere" and its significance in human life is of particular interest. Knowledge, he argued, is a form of collective consciousness and arises from the interaction of many people, the collision of many conscious minds. Without society (the "supraindividual" sphere), which allows traditions to be handed down, human beings would never have emerged from the animal state. In religious experience, too, this sphere is of decisive importance: through it alone can the individual come to know God and become a vessel for the divine truth. The way to God leads not through individualistic self-perfection or solitary asceticism, but through the strict observance of the traditional norms and conventions of social life. For Chaadaev this even included care for one's personal appearance and surroundings and the conscientious observance of religious ritual, which he called the "discipline of the soul." The effort to "fuse" with God was identified with the striving after complete sociality: "man has no other mission," Chaadaev wrote, "than the annihilation of his personal being and the substitution for it of a perfectly social or impersonal being."[3]

Chaadaev's ideal of absolute sociality can only be properly understood if it is clearly distinguished from the longing to "merge with the people" that is a frequent motif in the works of Russian thinkers concerned with the problem of alienation. Chaadaev's emphasis on sociality did not preclude a defense of social hierarchy or an espousal of a typically aristocratic, elitist theory of knowledge. The common people, he wrote, have nothing to do with Reason, nor can their voice be equated with the voice of God. The guardian of revealed truths is the Church, a social organism whose role is to mediate between the congregation and God. If God were to vouchsafe another Revelation, he would make use not of the common people but of chosen individuals with special spiritual qualities. Chaadaev criticized the Reformation mainly for its individualistic egalitarianism and its belittlement of the role of the Church. His dislike of mystical trends was based on similar arguments. If we assume that the essence of mysticism is to strive after direct, individual contact with God, and thus to bypass the alienated, institutionalized forms of religion, we must treat Chaadaev as a determined opponent of mysticism.

At the root of Chaadaev's philosophy of history were his beliefs in a "universal mind"—a collective consciousness evolving within the historical process—and in the importance of the social and organizational functions of the Church. His was a conscious attempt to return to a religious interpretation of history, which had been secularized by the Enlightenment. Again in contrast to Enlightenment historians, Chaadaev held that men's voluntary acts play a negligible role in history. Man's actions are subordinated to a

---

3. P. Chaadaev, *Philosophical Letters and Apology of a Madman*, trans. and introduced by Mary-Barbara Zeldin (Knoxville, Tenn., 1969), p. 136.

superior supraindividual force—the masses obey it blindly, like "inanimate atoms," whereas chosen individuals are conscious instruments in its service. Man can be called truly great and free when he realizes the Creator's design and identifies his own will with the superior will animating history. Unlike the traditional Providentialists, Chaadaev thus attempted to reconcile the notion of a transcendent Providence with an immanentist philosophy of history. The force implementing the Creator's design is also the inner pattern that governs the historical process and transforms chaotic happenings into history—into a meaningful process directed to a goal. The instruments of history are individuals and nations endowed with what Chaadaev called supraindividual "moral personalities." Their mission is to rise toward universality—and isolated nations locked up in their superstitions cannot be such historical nations. Since the time of Christ the substance of history has been Christianity, whose purest manifestation is Catholicism. Chaadaev called the papacy "a visible symbol of unity" and at the same time a symbol of the worldwide reunion of the future: in the Middle Ages the papacy had helped to weld Europe into one great Christian nation, but the Renaissance and Reformation had destroyed this unity and were responsible for mankind's relapse into the social atomization of paganism. Fortunately, this spiritual crisis was drawing to a close: Christendom had passed through all the phases of corruption that were an inseparable aspect of freedom, but it had not—and indeed could not—collapse. Even now, Chaadaev wrote, some great turning point was felt to be near. Having outlived its political role, Christianity was becoming social, and mankind was entering the last phase of the establishment of the Kingdom of Heaven upon earth.

RUSSIA'S PAST AND FUTURE

Chaadaev's view of Russia is closely bound up with his metaphysics and philosophy of history. In the first of the *Philosophical Letters*, which was devoted to Russia, he attempted to analyze what it was he found lacking in his native country. It was a land, he argued, that appeared to have been overlooked by Providence. It belonged neither to the East nor to the West, was without historical continuity, and lacked a "moral personality." Russians are only a collection of unrelated individuals; in their heads everything is "individual, unsettled, and fragmentary." They have no sense of permanency and resemble homeless spirits condemned to creative impotence. In their own families they feel like strangers; in their own homes they behave like visitors; and thought they live in cities, they are nomads. The moral atmosphere of the West—the ideas of duty, justice, right, and order—is unknown in Russia, as is the Western syllogism (logic and methodical thinking). Russia does not belong to the moral sphere; her daily life has not yet attained a firm and definite form, but is in a state of permanent ferment resembling the original chaos preceding the present state of our planet. Such people cannot contribute to the evolution of the universal consciousness and are incapable of real progress; they exist only to teach the world a great lesson. In the following paragraph, this despairing accusation from the first *Philosophical Letter* reaches its climax:

We Russians, like illegitimate children, come to this world without patrimony, without any links with people who lived on the earth before us; we have in our hearts none of those lessons which have preceded our own existence. Each one of us must himself once again tie the broken thread of the family. What is habit, instinct among other peoples, we must get into our heads by hammer-strokes. Our memories go no further back than yesterday; we are, as it were, strangers to ourselves. We walk through time so singly that as we advance the past escapes us forever. This is a natural result of a culture based wholly on borrowing and imitation. There is among us no inward development, no natural progress; new ideas throw out the old ones because they do not arise from the latter, but come among us from Heaven knows where. Since we accept only ready-made ideas, the indelible traces which a progressive movement of ideas engraves on the mind and which give ideas their forcefulness make no furrow on our intellect. We grow, but we do not mature; we advance, but obliquely, that is in a direction which does not lead to the goal. (. . .) Isolated in the world, we have given nothing to the world, we have taken nothing from the world; we have not added a single idea to the mass of human ideas; we have contributed nothing to the progress of the human spirit. And we have disfigured everything we have touched of that progress.[4]

In the final pages of this letter Chaadaev tries to analyze the reasons for this desperate condition. The main cause, he suggests, is Russia's isolation, both national and religious. This in turn had its roots in the Schism, the separation of Orthodoxy from the universal Church. While the nations of Europe traversed the centuries hand in hand, worshiped the Almighty in one language, and together fought to free Jerusalem, Russia from the beginning found

4. *Ibid.*, pp. 37, 41.

herself outside this great community. In order to rise from the state of "empirical vegetation" to a spiritual life she would have to repeat the entire past development of Europe from the beginning.

Of great interest when taken in conjunction with the argument of the first of the *Philosophical Letters* is the fragment on serfdom in the second. Chaadaev regarded serfdom as the decisive influence in Russian society, the source of its unhealthy atmosphere and paralysis. In the West the Church had abolished serfdom, whereas in Russia she had presided over its introduction without a murmur of protest. "This circumstance alone," he wrote, "could lead one to doubt that Orthodoxy with which we adorn ourselves."[5]

Some elements in Chaadaev's view of Russia can be traced back to the writings of the French traditionalists. De Bonald, too, wrote that Russia, lying between Europe and Asia, was still an unformed society; he called the Russian character intrinsically "nomadic" and compared the houses of the Muscovites to Scythian chariots from which the wheels had been removed. De Maistre, who lived in Russia for many years, called her a country ignorant of certain universal truths that were the fruits of an ancient civilization, and also ascribed this ignorance to the isolation following the religious Schism. The only remedy, he suggested, was for Russia to rejoin the Catholic community.[6] De Maistre's views circulated among the Russian aristocracy and may have helped to form the ideas developed by Chaadaev in the first of his *Philosophical Letters*.[7]

The similarities between Chaadaev's views and those of the French traditionalists (and to a lesser degree, of the German conservative romanticists) are not merely superficial; they derive from the system of values accepted by all these thinkers. The leitmotivs in Chaadaev's philosophy—the critique of individualism and of eighteenth-century rationalism and empiricism; the conception of society as a whole transcending its individual parts; the defense of tradition and historical continuity; the yearning for the spiritual unity of medieval Christendom—all had their more or less exact counterparts in the ideologies of the European conservatives. In the European context, therefore, we would have to call Chaadaev a conservative. Paradoxically, we cannot call him a conservative in the Russian context, especially if we consider that he himself pointed

5. *Ibid.*, p. 58.
6. See C. Quénet, *Tchaadaev et les lettres philosophiques* (Paris, 1931), pp. 155–62.
7. See M. Stepanov, "Joseph de Maistre v Rossii," *Literaturnoe nasledstvo*, nos. 29–30 (M, 1937), p. 618.

out the absence in Russia of such basic prerequisites of conservatism as a sense of permanency, tradition, and historical roots.[8]

In order to understand Chaadaev, we must remember that his ideas were imbued with a spirit of opposition to the "Orthodox autocratic, and national" Russia of Nicholas I. The first of the *Letters* was a challenge to the official ideology, which proclaimed that the West was rotten whereas prosperous Russia was a "sheet anchor" for the human race. The Chief of Gendarmes, Benckendorff, boasted: "Russia's past is admirable; her present situation is more than wonderful; as for her future, this exceeds even the boldest expectations." It is not surprising, therefore, that the publication of the "Letter" caused a violent reaction. The emperor personally intervened to have Chaadaev declared insane and placed under police and medical supervision. The periodical *Telescope* was closed down, and its editor, N. I. Nadezhdin, was banished to Ust-Sysolsk.

From Herzen's vivid account we know what effect the "Letter" had on the most radical sections of the young intelligentsia. It was "a shot that rang out in the dark night; whether it was something foundering that proclaimed its own wreck, whether it was a signal, a cry for help, whether it was news of the dawn or news that there would not be one—it was all the same: one had to wake up."[9]

Several years elapsed between the composition of the first of the *Philosophical Letters* (1829) and its publication (1836), and during this time Chaadaev's views underwent certain changes. The July Revolution in France was a shock that undermined his faith in Europe and tempered his pessimistic view of Russia. Under the influence of discussions with the future Slavophiles, above all with Ivan Kireevsky, he too began to see Russia as a providential force destined for a special mission, and for this reason kept apart from the great historical family of nations. The result was the *Apology of a Madman (Apologie d'un fou)*, written in 1837, in which Chaadaev tried to redefine his views of Russia and also to some extent to jusify himself in view of the violent reaction to the first "Letter."

Chaadaev now admitted that his interpretation of Russian history had been too severe; though he continued to adhere to his main theses, he drew different conclusions from them. He reaffirmed that

8. Very similar was the case of the Marquis de Custine, a staunch European conservative who came to Russia in 1839 and found her deeply repulsive—despite Russia's reputation for being the mainstay of conservatism in Europe. See George F. Kennan, *The Marquis de Custine and His "Russia in 1839"* (Princeton, N.J., 1971).

9. Alexander Herzen, *My Past and Thoughts*, trans. by Constance Garnett (London, 1927), vol. 2, p. 261.

Russia was a country without history and that its past revealed a lack of spontaneous internal development. If she had been a historical nation, his argument ran, the Petrine reforms would have proved impossible, for ancient and deep-rooted traditions would have offered resistance to the emperor's arbitrary will. As it was, Peter's legislation did not transgress against "historicity," since Russia was only "a blank sheet of paper." [10] It is worth noting that this argument can be seen as a concealed attempt to convince Peter's heir that only the view of Russia as a country without history could justify the violence of his reforms and, consequently, the legitimacy of his arbitrary and bureaucratic despotism.

"I love my country," Chaadaev wrote, "as Peter the Great taught me to love it." [11] Russia's isolation, he now emphasized, was not her fault, but the result of her geographical situation. If she had no history, this could also be regarded as something of a privilege. Fettered by their own traditions, by their splendid history, the nations of Europe found it an effort to construct their future and were constantly struggling against the forces of the past. In Russia, on the other hand, it is enough for some mighty ruler to give vent to his will, and all convictions collapse, all minds open to receive the new ideas. In constructing their future, the Russian people can make use of the experience of European nations while avoiding their mistakes: they can be guided solely by "the voice of enlightened reason and conscious will." "History is no longer ours, granted," Chaadaev wrote, "but knowledge is ours; we cannot repeat all the achievements of the human spirit, but we can take part in its future achievements. The past is no longer in our power, but the future is ours." [12] These were the arguments on which Chaadaev based his conviction that Russia was destined "to resolve the greater part of the social problems, to perfect the greater part of the ideas which have arisen in older societies, to pronounce judgment on the most serious questions which trouble the human race." [13]

The *Apology of a Madman* brings the tragic paradox of Chaadaev

10. The Polish poet Adam Mickiewicz also compared Russia to a blank sheet of paper: "This level plain lies open, waste and white/ a wide-spread page prepared for God to write" (translated by G. R. Noyes). Numerous parallels between Chaadaev's first *Letter* and passages dealing with Russia in *Forefather's Eve*, Part 3 ("Digressions"), are discussed in Chapter 1 of W. Lednicki's *Russia, Poland and the West* (New York, 1954). Lednicki suggests that Mickiewicz might have met Chaadaev during his stay in Russia and that passages in the "Digression" echoed their conversations.

11. Chaadaev, *Philosophical Letters*, p. 173.

12. *Ibid.*, pp. 174–75.

13. *Ibid.*, p. 174.

into sharp focus. The man whose philosophical system recognized the inheritance of ideas through a supraindividual universal mind as the "fundamental fact of psychology," and who was a whole-hearted opponent of Locke's empiricism, was at the same time forced to argue that the minds of his countrymen were a "blank sheet of paper" and their country a land without an inheritance. In the *Philosophical Letters* he had considered this to be a tragedy, but in the *Apology of a Madman* he came to the conclusion that the lack of a heritage could also be viewed as a privilege that offered Russia a unique opportunity.

The view of Russia as a country where nothing had as yet been accomplished and everything remained to be done was not a new one: it had been put forward by Leibniz after the Petrine reforms and by Diderot in connection with the legislation of Catherine the Great.[14] There is dramatic irony in the fact that Chaadaev adopted this view in spite of himself, as it were—it contradicted his own philosophy, which represented a sharp reaction against anti-histori-cal rationalism, and also his belief in a conservative system of values. The theory as he proposed it could be used to justify not only en-lightened absolutism (as its author intended) but also the hopes of revolutionary radicals. Herzen, for instance, was echoing Chaadaev when he wrote that since there was nothing in their past for Rus-sians to love, social revolution would not encounter any serious obstacles.

CHAADAEV'S PLACE IN RUSSIAN INTELLECTUAL HISTORY

The author of the *Philosophical Letters* is without doubt one of the most striking personalities in the history of Russian ideas. Although he appears to be an isolated thinker, standing aloof from the main currents of Russian intellectual life, he nevertheless was the first to formulate—in drastic terms—a number of basic problems that were later taken up by thinkers representing very different world views: by Slavophiles and Westernizers, Herzen and Dostoev-sky, Chernyshevsky and Soloviev. He was an admirer of the West who was repelled by liberal and bourgeois Europe; an opponent of revolution who provided intellectual stimulus for revolutionaries; a religious thinker who was accepted by the anti- or at least non-religious progressive intelligentsia that followed Herzen in regard-

14. See L. Richter, *Leibniz und sein Russlandbild* (Berlin, 1946). On Diderot see above, p. 3.

ing him as a symbol of protest against the stifling atmosphere of autocratic Russia.

In the dispute between Slavophiles and Westernizers, Chaadaev's position was equally untypical. He was an ardent Westernizer; but the Western Europe he admired was not that of the democratic and liberal Westernizers of the 1840's, but that of the old aristocratic order before the age of revolutions. Liberalism and revolutionism were to him symptoms of the crisis of European civilization. The Westernizers of the 1840's experienced the formative influence of Hegelianism, and their later philosophical evolution was toward materialism and atheism. Chaadaev, on the other hand (like the Slavophiles), founded his hopes on a future religious renaissance and eagerly welcomed the anti-Hegelian "philosophy of revelation" expounded by Schelling in his last years.

In a certain sense, Slavophilism may be interpreted as a "reply to Chaadaev." Not Russia, but revolutionary and individualistic Europe, the Slavophiles insisted, was the land of disinherited people, unconnected by any bonds and with no traditions to lean on. If Russians felt "strangers to themselves," this was only because they had been torn away from their own foundations by the artificial process of Westernization. It was true that Russians had no history and no traditions, that they had no connecting links between the generations, and that they lived like nomads without a sense of permanency; but it was true only of the Westernized elite, who had been uprooted and alienated from the common people. The remedy, however, was to be sought not in Europe but in reintegration with the common people, in a return to their own history and religion and a reconstruction of the distinctive forms of national life that had been weakened by Western influences. Such a process of reintegration was possible, the Slavophiles contended, because the Russian people, unnoticed by Chaadaev, had remained faithful to their tradition and Orthodox faith.

CHAPTER 6

THE SLAVOPHILES

The term "Slavophilism" was originally used as a gibe to underline a certain narrow tribal particularism that was felt to be typical of the opponents of Russian Westernism. The term "Westernism" (*zapadnichestvo*) had similar origins; it was first coined by the Slavophiles to draw attention to their opponents' alleged national apostasy. Both terms, however, could be interpreted positively and were finally accepted by the ideologists of each side as something in the nature of a challenge.

The etymological meaning of "Slavophilism" is "love of Slavs." In Russian historical literature, however, this term has come to be applied in a more narrow sense to a group of ideologists belonging to the conservative nobility, whose outlook became formed in the late 1830's in opposition to the trend known as "Westernism." Moreover, Slavophilism denoted in this case not so much a feeling of solidarity with brother Slavs as a cultivation of the native and primarily Slavic elements in the social life and culture of ancient Russia. An interest in the fate of the non-Russian Slavs only began to play a role in Russian Slavophilism at the time of the Crimean War; in the 1840's only Khomiakov could be called a "Slavophile" in the etymological meaning of the word.[1]

The most outstanding thinkers of Slavophilism were IVAN KIREEVSKY (1806–56), ALEKSEI KHOMIAKOV (1804–60), KONSTANTIN AKSAKOV (1817–60) and YURY SAMARIN (1819–76). Kireevsky (who was associated with the Wisdom-lovers in his youth) was, as a philosopher, chiefly responsible for the formulation of the Slavophile philosophy of man and of history. Khomiakov, a man of wide interests and a strong and colorful personality (during his career he was a cavalry officer, poet, publicist, philosopher, and inventor), was

1. The most important American contributions to the study of Russian Slavophilism are N. V. Riasanovsky, *Russia and the West in the Teaching of the Slavophiles* (Cambridge, Mass., 1952); P. Christoff, *An Introduction to Nineteenth-Century Russian Slavophilism: A Study in Ideas*, vol. 1, *A. S. Khomiakov* (The Hague, 1961), vol. 2, *I. V. Kireevskij* (The Hague, 1972); A. Gleason, *European and Muscovite: Ivan Kireevsky and the Origins of Slavophilism* (Cambridge, Mass., 1972).

above all a lay theologian and the creator of Slavophile ecclesiology. Aksakov and Samarin, who were known as the "younger Slavophiles," were both fascinated by Hegel in their youth. At the beginning of the forties they were what has been termed "Orthodox Christian Hegelians,"[2] but they abandoned Hegelianism when they decided that it could not be reconciled with Slavophile ideas. Within the Slavophile movement, however, Aksakov and Samarin represented diametrically opposing trends. Aksakov, who had studied history and philology, was an extreme utopian idealist, with a fanatical belief in the virtues of the common people and "folk principles"; he even went so far as to grow a beard and wear the traditional Russian peasant coat, although (according to Chaadaev) this merely led to his being mistaken for a Persian. Samarin, on the other hand, was a sober politician not given to moralizing; when in later years he played an active part in drawing up and putting into effect the land reforms of 1861, he was quick to see how the Slavophile cult of the common people could serve the political interests of the nobility.

We should also note the names of three other Slavophiles who did not, however, make any important theoretical contributions to the movement's doctrine. These are Petr Kireevsky (Ivan's brother), a folklorist and collector of Russian folk songs; Aleksandr Koshelev, a politician who in the 1860's represented the right wing of gentry liberalism; and Ivan Aksakov (Konstantin's brother), who was to become one of the leading representatives of Russian Pan-Slavism.

THE SLAVOPHILES' PHILOSOPHY OF
HISTORY AND SOCIAL IDEAS

The central issue of Slavophile ideology was Russia's relationship to Western Europe, which the Slavophile's examined in the light of an all-embracing philosophy of history. The principal tenets of their philosophy were formulated in 1839 in Kireevsky's unpublished article "A Reply to Khomiakov," and were expanded in Kireevsky's long essay *On the Character of European Civilization and Its Relationship to Russian Civilization* (1952).

The fabric of European civilization, Kireevsky argued, was made up of three strands: Christianity, the young barbarian races who destroyed the Roman Empire, and the classical heritage. Russia's exclusion from the Roman heritage was the essential feature dis-

2. Cf. D. I. Tschiževskij, *Gegiel w Rossii* (Paris, 1939).

tinguishing her from the West. In the pre-Slavophile stage of his intellectual development[3] Kireevsky had regarded this circumstance as regrettable, but as a Slavophile he came to see it as a blessing. He saw ancient Rome as a rationalist civilization that represented "the triumph of naked and pure reason relying on itself alone and recognizing nothing above or outside itself."[4] That was why the Romans had excelled mainly in the sphere of jurisprudence, in the pernicious rationalization and formalization of vital social bonds. The juridical rationalism of the Roman state had appeared to hold society together, but it had actually torn apart its organic unifying bonds. Roman society had been merely an aggregation of rationally thinking individuals motivated by personal advantage and knowing no other social bond than that of common business interests. The state, or "universal" sphere, had split off from the sphere of private, antagonistic interests and had risen above it as an alienated, external force that chained people together but did not unite them. Having inherited this pagan rationalism, Western Europe found its evolution bound to be a constant struggle of mutually antagonistic interests; Russia, on the other hand, had been spared this fatal heritage and was therefore established on purely Christian principles that were in complete harmony with the spirit of the Slavic peasant commune.

"Private and social life in the West," Kireevsky wrote, "are based on the concept of an individual and separate independence that presupposes the isolation of the individual. Hence the external formal relations of private property and all types of legal conventions are sacred and of greater importance than human beings."[5] In this world, there could only be an external and artificial unity precluding freedom; that is why European history had (in Khomiakov's succinct phrase) been the history of the struggle between "unity without freedom" and "freedom without unity." According to Khomiakov, the first principle was embodied in the Catholic Church, which established papal absolutism, exchanged the bond of love for institutionalized bonds, and itself came to resemble a

---

3. That is, during the period that Kireevsky was editor of the periodical *The European* (1832). At this time his outlook—which was influenced by the philosophical romanticism of the Wisdom-lovers—was clearly pro-Western (as the title of the periodical suggests). His article "The Nineteenth Century," published in *The European*, aroused the suspicions of the emperor himself and led to the suppression of the periodical.

4. I. V. Kireevsky, *Polnoe sobranie sochinenii*, ed. M. O. Gershenzon (2 vols.; M, 1911), vol. 1, p. 111.

5. *Ibid.*, p. 113.

hierarchical and authoritarian state. The second principle found expression in Protestantism, which was justified as a negative reaction but lacked constructive force. Further stages in Europe's spiritual evolution listed by Khomiakov were the philosophy of the Enlightenment, which paved the way for the French Revolution, and German idealism, which ultimately led to Feuerbach's deification of man and Stirner's apotheosis of egoism. This spiritual evolution was accompanied by appropriate social changes, such as the growing atomization of society and its increasing rationalization. Atomization, in turn, led logically to the idea of a "contract" as the only rational bond linking isolated autonomous individuals. The "social contract" thus was clearly not the "brainchild of the encyclopedists but a concrete ideal that had once been the unconscious and was now the conscious goal of all Western nations" (Kireevsky). Organic communities were replaced by associations based on calculations, and human energy was now entirely redirected to the outside, to feverish and restless activity. This soulless "logicotechnical" civilization was governed by the mechanism of industrial production.

"Only one serious thing," Kireevsky wrote, "was left to man, and that was industry. For him the reality of being survived only in his physical person. Industry rules the world without faith or poetry. In our times it unites and divides people. It determines one's fatherland, it delineates classes, it lies at the base of state structures, it moves nations, it declares war, makes peace, changes *mores*, gives direction to science, and determines the character of culture. Men bow down before it and erect temples to it. It is the real deity in which people sincerely believe and to which they submit. Unselfish activity has become inconceivable; it has acquired the same significance in the contemporary world as chivalry had in the time of Cervantes."[6]

In ancient, pre-Petrine Russia, the Slavophiles believed that they had found an entirely different form of social evolution. Orthodox Christianity—a form of Christianity that had not been infected by Pagan rationalism or the secular ambitions of Catholicism—had contributed a principle unknown to the West, that of *sobornost'*[7] or "conciliarism" (Khomiakov). This was a form of true fellowship, a "free unity" of believers that precluded both self-willed individual-

---

6. *Ibid.*, p. 246. (Quoted from J. Edie et al., *Russian Philosophy* [3 vols.; Chicago, 1965], vol. 1, p. 195; the last sentence has been retranslated.)

7. The word *sobornost'* comes from the noun *sobor* (council) and the verb *sobirat'* (collect, connect, unite).

ism and its restraint by coercion. The relationship between the common people and the ruler it had "called" to power (a reference to the "calling of the Varangians") was based on mutual trust. The disintegrating egoism of private ownership as a privilege divorced from any duties was unknown, and so was the rigid division into estates and the ensuing antagonisms. In ancient Russia the basic social unit was the village commune (*obshchina*), which was founded on the common use of land, mutual agreement, and community of custom, and which was governed by the *mir*—a council of elders who settled disputes in accordance with hallowed traditions and were guided by the principle of unanimity rather than the mechanical majority of a ballot. Society was held together by what was primarily a moral bond—a bond of convictions—that united the entire land of Rus' into one great *mir*, a nationwide community of faith, land, and custom.

At first glance it might seem that there is no room in this picture for an absolute ruler or a strong centralized government. In fact, however, the Slavophile interpretation of Russian history had little in common with the Decembrists' idealization of "ancient Russian freedom" or with Lelewel's conception of Slavic communalism. In contrast to these conceptions, the Slavophile ideal of "ancient Russian freedom" had nothing in common with "republican liberty." This fact emerges most clearly in the historical writings of Konstantin Aksakov. Republican liberty, he argued, was political freedom, which presupposed the people's active participation in political affairs; ancient Russian freedom, on the other hand, meant *freedom from politics*—the right to live according to unwritten laws of faith and tradition, and the right to full self-realization in a moral sphere on which the state would not impinge.

This theory rested on a distinction the Slavophiles made between two kinds of truth: the "inner" and the "external" truth. The inner truth is in the individual the voice of conscience, and in society the entire body of values enshrined in religion, tradition, and customs—in a word, all values that together form an inner unifying force and help to forge social bonds based on shared moral convictions. The external truth, on the other hand, is represented by law and the state, which are essentially conventional, artificial, and "external"—all the negative qualities that Kireevsky and Khomiakov ascribed to institutions and social bonds that had undergone a rationalizing and formalizing process. Aksakov went even further than the other Slavophiles in regarding *all* forms of legal and political relations as inherently evil; at their opposite pole was the communal principle, embodied in the village commune, based (in Aksakov's view) purely on trust and unanimity and not on any legal guarantees or conditions and agreements characteristic of a rational contract. For Aksakov the difference between Russia and the West was that in Russia the state had not been raised to the "principle" on which social organization was largely founded. When the frailty of human nature and the demands of defense appeared to make political organization necessary, Russians "called" their rulers from "beyond the sea"[8] in order to avoid doing injury to the "inner truth" by evolving their own statehood; Russian tsars were given absolute powers so that the people might shun all contacts with the "external truth" and all participation in affairs of state. Relations between "land" (that is the common people who lived by the light of the inner truth) and state rested upon the principle of mutual noninterference. Of its own free will the state consulted the people, who presented their point of view at Land Assemblies but left the final decision in the monarch's hands. The people could be sure of complete freedom to live and think as they pleased, while the monarch had complete freedom of action in the political sphere. This relationship depended entirely on moral convictions rather than legal guarantees, and it was this that constituted Russia's superiority to Western Europe. "A guarantee is an evil," Aksakov wrote. "Where it is necessary, good is absent; and life where good is absent had better disintegrate than continue with the aid of evil."[9] Aksakov conceded that there was often a wide gap between ideal and reality, but ascribed this entirely to human imperfections. He strongly condemned rulers who tried to interfere in the inner life of the "land," but even in the case of Ivan the Terrible, whose excesses he condemned, he would not allow that the "land" had the right to resistance and he praised its long-suffering loyalty.

A paradoxical aspect of Aksakov's argument is that he subconsciously adopted and applied to Russia's past one of the chief assumptions of Western European liberal doctrine—the principle of the total separation of the political and social spheres. At the same time he rejected both liberal constitutionalism and the very content of the liberal ideal of freedom. Aksakov's interpretation of the freedom of the "land" is not to be confused with the freedom of the

8. What Aksakov had in mind was the legend about the "calling of the Varangians" from Nestor's *Primary Chronicle*, according to which the Kievan state was founded by "Norman" (or Norse) princes who were invited by the quarreling local tribes to rule over them.

9. K. S. Aksakov, *Polnoe sobranie sochinenii* (3 vols.; M, 1861–80), vol. 1, pp. 9, 10.

individual, since in his interpretation freedom only applied to the "land" as a whole; it was not the freedom of the individual in the community, but the community's freedom from outside interference in matters of faith, traditions, or customs. This noninterference had nothing to do with the liberal doctrine of *laissez-faire*, since, according to Aksakov, the moral principles of the "land" rendered economic individualism out of the question. Even his call for freedom of speech was not a truly liberal postulate since it did not envisage the acceptance of pluralistic beliefs or of minority oppositions within society. While demanding freedom in the nonpolitical sphere, Aksakov wanted every individual to submit totally to his *mir*—a submission, moreover, that was to be "according to conscience" and not only "according to law." His ideal was a "free unity" based on a total unanimity that would reduce external constraints to a minimum but at the same time exclude individual autonomy and any departure from communal traditions.

The greatest difficulty faced by the Slavophiles in their interpretation of Russian history was to find an adequate explanation for the Petrine reforms. How was it possible, they had to ask themselves, that the truly Christian community of ancient Russia gave way before the onslaught of an inferior civilization based on the "external truth"? The fault, they suggested, lay not with the people but with the state and those members of the elite who were dazzled by the purely external achievements of European nations. A civilization based on rationalist criteria can evolve faster and more easily than one based on Christian principles, for its development does not depend on the inner perfection of its human potential; therefore Europe outstripped Russia in the material sphere and built a civilization whose technical achievements aroused the envy of Peter and his supporters.

The Petrine reforms, according to the Slavophiles, cut the links between Russia's upper strata and the common people.[10] A leitmotiv of Slavophile ideology is the consequent cleavage in Russian life, the antithesis between the people (*narod*) and society (*obshchestvo*) —the enlightened elite that had adopted Western ways. The people cultivated stable customs, whereas society bowed to the caprice of

10. The Slavophiles maintained that before Peter the higher estates were an organic part of the "people." In fact, by "people" they meant all sections of society who had remained faithful to the old tradition—for instance the old Moscow merchant families were part of the "people," whereas Westernized merchants belonged to "society."

fashion; the people had preserved the patriarchal family, whereas society was witnessing the breakup of family ties; the people had remained faithful to ancient Russian traditions, whereas society was an artificial product of the Petrine reforms. Westernized Russians had become "colonizers in their own country" (Khomiakov). Through being torn away from their popular roots, they had lost their sense of historical attachment and had become what Chaadaev had accused them of being: men without a fatherland, strangers in their own country, homeless wanderers. The return of the enlightened sections of society to the fold of Orthodoxy and the "native principles" preserved in the present village commune seemed, from this vantage point, to offer the only hope of a cure for Russia.

THE CONCEPT OF THE "INTEGRAL PERSONALITY" AND "NEW PRINCIPLES IN PHILOSOPHY"

It was suggested earlier that Slavophile ideology could be interpreted as a reply to Chaadaev's *Philosophical Letters*.[11] From a wider perspective, one might say that it was a reaction to processes taking place in the awareness of the intellectual elite—the generation of "superfluous men" who lived during the reign of Nicholas I and were immortalized in Turgenev's novels. Herzen aptly defined this reign as a "strange age of external constraint and inner liberation."[12] Despite the government's constant attempts to ward off "infection" from Europe, the Russia of Nicholas experienced to an unusual degree the impact of cultural influences from Western Europe. Literature and philosophy became increasingly powerful tools in the liberation of the individual from the pressure of received truths imbibed at the breast and accepted unreflectively. The struggle for emancipation that would not be played out in the political arena became "introverted" and found an outlet in philosophical exaltation and the cult of introspection, accompanied by a sense of isolation, alienation, and inner fragmentation. The articles and letters of the young Bakunin, Herzen, Stankevich, and Belinsky are filled with complaints about the excessive reflection that kills all spontaneity, about inner dualism, about "spectrality" and Hamlet-like self-analysis. The Chaadaevian motif of alienation and homelessness also makes an appearance: "a wanderer in Europe, a stranger at home and a stranger abroad" is how Herzen described

11. See the end of the chapter on Chaadaev, p. 91.
12. A. Herzen, *Sobranie sochinenii* (30 vols.; M, 1954–65), vol. 14, p. 157.

the hero of his novel;[13] and Ogarev echoed this with his *"Ich bin ein Fremdling überall"*—a homeless wanderer from country to country.[14]

For the Slavophiles these moods were a symptom of the "spiritual malady" that resulted from the cleavage between "polite society" and the common people. They welcomed this symptom, however, as evidence that alienation was not accepted as something normal. Their aim was to help the "Russian Hamlets" overcome their alienation and inner dualism by showing them the ideal of the *tsel'naia lichnost'*, the integral personality.

In their philosophy of man and their epistemology, the Slavophiles (especially I. Kireevsky) were largely concerned with analyzing the destructive influence of rationalism. Rationalism, they argued, is the main factor in social disintegration, and also destroys the inner wholeness of the human personality. The ideal, untainted personality is an integral structure with an "inner focus." This "inner focus" helps to harmonize the separate psychic powers and safeguards the inner unity and wholeness, or "integrality" (*tsel'nost'*), of the spirit. The unifying principle is concealed but can be grasped by means of inner concentration; it is only this "vital focus hidden from the ordinary condition of the human soul" but accessible to those who seek it that makes the psyche something more than an aggregate of heterogeneous functions. Natural reason, or the capacity for abstract thought, is only one of the mental powers and by no means the highest: its one-sided development impoverishes man's perceptive faculties by weakening his capacity for immediate intuitive understanding of the truth. The cult of reason is responsible for breaking up the psyche into a number of separate and unconnected faculties, each of which lays claim to autonomy. The resulting inner conflict corresponds to the conflict between different kinds of sectional party interests in societies founded on rationalistic principles. Inner divisions remain, even when reason succeeds in dominating the other faculties: the autocratic rule of reason intensifies the disintegration of the psyche, just as rationally conceived social bonds "chain men together but do not unite them" and thus intensify social atomization. "The tyranny of reason in the sphere of philosophy, faith, and conscience," wrote Samarin, "has its practical counterpart in the tyranny of the central government in the sphere of social relations."[15]

13. Beltov, the hero of *Who Was Guilty?*.
14. In his poem "Humor."
15. Yury Samarin, *Sochineniia* (M, 1877), vol. 1, pp. 401–2.

Thus, against the principle of autonomy the Slavophiles set the ideal of "integrality," the precondition of which they found in religious faith uncontaminated by rationalism. Only faith, they claimed, could ensure the wholeness of the psyche. Faith helped to fuse "the separate psychic powers . . . into one living unity, thus restoring the essential personality in all its primary indivisibility." Thanks to Orthodoxy, Russians were still capable of attaining this kind of inner integration. In their search for truth they were guided not by natural reason but by "integral reason," which represented the harmonious unity of all the psychic powers. The inhabitants of Western Europe, on the other hand, had long since lost their inner wholeness, their capacity for inner concentration, and their grasp on the profound current of spiritual life. Different spheres of life— the intellectual, moral, economic, and religious spheres—had become separated and were in conflict with each other. This was responsible for the amorality of Western civilization, which could continue to advance even when the inner psychic powers had become weakened, when total havoc reigned in the sphere of moral values. At the same time Western civilization suffered from a tragic dilemma: the "division of life as a whole and that of all the separate spheres of individual and social being."[16]

The Slavophiles emphasized that their conception of the "integral personality" was only a continuation of the philosophy of the Greek Church Fathers, to whose writings Kireevsky had been introduced by Father Makary, a learned monk from the famous Optina Pustyn Cloister. By acknowledging their debt to Eastern Patristics, the Slavophiles were trying to stress their roots; but it must be pointed out that their handling of this tradition was influenced by their reading of the German conservative romantics, with whom they had much in common. The idea of the "integral personality" is closely related to the typically romantic critique of rationalism, as is the theory of knowledge expounded by Kireevsky in an essay with the significant title *On the Necessity and Possibility of New Principles in Philosophy* (1856).

"Logical thinking, when separated from the other cognitive faculties," Kireevsky declared, "is a natural attribute of the mind that has lost its own wholeness.[17] Rationalism acts as a disintegrating force because it transforms reality into an aggregate of isolated fragments bound together only by a network of abstract relationships. Reason is a purely cognitive faculty that can only grasp abstract no-

16. Kireevsky, *Pol. sob. soch.*, vol. 1, p. 218.
17. *Ibid.*, p. 276.

tions and relationships; the substantial, on the other hand, can only be comprehended by a faculty that is itself substantial—in other words by the whole psyche. This kind of understanding presupposes a vital and *immediate* connection between the knower and the object of knowledge. By isolating the knower from reality and setting him up in opposition to it, rationalism casts doubt upon the reality and objective nature of the universe. True understanding, therefore, cannot be content to define relationships but must attempt to penetrate to the substantial essence of things, must be a kind of *revelation* or *immediate* cognition. Only *believing reason*, as Kireevsky called it, can achieve direct contact with God, the supreme principle of the oneness of the universe.

Not all individuals possess the capacity for true understanding to the same degree. The main weakness of Protestantism (and later of the Cartesian system), Kireevsky suggested, was that it ignored the existence of a spiritual hierarchy and attempted to find a basis for the perception of truth "in that part of human reason common to every individual." Philosophy inspired by Protestantism therefore had to "restrict itself to the domain of logical reason shared by every man, regardless of his moral worth. The concentration of all spiritual forces into a single power, the integrity of mind essential for attaining integral truth, could not be within everyone's reach."[18]

At first sight this characteristically elitist theory of knowledge seems to be incompatible with the elements of sociologism that are an unmistakable feature of Slavophile theories. Kireevsky, for instance, held that "everything essential in the human soul grows in it socially,"[19] that true faith (and therefore knowledge) could not be experienced by an individual in isolation, and that the authentic Orthodox faith was preserved only among the common people and not among the demoralized elite. In fact there is no real contradiction. The Slavophiles' "spiritual hierarchy" was not a hierarchy of talent or of social status; at its apex were to be found men of unusually strong faith bound by exceptionally strong ties to the national community and the fellowship of the Church.

An application of these ideas is to be found in Khomiakov's theory of knowledge, which assumes that only the organic fellowship of *sobornost'* makes true understanding possible. The organic root of understanding, he wrote, is *free will* and *faith*, and the degree of their intensity reflects the strength of the social bond connecting the individual to the collective. "The isolated individual,"

18. *Ibid.,* p. 230.   19. *Ibid.,* p. 254.

on the other hand, "represents absolute impotence and unalleviated inner division."[20] An individual can comprehend the truth only insofar as he is united to the Church in loving fellowship and thus becomes an organ of a consciousness transcending the individual (*sobornost' soznaniia.*) Thus truth, which is "seemingly accessible to only a few, is in fact created and shared by all."[21]

Only the Orthodox Church had preserved this supraindividual Christian consciousness in all its purity. Western European thought was everywhere infected by the incurable disease of rationalism. Kireevsky and Khomiakov approved of Hegel's criticism of Enlightenment intellect (*Verstand*) but felt that Hegel's own dialectical reason (*Vernunft*) was no less rationalistic and even more dangerous. Khomiakov called Hegel the most complete rationalist of modern times, a thinker who had transformed "living reality" into a "dialectic of incorporeal notions" and had exhausted the potentialities of cognitive rationalism by taking it to its logical conclusions. In Europe, the thinker who had realized the one-sidedness of philosophical reason was the aged Schelling, who had evolved his religious philosophy of revelation[22] in opposition to Hegelianism. Although the Slavophiles approved of Schelling, Kireevsky criticized the philosophy of revelation for confining itself to a merely negative critique of rationalism. The dilemma, as he saw it, was that a new, positive philosophy required true religious faith, whereas Western Christianity was itself infected by rationalism. Although Schelling was aware of this, and had attempted to cleanse Christianity of the deposits of rationalism, it was "a lamentable task to invent a faith for oneself."[23]

It was logical to infer from these arguments that only Orthodox Russia could give birth to a new and truly Christian philosophy capable of transforming European intellectual life. The Slavophiles felt that they themselves—and particularly Kireevsky and Khomiakov—had been responsible for formulating the basic principles of this new philosophy.

20. A. S. Khomiakov, *Polnoe sobranie sochinenii* (4th ed.: M, 1914), vol. 1, p. 161.

21. *Ibid.*, p. 283.

22. In 1841 the elderly Schelling was summoned to Berlin by Frederick William IV and there began his lectures on the "philosophy of revelation," which were supposed to reconcile religion and philosophy and counteract the growing influence of the Hegelian Left. Schelling called his philosophy "positive" and contrasted it with Hegelian rationalism, which he called a "negative" philosophy that was confined to the sphere of pure logical thought.

23. Kireevsky, *Pol. sob. soch.*, vol. 1, p. 262.

SLAVOPHILE ECCLESIOLOGY

The notion of *conciliarism* formed a bridge between Khomiakov's epistemological views and his theology—or, more accurately, his ecclesiology. In his essay *The Church Is One*, Khomiakov described the Church as neither "institution nor doctrine" but a "living organism of truth and love" pervaded by the spirit of *sobornost'*. This spirit of "free unity" made the Church an ideal social organism, an antidote to the social atomization and spiritual disintegration of the contemporary world.

Khomiakov's views on the role of the Church took as their starting point Slavophile criticism of Catholicism and Protestantism, which was mentioned earlier in connection with the Slavophile philosophy of history. He accused the Roman Catholic Church of choosing a material unity symbolized in the person of the pope, and thereby replacing the unity of love by utilitarian calculations (indulgences) and blind submission to authority.

Protestantism, on the other hand, abolished all outward symbols of the religious bond and became a religion of lonely individuals lost in an atomized society. For the *materialistic* rationalism of the Roman Church the Protestants substituted *idealistic* rationalism. Whereas Catholicism became set in reified concrete forms, Protestantism wasted itself in empty subjectivism; the Catholic spirit expressed itself most strongly in the antiindividualistic conservatism of de Maistre, whereas Protestant individualism turned into atheism and culminated in the nihilism of Max Stirner. The West, according to Khomiakov, was dominated by a secular version of Protestant individualism, even in countries that had remained formally true to Catholicism. At the same time the ancient Catholic principle of "unity without freedom" had taken on a new guise and drawn fresh strength from contemporary socialism, which, according to Khomiakov, was in fact an attempt to overcome social atomization by imposing a new kind of all-embracing authoritarian unity modeled on medieval Catholicism. This notion, which was clearly formed under the influence of Saint-Simonian ideas, later in turn influenced Dostoevsky, who in several works (*The Idiot*, *The Diary of a Writer*, and above all "The Legend of the Grand Inquisitor" in *The Brothers Karamazov*) set out to show that the Roman Catholic Church and socialism were closely related.

For Khomiakov Orthodoxy was the sole repository of the spirit of *sobornost'* and therefore the only true Church. In his description of this Church—or rather of his idealized vision of Orthodoxy—Khomiakov was influenced in many points by J. A. Möhler, a Romantic

Catholic theologian from Tübingen who claimed that contemporary Catholicism had degenerated into papism and that the ecumenical council and not the pope was the highest organ of the Church.[24] Möhler's description of the council as "unity in multiplicity" was close to Khomiakov's definition of *sobornost'* as "unity in freedom." In the Orthodox Church, Khomiakov argued, this unity was safeguarded by the far-reaching internalization of tradition, which expressed the supraindividual and suprarational consciousness of the community. This was a *real* unity, based on organic bonds at a prereflective stage of development and not subject to rationalization, and at the same time a *free* unity, not imposed from outside but regulated by norms in which members of the Church community saw reflected their own nature. In this Church there was no room for authority, since authority was always something external; nor was there room for individualism or subjectivism, since the awareness of individuals was not cut off from the supraindividual consciousness of the community. On the other hand, this collective consciousness was *internalized* by individuals and did not become alienated in the shape of institutionalized reified forms; in a fellowship of this kind, the measure of truth was not the authority of the pope or the Scriptures, but the extent to which harmony was achieved with the collective consciousness of the Church evolving historically as a supraindividual whole embracing the entire body of believers, laity as well as clergy. To be part of this transcendent whole was the only way to true understanding—hence Orthodox Russians were privileged when compared to the inhabitants of Western Europe.

Khomiakov was aware that there was a wide gap between his ideal vision of the Russian Church and reality: he himself once noted that his ecclesiology only showed the "ideal essence" and not the "empirical reality" of Orthodoxy.[25] The fate of his own theological

24. See S. Bolshakoff, *The Doctrine of the Unity of the Church in the Works of Khomyakov and Moehler* (London, 1946).

25. This, of course, made Khomiakov's attempts to convert others somewhat difficult. He often set out his theological views in his correspondence with various notables, including the Jansenist Bishop Looss and the Protestant theologian Bunsen. His most important letters are those addressed to the Anglican theologian William Palmer, a Fellow of Magdalen College, member of the Oxford Movement, and friend of Cardinal Newman. Under Khomiakov's influence, Palmer came to the conclusion that in the dispute with Rome, the Eastern Church had been in the right. He was very close to conversion, but the attitude of the Hierarchy, whom he came to know during his three visits to Russia, decided him against it. In the end Palmer, like Newman, embraced Catholicism, but insisted on the right to retain his own private views on the Schism. Khomiakov's correspondence with Palmer has been published by W. J. Birkbeck, *Russia and the English Church* (London, 1917).

writings is an illustration of this gap. They had to be printed abroad (mainly in French) and were strictly prohibited in Russia until 1879, when the Holy Synod finally sanctioned their publication. Even then the Russian edition had to be prefaced by a statement explaining that "the vagueness and want of precision of certain phrases are the result of the author's lack of specific theological training." From the point of view of the Synod, conciliarism was a dangerous principle leading to the questioning of church authority and neglect of external, institutionalized forms of religious ritual.

In his Preface to the posthumous edition of Khomiakov's theological work, Samarin called his friend and teacher a Doctor of the Church who had made an epochal contribution to Orthodox Christianity, and suggested that future generations would regard this as self-evident. Although this prophesy was not to be fulfilled, it is nevertheless true that Khomiakov's influence on Russian religious thought was very considerable. The large group of "lay theologians" who were active at the beginning of the twentieth century (Bulgakov, Berdiaev, L. Karsavin, and S. Frank, among others) examined Orthodoxy in the light of Khomiakov's ideas and developed various motifs borrowed from his writings. It must be pointed out, however, that Khomiakov's role was more important in attracting intellectuals to the Church than in influencing the outlook of the Russian clergy. The Orthodox hierarchy only refrained from attacking his ideas because they were reluctant to offend believers among the intelligentsia. The fact that many of Khomiakov's views seemed to the Orthodox clergy to smack of Protestant liberalism and Catholic modernism only deepened this mistrust. In a brochure published at the Sergeevskaia Lavra Monastery, the Orthodox theologian Father Pavel Florensky accused Khomiakov of rejecting ecclesiastical authority, obligatory canons, and the "principle of fear," and even questioned his political loyalty.[26]

SLAVOPHILISM AS CONSERVATIVE UTOPIANISM

It is understandable that the Slavophiles were inclined to exaggerate the "native" and "essentially Russian" character of their views. Yet seen in historical perspective, Slavophile ideology was clearly only an interesting offshoot of European conservative romanticism. In particular, there are striking affinities with the ideas of such German romantic thinkers as Friedrich Jacobi (the concept of "believing reason"), Schelling (the critique of Hegelian ration-

26. P. A. Florensky, *Okolo Khomiakova* (Sergeev Posad, 1916).

alism), Möhler ("unity in multiplicity"), Adam Müller (the harmful influence of Roman civilization on the history of Christendom),
and Friedrich Schlegel (rationalism as the cause of the disintegration of the psyche). The most striking parallels are to be found between the history of philosophy of Ivan Kireevsky and that of Franz
von Baader, who like the Slavophiles looked to Orthodox Russia for
future salvation.[27] Although there is no doubt that the Slavophile
theorists, especially Kireevsky and Khomiakov, were well acquainted
with the works of the German philosophers, one should not dismiss
these similarities as a matter of influence only. At a fundamental
level they were a function of social developments in the two
countries. Though at different levels of development, both Russia
and Germany were economically backward and faced the need to
modernize at a time when capitalism had already become established
in the more advanced countries of Europe. In these latter countries
the new social and political system had already begun to reveal its
negative features and had already come under attack by critics on
the right as well as the left; this gave German and Russian conservative thinkers a wider perspective, and made it easier for them
to idealize the patriarchal traditions and archaic social structures
that in their countries had shown an obstinate vitality.

Slavophile criticism of Western Europe was therefore essentially,
thought not solely, a critique of capitalist civilization from a romantic conservative point of view. In this instance, however, conservatism cannot be equated with the acceptance of the status quo in
Russia and suspicion of any kind of change; it was less defense of the
present than romantic nostalgia for a lost ideal. In this sense it is
possible to call Slavophile philosophy conservative utopianism:
utopianism because it was a comprehensive and detailed vision of
a social ideal, sharply contrasted to existing realities; and *conservative*, or even reactionary, because it was an ideal located in the
past. This utopianism also had a strongly compensatory element,
for dreams of a lost harmonious world always conceal some sense of
alienation or deprivation. As the educated offspring of old aristocratic families, the Slavophiles were too closely bound up with old
Russian patriarchal traditions, and at the same time too much
influenced by Western culture, to feel happy in the outwardly
Westernized authoritarian bureaucracy of Nicholas I.

The Slavophile utopia was not, of course, a utopia in the sense
of a carefully thought-out model of a future society. It was a vision
based on the concrete experience of that segment of the hereditary

27. See E. Susini, *Lettres inédites de Franz von Baader* (Paris, 1942), pp. 456–61.

nobility whose lives followed a firmly traditional social pattern. That is why Slavophilism contains many elements of what might be called "presociological" thought. The typology adopted by the nineteenth-century German sociologist Ferdinand Tönnies in his classic study *Community and Society* is of particular assistance in clarifying these elements. The Slavophile antithesis of Russia and Europe, of "people" and "society," and of Christian and rationalist civilizations corresponds almost exactly to the distinction Tönnies makes between *Gemeinschaft* and *Gesellschaft, community* and *society*.[28] In my first article published in the United States I wrote about this as follows:

It is significant that even the terminology was very similar. The Slavophiles saw contemporary Russia as a country split between the people, the folk, which remained true to the old "community principles" (*obščinnoe načalo*), and "society," an aggregate of individuals separated from the people and living a conventional and artificial life. This concept of "society" is almost identical with Tönnies' *Gesellschaft*; the Slavophile concepts of folk and "community principles" has essentially the same content as Tönnies' *Volkstum* and *Gemeinschaft*. Members of the community, according to Tönnies, are endowed with "natural will" (*Wesenwille*); "society" is composed of people endowed with "rational will" (*Kürwille*). This conception had its counterpart in the Slavophile conception of the organic "togetherness" of man's spiritual forces as opposed to calculated rationalism. "Community" was described by Tönnes and the Slavophiles as a living organism: "society" was presented as a mechanical artifact, a mere sum of isolated individuals. Tönnies and the Slavophiles alike insisted that real community is based on mutual understanding, concord, and unanimity (*Eintracht*), while society is characterized by inner conflict, mutual tension, and the rule of a mechanical, quantitative majority, which presupposes an internal atomization and disintegration of organic social ties. Community is an enlarged family; in society, human relationships assume a contractual form. The collective will of the community expresses itself as common belief and common custom; in "society" these great unifying spiritual factors are replaced by public opinion, always accidental and unstable. The modern bureaucratic state was regarded by Tönnies as a phenomenon of *Gesellschaft*; the same conceptions, the same characteristic pair of opposite categories—*Volkstum* and *Staatstum, narod* and *gosudarstvo*— were constantly used by the Slavophiles, to whom the bureaucratic state appeared to be a soulless machine, a product of the artificial Westernization of Russia. There is no need to multiply these similarities. It may be

28. See A. Walicki, *The Slavophile Controversy* (Oxford, 1975), pp. 168–78, 265–66. Here there is also a comparison between Slavophile ideas and the interpretation of the rationalization of social relations in the historical sociology of Max Weber.

interesting, however, to indicate that they can be found even among the purely historical generalizations of Tönnies and the Slavophiles. The latter believed, as we know, that Old Russia could preserve, let us say, the pure form of *Gemeinschaft* because she was not encumbered by the heritage of rationalistic Roman culture, especially that of Roman law, which was so powerful a force in the process of disintegration and dissolution of "community principles" in the West. Tönnies subscribed to this view when he wrote that "a rational scientific law was made possible only through the emancipation of the individuals from all organic social ties," and that "the assimilation of Roman Law has served and still serves to further the development of *Gesellschaft* in a large part of the Christian-German world."[29]

Attention has been drawn to these parallels between Slavophile ideas and those of Tönnies, not because of any desire to claim for Slavophile theory a degree of scientific importance it does not possess, but because Tönnies's typology provides conceptual tools for a better interpretation of the social content of Slavophilism. Romantic conservatism of the first half of the nineteenth century, wrote Karl Mannheim in his work on the German conservatives,[30] was an ideological defense of *community* against *society*. The Slavophiles provide an excellent example of the accuracy of this comment.

It is worth noting that Tönnies's view on the role of juridical rationalism in European history has been brilliantly corroborated by Max Weber in his powerful analysis of the progressive rationalization of economic production, human behavior, and social institutions of the West. "The tremendous aftereffect of Roman Law, as transformed by the late Roman bureaucratic state," Weber wrote, "stands out in nothing more clearly than in the fact that everywhere the evolution of political management in the direction of the evolving national state has been borne by trained jurists." It has been the work of jurists to give birth to the modern Occidental state as well as to the Occidental Churches." This evolution, according to Weber, was "peculiar to the Occident" and had no analogy anywhere else in the world.[31] The Russian Slavophiles would have subscribed wholeheartedly to this view.

Despite its obvious conservatism, Slavophile ideology aroused the

29. A. Walicki, "Personality and Society in the Ideology of the Russian Slavophiles. A Study in the Sociology of Knowledge," *California Slavic Studies*, 2 (1963), pp. 7–8. Tönnies is quoted from F. Tönnies, *Community and Society*, trans. and ed. by Charles P. Loomis (East Lansing, Mich., 1957), pp. 202–3.

30. See K. Mannheim, "Conservative Thought," in *Essays on Sociology and Social Psychology* (London, 1953), p. 89.

31. Cf. Max Weber, *Essays on Sociology*, ed. by H. H. Gerth and C. Wright Mills (New York, 1958), pp. 93–94, 299.

suspicions of the government. Nicholas I thought of himself as the heir to Peter the Great and wanted to be a European emperor rather than an ancient Russian tsar. His veneration for Orthodoxy and pure national principles notwithstanding, Nicholas had no intention of changing his methods of government to suit the requirements of religion or traditional customs. Moreover, he had some grounds for suspecting that the demand for an organic relationship between law and custom was an attempt to impose restrictions on autocracy. The Central Censor's Office struck the right note in its special report to the emperor on Kireevsky's article "On the Character of European Civilization," published in 1852 in the *Moscow Miscellany*: "It is not clear what Kireevsky means by the integrity of Orthodox Russia; it is obvious, however, that in his apparently loyal article he fails to do justice to the immortal services of the Great Russian Reformer and his imperial heirs, who were untiring in their efforts to bring Western civilization to their subjects and only by this means were able to raise the power and glory of our Fatherland to their present splendor."[32] Comments on articles by other authors in the Slavophile *Moscow Miscellany* (*Moskovskii Sbornik*, 1852) were of a similar nature. As a result, further publication was forbidden and five of the principal contributors (including Kireevsky) were placed under police surveillance and ordered to obtain special permission from the Central Censor's Office for any further publications.

Nicholas rightly sensed that there was a difference between his own conservatism and that of the Slavophiles. The Slavophile vision of ancient Russia—its idealization of the Land Assemblies and the notion of the separation of "Land" and "State"—embodied the ideals of the boyar opposition to absolutism. Kireevsky's critiques of rationalism was directed not only at the bourgeois rationalism of merchants and manufacturers, but also at the bureaucratic rationalism of absolute monarchy. The most uncompromising of the Slavophiles in this respect was Kostantin Aksakov, in whose antithesis of "state" and "community" (the land) the organs of government were dismissed as representing only an "external truth," "the principle of slavery and external coercion."

Lacking their own journal, the Slavophiles now published their articles in *The Muscovite* (*Moskvitanin*), edited by the historian NIKOLAI POGODIN (1800–75) in collaboration with the literary critic STEPAN SHEVYREV (1806–64). As Pogodin and Shevyrev also criticized the "pernicious influences" emanating from the West (Shevyrev was responsible for coining the phrase "rotten West"), contem-

32. Tsentr. Gos. Istorich, Arkhiv SSSR, fond. 772, op. 1.

poraries were apt to identify the Slavophiles wtih the *"Muscovite party."* The inference was not entirely sound: unlike the Slavophiles, Pogodin showed no interest in the peasant commune, did not criticize the Petrine reforms, and did not draw contrasting pictures of Moscow and St. Petersburg. Quite the contrary, he eulogized Peter the Great as the founder of the modern Russian state, portrayed Westernization as an essential stage, and held that the violence with which the reforms had been carried out was a characteristic expression of the spirit of Russian history, in which the State had always been the sole creative force, molding a passive nation according to its arbitrary will. What was specifically Russian for Pogodin was not the commune, or the spirit of fellowship in Orthodoxy, but the uncompromising nature of absolutism, whose strength was rooted in the boundless "humility" of the common people. His interpretation of history left no room for the Slavophile antithesis of ancient and modern Russia: by consolidating absolutism, he argued, Peter the Great had strengthened Russia's "native principle" instead of weakening it.

The differences dividing the Slavophiles from the exponents of the official ideology of "Orthodoxy, autocracy, and nationality[33] were therefore quite fundamental. Despite the conservative and backward-looking character of their social ideals, the Slavophiles made a truly creative contribution to the ideological disputes of the 1840's. That their ideals were capable of providing intellectual stimulus is shown by the influence they had on Herzen's "Russian socialism" and on the writings of Dostoevsky and Soloviev.

THE DISINTEGRATION OF SLAVOPHILISM

Slavophile utopianism was the product of an age in which Russian social thought could not be expressed or tested in the political arena. This situation changed after Russia's defeat in the Crimean War and the death of Nicholas I. Alexander II undertook certain overdue reforms (see chapter 11), including the easing of censorship restrictions on literature and the press. Contemporaries referred to these changes as the "thaw," and although this thaw was interrupted by attacks of frost and did not entail any basic changes in the authoritarian structure of government, it was enough to

33. This "triune" slogan, formulated by S. Uvarov, the minister of education, was the motto of Official Nationality during the reign of Nicholas I. On the ideology of Official Nationality, see N. V. Riasanovsky, *Nicholas I and Official Nationality in Russia* (Berkeley, Calif., 1959).

change the general climate of opinion. A new element was the widespread conviction that ordinary citizens had the right to express their views on affairs of state and to influence the direction of the reforms introduced by the government. There was also a growing feeling that abstract philosophical discussions must now give way to a realistic program of action. In this context, the romantic utopianism of the Slavophiles slowly began to disintegrate in favor of practical considerations that ultimately turned out to reflect the concrete class interests of the gentry. Those who now came to the fore were men with a gift for practical leadership, such as Ivan Aksakov, Samarin, and Koshelev.

In its transition from philosophy to politics Slavophilism split into two trends—a conservative reformism on the one hand, and Pan-Slavism on the other. Even within Slavophile reformism there were two trends, represented by Samarin and Koshelev, whose careers were almost identical. Both took part in the preparations for the emancipation act; after the defeat of the Polish uprising of 1863, both were sent on important government missions to Poland; and finally both were active in the *Zemstvos*. Their debt to Slavophile ideology is apparent in their defense of the village commune, although the arguments they used scarcely recall Konstantin Aksakov's idealized picture of the *obshchina* as a truly Christian social organism. Samarin and Koshelev regarded the commune as a useful instrument for exercising control over the peasants, facilitating the collection of taxes and redemption payments, and ensuring a source of cheap farm labor to the landowners. The land reform model they proposed (which was actually implemented by the government) was essentially a deliberate adaptation of the Prussian model—Samarin even wrote a detailed monograph entitled *The Abolition of Serfdom and the Structure of Peasant and Landowner Relations in Prussia*. Both men accepted the need for capitalist development in Russia (thus abandoning romantic anticapitalist utopianism) but feared that its uncontrolled expansion might result in social unrest; this danger could be tempered, they felt, by the institution of the commune and the active interference of a strong central government. The difference between the two men was that Samarin consistently opposed all types of representative institutions, whereas Koshelev was in favor of an all-Russian Land Assembly with advisory powers to be convened in Moscow, where it would act as a conterpoise to the Petersburg bureaucracy.

The events that provided the immediate stimulus for the transformation of Slavophilism into Pan-Slavism were of course, the

Crimean War and the resulting interest in the fate of the Southern Slavs. Khomiakov, who unlike the other Slavophile theorists had always been interested in his brother Slavs (and wrote about them in his three-volume *Notes on Universal History*), was not the only one to cry out: "Let the standards fly, let the trumpets sound!" One of the documents preserved in the Moscow archives is Konstantin Aksakov's memorial *On the Eastern Question*, which shows that he, too—until shortly before a determined pacifist entirely uninterested in the fate of the Slavs under Turkish rule—was affected by the mood of the times and proclaimed that the "holy aim" of the Crimean War was to conquer Constantinople and unite the Slavs under the rule of the Russian tsar. Russia's defeat dashed these hopes, but the Slavic question continued to be eagerly debated in nationalist circles.

Slavophile ideology could not be pressed into the service of Pan-Slavism without undergoing certain essential changes. The inner regeneration of Russian society in the spirit of Christian and ancient Russian principles now seemed less important than the external expansion of the Russian state. This idea harmonized with the wave of chauvinism that swept over Russia after the Polish uprising of 1863: when the insurrection was crushed, Slavophile doctrine provided a whole range of arguments justifying the harsh treatment of the Poles as the struggle of the "popular," Slavic element with the aristocratic "Latinism" of the Polish gentry.

The leading figure in the transformation of Slavophilism into Pan-Slavism was IVAN AKSAKOV (1823–86), an influential but hardly original thinker.[34] In the forties and fifties he was the least orthodox of the Slavophiles and the most susceptible to liberal and democratic ideas; later, however, under the impact of the insurrection in Poland and the growing strength of the revolutionary movement in Russia, he became bitterly hostile toward even the slightest manifestation of liberalism. Perhaps Aksakov's most characteristic feature was his obstinate adherence to the letter of Slavophilism despite his almost complete (though not conscious) jettisoning of its anticapitalist spirit. This found symbolic expression when he became president of one of the leading Moscow banks (in 1874). Not that anti-capitalist elements simply disappeared without trace—what

34. The Slavic Philanthropic Society—a Pan-Slavic organization led by Ivan Aksakov—reached the height of its influence during the Russo-Turkish war of 1877–78. After Bulgaria gained independence, some local election committees even put forward Aksakov as a candidate for the Bulgarian throne. On the development of Slavophilism after the Crimean War, see Frank Fadner, *Seventy Years of Pan-Slavism in Russia: Karazin to Danilevskii* (Washington, D.C., 1962).

happened is that they suffered a characteristic transformation into anti-Semitism ("the socialism of fools," as August Bebel called it), which figured largely in Aksakov's views after 1861 and clearly set him apart from the founders of Slavophilism.

Ivan Aksakov's articles on the Slavic question contain all the typical Pan-Slavist stereotypes: the antithesis of Slavdom and Western Europe; aggressive hostility toward Austria; the accusation that the Poles were the "renegades of Slavdom"; demands for the conquest of Constantinople and the establishment of a powerful federation of Slavic nations "under the wing of the Russian eagle." Despite his immense loyalty to his brother, it is immediately obvious that Ivan Aksakov's view of Russia as a nation with a powerful instinct for statehood, with expansionist and hegemonic tendencies, differed greatly from Konstantin Aksakov's idyllic vision of an apolitical nation devoted to a quiet Christian existence in small rural communes. Ivan's great-power chauvinism brought him closer to Pogodin, who earlier had made vain attempts to interest Nicholas and his foreign ministry in Pan-Slavic ideas. Like Pogodin, Aksakov opposed the "legitimist superstition" and wanted to inject "national" sap into the empire by subordinating domestic policy to Russian nationalism and foreign policy to Pan-Slavism. The new political atmosphere allowed him to act more openly than Pogodin, so that he was not afraid to criticize the government and to appeal directly to the more nationalistic section of public opinion.

To recapitulate: the classical Slavophilism of the 1840's was a romantic conservative utopianism, and a reactionary one insofar as it was based on backward-looking ideals. Yet despite expressing a conservative system of values, it went beyond the immediate and selfish class interests of the gentry. As an intellectual doctrine, classical Slavophilism helped to raise the level of philosophical discussion in Russia and stimulated both moral questioning and a critical attitude to existing social realities. The transition of Slavophilism from the philosophical-utopian stage to the practical-political one resulted in greater "realism" but also intellectual impoverishment; it overshadowed or even eliminated retrospective utopianism, but at the same time strengthened the community of interest between the theorists of Slavophilism and reactionary social forces. From the point of view of the historian of ideas, therefore, the Slavophiles are more interesting in the 1840's than later, when they had obtained their own journals and could take an active part in political affairs.

CHAPTER 7

THE RUSSIAN HEGELIANS—FROM "RECONCILIATION WITH REALITY" TO "PHILOSOPHY OF ACTION"

One of the characteristic aspects of the 1840's[1] in Russia was the fascination exerted by Hegelian philosophy. Hegel's works, Herzen wrote, "were discussed . . . incessantly; there was not a paragraph in the three parts of the *Logic*, in the two of the *Aesthetics*, in the *Encyclopaedia*, etc. that had not been the subject of desperate disputes for several nights running. People who loved each other avoided each other for weeks at a time because they disagreed about the definition of "all-embracing spirit," or had taken as a personal insult an opinion on the "absolute personality and its existence in itself." Every insignificant pamphlet of German philosophy published in Berlin or even a provincial or district town was ordered and read to tatters and smudges; the leaves fell out in a few days if only there was a mention of Hegel in it."[2]

The impact of Hegelian philosophy in Russia, as well as in Poland, cannot be compared to that of any other Western thinker; its influence was both widespread and profound; it reached to distant provincial centers and left its mark in Russian literature. In many instances this was only a superficial intellectual fashion; but seen as a whole, it was a phenomenon with far-reaching consequences.

First, the reception of Hegelian philosophy was the natural culmination of a period in Russian intellectual history which deserves to be called the "philosophical epoch." It was the epoch when the progressive intelligentsia, bitterly disappointed by the failure of the

1. The "period of the forties" in Russian historical literature usually refers to the years 1838–48, which Pavel Annenkov in his memoirs called "a marvelous decade." A most stimulating analysis of the intellectual history of this period can be found in the chapter entitled "A Remarkable Decade" in Isaiah Berlin, *Russian Thinkers* (New York, 1978).

2. Alexander Herzen, *My Past and Thoughts*, trans. by Constance Garnett (London, 1927), vol. 2, p. 115.

Decembrist uprising, lost faith in the efficacy of political action. Instead, intellectuals became preoccupied with philosophical problems, such as the meaning of history, the individual's relationship
to supraindividual social and cultural structures, and Russia's place
in universal history. In Russia, as in Germany, philosophical speculation had a compensatory function for men of intellectual vigor
living in a society where public life was almost totally paralyzed.

Second, Hegelian philosophy was welcomed as an antidote to romanticism. To begin with, it recommended itself as the antithesis
of introspective "day-dreaming" and attitudes of romantic revolt
inspired by Byron and Schiller; in this context Hegelianism was
largely interpreted as a philosophy of "reconciliation with reality."
Somewhat later it was seen as a powerful tool in the struggle against
romantic irrationalism and conservatism, represented in Russia
by the Slavophiles. At the same time (here the Left Hegelians in
Germany were not without influence) the need began to be felt to
master and transcend the Hegelian system; this in turn led to a
transformation of the philosophy of reconciliation with reality into
the philosophy of rational and conscious action.

Third, and last, both the "reconciliation with reality" and the
"philosophy of action" seemed to supply answers to moral and philosophical dilemmas that had tormented the "superfluous men"
mentioned earlier in connection with the Slavophile movement. For
educated Russians who suffered from their own alienation and inner dualism, Hegelianism was above all a philosophy of *reintegration*, of overcoming one's alienation either through a conscious
adaptation to existing reality or through efforts to change it. In the
latter variant, philosophy rehabilitated political action, which earlier had been despised, and ushered in the "translation of thought
into action."

NIKOLAI STANKEVICH

In the 1830's the chief center of Russian Hegelianism was the
Stankevich circle. The importance of its contribution to the evolution of progressive thought in the reign of Nicholas I can be
compared to that of the Wisdom-lovers to the formation of Slavophile ideology.

NIKOLAI STANKEVICH (1813–40) was a thoroughly typical representative of the younger progressive intelligentsia of noble birth.
In Annenkov's words, he "personified the *youthfulness* of one of
the stages of our development; he united all the best and noblest

characteristics, aspirations, and hopes of his companions."[3] His circle counted among its members the radical democrat Belinsky, the liberals Granovsky and Botkin, the anarchist Bakunin, and even the Slavophile Konstantin Aksakov. Herzen, the founder of "Russian socialism," was one of Stankevich's friends. In their later reminiscences, all these very different men recalled Stankevich with equal affection. Ivan Turgenev, whose novels are both a literary monument to the "superfluous men" and an indictment of their weakness, confessed that his association with Stankevich marked the beginning of his spiritual development.

Stankevich's early interests concentrated on the romantic philosophy of nature (especially the *Naturphilosophie* of Schelling) that had fascinated the Moscow Wisdom-lovers. Stankevich defined the nature of being as *creativity*, and *love* as its animating spirit. He was primarily concerned to overcome subjective aestheticism (*Schönseeligkeit*)—to free himself from the "oppressiveness of the particular" and to find support in the sphere of the "universal." At first he saw this as a question of religious identification of the self with God and with a pantheistically conceived nature. Under Hegel's influence, the nature of the problem changed almost imperceptibly until it came to express the conflict between personality and history, between the subjective aspirations of the individual and historical necessity. Although Stankevich did not formulate the need for reconciliation with Russian reality in so many words, there is no doubt that Hegelian philosophy provided him with arguments in favor of the rejection of romantic poses of revolt and "irrational" attempts to change the existing order. In one of his letters, which were in themselves miniature philosophical essays, he wrote: "The world is governed by reason, by the spirit—that sets my mind entirely at rest."[4]

This comment was not, however, Stankevich's last word. In spite of the advancing ravages of consumption, his mind was astonishingly active to the very end of his life. In his intellectual development he appeared often to anticipate many of the ideas of the Russian philosophical left. In the last year of his life, for instance, he read the early works of Feuerbach and the Polish philosopher August Ciezkowski's *Prolegomena zur Historiosophie* (Berlin, 1838). This led him to postulate (following Cieszkowski) the "translation

3. N. V. Stankevich, *Perepiska ego i biografiia napisannaia P. V. Annenkovym* (M, 1857), pp. 236, 237. The most comprehensive recent monograph on Stankevich in English is Edward J. Brown, *Stankevich and His Moscow Circle* (Stanford, Calif., 1966).

4. Stankevich, *Perepiska*, p. 342.

of philosophy into action" and to link this to a rehabilitation of the feelings and senses, as called for by Feuerbach. Death prevented Stankevich from developing his ideas, but any account of the intellectual evolution of Bakunin and Belinsky, of Herzen and Ogarev should note the part played by Stankevich in pointing out the way shortly to be followed by his friends.

MIKHAIL BAKUNIN

After Stankevich went abroad in 1837, the leadership of his circle was taken over by MIKHAIL BAKUNIN (1814–76). Bakunin's enthusiastic proselytism and his devotion to philosophy, which verged upon a fanatical intolerance of views he did not share, became almost legendary. For the young Bakunin, philosophy was the way to salvation and a substitute for religion; the desired trip to Berlin in 1840 was to him a journey to the "new Jerusalem."

At first Bakunin's interpretation of Hegel was influenced by the mysticism of the German romantics. He concentrated largely on the issue that traditionally occupied the mystics, namely man's separation from God. Salvation, he thought, depended on killing the "individual self" and liberating the element of infinity locked up within it. The way to achieve this salvation seemed to be at first through love and later (under the influence of Hegel) through total reconciliation with reality. Being the will of God, Bakunin argued, reality must be rational; everything in it is good and nothing evil, for the very distinction between good and evil (the "moral standpoint") is the result of the Fall: "Whoever hates reality hates God and does not know him." Poetry, religion, and philosophy help to reconcile man to God; anyone who has passed through these stages of development attains perfection: "Reality becomes his absolute good and God's will his own conscious will." In order to achieve this identification with the divine—to become "the spirit personified"—it is necessary first to pass through "the torment of reflection and abstraction," to experience the "independent development and purgation of the mind" that makes it possible to cleanse oneself of "spectrality." It is characteristic of Bakunin at this time that he substituted such mystical terms as "torment" and "purgation" for the Hegelian "negation"; in his interpretation, the dialectical drama of the Spirit became a kind of pilgrim's progress toward "the Kingdom of God," and philosophy a substitute for religion.

In his *Foreword to Hegel's School Addresses*, published in 1838,

Bakunin proclaimed the "reconciliation with reality in all respects and in all spheres of life." The separation from reality, he argued, was a disease, the "inevitable consequence of the abstraction and spectrality of the limited intellect (*Vernunft*), which recognizes nothing concrete and transforms every manifestation of life into death." Schiller's *Schönseeligkeit*, the subjective philosophy of Kant and Fichte, and Byron's rebellious poetry had been successive stages of this disease. The revolt of the intellect led to the Revolution in France, a country that was mortally sick, a symbol of barren negation, of "vast spiritual emptiness." "Reconciliation with reality in all respects and in all spheres of life," Bakunin concluded, "is the first task of the age. Hegel and Goethe were the leaders in this process of reconciliation, in the return from the state of death to life." The discrepancy between this article, which was generally accepted as a manifesto of Russian Hegelianism, and Hegel's own intentions is quite obvious. For instance (to give just one example), Hegel traced his philosophy back to the Reformation, which Bakunin (following the conservative romantics sympathetic to Catholicism) regarded as the original source of the "disease of the spirit."

Nevertheless, Bakunin's views did not spring from an authentically conservative outlook. Bakunin was a typical representative of the unattached intelligentsia—that is, members of the gentry who had become alienated from their own class and were therefore ready to adopt new world views associated with a different social background. His later philosophical evolution provides telling testimony of this. In Germany his ideas began to develop with such rapidity that they gave the impression of sudden leaps from one extreme to another.

The inner logic of Bakunin's ideas led him to a gradual affirmation of the active element in personality and a rejection of the contemplative ideal. Paradoxically, even his temporary recognition of the personal nature of God and the immortality of the soul was a step in this direction; the immortality of the soul seemed to be a metaphysical guarantee of the preservation of individuality, an affirmation of the autonomy and activity of the psyche. The idea of man's fusion with God gave way almost imperceptibly to the idea of setting free the divine element in *man*. In any case, Bakunin's new conception of God lent support to revolutionary negation and the philosophy of action rather than to reconciliation with reality: "God himself [is] nothing other than the miraculous creation of oneself . . . a creation that in order to be truly understood and grasped must be constantly understood anew—and it is the nature of action to be a constant affirmation of God-in-oneself."[5]

The notion of "action" was not new in Bakunin's world view. However, in the thirties, when he was under the influence of Fichte and had not yet read Hegel, he used the word only in connection with "spiritual acts." He criticized Belinsky for his "Robespierrian" interpretation of Fichte and for taking the postulate of action literally. Now, in 1842, Bakunin himself understood action as active participation in the revolutionary transformation of reality.

Bakunin's famous article "The Reaction in Germany" (published in 1842 in Arnold Ruge's *Deutsche Jahrbücher für Wissenschaft und Kunst*)[6] elaborates further the theoretical foundations of the revolutionary philosophy of action. The publication of the article coincided with Bakunin's decision to remain in Germany rather than return to Russia and to abandon philosophy for politics. The article was directed against the *juste-milieu*, against the "eclectic compromisers" who strove for the reconciliation of opposing sides. It was one of the first serious attempts at a radical left-wing interpretation of Hegelianism—at demonstrating what Herzen called "the algebra of revolution" through the Hegelian dialectic. Bakunin considered Hegel's greatest contribution to be his concept of the struggle of opposites and his recognition of "the absolute legitimacy of negation." In fact, Bakunin departed from the Hegelian interpretation of negation by rejecting the moment of mediation between the opposites. In contrast to Hegel, he saw transcending (*Aufhebung*), i.e. the final result of dialectic process, not as negating and preserving at the same time, but as a complete destruction of the past. The essence of contradiction, he argued, is not an equilibrium of the two opposites but "the preponderance of the negative," whose role is decisive. As the element determining the existence of the positive, the negative alone includes within itself the totality of the contradiction and so alone has absolute legitimacy. From this it follows that the creation of the future demands the destruction of the existing reality. Bakunin closed his article with the famous sentence: "The joy of destruction is also a creative joy" (*Die Lust der Zerstörung ist auch eine schaffende Lust*).

Bakunin signed his article with the French pseudonym "Jules Elysard." This had symbolic significance and was meant to show that he now rejected his recent Francophobia and sympathized with

5. N. Bakunin, *Sobranie sochinenii i pisem* (M, 1934–36), vol. 3, pp. 111, 112.
6. English translation in J. Edie et al., *Russian Philosophy* (3 vols.; Chicago, 1965), vol. 1, pp. 385–406.

France as the land of "action" and revolution. Many progressive thinkers (including the young Marx) were at that time attracted by the possibility of a future fusion of the German and French elements, of philosophy and political action. The idea of a "Franco-German intellectual alliance" was proclaimed also by Arnold Ruge, the editor of the *Deutsche Jahrbücher* and the leader of the Left Hegelians. In a short editorial note he therefore presented the article by Jules Elysard as a new and striking fact, namely "a Frenchman who understands German philosophy and . . . will induce certain [German] sluggards to arise from their bed of laurels." This example, Ruge suggested, should encourage Germans to give up their "boastfulness in the realm of theory" and to become Frenchmen.

VISSARION BELINSKY

The chief personality among the philosophical Left in the 1830's and 1840's was undoubtedly the remarkable literary critic VISSARION BELINSKY (1811–48). His philosophical explorations found an outlet in essays of literary criticism that had an unprecedented and indeed unparalleled influence in nineteenth-century literature.[7] Through these essays the issues discussed in the Stankevich circle reached a much wider audience. It is no exaggeration to say that Belinsky's dramatic intellectual evolution influenced the outlook of an entire generation.

Unlike his gentry friends, Belinsky, who was the son of a provincial doctor, had to support himself entirely by his own work and was often in financial difficulties. He was not allowed to complete his studies at Moscow University, ostensibly on grounds of "ill health and mediocre talent," but really because he had written a play [*Dmitry Kalinin*, a Schillerian tragedy attacking serfdom] that he was naive enough to submit to the university censors. The strong sense of human dignity that was such an outstanding feature of Belinsky's personality was formed early and had nothing aristocratic about it. It evolved in protest against the circumstances of his youth —the primitive corporal punishment used at his school, his brutal family life, and the humiliations encountered everywhere in an oppressive society. Last but not least, it was formed under the in-

7. See V. Terras, *Belinskij and Russian Literary Criticism: The Heritage of Organic Aesthetics* (Madison, Wisc., 1974). On Belinsky's and Bakunin's roles in the crisis of Hegelian "Absolute Idealism," see J. Billig, *Der Zusammenbruch des Deutschen Idealismus bei den Russichen Romantikern Bjelinski, Bakunin* (Berlin, 1930); and A. Koyré, *Etudes sur l'histoire de la pensée philosophique en Russie* (Paris, 1950).

fluence of the glaring contrast between literature, his greatest passion from childhood, and his entire daily environment.

The young Belinsky's world view was a characteristic mélange of philosophical romanticism (derived from Schelling) and rationalist faith in the power of education. He was fascinated by the rebellious courage of the heroes of Schiller's tragedies, and at the same time he was led by hatred of social injustice to look for a philosophy that would validate protest and struggle. His ideological drama began in 1836, when he believed that he had found such a philosophy in Fichte's voluntaristic, activistic idealism.

In Fichte's conception of an all-powerful Ego that nothing can crush once it has accepted its vocation, Belinsky saw a sanction of rebellion, even solitary rebellion; as he himself put it, in the new theory he "smelt blood." However, his ingrained *realism* made him suspect that heroic voluntarism was only an illusory solution and that "an abstract ideal taken in isolation from its geographical and historical conditions of development"[8] was doomed to be shattered when it came into contact with the stern laws of reality.

Toward the end of 1837, Belinsky came across a formulation of the problem tormenting him in Hegel's famous thesis that "the real is rational and the rational is real." According to this thesis, the "reason" of social reality is the law governing the movement of the Absolute, a law that is unaffected by the subjective pretensions of individuals. The individual's revolt against historical Reason is inevitably motivated by a partial—and therefore merely apparent—understanding, by subjective and ultimately irrational notions. For Belinsky this argument was a dispensation from the moral duty to protest—something that enabled him to reject the heavy burden of responsibility. "Force is law and law is force," he wrote in a letter to Stankevich. "No, I cannot describe the feeling of relief it gave me to hear these words: it was a liberation."[9] After thus paying homage to Historical Reason and accepting that "freedom is not license but action in accordance with the laws of necessity," Belinsky, like Bakunin, proclaimed his "reconciliation with reality."

In fact, Belinsky's reconciliation was an act of tragic self-denial. The enthusiastic glorification of Russian reality in his articles at that time did not adequately reflect his state of mind. This is clear from his private letters, where he spoke his mind more openly and revealed the painful doubts troubling him. He admitted that he had "forced" himself into reconciliation against his own nature,

8. V. G. Belinsky, *Polnoe sobranie sochinenii* (M, 1953–59), vol. 11, p. 385.
9. *Ibid.*, p. 386.

and by pushing aside his own "subjectivity." He believed that submitting to the inflexible laws of "rational necessity" would help him to gain a firm foothold on life, to become a "real" man rather than a "spectral" being.

In Bakunin's case, reconciliation with reality was based on a conservative romantic and mystical interpretation of Hegelianism. In Belinsky's writings, too, we find elements of romantic conservatism (for instance, the cult of "immediacy" and of irrational elements in national tradition); but on the whole, antiromantic motifs, such as emphasis on prosaic virtues, and rehabilitation of commonplace, "kitchen-sink" reality are more characteristic of him. For Bakunin, true reconciliation with reality was only possible through the mystical identification of the self with the divine essence of the universe. Belinsky was not so exacting: he was content to adopt the role of a man who did not indulge in sophistries but had both his feet firmly planted on the ground. His vindication of the "ordinary"—of simplicity and normality—expressed his desire to break away from the stifling atmosphere of the Stankevich circle, which he compared to a desert island. "Real life" as an ideal was to be an antidote to the vicious circle of "reflection," to the interminable epistolary confessions and endless games of self-analysis. Any useful participation in society, however limited in scope, was better than "rotten reflection pretending to be idealism," Belinsky maintained.

Belinsky seems to have abandoned reconciliation precisely because it did not—in fact could not—give him what he had expected from it. Far from providing him with a basis for reintegration, it intensified his feelings of alienation, his sense of being a specter rather than a real man. Having concluded that for him personally "rational reality" was something unattainable, Belinsky consoled himself for a time with belief in the rationality of the historical process as a whole—in a total "harmony" in which even dissonances have their place. However, these "philosophical consolations" could not arrest the influx of new ideas. In the years 1840–41 (when Stankevich and Bakunin were first beginning to toy with the idea of a "philosophy of action"), Belinsky underwent a profound process of inner liberation. This liberation came about as part of the struggle for the rights of the individual, for the radical reassessment of the antipersonalist implication of the idea of historical necessity, and for the vindication of *active* participation in history.

At first Belinsky rejected the "philosophy of reconciliation" on moral rather than theoretical grounds. In March 1841 he summed up his new attitude to Hegel in a letter to Botkin:

I thank you most humbly, Egor Fedorovich [Hegel], I acknowledge your philosophical prowess, but with all due respect to your philosophical cap and gown, I have the honor to inform you that if I should succeed in climbing to the highest rung of the ladder of progress, even then I would ask you to render me an account of all the victims of life and history, of all the victims of chance, superstition, the Inquisition, Philip II, and so forth. Otherwise I should hurl myself head first from that very top rung. I do not want happiness, even as a gift, if I cannot be easy about the fate of all my brethren, my own flesh and blood. They say that there can be no harmony without dissonance; that may be all very pleasant and proper for music lovers, but certainly not for those who have been picked out to express the idea of dissonance by their fate. . . . What good is it to me to know that reason will ultimately be victorious and that the future will be beautiful, if I was forced by fate to witness the triumph of chance, irrationality, and brute force.[10]

This emotional stand was not enough for Belinsky; his Hegelian training had not been in vain and he now felt he had to find an *objective, historical justification* for his protest. He was aided in this by his sense of solidarity with the masses, which helped him transcend his tragic sense of loneliness. The widespread public response to his articles and the growing force of public opposition to tsarist policies gave him the desired feeling that he was at last overcoming his "spectrality." He regained his faith in history—yet no longer as belief in the rational and historical justification of everything existing, but as belief in the rationality of general historical development.

One of the essential components of the mature Belinsky's world view was his dialectical historicism, which led him to conceive progress as a law of history enacting itself in unremitting criticism and negation of fixed, anachronistic social patterns. Belinsky's dialectic was rationalistic (like Hegel's and unlike Schelling's). The essence of history, for him, was the movement of reason: "Reason does not recognize a truth, theory, or phenomenon as real unless it finds itself to be an intrinsic part of it."[11] Reason now demanded the total emancipation of the individual, just as the notion of "rational reality" implied the negation of existing reality. This shift of emphasis enabled Belinsky to reexamine his attitude to the French Enlightenment and to take as his new heroes mainly "destroyers of the old" such as "Voltaire, the encyclopedists, and the Terrorists." At the same time he made clear his rejection of anti-historical Enlightenment rationalism. "Do not suppose," he wrote to a friend,

10. *Ibid.*, vol. 12, pp. 22–23.   11. *Ibid.*, vol. 6, p. 279.

"that I base my arguments on abstract reason [*rassudok*]; no, I do not deny the past, I do not deny history, I perceive in them the inevitable and rational unfolding of the idea; I want a golden age, but not that of the past, not an unconscious golden age on the level of the brutes, but one prepared by society, law, marriage, in a word by everything that once was necessary and rational, but now has become stupid and trivial."[12]

His dialectical view of history showed Belinsky a way of reconciling the tragic conflict between the individual's struggle for change and established social norms. It ought to be possible, he suggested, to play an active part in the transformation of nature and history through an understanding of the laws governing these forces. Aware of the utopian character of many progressive ideals, he tried to anchor them in reality, to show that they were an inevitable part of the historical process. He attempted to formulate a "philosophy of action" that would be free of Fichte's subjectivism, that would resolve Kant's and Schiller's dualism of ethics and necessity, and that would heal the split between the abstract ideal and the concrete, objective world. The difficulty confronting him was the lack of objective criteria of historical progress; this posed the threat of an unintended subjectivism in which Historical Reason would be equated with the reasoner's own reason—i.e. with the ideas of the ideological avant-garde of the Russian intelligentsia.

Belinsky's intellectual evolution followed the prevailing trend in European thought and in particular that of the Hegelian Left in Germany, which by emphasizing Hegel's links with the rationalist heritage of the Enlightenment, was trying to bring about a synthesis of German philosophy and French revolutionary thought, to combine German "thought" with French "action." Belinsky stressed that his rejection of the philosophy of reconciliation did not imply a complete break with Hegelianism. "Hegel," he wrote in a passage that paraphrased certain ideas first put forward by Engels, "turned philosophy into a science. His method of speculative thought is the greatest contribution made by the greatest thinker the modern world has known. This method is so unfailing and superior that it alone can serve as a tool for demolishing those propositions of his philosophy which are now inadequate or erroneous."[13]

One of the characteristic motifs in Belinsky's world view after

12. *Ibid.*, vol. 12, p. 71,

13. *Ibid.*, vol. 7, pp. 49–50. These words clearly demonstrate the influence of the young Engels's brochure *Schelling and Revelation*. Belinsky knew about this work through an article by Botkin on German literature in *Notes of the Fatherland* (1843), which repeated almost word for word whole passages from Engels's pamphlet.

his rejection of reconciliation was his defense of the particular (the real, living individual) against the tyranny of the universal (the Absolute, Reason, and the Spirit). On a number of issues this brought him close to materialism as a philosophical system that saw mankind as a collection of individual, sensual human beings. This emphasis that men are creatures of flesh and blood was characteristic of the anthropological materialism of Ludwig Feuerbach, whose *Essence of Christianity* made a deep impression on Belinsky (although he only knew it from hearsay). In the *Review of Russian Literature for the Year 1846*, for instance, Belinsky declared that personality is "a man with a body, or rather a man who is a man thanks to his body," and that "a mind without a body, a mind without a face, a mind that does not work on the blood and is not affected by it, is mere fantasy, a lifeless abstraction."[14]

It is worth pointing out that Belinsky was at least partially acquainted with the early works of Marx and Engels. As early as 1843 he read a summary of Engels' pamphlet *Schelling und die Offenbarung*, and two years later he came across essays by Marx ("On the Jewish Question" and "A Contribution to a Critique of the Hegelian Philosophy of Right") and an article by Engels ("A Contribution to a Critique of Political Economy") in the *Deutsch-Französische Jahrbücher für 1844*.

Belinsky's literary criticism was also affected by his break with the philosophy of reconciliation. Before this break he had dismissed "subjective" literature as an irrational rebellion against reality on behalf of an ideal fabricated by the narrow "abstract reason" of the individual. Schiller was for him at this time the personification of empty daydreaming aestheticism, of abstraction lacking a foothold in reality. His "Gods" were "Olympian" Goethe and Pushkin, great "objective" poets who refrained from judging reality. Of the later Pushkin he wrote that the poet "had found his way out of the aesthetic impasse to the harmony of an enlightened spirit reconciled with reality." After himself rejecting this reconciliation, Belinsky again acknowledged the value of what he called "subjective" literature, that is works expressing protest against existing social realities. At the same time he worked out a new and more sophisticated definition of "subjectivity" as a viewpoint transcending "objectivity" and not merely rejecting it; this "subjectivity" does not distort reality but reproduces it faithfully and judges it not from the point of view of the artist's whim, but in accordance with the forward-moving trend within society. Through his literary criti-

14. Belinsky, *Pol. sob. soch.*, vol. 10, p. 27.

cism Belinsky thus popularized the role of ideologically committed and realistic writing.

Belinsky insisted that realistic literature (he used the term "natural school" in literature) must provide a true and faithful picture of reality, but he also warned against confusing a faithful portrait with a mere copy. The true rendering of reality requires the revelation of the universal in the particular, the portrayal of *typical* phenomena that contain the essence of the infinite variety of life—universality distilled from an apparent chaos of facts. Since artistic generalization of this kind implies some form of value judgment, Belinsky concluded that there is no such thing as "pure art, since every work of art is tendentious." The difference between "objective" and "subjective" literature consists solely in the fact that the former affirms reality whereas the latter adopts a critical, active stance toward it.

Belinsky emphasized that universality in a work of art should not be confused with a "logical syllogism" or "schematic abstraction." This would be transgressing against the nature of art, which he defined as "thinking in images." Artistic generalization must obtain its effects through vital, concrete images working directly on the feelings and imagination of the reader—otherwise it is nothing but "vague rhetoric."

This theory represents a lasting achievement of Russian aesthetics and at the same time sums up the rich experience of the "Gogol period in Russian literature" (Belinsky's own expression).

ALEKSANDR HERZEN

Unlike Stankevich, Bakunin, or Belinsky, ALEKSANDR HERZEN (1812–70)[15] and his closest friend, Nikolai Ogarev, thought of themselves even as adolescents as the continuators of the revolutionary traditions of the Decembrists. Herzen relates how in the summer of 1827 (or 1828), during a walk in the countryside near Moscow, the two youths embraced each other and swore to devote their lives to the struggle for liberty. While attending Moscow University they founded a study circle that was to prepare them for the pursuit of this ideal. In his memoirs (written much later as an émigré) Herzen compared this circle with the Stankevich one: "They did not like

15. Herzen was the illegitimate but much loved son of Ivan Iakovlev, a rich and cultured nobleman who was an admirer of Voltaire, and a German mother (Louise Haag). He was called "Herzen" by his father (from the German *das Herz*—"heart"). The best American book on Herzen is M. Malia, *Alexander Herzen and the Birth of the Russian Intelligentsia* (Cambridge, Mass., 1961).

our almost exclusively political interests, while we did not like their almost exclusive interest in abstractions. They considered us to be Frondists and Frenchmen, while we thought of them as abstract sentimentalists and Germans." [16]

On closer examination this version of events does not entirely fit the facts. Despite their cult of the Decembrists and undoubted opposition to tsarism, Herzen and Ogarev were hardly less devoted to sentimentalism and abstraction than Stankevich. In the young Herzen's world view French influences (those of the Saint-Simonians, Ballanche, Buchez, and Pierre Leroux) coexisted side by side with equally influential ideas borrowed from Schelling and German romantic literature and philosophy. What attracted the young Herzen to Saint-Simonianism was not so much its political aspects as its philosophy of history and its revelation of a new religion, a new "organic epoch." The tsarist police were not, however, interested in such subtle distinctions. In July 1834 Herzen and Ogarev were arrested, and after a slow investigation lasting nine months were condemned to banishment. Herzen spent more than five years in the provinces—two years in Viatka and three in Vladimir. His compulsory service as a clerk gave him firsthand knowledge of the venal world of the tsarist bureaucracy and the brutality of the serfowners. At this time he became interested in religion and even mysticism. This fervor was partly the outcome of his correspondence with his extremely devout cousin Natalia Zakharina, whom he married secretly in 1838 in highly romantic circumstances (an elopement was arranged by friends).

Herzen returned from exile at the beginning of 1840, when the influence of Hegelian philosophy was at its peak. When he met the members of the Stankevich circle he was shocked by the gospel of reconciliation preached by Bakunin and Belinsky, which he considered a form of moral suicide. Nevertheless, since the philosophy of reconciliation claimed to have the authority of Hegel—the last word in "science"—behind it, Herzen was sufficiently interested to undertake a deep and systematic study of Hegelian philosophy. In the course of his work, he came to the conclusion that Bakunin's and Belinsky's interpretation was erroneous and that the best counterarguments were provided by Hegel himself. On the other hand, he perceived elements in Hegelianism that—if interpreted formalistically—could give rise to a cult of Historical Reason as an impersonal and cruel force, both alien to man and outside him. Herzen

16. Alexander Herzen, *My Past and Thoughts*, trans. by Constance Garnett (London, 1927), vol. 2, p. 114.

therefore undertook a reinterpretation (and critique) of Hegelianism that would vindicate independent action and the autonomy of the personality, two values he considered to be interdependent: "Action—is the personality itself," [17] he wrote in his essay "Buddhism in Science."

Reflection on Hegel opened a new chapter in Herzen's intellectual evolution and helped him outgrow his youthful romanticism and religiosity. New personal tragedies—another year's exile (1841–42; this time to Novgorod) as a result of careless phrases in his private correspondence, and the death of three of his children in rapid succession—did not bring about another attack of religious fervor but, on the contrary, helped to consolidate his new and "realistic" view of the world. In 1842 Herzen was ready to accept the main theses of Feuerbach's critique of religion and the atheistic conclusions to which they led.

The fruit of his reflections was an essay cycle, *Dilettantism in Science* (1843), of which the most important essay was the fourth, entitled "Buddhism in Science," in which Herzen put forward an interesting theory linking action and personality. The main influences in these essays (apart from Hegel, of course) were August Cieszkowski and Ludwig Feuerbach. Herzen had come across Cieszkowski's *Prolegomena zur Historiosophie* in Vladimir, even before he undertook his study of Hegel.[18]

Following Cieszkowski, Herzen divided history into three great epochs, corresponding to the three dialectical moments in the evolution of the mind: the age of natural immediacy, the age of thought, and the age of action. In the first epoch individuals exist in a world of particular interests and cannot attain universality; their existence is individual but they lack awareness and are at the mercy of blind forces. The negation of the moment of natural immediacy comes with the advent of thought or science; thanks to science, individuality renounces itself in order to become a vessel of the impersonal truth and is thus raised to the sphere of the universal. This is not the ultimate aim, however: "To perish in the state of natural

17. *Russian Philosophy*, vol. 1, p. 332.
18. In a letter to A. L. Witberg (July 1838) Herzen wrote about the *Prolegomena*: "It is surprising to what an extent I am in agreement with the author on all major points. That means that my ideas are correct, and I shall therefore work on them." A. I. Herzen, *Sobranie sochinenii* (30 vols.; M, 1954–65), vol. 22, p. 38. Cieszkowski's pioneer role in transforming Hegelianism into a "philosophy of action" (or "philosophy of praxis") is analyzed at length in N. Lobkowicz, *Theory and Practice: History of a Concept from Aristotle to Marx* (Notre Dame, Ind., 1967), pp. 193–206, 218–21. On Cieszkowski's influence on Herzen, see A. Walicki, "Cieszkowski und Herzen," in the collection *Hegel bei den Slaven* (Prague, 1967).

immediacy is to rise again in the mind and not to perish in the infinity of nothingness as the Buddhists do."[19] The abstract impersonality of science is in turn negated by conscious action; having transcended its immediacy, the self realizes itself in action, bringing rationality and freedom to the historical process. In Herzen's argument, therefore, personality is not just an instrument, but the ultimate goal of all development. For the "formalists," or "Buddhists in science," as Herzen called them, it was enough to raise individuality to the sphere of the supraindividual or impersonal; they annihilated the self and were not interested in its rebirth or in self-realization through participation in history. Herzen conceded that this was not merely a matter of misinterpretation, but that Hegel himself was largely responsible for this "Buddhist" reading of his philosophy. He agreed with Cieszkowski that Hegelianism was the highest achievement of abstract thought, and therefore the prologue to the negation of the negation, when thought would be transcended in action. As a child of the "age of thought," Hegel was absorbed in the sphere of the universal—of logic—and had overlooked the concrete demands of the self; but now the "personality ignored by science demands its rights, demands a full and passionate life which can only be satisfied by free and creative action."

Herzen's attacks were directed not only against Hegel's "contemplativism" but also against his "pan-logism," i.e. his identification of the laws of history with those of logic. Apart from the capacity for logical reasoning, Herzen argued, man possesses will, which "may be called positive, creative reason." This Fichtean emphasis on the will was clearly taken over from Cieszkowski, who opposed Hegelian logic by the "entirely practical sphere of the will." In Herzen's view, the future age of action rather than the age of thought (which culminated in Hegelian philosophy) was to be the epoch of true history. In Herzen's conception, nature—where "everything is particular, individual, and separate"—corresponds to the moment of natural immediacy, whereas logic (in the Hegelian sense) is the moment of thought that negates immediacy; the moment of action, which would in its turn negate the previous negation of logic, would express itself in history, which "transcends nature and logic and recreates them afresh." It is worth noting that in terms of the Hegelian triad, action here represents a dialectical return to immediacy. This was important to Herzen, who proposed

19. All quotations from "Buddhism in Science" are from Herzen, *Sob. soch.*, vol. 3, pp. 64–88.

something like a rehabilitation of nature and natural immediacy; he emphasized that, as part of nature, man is not only a thinking being but a creature capable of feeling, passion, and sensuality. Here Herzen used arguments borrowed from Feuerbach to support his own. *Dilettantism in Science* was, in fact, an attempt to reinterpret Hegelian motifs in the spirit of Feuerbach's anthropotheism. Both Herzen and Feuerbach formulated their ideal in identical terms: reconciliation of the particular and the universal, existence and essence, heart and reason, individual and genus. Undue importance should not, however, be attached to this similarity of phrasing. Feuerbachian philosophy was only a passing stage in Herzen's intellectual evolution, and the role it played was important but subordinate. The personalist ideal put forward by Herzen assumed a synthesis of materialism and idealism—of nature, in which "everything is particular," and logic, the sphere of the universal. This ideal was to be realized through the much-desired reconciliation of the Feuerbachian "man of flesh and blood" with Hegel's rationalist universalism.

Herzen's chief philosophical work, the *Letters on the Study of Nature* (1845), would appear to be concerned with entirely different issues. It opens with a strictly epistemological problem—a discussion of empiricism (identified with materialism) and idealism (or speculative philosophy) as two different ways of understanding reality. Herzen argues that the study of nature requires a knowledge of philosophy, and that philosophy cannot exist in isolation from the study of nature. Experimental and speculative philosophy are two separate aspects of the same body of knowledge: speculation on its own (apart from "empiria") and "empiria" unsupported by speculation are doomed to failure.

On closer examination it becomes clear that the argument about the relative merits of empiricism and idealism is of practical consequence and has some bearing on the ethical and sociohistorical problems that interested Herzen and the rest of the Russian philosophical Left. Empiricism (materialism), Herzen argues, proceeds from the particular and is incapable of organic synthesis; therefore it views society as the abstract sum of individuals and personality as the sum of mechanical processes and material particles. Idealism, on the other hand, proceeds from the universal, from the "idea" or impersonal "Reason," and is likely to overlook the concrete, individual human being. The conclusion of the essay—that "empiria" and idealism should combine and supplement each other—accords with the postulate for the harmonious "reconciliation of the particular and the universal" that was expounded in detail in "Buddhism in Science."

Herzen agreed with Hegel that the logical process of the evolution of self-consciousness is essentially identical with the historical process; the difference is merely that logic describes this process in a form entirely purged of all fortuitous elements. In order to understand any important philosophical problem, it is therefore essential to show its history and to grasp the inner connection between the logic of actual movement and cognitive logic. The *Letters on the Study of Nature* were an attempt to follow this method, and present an outline of the history of philosophy in relation to the historical evolution of Europe from antiquity to modern times.

In Herzen's dialectical view of history (as in Cieszkowski's analogical scheme) antiquity corresponds to the moment of natural immediacy. Christianity initiated the epoch of idealism, of the rejection of nature, of painful dualism and reflection. Herzen did not believe that the Reformation brought about any essential changes; unlike Hegel, he looked on post-Reformation Europe not as the beginning of a qualitatively new age but merely as the last stage of the Middle Ages. German idealism (including Hegelian philosophy) he dismissed as "the scholasticism of the Protestant world." Hegel, Herzen thought, had halted on the threshold of a new historical epoch—the "age of action"—whose role it would be to achieve a synthesis of the ancient and Christian worlds.

In Herzen's scheme this synthesis corresponded to the synthesis of materialism and idealism. For Herzen (as for Feuerbach) idealism represented a continuation of Christian theology, whereas materialism represented the rehabilitation of the natural immediacy of the ancient world. The rediscovery of Greek and Roman civilization during the Renaissance foreshadowed the future synthesis. The Renaissance led to the rebirth of materialism and the victorious forward march of empirical inquiry, whereas the Reformation encouraged the development of idealism, which culminated in the philosophy of Hegel. The task of the new age was to bring about a synthesis of Bacon (the father of modern empiricism) and Descartes (the father of idealism)—a synthesis of enlightened materialism and Hegelian idealism. This synthesis would benefit not only science but also—even chiefly—the development of the human personality. Like the Saint-Simonians, whom he had read avidly in his youth, Herzen assumed that there was a close connection between synthetic and analytic modes of thought (idealism and empiricism) and processes of social integration or disintegration. The renaissance of materialism and the growing emphasis on analytical and empirical inquiry from the Renaissance to the Enlightenment was the counterpart of the growing assertion of the self against the tyranny of tradition and authority. This process was beneficial but also posed certain problems. An undesirable side effect of the domination of a one-sided empiricism was social atomization or even the disintegration of the personality. Processes of disintegration had culminated in the philosophy of Hume, which deprived the personality of its substantial foundations and reduced it to a bundle of sensations and a sequence of moments in time.

"*Consummatum est!*," Herzen wrote. "The role of materialism as a logical moment has ended: in the sphere of theory it was not possible to advance any further. The world disintegrated into an infinite multiplicity of individual phenomena, our ego disintegrated into an infinite multiplicity of individual sensations. . . . The reality of reason, mind, substance, causality, even the awareness of self—all disappeared. . . . The vacuum that was the outcome of Hume's philosophy must have given the human consciousness a severe shock."[20] This quotation explains Herzen's reluctance to make materialism into a cornerstone of his theory of personality. Since he equated materialism with empiricism and naturalistic materialism, he wished to protect the human personality against the latter's "anatomical" and atomistic mode of thought. Idealism was to help in this defense.

Herzen did not complete his history of philosophy in the *Letters on the Study of Nature,* but there are good grounds for supposing that later letters would have been devoted to the philosophy of Hegel and Feuerbach. The main outline of his conception is clear: in the postulated synthesis of materialism (empiricism) and objective idealism, materialism was to protect the personality against the tyranny of "logic," i.e. against the hypostatization of universals and the demand for the absolute submission of the self. Idealism, on the other hand, was to defend the personality against disintegration, to organize the environment into a rational structure and to prevent a situation where there were "atoms, phenomena, a mass of fortuitous facts, but no harmony, no wholeness, and no ordered universe."[21]

It is interesting to note that as far as methodology is concerned, Herzen was convinced of the superiority of idealism. The greatest

20. *Ibid.,* p. 304.
21. *Ibid.,* p. 307.

methodological achievement of idealism, in his opinion, was the dialectic, which made it possible to see reality in all its dimensions—not statically but as a process with internal contradictions and relationships. When Herzen wrote of a synthesis of empiricism (materialism) and idealism, what he had in mind was in fact a synthesis of materialism and dialectics. That is why Lenin said of him (the quotation also applied to Belinsky) that in his *Letters on the Study of Nature* Herzen "came right up to dialectical materialism, and halted before historical materialism."[22]

22. V. I. Lenin, "In Memory of Herzen," in *Collected Works* (Eng.-lang. ed.; M, 1960–66), vol. 18, p. 26.

CHAPTER 8

BELINSKY
AND DIFFERENT VARIANTS
OF WESTERNISM

In contrast to the Slavophiles, their opponents, the so-called "Westernizers" (*zapadniki*), did not form a homogeneous movement with a single cohesive ideology and social philosophy. Westernism was only a loose alliance of potentially divergent trends, a platform where democrats and liberals in the 1840's found common ground in their opposition to Slavophilism. The controversial issue that divided the two groups was the "idea of personality," the key issue for the Philosophical Left, which the Slavophiles attacked as a Western misconception, the result of the false road taken by Western Europe. Slavophilism was therefore a philosophy that demanded an answer, especially since in the early 1840's the Slavophiles had already contributed an original interpretation of Russian history. The Westernizers, as Herzen later admitted, were increasingly aware of the need to "master the themes and issues put into circulation by the Slavophiles."[1]

Contemporary commentators were unanimous in ascribing the main role in the public debate with the Slavophiles to Belinsky. Herzen confined himself to private discussions, which he sometimes noted down in his *Diary*. In his philosophical ideas—and especially in his conception of "action" and "personality"—he was a determined opponent of the Slavophiles, but he was not an unequivocal supporter of "Europeanism." He was impressed, to some extent, by Slavophile criticism of Western Europe, which seemed to him to have much in common with socialist criticisms of capitalism. Herzen clearly felt that Belinsky's attitude to the Slavophiles was too hostile. This is shown by an entry in his *Diary* for May 1844.

Belinsky says: "I am a Jew by nature and cannot sup at one table with the Philistines"; he suffers, and because of his suffering he wants to hate

1. P. V. Annenkov, *Literaturnye vospominaniia* (M, 1960), p. 293.

and revile the Philistines who have done nothing to deserve it. For Belinsky the Slavophiles are the Philistines: I do not agree with them myself, but Belinsky refuses to accept the truth in the *fatras* of their nonsense. He cannot understand the Slavic world; they drive him to despair but he is not right; he has no presentiment of the life of the coming century. . . . A strange situation, a kind of involuntary *juste milieu* on the Slavophile issue: in their eyes [i.e. the Slavophiles'] I am a man of the West and in the eyes of their enemies a man of the East. This means that such one-sided labels have become obsolete.[2]

BELINSKY'S WESTERNISM
Ancient and Modern Russia

In his philosophical interpretation of Russian history, Belinsky was concerned with the same issues that interested the Slavophiles, above all with the role of Peter the Great and the antithesis of pre- and postreform Russia. In his analysis, he made use of a dialectical scheme current among the Russian Hegelians, although he was the first to apply it to Russian history. Individuals as well as whole nations, he argued, pass through three evolutionary stages: the first is the stage of "natural immediacy"; the second is that of the abstract universalism of reason, with its "torments of reflection" and painful cleavage between immediacy and consciousness; the third is that of "rational reality," which is founded on the "harmonious reconciliation of the immediate and conscious elements."[3]

Belinsky developed this idea in detail as early as 1841, in his long essay on "The Deeds of Peter the Great," in which he wrote: "There is a difference between a nation in its natural, immediate, and patriarchal state, and this same nation in the rational movement of its historical development."[4] In the earlier state, he suggested, a nation cannot really properly be called a nation (*natsiia*), but only a people (*narod*). The choice of terms was important to Belinsky: during the reign of Nicholas the word *narodnost'*, used—or rather misused—by the exponents of Official Nationality, had a distinctly conservative flavor; *natsional'nost'*, on the other hand, thanks to its foreign derivation evoked the French Revolution and echoes of bourgeois democratic national movements.

Belinsky's picture of pre-Petrine Russia was surprisingly similar to that presented by the Slavophiles, although his conclusions were quite different from theirs. Before Peter the Russian people (i.e.

---

2. A. I. Herzen, *Sobranie sochinenii* (30 vols.; M, 1954–65), vol. 2, p. 354.
3. V. G. Belinsky, *Polnoe sobranie sochinenii* (M, 1953–59), vol. 5, p. 308.
4. *Ibid.*, p. 135.

the nation in the age of immediacy) had been a close-knit community held together by faith and custom—i.e. by the unreflective approval of tradition idealized by the Slavophiles. These very qualities, however, allowed no room for the emergence of rational thought or individuality, and thus prevented dynamic social change.

Before Russians could be transformed into a nation it was necessary to break up their stagnating society. With considerable dialectical skill Belinsky argued that the emergence of every modern nation was accompanied by an apparently contradictory phenomenon —namely the cleavage between the upper and lower strata of society that so disturbed the Slavophiles. He regarded this as confirmation of certain general rules applying to the formation of modern nation-states: "In the modern world," he wrote, "all the elements within society operate in isolation, each one separately and independently . . . in order to develop all the more fully and perfectly . . . and to become fused once more into a new and homogeneous whole on a higher level than the original undifferentiated homogeneity." In his polemics with the Slavophiles, who regarded the cleavage between the cultivated elite and the common people as the prime evil of post-Petrine Russia, Belinsky argued that "the gulf between society and the people will disappear in the course of time, with the progress of civilization." This meant "raising the people to the level of society," he was anxious to stress, and not "forcing society back to the level of the people," which was the Slavophiles' remedy. The Petrine reforms, which had been responsible for this social gulf, were therefore, in Belinsky's view, the first and decisive step toward modern Russia. "Before Peter the Great, Russia was merely a people [*narod*]; she became a nation [*natsiia*] thanks to the changes initiated by the reformer."[5]

The Petrine reforms thus represented the radical negation of the natural immediacy of ancient Russia; in accordance with the dialectical process, however, this antithesis had to be followed by a synthesis—that is, a dialectical return to "immediacy" on a higher plane. Peter the Great negated ancient Russian immediacy in the name of the universal human values represented by European civilization; these universal values had in turn to assume national form so that the negation of immediate instinctive nationality could lead to the positive emergence of a new conscious national awareness. This, in fact, is what happened in Russia. The Napoleonic campaign of 1812 was, in Belinsky's view, the catalyst that helped to form this new national consciousness, which found expression in

5. *Ibid.*, p. 124.

the poetry of Pushkin—the first great Russian poet, in whose work the national and universal elements were organically fused.

It would appear, from this argument, that the stage of negation of the national on behalf of the universal initiated by Peter could now be considered a closed chapter. In his "Review of Russian Literature for the Year 1846," Belinsky in fact expressly supported this view and even conceded that the Slavophiles deserved credit for certain aspects of their criticism of Westernization. He appeared to be struck most forcibly by their comments on the cleavage in Russian life and the lack of moral unity—in other words, by their criticism of the "superfluous men" and of "society torn forcibly away from its immediacy."[6] Belinsky, with his own painful experiences in mind, was ready to agree that the consequence of loss of immediacy was alienation; he did not believe, however, that it was possible to return to an earlier stage of social development. Using Hegelian arguments to prove that Peter's reforms had been historically inevitable, he pointed out the utopian character of the Slavophiles' program and accused them of misinterpreting the concept of independent development: "To bypass the period of reforms, to leap over it, as it were, and to return to the preceding stage —is that what they call distinctive development? A really ridiculous idea, if only because it cannot be done, just as one cannot change the order of the seasons or force winter to come after spring, or autumn to precede summer."[7]

Although Belinsky argued that the period of reforms had run its course, this did not mean that he no longer admired the type of historical leader represented by Peter. On the contrary, he continued to regard him as the personification of the idea of rational and conscious activity, without the faults of either unreflective traditionalism or "rotten reflection." In 1847 he wrote to Kavelin: "Peter is my philosophy, my religion, my revelation in everything that concerns Russia. He is an example to great and small, to all who want to achieve something, to be in any way useful. Without the immediate element everything is rotten, abstract, and lifeless, but where there is nothing but immediacy everything is wild and nonsensical."[8]

Narodnost' and Natsional'nost' in Literature

Belinsky's Westernism played perhaps an even more prominent role in his literary criticism. In his critical debut in 1834 (in the

6. *Ibid.*, vol. 11, p. 526. 8. *Ibid.*, vol. 12, p. 433.
7. *Ibid.*, vol. 10, p. 19.

article "Literary Reveries"), he maintained outright that Russia was still without a literature of her own. His justification of this extreme point of view echoed the argument used by Chaadaev to show that Russia was a country without history: what was known as Russian literature, Belinsky wrote, was an imitative product without historical continuity or internal organic development. Some years later he modified this view, but to the end of his life he would only recognize European-influenced literature, founded, according to him, by Lomonosov—the "Peter the Great of Russian letters." He was convinced that everything valuable in Russian writing owed its existence to Westernization, and that anything that came before hardly deserved to be called literature.

To the Slavophiles these views were of course proof of Belinsky's ignorance and of his contempt for Russia's "native" cultural roots. They were equally shocked by his attitude toward folk poetry. He was ready to concede that it had its merits as a reminder of the "childhood of mankind," "the age of natural immediacy when all was clear and no oppressive thoughts or uneasy questions disturbed us," but at the same time he wholeheartedly disliked all forms of "folk-mania." In his polemics he stressed the difference between unsophisticated popular writing (*prostonarodnost'*) and national individuality; in the heat of the argument he went so far as to claim that "one short verse by a sophisticated artist is of incomparably greater value than the entire body of folk poetry."[9]

Writers who wished to express the true national spirit in their works were warned by Belinsky not to look for inspiration to folk poetry. Popular ballads were only capable of conveying the restricted particularism of tribal existence, whereas nations came about as a result of "individualization," which required the negation of tribal particularism. The Petrine reforms, which broke with natural immediacy, represented such a negation. Their role was to bring Russia closer to the nations of Europe, which at that time were the only "historical nations" and true representatives of humanity.

The Hegelian notion of "historical nation" had an important place in Belinsky's criticism. Although he frequently reaffirmed his faith in the great potential of the Russian "substance," he also stressed that this potential could not be realized without "historical soil," and that since the Russian nation "was still at the very early stage of its evolution" it could not claim to have "world-historical significance" in the intellectual life of mankind. That is why he

9. *Ibid.*, vol. 5, p. 309.

argued that an old Russian epic such as the "Lay of the Host of Igor" was lacking in universal values and could not stand comparison with the medieval epics of chivalry. Even the work of his own favorite, Gogol (he maintained in a polemic with Konstantin Aksakov), was without universal significance and could not be compared to the work of such "world-historical" artists as James Fenimore Cooper and George Sand, let alone Homer and Shakespeare (to whom Aksakov had compared Gogol).[10]

Nevertheless Belinsky was untiring in his efforts to further the cause of a national literature and was convinced that in future it would achieve universal significance. What he meant by "national character," however, was influenced by his Westernism. He suggested that Pushkin was a truly national poet in *Evgeny Onegin* but not in his verse tales, which represented a conscious attempt to recreate the style and content of folk poetry. Of Lermontov's "Song of the Merchant Kalashnikov" Belinsky wrote that though it was a work of great talent, it had exhausted all the potentialities of this kind of poetry, so that other poets would therefore do well not to try and imitate it.

Though he had his reservations about folk songs and ballads, there was no doubt about Belinsky's special hostility to "pseudo-romantic imitations of the folk style" that identified nationality with the external attributes of popular traditions and recommended that literature reproduce the life and language of the most backward sections of society.[11] "Nationality," he wrote, "is not a homespun coat, bast slippers, cheap vodka, or sour cabbage."[12] Whatever the Slavophiles might claim, the real national character of Russia was represented by the cultivated elite and not by the common people. "If the national character of poetry is one of its greatest values," Belinsky wrote, "then truly national works should undoubtedly be sought among those depicting the social groups that emerged after the reforms of Peter the Great and adopted a civilized way of life."[13]

In his uncompromising opposition to these "homespun-slippery" notions, Belinsky represented an extreme form of Westernism that occasionally disturbed even his closest friends. Herzen, for instance, thought some of his statements rash, smacking of contempt for

10. *Ibid.*, vol. 5, p. 649.
11. This type of literature was encouraged by the government: *narod* in Russian means both "nation" and "people," so that the "narodnost' " of the triune slogan of Official Nationality conveniently covered a wide semantic field.
12. Belinsky, *Pol. sob. soch.*, vol. 7, p. 435.
13. *Ibid.*

people in homespun coats and bast slippers; he told Annenkov that there were times when he found it difficult to defend Belinsky against the attacks of the Slavophiles. Reservations of this kind (shared also by Granovsky) reflected the complexes of the educated progressive gentry, who were afraid of seeming to parade their social superiority. Thanks to his plebeian origins Belinsky did not suffer from such scruples. He knew that it was not the common people he despised, but the ignorance and backwardness idealized in the state-propagated doctrine of Official Nationality. When such works as Grigorovich's *Anton the Unfortunate* and Turgenev's *Sportsman's Sketches* began to appear in the second half of the 1840's—books that did not idealize native backwardness but looked at social conditions in the Russian village with a critical eye—Belinsky greeted them enthusiastically and defended them against pseudoaristocratic readers who complained of the "invasion of peasants in literature."

Belinsky's celebrated "Letter to Gogol," written on July 15, 1847, in the Lower Silesian spa of Salzbrunn—when he was already mortally ill—sums up admirably his conception of the national and universal mission of literature. Belinsky wrote this letter in reply to Gogol's *Selected Passages from Correspondence with Friends*. In this book the author of the *Government Inspector* and *Dead Souls* had turned his back on his previous writings and had undertaken a justification of Orthodoxy and the entire tsarist system. For Belinsky this meant a betrayal of the noble mission of the Russian writer, his country's only champion against the "gloom of autocracy, Orthodoxy, and the pseudofolk style." His attack was impassioned: "Devotee of the knout," he addressed Gogol, "apostle of uncouthness, defender of obscurantism and backwardness, glorifier of the Tartar way of life—what are you doing? Look down at your feet! You are standing of the edge of an abyss."[14]

This was not an outburst of uncontrolled anger but the "fanaticism of truth"—an attempt to win back the author's soul. Belinsky still hoped that Gogol would see that he was mistaken and repair the damage with new masterpieces. He tried to convince him that "Russia sees that her salvation lies not in mysticism, or in asceticism, or in pietism, but in the progress of civilization, education, humanitarian values. What she needs are not sermons (she has heard enough of them) or prayers (she has babbled enough of them) but the awakening of human dignity which has been dragged through mud and dirt for so many centuries." The Russian people, he continued, have many positive characteristics that "perhaps contain

14. *Ibid.*, vol. 10, p. 214.

the germ of [their] future historical greatness." But this great potential will not be realized unless the conditions that destroy human dignity are removed.

After Belinsky's death illegal copies of the "Letter to Gogol" were distributed throughout Russia and helped to awaken and sustain moods of opposition. Legal publication of the entire letter was only permitted after 1905.

The Polemic with Maikov

It was a characteristic aspect of Belinsky's Westernism that he stressed the close connection between the emancipation of the individual and the emergence of modern nations from the constraints of "natural immediacy." This was shown very clearly by his angry response to an article by a talented young literary critic, VALERIAN MAIKOV (1823–47), who maintained that the emancipation of the individual meant the progressive shedding of national features.

Maikov was one of the first Russian pre-positivists and had not passed through the stage of enthusiasm for dialectical philosophy that was the common experience of the "superfluous" generation. He had been a member of the Petrashevsky circle,[15] but believed in the benefits of science rather than the utopian socialism of Fourier. In the controversy between "socialists" and "economists" (i.e. the representatives of liberal political economy), he tended to side with the latter. He called Belinsky a "semiromantic," not trained in sober logical reasoning. In particular he thought him inconsistent and illogical on the problem of nationality; he himself was convinced that the ideal of the autonomous personality imbued by universal values was incompatible with national features. "There is only one true civilization," he wrote, "just as there is only one truth, and one good; therefore the fewer specific features there are in the civilization of a particular nation, the more civilized it is."[16] "Nationality" implied the subordination of the individual to the community, whose character was determined by external factors, whereas the flowering of personality depended on the autonomy of the individual.

The difficulty in this line of reasoning was to explain how the ideas of great emancipated individuals became diffused among the masses and pushed them forward toward a universal ideal of progress. Maikov suggested that this movement of ideas was the work of an educated minority who represented the active, progressive part

15. See Chapter 9 below.
16. V. N. Maikov, *Kriticheskie opyty* (St. Petersburg, 1891), p. 389.

of the nation. Participants in the great ideological discussion of the 1840's presumably had no difficulty in identifying Maikov's active minority with the Westernized "society" that had emerged after the Petrine reforms, whereas the passive majority was clearly just another version of the common people idealized by the Slavophiles. Maikov's law was therefore essentially a universalization of the Westernist view on the role of this "society" in Russian history (a view shared by Belinsky). Not having Belinsky's dialectical understanding of this process, however, Maikov proposed it as a universally valid law and identified the overcoming of immediate national particularism with the elimination of nationality as such.

Maikov's views were expressed in a long article on the poetry of V. V. Koltsov that was, in fact, a hidden polemic with Belinsky. The latter reacted sharply. In the "Review of Russian Literature for the Year 1846" he made it clear that he disagreed utterly with the views of the "humanist cosmopolitans" (Maikov was not mentioned by name). "Nationalities," Belinsky wrote, "are the individualities of mankind. Without nations mankind would be a lifeless abstraction, a word without content, a meaningless sound. In this respect I would rather join the Slavophiles than stay with the humanist cosmopolitans because even if the former make mistakes they err like living human beings, whereas the latter make even the truth sound like the embodiment of some abstract logic. . . ."[17]

Belinsky's declaration alarmed some of his friends, who suspected him of succumbing to Slavophile influences. In fact, in his argument with Maikov, Belinsky was merely defending views he had formulated in the early forties (in articles on folk poetry), where he had made it clear that he was opposed both to the "nationalists" who stood for form without content and to the "supporters of undifferentiated universality" who wanted to divorce the universal content from its national form.

The minority [Belinsky argued], always reflects the majority, both in the positive and in the negative sense. . . . In the same way, great men are always children of their country, sons of their nation, for they are great just because they are representatives of their nation. The struggle between the individual genius and the masses is not a struggle between the universal element and nationality, but simply a struggle between the new and the old, between idea and empiricism, between reason and superstition. Folkways are founded on habit; the masses accept as reasonable, just, and useful whatever they have become accustomed to and fervently defend those *old* things that a century or less before they op-

17. Belinsky, *Pol. sob. soch.*, vol. 10, p. 29.

posed equally fervently as *new*. Their resistance to genius is a necessary factor: it is a form of trial to which they subject him.[18]

An analysis of this argument suggests that Belinsky and Maikov were at least in agreement on one vital issue dividing Westernizers and Slavophiles: both regarded the masses as a conservative force and believed that progress was accomplished through individuals. On this issue Belinsky was sometimes doubtful, but he never abandoned the Westernist position. In the last year of his life (after Maikov's death), when the conflict with the Slavophiles had reached its climax (in connection with Samarin's article "On the Opinions of the *Contemporary*"),[19] he expressly rejected the "mystical faith in the people"—upheld by the Slavophiles as well as Herzen and Bakunin—in favor of an uncompromising reaffirmation of the contribution to progress made by outstanding individuals and the educated elite.

The Dispute over Capitalism

The Westernizers emphasized the positive role of Western influences in the modernization of Russia and wished this process to continue. This did not mean, however, that they automatically accepted the capitalist system, whose obvious shortcomings were already being widely discussed and criticized in Western European progressive circles. Belinsky's own outlook can best be described as a combination of belief in bourgeois democracy and dislike of the bourgeoisie itself, along with a vague, undefined trust in the the "idea of socialism." There was nothing strange about this mixture—any sincere democrat in a backward part of Europe who followed events in the more advanced countries would have found it difficult to be an apologist for the bourgeoisie and was bound to sympathize in one way or another with the aspirations of the downtrodden masses.

Belinsky expressed his own sympathies in an interesting article on Eugène Sue's *Les Mystères de Paris* (1844).[20] His ideological position, however, was complicated by the fact that in Russia criticism of the bourgeoisie and belief in the common people were the pre-

18. *Ibid.*, p. 31.
19. See below, p. 149.
20. Here he wrote: "The people is like a child: but this child is growing rapidly and will soon become a man in full possession of his physical and mental powers. Misfortune has taught it sense and has shown up the trashy constitution in its proper light. . . . The people is still weak, but it is the only force in France to have preserved the flame of national life and the fresh enthusiasm of convictions which has been extinguished in the educated classes." Belinsky, *Pol. sob. soch.*, vol. 8, p. 173.

rogative of the Slavophiles, for they undermined confidence in social reconstruction along European lines and hence seemed to be
incompatible with Westernism.

The problem of capitalism acquired more concrete meaning for
Belinsky when he went abroad for medical reasons at the beginning
of May 1847. From Salzbrunn in Lower Silesia he wrote to Botkin
that he now understood for the first time "the terrible meaning of
the words pauperization and proletariat." At the same time he was
becoming critical of the one-sided evaluation of the bourgeoisie by
the French utopian socialists, and especially by Louis Blanc, whose
History of the French Revolution he had started to read. "For
Blanc," he wrote to Botkin in July 1847, "the bourgeoisie has been
the arch-enemy and has conspired against the happiness of mankind since before the creation; and yet his own work proves that
without the *bourgeoisie* we would not have had the revolution he
is so enthusiastic about, and that all the successes of that class were
the fruit of its own labor."[21]

When Belinsky arrived in Paris in July 1847, the heated discussion of the role of the bourgeoisie raging among his Russian friends
already there had reached its climax. Herzen and Bakunin were
totally opposed to the bourgeoisie and thought that Russia's future
depended on the peasants and the intelligentsia, whom they considered to be classless; on the other side were Sazonov and Annenkov. Herzen's viewpoint, formulated in the *Letters from the Avenue
Marigny* (published in the *Contemporary—Sovremennik*), caused
a good deal of consternation among the Westernizers in Moscow
and St. Petersburg. Herzen's most determined opponent was VAS-
SILY BOTKIN (1811–69), himself the son of a merchant. In the 1840's,
Botkin, who had been a member of the Stankevich circle, worked
out a "practical philosophy" of his own in which he substituted the
"iron law" of bourgeois political economy for the Hegelian *Weltgeist*. "The important thing is not to attack the existing state of
affairs," he wrote in 1846, "but to find out what causes it; in short,
to discover the laws governing the world of industry."[22] Applying
this principle to Russia, Botkin came to an unambiguous conclusion: "Heaven grant us our own bourgeoisie!"

Belinsky's immediate reaction to conditions in bourgeois France
was not unlike Herzen's. On his return to Russia, however, he had
time to reconsider his one-sided condemnation. He stressed the
bourgeoisie's historical role and carefully distinguished between

21. *Ibid.*, vol. 12, p. 385.
22. *P. V. Annenkov i ego druz'ia* (St. Petersburg, 1892), p. 525.

the "big capitalists who must be fought as the plague or cholera of contemporary France" and the rest of the middle class. Industry, he admitted, was not only the source of all evil, but also the source of public prosperity.[23] Later still, just before his death, he wrote to Annenkov:

The entire future of France lies in the hands of the bourgeoisie; all progress depends on it alone; the people can only play a passive auxiliary role in historical events. When I said in Paris that Russia needed a new Peter the Great, our believing friend [Bakunin] attacked this idea as heresy and maintained that the people must manage their own affairs. What a naive, arcadian idea! . . . Our believing friend also tried to convince me that Heaven should preserve Russia from the bourgeoisie. And yet it has become obvious that the process of internal civic development will begin in Russia only when our gentry as become transformed into a bourgeoisie. Poland is the best example of what happens to a state without a bourgeoisie in full enjoyment of its rights.[24]

Nevertheless, the similarity between Belinsky's views and those of Botkin and Annenkov was only superficial. Belinsky became reconciled to the bourgeoisie because it represented a specific case of historical necessity; his acceptance sprang not from spontaneous sympathy but from a wish to avoid a charge of quixotic subjectivism. It is characteristic that he supported Herzen and Bakunin in Paris but changed his mind when he returned home and was confronted by the gloomy realities of tsarist Russia. He became firmly convinced that socialism in Russia must remain a remote dream as long as the country had to pass through so many urgent reforms long since introduced in Western Europe. Because of Russia's backwardness, the masses were largely an inert peasantry kept in patriarchal subjection, among whom it was difficult to discern the nucleus of a proletariat or a force capable of building a system superior to capitalism. Belinsky was aware of the main internal contradictions of capitalism and of its transitional character, but he understood clearly its superiority as a social system over the semifeudal Russia of Nicholas I. This clearsighted understanding—as well as his consistent desire to see the process of Westernization completed by the adoption in Russia of bourgeois democratic reforms—was a positive aspect of Belinsky's Westernism. This was emphasized by Plekhanov, who wrote that Belinsky had the "intuition of a sociological genius" and a profound understanding of the basic principles of social development.

23. Belinsky, *Pol. sob. soch.*, vol. 12, pp. 448, 449.
24. *Ibid.*, pp. 467–68.

THE LIBERAL WESTERNIZERS

Using political categories, one might call Belinsky's brand of Westernism democratic, and Annenkov's and Botkin's liberal. In the forties this distinction was not yet obvious. A definite split did not take place until the sixties, when the radical democrats (followers of the Belinsky tradition) represented the popular interest, whereas the liberals supported restricted reforms that would not affect the privileged position of the gentry. During Belinsky's lifetime, democrats and liberals differed mainly in their attitudes to religion (the liberals among the Westernizers rejecting Herzen's and Belinsky's atheism), in their assessments of the French Revolution (Belinsky's sympathies being with the Jacobins, whom Granovsky condemned), and in their attitudes to art (the liberals supporting "art for art's sake," the democrats, led by Belinsky, demanding social commitment). Although these differences sometimes led to angry and painful quarrels, they did not undermine the sense of common political aims.

Timofey Granovsky

One of the important representatives of liberal Westernism in the 1840's was TIMOFEY GRANOVSKY (1813–55), a former member of the Stankevich circle and professor of European history at Moscow University.

Granovsky's impact stemmed not so much from his writings as from his direct contact with audiences; his most important contribution to the cause of Westernism was an enormously popular course of public lectures on the Middle Ages held at Moscow University in 1842. "Granovsky," wrote Herzen, "turned the lecture hall into a drawing room, a meeting place of the *beau monde*." The end of the first course of lectures was greeted by a spontaneous ovation; ladies and "young people with flushed cheeks" wept; "amid prolonged clapping, there were enthusiastic shouts and requests for the lecturer's likeness."[25]

Granovsky's lectures were decidedly anti-Slavophile in content. This did not escape the notice of the Slavophiles and the apologists of Official Nationality, who hastened to counter Granovsky's impact with a course of public lectures on early Russian literature given by Shevyrev.

In his polemics with the Slavophiles, Granovsky, like Belinsky, concentrated on a critique of their idealization of the common peo-

25. Alexander Herzen, *My Past and Thoughts*, trans. by Constance Garnett (London, 1927), vol. 2, p. 245.

ple. "A large party," he wrote, "has hoisted the standard of popular traditions in our time, exalting it as an expression of infallible collective reason." According to Granovsky, this trend, inspired by the German romantics, was hostile to any sign of progress in science or social relations.

The masses, like nature or the Scandinavian god Thor, are thoughtlessly cruel or thoughtlessly good-natured. They become apathetic under the burden of historical and natural determinations that only the thinking individual can throw off. This individualization of the masses through the power of ideas is the essence of historical progress. The goal of history is the moral, enlightened individual, emancipated from the fatalist pressure of external determinations, and a society founded on his postulates.[26]

With its emphasis on the autonomous personality and emancipation from the "determinations of immediacy," this quotation surely expresses the quintessence of the Westernizing philosophy of history as expounded by Belinsky and Herzen. Another liberal Westernizer was to take this thesis and apply it to Russian history. This was Granovsky's friend and disciple, the young Moscow historian KONSTANTIN KAVELIN (1818–85).

Konstantin Kavelin

Kavelin's essay entitled "A Brief Survey of Juridical Relations in Ancient Russia" was published with Belinsky's "Survey of Russian Literature for the Year 1846" in the first issue of the *Contemporary* in 1847, and fully deserved to become known as the true manifesto of the "Western party." Belinsky himself was greatly impressed by it and even called it the first philosophical interpretation of Russian history, undervaluing his own work in the field.

In his essay Kavelin developed the argument that the historical process in Russia consisted in the gradual replacement of community relations founded on kinship and custom with a system based on political and juridical legislation, and in the corresponding emancipation of the individual from traditional patriarchal bonds. This involved the dissolution of physical nationality dependent on outward and unchanging forms, and the gradual emergence of a spiritual nationality—nationality as a specific moral attribute to national existence and not as a mere matter of external physical features. This process achieved its climax in the Petrine reforms: "Not until the eighteenth century," Kavelin proclaimed to the out-

26. T. N. Granovsky, *Sochineniia* (M, 1900), p. 455.

raged Slavophiles, "did Russia begin to live on an intellectual and moral plane."

In the person of Peter the Great, individuality in Russia entered upon its absolute rights, after throwing off the shackles of immediate, natural, and exclusively national determinations and subordinating them to itself. Both in his private life and in his political measures Peter represented the completion of the first phase in the realization of the personality principle in Russian history.[27]

In reply to Kavelin's essay and Belinsky's article published in the same issue of the *Contemporary*, Yury Samarin published a hostile review in the Slavophile *Muscovite* entitled "On the Historical and Literary Views of the *Contemporary*." In it Samarin accused Kavelin of equating personality with Western European individualism, failing to make a distinction between the peasant commune and the clan or kinship group, and exaggerating the positive role of the centralized state. He was especially indignant at Kavelin's attempt to rehabilitate Ivan the Terrible by presenting his brutal struggle against the boyars as a consistent effort to replace hereditary privileges by personal merit. The meaning of Russian history, Samarin suggested, lay not in the development of the personality principle but in the preservation of the Christian community principle, which was now attracting the attention of the West. To prove this point, Samarin drew attention to the interest in things Slavic that had been greatly stimulated by the Paris lectures of the Polish poet Adam Mickiewicz: "In response to [his] eloquent appeal many eyes, those of George Sand among them, have turned toward the Slavic world conceived as a world based on the community principle; they have turned to us not from mere curiosity, but with a certain sympathy and expectation."[28]

An examination of Kavelin's and Belinsky's views on Russian history shows that there was no essential difference between them: both believed that the historical process in Russia consisted essentially in the emancipation of the individual through the rationalization of social relations; both argued that nations developed from the stage of natural immediacy to that of a fully modern "spiritual" nationality. Kavelin, however, placed special emphasis on the role played in this process by the juridical and state apparatus: the emergence of the centralized Muscovite state, he suggested, was the decisive moment in the rationalization of social relations in Russia,

27. K. D. Kavelin, *Sobranie sochinenii* (St. Petersburg, 1897), vol. 1, p. 58.
28. Yury Samarin, *Sochineniia* (M, 1877), vol. 1, p. 39.

and therefore also in the emancipation of the personality from the fetters of traditionalism. This view—which sprang from Kavelin's interpretation of sixteenth-century Muscovite autocracy in terms of the rationalistic Hegelian state—was later to be developed as the basic thesis of the "etatist" school of Russian historiography. This school, one of whose representatives was the eminent historian S. Soloviev, argued that in Russia the state had always been the leading organizer of society and the main agent of progress, and concluded that in future, too, it must be responsible for the nature and implementation of reforms.

Boris Chicherin

The leading theorist of the "etatist" school was BORIS CHICHERIN (1828–1904), philosopher, historian, jurist, and ideologist of right-wing gentry liberalism in the second half of the nineteenth century. Chicherin was taught by Granovsky and Kavelin and was also a Hegelian, linked by many associations with the Hegelian period of the forties (although his own contribution was made later). His philosophical work will be discussed in a later chapter; at present we are only concerned with giving a general outline of his position as a Westernizer.[29]

The Westernism expounded by Chicherin was a blend of the Hegelian cult of the powerful state and juridical order with the economic liberalism of the school of Say and Bastiat. This enabled Chicherin to defend the historical role of Russian autocracy (which, like Kavelin, he interpreted in terms of the Hegelian state) while at the same time speaking up in favor of capitalism and civil rights. The weakness of the state apparatus, his argument ran, and the demands of defense and unification of Russian territory were responsible for the fact that in the sixteenth and seventeenth centuries the Muscovite state was forced to deprive the members of all estates of their personal freedom. After political consolidation this process was reversed, beginning with the emancipation of the gentry (The Manifesto on Gentry Liberty, 1762), and it had to lead inevitably to the emancipation of the peasants and the granting of civil rights to wider sections of the population. In this way Chicherin established the historical legitimacy and necessity of liberal measures, while at the same time stipulating that reforms must be gradual and directed by the country's legal government, since their

29. A stimulating analysis of Chicherin's Westernism is contained in Leonard B. Schapiro, *Rationalism and Nationalism in Russian Nineteenth-Century Political Thought* (New Haven, Conn., 1967).

success—and indeed their initiation—depended on the stability and strength of the state.

Following Hegel, Chicherin made a sharp distinction between state and society but tended to interpret all social bonds as contractual bonds. His theory on the origins of the village commune gained wide acceptance: the present-day Russian commune, he argued, had nothing in common with a primitive patriarchal kinship organization; it arose in the sixteenth century, not as an "organic" product of the common people, but as an artificial product of the centralized state that wished to streamline its fiscal policies by forcing villagers to adopt a system of collective responsibility for all kinds of taxes and labor obligations.[30]

In 1856 this argument, which enraged the Slavophiles, initiated a long-drawn-out polemic between the Slavophile *Russian Conversation (Russkaia Beseda)* and the liberal *Russian Messenger (Russkii Vestnik)*. The controversy had a topical significance, since the basic argument was about whether the village commune was to continue to function or was to be abolished together with the institutions of serfdom and the *corvée*. Chicherin was of course a determined opponent of the *obshchina*: he was convinced—and repeated the argument to the end of his life—that as an institution hampering the normal functioning of economic laws and setting up a state within the state, the peasant commune was the greatest obstacle to the consistent Westernization of Russia.

As a politician Chicherin was less antagonistic to the Slavophiles —with whom he found much common ground on practical issues— than to the democratic opposition and in particular the revolutionary movement. His career provides a good example of the evolution of Russian gentry liberalism. Granovsky and the young Kavelin had been close to Belinsky, but although Chicherin had been their student, the Belinsky tradition was alien to him and he actively opposed its continuators.

30. This view was not correct, but it drew attention to the fact that the commune self-government was a very useful institution allowing the central government to exercise control over the villages. In the 1860's, therefore, Kavelin (unlike Chicherin) advocated its retention. The commune, he argued, slows down the development of agriculture, but at the same time it acts as a talisman that protects the peasants against social upheavals.

CHAPTER 9

THE PETRASHEVTSY

On December 22, 1849, the inhabitants of St. Petersburg were witness to a curious spectacle: twenty-one political prisoners were brought from the Peter and Paul Fortress to Semenovsky Square and lined up in front of a scaffold draped in crepe. An official read out the death sentences, a priest called on the prisoners to repent, and soldiers dressed each man in the white cloak and hood traditionally associated with executions. The first three men were tied to posts, their faces were covered, the drums began to roll, and the command was given for the soldiers to shoulder arms—but at that very moment an imperial adjutant appeared with a last-minute reprieve. The death sentences were commuted to hard labor in Siberia, prison, or banishment. The condemned men were now ordered to kneel on the scaffold and executioners in colorful robes began the symbolic ceremonial of breaking swords over their bare heads. The leading prisoner was immediately placed in shackles and put in the covered cart that was to take him to Siberia.

This was the method chosen by Nicholas I to deal with the secret discussion groups active in St. Petersburg in the years 1845–49. The main circle from which most of the others had branched off was founded and led by MIKHAIL BUTASHEVICH-PETRASHEVSKY (1821–66). It was he who was publicly shackled in Semenovsky Square; the other two men who had to face the firing squad were two officers, N. P. Gridoriev and N. A. Mombelli, whom Nicholas could not forgive for "staining the honor of an officer." Among the remaining eighteen "Petrashevtsy" who had to go through the agony of waiting for their own execution was a young man who was to become one of the greatest writers of the nineteenth century—Fyodor Dostoevsky.

THE SOCIAL AND POLITICAL IDEAS
OF THE PETRASHEVTSY

Unable to find any evidence of intention to overthrow the state, the imperial investigating commission characterized the Petrashevsky movement as a "conspiracy of ideas." For Nicholas I, who was terrified by the recent revolutions in Western Europe, this accusation was sufficiently serious to warrant the most severe punishment. The suspicious terror aroused in government circles in Russia at that time by the mere shadow of ideas is shown by the fact that the main crime of which Dostoevsky was accused was reading aloud Belinsky's famous letter to Gogol at a meeting of the Petrashevsky circle.

The Petrashevtsy took the study of ideas very seriously. They began collecting books and shortly had the largest multilingual library of works on philosophy, economics, and sociopolitical thought in Russia. They were particularly interested in the French socialists, including Fourier and his followers (especially V. Considérant), Blanc, Proudhon, and Leroux. Books they had read, as well as their own ideas and plans, were systematically discussed at their meetings. The regular Friday gatherings were attended not only by members but by a large circle of invited guests. Unlike the meetings of the Stankevich circle, these were not spontaneous discussions among close friends, but organized regular encounters of people (who often did not even know each other) brought together by a community of interests and the wish to bring about much-needed reforms. Several hundred persons are known to have taken part in the discussions, so that their influence was considerable. The Petrashevtsy represented a far wider social spectrum than the homogeneous Decembrist movement, which had drawn its main support from the officer class. The circle included rich landowners and a number of eminent writers and professors,[1] but according to the report of I. Liprandi (an official of the Ministry of Internal Affairs) there were also "half-baked students, merchants, and even petty tobacconists."

The most important venture undertaken by the Petrashevtsy to propagate their ideas in print was a *Pocket Dictionary of Foreign Terms*,[2] two installments of which were published in 1845 and 1846. The first number was edited by the literary critic Valerian Maikov (with Petrashevsky's help), but the second, which was far more openly ideological in character, was edited by Petrashevsky alone. Many entries in the dictionary were in fact short articles skillfully slipping in various forbidden ideas. The entries "Nature,"

1. Other members of the Petrashevtsy included the poet A. Pleshcheev, the poet Apollon Maikov, Apollon's brother Valerian, the eminent economist V. A. Muliutin, and the young M. E. Saltykov-Shchedrin (the future satirist).

2. Owing to the intervention of the censor's office, the dictionary had to terminate with the letter "o."

"Naturalism," and "Natural Philosophy" were used by Petrashevsky to expound his philosophical views; "Owenism," "Organization of Production," "Neo-Christianism," and "Normal State" were
used to present socialist ideas; "Neology" and "Innovation" contained reflections on the role of revolutionary change in history;
and a number of other entries, such as "Nation" and "Opposition,"
set out the author's political convictions. The authorities realized
too late what was happening—Uvarov, the minister of education,
issued a severe reprimand to the censor and ordered the confiscation
of the *Dictionary*, but it was too late to prevent the sale of the entire
edition.

The prevailing mood of the discussion groups was socialist, and
several members even thought of themselves as "communists." The
teaching of the French utopian socialist Fourier enjoyed special
popularity. Petrashevsky himself was a convinced disciple of Fourierism and in 1847 even attempted to transform one of his villages
into a "phalanstery"—a self-supporting Fourierite commune. His
suspicious peasants, however, put an end to the scheme by setting
fire to the buildings that were to house their utopian community.
At a banquet to celebrate Fourier's birthday organized by the most
active Petrashevtsy in April 1849, speeches were made by Petrashevsky himself, as well as by Aleksandr Khanykov, Dmitry Akhsharumov, and Hipolit Desbout. Khanykov presumably expressed the
assembled company's general mood of enthusiasm and faith in the
future regeneration of the world as foretold by Fourier when he
called the occasion an "event foreshadowing the metamorphosis of
our entire planet and the people dwelling on it." "The transformation is at hand," he is said to have called out, and Akhsharumov answered him: "We shall begin the task of transformation here, in
Russia, and the whole world will complete it."[3]

What attracted the Petrashevtsy to Fourier's social philosophy
was his defense of the laws of nature, of the free and harmonious
play of human passions—his vision of a social system that would
release human nature from all artificial restraints and allow human
beings to lead "normal" lives for the first time in history. In this
respect, their Fourierism was only another embodiment of the idea
of the full emancipation and harmonious development of the personality central to the views of the Russian Westernizers. In view of
their characteristically sharp criticism of Western European capitalism, however, it would be an error to classify the Petrashevtsy

3. *Filosofskie i obschestvenno-politicheski proizvedeniia petrashevtsev* (M, 1953),
pp. 514, 691.

as Westernizers. Petrashevsky himself said that capitalism was against human nature because it stimulated antisocial instincts and benefitted only the rich while pauperizing the poor. Socialism, on the other hand, was for him not "an invention of modern times, a cunning trick thought up in the nineteenth century," but something that had "always been a part of human nature and would remain part of it as long as humanity retained the capacity to evolve and perfect itself." Liberalism he dismissed as a doctrine defending capitalism, and therefore "the direct opposite" of socialism.[4]

These beliefs could be reconciled with different political programs. A. P. Beklemishev and N. Ia. Danilevsky (the future Pan-Slavist) thought that Fourierism was an apolitical doctrine the Russian government ought to adopt it in its own interest; Beklemishev suggested, for instance, that Fourierist associations could help to bring about a peaceful solution to the conflict between peasants and landowners. Views of this kind were, however, untypical—the overwhelming majority of the Petrashevtsy loathed autocracy and combined belief in socialist ideas with dreams of a democratic republic or, at least, a constitutional monarchy that would guarantee freedom of speech, a free press, and legal reforms, and that would reduce state interference in the private sphere. What was original about the Petrashevsky movement, in fact, was its adoption of a program blending socialist ideas with the struggle for democratic rights.

When it came to putting their program into action, the Petrashevtsy, unlike Fourier and his followers in France, did not condemn or dismiss the possibility of overthrowing the government by force. In practice, however, they believed that there was little hope of a victorious revolution in Russia, and they were afraid that a revolutionary movement might turn into another primitive Jacquerie, like the Pugachev revolt. Hence they adopted a policy of legal struggle for partial reforms. Petrashevsky, who was more faithful to the spirit of Fourierism, supported reformism on principle: "Fourierism," he wrote, "leads gradually and naturally to the same goal that communism wants to introduce at once and by force. . . . It does not aspire to lose in one brief moment of diseased and feverish upheaval—no matter how magnificent—the results of thousands of years of human effort."[5] Petrashevsky therefore placed greater emphasis on juridical reforms—which would provide at least mini-

4. This view largely concerned economic liberalism as a doctrine advocating unrestricted competition and opposing government interference in the economic sphere.
5. *Filosofskie i obshchestvenno-politicheskie proizvedeniia petrashevtsev*, p. 379.

mal conditions for the legal struggle for social reforms—than on the abolition of serfdom and the granting of land to the peasants, although he was fully aware of the extreme importance of these latter measures.

The reformist camp was opposed by a radical group led by NIKOLAI SPESHNEV (1821–82), the prototype of Stavrogin in Dostoevsky's *Possessed*. His aim was to convert the movement into a revolutionary organization that would prepare the ground for an armed revolt appealing—unlike the Decembrists—directly to the peasants. Speshnev was not a follower of Fourier but thought of himself as a communist: his reading included Dézamy, Weitling, and Marx's *Poverty of Philosophy*. While traveling abroad he established contact with democratic Polish émigré circles.

It was characteristic of the most active Petrashevtsy (among them Petrashevsky himself and Speshnev) that they looked beyond limited national goals and saw cosmopolitanism as a necessary precondition of true progressivism. Petrashevsky's views on the subject, expressed in the entry for "Nation" in the *Pocket Dictionary of Foreign Terms*, did not differ from Maikov's. Elsewhere he wrote that socialism "is a cosmopolitan doctrine standing above nationalities—for the socialist, national differences disappear and only people are left."[6] Though it was not part of the Petrashevtsy's program to encourage the artificial disappearance of national differences, they proclaimed the absolute primacy of universalist aims (although they approved of the principle of self-determination for the subject nations of the Russian empire). At one of their meetings, a leading Polish member, Jan Jastrzębski, declared that he was "body and soul a Pole and would give the last drop of his blood for Polish independence, but if he was convinced that Polish independence would harm the evolution of the universal idea, he would be the first to cut off its head with one blow of the ax."[7]

In the history of the progressive movement in Russia the Petrashevtsy hold a distinct place as an intermediate link between the gentry revolutionaries and the radical movements of the second half of the nineteenth century, in which the nonnoble intelligentsia played a leading part. A typical survival of Decembrist ideas was the tendency of certain Petrashevtsy (Khanykov, for instance) to idealize the "republicanism" of ancient Russia. On the other hand, comparisons between the village commune and Fourier's "phalanstery," and the suggestion that the village was an embryonic socialist com-

6. *Ibid.*, p. 432.
7. *Delo petrashevtsev* (M-L, 1951), vol. 3, p. 431.

munity (views of this kind were expressed by Petrashevsky, Golov-
insky, Khanykov, and Balasoglo), clearly foreshadowed Populist
ideas. The social philosophy of the Petrashevtsy, with its reinstatement of the Enlightenment view of human nature and "natural"
social relations, paved the way for the "enlighteners" of the 1860's.
Finally, the role of the Petrashevtsy in pioneering socialist ideas in
Russia can hardly be overestimated: it is significant, for instance,
that the young Chernyshevsky first absorbed socialist ideas from
Khanykov in discussion-group meetings that took place at the home
of Irinarkh Vvedensky, a friend and in many respects a disciple of
Petrashevsky himself.

THE PHILOSOPHICAL IDEAS OF THE PETRASHEVTSY

The transitional nature of the Petrashevsky movement is also
apparent in their philosophical views. The movement came at a
time when philosophical idealism in Europe was giving way to naturalism, as manifested in biological materialism and the positivist
cult of science. In Russia, too, the "age of philosophy" was drawing
to a close. Leading Russian thinkers such as Belinsky and Herzen
were moving beyond Hegelian idealism with the help of Feuerbach's
materialist philosophy.

The entry on "Naturalism" in the second installment of the
Pocket Dictionary of Foreign Terms can be regarded as Petrashevsky's most succinct lecture on philosophy. The term "naturalism,"
the entry reads,

means a science which holds that by thought alone, without the help of
tradition, revelation, or divine intervention, man can achieve in real
life a state of permanent happiness through the total and independent
development of all his natural faculties. In the lower phases of its evolution, naturalism considers the appearance of the divine element in
positive religions to be a falsehood, the result of human rather than
divine action. In its further evolution, this science—having absorbed
pantheism and materialism—conceives divinity as the supreme and all-
embracing expression of human understanding, moves toward atheism,
and finally becomes transformed into anthropotheism—the science that
proclaims that the only supreme being is man himself as a part of nature.
At this stage of its rational evolution, naturalism considers the universal
fact of the recognition of God in positive religions to be a result of man's
deification of his own personality and the universal laws of his intellect;
it considers all religions that reflected the historical evolution of man-

kind to be a gradual preparation for anthropotheism, or—in other words —total self-knowledge and awareness of the vital laws of nature.[8]

This was no doubt the brand of philosophy favored by Petrashevsky himself, just as there is little doubt that "anthropotheism" in this context stands for the philosophy of Feuerbach. The category of "nature" in Petrashevsky's philosophy was not derived from eighteenth-century rationalism, which he considered to be a lower phase of naturalism. An intermediate phase, superior to the latter in his view, was Fourier's materialistic pantheism and Hegel's idealistic pantheism, in which God was conceived as the "universal and supreme formula of human understanding" (Petrashevsky saw nothing contradictory in regarding Hegelianism as a phase of "naturalism," because he thought of the latter as the antithesis of supranaturalism, i.e. the standpoint Hegel combated in the name of the immanence of God). The highest phase of "naturalism," represented by Feuerbach, was seen therefore as a culmination of the development of German philosophy.

Speshnev's conception was similar, although he thought atheism rather than anthropotheism was the final negation of "supranaturalism." In a long letter to the Polish émigré Edmund Chojecki we find the following passage:

The whole of nineteenth-century German idealism—the great body of German philosophy from Fichte onward—strives solely toward anthropotheism until, having achieved its culmination in the person of its last standard-bearer and chorus leader—Feuerbach, to be precise—it calls out with him: *Homo homini deus est*, "Man has become a god to men." This doctrine, which originated in Germany, also spread among other nations, though not, of course, as widely as in its homeland. I am thinking here not of those who slavishly imitated Hegelian philosophy outside Germany, but only of the independent intellect of Proudhon in France and Kamieński in Poland. Both were trained in Hegelianism, and the fact that in the case of both these neighbors of Germany Hegelianism appeared as anthropotheism (and moreover at the same time as in Germany), and that both came to this point not knowing Feuerbach, just as Feuerbach did not know them, demonstrates most convincingly that the premises of the deification of man are to be found in Hegel himself, and that the Feuerbachian school is his legitimate heir in Germany.[9]

8. *Filosofskie . . . proizvedeniia petrashevtsev*, pp. 183–84.

9. *Ibid.*, pp. 494–95. Henryk Kamieński (1813–65), philosopher and important ideologist of the radical wing of the Polish national-liberation movement, wrote the book *Philosophy of the Material Economy of Human Society* (in Polish, two vols.; Poznan, 1843–45). He claimed in it that working, historically developing mankind was the only Absolute for man.

Feuerbach's "anthropotheism" depended on his "substitution of the human for the divine being," and his promotion of "anthropology to the rank of theology." "The Christian religion," Feuerbach wrote, "linked the name of man and the divine name in one name, that of God-Man, and in doing so, raised the name of man to the dignity of being an attribute of the supreme being. In keeping with the true state of affairs, the new philosophy transformed attribute into substance, predicate into subject."[10] The God-Man was thus replaced by the Man-God: "God is man, man is God."[11] Feuerbach expected his message to have a liberating effect—man would straighten his limbs and be reborn, he would reassimilate the divine element that had become alienated from him and focused in the Kingdom of Heaven. At the same time he lost no opportunity of stressing that man as a creature with a body was also subject to the laws of nature. This arose from his violent opposition to spiritualism, which only valued the soul, and Hegelian idealism, which saw man only as a thinking being. Anthropotheism was to be a rehabilitation of nature and of man as a part of that nature, a sensual and passionate being of flesh and blood.

This brief comment makes it easier to understand the combination of Feuerbachian and Fourierist elements so characteristic of the ideology of the Petrashevtsy. It was easy to reject Fourier's pantheistic fantasies and replace them by anthropotheism, since Feuerbach agreed with Fourier on issues that were of prime importance to the Petrashevtsy: the rehabilitation of nature and sensuality, the free and harmonious development of the passions, and the vision of a renaissance of mankind founded on the liberation of human nature and the flowering of all its potentialities. Akhsharumov's speech at the banquet in honor of Fourier is a good example of the organic fusion of Fourierism with the "anthropotheistic" motif of the "restoration of divine attributes to man:

We ought to remember what a great task we have undertaken: to restore the laws of nature trampled underfoot by ignorance, to reinstate the divine aspect of man in all its greatness, to liberate and organize his lofty and harmonious passions, which have been curbed and inhibited. To tear down towns and capital cities; to use their bricks and mortar to erect other buildings; to transform a life full of pain, unhappiness, poverty, shame, and humiliation into a life full of splendor, harmony, joy, wealth, and happiness; to cover the face of the earth with palaces and

10. L. Feuerbach, *Vorläufige Thesen zur Reform der Philosophie* (1842).
11. L. Feuerbach, *The Essence of Christianity*, trans. George Eliot, introduced by Karl Barth (New York, 1957).

fruits; to adorn it with flowers—behold, that is our goal, our great goal, the greatest of all goals that the earth has ever known." [12]

As this passage shows, Feuerbach's materialism (unlike the vulgarized version developed by Vogt and Moleschott, for which it paved the way) was not bound to be accompanied by positivist "sober-mindedness." On the contrary, it bore the stamp of the age of "social romanticism," [13] of intense faith in the universal and total regeneration of mankind. On the other hand, Feuerbachian philosophy also contained a tendency that might be called prepositivism. If the key to an understanding of philosophy (that is idealist philosophy) is theology, and the key to an understanding of theology is anthropology, then the study of human nature must be the most important branch of knowledge. But if we accept that man is a part of nature, subject to the strict causality of universal laws, then the study of human nature is part of the natural sciences and requires the use of scientific methods. This line of reasoning explains why the Petrashevtsy placed so much reliance on the natural sciences, were convinced of the need to study human physiology and psychology, and were generally sympathetic to positivist trends in European thought. This "prepositivism" was especially apparent in the articles by the publicist Valerian Maikov, who was one of the first men in Russia to study the works of Comte, Littré, and John Stuart Mill.

It seems pertinent to ask why this prepositivist tendency did not oust the romantic flights of anthropotheism and utopian socialism in the Petrashevtsy's thought. It probably would have done so in the long run, but their discussion groups were only active for a couple of years, too short a time for members to become aware of the potentially conflicting elements in these two trends. A characteristic expression of this duality was Mombelli's declaration that people would not become "gods on earth" until they had divested themselves entirely of "superstitions and prejudice." [14] This argument —which echoes Feuerbach's conviction that men would only be free when they had rejected all illusions—would seem to lead naturally to the conclusion that "superstitions" could only be fought through the use of strict scientific reasoning and through constant reference

12. *Filosofskie . . . proizvedeniia petrashevtsev*, p. 690.
13. The term applied to various social and religious conceptions of a rebirth of mankind so popular in France in the period 1815-48. One of these was Fourierism, especially the maximalistic ideas of Fourier himself, which easily passed into pure fantasy.
14. *Filosofskie . . . proizvedeniia petrashevtsev*, p. 623.

to the latest discoveries of the natural sciences. In this way the Petrashevtsy became the direct precursors of the rationalism of the sixties, including the "realism" of Dmitry Pisarev. Their world view harmonized with the prevailing trend in Russian literature— at that time represented by the "natural school"—which emphasized the cognitive function of art and favored literary works that would provide a "physiological analysis" of society. The psychologism of the young Dostoevsky also derived from the Petrashevtsy's postulate of a psychological analysis of human nature.

In order to define the Petrashevtsy's role in the history of Russian thought, it is necessary to consider the reception of their ideas in the mature writings of Dostoevsky. The polemic with socialism that forms a background to all his great novels is to a large extent an argument carried on with the ideas of the companions of his youth. The main theme of this polemic—the argument that socialism was founded not so much on the desire for social justice as on the vainglorious attempt to put man in the place of God—was no doubt influenced by the anthropotheism Dostoevsky heard about at the discussion groups he attended in his youth.

CHAPTER 10

THE ORIGINS
OF "RUSSIAN SOCIALISM"

Herzen's "Russian socialism" grew out of the polemics on the roles of Russia and Europe conducted in the 1840's by the Slavophiles and the Westernizers. The Slavophiles claimed to represent the intrinsically "Russian principles" embodied in the village commune, and rejected the rationalism and individualism that, for them, were the hallmarks of Western civilization. The Westernizers, for their part, defended the autonomy of both reason and personality and argued that the emancipation of the individual was closely bound up with the rationalization of social relations. The history of modern Europe seemed to offer a prototype of the individual's emancipation from external authority and unquestioned traditions, so that it was logical for Westernizers to accept the principle of bourgeois development.

Herzen's doubts about the correctness of this latter conclusion gave rise to his "Russian socialism." As a convinced believer in the personality principle, Herzen supported the Westernizers; but even in the first half of the 1840's he was sufficiently influenced by socialist criticisms of capitalism to doubt whether the "Western" way would really lead to the victory of this principle. His first personal contacts with Western Europe convinced him that it was in the grip of a severe crisis and that Russia ought to look for its own, "native" evolutionary road. This was, of course, tantamount to a complete break with Westernism.

THE EVOLUTION OF HERZEN'S VIEWS
The Crisis of Belief

After leaving Russia in January 1847, Herzen made for Paris. Brought up under the influence of French culture from his earliest years, his arrival in the "political and social" capital of Europe meant the fulfillment of a dream. Disillusionment set in quickly:

even his first letter to his Moscow friends showed that the middle-class vulgarity of the Paris theater had shocked his aesthetic sensibilities. This aesthetic revulsion, which was not without a tinge of aristocratic superiority, was accompanied by a deep moral revulsion. In his *Letters from the Avenue Marigny* (1847), Herzen defined the social role of the bourgeoisie thus:

> The bourgeoisie has no great past and no future. It was good only for a moment, as a negation, as a transition, as an opposite, when it was fighting for the recognition of its rights. . . . The aristocracy had its own social religion; you cannot replace the dogma of patriotism, the tradition of courage, and the shrine of honor by the rules of political economy. There is indeed a religion that is the opposite of feudalism, but the place of the bourgeoisie is between these two religions.[1]

The religion that was the opposite of feudalism was, of course, socialism, the only worthy adversary, in Herzen's view, of the social religion of the nobility. On the other hand, in the 1848 revolutions socialism was defeated, and the bourgeoisie once again emerged victorious. It seemed to Herzen that the failure of the revolutions sealed the fate of Europe, that the bourgeoisie was safely established for many years, and that even Western socialists had become imbued with bourgeois traits—which was why they had failed to seize their great chance. This left Slavdom—and above all Russia—as the last hope of mankind. Herzen now came to see Europe as the reincarnation of Rome in its decline, the European socialists as the persecuted early Christians, and the Slavs as the barbarian tribes who were destined to destroy the Roman empire and make their own contribution to history, while at the same time becoming standard-bearers of the Christian ideals taken over from Rome.

Herzen's loss of faith in Westernism led him to reappraise Hegelian philosophy. When he left Russia he still thought of himself as a Hegelian, albeit in a very broad sense of the word; he may have attacked man's submission to the *Weltgeist* and put forward a voluntaristic and personalistic interpretation of Hegelian philosophy, but he still retained his faith in the inevitable forward march of history and the rationality of the historical process as a whole. The triumph of the bourgeoisie in 1848—in fact the very existence of the bourgeoisie—undermined this optimism. The fact that the "social religion" of the aristocracy had been replaced not by the noble faith of socialism but by the mundane and aesthetically repulsive world of shopkeepers seemed to him a glaring contradiction of historical reason.

1. A. I. Herzen, *Sobranie sochinenii* (30 vols.; M, 1954–65), vol. 5, p. 34.

The crisis of belief Herzen experienced at this time bore fruit is one of his most interesting works, *From the Other Shore*, published in German in 1850. In it the former Hegelian proclaimed that history had no goal, that it was an eternal improvisation, and that each generation was an end in itself. History was guided not by reason but by chance and blind forces. Therefore, "to subordinate the individual to society, nation, humanity, and an abstract ideal is to go on making human sacrifices, to slaughter the lamb in order to placate the Almighty, to crucify the innocent for the guilty."[2]

Although history could not be called "rational," this did not mean that it was not subject to the laws of cause and effect. Only a moralist or sentimentalist would resent history, since whatever happened was clearly necessary. "Necessity," on the other hand, should not be confused with "rationality"—on the contrary, it was often unreasonable. History was in the grip of blind forces of nature that were necessary in a causal sense, but that did not imply any kind of teleological order. History "rarely repeats itself . . . she uses every chance, every coincidence, she knocks simultaneously at a thousand gates—who knows which may open?"[3] In history nothing was predetermined and therefore everything was possible.

This new interpretation led inevitably to a questioning of accepted myths: It now appeared to Herzen that to believe in inevitable historical progress was to believe in "a Moloch who, . . . as a consolation to the exhausted, doomed multitudes crying *morituri te salutant,* gives back only the mocking answer that after their death all will be beautiful on earth."[4] After asking what slogans and banners he should now support, Herzen declared simply that he was not looking for a banner, but trying to get rid of one. His new advice was unambiguous: "If only people wanted to save themselves instead of saving the world, to liberate themselves instead of liberating humanity, how much they would do for the salvation of the world and the liberation of humanity."[5]

This was not the final answer, however. Although Herzen now proclaimed the total destruction of all myths and "faiths," he was already preparing to take up a new one—faith in Russia and Slavdom, in a "Russian socialism" based on the village commune idealized by the Slavophiles. This faith derived from a voluntaristic

2. Alexander Herzen, *From the Other Shore, and the Russian People and Socialism,* trans. by Moura Budberg, introduced by Isaiah Berlin (London, 1956), pp. 134–35.
3. *Ibid.,* p. 34.   5. *Ibid.,* p. 128.
4. *Ibid.,* p. 36.

philosophy of history that enabled Herzen to reject the Russian Westernizers' conviction that Russia must pass through the same historical evolution that Western Europe had experienced before her. Although the premises on which "Russian socialism" was founded contradicted the extreme skepticism and pessimism of *From the Other Shore* and its clear message of noncommitment, this contradiction should be seen in dialectical terms. Herzen's pessimism was that of a Westernizer who had lost his faith in the future of Europe. In a discussion between a skeptical observer "from outside" and a disillusioned but emotionally committed idealist, Herzen himself called his despair "the whim of a sulky lover." Intellectually he supported the skeptic, but in practice he preferred the position of the idealist whose loss of faith in Europe drove him to place his hopes elsewhere: "I can see judgment, execution, death, but I can see neither resurrection nor mercy. This part of the world has done what it had to do; now its strength is exhausted; the people living in this zone have accomplished their mission, they grow dull and backward. The stream of history has evidently found another bed—that is where I am going."[6]

"Russian Socialism"

Herzen expounded his conception of "Russian Socialism" mainly in French, in a number of brochures intended primarily for the Western European reader. These included *La Russie* (1849, an open letter to the German socialist Georg Herwegh), *Lettre d'un Russe à Mazzini* (1849), *Du développement des idées révolutionnaires en Russie* (1850), *Le Peuple russe et le socialisme* (1851, an open letter to J. Michelet), *To the Editors of the Polish Democrat* (1853, in Polish), and *La Russie et le vieux monde* (1854, letters to W. Linton). Herzen wrote these works from abroad, since he had decided to emigrate in order to found an independent Russian press. The Free Russian Press, which he set up in 1853 with the help of the Polish Democratic Society, published the *Poliarnaia Zvezda (North Star*, 1855), whose title harked back to the Decembrists' almanac published in 1823–25. From 1857, the Press also published the periodical *Kolokol (The Bell)*. Although it was strictly prohibited inside Russia and frequently confiscated, *The Bell* soon gained great popularity and influence there; it was read by a wide cross section of the population, from high school students to members of the imperial court.

Herzen's Russian socialism represented an original attempt to

6. *Ibid.*, p. 78.

formulate a philosophy of Russian history combining elements borrowed from the Slavophiles, Chaadaev, and the Westernizers of the 1840's (in particular Belinsky and Kavelin). From the Slavophiles, Herzen took over the view of the village commune as the embryonic stage of a new and higher social form and the conviction that collectivism (in Herzen's terminology "socialism" or even "communism") was a feature native to the Russian people. "Has not the socialism that divides Europe so deeply and so decisively into two hostile camps been recognized by the Slavophiles just as it has by us? It is a bridge on which we can join hands."[7] Like the Slavophiles, Herzen stressed that the Russian people had not been corrupted by the Roman juridical heritage or the individualistic view of property relations associated with it. Like them he valued the self-government principle of the commune and the unaffected spontaneity of relations between its members, who were not governed by contracts or codified laws. Finally, Herzen believed with the Slavophiles that the Orthodox faith in Russia was "more faithful to the teachings of the Gospels than Catholicism," and that thanks to their religious isolation the Russian people had been spared contact with the sick civilization of Western Europe. Only this isolation had enabled peasants in Russia to preserve their commune, which in turn had saved them from both "Mongolian barbarism" and "imperial civilization" and had helped them to avoid the "temptations of power" and to survive "to see the emergence of socialism in Europe."[8] What in Europe had been the culmination of a long process of intellectual development in Russia was the fruit of "natural immediacy." Europe, which was so proud of its civilization, Herzen concluded, had much to learn from the Russian peasant in his primitive hut, who had remained faithful to the community principle and to the "antediluvian" view that every man had a right to a share of the earth and its fruits.

The Pan-Slavic elements in Herzen's writings at this time—which so irritated Karl Marx and other West European radicals—can also be traced to Slavophile influences. In the 1840's the Slavophiles had not yet embraced Pan-Slavism, although a Pan-Slavic note had already been sounded by Khomiakov in his philosophy of history. Herzen held frequent discussions with Khomiakov. Herzens' *Diary* entries for 1844 show that Slavophile influence was greatly reinforced by Mickiewicz's Paris lectures on Slavic literature; in Mickiewicz, too, Herzen found criticism of Europe's ra-

7. Herzen, *Sob. soch.*, vol. 7, p. 118.
8. *Ibid.*, p. 288.

tionalistic civilization, the notion that the Slavic nations were the "men of the future," and even an analogy between the Slavic commune and socialist conceptions.[9]

The element taken over from Chaadaev was the view of Russia as a "country without history" and the conviction (in line with Chaadaev's *Apology of a Madman*) that this was a matter for congratulation, since it made possible the construction of a future without concern for the past. The absence of deep-rooted traditions (apart from the village commune, which had remained outside history, as it were) and the lack of a "ballast of history" that might have proved a burden to the present generation suggested to Herzen that Russia would find it easy to make a radical break with the "old world." The Russian monarchy was not part of the European royal tradition; the bureaucratic and alien regime imposed on Russia was a Napoleonic type of despotism and could not even be called conservative, since it destroyed tradition instead of protecting it. Modern Russian history began with the "negation of the past" forced through by Peter the Great, which destroyed "all traditions so thoroughly that no human effort would be capable of restoring them."[10] Educated Russians had nothing in common with their country's past; brought up in a cosmopolitan atmosphere and not fettered by any historical traditions, they were the most independent men in Europe. "We are free," Herzen wrote, "because we start with ourselves . . . we are independent because we possess nothing; we have hardly anything to love, all our memories are steeped in bitterness."[11] Therefore Russians had everything to gain and nothing to lose in a social upheaval. In fact, in a travesty of Marx's comment on the proletariat, one might say that Herzen regarded Russia as a proletarian among countries, which had nothing to lose in a revolution but its chains.

There was one other dynamic country that was not held back by its feudal past: "Just look at these two enormous land masses stretching out on both sides of Europe. Why are they so huge? What are they preparing for? What does this devouring appetite for action, for expansion mean? These two worlds that are so unlike, but in whom one cannot but perceive certain analogies, are the United States and Russia."[12] In 1835 de Tocqueville had already

9. See A. Walicki, "The Paris Lectures of Mickiewicz and Russian Slavophilism," *The Slavonic and East European Review*, 46, no. 106 (Jan. 1968).
10. Herzen, *Sob. soch.*, vol. 7, p. 332.
11. *Ibid.*
12. *Ibid.*, vol. 12, pp. 136–39.

suggested that the future belonged to America and Russia. Herzen agreed, but with the proviso that only Russia would contribute a truly new principle to the history of mankind. America, he wrote, only appeared to be without a history—in reality she was merely Protestant Europe transposed to a new continent. Above all she lacked the Russian "courage of negation" that Herzen described with such a mixture of pride and bitterness in his open letter to Michelet:

There are already enough impositions that we are forced to endure, without our making the position worse by imposing new ones on ourselves of our own free will . . . we bow to brute force; we are slaves because we have no way of freeing ourselves; but whatever happens, we shall accept nothing from the enemy camp.

Russia will never be Protestant.

Russia will never choose the *juste-milieu*.

Russia will not stage a revolution with the sole aim of ridding herself of Tsar Nicholas only to replace him by a multitude of other Tsars— Tsar-deputies, Tsar-tribunals, Tsar-policemen, Tsar-laws.[13]

In his articles at this time, Herzen did not suggest that the absence of history combined with the native communism of the Russian peasant were sufficiently strong in themselves to bring about the expected and desired social upheaval. Left to itself, the village commune was a static and conservative institution that stifled individuality and personal independence. In his concern for individual freedom, at least, Herzen remained consistently faithful to his earlier ideals. What was needed, therefore, was an active force capable of awakening the peasant and breathing new life into the commune. This force was the "principle of individualism," embodied for the first time in Peter the Great, the "crowned revolutionary," the tsar-Jacobin who had denied tradition and nationality.[14]

This view of Peter the Great clearly harked back to the Westernizing conceptions of the forties: to Belinsky's argument that the Petrine reforms had contributed a dynamic element to Russian reality, and to Kavelin's interpretation of the reforms as "the first phase in the realization of the personality principle in Russian history." Throughout the eighteenth century, Herzen argued, the tsarist system had exerted a civilizing influence and had encouraged the emancipation of the individual by creating a Westernized elite that began by supporting the government but later turned against it. The turning point was the Decembrist uprising: whereas Peter's

13. Herzen, *From the Other Shore*, p. 200.
14. Herzen, *Sob. soch.*, vol. 12, p. 156.

autocracy had been a "progressive dictatorship," the bureaucratic and "German" despotism in post-Decembrist Russia became an unmistakably reactionary force. This meant that the new carriers of the personality principle were the enlightened gentry, who had helped the government create "a European state within the Slavic state," and who had experienced all the successive phases of the evolution of European self-consciousness.[15] Herzen made the point that in Russia the "educated middle class"—and indeed anyone who was "no longer part of the common people"—should be considered part of the gentry. The section of society that was to be the "hotbed and intellectual focus of the future revolution"[16] was, therefore, not the gentry as a landowning class but its educated members—the intelligentsia of the gentry—whose "universalist upbringing" had uprooted them from the "immoral soil" and, by alienating them from their own social class, turned them into opponents of official Russia.[17]

The future of Russia thus depended on whether it would prove possible to fuse the communism of the common man with the personality principle represented by the intelligentsia. For Herzen, this was tantamount to fusing native Russian principles with European achievements, especially with the individual liberty characteristic of the Anglo-Saxon countries. As the carrier of the personality principle, the Russian intelligentsia was a product of Westernization and heir to European civilization. Although certain quotations taken out of context have been used to suggest otherwise, Herzen's Russian socialism was to be not merely the antithesis of Europe but also a synthesis preserving everything that was best in the European heritage.

Herzen did not suppose that Russian socialism was historically inevitable. There were other possibilities, he suggested: perhaps communism, that "Russian despotism in reverse," would be victorious; perhaps the tsarist system would transform itself into a "social and democratic despotism."[18] Or perhaps Russia would swoop on Europe, destroy the civilized nations, and perish together with them in a universal holocaust. History, Herzen stressed, had no predestined paths; it allowed humanity to select one among a number of possible choices and to fight for its implementation.

The motto of Russian socialism—"preserve the community while liberating the individual"[19]—was essentially a restatement of Her-

15. *Ibid.*, vol. 7, p. 297.　　17. *Ibid.*, vol. 12, pp. 155, 188–89.
16. *Ibid.*, vol. 6, p. 215.　　18. *Ibid.*, p. 197.
19. *Ibid.*, p. 156: "Conserver la commune et rendre l'individu libre."

zen's long-standing concern with the problem of achieving freedom without alienation, of reconciling a sense of autonomy with a sense of belonging. In the 1840's he had postulated the reconciliation of the particular with the universal in Hegelian terms; a few years later the same problem occurred in a different context, but we may safely assume that in both instances Herzen was concerned with satisfying the same psychological need.

Criticism of the "Old World"

Herzen's renewed interest in Russia's past and future was closely linked to his bitter disappointment in the "old world." He was a discerning critic of bourgeois society, even if his strictures were not always fair. The modern reader is struck especially by certain far-sighted observations that seem to anticipate criticism of a complex phenomenon we have come to refer to as "mass culture." Herzen's most interesting comments in this respect are to be found in a series of articles entitled *Ends and Beginnings*, in which he conducted a polemic with Ivan Turgenev, who had become the moral authority for liberal Westernizers in Russia.

For Herzen the year 1848 marked a turning point, the beginning of the end, the *ne plus ultra* of European civilization. It also marked the collapse of all ideals—of progress, of republicanism and of democracy. Philosophy was no longer absolute, and the constitution had turned out to be a lie. The West had abandoned its ideals, its belief in various utopian solutions capable of arousing men to action. All that remained were conflicting national interests and naked power struggles.

This was so, Herzen thought, because the nations of the West had nearly attained their maturity and were close to the state of stability that marks the completion of the evolutionary process. The representative of this "age of maturity" was the *middle class*. The victorious emergence of the middle class was the victory of a "thousand-headed hydra that would listen to everything, look at everything, wear everything, and devour everything"; it was the victory of the "despotic crowd," of that "conglomerated mediocrity" which so disturbed John Stuart Mill.[20] There were good reasons, however, for this victory; the crowd that "buys everything and therefore controls everything," that breaks all dams, fills everything, and overflows its banks," that "is satisfied with anything and for which nothing is enough"—this crowd was proof of the success and power of the middle class. It might destroy beauty and obliterate

20. *Ibid.*, vol. 16, p. 141.

individuality, but it enhanced prosperity. Like wares for sale, people became a wholesale product: commonplace, shoddier, and worse as individuals, but more numerous and powerful *en masse*. It was for the sake of this upward mobility of the masses that the "middle class was justified in gaining its victories. You cannot tell a hungry man, 'hunger becomes you better; don't look for food.' "[21]

This diagnosis clearly sets Herzen apart from the ideologists of Russian Populism. To the Populists, who followed Marx in this respect, capitalism meant the forced expropriation and proletarianization of the small producer and the growing contrast between "national wealth" and mass poverty. It is difficult to conceive of a notion more alien to the Populists than that of capitalism as a state of stability and balance achieved thanks to the social advancement of the masses. They were horrified by the cruelty of primitive accumulation and the high price paid for industrial expansion. Herzen, on the other hand, in his somewhat aristocratic, Tocquevillian criticism of middle-class civilization, looked at capitalism from the opposite pole, as it were—from the point of view of the end-product of industrialization, i.e. cheap production and mass consumption, and their social consequences. Countering arguments on the growing impoverishment of the proletariat, he suggested that in Western Europe a worker was a member of the middle class *in spe*—a concept of some originality in the 1860's.

Freedom and Necessity

As was mentioned earlier, Herzen's theory of "Russian socialism" was preceded by an intensification of the voluntaristic elements in his world view. Both before and after 1848, he rebelled against a teleologically conceived historical necessity, against allegedly objective laws of history that appeared to force individuals and nations to take a predetermined path. He developed his new ideas in the book *From the Other Shore*: here his passionate denial of the "rationality" of the historical process and his emphasis on the role of accident and "improvization" were expressions not only of the collapse of his previous optimistic view of history but also of the urge to create a philosophy of history that would leave a larger margin for free and conscious personal choice.

At the same time, certain themes associated with philosophical naturalism also made their appearance in *From the Other Shore*. Having rejected belief in the guidance of events by a rational spirit, Herzen now turned history into a battleground where man strug-

21. *Ibid.*, p. 138.

gled against the blind forces of nature. Some years earlier, in his philosophy of action, Herzen had been drawn to the naturalism of Feuerbach as a philosophy that defended natural immediacy against the one-sided domination of the universal. But after 1848, under the influence of positivist trends in Europe, he came to regard naturalism as a philosophy that demanded a scientific explanation of all phenomena. In the 1860's, he therefore attempted (especially in *Ends and Beginnings*) to provide a scientific groundwork for his theory of Russian socialism. By emphasizing that his conceptions were supported by the "natural, physiological approach to history," he was in fact trying to cut the ground from under his opponents' feet.

In support of his own theories Herzen now stressed the *multiplicity of evolutionary choice in nature*, which (he insisted) was proof that there was no "law of physiology" requiring Russia to develop along the same lines as Europe: "The overall evolutionary design permits an infinite number of unforseen modifications like the elephant's trunk or the camel's hump."[22] Different animal species evolved until they achieved their final form. By analogy, Europe had evolved into its finished form—the bourgeois state. Russia, on the other hand, was an organism whose evolution was not yet completed and whose future shape was still uncertain. Western Europe had adapted itself to the bourgeois system, just as fish had adapted themselves to life in water and breathing through gills; this did not mean that Russia's fate was already determined, even if she showed certain early symptoms of capitalist developments. Herzen used the evolution of the duck to illustrate this point: "There was a moment of hesitation when the aorta did not form a downward loop but branched outwards, showing a certain tendency to form gills; however, backed by its psysiological inheritance, habit, and evolutionary opportunity, the duck did not remain at the stage of the less complex system of respiratory organs but developed lungs."[23] With such examples drawn from natural history, Herzen argued against that naturalistic conception of social evolution based on a unilinear and Eurocentric idea of progress.

The term "naturalism" does not, however, adequately sum up Herzen's philosophical position after 1848. His naturalistic philosophy of history played a subordinate role in his world view: what is more, every attempt to extend its range was bound to lead to a clash with the paramount values of the philosophy of action and the belief in a universal ideal, which also played an important part

22. *Ibid.*, p. 196.   23. *Ibid.*, pp. 196–97.

in his arguments on behalf of Russian socialism. Thinking men must oppose the development of capitalism in Russia, he insisted, because humanity had already found a higher ideal—the ideal of socialism—and "the work done, the effect achieved, have been done and achieved on behalf of all who understand them; that is the solidarity of progress, humanity's coming of age."[24] This argument, of course, ran counter to the naturalistic premises of the philosophy of history put forward in *Ends and Beginnings*, which assumed that there was no such thing as "solidarity of progress": frog and hen evolved along different lines, and so did Russia and Western Europe; there was no common yardstick by which their development could be measured; each species developed its own "entelechy" and forged ahead according to the laws of its own "organic natural teleology."

Furthermore, the naturalistic philosophy of history was based on a strictly "physiological" determinism and thus clashed with Herzen's conviction that human beings were, or should be, masters of their own fate. If historical evolution was only an "extension of organic evolution," and if the development of a given nation could be compared (as Herzen compared it) to the evolution of a reptile or bird whose final shape was predetermined (even taking into account all possible permutations) by the properties of the embryo or egg, then it was hardly possible to talk of the "sovereign independence of the individual" or of the conscious and creative guidance of the course of history.

During his years as a political émigré, Herzen was too absorbed by his day-to-day political work to have time to consider and systematize his theoretical views. It must occasionally have occurred to him, however, that a naturalistic philosophy of history and a positive belief in scientific solutions could not easily be reconciled with earlier and more essential elements in his world view. In his later years, at least, he showed increasingly that he was aware of this potential conflict.

An interesting document in this respect is the letter to his son (who was a naturalist) written in 1868 with a view to publication and usually referred to as the *Letter on Free Will*. This document shows that Herzen's ideas had changed significantly, and in particular that he had come to question the adequacy of the natural sciences as a tool for understanding social developments, especially the philosophy of history. "Physiology," Herzen wrote to his son, "has more than adequately fulfilled its task by taking man apart

24. *Ibid.*, vol. 12, p. 186.

into innumerable actions and reactions and reducing him to a web, a welter of reflexes. Now it should allow sociology to recreate him in his totality. Sociology will snatch man from the dissecting room and restore him to history."[25]

The fundamental difference between a naturalistic and sociological conception of man, Herzen argued, lies in the issue of free will. From the "physiological" point of view a sense of free will is only a delusion, whereas from the point of view of sociology it has far greater significance. In contrast to the physiological self, which is only a certain "fluid form of organic functions," the sociological self "postulates the existence of consciousness, and the conscious self can neither react to stimuli nor engage in activity unless it assumes that it is free, i.e. that within certain limits it has the choice of doing or not doing something." This sense of freedom is a necessary attribute of the consciousness of men who have "awoken from a brutish dream" and become the substance of history. The idea of freedom, therefore, must be understood as the "phenomenological necessity of human reason, as a psychological reality."[26]

It is fairly obvious that Herzen's line of argument did not aim to do away with the contradiction between physiological determinism and human freedom—on the contrary, this contradiction was raised to the status of an insoluble Kantian antinomy. Not only did Herzen put aside the notion of the reconciliation of theory and practice he had held in the forties, but he now found philosophical arguments in favor of the very dualism—the split between "theoretical" and "practical" reason—he had once opposed. Nevertheless, Herzen followed Kant in recognizing the primacy of "practical reason" and thus remained faithful to the basic intentions of his philosophy of action. Objective truth—the thing in itself—was still the *magnum ignotum,* but at least moral freedom was an "anthropological reality." As such, it was no less real to human beings than time or space.

For all its weaknesses, this solution encouraged the rejection of all theories that advised radicals in the name of "objective laws" of physiology, history, or economics to become reconciled to inevitable facts and abandon the struggle to realize their "utopian" aims. At a time when science was frequently quoted in support of the thesis that socialism would only be possible in Russia in the distant future, Herzen's interpretation of the problem of freedom and necessity had great appeal to the majority of Russian socialists. In fact, it was this theory that was at the root of the so-called "sub-

25. *Ibid.,* vol. 20, p. 439.   26. *Ibid.,* p. 443.

jective" method in sociology developed at about the same time by Petr Lavrov and Nikolai Mikhailovsky, the leading theorists of Russian Populism.

To an Old Comrade

Herzen's political outlook was to undergo yet another significant shift after the Russian reforms of the sixties. Before the death of Tsar Nicholas I, as an armchair philosopher unable to influence the course of events, Herzen found it easy to preach unswerving radicalism, prophesy imminent disaster, and proclaim proudly that Russia would never choose the *juste-milieu*. After 1855 he was more willing to compromise: he appealed to the new emperor to take the chance of furthering "bloodless progress"; he welcomed every step forward, however minor; he adopted a number of "half measures" or "makeshift" postulates in his political program; and he was even ready to accept the continued existence of the monarchy provided the most urgent reforms were put into effect. Thanks to this change of front, Herzen now found supporters among a far wider cross section of society—among people who were in favor of reforms but certainly not of revolutionary changes. At the same time, under the impact of its large readership *The Bell* was inevitably obliged to become a mouthpiece of public opinion; this introduced an eclectic note, and a compliance with currently prevailing moods and the accepted views of the "reform camp" in the widest sense of the word.

Understandably enough, all this brought about a rapprochement between Herzen and the Russian liberals, which was further encouraged by certain differences Herzen had with the radicals. Herzen felt that Chernyshevsky and Dobroliubov were too sharp in their rejection of the liberal traditions of the progressive gentry, and guilty of a dogmatic judgment in their dismissal of the "superfluous" generation of the 1840's.[27] These differences, however, should not be exaggerated: on all political issues Herzen sided with Chernyshevsky's young radicals rather than with the gentry liberals. When the first revolutionary organization since the Decembrist movement was set up in 1861, it included among its founders Herzen and Ogarev as well as Chernyshevsky, and it called itself "Land and Freedom" (*Zemlia i Volia*) after the motto of Herzen's *The Bell*.

Soon, however, events were to put an end to Herzen's great popularity and widespread influence inside Russia. The most important

27. See below, pp. 206–8.

of these events was the Polish uprising of 1863. Herzen had always accepted as "dogma" the Polish nation's unquestionable right to independence and the "need for a revolutionary Russo-Polish alliance." By his unswerving loyalty to this principle in 1863, Lenin was to write later, he saved the "honor of Russian democracy." Although he had serious doubts about the likelihood of its success, Herzen at once put his entire moral and political authority behind the insurrection and placed his energy and journalistic talent at the disposal of the Polish cause. His pessimistic forecasts were soon to be proved correct. In Russia the uprising stimulated a wave of chauvinism that—thanks to the government's skillful propaganda and the violently anti-Polish campaign unleashed by the nationalistic press (led by Katkov's *Moscow News*)—even affected certain sections of progressive circles. Formerly enthusiastic readers of *The Bell* became susceptible to demagogic arguments portraying the uprising as a reactionary movement among the gentry aimed at imposing Polish rule over the Ukraine and Belorussia and at preventing land reform in Poland. Objective observers who understood the justice of the Polish demands and agreed with Herzen were forced to remain silent while *The Bell* was loudly attacked (from all sides) for its betrayal not only of the national interest but even of socialism and democracy. Its circulation fell rapidly and never again reached its previous high level.

After the uprising had been quelled and passions had died down, further disappointments were in store for Herzen. In particular he was embittered by misunderstandings and quarrels with the group known as the "young emigration." There were many grounds for mutual suspicion. The young radical *raznochintsy* accused Herzen of aristocratic high-handedness, lukewarm liberalism, and a reluctance to make personal sacrifices for the sake of revolution. Herzen, for his part, accused them of political recklessness and dishonest tricks in obtaining money for irresponsible ventures. He was offended by their lack of manners and "unceremonious brusqueness" which showed, he thought, that they had not succeeded in shaking off the bad habits of their early environment. Despite many attempts to reach some kind of mutual rapprochement, a final split proved unavoidable.

Herzen's bitterness and sense of isolation were aggravated by the fact that his attitude to the young émigrés was not always understood by his closest collaborators. Bakunin's authority and influence increased rapidly, although his views were sharply attacked by the Russian Section of the First International. Even Ogarev felt more at home among the young émigrés than Herzen did (indeed, he largely shared their views). In the year before Herzen's death this difference once more became sharply accentuated in the Nechaev affair.[28] Despite appeals by both Bakunin and Ogarev, Herzen refused to hand over money to Nechaev that had been left with him by a certain Bakhmetiev for use in the revolutionary cause. The outcome of the Nechaev affair convinced even Bakunin that his friend's skepticism had been justified, but by then Herzen was no longer alive.

Herzen's critical and profoundly skeptical view of the Russian revolutionaries of the late sixties, as well as his intimate knowledge of the organizational successes of the labor movement in Western Europe, prompted him to change his mind once more. He analyzed the motives that led him to this in the cycle *Letters to an Old Comrade* (1869), ostensibly addressed to Bakunin but essentially a polemic against the views he himself had held after the tragic events of 1848–49, when his disappointment with Western Europe was at its height.

The doctrine of Russian Socialism stemmed from Herzen's unusually strong conviction that his own age was some kind of decisive turning point. It seemed to him that the old world was about to collapse and that Western Europe, like ancient Rome, would go under in a great historical catastrophe in which the Russians would play the role of the new barbarians. In his *Letters to an Old Comrade*, this catastrophic vision has given way to a far more moderate judgment. In fact, Herzen no longer prophesies the imminent collapse of bourgeois society: the newly emerging world is not yet complete, he argues, and the old order is still soundly established on strong moral as well as material foundations; attempts to overthrow it by

28. Sergei Nechaev (1847–82), the founder of the highly centralized and clandestine revolutionary organization known as "The People's Vengeance," pretended to be a representative of the International and a member of an All-Russian Revolutionary Committee; he was helped in this by Bakunin, who gave him a special warrant with the stamp of a nonexistent "Alliance Révolutionnaire Européenne, Comité Général." Nechaev's *Revolutionary Catechism* advocated ruthless and unscrupulous methods of struggle. The revolutionary, it declared, despises and hates the existing social ethic: "for him, everything that allows the triumph of the revolution is moral, and everything that stands in its way is immoral" (quoted in F. Venturi, *Roots of Revolution* [London, 1960], p. 366). This rule was applied in the case of Ivan Ivanov, a member of Nechaev's organization, who was "sentenced to death" and killed in 1869 because he suspected Nechaev's credentials and protested against his methods. His assassination enabled the police to pick up the trail of "The People's Vengeance" and to arrest its members. The trial in St. Petersburg in 1871 aroused great indignation in both Russia and the West. The reactionary press (and also Dostoevsky in *The Possessed*) utilized it to discredit the revolutionary movement as a whole.

force will only result in ruin, stagnation, and disorder. "After you have blown up bourgeois society, when the smoke has settled and the ruins have cleared away, what will emerge—with certain modification—is just *another form of bourgeois society*."[29]

This new view of the future involved a characteristic shift in Herzen's philosophy of history from voluntarism to renewed emphasis on necessity and the internal consistency of historical processes. Every historical formation, he now argued, was once the "supreme truth" of its age: "Private property, Church, State—all were once powerful training grounds serving the liberation and development of mankind; they will be left behind when they cease to be necessary."[30] Only enterprises that were in harmony with the internal rhythm of historical evolution were likely to succeed. In the heat of the argument with Bakunin, Herzen went so far as to quote Hegel's paradox that even slavery could be a step toward freedom.

Herzen accepted the decisive role played by economic processes, but unlike Bakunin concluded that social changes must ripen slowly and could only be accelerated to the extent that a midwife helps to hurry up the birth of a child. His determinism was not, however, purely mechanical and only appeared to contradict his earlier view put forward in the *Letter on Free Will*: it was not a return to Hegelian idealism, but neither was it a concession to "economism," which assumed that changes took place automatically, without the participation of human will or consciousness. Economic changes, Herzen argued, make headway *solely* by impressing the will and consciousness of the masses, so that will and consciousness form an indispensable link of the chain we call the historical process. Bakunin's revolutionary anarchism was unacceptable not because it exaggerated the role of human will and consciousness in history, but on the contrary because it ignored them and attempted to impose the revolutionary's own will on the masses. This "petrograndism," as Herzen called it, could at best lead to the "galley slave equality" of Babeauf, or the "communist serfdom" of Cabet. Herzen's new view of history entailed not belief in *"objective"* (or in other words immutable) laws determining the movement of events, but only recognition of the fact that the conscious will of even the most emancipated individual is of far less significance than the historically conditioned consciousness and will of the masses.

The practical implication of this view was that Herzen came

29. Herzen, *Sob. soch.*, vol. 20, part 2, p. 577.
30. *Ibid.*, p. 580.

to favor gradual reform rather than revolution. Since economic changes (and the changes in outlook accompanying them) take place gradually, and "it is not possible to liberate people further in their external circumstances than their *inner* freedom permits,"[31] the most urgent task was to influence the consciousness of the masses, to hasten—but without omitting necessary stages—the process of "inner liberation." Argument ought to replace "crude force," Herzen wrote; "apostles are of more use to us than officers of the advance guard."[32] He was determined to make his meaning quite clear: "I do not believe in the old revolutionary ways and try to understand the *human pace* in the past and in the present; this means not being left behind but not running ahead either, far ahead where people will not and cannot keep up with me."[33]

This reappraisal was part of Herzen's renewal of faith in Europe and, in particular, in the European working class. In the *Letters to an Old Comrade* Herzen made several references to the International Workingmen's Association, suggesting that it was an early bud of the new system growing within the body of the old world. This "turning of his gaze to the International,"[34] as Lenin described it, was not inconsistent with his rejection of the "old revolutionary ways"; Herzen's reaction to the First International was influenced by Bakunin, who accused it of recognizing the bourgeois state and abandoning revolution in favor of legal and peaceful opposition. The difference, of course, was that what Bakunin found grounds for criticism Herzen found grounds for approval. Thus we can see that the *Letters to an Old Comrade* represented, at least partially, a rejection of Russian socialism: though they did not assume that progress could only be in one direction—obliging Russia to pass through a capitalist phase—they nevertheless rejected the historical diagnosis of Russia as "the chosen people of the social revolution."[35]

After the 1905 Revolution, the *Letters* were interpreted in liberal circles as evidence of Herzen's conversion to the liberal point of view—although it is difficult to agree with this conclusion. Herzen neither embraced bourgeois reformism nor gave up the ideal of a total and worldwide transformation of society. What he attempted to do was to reconcile the conception of such a radical transforma-

31. *Ibid.*, pp. 589–90.
32. *Ibid.*, pp. 592–93.
33. *Ibid.*, p. 586.
34. V. I. Lenin, *Collected Works* (Eng.-lang. ed.; M, 1960–66), vol. 18, p. 27.
35. A phrase used by Engels in his afterword to the article "On Social Relations in Russia" (1894).

tion with historical and cultural continuity. If he was now reluctant to "burn to the ground the whole field of history,"[36] it was because he no longer believed this would bring about a real and revolutionary eradication of evil: the scorched fields would become overgrown with weeds and the realization of the humanist ideals of the revolution would be doomed to failure or at least greatly delayed.

In any case, the *Letters to an Old Comrade* do not change Herzen's place in Russian intellectual history. As a political leader he represented a link between the Decembrists and the "superfluous men" (gentry revolutionaries and gentry liberals), on the one hand, and the radicals democrats of the sixties, on the other. As a theorist he stood between the Westernizers and Slavophiles of the forties and the ideologists of Populism.

NIKOLAI OGAREV

The loose definition applied to Herzen above is equally true of his closest friend and collaborator, NIKOLAI OGAREV (1813–77). His career and Herzen's were closely parallel from their student days to later years in emigration. In their youth they went through a romantic phase of friendship founded on mutual sympathy and shared ideals (to which they swore allegiance on the Vorobov Hills). They were students at Moscow University at the same time and together founded a student study circle in which they discussed the ideas of the Saint-Simonians and other exponents of the "new palingenetic period of history." In 1834, Ogarev was arrested with Herzen and banished to Panza Province. On his return, he, like Herzen, eagerly took up German philosophy; he studied in Germany from 1841 to 1846. Although the two friends were separated at this time, Ogarev's intellectual evolution continued to be strikingly similar to Herzen's: like the latter he began to feel his way toward a "philosophy of action," tried to "overcome" Hegelian idealism, and carefully read the works of Feuerbach (indeed, it was Ogarev who introduced Feuerbach to Herzen and his other Moscow friends during a brief visit to Russia in 1842). Afterwards the two friends' paths diverged for a time: while Herzen was beginning to work out the theory of Russian socialism abroad, Ogarev settled on his estates, freed his peasants, and tried out a number of innovations aimed at raising the standard of living in the countryside by rational farming methods. However, as soon as Ogarev was able to obtain a passport (after the death of Nicholas I) he left Russia and joined Herzen at the

36. Herzen, *Sob. soch*, vol. 20, p. 589.

Free Russian Press. He became joint editor of *The Bell* and shared in all its successes and failures.

As a political thinker, Ogarev in principle shared Herzen's outlook, although on a number of issues he differed over details or even disagreed with his friend. Although he also wrote poetry, Ogarev was primarily interested in practical problems such as the organization of the revolutionary movement and the economic aspects of Russian socialism. Even in 1857, when, like Herzen, he still believed it possible to achieve essential democratic and social reforms without the use of force, he wrote about the advisability of organizing a secret society in Russia (*Zapiska o tainom obshchestve*). Disappointed by the limited scope of the land reforms introduced by Alexander II, he devised plans for overthrowing the government by means of a military-cum-peasant revolution. These plans were based on a careful study of the lessons of the Decembrist revolt and antifeudal peasant rebellions: the army was to make the first move and supply the disciplinary backbone, whereas the armed peasants would provide the battalions.

Ogarev was more readily inclined to appeal to the revolutionary peasantry than Herzen, who was more skeptical of the chance of a peasant revolution and who tended to stress the need for preserving the cultural achievements of the educated elite. Ogarev also found it easier to get on with ordinary rank-and-file sympathizers and in 1862 undertook to edit a new periodical—*Obshchee Veche*—intended for a more plebeian readership than *The Bell* (peasants, workers, soldiers, and Old Believers). One of Ogarev's letters in the sixties gives a characteristic insight into this aspect of his personality: "If a Pugachev were to appear I should volunteer to be his adjutant, because the Polish gentry does not arouse even one hundredth of the hatred in me that the Russian gentry does—paltry, despicable, and inevitably committed to the Russian government."[37]

If Herzen was concerned to establish the historiosophical groundwork of Russian socialism, Ogarev was more interested in socialism's economic aspects. With the help of a detailed analysis of concrete economic factors, he attempted to prove that in Russia capitalism was an artificial phenomenon and had no hope of success. The existence of the peasant commune, on the other hand, showed that socialism was not a mere "literary idea"—as in Western Europe, which was corroded by economic individualism—but a notion with real roots in the agricultural economy and in folkways, requiring only a transition from communal ownership of the land to com-

37. *Literaturnoe nasledstvo*, vol. 61 (M, 1958), p. 824.

munal cultivation to become established. The Russian peasantry's spontaneous inclination toward socialism was a guarantee that a federal system of government could be established, thus avoiding centralization or regimentation from above, which were the main weaknesses of the revolutionary communism of Babeuf.

Ogarev was well aware that what he was discussing was agrarian socialism, and he was consistent in the conclusions he drew from this. For instance, he declared that towns were unnecessary in Russia, he accused Chernyshevsky of representing "urban" socialism, and he reproached socialists in Western Europe for not understanding that the abolition of private ownership of the land was a *conditio sine qua non* of a socialist system.

Ogarev's philosophical views evolved from the religiously tinged romantic idealism of his youth by way of Hegelianism to materialism and atheism. He was also influenced by positivism: the distinction between materialism and positivism, he suggested, was that the latter system did not attempt to define the universal "principle" of existence, which for the materialist was matter; in practice, however, he felt this to be of little importance, since both systems were grounded in "positive knowledge." In Ogarev's views on society mechanistic materialism was combined with historical idealism: on the one hand, he stressed that the historical process is part of natural history; on the other, he shared the Enlightenment's view that the prime mover of progress is the development and dissemination of scientific knowledge. Hegelian influence can be traced in his belief that the course of progress was along a spiral rather than a linear path. Also characteristic of Ogarev was a strict "physiological" determinism formed under the influence of the eminent Russian physiologist I. M. Sechenov; in keeping with the latter's teaching, he rejected free will as an idealistic superstition and attempted to replace the "fatalism of predestination" by the "fatalism of cause and effect."

This standpoint differed from the more complex conception put forward by Herzen in his *Letter on Free Will*. Despite his determinism, however, Ogarev tended (rather more than Herzen) toward voluntarism in his political activities. One aspect of this was his lack of critical distance from the political adventurer Nechaev. Today we know that Ogarev collaborated closely with Nechaev and wrote most of the proclamations circulated by the latter's organization. It is also interesting to note that Ogarev supported Bakunin in the discussion Herzen undertook in the *Letters to an Old Comrade*.

CHAPTER 11

NIKOLAI CHERNYSHEVSKY
AND THE "ENLIGHTENERS"
OF THE SIXTIES

When Russian historians write about "the sixties," what they usually have in mind is not the actual decade from 1860 to 1870 but a crucial period in modern Russian history beginning in 1855 with Russia's defeat in the Crimean War and ending in 1866 with Karakozov's unsuccessful attempt on the life of Tsar Alexander II. The key year of this decade was 1861, which not only saw the proclamation of the emancipation and land-settlement edicts, but also marked the high tide of the tense revolutionary mood of the previous two years. The first all-Russian revolutionary society, "Land and Freedom" (*Zemlia i Volia*), was also founded at the end of 1861. By 1862 the chances of a successful revolution began to recede, and reaction was strengthened by the mood of chauvinism following the Polish insurrection of 1863. The government nevertheless continued to carry out social reforms: early in 1864 local self-government institutions known as *zemstvo* assemblies were set up, and later in 1864 far-reaching legal reforms were introduced. At the same time, however, radicals pressing for further changes were persecuted with increasing vigor and the general climate of opinion became unfavorable to the democratic camp. After Dmitry Karakozov's attempt on the emperor's life, a hysterical campaign against "nihilists" was unleashed by both the liberal and the conservative press.

The land reform of 1861 did not go far enough: it failed to satisfy the peasants' hunger for land, took away some of the acreage peasants had previously cultivated, and burdened them with heavy redemption payments to cover the compensation paid by the government to former serf owners. In short, the agrarian problem was not finally solved and the structure of tsarist absolutism remained unchanged. However, even granting all this, the fact remains that Russia now embarked on a phase of rapid capitalist development and that profound changes took place in the country's intellectual climate.

After the disastrous defeat at Sevastopol—a defeat all the more galling in view of the undoubted heroism of the Russian army—the feudal and bureaucratic empire that until recently had seemed to be the most powerful support of the Holy Alliance was seen to be nothing but a giant with feet of clay. The death of Nicholas I, who had symbolized all the evil of the old regime, was welcomed by most with a sense of relief and the hope that the new emperor's reign would usher in an age of political and social change. Even government circles realized that certain reforms—chief among them a solution to the peasant problem—were long overdue. Alexander II felt compelled to embark on a course of partial concessions, which included sounding out public opinion on ways of introducing the most urgent reforms without detriment to the existing system. The period of great hopes and spontaneous civic activity that followed Alexander's accession to the throne became known as the "thaw."

The government's new policies were both inconsistent and fragmentary, thus arousing mingled hopes and doubts. The concessions went far enough, however, to help bring about a superb flowering of social thought—the "golden age" of serious Russian journalism. The outburst of creativity after 1855 is particularly striking when we contrast it with the almost total stagnation of the last seven years of the reign of Nicholas I, the years after the death of Belinsky, Herzen's emigration, and the trial of the Petrashevtsy. From 1848 to 1855 the reform movement was deprived of men of ideas; under the impact of the revolutionary tide in Europe, the authorities increased their persecution of all independent thought, the press languished under a repressive censorship, and the universities were treated as centers spreading infection. So fearful were the authorities of the specter of "intellectual unrest" that they closed down the university philosophy departments and handed over the teaching of philosophy to Orthodox theologians. The vivid memory of the unrelieved repression of these last years gave rise to exaggerated faith in the new emperor's liberalism; there was widespread hope that progress would be achieved by the willing cooperation of government and public, without disorder or outbreaks of violence. Representatives of almost all social and political trends appeared to be united in a general desire for reform and for the liberalization of public life. The emperor's announcement of the impending emancipation edict was greated with enthusiasm. "Man of Galilee, you have triumphed!," was how Herzen put it.

This mood of high-minded optimism and national harmony was soon over. The inner logic of events brought about a growing polarization of attitudes: as democratic circles became increasingly disappointed in the government's actions, they also became increasingly susceptible to revolutionary ideas. In the political field, the most important change was the emergence of a strong and separate radical camp. The alliance of radical democrats and liberals broke up when it became clear that they differed not only on the methods to be used to achieve social change, but also on ultimate aims. Liberals as well as radicals were working for changes within the capitalist system, but each represented different interests. As Russia lacked a strong bourgeoisie capable of challenging absolutism, neither liberals nor radical democrats can be called spokesmen of the bourgeoisie in the strict sense of the word. The liberals were "gentry liberals" who represented the reformist tendency of that section of the landowning class anxious to adapt itself to the new age; the radical movement, by contrast, expressed the desires and interests of the "people" in the widest possible meaning of the word —in Russia this of course meant the peasantry.

The statement that the radical democrats represented the interests of the peasantry should not be understood too literally. The Russian peasants were not in a position to engage directly in the ideological struggle. Members of the democratic groups came not from the peasantry as such but from the *raznochintsy*, men of mixed, non-noble background, who were mostly sons of petty officials, priests, or impoverished gentry families, and who had to earn their living by their brains. The emergence of this new group in public life brought about a significant intellectual and cultural revolution.

Among Russian Marxists the dominant ideology of the radical democrats of the sixties came to be known as *prosvetitel'stvo*—a term for which it is difficult to find any other translation than "enlightenment," which must, of course, also make do for the eighteenth-century Russian Enlightenment. The representatives of the movement were simply referred to as "enlighteners" (*prosvetiteli*). Plekhanov stressed the connection between the "enlightenment" of the sixties and eighteenth-century historical idealism. For Lenin *prosvetitel'stvo* was chiefly a democratic ideology supporting bourgeois progress and attacking the survivals of feudalism. The common element in both Plekhanov's and Lenin's views was the movement's links with eighteenth-century rationalism, although Plekhanov drew attention to the theoretical weakness of this rationalism, whereas Lenin stressed its progressive and antifeudal function.

The similarity between the "enlightenment" of the sixties and French eighteenth-century Enlightenment philosophy can also be traced in philosophical attitudes ("human nature" as opposed to various feudal "superstitions") and in the movement's philosophical style, which was deliberately critical, aggressive, and always eager to underline the contrast between "what was" and "what should be." The "enlighteners" themselves were aware of this. As one of them, Nikolai Shelgunov, wrote:

> The sixties were a period of unusual spiritual intensity, of remarkable concentration of mental effort and remarkable sharpening of our critical faculties. . . . There was not a single field of knowledge that the critical faculty did not penetrate, not a single social phenomenon untouched by it. Earth and heaven, paradise and hell, problems of personal and public happiness, the peasant's hut and the nobleman's mansion—all these were scrutinized and subjected to critical appraisal. . . . The intellectual revolution we experienced in the sixties was not less in scope than the one France experienced after the middle of the eighteenth century.[1]

CHERNYSHEVSKY'S ANTHROPOLOGICAL MATERIALISM

Biographical Note

The key figure of the "sixties" was undoubtedly NIKOLAI CHERNYSHEVSKY (1828–89).[2] The son of a priest at the Church of St. Sergius in the city of Saratov, he was intended for the priesthood but, after graduating from the seminary, entered the faculty of history and philology at St. Petersburg University instead of continuing his theological studies. At the university he immediately plunged into the study of prohibited books that were not available in public libraries. At the time of the 1848 revolutions he eagerly read French and German newspapers in order to be abreast of the latest happenings. Aleksandr Khanykov (one of the Petrashevtsy) introduced him to Fourier and utopian socialism. With his characteristic thoroughness, Chernyshevsky set out to master the chief works of Fourier and Saint-Simon, Cabet, Leroux, Considérant, Proudhon, and Blanc. His ideas on literature and the arts were

1. Quoted from *V. I. Lenin i russkaia obshchestvenno-politicheskaia mysl' XIX-nachala XX veka* (L, 1969), p. 42.
2. Three books on him have recently been published in English: F. B. Randall, *N. G. Chernyshevskii* (New York, 1967); W. F. Woehrlin, *Chernyshevskii: The Man and the Journalist* (Cambridge, Mass., 1971); N. G. Pereira, *The Thought and Teachings of N. G. Černyševskii* (The Hague, 1975).

formed under the marked influence of Belinsky. Another formative influence on the young Chernyshevsky was the discussions held at the home of Irinarkh Vvedensky, who taught Russian literature at the Artillery School. Vvedensky had been a friend of Petrashevsky and thus represented another link between Chernyshevsky and the Petrashevsky circle.

To begin with, Chernyshevsky attempted to reconcile "the ideas of the socialists and communists, the radical republicans and montagnards" with his Christian faith; in 1848, for instance, he prayed for the souls of the defeated revolutionaries condemned to death. Later, under the influence of the Saint-Simonians and Pierre Leroux, he tried to link utopian socialism to the concept of a "new Christianity," of a "new Messiah, a new religion, and a new world." Later still, new doubts assailed him. "The methods adopted by Jesus Christ were not, perhaps, the right ones," he wrote in his diary. It might have been more useful if he had invented a self-regulating mechanism, a kind of *perpetuum mobile* that would have freed mankind from the burden of worrying about its daily bread.[3]

Comments of this kind suggest that the young Chernyshevsky's Christianity sprang not from a transcendental experience, but from a passionate belief in the Kingdom of God on earth. This belief easily underwent a process of secularization: from concluding, after Feuerbach, that the secret of theology was anthropology, it was an easy step to interpreting the Kingdom of God on earth as a kingdom of emancipated human beings in full control of their fate.

After graduating from the university in 1851, Chernyshevsky was appointed to a post as teacher of literature at the Saratov Lycée. He was a talented teacher and soon became popular with his students. His radical views created difficulties for him, however, and he left his native Saratov for St. Petersburg after only two years, in 1853. In St. Petersburg, Chernyshevsky set about writing a master's dissertation entitled *The Aesthetic Relations Between Art and Reality*.[4] He also began to contribute articles and literary criticism to the press, and in 1855 he joined the editorial staff of Nekrasov's *Contemporary*. After Belinsky's death the *Contemporary* had come under the influence of a group of liberal critics of aestheticist leanings (A. V. Druzhinin, P. V. Annenkov. and V. P. Botkin), so that it no longer represented a homogeneous and well-defined ideological line. With the addition of Chernyshevsky,

3. See Chernyshevsky's *Diary* for the years 1848–50.
4. In prerevolutionary Russia the degree of "master" entitled one to hold a professorial appointment.

though, it once again took up the cudgels on behalf of an ideologically committed, critical realism.

Chernyshevsky wrote most of his literary criticism between 1854 and 1857. In the fall of 1857 he handed over the editorship of the literary section of the *Contemporary* to his younger colleague Nikolai Dobroliubov in order to devote himself to history, philosophy, and political economy. In the articles he wrote subsequently he put down the basic principles of a new and revolutionary radicalism that departed totally from the world view of the Russian liberals and their gentry sympathizers. In his "The Anthropological Principle in Philosophy" (1860), Chernyshevsky expounded his views on philosophy and ethics; in "Capital and Labor" (1859), the lengthy "Notes on the Founding of Political Economy by J. S. Mill" (1860),[5] and other economic articles, he subjected economic liberalism to critical analysis from the point of view of the "political economy of the working masses." In many articles, and especially in the "Critique of Philosophical Prejudices Regarding the Communal Ownership of the Land" (1858), he defended the peasant commune against attacks by the advocates of capitalist development. Of special interest are a group of articles dealing with the revolutions in France ("Cavaignac," "The Party Struggle in France in the Reigns of Louis XVIII and Charles X," "The July Monarchy," etc.). In his work at this time Chernyshevsky stressed the vacillation and cowardice of the liberal politicians and attacked the half measures they proposed; he also contrasted the liberals' program, with its emphasis on the issue of political liberties (which, he argued, largely benefited the economically prosperous sections of society), with that of the radicals, with its emphasis on the welfare of the people. It should be noted that the outlook of an entire generation of Russian revolutionaries was formed by these articles.

As the revolutionary mood in Russia gained momentum, Chernyshevsky's role as the intellectual leader of the radical camp grew in importance. His rooms were a meeting place of revolutionary activists (among whom were N. Shelgunov, M. Mikhailov, N. Utin, and the brothers Serno-Solovievich), and students came to see him to discuss their political demonstrations. According to M. Sleptsov, Chernyshevsky showed great interest in the work of the revolutionary *Zemlia i Volia* society, which also benefited from his advice. Even a revolutionary society of Polish officers, founded by Zygmunt Sierakowski, a close friend of Chernyshevsky, was under his influence (one of the members of the society was Jarosław Dąbrowski,

5. These were highly praised by Marx.

who was to suffer a heroic death as the commander-in-chief of the Paris Commune).

Chernyshevsky was thoroughly at home with conspiratorial methods of struggle and was an expert at covering his tracks. As a result, we know very little of his links with the revolutionary organizations; indeed, there is no evidence that he was a member of the *Zemlia i Volia* group. We do know, however, that he was responsible for the proclamation "To the Peasants of the Landlords, Greetings from Their Well-wishers," which explained the shortcomings of the emancipation act.[6] It also seems likely that he was the main source of inspiration of the secret periodical *Great Russian (Velikorus'*, 1861), which appealed to the educated sections of society to take social and political reform into their own hands.

The tsarist authorities had long been eager to get rid of this thorn in their flesh and were glad to find a suitable pretext in an intercepted letter from Herzen that appeared to provide evidence of Chernyshevsky's contacts with Russian émigré circles in London. In July 1862 he was arrested and held in custody in the Peter and Paul Fortress. No incriminating papers were found in his rooms, however, and hopes that he would break down in prison proved misplaced. The prosecution was therefore forced to base its case on circumstantial evidence and forged documents and testimony. The trial dragged on for almost two years before Chernyshevsky was condemned, despite insufficient evidence, to fourteen years' hard labor and banishment for life to Siberia. The emperor confirmed the sentence, but halved the period of hard labor to seven years.

While he was in prison Chernyshevsky wrote his famous novel *What Is to Be Done?* This paints an idealized portrait of the generation of "new men," the radicals of the sixties, who represented a new morality as well as a new rationalist and materialist outlook. The novel's heroes—Lopukhov, Kirsanov, and Vera Pavlovna—stand above social conventions, being guided not by irrational beliefs but by positive self-interest or "rational egoism," i.e. the identification of their own interests with the interests and welfare of society as a whole. An entire section of the book is devoted to a rather curious character, the revolutionary Rakhmetov, a "superior nature"

6. For reasons that have never been established, this proclamation, which was written on the eve of the emancipation edict, was not printed. Perhaps the peasant uprising in Bezdna convinced Chernyshevsky that the former serfs themselves understood that they had been cheated of part of their land, or perhaps he felt that in the absence of an organized revolutionary movement the proclamation would only unleash undisciplined riots directed against the entire educated elite rather than just the landowner class.

whose devotion to the common good is even greater than that of Chernyshevsky's other heroes. Although Rakhmetov is a scion of the wealthy gentry, he is familiar with the people's lot, has measured the whole of Russia on foot, and has worked at cutting timber, quarrying stone, and hauling riverboats. He is one of a select band, the "salt of the earth": in order to train his willpower and resistance to pain, this perfect knight of the revolution even sleeps on a bed of nails.

Thanks to a strange oversight on the part of the censors, *What Is to Be Done?* was allowed to be serialized in the *Contemporary*. The authorities realized their mistake too late. The censor concerned was dismissed and new editions of the novel were forbidden, but these measures were not enough to halt its impact. The issues of the *Contemporary* in which it had been printed were preserved with immense piety, as though they were family heirlooms. For many members of the younger generation the novel became a true "encyclopedia of life and knowledge." In her memoirs, Lenin's wife, Nadezhda Krupskaya, relates that her husband recalled the work in every slight detail. Plekhanov was not exaggerating when he declared that "since the introduction of printing presses into Russia no printed work has had such a great success in Russia as Chernyshevsky's *What Is to Be Done?*" [7]

Chernyshevsky spent his first years of exile near the Chinese frontier. Having obtained a medical certificate exempting him from work in the mines, he devoted himself to writing and research. The autobiographical novel *The Prologue*, written at this time, throws an interesting light on Russian history in the revolutionary sixties. After he had served the first seven years of his sentence, he was bitterly disappointed to find that the place where he was to spend the rest of his life in exile was an isolated Yakut settlement lost in the taiga of eastern Siberia. He faced this new disappointment bravely, and three years later firmly dismissed a suggestion that he appeal for a remission of his sentence.

One of the reasons for Chernyshevsky's banishment to such a remote place was the authorities' fear of a forcible rescue attempt, something that was often discussed in revolutionary circles. The first such attempt was made by the exiled revolutionary Herman Lopatin, a friend of Marx.[8] An equally unsuccessful attempt was

---

7. G. V. Plekhanov, *Izbrannye filosofskie proizvedeniia* (M, 1956–58), vol. 4, p. 160.
8. Lopatin decided to try and help Chernyshevsky escape under the influence of his conversations with Marx, who often said that "of all contemporary economists Chernyshevsky is the only original mind; the others are just ordinary compilers" (G. A. Lopatin, *Avtobiografiia* [Petrograd, 1922], p. 71).

undertaken in 1875 by the radical Populist Hipolit Myshkin. Chernyshevsky's situation did not improve until the 1880's. In 1883 he was given permission to settle in Astrakhan with his family, and in 1889, shortly before his death, he was allowed to return to his native Saratov.

Aesthetics

Chernyshevsky's master's dissertation on *The Aesthetic Relations Between Art and Reality* contains the first mature exposition of his world view. Chernyshevsky's highest philosophical authority was Ludwig Feuerbach. In view of the censorship he could not at first openly refer to Feuerbach; but he did so after his return from banishment, in his preface to the third edition of the thesis, published in 1888.[9] There he wrote that "the author made no claim whatever to saying anything new of his own. He wished merely to interpret Feuerbach's ideas in application to aesthetics."[10]

In making this disclaimer, Chernyshevsky was, of course, being unduly modest. To begin with, his aesthetics do not derive entirely from Feuerbachian philosophy; moreover, Feuerbach did not actually write about aesthetics, so that the application of his ideas to aesthetic arguments was in itself something novel and original.

Following Plekhanov, most scholars have argued that Feuerbachian influence is most apparent in Chernyshevsky's thesis that the purpose of his aesthetics was to provide "a defense of reality against fantasy." This point of view is only partly correct: the materialist assumption concerning the primacy of reality over art has nothing *specifically* Feuerbachian about it. What was original in Feuerbach's philosophy—and Chernyshevsky's aesthetics—was something different, namely the fusion of materialism and anthropocentrism.

The "anthropocentric" theme in Chernyshevsky's thought is most apparent in his theory of beauty. Beauty, he argued, is something objective, and a matter of content rather than form. Hegel understood this when he called beauty a manifestation of the Absolute spirit. But the Hegelian conception of the Absolute was overthrown by Feuerbach, who demonstrated that man himself was the only absolute value. From this thesis Feuerbach drew the conclusion that for man "the supreme good, the supreme being" is life itself: "Man makes a god or divine being of what his life de-

9. It was the mention of Feuerbach that prevented this edition from receiving the censor's imprimatur.

10. N. S. Chernyshevsky, *Selected Philosophical Essays* (M, 1953), p. 416.

pends on only because to him life is a divine being, a divine possession or thing."[11] These ideas of Feuerbach are clearly at the root
of Chernyshevsky's definition of beauty, which reads as follows:
"Beauty is life; beautiful is that being in which we see life as it
should be according to our conceptions; beautiful is the object
which expresses life, or reminds us of life."[12]

Immediately after this definition of beauty in general, Chernyshevsky undertook a detailed analysis of the aristocratic and
peasant ideals of feminine beauty. A man of the people, he pointed
out, regards as beautiful everything that is a sign of robust health
and balanced physical development; an aristocratic beauty, on the
other hand, must be pale, weak, and sickly—all signs of a life of
leisure and indeed of an incapacity for work. This argument goes
beyond Feuerbachian "anthropologism" and shows an understanding of the relationship between the aesthetic imagination and the
social circumstances that help to determine it. Nevertheless, Chernyshevsky went on to insist that only one aesthetic ideal can be
considered "true" and "natural." The aristocratic ideal is "the artificial product of an artificial life," and only the ideal of men living
in "normal" conditions (i.e. laboring and in touch with nature) is in
harmony with man's true nature. This switch from historical relativism to normative aesthetics was of course important to Chernyshevsky, since it enabled him to justify the aesthetic ideals of
the common man and the demand for the widest possible democratization of art.

The notion "life" also has two different meanings attached to it
in the dissertation. In the first, narrow sense of the word, life appears to mean the abundance and richness of vital forces. More
characteristic, however, is a wider meaning that also embraces the
moral sphere. "True life is the life of the heart and mind,"[13] Chernyshevsky wrote, and the supreme ideal of beauty is thus a human
being in the full flowering of his faculties—a definition that comes
close to the great humanist tradition in Germany represented by
Goethe, Schiller, and Hegel. It is true that Chernyshevsky rejected
Hegel's and Vischer's thesis concerning the superiority of artistic
to natural beauty; but he did agree with them that beauty in nature
is significant only insofar as it relates to man. "Oh, how good
Hegelian aesthetics would be if this idea, beautifully developed in

11. L. Feuerbach, *Lectures on the Essence of Religion*, trans. Ralph Manheim
(New York, 1967), p. 52.
12. Chernyshevsky, *Selected Philosophical Essays*, p. 287.
13. *Ibid.*, p. 288.

it, were the basic one, instead of the fantastic search for the perfect manifestation of the Idea!"[14]

The reinstatement of matter, which in Chernyshevsky's aesthetics takes the form of a rehabilitation of the beauties of nature, was linked to a characteristically Feuerbachian "rehabilitation of the individual." In the Hegelian view, only ideas are truly real; individuals seen in isolation from the "universal" (the Idea or Spirit) are pure abstraction. For Feuerbach, on the other hand, it is individuals that are real, and the universal that is an abstraction. Chernyshevsky—who was in complete agreement with Feuerbach—set out to demonstrate in his thesis that "for man the general is only a pale and lifeless extract of the individual."[15] When applied to aesthetics, this belief was bound to lead to a denial of the generalizing function of art, to the view that the "universal types" allegedly created by literature are actually only copies of individual human types, and that in real life we meet typical characters who are far truer and more attractive than the "generalizations" of literature and art. Art in this view can only be a surrogate for reality. As has been aptly pointed out, this was a "reaction, typical of Feuerbachian materialism against Hegelian abstraction (the "universal") and led to the metaphysical antithesis in which the universal was identified with abstraction and the particular with concrete reality."[16]

Chernyshevsky's dissertation must therefore be seen as a passionate defense of individuality, of the concrete human being ignored by the idealist philosophers, who had treated man as a mere instrument of the Absolute. Where Chernyshevsky went astray was in the excessive oversimplification and abstract rationalism of his arguments. He failed to see the dialectical relationship between art and reality and, like Feuerbach, treated the comprehension of reality as a mechanical act not unlike the passive reflection of external objects in a mirror. The theory that resulted from this would have served better to underpin a naturalistic rather than a realistic conception of art. It ran counter to Chernyshevsky's own critical perception and clearly conflicted with the views on the role and significance of art put forward elsewhere in the dissertation. The function of art, he wrote, is not only to reproduce reality, but also to explain and evaluate it—to "pass judgment" on the real-life phenomena that have been recreated. In the light of this definition,

14. *Ibid.*, p. 290.
15. *Ibid.*, pp. 349–50.
16. A. Lavretsky, *Belinsky, Chernyshevsky, Dobroliubov v bor'be za realizm* (M, 1941), p. 221.

art cannot be a surrogate, for a surrogate of real-life phenomena cannot add to our knowledge of reality or help us to pass judgment on it.

When Pisarev said that Chernyshevsky's thesis stood for the "total abolition of aesthetics," he showed that he had quite misunderstood its central argument. The thesis was not directed against aesthetics as such, but against aestheticism. Because man's spiritual and material natures are one, Chernyshevsky argued, purely spiritual activity springing solely from the aspiration toward beauty is inconceivable. Love of beauty is disinterested, but it never appears in isolation from other human aspirations or needs; therefore, the sphere of art cannot be narrowed down to the sphere of aesthetic beauty. Chernyshevsky did not intend to belittle the role of art; quite the contrary, he thought "art for art's sake" was a dangerous theory just because it might lead to art's being relegated to an unimportant margin of human life. An artist who created solely for the sake of beauty would be an incomplete, and indeed crippled, human being.

From the first, Chernyshevsky's aesthetic notions suffered from one-sided interpretations and misunderstandings. They were attacked not only by critics who defended uncommitted "pure art" (Druzhinin, Annenkov, Botkin) but also by the great Russian realist novelists. Turgenev, who was particularly incensed by them, called *The Aesthetic Relations Between Art and Reality* the "stillborn offspring of blind malice and stupidity." Despite numerous hostile critics and frequently misguided supporters (e.g. Pisarev), Chernyshevsky's aesthetic ideas exerted a considerable influence on Russian literature and art. The main theses of the *Aesthetic Relations* were adopted as the fundamental tenets of progressive Russian criticism, and radical as well as Populist writers (Nekrasov, Saltykov-Shchedrin, Gleb Uspensky, and Vladimir Korolenko) tried to apply Chernyshevsky's ideas to their own creative work. Ilya Repin, the most accomplished of the nineteenth-century Russian realist painters, wrote in his memoirs that young painters, too, read Chernyshevsky with keen inerest. One of the leading advocates of Chernyshevsky's aesthetics was Vladimir Stasov, the chief Russian theorist of realism in the visual arts.

The Anthropological Principle

The title of Chernyshevsky's main philosophical work—"The Anthropological Principle in Philosophy" (1860)—pays homage to Feuerbach's "anthropologism." For Chernyshevsky the "anthropological principle" supplied the theoretical foundation for the integral wholeness of man, the abolition of the eternal dualism of body and soul. He formulated his ideas as follows: "What is this anthropological principle in the moral sciences? . . . It is that man must be regarded as a single being having only one nature; that a human life must not be cut into two halves, each belonging to a different nature; that every aspect of a man's activity must be regarded as the activity of his whole organism, from head to foot inclusively, or if it is the special function of some particular organ of the human organism we are dealing with, that organ must be regarded in its natural connection with the entire organism." [17]

An interesting supplement to the "Anthropological Principle" is the article on the "Character of Human Knowledge," written after Chernyshevsky's return from Siberia. In this article he put forward an epistemological theory based on a conception of the human organism as both knower and object of knowledge—and thus positing the indivisibility of matter and consciousness. For man, the "Archimedes principle" on which everything rests, he suggested, is not "I think" but "I am"; since our knowledge of our own existence is immediate and not open to doubt, our knowledge of the material world of which we form a small part is equally reliable.

Chernyshevsky did not take this theory of the oneness of human nature a step further to the conclusion that all human characteristics can be explained in terms of physiological properties. Psychology cannot be explained in terms of physiology, he declared, any more than physiology can be explained in terms of chemistry, or chemistry in terms of physics, because in such cases a quantitative difference becomes a qualitative difference. The important thing, he stressed, is to stop man from being "split up," and to prevent any one of his functions (either "spirit" or "nature") from being raised to the rank of an absolute. Man is an indivisible being, and only as such can he represent an absolute value to other men.

It was these arguments that underpinned Chernyshevsky's ethical theory of "rational egoism," which was based on the premise that—however interpreted—the guiding principle of men's conduct is egoism. In the normative sphere this theory gave preference to utilitarianism, rationalism, and egalitarianism. It postulated that the standard by which human actions must be judged is the benefit they bring—that good is not a value in itself but only a lasting benefit, "a very beneficial benefit." Egoism may be rational or ir-

17. Chernyshevsky, *Selected Philosophical Essays*, pp. 132–33.

rational, numerous cases of apparent unselfishness and self-sacrifice being in fact expressions of a rational conception of egoism: "To argue that a heroic act was at the same time a wise one, that a noble deed was not a reckless one, does not in our opinion, mean belittling heroism and nobility."[18] The rational egoist accepts other people's right to be egoists because he accepts that all men are equal; in controversial issues, where there is no unanimity, he is guided by the principle of the greatest good of the greatest number: "The interests of mankind as a whole stand higher than the interests of an individual nation; the common interests of a whole nation are higher than the interests of an individual class; the interests of a large class are higher than the interests of a small one."[19] Egoism that is truly rational makes men understand that they have interests in common and ought to help each other. This is what Feuerbach had in mind when he wrote "To be an individuality means to be an egoist and therefore—willingly or unwillingly—a *communist.*"[20] Chernyshevsky could have used this sentence as the motto for his novel *What Is to Be Done?*, a story of "rational egoists" who also believe in a socialist system.

Even from this short account it becomes clear that this "rational egoism" differs widely from what we normally understand by egoism. Chernyshevsky used the term "egoism" for his ethical theory as a challenge to those who, in the name of transcendent values, condemned as "egoism" all attempts by the oppressed to better their lot; it was a symbol of his distrust of ideologies that called on men to sacrifice themselves for the sake of allegedly higher aims— higher, that is, than man himself conceived as a living concrete human individual.

As early as the Enlightenment the materialist philosophers— Helvetius and Holbach—regarded rational egoism as a logical outcome of materalism. Chernyshevsky extended the theoretical foundations of "rational egoism" by a Feuerbachian critique of such idealistic hypostases as supra-individual Reason or Spirit. Feuerbach claimed that the universal did not have a separate independent existence; it existed only as a "predicate of the individual." This led to the rejection of organicist and historicist theories treating society as a supra-individual organic whole subject to rational laws of historical necessity. "The life of society," Chernyshevsky wrote,

18. *Ibid.,* p. 123.
19. *Ibid.,* p. 125.
20. See L. Feuerbach, *Das Wesen des Christenthums in Beziehung auf den "Einzigen und sein Eigentum."*

"is the sum of individual lives."[21] The laws to which man is subject are the laws of nature—laws of his own organism. He dismissed as unscientific the suggestion that there might be separate laws governing the evolution of society on the lines of Hegel's Historical Reason: society was not a biological organism and therefore could not behave like a real being.

In his article "What Caused the Downfall of Rome?," Chernyshevsky again returned to the same theme. Apropos of Herzen's comments on the "senility" of Western Europe and the "youth and robust energy" of the Russian nation, he suggested that to talk of societies growing, maturing, and aging was sheer anthropomorphism. Since civilizations are not organisms, they cannot experience a process of organic evolution; therefore one cannot talk of the inevitable decline of civilizations as if they were human beings subject to the laws of mortality. Chernyshevsky was especially impassioned in his attacks on Hegel's notion of the "rational necessity" of historical processes. There is no such thing as Historical Reason, he declared; "rationality" is introduced to history by rational human beings, by men creating knowledge: "Progress is the fruit of knowledge."[22] It is not guaranteed as the inevitable outcome of history; its achievements are fragile, just as fragile as human life and human intellectual achievements. The fall of Rome in fact was an excellent example of the fragile nature of progress, for it illustrated the downfall of a civilization under the impact of barbarian invaders.

This interpretation could give rise to pessimistic as well as optimistic conclusions. If we accept that progress is not inevitable, then the course of events can be determined by mere coincidence; on the other hand, no "rational necessity" can stand in the way of human effort to impose a rational shape on history. It may be very difficult to bring about "what should be," but it can never be ruled out altogether. Chernyshevsky thought that objective, scientific criteria determining "what should be" could be deduced from the laws governing "human nature," the totality of man's "natural" (i.e. material and spiritual) needs. From the "anthropological" point of view, he argued, human nature is constant; what varies are "artificial" needs arising out of man's partial denaturalization in conditions that are no longer "normal." By means of this Feuerbachian argument Chernyshevsky arrived back at the abstract ra-

21. N. S. Chernyshevsky, *Izbrannye filosofskie sochineniia* (L, 1950–51), vol. 2, p. 484.
22. *Ibid.*, vol. 3, p. 314.

tionalism of the "natural law" of the Enlightenment. This was undoubtedly a departure from the dialectical and historical view that Belinsky had worked out with such difficulty, but there were good historical reasons for this. The radical democrats of the sixties— representatives of the critical "intellect" of a new, emerging social force—preferred absolute criteria to historical arguments that were inevitably relative. After breaking with the conservative interpretations of Hegelianism, Belinsky, too, reaffirmed the ideals of Voltaire and the Encyclopedists; Chernyshevsky went even further in this direction because, like the French Enlightenment philosophers, he lived under an absolutist system that was experiencing a crisis, and in such conditions appeals to "human nature," reason, and a rationally based autonomous morality have greater resonance than appeals to history.

Russia's Future Development

Criticism of blind reverence for Necessity and the transcendent Laws of History is one of the characteristic and recurring motifs in Chernyshevsky's thought. Even in his aesthetics, he criticized the Hegelian conception of tragedy because it raised historical necessity to the rank of an absolute principle. In fact, this tendency did not always lead him to such sweeping conclusions as those put forward in the "Downfall of Rome." Other articles show that his rejection of idealistic hypostases did not mean that he considered it pointless to look for objective laws of social change.

Of particular interest in this respect is his article "A Critique of Philosophical Prejudices Against the Communal Ownership of the Land" (1858). Although he declared that there were no features typical of society that could not be deduced from the characteristics of individuals. Chernyshevsky nevertheless posited the existence of a universal evolutionary law, which he summed up as follows: "As far as form is concerned, the highest stage of development everywhere represents a return to the first stage which—at the intermediate stage—was replaced by its opposite."[23] Since individuals can "skip" the intermediate stage, he argued, why should not societies —which are only aggregates of individuals—be able to do so as well? If individuals can evolve at a faster pace symbolized in the progression 1, 4, 64, . . . , then social development can follow the formula 1A, 4A, 64A, ...

This argument was used by Chernyshevsky to prove that Russia

23. *Ibid.*, vol. 2, p. 473.

could bypass the capitalist stage and that the communal ownership of the land could serve as a basis for the socialist development of agriculture. In many respects Chernyshevsky's arguments in support of this thesis were in advance of those used by the diffusionists in their polemics with the evolutionists. The factor speeding up social change, he suggested, was cultural contact "between the man who is yet to attain a higher stage in a given process and the man who has already attained this stage."[24] In this accelerated process the intermediate stages only existed theoretically, as logical moments of change. If they achieved real existence, it was only on such an infinitesimal scale that no practical significance could be attached to them. The evolution of forms of ownership progressed from the communal property of the tribe through private ownership (which reached its culmination under capitalism) to modern communal ownership by associations; Chernyshevsky had no doubt that this last stage would soon replace capitalist property relations in the developed countries. Communal landholdings in Russia, Chernyshevsky thought, were a form of ownership corresponding to the first phase of the universal development of mankind; since a direct transition to the third phase—that of postcapitalist collectivism—seemed likely, there was no point in abolishing the village commune and thus destroying the collectivist traditions alive among the Russian people. On the contrary, attempts should be made to modernize the commune and to transform it along rational lines into an association similar to the workers' associations existing in Western Europe.

The issue of capitalist versus noncapitalist development is today one of the chief problems engaging the attention of economists and social scientists, and has obvious practical signification for the Third World countries. In relation to Russia, Herzen raised this issue some years before Chernyshevsky, but the latter was the first to formulate a general theory of accelerated social change based on noncapitalist methods.

It is interesting to note that the importance of the problem was recognized by Marx, who made a careful study of the "Philosophical Prejudices Against the Communal Ownership of the Land." It is even highly probable that this article influenced his views on the future development of Russia.[25] For instance, in his detailed drafts

24. *Ibid.*, p. 482.
25. See V. N. Shteyn, *Ocherki razvitiia russkoi obshchestvenno-ekonomicheskoi mysli XIX–XX vekov* (L, 1948), p. 236.

for a letter to Vera Zasulich dated March 8, 1881,[26] Marx argued that the situation in Russia was exceptionally favorable, since primitive communism had survived to see the day when economic, technical, and intellectual conditions in the West were ripe for modern communism. Russia was not an isolated country but part of the international market economy, and she could thus take advantage of all the achievements of modern civilization and technology, assimilating the fruits of capitalist production but rejecting its *modus operandi*. In these circumstances, there was no reason why Russia should have to go through the capitalist stage; an argument that could be used against the advocates of capitalism, who alleged that no stage could be bypassed, was that Russian capitalism itself was skipping various phases by adopting the finished products of foreign capitalism in the form of modern machinery, railways, and a banking system. The similarity with Chernyshevsky's arguments is striking.

Chernyshevsky's Place in the History of Russian Ideas

The Chernyshevsky tradition was continued in the 1870's by the revolutionary Populists. Chernyshevsky himself might be called a Populist in the broad sense of the word, but if we want to establish his place in the history of Russian revolutionary ideas we must not overlook the important differences that divided him from classical Populism.

Populist elements in Chernyshevsky's ideology were his defense of the peasant commune and noncapitalist development. Unlike the later theorists of Populism (especially N. K. Mikhailovsky), Chernyshevsky did not romanticize the "natural economy of the common people" or ancient "native" folkways; not surprisingly, he could not agree with the historian A. Shchapov, who regarded commune self-government as an invaluable survival of ancient Russia and a guardian of patriarchal traditions. Whereas Mikhailovsky thought of the commune as the embryo of a new civilization that would be both different from and qualitatively superior to capitalism, Chernyshevsky felt that the commune represented an evolutionary stage incomparably lower than capitalist property relations. The essential difference was that Chernyshevsky hoped Russia would be able to *catch up* with Western Europe by building on the latter's achievements and that she would overtake her and become a model for others: "Europe has her own understanding—an understanding

26. For an analysis of these drafts see A. Walicki, *The Controversy over Capitalism: Studies in the Social Philosophy of the Russian Populists* (Oxford, 1969), pp. 189–92.

that is much better developed than ours—and need not look to us for either theory or assistance."[27] While the Populists of the seventies hoped that Russia would take a course quite different from that of Western Europe, Chernyshevsky insisted that the Westernization of Russia ought to be completed by the eradication of "Asiatic conditions, the Asiatic social structure, and Asiatic habits."[28]

Another characteristic difference concerned the relative importance of social and political goals. The Populists of the seventies equated political revolution with bourgeois revolution, and a parliamentary system with government of the bourgeoisie; this led them to conclude that extending political democracy would only benefit the privileged classes and thus contribute still further to the impoverishment of the masses. At one stage Chernyshevsky shared this belief: "Tsar or no tsar, constitution or no constitution, it makes no difference," he wrote as a young man. What matters is "how to prevent the situation in which one class sucks the blood of another."[29] As late as 1858 he suggested that democracy was a function of the people's prosperity and that therefore Siberia whose population was relatively well off, was more "democratic" than England, which was suffering from "pauperization."[30] Soon afterwards, however (during the revolutionary years 1859–61), he returned to this problem and came to entirely different conclusions. Undemocratic methods used to prepare the abolition of serfdom convinced him that political freedom was in Russia a necessary condition of true social progress. Thus in his "Letters Without Addressee" (1862) he sided with the gentry liberals of Tver', who demanded a liberal constitution for Russia.[31]

This shift in Chernyshevsky's position resulted from his conclusion that the greatest evil in Russia was *autocracy*—which because of the censorship he was obliged to refer to as "bureaucracy."

27. Chernyshevsky, *Izbr. fil. soch.*, vol. 3, p. 336.

28. *Ibid.*, vol. 2, p. 668.

29. *Ibid.*, vol. 3, p. 821.

30. See Chernyshevsky's article "The Party Struggle in France in the Reigns of Louis XVIII and Charles X."

31. The "Letters Without Addressee" were intended for the February number of the *Contemporary* (1861), but the censor stopped their publication. Despite the title, they were clearly addressed to Alexander II. Chernyshevsky confessed that he himself hardly believed it likely that he would be able to convince the emperor of the need to place limits on his own absolute powers. Presumably, the real aim of the "Letters" was to convince the journal's educated readers that they must exert pressure on the government. In the same year the clandestine journal *Great Russian* (*Velikorus'*) made similar proposals advocating a campaign of this kind. For an analysis of the position of the gentry liberals of Tver', see T. Emmons, *The Russian Landed Gentry and the Peasant Emancipation of 1861* (Cambridge, Eng., 1968).

In the absence of political freedom, he pointed out, the central-ized bureaucratic government hampers normal social development, stifles public opinion, and ignores the advice of experts. "In the bureaucratic system, the understanding, knowledge, and experience of the men entrusted with responsibility are completely superfluous. These men act like machines without minds of their own; they carry out their responsibilities on the basis of chance information or con-jectures concerning the views held on a given subject by this or that person, who has nothing to do with it."[32] Political forms cannot be a matter of indifference, was Chernyshevsky's conclusion; if new content is poured into an old form it will absorb the odor of old age. "Social" democracy is therefore inseparable from "political" democracy.

Many other differences of this kind could be found. They reflect the gap between the "sixties," which were largely committed to "bourgeois" reforms, and the "seventies," which witnessed a grow-ing awareness of the tragic contradictions inherent in capitalist prog-ress. Chernyshevsky's main enemy was the old semifeudal social structure; to the end of his life he remained faithful to Westernist ideals and attacked Russian backwardness in the name of European science, civilization, and political liberty. Coming after the land reform, the Populists had a different perspective: horrified by the prospect of the capitalist expropriation of the small producers, they idealized Russian backwardness, dismissed capitalist development as retrogression, and looked for a way forward that would allow Russia to embark on a separate and "native" course. Chernyshev-sky, on the other hand, continued to stand firm for the "enlightened" and rationalist ideals of radical bourgeois democracy—despite his warm sympathy for socialist thinkers. Because his ideological heri-tage did not include an idealization of archaic social structures, it could be embraced not only by the Populists but also by the Russian Marxists. Plekhanov, who was wholeheartedly committed to fighting Populist ideas, thought of Chernyshevsky with the greatest respect, although he never forgot to stress to what extent his ideas differed from those of Marxism. Lenin, too (in a conversation with Valenti-nov in 1904), said that Chernyshevsky had been his favorite author when he was a young man: "Under his influence hundreds of young people became revolutionaries . . . he cast his spell over my brother, for instance, and over me too. He cut a very deep furrow in me."[33]

32. Chernyshevsky, *Izbr. fil. soch.*, vol. 3, pp. 511, 513–14.
33. See N. Valentinov, *Vstrechi s V. I. Leninym* (New York, 1953).

NIKOLAI DOBROLIUBOV AND THE DISPUTE
OVER THE "SUPERFLUOUS MEN"

Chernyshevsky's most talented disciple and closest friend was NIKOLAI DOBROLIUBOV (1836–61). Not only the outlooks but the personal histories of both men were strikingly similar: Dobroliubov, too, was the son of a provincial priest (in Nizhnii Novgorod), attended a theological seminary, and came under the powerful influence of progressive Russian literature and literary criticism. There were important differences as well, but these can largely be attributed to the fact that Dobroliubov's intellectual development was more rapid and less complex than Chernyshevsky's since the way had already been paved by the older man.

It is a characteristic fact that the liberal writers of his day found the younger critic far more irritating. "You are an ordinary viper," Turgenev once told Chernyshevsky, "but Dobroliubov is a cobra."[34] In another conversation, also with Chernyshevsky, Kavelin made a similar distinction: "You have something in common with us [that is, the liberals of the forties]; you also have something in common with Dobroliubov's generation, but we have nothing in common at all—it would seem—with Dobroliubov. What can we do about it? We regret it, but it is all part of progress."[35]

There is a good deal of truth in Kavelin's remark. Chernyshevsky, like the "men of the forties," had lived through the period of intense philosophical speculation and had studied Hegel. Dobroliubov, on the other hand, was totally uninterested in the problems raised by idealist philosophy and only read the Young Hegelians and Feuerbach for the sake of their atheist arguments. On political issues he was sometimes more uncompromising than his older teacher. It was he who brought about the split on the editorial board of the *Contemporary*, despite Nekrasov's efforts to prevent a final break. After reading Dobroliubov's article "When Will the True Day Come?" (1860), Turgenev told Nekrasov that either Dobroliubov must go or he, Turgenev, would. Nekrasov chose Dobroliubov, and Turgenev—followed by Tolstoy, Goncharov, and D. Grigorovich—severed his connection with the periodical.

Although Dobroliubov regarded Chernyshevsky as his highest

34. Quoted in V. Poliansky [P. I. Lebedev], *A. A. Dobroliubov, Mirovozzrenie i kriticheskaia deiatel'nost'* (M, 1933), p. 18.
35. *Ibid.*, p. 9. On the split between the generation of "the forties" and that of "the sixties," see E. Lampert, *Sons Against Fathers* (Oxford, 1965); and I. Berlin, "Fathers and Children," in his *Russian Thinkers* (New York, 1978).

authority on philosophical matters, he differed from him on certain details. Like Chernyshevsky, he believed in the "anthropological principle"; and though a materialist, he rejected the "vulgar" materialism of Büchner and Moleschott (unlike Pisarev). At the same time, however, he attached less importance to philosophy and history than to the natural sciences, so that his world view was more inclined toward naturalism.

In his social philosophy Dobroliubov was a typical "enlightener" who judged historical phenomena according to the unchanging standards of a rational "human nature." The disturbing gulf between his rational, commonsense ideal and reality led him to ask: "Where is the source of that incomprehensible dissonance between things as they ought to be, according to the natural rational course of events, and things as they actually are?"[36] To say that he regarded lack of education and the exploited majority's insufficient understanding of its strength and natural rights as the only source of this dissonance would be an oversimplification; on the other hand, arguments along these lines were typical of him. He had a rather naive view of the class struggle as the struggle of "working people" (representing the "natural" needs and ideals of humanity) against "spongers" (whose very existence was a deviation from the "natural" norm). "Humanity's natural inclination," he wrote, "reduced to the simplest terms, can be put in a few words: 'Everyone should prosper.' In endeavoring to reach this goal people were at first bound, in the nature of things, to move away from it; by trying to look after his own well-being, every man interfered with that of others; no one knew how to arrange matters otherwise."[37]

Dobroliubov also differed somewhat from Chernyshevsky in his view on the role of the masses. Like the Westernizers of the forties, Chernyshevsky regarded the common people as an essentially conservative force acting from habit; nonetheless he differed from the liberals in believing that in exceptional circumstances the masses were capable of deviating from routine and playing a creative part in history (making a revolution for instance; see his article "Could This Be the Beginning of Change?"). Dobroliubov went further than this; in his article "A Contribution to a Character Sketch of the Russian People" (1860), he stressed the common people's ability to break out of the daily rut, their characteristic love of liberty, their noble emotions, and their inexhaustible store of creative

36. N. Dobroliubov, *Sobranie sochinenii* (M-L, 1961–64), vol. 7, p. 247.
37. *Ibid.*, vol. 6, p. 307.

energy. This idealized view would have been quite foreign to Chernyshevsky.

Dobroliubov called his own type of literary criticism "real criticism"—"real" presumably because it consisted first in analyzing a literary work as if it were an objective sociological document and then in drawing conclusions that entirely disregarded the author's subjective intentions. Dobroliubov frequently and indeed ostentatiously rejected the critic's normative role and condemned attempts to judge literary works by previously established critical standards; what he himself prized most highly was not ideological content but the faithful reproduction of reality.

Some of the critic's formulations suggest that the role of "real criticism" was only to show how accurately a given work measured up to reality and not to assess the merit of literary works or "pronounce judgment on the aspects of reality reproduced in them," as Chernyshevsky had demanded. This, however, would be too hasty a conclusion. Dobroliubov was quite sincere in rejecting "diverse maxims and judgments based on God knows what theories": this was his reaction to the obtrusive moralizing and didacticism that were the hallmarks of the liberal "literature of exposure"; it was also his way of declaring his indifference to judgments based on various aesthetic canons. At the same time there was no doubt in his mind that there are "natural rules deriving from the nature of things," that "we know certain axioms without which thinking is impossible," certain "general concepts and rules which every man undoubtedly takes into consideration when arguing on no matter what theme."[38] The system of these axioms and norms is what Dobroliubov called "human nature." His condemnation of subjective judgments sprang, therefore, from a firm belief in the existence of an entirely objective and absolute system of values; he demanded that the writer confine himself to showing "facts," because he was convinced that facts contained their own meaning and that the presentation of unadorned and undisguised reality must itself suggest an appropriate judgment to the reader. Indeed only strict adherence to facts would liberate men's minds from the "unnatural notions that make it difficult to bring about the universal welfare."[39]

Despite Dobroliubov's rejection of aesthetic canons, the criterion of "human nature," when applied to literature, certainly implied

38. *Ibid.*, p. 304.
39. *Ibid.*, p. 309.

the superiority of uncompromising realism and the rejection—or at best neglect—of all literary conventions. Realism in literature, Dobroliubov wrote, is one of the "incontrovertible and universally recognized axioms."[40] Moreover, insisting on the criterion of conformity with human nature and "natural" human needs led, in Dobroliubov's interpretation, to a view of literature as a "handmaiden whose importance depends on propaganda and . . . who is judged by what she advocates and how."[41] "We judge the merit of a writer or a particular work," he wrote, "by the extent to which it expresses the natural aspirations of a given epoch or nation."[42] It was only a short step from this to the concrete identification of "natural" aspirations and ideals with the aspirations and ideals of the common man. In the essay on "The Role of the Folk Element in the Development of Russian Literature" (1858), the critic interpreted the history of Russian literature as a gradual process of drawing closer to "naturalness" and "narodnost'," and concluded with an appeal for a "people's party" in literature.

From a historical perspective, the weakness of Dobroliubov's theoretical assumptions are unmistakable: his method relied on the one hand on an anachronistic eighteenth-century conception of human nature, and on the other on a positivistic (in the broad sense of the word) illusion about the objective nature of "facts." But this illusion did not lead Dobroliubov to bow down before facts— on the contrary, his faith in "human nature" as an immutable and absolute frame of reference for normative judgments gave him a self-confidence that made him very different from the self-questioning liberals of the forties he criticized. Dobroliubov's "facts" acquired a new revolutionary meaning, reinforced by his conviction that this meaning was an inseparable aspect of the facts themselves. In the light of his articles it appeared that Russian reality was against human nature itself, and that this was shown by objective facts registered in the works of almost all realist writers, even those who were far from radical. All this made a great impression, of course, and transformed literary criticism into a powerful tool helping to radicalize the social consciousness.

Dobroliubov's favorite theme was the problem of the "two generations," or more accurately of the two social forces involved in the reform movement. His articles were an expression of the insight gained by the younger generation of radical democrats,

40. *Ibid.*, p. 305.
41. *Ibid.*, p. 309.
42. *Ibid.*, p. 307.

who were clearly aware of the gulf that divided them from the liberal gentry, who had until recently borne the main burden of opposition. Following Chernyshevsky,[43] Dobroliubov set out to draw a close parallel between the lack of determination of the liberal opposition of his day and the psychological type of the "man of the forties." Lacking roots in a concrete social force, he argued, the "superfluous men" were incapable of action and preferred to be passive observers mouthing approval of the reforms initiated by the government. The new age needed "new men," and such men had already begun to appear. The liberal idealists, torn by inner conflict and paralyzed by "reflection," were being replaced by "real men with strong nerves and a healthy imagination."[44]

These quotations come from "Last Year's Literary Trifles," an article published in 1859. In it Dobroliubov skillfully combined impassioned criticism of liberal publicists and the so-called "literature of exposure" with reflections on the "men of the forties" as the precursors of modern Russian liberalism. Although the "muckrakers" denounced various social evils, he wrote, their criticism was superficial and the remedies they proposed were mere palliatives. In fact, the liberals were afraid of consistent radical exposure because they themselves were a product of the very social realities they were attempting to denounce.

Dobroliubov developed these ideas in his trenchant article "What is Oblomovism?" published in the same year. In it Oblomov, the hero of Goncharov's famous novel, is shown from an unexpected angle as the last of the "superfluous men" in Russian literature—brother, or at least close relative, of Pushkin's Eugene Onegin, Lermontov's Pechorin, Herzen's Beltov, and Turgenev's Rudin and Hamlet of Shchigrovsk. There were certain individual differences, Dobroliubov conceded, between the indolent and totally apathetic Oblomov and the tragic figure of Pechorin, whom Lermontov had made into a "hero of our time"; nevertheless, all "superfluous men" were organically incapable of real action, for they had all been brought up in the demoralizing hothouse conditions of privilege, indolence, and lack of responsibility. They had no right to a halo of glory, for every one of them suffered from the paralysis of "Oblomovism." This was indeed a severe settling of accounts with the entire culture and traditions of the enlightened liberal gentry.

43. Chernyshevsky discussed the issue of the "superfluous men" in his article "Russkii chelovek na Rendez-vous" (1858).
44. Dobroliubov, *Sob. soch.*, vol. 4, p. 73.

The severity of this attack evoked protests on more than one front. The liberals reiterated the view, upheld by Annenkov in his polemic with Chernyshevsky, that the "idealist of the forties" criticized by the radical democrats was "the only moral type in the contemporary world."[45] It is significant that Herzen, too, hastened to the defense of the superfluous men. In his article "Very Dangerous!" he even suggested that by criticizing the liberal press and the liberal traditions of the Russian intelligentsia the "buffoons" of the *Contemporary* were abetting the tsarist regime and deserved to be decorated for their services to absolutism. The editors of the *Contemporary* were taken aback to find themselves the target of an attack from such a source—even Dobroliubov had always regarded Herzen (as well as Belinsky) as a "superior nature" whom his criticism did not concern. Chernyshevsky thought it essential to go to London in order to clear up the misunderstanding in person. He returned with little to show for his pains, convinced that Herzen was a man of the past. The misunderstanding had been cleared up, but the difference of opinion remained. This is shown by the fact that, even after his conversation with Chernyshevsky, Herzen published another article ("Superfluous Men and Angry Men"), milder in tone, but condemning Dobroliubov's dismissal of the generation of the forties as prejudiced and unhistorical.

Dobroliubov's uncompromising criticism of Russian society, and his equally severe strictures of men who until recently had been regarded as Russia's "finest sons," were paralleled by his determination to find praiseworthy aspects of Russian life, new models worthy of imitation and new literary heroes.

In his article "When Will the True Day Come?" he sketched a vivid portrait of a "strong nature," a man of action capable of impelling his country forward along the path of progress. This "strong nature" was Insarov, the hero of Turgenev's novel *On the Eve*, a Bulgarian fighting against the Turks for his country's freedom. The source of Insarov's firmness and energy, Dobroliubov suggested, was his absolute lack of any connection with what he was trying to oppose. Although Russia was not a conquered nation, she had been subjugated by her "domestic Turks" and needed men like Insarov. Such men would soon arise, according to the optimistic conclusion of the article.

The article "A Ray of Light in the Kingdom of Darkness" (1860) shows another kind of revolutionary protest. The character of

45. P. V. Annenkov, *Vospominaniia i kriticheskie ocherki* (St. Petersburg, 1879), vol. 2, pp. 170–72.

Catherine in Ostrovsky's play *The Storm* was interpreted by Dobroliubov as a symbol of elemental revolt gathering strength among the masses, a sign of the approaching "storm." Catherine's fate, he argued, was intended to convince the audience that the "vital Russian nature" could no longer accept the somber reality of the "kingdom of darkness," that protest must erupt among the subjugated masses. This interpretation does not necessarily arise out of the play, but thanks to Dobroliubov it has become permanently associated with it.

While he was writing his articles on Turgenev and Ostrovsky, Dobroliubov was already suffering from advanced tuberculosis. In the summer of 1860 his friends persuaded him to go to Italy, for the sake of his health. There, too, he continued to work hard; the fruits of his stay were an impressive cycle of articles analyzing the successes and defeats of the Italian national independence movement. On his return to St. Petersburg in August 1861 it became clear that the change of climate had not brought about the hoped-for improvement in his health. He died shortly afterwards, in November of the same year.

DMITRY PISAREV AND "NIHILISM"

After the death of Dobroliubov and Chernyshevsky's imprisonment, the most influential literary critic in Russia was DMITRY PISAREV (1840–68).[46] Although he, like Dobroliubov, developed ideas put forward by Chernyshevsky, he gave them his own personal slant and arrived at conclusions very different from Dobroliubov's; indeed, Pisarev once wrote that if he had ever met Dobroliubov they probably would not have agreed on a single issue.[47]

The intellectual trend represented by Pisarev in his articles for the periodical *Russian Word* (*Russkoe Slovo*) was often referred to as "nihilism." This word, which had been given wide currency by Turgenev's novel *Fathers and Sons*, was not at first a term of abuse, although that is the meaning imposed on it by right-wing critics. Originally it simply meant a radical rejection of all estab-

46. Unlike either Chernyshevsky or Dobroliubov, Pisarev came from the gentry. In his first articles he defended "pure art" and a moderate liberalism. It was in 1861 that his views became more radical. The most comprehensive Western work on Pisarev is A. Coquart, *Dmitry Pisarev et l'idéologie du nihilisme russe* (Paris, 1946). In the book by a Soviet scholar, A. I. Novikov, *Nigilism i nigilisty* (L, 1972), Russian "nihilism" of the 1860's is analyzed in the perspective of the further development of nihilist ideas in Russian and Western thought.

47. D. I. Pisarev, *Sochineniia* (M, 1955–56), vol. 3, p. 35.

lished authorities, the determination to recognize nothing (*nihil*) that could not be justified by rational argument. In *Fathers and Sons*, Bazarov (who represents the generation of the "sons") himself adopted the label "nihilist"; Pisarev was a great admirer of Turgenev's hero and held him up as a model to the younger generation. Like Bazarov, Pisarev thought that the emancipation of the individual from the irrational bonds imposed by society, family, and religion (the central idea of nihilism) would be largely accomplished through the popularization of the natural sciences. At the same time, he had an exaggerated faith in the utilitarian ethics of "rational egoism." He used his articles to advocate the attitudes of "thinking realists" (whose literary prototype was Bazarov) and to attack "aesthetics"—by which he meant the aestheticizing postures of the gentry liberals.

In the course of time, mainly under the influence of the right-wing press, the label "nihilists" also became attached to the revolutionaries of the seventies (especially the terrorists, although they persistently rejected the label, reserving it exclusively for "Pisarevites"). The distinction is emphasized by the revolutionary Populist Sergei Kravchinsky, author of a successful attempt on the life of chief of police Mezentsev, who wrote in his book *Underground Russia*: "It would be difficult to imagine a sharper contrast. The nihilist's objective is personal happiness at any price, his ideal is the 'rational' existence of the 'thinking realist.' The revolutionary's object, on the other hand, is the happiness of others; for this he is ready to sacrifice his own. His ideal is a life full of suffering and a martyr's death."[48] There is, of course, some oversimplification in this comment; elsewhere Kravchinsky emphasized that the nihilists were not calculating egoists and quoted a characteristic statement made by V. Zaitsev, one of Pisarev's closest collaborators: "We were convinced that we were fighting for the happiness of mankind, and every one of us would gladly have given his head for Moleschott and Darwin."[49] Nevertheless, the fact remains that the nihilism of the sixties was not a revolutionary movement; no doubt by its attacks on established authorities it helped to radicalize public opinion, but it did not advocate revolutionary methods of struggle or lead automatically toward revolutionary goals.

This conclusion would appear to be contradicted by an apparently significant episode in Pisarev's life that led to his imprison-

48. Serge Kravchinsky, *Underground Russia: Revolutionary Profiles and Sketches from Life*, with a preface by P. Lavrov (2d ed.; London, 1883).
49. *Ibid.*

ment for four-and-a-half years in the Peter and Paul Fortress. In June 1862, Pisarev approached Petr Ballod, a student who was running an illegal printing press, and asked him to print a proc- lamation he had written. This was a defense of Herzen against at- tacks contained in two pamphlets written in French by Baron Fircks, a tsarist agent in Belgium who used the pseudonym Schedo- Ferroti. The final words of the proclamation sound like a call to revolution:

> The Romanov dynasty and the Petersburg bureaucracy must disap- pear. They will not be saved by ministers like Valuiev or litterateurs like Schedo-Ferroti.
> That which is dead and decaying will come crashing down into the grave on its own; our role is merely to give it the final impetus and bury the stinking corpses in the mud.[50]

Ballod was arrested before the proclamation could be printed, and Pisarev, too, was detained. During interrogation Pisarev tried to defend himself by citing his nervous condition resulting from a broken engagement and the government's reactionary measures (the closing of Sunday schools, and the temporary suspension of the *Contemporary* and *Russian Word*). Even taking his explanations at their face value, it is possible that under different circumstances Pisarev might have joined the revolutionary camp. As it turned out, this proclamation was to remain an isolated episode in his life. In articles published both before and after his arrest (in prison he was allowed to read books and write articles), Pisarev gave his un- equivocal support to nonrevolutionary methods of struggle. He was convinced that, for the time being at any rate, a sober, realistic view of the situation would make it clear that a successful revolu- tion was quite unlikely; and though revolution might be unavoid- able in certain circumstances, it was a form of struggle that "think- ing realists" should only adopt as a last resort. In his programmatic article "The Realists," Pisarev contrasted "mechanical influences" (by which he meant revolution) with "chemical influences" (that is, the struggle for a new and "realistic" outlook, and the systematic and legal struggle for reforms). In contrast to Dobroliubov, there- fore, Pisarev may be called not a revolutionary democrat but rather a radical advocate of patient organic work for progress.

This distinction becomes very clear when we examine Pisarev's attitude toward Dobroliubov's favorite literary characters. Turge- nev's Insarov (*On the Eve*), for instance, he accused of being un-

50. Pisarev, *Soch.*, vol. 2, p. 126.

realistic, stiff, and bombastic. He also disagreed with Dobroliubov's view of Catherine in Ostrovsky's *The Storm*, maintaining that her rebellion was purely emotional and irrational, and therefore without positive value. By his enthusiastic praise for Catherine, Pisarev contended, Dobroliubov had abandoned the "realistic" point of view and had unwittingly given his support to "aesthetics."

The difference of outlook between the two men had its underlying source in their philosophical convictions. Both were materialists in their general view of the world, but idealists in their interpretation of history. Pisarev's materialism had characteristic elements of positivism (e.g. his view of agnosticism as a radical defense against metaphysics) and was as extremist as his historical idealism. It is interesting to note, for instance, that it was not Feuerbachian materialism but the vulgarized naturalistic version of it put forth by Büchner, Vogt, and Moleschott that most appealed to him. At the same time, his rather naive rationalistic idealism led him to identify progress with the advance of scientific knowledge, thus turning science into a veritable demiurge of history. Dobroliubov also believed in science, but his idealization of simple folk as the representatives of an unchanging human nature led him to put some stress on the role of the masses. Pisarev, on the other hand, continued the line of thinkers in Russia who believed that the only progressive force was the educated minority and who regarded all purely "natural" and spontaneous acts with considerable skepticism.

An interesting exposition of Pisarev's view on the issue of the "new men" and the positive hero may also be found in an article on Chernyshevsky's *What Is to Be Done?* published in 1865 under the title "A New Type" (reissued later as "The Thinking Proletariat"). What at first sight seems surprising in this article is Pisarev's praise for the mysterious revolutionary Rakhmetov, whom he calls a successful portrait of an "unusual man" infinitely superior (apart from his asceticism) to Turgenev's Insarov. This view should not be regarded as inconsistent with Pisarev's program of organic reforms, rather it should be taken as showing that in his case "nonrevolutionary" was not synonymous with "antirevolutionary." Rakhmetov, Pisarev wrote, was an unusual man whose activities could only find full scope in unusual circumstances that could not be planned or foreseen; only the distant future would reveal what were to be the fruits of this man's work. For the time being, however, ordinary people needed models to look up to in their everyday lives. The other leading characters of Chernyshevsky's novel—Lopuchov, Kirsanov, and Vera Pavlovna—provided models of this kind.

Pisarev's favorite literary hero—the best example of a "thinking realist"—was Turgenev's Bazarov, to whom he devoted two essays, "Bazarov" (written in 1862) and the longer "The Realists" (written in prison in 1864). The difference in viewpoint between the two pieces is striking. In the first, Pisarev revealed his obvious fascination with the ideal of the emancipated autonomous individual and represented Bazarov as a man who had rejected all "principles" or norms, thought only of himself, and was incapable of any form of self-sacrifice: "He is guided only by his own whim or calculation. He recognizes no regulator—whether above him, outside him, or within him—no moral law, no principle. He has no noble aims and for all that represents a powerful force."[51] For Pisarev this absolute self-affirmation of the individual ego was synonymous with the emancipation of the individual, and was therefore praiseworthy as a necessary prerequisite of critical understanding.

In "The Realists" this viewpoint was strikingly modified. Immoral individualism was replaced by a utilitarianism that, though rooted in an individualistic world view, was closely bound up with the idea of work for the common good. A close analysis of his own position, Pisarev now argued, would show that the thinking individual owes everything to society and that a sense of honor should make him pay his debt: every honest man ought therefore to contribute as far as he is able to the solution of the "unavoidable problem of the hungry and the naked"; "apart from this problem there is nothing worthy of our efforts, thoughts, or exertions."[52] In his new character sketch of Bazarov, Pisarev now placed emphasis not on the importance of the pleasure motive but on social goals, not on the joyful emancipation from restrictive bonds but on the willing subordination to the rigor of critical reflection and the taste for steadfast, "socially useful" work. Of course, Pisarev did not consider this to be inconsistent with egoism: Bazarov was motivated by egoism, but by the egoism of a "thinking realist" and not that of an "aesthete."

Although he placed such stress on efforts to improve the lot of "the hungry and the naked," Pisarev was not a socialist; "thinking realists" in his eyes were to be found not only among the democratic intelligentsia, but also among enlightened capitalists, whom

51. *Ibid.*, p. 11.
52. *Ibid.*, vol. 3, p. 105.

he called "thinking leaders of work among the masses." This attitude stemmed not only from the fact that he placed little hope in
the masses, but also from the fact that he knew more about the role
of industrialization and technological advance than Dobroliubov.
In the Russia of his time, he felt, men like Bazarov would only appear among the intelligentsia; the masses were still the passive raw
material of history and were likely to remain so for a long time to
come. Only the educated and financially independent strata of
society were capable of organizing the labor of the masses along
rational lines and increasing productivity by the application of
the latest scientific and technological advances.

"Nihilism" in the sense of a revolt against established authorities
thus took second place to a constructive and politically moderate
positivist program concentrating on the foundations of future prosperity. Only in its view of art or "aesthetics"—which Pisarev said
had become "a veritable nightmare" to him—was the later article
more "nihilistic." In the earlier one Pisarev had not identified himself with his favorite hero's comments that Pushkin was not "worth
reading" or that "Raphael was not worth a brass farthing." He
called these comments a possibly justifiable reaction against the
aestheticism of the generation of the "fathers," but also an example
of "ridiculous overreaction" and even of "narrow-minded intellectual despotism." In the later "Realists," Pisarev withdrew even
these reservations. In his puritan radicalism he even declared that
to waste human energy on the creation and consumption of artistic
pleasures contradicted the principle of "the economy of material
and intellectual forces." Novels, he allowed, might have a certain
didactic value, but he was doubtful about the role of poetry and
quite vehement about the total uselessness of music and the visual
arts, about which he wrote: "I can see no reason for believing that
these art forms can make any contribution whatsoever to raising
the intellectual or moral standards of humanity." [53]

These ideas, which were characteristic of the general line of the
periodical *Russian Word*, were developed by Pisarev in his critical
essay "Pushkin and Belinsky" (1865), and in an article with the
self-explanatory title "The Destruction of Aesthetics" (1865). The
first of these was a vehement and even brutal attack on both the
cult of Pushkin led by Apollon Grigoriev and the liberal critics'
defense of art for art's sake. Pisarev also took exception to the high
praise of Pushkin in Belinsky's writings and called even him a

53. *Ibid.*, p. 114.

"semi-aesthete." The second essay—"The Destruction of Aesthetics"
—was a one-sided "nihilistic" interpretation of Chernyshevsky's
aesthetic theories.

An important part of Pisarev's work was his popular articles on
the natural sciences, which he regarded as the most efficient instrument for spreading "realism." He was one of the first men in Russia
to write of Darwin and the theory of evolution, and his contribution
in this field was praised by the botanist K. Timiryazev, Russia's
most eminent champion of Darwinism. Pisarev's articles, written
with considerable verve and a vivacious and colorful style, were
read by high school students all over Russia. In some of his articles on animal life he succeeded in combining popularization of
sciences and materialist philosophy with witty and satiricial comment (by analogy) on human society.

There are grounds for supposing that if Pisarev had not died at
an early age he would have arrived at a more balanced viewpoint,
closer to that of Chernyshevsky and the contributors to the *Contemporary*. The tone of his last articles seems to lend credence to
this view. Further evidence for a change of outlook is the fact that
after leaving prison (in November 1866) he made approaches to
Nekrasov and Saltykov-Shchedrin, who had taken over the periodical *Notes of the Fatherland* after the *Contemporary* was closed
down. Unfortunately, Pisarev did not have long to live: he drowned
in June 1868 while bathing in the Baltic near Riga.

CRITICS OF THE "ENLIGHTENERS":
APOLLON GRIGORIEV AND NIKOLAI STRAKHOV

Enlightenment-style rationalism in various forms was prominent
in progressive circles in the 1860's. In the domain of philosophy,
materialism was able to make headway because there were no professional philosophers at Russian universities. It is significant that the
most serious critic of Chernyshevsky's *Anthropological Principle*
was a theologian, PAMPHILUS YURKEVICH (1827–74), a professor at
the Kiev Theological Academy. His articles "A Contribution to
the Science of the Human Spirit" and "Against Materialism" attracted the notice of influential conservatives, who had him pro-
moted to the chair of philosophy at Moscow University. Yurkevich's Platonic idealism was, however, too reminiscent of traditional
Christian apologetics to have any wider influence in secular circles.

Of greater interest and far greater intellectual and cultural potential was the critical reaction to the "enlighteners" of the *poch-venniki* group—advocates of a "return to the soil" (from *pochva*, the Russian word for "soil"). This group's call clearly harked back to Slavophilism; and indeed, the ideologists of the group treated the conflict with the "enlighteners" as part of the wider polemic on the relationship between Russia and Europe, thus continuing the philosophical discussions of the forties in a new context. Quantitatively speaking, the influence of the group was negligible, but their contribution to Russian culture was nevertheless of great importance, largely because of the seminal role of their ideas in the work of Dostoevsky.[54]

The main ideologist of the *pochvenniki* was the romantic poet and literary critic APOLLON GRIGORIEV (1822–64). His own romantic nationalism, however, differed from that of the Slavophiles, whom he accused of an idealization of Russia's ancient boyars. He believed that vital national principles had been best preserved among social groups unaffected by serfdom, and should therefore be sought not among the patriarchal peasantry but among the conservative merchant class, which he called "the eternal quintessence of ancient Russia." The Slavophiles, for their part, were rightly suspicious both of Grigoriev's extravagant "aestheticizing" romanticism, which even colored his attitude to religion, and of his romantic delight in the diversity of national cultures with their "scents" and "colors," which smacked of relativism and was difficult to reconcile with a "truly Christian" system of values.

Perhaps the most outstanding feature of Grigoriev's personality was his deep-rooted dislike of all "artificiality," of schematic fetters and lifelessness—of anything that was "made" rather than "created," to use his own distinction. He violently opposed all rationalist theories in the name of "immediate" intuitive knowledge, and set "life," "organicity," and "history" against "theory" and "logic." His own philosophy he summed up in the following sentence: "Not reason itself with its logical exigencies and the theories they give rise to, but reason and its logical exigencies plus life and its organic manifestations."[55]

One of the most dangerous theories, according to Grigoriev, was Hegelian philosophy. In his critique of Hegelianism he attempted to explain how the "enlighteners" had acquired their dominant position in Russian intellectual life and how Belinsky's Hegelian ideas had paved the way for the enlightenment-style rationalism

54. See below, pp. 311, 319–20, 323.
55. A. A. Grigoriev, *Sochineniia* (St. Petersburg, 1876), vol. 1, p. 624.

of Chernyshevsky and Dobroliubov.[56] Against the "historical criticism" represented by the mature Belinsky he proposed to set something he called "organic criticism." This antithesis was based on a differentiation between a "sense of history" (i.e. the conservative historicism that arose in reaction against eighteenth-century rationalism) and the Left Hegelian "historical view" (i.e. the historicist theory—put forward by Belinsky among others—of infinite and universal progress). Grigoriev dismissed the latter as another variant of the eighteenth-century standpoint. The danger of this theory, he argued, was that it represented a peculiar combination of fatalism and relativism, according to which neither individuals nor nations were responsible for their own lives but were merely "transient moments," instruments of the universal spirit. Hegel himself, the founder of the "historical view," possessed a "sense of history"; but in his disciples that sense had disappeared altogether, so that they were left with nothing but a dogmatic teleological "theory of history," an abstract model of evolution implementing a preestablished plan. This theory, like all variants of rationalism, implied that there was an "abstract Spirit of mankind," a notion that Grigoriev dismissed as illusory, since in his view only concrete individualties—either individual human beings or collective individualities—could claim to be real.[57]

Grigoriev's main objection to the "historical view" (and "historical criticism") can be summed up under three headings. First, he accused its representatives of putting an absolute value on every "last word' of progress, of reducing the rich variety of life to a simplified pattern of "gradual approximations" to the currently accepted norm. Second, he felt that the belief of the representatives of the "historical view" in the universal and inevitable nature of progress led them to undervalue national "distinctiveness," to overlook the importance of the specific individual and unrepeatable phenomenon, and to ignore anything that could not be explained by universal laws. Third, by identifying their own consciousness with immanent Historical Reason, they were guilty of attempting to seek conscious control over life, of claiming the right to force it

56. Grigoriev's attitude toward Belinsky was complicated. He distinguished two trends in Belinsky's work, one leading down to himself, the other leading straight to the "enlighteners" of the sixties. He criticized Belinsky as the theorist of the "natural school," but he accepted his interpretation of Pushkin and at the same time praised the writings of the "reconciliation with reality" and Schellingian periods of the 1830's, while attacking him as a Left Hegelian.

57. See Grigoriev's article "Vzgliad na osnovy, znachenie i priemy sovremennoi kritiki iskusstva" (1858), in *Soch.*, vol. 1.

into a Procrustean bed of logic and slice into its living tissues with a scalpel in the conceited belief that such an operation would prove salutary. This was an absurd and harmful claim, Grigoriev declared. It failed to take account of the fact that life was directed by divine creativity—that "vital focus of the supreme laws of life itself"[58] —and that therefore man must listen to the irrational pulse of life instead of trying to control it.

Grigoriev attributed the merit of transcending the "historical view" to the later Schelling, whose insistence on the personality of God in his "philosophy of revelation" had once more reinstated human individuality as an absolute value, and who had laid the basis for the view that nations, too, were endowed with unique irrational and exclusive personalities unaffected by the so-called universal laws of human evolution.

"Nations," Grigoriev wrote, are organisms each of which "is self-contained, is governed by its own necessity, is permitted to live in its own way according to laws specific to itself, and need not serve as a transitional form for any other organism."[59]

The basic premise of Grigoriev's "organic criticism" was "faith in the fact that life is an organic whole."[60] This naturally led to a preference for "organic phenomena" in culture, i.e. for works rooted in the native soil. Nevertheless, for Grigoriev (unlike the Slavophiles) a "return to the soil" did not mean a rejection of Western values or the denial of the personality principle. In his view not only the "meek" type idealized by the Slavophiles but also his opposite, the "predatory" type who represented individualism, had his roots in the Russian soil. An organic synthesis of respect for tradition and the personality principle, of spontaneous plant-like growth and sophisticated rational consciousness—in fact, of Slavophilism and Westernism—was not inherently impossible. Such a synthesis, Grigoriev thought, had already taken place in the work of Pushkin and would come about in society as well, for a great poet was always the most perfect spiritual organ of his people and an infallible harbinger of its future.

Holding views of this kind, it is not surprising that Grigoriev took an original stand on the question of the "superfluous men" in Russian life and literature. The "superfluous men" had indeed been uprooted from the soil and condemned to inner duality, he admitted, but this process had been necessary in order to enrich

58. *Ibid.*, p. 205.
59. *Ibid.*, p. 210.
60. *Ibid.*, p. 223.

the soil and help it to assimilate European elements and the personality principle. The "superfluous men" had torn themselves away from the soil, but their destiny had been to return home not only as repentant prodigals but also as men who had brought back new and valuable experiences gathered during their "wanderings." Grigoriev's favorite confirmation of this thesis was the development of Lavretsky, the hero of Turgenev's *House of Gentlefolk*. In fact, he interpreted the ideological evolution of the most outstanding Russian writers, beginning with Pushkin and ending with Dostoevsky, as a similar process of "striking roots," or of a return to the native soil.

In the controversies of the sixties, therefore, Grigoriev warmly supported the "superfluous men" against their detractor Dobroliubov. When the latter set out to prove in his article "What Is Oblomovism" that the "superfluous men" were themselves rooted in the serf system they appeared to attack, Grigoriev reversed the argument to claim that this very "rootedness" was a point in their favor against the "rootless theoreticians." The apathetic village of Oblomovka became a symbol of the "true mother" whom Dobroliubov had "bespattered with saliva like a mad dog." [61] The rule "love work and avoid indolence," Grigoriev wrote, is entirely correct and praiseworthy in the abstract; however, as soon as we make use of it in order to "dissect, as with a scalpel, what is called Oblomovka and Oblomovism, then if we are living beings, organic products of soil and nationality, Oblomovism, that poor wronged creature, makes its voice heard in ourselves." [62]

Central to Grigoriev's thought was a specific conception of national features of literature, which he set against both the subordination of literature to social and political ends and the ideal of art for art's sake. This enabled him to reconcile romantic aestheticism with support for realistic tendencies, a cult of the great romantic poets (in addition to Pushkin, he admired Mickiewicz and Byron) with understanding and sympathy for the poetry of Nekrasov. Since there was room for the folk element in his conception of nationality, he was on the whole inclined to welcome the democratization of literature—both the tendency for writers to be drawn from a wider background and the tendency for literature to penetrate more profound levels of national life. It must be remembered, however, that the concept of nationality in Grigoriev's world view was linked to a romantic irrationalism and a conservative view of history in

61. A. A. Grigoriev, *Vospominaniia (i vospominaniia o nem)* (M-L, 1930), p. 212.
62. Grigoriev, *Soch.*, vol. 1, p. 415.

which "organicity" was set against rational thought and conscious attempts to shape reality. This, of course, prevented him from understanding that the "theorists" he criticized—Chernyshevsky, Dobroliubov, and Pisarev—were in fact also organic products of the Russian soil.

The other leading ideologist of the "return to the soil" movement was NIKOLAI STRAKHOV (1828–96), a scientist by training and a close friend of Dostoevsky and later of Tolstoy.[63] The notion central to his thought was that nature and society form an organic whole. Strakhov believed that Hegelian philosophy provided the theoretical foundations of this holistic vision of the world. His interpretation of this philosophy was, of course, different from Grigoriev's: he regarded Hegelianism not as a form of rationalism but as the "purest mysticism," related to the mysticism of Baader, Meister Eckhart, and Angelus Silesius.[64] It is hardly surprising that he found it possible to reconcile Hegelianism thus conceived with Orthodox theism and Slavophile irrationalism.

Strakhov devoted his whole life to fighting various manifestations of atomistic and mechanistic theories, which he felt were symptoms of the sickness of Western civilization and provided the ideological foundations of the nihilism, revolutionism, and fashionable "enlightenment" of the sixties. He regarded Feuerbachian philosophy as the counterpart of atomistic conceptions in the natural sciences. The quintessence of Feuerbachian ideas, he wrote, is the lack of unity: "There is no unity, no wholeness in the world; there is only multiplicity and parts. There is no center, no connecting link in the world; the center of everything is in the thing itself, everything exists because it is separate and not connected with any others. Every point in space, every atom exists separately, by itself, and that is true existence."[65] The article from which this quotation is taken was written in 1864. Though writing about Feuerbach, there is no doubt that Strakhov also had in mind his Russian disciple Nikolai Chernyshevsky.

Strakhov's main work was a book called *The World as a Whole* (1872). In it he set out his own philosophy of nature and a detailed critique of ideas popularized by Pisarev in his articles (materialism, atomistic and mechanistic natural history, Darwin's evolutionary theory). The world is a whole, Strakhov argued. Moreover, it is a

63. See L. Gerstein, *Nikolai Strakhov* (Cambridge, Mass., 1971).
64. See D. I. Tschiževskij, *Gegiel w Rossii* (Paris, 1939), p. 273.
65. N. N. Strakhov, *Bor'ba s Zapadom v nashei literature* (St. Petersburg, 1883), vol. 2, p. 92.

whole imbued by spirit, and its various parts are in fact embodiments of the spirit at different stages. No single part is separate or autonomous; everything is connected with everything else, nothing exists "by itself," everything is fluid, as Heraclitus would say. The unity of the world has a harmonious and organic character; the parts that compose it are not only linked together but also subordinated to each other to form a hierarchical structure. Last of all, this world has a center and that center is man, nature's finest achievement and the "nodal point of being," the "chief phenomenon and chief organ of the world." Man, however, constantly aspires to become separated from the whole, to cut the umbilical cord that links him to the organic unity of creation.[66]

Strakhov of course condemned these centrifugal tendencies. The world around him filled him with misgivings, for it seemed to be the battleground of powerful forces of disintegration. In order to counteract these forces he called for a reaffirmation of the "organic" principle in human existence, expressed through religious feeling, ties with the "native soil," and a sense of nationality.

66. N. N. Strakhov, *Mir kak tseloe* (2d ed.; St. Petersburg, 1892), pp. vii–ix.

CHAPTER 12

POPULIST IDEOLOGIES

INTRODUCTION

The term "Populism" has had several different meanings attached to it.[1] In the broadest sense of the word, "Populism" is the name given to all Russian democratic ideologies—revolutionary as well as reformist—that expressed the interests of the peasants and small producers and advocated the view that Russia could skip the capitalist stage of development. If we accept this definition, then Populism is a very broad, internally differentiated movement with a long history extending from Herzen and Chernyshevsky to the Social Revolutionaries in the twentieth century.

In the narrow historical meaning—that used by the Russian revolutionaries of the 1870's—the term "Populism" is applied to a single trend within Russian radicalism, a trend that made its appearance in the mid-1870's after the experiences of the first "go to the people" movement, and that differed from other revolutionary trends by its advocacy of "the hegemony of the masses over the educated elite." In this sense of the word, "Populism" was opposed to the "abstract intellectualism" of those revolutionaries who tried to teach the peasants instead of learning from them, and who wanted to impose on the peasants the ideals of Western socialism instead of listening to what they had to say and acting in their real interests. From the point of view of the methods of struggle advocated, the "Populists" (in the second meaning of the word) were opposed to the members of the *Narodnaia Volya* ("People's Will") organization[2]—the Populist revolutionary organization formed in 1879—because unlike the latter they advocated action solely among the

1. This is discussed in some detail in A. Walicki, *The Controversy over Capitalism* (Oxford, 1969), pp. 1–28. See also R. Pipes, "Narodnichestvo: A Semantic Inquiry," *Slavic Review*, 23, no. 3 (Sep. 1964). The most comprehensive recent history of the populist revolutionary movement is F. Venturi, *Roots of Revolution: A History of the Populist and Socialist Movements in Nineteenth-Century Russia* (London, 1960).

2. The best monograph on the ideas of the "People's Will" is V. A. Tvardovskaia, *Sotsialisticheskaia mysl Rossii na rubezhe 1870–1880–kh godov* (M, 1969).

people and through the people, condemning revolutionary plots, individual terror, and attempts to seize power by professional revolutionary organizations.

The use of the term "Populism" in this chapter tends to follow the first of the definitions outlined above, albeit in a slightly narrower and more restricted meaning. The author would like to suggest that "Populism" should be understood not as a specific trend in revolutionary thought, but as a dynamic ideological structure within which many positions were possible. The significant feature of this ideology was that it combined bourgeois democratic radicalism with opposition to capitalism as a social system. This opposition was expressed in various forms of "socialism," but in fact was closer to something that Lenin labeled "economic romanticism" —a backward-looking utopia idealizing precapitalist economic and social relations. In this sense of the word Populism gained ground in Russia only in the 1870's, when there was widespread disillusionment in the progressive role of capitalist development. Chernyshevsky might be called a Populist *in statu nascendi*: he formulated the basic theses of the Populist conception of noncapitalist development, but primarily he belonged to the "enlighteners," whom Lenin called advocates of radical bourgeois democracy fighting against the remnants of feudalism. The Populists, on the other hand (Lenin stressed), took an important step forward compared with the "enlighteners" because they realized what tragic consequences capitalism would have for the masses. The "enlighteners" dominated the democratic movement at the time of the struggle for the abolition of serfdom, whereas Populism came to maturity in postreform Russia in reaction against the rapid development of capitalism. Both "enlighteners" and Populists represented the broad masses, which in nineteenth-century Russia meant the peasantry above all; that was why the former movement could be regarded as the base from which the latter sprang. However, the Populists, unlike the "enlighteners," combined antifeudal bourgeois-democratic radicalism with a petty-bourgeois reaction against bourgeois progress. That was why the "heritage of the sixties" (Lenin's term) was unambiguously progressive, whereas the heritage of Populism was in this respect equivocal. The Populist is a Janus, Lenin wrote, "looking with one face to the past and the other to the future."[3] The backward-looking face of Janus was Populist socialism; Lenin frequently stressed that the Populists' socialist theories were

3. V. I. Lenin, *Collected Works* (Eng.-lang. ed.; M, 1960–66), vol. 2, p. 507.

petty-bourgeois (in the Marxist use of the term), reactionary, and hopelessly influenced by "economic romanticism."[4]

The years 1868–70 can be selected as the period marking the emergence of classical Populism. Many of the younger radicals turned away from Pisarev's "realism" at this time and rejected positivist belief in the all-liberating mission of science. In 1868 Bakunin published his famous article (in the émigré journal *Narodnoe Delo* [*People's Cause*]) calling on young Russians to leave the universities and "go to the people." Three classic documents of Populism were published a year later. These were Lavrov's *Historical Letters*, Mikhailovsky's treatise *What Is Progress?*, and Flerovsky's book *The Situation of the Working Class in Russia*. The first two called into question the optimistic belief in progress so characteristic of the "enlighteners," pointed out the painful contradictions of the historical process, and threw doubt on the conception of unidirectional evolution used to justify the view that Russia must follow the general pattern of European capitalist development. Flerovsky, in his turn, painted a vivid picture of the growing destitution of the peasantry following the introduction of capitalist social relations in agriculture; the conclusion he drew was that everything possible should be done to prevent capitalism from making further headway and to utilize, instead, the potentialities of the peasant commune. In the same year that these important documents appeared, the Populist revolutionary movement also began to emerge. What was specifically Populist about these particular revolutionary cells was their determination to put the main emphasis on the struggle against the further development of capitalism inside Russia.

If we view "classical Populism" as conceiving of capitalism as "enemy number one," we should add that the classical Populism of the 1870's was not only influenced but, in a sense, called into being by Marxism. It was not by chance that this phase of Russian Populist thought began after the publication of the first volume of *Capital* (1869), and that, to Marx's surprise, the first translation of *Capital* came out in Russia (1872), thanks to the efforts of the Populists (the translation was begun by Herman Lopatin, who was a personal friend of Marx, and completed by Nicholas Danielson, who thought Marxism to be perfectly compatible with Populism).

4. It should be noted that Lenin himself pointed out that he was using the term "reactionary" in the "historico-philosophical" sense and was only referring to the error of theoreticians who used obsolete social relations as a model for their theoretical constructs (*Collected Works*, vol. 2, p. 217).

To put it briefly, the Russian democrats were so much impressed by *Capital*, especially by the description of the atrocities of primitive accumulation, that they decided to do everything to avoid capitalist development in Russia, thus becoming full-fledged, "classical" Populists.

We may thus say that Russian Populism was not only a reaction against capitalism inside Russia (and not even a reaction to the "demonstration effect" of capitalism in the West) but also, and perhaps foremost, a Russian response to the *image* of capitalist development in Western socialist thought. It was a reaction to Western socialism by the democratic intelligentsia in a backward peasant country at an early stage of capitalist development. And it is quite understandable that it had to be, first of all, a reaction to Marxism—for, after all, Marx was by then the leading figure of European socialism and the author of the most authoritative book on the development of capitalism.

FROM "GO TO THE PEOPLE" TO THE "PEOPLE'S WILL"

The anticapitalist character of Populist ideology can be seen most clearly in its distrust of parliamentary institutions and ostentatious indifference to "political" forms. The Populists identified "socialist" revolution with social revolution, or the radical transformation of the economic base of society. The "political" struggle, on the other hand—i.e. the struggle for political freedom aiming at the overthrow of autocracy—was dismissed as a merely "bourgeois" revolution to be ignored by true socialists. Socialism was thus conceived as the antithesis of "political struggle"; it was even suggested that a liberal constitution would strengthen the possessing classes and ruin the chances of the socialists for many years to come. Although today this seems to us a curious paradox, Populists regarded themselves as being "apolitical" and saw this as a guarantee that their socialism had not been contaminated by bourgeois values. Sometimes they took this position because they were ready to collaborate with the government provided it decided to push through the necessary social reforms; more often, though, they took this line because they believed that the overthrow of tsarist autocracy without a change in the social system would only lead to government of the bourgeoisie and the worsening of the economic lot of the masses.

The problem of the relationship between political and social goals was not a new one. In the sixties it had exercised Herzen and Bakunin, although the distinction they had made between the two types of goals was neither so radical nor so principled as that made in the following decade. The first "Land and Freedom" organization (set up in 1862–63 under the inspiration of Chernyshevsky, Herzen, and Ogarev) had political goals, such as the convocation of a Land Assembly, and did not regard that fact as a defection from its social goals. The consistent rejection of the political struggle did not become widespread in the Populist movement until the early seventies.

This rejection occurred for a number of reasons. Of these the most immediately obvious was the influence of Bakunin, who by then had become the leader and chief theorist of international anarchism. He opposed Marx and the German Social Democratic party on the grounds that fighting for universal suffrage or seats in a bourgeois parliament was unworthy of a socialist, was a form of capitulation to petty-bourgeois radicalism.

Another factor was the state of mind of the "conscience-stricken gentry" (a term coined by Mikhailovsky), which was brilliantly portrayed in Lavrov's *Historical Letters*. Members of the Chaikovsky Circle[5] the largest Populist organization at the beginning of the seventies—were particularly prone to intense ethical self-questioning. For these young men the rejection of the political struggle was a way of paying their debt to the people for whom political freedom was felt to be meaningless. Mikhailovsky, who in his legally published articles showed a gift for formulating the current problems and dilemmas of the revolutionary movement in pithy terms, defined this mood as the victory of "conscience" (a sense of moral obligation) over "honor" (a sense of one's own rights). In a fine article on Dostoevsky's *Possessed* published at the beginning of 1873, just before the first "go to the people" movement, he wrote:

For the man who has tasted the fruit of the universal human tree of knowledge nothing is more attractive than political freedom, freedom of conscience, freedom of speech and of the press, the free exchange of ideas, the right of free assembly, and so on. And naturally we want all this. But if all the rights arising out of this freedom are merely to allow us to go on playing the role of a colorful and scented blossom, then we reject these rights and this freedom! A curse upon them, if all they do is increase our debt to the people instead of helping us to discharge it! . . . By accepting the priority of social over political reform we relinquish the demand for further rights and greater freedom, acknowledging these

5. The circle took its name from N. V. Chaikovsky, but its real founder was N. A. Natanson.

to be instruments for the exploitation of the people and a further aggravation of our guilt.[6]

Finally, and most importantly, there was a growing realization that political freedom modeled on the English system was bound up with the development of capitalism, which was felt to be a retrogressive step—at least in Russia. Two books played an important part in creating the Populist image of capitalism and bourgeois political freedom—*The Situation of the Working Class in Russia* (1869), and *The Alphabet of the Social Sciences* (1871). Both were written by the economist V. Bervi-Flerovsky, who was connected with what were then the two main centers of the Populist movement—the Chaikovsky and Dolgushin circles.[7] Young Populists were also greatly impressed by Mikhailovsky's article "What is Progress?," and by Eliseev's attacks on the "plutocracy" and his dismissal of parliamentary government as a convenient tool of the bourgeoisie.[8] Last but not least, there was the influence of Marx, the first volume of whose *Capital* was widely known in Populist circles even before the publication of its Russian edition in 1872 (the censor thought it harmless because it only concerned Western Europe). Marx himself (unlike Bakunin) never neglected the political struggle; but the Populist revolutionaries had little difficulty in making their own interpretation of his work, his thesis that the political superstructure always serves the interests of the ruling class and his acute analysis of the "formal" nature of bourgeois democracy being taken as powerful arguments in favor of the Populist view that social and economic changes should be given priority.

The Populists' rejection of political struggle was therefore part of their endeavor to prove that they were completely free from bourgeois illusions, and that their chief enemy was capitalism. It is thus understandable that as capitalist processes accelerated in the Russian countryside, the Populists reacted by bringing into the foreground the anticapitalist and antibourgeois aspects of their ideology, and by increasingly idealizing the allegedly socialist nature of commune self-government.

The real explosion of this romantic faith in the socialist instincts

6. N. K. Mikhailovsky, *Polnoe sobranie sochinenii* (5th ed.; St. Petersburg, 1911), vol. 1, pp. 870–72.

7. The founder of the Dolgushin Circle organized in St. Petersburg in the fall of 1869 was A. V. Dolgushin.

8. See the article by G. Z. Eliseev "Plutocracy and Its Social Base," published in *Notes of the Fatherland*, no. 2 (1872), and reprinted in N. K. Karataev, ed., *Narodnicheskaia ekonomicheskaia literatura* (M, 1958), pp. 125–59. Eliseev based his analysis of government by "plutocracy" on Marx's *Capital*.

of the Russian peasantry was the great Populist crusade of 1873–74. Following the example of members of the Chaikovsky and Dolgushin circles, hundreds and thousands of young men and women decided to "go to the people." Clad in peasant clothes, without having made any previous arrangements, very often without even having consulted each other, they went to the villages in order to taste the authentic, healthy, and simple life.

The enthusiasm that accompanied this "collective act of Rousseauism," as Venturi has called it,[9] was by all accounts something unprecedented and unique. "Nothing similar had been seen before or since," wrote Sergei Kravchinsky. "It was a revelation, rather than a propaganda. At first the book, or the individual, could be traced out, that had impelled such or such person to join the movement; but after some time this became impossible. It was a powerful cry which arose no one knew where, and summoned the ardent to the great work of the redemption of the country and of humanity."[10]

Among the participants in the movement a distinction is usually made between the followers of Bakunin and the followers of Lavrov. The differences between the two groups began to be apparent in the late 1860's—even before the "go to the people" movement —during an interesting controversy over the value of education and science from the point of view of the revolutionary cause. In an 1868 article in the émigré journal *The People's Cause*, Bakunin had called on Russian students to give up their studies, since they were merely a form of exploitation. In a revolutionary epoch, he argued, there is no time for learning; revolutionaries have no need of the official learning that serves the interests of the ruling classes and aggravates social inequalities. Lavrov, who was much closer to the rationalist heritage of the "enlighteners," thought it necessary to dissociate himself from Bakunin's view. This he did most succinctly in an article "Knowledge and Revolution" published in the first number of his émigré journal *Forward* (1873). In their practical work the Lavrovites, who were known as "propagandists," emphasized revolutionary propaganda: by enlightening the peasants they hoped to prepare them for socialism. The Bakuninites, on the other hand, were known as "rebels," for they went to the villages not to teach their inhabitants but to stir them into spontaneous and immediate revolt.

9. See Venturi, *Roots of Revolution*, p. 503.

10. S. Kravchinsky, *Underground Russia, Revolutionary Profiles and Sketches from Life*, with a preface by P. Lavrov (2d ed.; London, 1883), pp. 25–26.

The results of the Populist crusade were very disappointing, and the police made massive arrests. Very often the young enthusiasts were handed over to the gendarmes by the very people they had wished to prepare for revolution. The Russian peasantry turned out to be less receptive to socialist ideas and more reluctant to revolt than the town-bred intellectuals had believed. The Populist movement had gained its first important experience: appropriate conclusions now had to be drawn from it.

The program of the revolutionary "Land and Freedom" organization, founded at the end of 1876, was based on the experiences of both the "rebels" and the "propagandists." Their common platform was the conviction that revolutionaries should act only among and through the people. The main reasons for their previous lack of success were felt to be the Bakuninites' exaggeration of the peasants' readiness to revolt and the excessively abstract nature of socialist propaganda. This latter reproach was directed mainly against the Lavrovites, but it was not without relevance to the Bakuninite "rebels," whom experience had convinced that it was wrong to begin revolutionary agitation among the peasants by a general attack on the foundations of the existing social order. To avoid these errors in the future, the program of "Land and Freedom" put forth only goals that could be "realized in the immediate future," i.e. goals that harmonized with the peasants' immediate interests. It is not enough, declared Kravchinsky, to give up German dress and go to the villages in peasant clothes; not the socialists only but socialism itself should be the homespun variety of the Russian peasant.[11] It was this attempt to jettison their abstract intellectualism and utopianism and make their socialist program more attractive and comprehensible to the masses that gave prominence to the name *narodnichestvo*, which previously had been rarely used.

Armed with a new program, the "Land and Freedom" revolutionaries started a new popular crusade, much better organized than the first one. According to Vera Figner, the new organization tended from the very first to replace "federalist" principles by centralism and effective leadership.[12] The conditions of underground activity reinforced this tendency until, finally, "Land and Freedom" became transformed into the "militant centralized organization" that Lenin (in *What Is to Be Done?*) held up as an example for Russian revolutionary Marxists to follow.

The postulate of a strong centralized organization had been put

---

11. See B. P. Kozmin, *Iz istorii revoliutsionnoi mysli v Rossii* (M, 1961), p. 642.
12. V. Figner, *Polnoe sobranie sochinenii* (M, 1932), vol. 1, p. 105.

forward long before by Petr Tkachev.[13] His ideas, however, known under the name of "Jacobinism" or "Blanquism," because of their emphasis on the role of a revolutionary elite, were incompatible with the generally accepted principle of action through the people, let alone the *narodnichestvo* of "Land and Freedom." What he recommended was a conspiracy of professional revolutionaries who would aim, first of all, at the seizure of political power. He regarded the Populist crusades as a tremendous waste of energy and recommended instead a return to the methods of Nechaev,[14] with whom he had collaborated in the late 1860's. He also thought that much could be learned from the Western European revolutionary conspiracies of the first half of the nineteenth century, and he particularly extolled the experience and conspiratorial skill of the Poles. His closest collaborators while he was an émigré were, in fact, two Poles: Karol Janicki and Kasper Turski.[15]

The masses, Tkachev contended, were incapable of liberating themselves by their own efforts. Their support was necessary for the victory of the revolution, but their role was the purely negative one of a destructive force. The decisive role would be played by the strong leadership and well-organized intervention of a revolutionary vanguard who would know how to exploit the chaos caused by popular uprisings. Preparatory work among the people made no sense; it was simply a way of shirking genuine revolutionary involvement, a convenient dodge thought up by "reactionary revolutionaries." Revolution in Russia could not be postponed, for its chance of success was lessening daily. So far the Russian state was "absolutely absurd and absurdly absolute," lacking any genuine support and "suspended in thin air."[16] Soon it would become "constitutional and moderate" and gain the support of sections of society that would not dream of defending it at present. As long as the Russian bourgeoisie was weak and capitalism in its early stage,

13. See below, pp. 244–52.
14. See above, p. 177, note 28.
15. Kasper Turski was a co-founder of the Polish Social-Democratic Society, established in Zurich in 1872, and affiliated with the International. In 1877–78 he was in close contact with Walery Wróblewski, the Polish general of the Paris Commune, helping to arrange his illegal trip to Russia. Wróblewski was a member of the International and a personal friend of Marx and Engels. Knowing Engels's critical attitude toward Tkachev, Wróblewski preferred to conceal from him (and from Marx) his contacts with Tkachev's group. See J. W. Borejsza, *W kręgu wielkich wygnańców 1848–1895* (Warsaw, 1963), pp. 68–69, 123–24. On Turski see K. Pietkiewicz, "Kasper Michal Turski," *Niepodległość*, 1 (1930), pp. 103–13.
16. An expression used by Tkachev in his "Open Letter to Engels" (see p. 251).

it was possible to map out another future for Russia; soon it might be too late.

This diagnosis suited the mood of the impatient Bakuninites, always eager to engage in direct revolutionary action; on the other hand, Tkachev's views of the masses and of the society of the future molded by the totalitarian revolutionary state were a far cry from the Bakuninites' belief in spontaneity and their ideal of a free federation of self-governing communes. Tkachev, for his part, was convinced that the peasant communes could not give rise to socialism: according to him, the autarchic and self-contained rural communities were among the most conservative and static forms of social organization and contained no germ of any progressive development. Collectivism—the "innate communism" of the Russian peasantry—could no doubt greatly facilitate the revolutionary transformation of society, but it did not constitute an adequate basis for socialism. The people alone would not be able to found a dynamic, progressive society; they would not even be able to remain true to their old ideals and defend them against hostile social forces. The task of the revolutionary vanguard thus could not be restricted to the overthrow of absolutism. The revolutionary party, Tkachev concluded, should take over and strengthen the absolute power of the Russian state in order to turn it into a powerful instrument of revolutionary dictatorship and utilize it for a thorough transformation of all aspects of society. The authority of the revolutionary party running the revolutionary state should replace for the Russian people the authority of its "mythical tsar."

Members of "Land and Freedom" were, as a rule, violently opposed to Tkachev. They accused him of compromising the Russian revolutionary movement and betraying the cause of the people for the sake of his own political ambitions. Despite this, however, his influence accelerated the emergence of a new trend within "Land and Freedom" in which well-organized political struggle to overthrow autocracy was given priority over "work among the people."

This reluctant withdrawal from a purely "Populist" position (in the narrow, historical sense of the word) was the result both of the partial successes and of the overall failure of the second "go to the people" movement. The revolutionaries who had settled in remote villages as country doctors, teachers, or artisans in order to help the peasants in their daily life and organize their resistance to the landlords, *kulaks*, and local officials could rightly claim to have achieved far more than the "propagandists" of 1874; at the same time, however, they were forced to realize that they could not continue their work effectively under existing political conditions. It was this realization that led some to take the step from narrowly Populist methods of struggle to political terrorism. In January 1878, a young girl, Vera Zasulich, fired at General Trepov, governor of St. Petersburg, in order to avenge a revolutionary who had been flogged in prison. In May of the same year Colonel Heyking of the Gendarmerie was assassinated in Kiev. In August Sergei Kravchinsky stabbed to death General Mezentsev, chief of the secret police. On April 2, 1879, Alexander Soloviev made an unsuccessful attempt on the life of the tsar with the knowledge of the "Land and Freedom" organization, though without its help; a few weeks later the autonomous "Death of Liberty" terrorist organization was set up within "Land and Freedom."

The new trend was deplored by the orthodox Populists, who, led by Plekhanov,[17] accused the terrorists of abandoning work among the people and betraying the traditional principle of putting "social" goals first. Many leading members of "Land and Freedom" tried to remain true to the original tenets of Populism while not rejecting terrorism. A characteristic example of this was an important article by Kravchinsky published in the first number of the party's clandestine journal (in the fall of 1878). In it he tried to convince his comrades that the party's main forces should continue to work in the villages; terrorists, he wrote, were only a "defensive detachment whose role was to protect the revolutionaries working among the people against the treacherous blows of the enemy."[18]

However, neither Kravchinsky's article nor the new version of the party program worked out in 1878 could prevent a split in "Land and Freedom." At a secret general meeting of members in Voronezh (in June 1879) a temporary compromise was reached (facilitated by the fact that Plekhanov walked out of the meeting); but this was not enough to enable the "traditionalists" and "innovators" to resolve their differences. In October 1879 the split was formally recognized and "Land and Freedom" ceased to exist. The orthodox Populists, led by Plekhanov and joined—to the disappointment of the "innovators"—by Vera Zasulich, created a separate organization under the name of "Black Repartition" (*Chernyi*

17. See below, pp. 409–11.
18. The program of the journal *Land and Freedom*. Reprinted in Karataev, pp. 322–26.

Peredel), a name that referred to the popular dream of a just distribution of the land among the "black" people, i.e. the peasants. The "innovators" adopted the name *Narodnaia Volia*, which is generally glossed in English as "The People's Will," although it can mean both the will of the people and the freedom of the people. The new organization's program was the overthrow of absolutism and the establishment of a government in accordance with the people's will.

Thanks to the almost universal feeling that traditional methods of work among the people had failed to secure any lasting results, the "People's Will" easily took over the leadership of the revolutionary movement; by comparison, the "handful of members of the 'Black Repartition' did not represent any real revolutionary force."[19] What was new in the revolutionary theory of the "innovators" was their rejection of the traditional Populist emphasis on the priority of "social" over "political" goals, and their attempt to justify this change of front by reference to certain specific characteristics of the Russian state. The party's chief theorist, Lev Tikhomirov, put forward two main arguments in defense of the new line: one was rooted in the government's active encouragement of capitalist development in Russia, the other in the theory of the étatist school of historians (discussed in Chapter 8) that in Russian history the state had always been not a mere instrument of the existing social classes, but the creator of them, the supreme organizer of the whole of social life. Tikhomirov used this latter theory in support of his own thesis that in Russia the struggle against the possessing classes must necessarily turn into a political struggle against the state that had called these classes (including the bourgeoisie) into being and was their main source of strength.

The acceptance of the postulate of "political struggle" did not, of course, mean that there were no important differences in its interpretation. According to Plekhanov, there were two opposing tendencies within "The People's Will": one was the "constitutional tendency" represented by Zhelabov, the other the "Blanquist"[20] (or "Jacobin") tendency to which Tikhomirov himself inclined. Tikhomirov was not, it should be added, an altogether consistent "Blanquist"; he was outdistanced in this respect by another member

19. See L. Bazylov, *Działalność narodnictwa rosyjskego w latch 1878–1881* [*Russian Populism, 1878–1881*] (Wroclaw, 1960), p. 107.

20. Named thus after Auguste Blanqui (1805–81), a French revolutionary and radical thinker.

of the party's executive committee, Maria Oshanina, an ardent follower of Tkachev and a disciple of the veteran of Russian "Jacobinism," P. G. Zaichnevsky.

According to Zhelabov's "constitutional" interpretation, switching over to political struggle meant seeking an alliance with all sections of society interested in the overthrow of Russian absolutism—primarily, in practice, with the liberals. The aim of this alliance was to secure a representative government and democratic rights that would allow the socialists to carry on a legal struggle for the economic betterment of the peasants' and workers' lot. This view was supported by Mikhailovsky in his series "The Political Letters of a Socialist," published under a pseudonym in the journal *People's Will* in 1879. Mikhailovsky provided a theoretical basis for Zhelabov's ideas by arguing (in contradiction of views he himself had held not long before) that political freedom could be used as a weapon against the Russian bourgeoisie, which unlike the French bourgeoisie of the eighteenth century was luckily still too weak to impose its own rule after the overthrow of absolutism.

Tikhomirov's conception of "political struggle" was less precise because he was torn between traditional "Populism" and "Blanquism." Unlike Zhelabov, he stressed the seizure of power through the determined action of a revolutionary vanguard rather than a broad alliance with the liberals. On the other hand, he rejected Tkachev's idea of a long-term revolutionary dictatorship. Revolutionaries should seize power, he argued, but keep it only until a popular social revolution was under way.

Irrespective of these differences, all members of the party agreed that the quickest way to overthrow absolutism was to assassinate the tsar. All possible efforts were made to achieve this end. The first two attempts—a plot to blow up the emperor's train, and an explosion in the Winter Palace carefully prepared by Stepan Khalturin —failed, but the third was successful. On March 1, 1881, Alexander II was killed by a bomb thrown by a member of "The People's Will," the Russified Pole Ignacy Hryniewiecki. The result was a bitter disappointment to the revolutionaries: the assassination of the tsar was followed not by chaos and revolutionary disturbances but by the consolidation of autocracy. Instead of political freedom, there arose an even more reactionary government; and instead of the expected tremendous increase in the strength and popularity of the party, the arrest of its most important leaders put an effective end to its activities. The executive committee (or rather those of its members who had managed to escape arrest) addressed a letter to the new emperor (presumably drafted by Tikhomirov and modified in some details by Mikhailovsky) exhorting him to convene a National Assembly and thereby avoid a bloody revolution in the future. The letter ended with a solemn declaration that the revolutionary party would accept as binding all decisions of the freely elected Assembly, and would unconditionally renounce the use of force against the government. However, Alexander III preferred policies that precluded all hope for the peaceful evolution of the Russian monarchy.

Those who had taken part in the assassination attempt—Rysakov, Zhelabov, Mikhailov, Kibalchich, and Sofia Perokskaia—were hanged on April 3, 1881 (Hryniewiecki was killed by his own bomb). During the hearing only Rysakov—a youth of nineteen—broke down. The courageous behavior of the rest, especially the fortitude of Zhelabov and Perovskaia, amazed the judges and gained the admiration of the entire world.

PETR LAVROV

Biographical Note

PETR LAVROV (1823–1900), a leading Populist thinker and one of the most attractive figures in the nineteenth-century Russian revolutionary movement, came from a family of wealthy landowners.[21] He was educated in Mikhailov's Artillery Academy in St. Petersburg, and after graduation he taught mathematics at various military academies. His promotion was rapid, and by 1858 he had attained the rank of colonel. He was also interested in philosophy and sociology, and in 1860 published his first book, *Sketches in the Domain of Practical Philosophy (Ocherki voprosov prakticheskoi filosofii)*, in which he showed himself to be an adherent of "anthropologism." This book came to the attention of Chernyshevsky, who discussed it in his *Anthropological Principle in Philosophy*; he accused Lavrov of eclecticism but nevertheless expressed agreement with the general line of his argument.

At this time Lavrov was in close touch with the revolutionary leaders of the first "Land and Freedom" organization. In 1866 he was arrested during the wave of repression that followed Karakozov's attempt on the Tsar's life and sentenced to exile under police surveillance in Vologda Province. His essay cycle *Historical Letters*,

21. See P. Pomper, *Peter Lavrov and the Russian Revolutionary Movement* (Chicago, 1972). Lavrov's *Historical Letters* were translated and published with an introduction and notes by J. P. Scanlan (Berkeley, Calif., 1967).

published in the periodical *The Week* (*Nedelia*) in 1868–69, gained him immense popularity among young radicals. In February 1870 he was helped by the revolutionary Herman Lopatin to flee abroad, where he immediately made contact with the International Workingmen's Association, which he joined in the fall of the same year. He took part in the Paris Commune and was sent by the Commune Government to organize help in Belgium and England; this led to a lasting friendship with Marx and Engels. From 1873 to 1876 he published a revolutionary periodical, *Forward* (*Vpered*), first in Zurich and later (from 1874) in London. In it he condemned the Nechaev line that all means were permissible in the revolutionary struggle, warned against revolutionary adventurism, and emphasized the need for a lengthy and careful preparatory struggle. He shared the general Populist belief in the priority of social over political goals and agreed with Bakunin that the introduction of socialism could not be reconciled with the retention of the state apparatus; however (in contrast to the anarchists), this did not prevent him from being friendly with the German Social Democrats, who were anything but apolitical.

From the beginning, Lavrov was more radical than his followers in Russia. At a general meeting of his supporters held in Paris toward the end of 1876, discontent came to a head and resulted in a split, with Lavrov resigning the editorship of his journal. From the experiences of the "go to the people" movement, a section of his followers, especially the influential St. Petersburg group, drew conclusions that Lavrov himself could not accept. Having been disappointed in the peasants, this section now concentrated on propaganda among the workers; they were very careful in their approach and laid stress on long-term educational work rather than immediate revolutionary action (indeed, they were opposed to all premature disturbances, outbreaks of violence, or even strikes).[22] Lavrov, on the other hand, interpreted preparatory work for revolution in far wider terms than mere peaceful propaganda; though he approved of educational work among the workers, he still believed in the socialist potential of the peasant commune and thought that the future of Russia lay in agrarian socialism.

22. Toward the end of the 1870's they began to justify their decision by reference to Marx. The commune, they argued, is a reactionary institution and condemned to disappear: therefore a socialist revolution in Russia will only become possible after the establishment of capitalism and the emergence of a proletariat. See S. M. Levin, *Obshchestvennoe dvizhenie v Rossii v 60–70-e gody XIX veka* (M, 1958), pp. 378–83. In combination with the traditional Populist attitude to political struggle, this led to a curious "philosophy of inaction."

After the assassination of Alexander II, Lavrov joined "The People's Will" and together with Tikhomirov edited the party's journal from Geneva. With the decline of "The People's Will" he returned to scholarly work and published several books in the fields of historical sociology and the sociological philosophy of history. These included the *Essay on the History of Modern Thought* (*Opyt istorii mysli novogo vriemieni*) (Geneva 1888–94), *Problems in the Interpretation of History* (*Zadachi ponimania istorii*) (1898), and the posthumous *Important Stages in the History of Thought* (*Vazhneishie momenty istorii mysli*) (1903). The last two were published in Russia under the pseudonyms S. Arnoldi and A. Dolenga respectively. Before these works, though, he published (in 1880) a valuable study of the Paris Commune that was translated into many languages. In the years 1892–96 he edited a series of *Contributions to the History of the Russian Social Revolutionary Movement*.[23] He died in Paris, universally respected by socialists regardless of theoretical differences or political viewpoints.

The Historical Letters

The *Historical Letters* largely owed their popularity among young Russian radicals of the seventies to the immense impact of one essay, entitled "The Cost of Progress." "Mankind has paid dearly," Lavrov wrote, "so that a few thinkers sitting in their studies could discuss its progress." The personal development of "critically thinking individuals" from among the privileged cultivated minority has been purchased by the hard labor and terrible sufferings of generations of exploited men and women; each thought, each idea, "has been bought by the blood, sufferings, or toil of millions." The cultivated minority must never forget this debt and should make every effort to discharge it. Each ethical and critically thinking individual should say to himself: "I shall shed the responsibility for the bloody cost of my own development if I utilize this same development to diminish evil in the present and in the future."[24]

These words sum up perfectly the state of mind of those progressive members of the educated gentry who were tormented by feelings of guilt and eager to sacrifice their personal interests for the good of the masses. It was this younger "conscience-stricken" generation that, together with the more sober *raznochintsy*, was begin-

23. His own contribution to the *Materials* was the valuable monograph *Narodniki-propagandisty 1872–1878 godov*.

24. P. L. Lavrov, *Filosofiia i sotsiologiia* (M, 1965), vol. 2, p. 81 (English translation in J. Edie et al., *Russian Philosophy* [Chicago, 1965], vol. 2, p. 138).

ning to play a leading part in the radical movement. Lavrov's book put this generation's dilemma into words and at the same time set out to answer its questions. The most important of these was concerned with the nature of progress.

It was the conviction that their debt must be paid off which led young Populists to reject indignantly all theories claiming that progress was inevitable and inherent in the "natural" course of events. These theories seemed to them only too convenient as a way of justifying the uglier aspects of capitalism as part of the "objective laws of history" or the "iron laws of political economy." Dislike of this kind of "objectivism" that identified progress with "spontaneous" development and condemned as utopian all "subjective" ideals conflicting with this development led Lavrov and Mikhailovsky to formulate the views that came to be known as "subjective sociology." Populist "subjectivism" was much ridiculed by Plekhanov but deserves a fairer assessment.

The basic assumptions of "subjective sociology" (an unfortunate and not particularly accurate label) can be summed up under three headings. First, it was a defense of ethical standards, and implied that men had the right to judge everything from their own point of view and to protest even against the "objective laws of history"— that indeed they were obliged to protest against human suffering even where the situation seemed hopeless. Second, it was an epistemological and methodological standpoint that disputed the possibility of "objective" knowledge in the social sciences; "subjectivism" in this sense implied that historical and sociological knowledge could never be really objective because they were colored by the scholar's social position, his unconscious emotions, or consciously chosen ideals. Third, it was a philosophy of history that claimed that the "subjective factor"—human will and consciousness (expressed in the activity of a revolutionary party or in deliberate state intervention)—could effectively oppose the spontaneous-development trend and influence the course of history. For the Populist revolutionaries this last point was, of course, the most important; on it Lavrov based his "practical philosophy," which proclaimed that by forming a party and establishing a common program "critically thinking individuals" could become a significant force capable of changing reality and realizing their "subjective" aims.

To those of his readers who were looking for a definition of progress, Lavrov stated unequivocally: progress is not an objective or inevitable law of development. Such laws do not exist; historical events are always unique and unrepeatable. (Here Lavrov partly anticipated the theses of Windelband and Rickert.) In looking at history, therefore, the main problem is one of selection, of finding a criterion that will make it possible to pick out "what is important and meaningful" from the amorphous mass of historical data. Such a criterion must be subjective because it depends on the social ideal adopted by a particular scholar. All facts are classified and all historical events interpreted according to how they relate to this ideal. "In the historical perspective set by our moral ideal," Lavrov wrote, "we stand at the end of the historical process; the entire past is related to our ideal as a series of preparatory steps leading inevitably to a definite end."[25] According to this theory, therefore, progress is conceived as a category required to impose order onto the raw material of history and to impart a meaning to the chaotic mass of facts. In itself, history has no meaning; there are many meanings to be found in it, but all of them are imparted to it by men. Imposing a meaning on history also presupposes an ideal: not only in the sphere of historical understanding, but also in the sphere of historical action. Human history began, according to Lavrov, with the emergence of critically thinking individuals trying to shape the destiny of men by means of "criticism" and "idealization."[26] These two factors were necessary for those who wished to change the world: the first to destroy the old society, and the other to build a new one on the basis of specific ideals that were always to some extent utopian.

His own ideal Lavrov formulated as follows: "The physical, intellectual, and moral development of the individual; the incorporation of truth and justice in social institutions."[27] Or, more precisely: "Progress consists in the development of consciousness and in the incorporation of truth and justice in social institutions; it is a process that is being accomplished by means of the critical thought of individuals who aim at the transformation of their culture."[28] By culture Lavrov meant a static social structure based on religion, tradition, and folkways. With the emergence of critically

25. Lavrov, *Filosofiia*, vol. 2, p. 44 (*Russian Philosophy*, vol. 2, p. 131).
26. By "idealization" Lavrov meant something very close to "rationalization" in the Freudian sense, or to "ideology" in Karl Mannheim's use of this word. Idealization in this sense simply means the effort, usually unconscious, to hide one's real motivation and to interpret one's aspirations in terms of disinterested aims. "False" idealization serves to conceal aims of which people are ashamed, whereas "truly human" idealization helps to prepare the way for the realization of legitimate human needs.
27. Lavrov, *Filosofia*, vol. 2, p. 54 (*Russian Philosophy*, vol. 2, p. 34).
28. P. L. Lavrov, *Formula progressa N. K. Mikhailovskogo, Protivniki istorii. Nauchnye osnovy istorii tsivilizatsii* (St. Petersburg, 1906), p. 41.

thinking individuals there came about a gradual transformation of culture into civilization—that is, a dynamic social structure in which religion was replaced by science and custom by law. The development of civilization was no longer "organic," spontaneous, or unconscious but increasingly determined by the conscious activity of individuals.

This theory was a typical example of the rationalist's overestimation of intellectual factors in human history. In Russia it owed its great influence to the fact that—as Lavrov had intended—young Populist radicals identified themselves with the "critically thinking individuals" who were to influence history. On the other hand, the theory did not go well with the Populist idealization of the peasant commune and other ancient and patriarchal social bonds, which (in terms of Lavrov's theory) had to be recognized as belonging to the inferior static "culture." It is interesting in this context to note the similarity between Lavrov's ideas and the philosophy of history of the Westernizers of the forties. We find striking parallels with Belinsky's views on the growing role of the individual and of the rational consciousness in history, with Herzen's reflections on history as a process of individualization, and with Granovsky's theory of progress as the "individualization of the masses by means of thought." The close connection between Lavrov's thought and the philosophical themes of the forties is also shown by his early works on Hegelian philosophy: *Sketches in the Domain of Practical Philosophy*, and *Three Conversations on the Contemporary Meaning of Philosophy* (1861). Lavrov's "subjectivism"—like Belinsky's revolt against the tyranny of the *Weltgeist* and Herzen's philosophy of action—was initially directed against the fetishization of historical necessity and Hegel's tyranny of the "universal," rather than against positivistic naturalism. His philosophy of history drew its inspiration from Kant (progress conceived as a "regulative idea," as a postulate of practical reason), from the Left Hegelians (especially B. Bauer's "critical thought" as the prime mover of progress), and from the "anthropologism" of Feuerbach (anthropocentricity as opposed to "objectivism" and the "Absolute Spirit").

It is clear that Lavrov was the most extreme representative of the "Westernizing" wing of the Populist movement. We can also trace an obvious affinity between the views expressed in the *Historical Letters* and the rationalism of the "enlighteners" of the sixties, who, like Lavrov, overestimated the historical role of ideas and consequently of intellectual elites. Indeed, as a document of Populist ideology the *Letters* do not seem entirely consistent: they express admirably the ethical doubts of young radicals and also their sense of a historical mission; but they completely ignore one important aspect of classical Populism, namely its nostalgia for archaic social forms. Lavrov himself was too strongly bound up with the great progressive traditions of modern European humanism—represented in Russia by the Westernizers and "enlighteners"—to abandon them in favor of a backward-looking utopianism. Although he challenged the underlying concept of individualistic humanism—the free development of individuality—by insisting that this development had been bought by the "blood, sufferings, and toil of millions," in the last analysis his theory could be used to justify the ruthless course of history. If critical thought was the prime mover of social progress, then the price paid for it had not been wasted. If the flowering of individuality, together with the incorporation of truth and justice in social institutions, was the main criterion of progress, one was forced to conclude that European history had after all been a history of progress, and that the long process of mass exploitation and oppression was not to be altogether condemned—with the qualification, of course, that it was now high time to discharge the debt owed to the masses.

Sociological Conceptions

Under the influence of Marx, Lavrov paid more attention to the economic aspects of social processes in his later sociological writings. His basic ideas remained unchanged, but they were more fully worked out and systematized.[29]

Lavrov defined sociology as a science concerned with the solidarity of conscious individuals and describing concrete forms of cooperation. For Lavrov, "solidarity" was an indispensable condition of social life; but it had to be the solidarity of *conscious* individuals, since at the instinctual level (in a colony of polyps, for instance) it belonged to the realm of biology rather than sociology. Sociology has its theoretical as well as its practical aspect. It is a tool for investigating social evolution as an objective process but also has a normative role because it formulates social ideals and shows how they can be implemented. Because of this dual role, Lavrov repeatedly pointed out that his sociology could not be regarded in isolation from his socialism.

Lavrov divided the great variety of forms of social solidarity into three main types. The first was the unconscious solidarity of cus-

29. See P. A. Sorokin, "Osnovnye problemy sotsiologii P. L. Lavrova," in *P. L. Lavrov Stat'i, vospominaniia, materialy* (published by "Kolos," Petrograd, 1932).

tom[30] to which the individual submits under the pressure of necessity. The second was a purely "emotional solidarity" based on impulses not controlled by critical reflection. The third was "concious historical solidarity" resulting from a common effort to attain a consciously selected and rationally justified goal. This third type was the highest and most important form of social solidarity. It evolved later than the first two types and heralded the process of the transformation of static "culture" into dynamic "civilization." The appearance of this highest form of solidarity marked the end of prehistory and the beginning of true history in a given society.

Conscious solidarity was expressed through the community of "critically thinking" individuals, or in other words the intelligentsia, who were responsible for transforming culture by means of thought. The history of ideas therefore contained the quintessence of the historical process, and investigating "the most important moments in the history of thought" was the shortest way to understanding social evolution.

In his conception of the motive force of history Lavrov represented a pluralistic point of view. Social evolution, he thought, was stimulated by the individual's diverse needs, especially the need for food, the need to satisfy the mating and procreational instincts, and the needs for safety and for nervous stimulation (he regarded the need for the company of others as a peculiar variant of the latter). The most important of these *basic* biological needs was the need for food, which stimulated society's economic development. For Lavrov this thesis justified the priority of "economic" over "political" goals. However, he emphasized that apart from biological needs characteristic of man as a species, there were other needs; these he referred to as "historical categories," because they constituted what might be called the historical dimension of human existence. The most important of these was the disinterested "need for development" characteristic of "critically thinking individuals." Lavrov believed that this need was becoming more and more important and that its significance increased in direct proportion to the role played in a given society by conscious rational intervention.

This overall conception of history as a process in which culture became transformed into civilization was tied to the Saint-Simonian and Comtian notion of history as a succession of "organic" and

30. Lavrov uses the term "consciousness" in two different meanings: the first, wider meaning embraces "mental life" (in the definition of sociology as the science of the solidarity of conscious individuals); the narrower meaning only refers to reflective, critical consciousness, i.e. self-consciousness in the philosophical sense (in this sense the solidarity of custom is, of course, "unconscious").

"critical" phases. During the organic stages, which saw the emergence and maturation of specific forms of culture, the dominant
social mood was one of solidarity; critical stages, on the other hand,
were epochs of individualism and the destructive activity of "critical thought." Historical progress moved along a spiral in an acceler-
ating rhythm—its successive phases were growing shorter, and the
difference between organic and critical periods was constantly
diminishing. This was because historical evolution offered growing
opportunities to achieve a harmonious fusion of solidarity and
development, order and progress. Instead of swinging from one extreme to another, history was tending toward a state of "mobile
equilibrium" in which development would not conflict with existing forms of solidarity and the strengthening of solidarity would
not put a brake on development.

From the standpoint of the assumptions of the "subjective method," Lavrov's sociological writings appear to make considerable
concessions to "objectivism." It is true that he retained his emphasis on the role of critically thinking individuals and on the
normative role of sociology, but he jettisoned the very core of
"subjectivism"—the denial that objective knowledge in the social
sciences is possible. This was, however, a modification rather than
a radical structural change. Even in the *Historical Letters* Lavrov
made a distinction between history, which deals with what is unique
and unrepeatable, and sociology, which aims at discovering certain
overall laws of social development. A few years later, in his article
"On Method in Sociology," he clearly stated that in sociology (in
contrast to history) both methods—the subjective and the objective—
were justified and applicable. In time he even began to look for the
objective justification of social revolution in "historical necessity"
(by which he meant certain regular social processes established by
sociology). Of course, this was not a concession to "objectivism"
in the sense of the Hegelian idolization of history or to the liberals'
apologia for uncontrolled, "natural" development. It has been
rightly noted (by J. Hecker) that Lavrov's "subjective method" was
very close in this respect to the "anthropoteleological method" of
L. F. Ward, who stressed the superiority of artificial teleological
processes to "natural" ones without, however, denying the existence
of certain general laws of social evolution.[31]

Regardless of the theoretical cohesion or academic value of Lavrov's sociological theories, there is no doubt that they are of great

31. See J. F. Hecker, *Russian Sociology: A Contribution to the History of Sociological Thought and Theory* (New York, 1915), p. 118.

historical interest. Basically, they reveal Lavrov as an ideologist of the intelligentsia. Certain scholars have suggested that they are an expression of a specific "intellectual aristocratism"[32] (the apotheosis of "critically thinking individuals") or even of certain characteristic aspects of the gentry mentality (the view of the masses as an inert herd, combined with a sense of guilt).[33] Although this is partially true, such comments fail to draw attention to the fundamental difference between Lavrov's ideas and the apotheosis of intellectuals and scientists in the sociological theories of Auguste Comte. There is no hint in Lavrov's work of the Comtian vision of a new intellectual elite that would govern the hierarchically stratified society of the future. For the Russian thinker the intelligentsia was first and foremost the conscience of society—not an aristocracy of the intellect. Educated men who benefited from the gifts of civilization but were selfishly indifferent to the burning injustices of their time were for him "cultural savages" (*kulturnye dikari*)—individuals who had reverted to the prehistorical stage of uncivilized tribes, and to whom critical thought and the disinterested need for development were quite alien.

Thus, the author of the *Historical Letters* can be called an ideologist of the intelligentsia as an ethical category, i.e. in the nineteenth-century Russian meaning of the term intelligentsia. He was not a spokesman of professional intellectuals but an ideologist of intelligentsia as a community of human beings of superior moral and intellectual sensitivity committed to the struggle against social injustice.

PETR TKACHEV

The most serious challenge to Lavrov's views came from PETR TKACHEV (1844–86),[34] mentioned previously as the chief theorist of the "Jacobin" trend in Russian Populism. In the years 1868–69 he was active in the student movement and a close collaborator of Nechaev. With characteristic extremism, he is said to have declared

32. See Sorokin, "Osnovnye problemy," p. 286.
33. See G. Ladokha, "Istoricheskie i sotsiologischeskie vozzreniia P. L. Lavrova," in *Russkaia istoricheskaia literatura v klassovom osveshchenii*, ed. M. N. Pokrovsky (M, 1927), p. 422.
34. The most comprehensive monograph on him in any language is Deborah Hardy, *Petr Tkachev: The Critic as Jacobin* (Seattle, Wash., 1977). The author pays much attention to the differences distinguishing Tkachev's world view from those of the other Populist ideologists of the 1870's, and sets forth the thesis that he was in many respects much closer to the radicals of the 1860's.

that the radical rebirth of Russia required the extermination of anyone over twenty-five.[35] He was arrested in the spring of 1869, and after having been held in custody for two years awaiting trial was sentenced to sixteen months in prison and subsequent banishment to Siberia. Thanks to his mother's efforts in his behalf, exile was commuted to banishment to his family estates under police surveillance. In December 1873 Tkachev managed to flee to Zurich, where he tried to collaborate with Lavrov until it became clear that differences between them were too great. In 1874, shortly after attacking Lavrov's program in his pamphlet *The Role of Revolutionary Propaganda in Russia,* he broke off relations with him and joined the "Blanquist" *Cercle Slave,* which was headed by two Poles—Kasper Turski and Karol Janicki. In 1875 he published the journal *Tocsin (Nabat)* in which he expounded his ideas on the seizure of power by a revolutionary minority and the need for a strong centralized organization.

The fullest exposition of Tkachev's views is to be found in his essay "What Is the Party of Progress?" (1870)[36] written in answer to Lavrov's *Historical Letters.* Tkachev's criticism touches on the most sensitive points of Lavrov's doctrine and shows clearly the predicament of Populist thinkers who attempted to reconcile the flowering of individuality with the social advancement of the masses.

Tkachev's main criticism was that in the *Historical Letters* Lavrov had replaced the "real" notion of progress with a "formal" one that was completely useless as a criterion for classifying attitudes as reactionary or progressive: if all ideals are necessarily subjective, he argued, all ideologies, even reactionary ones, are entitled to call themselves progressive. To maintain that everything is important or unimportant, good or bad, only in relation to man is not an adequate argument; it is true that even the natural sciences cannot claim to know the "thing-in-itself," but it would be absurd to conclude from this that they, too, are merely "subjective." The same holds true for the theory of progress: it can attain to objectivity because there are some universally valid elementary and "self-evident" truths that may serve as an absolute yardstick against which to measure progress. "There exists an absolute criterion against

35. See Kozmin's introduction to P. N. Tkachev, *Izbrannye sochineniia na sotsialno-politicheskie temy,* ed. B. P. Kozmin (4 vols.; M, 1932), vol. 1, pp. 13–14.

36. The manuscript of this article, dated Sep. 16, 1870, was confiscated by the police and printed for the first time in Kozmin's edition of Tkachev's writings cited in the previous note: vol. 2, pp. 166–224. Tkachev's criticism of Lavrov was, however, known to his contemporaries from other articles.

which to check the validity of ideologies," Tkachev wrote. "There is, therefore, the possibility of an infallible ideology, that is, of an absolute, universally valid and obligatory formula of progress."[37]

Tkachev's rejection of the subjective method was not, however, entirely consistent. Though he dismissed relativism as an attitude endangering absolute faith in the rightness of one's cause, he did not himself reject all prescriptive norms and made no attempt to justify his ideal by certain objective laws of historical evolution. The notion of progress, he asserted, presupposes three elements: movement, direction, and goal. But only two of these elements are necessary to conjure up a clear notion of progress in the human mind. In the organic world of nature there is always movement in a definite direction; the goal in this case is identical with the direction of the movement. In social evolution it is not possible to find such steady movement in a given direction; contrary to the view of Spencer, the "historical process should not be treated as an organic process because there is no steady one-way direction in it, and *in itself* it is neither progressive nor retrogressive."[38] Thus the definition of social progress must make do with two elements, movement and goal; looking for a steady, objective direction in the movement of history is as nonsensical as trying to find deliberate goals in nature. Society's final and only goal (this was axiomatic to Tkachev) is the happiness of all its members; therefore in order to formulate an "absolute" definition of progress, it is first necessary to establish a scientific and objective definition of happiness.

Looking for such a definition, Tkachev made use of the "excellent and universal," "scientific and objective" definition of life he had found in Spencer's *Principles of Biology*. This indicates, he concluded, that happiness consists in the reconciliation or harmonious balance of man's needs and the means he has at his disposal to satisfy them. The problem, as Tkachev saw it, was that human needs were very diverse and that some could only be satisfied at the expense of others. The artificial needs of the "highly developed individualities" of the privileged minority were satisfied at the expense of the working masses, who were denied even the bare necessities of life. This was a good position from which to attack Lavrov: The fact that the "flowering of individuality" was an essential element of Lavrov's formula of progress, Tkachev argued, showed that he was basically a spokesman for the privileged minority, who as producers of ideas had become accustomed to thinking of themselves as "the

37. Tkachev, *Izbr. soch.*, vol. 2, p. 174.
38. *Ibid.*, p. 194.

salt of the earth, the lever of history, the creators of human happiness," and who regarded their very existence as sufficient proof of historical progress.[39] "From this point of view," Tkachev continued, "historical progress cannot indeed be denied: the salt of the earth has been multiplying and perfecting itself, so that progress is evident. This kind of progress, however, has nothing in common with social progress."[40] The personal development of "critically thinking individuals," as Lavrov himself pointed out, had been achieved at the cost of the masses, whose story was one of constant regress. When at last the situation of the masses became so unacceptable that the privileged minority found itself threatened by it, many pseudo-progressive theories were devised that—like Lavrov's—called for a fairer division of material and cultural riches. But all these theories "persist in openly defending the view that human individuality should remain at the high level of sophistication attained by the privileged minority and indeed, should develop further in the same direction."[41] This emphasis revealed the essentially reactionary nature of such theories. The "flowering of individuality" was a reactionary postulate because the happiness of society required the intellectual and moral leveling of individualities. Thus the main task facing the "party of progress" was to "stop the chaotic process of differentiation caused by the retrogressive movement of history, to reduce the existing multiplicity of individualities to one common denominator, one common level."[42]

To counter the formula of progress put forward in the *Historical Letters*, Tkachev proposed the following formula of his own:

To establish the fullest possible equality of individuals (this must not be confused with so-called political, juridical, or even economic equality—it should be an *organic physiological equality* stemming from the same education and from identical conditions of life), and to make sure that the needs of all individuals are in harmony with the means available to satisfy them—that is the final and only possible goal of human society, the supreme yardstick of historical progress. Everything that brings us nearer to this goal is progressive: everything that leads us further away from it is reactionary.[43]

In Tkachev's view, this formula followed logically from his definition of happiness as applied to society. The satisfaction of everyone's needs required the adjustment of these needs to "the existing level of labor productivity." Therefore society must con-

39. *Ibid.*, p. 218.
40. *Ibid.*, p. 219.
41. *Ibid.*, p. 205.
42. *Ibid.*, pp. 206–7.
43. *Ibid.*, p. 208.

trol and regulate the proliferation of needs and deliberately suppress any individual requirements that—at the existing level of economic development—could be satisfied only at other people's expense. Uniformity of needs is a prerequisite of a happy society, and the liquidation of the sophisticated culture of the elite is the price to be paid for it. Every differentiating process endangers the equilibrium between human needs and the level of production, thereby adding to the total sum of unhappiness. Compulsory egalitarianism, to which all true progressives aspire, means that individuals with greater needs who are unable to satisfy those needs at the expense of others are likely to be unhappy: their own happiness therefore requires the parity of their intellectual and moral development with that of other, less-developed members of society. Any increase in needs should be collective and planned to match an increase in production.

Tkachev's political theories clearly indicate that the "leveling of individuality" was a task that would fall to the revolutionary vanguard who, after seizing power, would organize a national system of child-rearing and education, and would deliberately restrain the development of outstanding individuals who threatened the accepted level of social equality. The revolution therefore would not end with the seizure of power, but would only be a prelude to the total future transformation of society.

The polemic with Lavrov was not only about means but also about ends. Cutting himself off from the tradition of Herzen and Chernyshevsky, Tkachev (in sharp contrast to Lavrov) flatly rejected the "personality principle." For him the ideal of a harmoniously developed, critically thinking personality was a supreme example of bourgeois individualism—an ideology that was antagonistic and alien to the common people. In one article he wrote that the principle of individualism had already been formulated by Protagoras and the Sophists, whose ideology reflected the urban bourgeois civilization of Athens; anti-individualism had an equally venerable and much more impressive genealogy, having been formulated by Plato, whose idealized image of ancient Sparta forcefully expressed the principle of the total subordination of the individual to the community.

These ideas divided Tkachev from the other Populist thinkers no less sharply than his "Jacobin" or "Blanquist" conceptions of revolutionary struggle. His theories cannot be said to fall within the scope of "bourgeois democratic" ideologies, even in the broadest view of this category. A belated disciple of Morelly, Babeuf, and Buonarroti, Tkachev was in Russia—and perhaps in the whole of nineteenth-century Europe—the most consistent and extreme spokesman of the "crude communism" that, to use the words of the young Marx, "negates the personality of man in every sphere." [44] It seems likely, as Kozmin has suggested, that the ominous vision of "Shigalev's system" in Dostoevsky's novel *The Possessed* was in fact an allusion to Tkachev's ideas on the "leveling of individualities." [45]

Tkachev's outright rejection of the importance of individuality was a specific solution to a characteristic dilemma facing Populist thinkers—namely, how to reconcile the value they placed on the archaic collectivism of the peasant commune with the postulate of individual freedom, or, to put it differently, how to reconcile the welfare of the people, which (according to Populist doctrine) demanded a stop to the process of Westernization, with the welfare of the intelligentsia, which was a product of westernization and vitally interested in its further progress. Unlike Herzen, Chernyshevsky, or Lavrov, Tkachev was convinced that the "individuality principle" (represented by the westernized elite) and the communal principle were mutually antagonistic and would not be reconciled until the full "leveling of individualities" had been achieved.

Tkachev combined his theory of progress with a specific "economic materialism" borrowed directly from Marx. After the preceding pages this must seem rather a surprising statement, and yet among Russian revolutionaries it was Tkachev who made the first serious attempt to assimilate some elements of Marxism. As early as 1865 he had written in the journal *Russian Word* that he supported the idea of "the well-known German exile Karl Marx," adding that "this idea has now become common to almost all thinking and honest men." Even earlier—at the end of 1863—he had expounded in print the notion of the dependence of all spheres of social life (the social superstructure) on the economic sphere. [46]

"Social life and all its manifestations, including literature, science, and religion, as well as political and juridical forms, are but the product of definite economic principles that lie at the roots of all these social phenomena." [47] This quotation from Tkachev was, of course, a paraphrase of the preface to Marx's *Critique of Politi-*

44. K. Marx, *Early Writings*, trans. and ed. T. B. Bottomore (London, 1963), p. 153 (Economic and Philosophical Manuscripts, Third Manuscript).

45. See B. P. Kozmin, *P. N. Tkachev i revoliutsionnoe dvizhenie 1860–kh godov* (M, 1922), p. 193. Dostoevsky could have become acquainted with Tkachev's conception of the "leveling of individuality" from the latter's article "The People of the Future" published in *Delo* in 1868.

46. See Kozmin, *Iz istorii revoliutsionnoi mysli v Rossii*, p. 374.

47. Tkachev, *Izbr. soch.*, vol. 5, p. 93.

cal Economy. It must be added that Tkachev did not stop at a declaration of principle: he also tried, more or less successfully, to apply these principles in his interpretation of ideological struggles past and present. He explained the Reformation, for instance, as a struggle between the feudal aristocracy and the rising bourgeoisie, and suggested that the emancipation of women was a necessary outcome of the advance of capitalism. In his polemic with Lavrov he attacked the latter's exaggerated emphasis on the role of "critically thinking individuals" and argued instead that the outcome of events was decided not by the human intellect or abstract knowledge but by "affective states stimulated by men's vital interests and thus having their roots in the sphere of economic relations."[48] This specific "economic materialism" did not amount to Marxism, but the Marxist influence in it was evident. It would be fair to describe it as a peculiar mixture of Marxism with a rather primitive utilitarian exaggeration of the role of direct economic motivation in individual behavior.

The interpretation of Tkachev's ideas poses an interesting problem. Economic materialism is a theory that, as a rule, appears in conjunction with a mechanically conceived determinism. How, then, is it possible that in Thachev's theories it coexisted side by side with his very voluntaristic conviction that the future of Russia depended on the will and determination of an active revolutionary minority?

In Marx's *Contribution to the Critique of Political Economy* Tkachev could read that no social formation was likely to disappear until the productive forces appropriate to it had achieved their full development. In the 1880's and 1890's Russian Marxists used to conclude from this that the socialist revolution in Russia would have to wait until Russian capitalism had exhausted all its potentialities for development. Tkachev naturally found this view unacceptable; he argued instead that revolution was possible *either after* the termination of the whole capitalist development cycle *or before* this cycle was even begun. Every economic principle, he wrote in 1868, has its own inner logic of development; just as in an argument we cannot jump from first premise to conclusion, so in economic development it is impossible to skip the intermediary phases.[49] It *is* possible, however, to start a completely new cycle, especially in epochs of transition when the old economic relations have outlived their time and the new ones are not yet firmly estab-

48. *Ibid.,* vol. 2, pp. 213–15 ("Rol' mysli v istorii").
49. *Ibid.,* vol. 1, pp. 260–62.

lished. Utopianism, Tkachev declared, is thus not something peculiar to the extreme radicals who try to replace existing economic
principles by new ones; the true utopians are the moderates who
wish to preserve the existing economic system while skipping some
of its natural phases and attempting to avoid some of its inevitable
results. The revolution in Russia could take place *either at once,*
while the old feudal system was exhausted and the new capitalist
formation had not yet taken root, *or in the distant future,* after
the country had passed through all the painful phases of capitalist
development. At present, Tkachev concluded, the future of the
country was still in the hands of the revolutionaries; tomorrow it
would be too late. A similar situation, he suggested, had existed in
Germany during the peasant wars. Here he disagreed with Engels,
who believed that the defeat of Thomas Müntzer, the German peasant leader, had been historically inevitable. Tkachev thought that
Müntzer might very well have won and that his victory would have
saved the German masses from the sufferings that awaited them
under capitalism.[50]

In 1874 Tkachev launched a sharp attack on Engels. The context
of this polemic was international rather than Russian: it arose out
of ideological differences between Bakunin and Marx and their
struggle for leadership in the First International. After the Nechaev
affair, in which the International had been involved by Bakunin, a
resolution was passed condemning Nechaev and expressing disapproval of conspiratorial methods. Tkachev, who was in a sense
Nechaev's disciple, interpreted this resolution as an attack on the
Russian revolutionary movement as a whole. In his famous "Open
Letter to Engels" (1874), he accused Engels of lacking revolutionary
fervor and defended his own ideas on the chances of revolution in
backward countries.[51] To accuse Engels of excessive regard for
legalism was to do him an injustice, but the second point—regarding Russia's readiness for socialist revolution—did reflect an
essential disagreement on fundamental issues. Engels certainly believed that an indispensable condition of socialism was the advanced
economic development of bourgeois society. "The bourgeoisie," he
wrote, "is just as necessary a precondition of the socialist revolution
as the proletariat itself. Hence a man who will say that this revolu-

50. *Ibid.* Engel's opinions on the chances of Müntzer's victory (diametrically
opposed to Tkachev's) were often quoted by Plekhanov, who used them as an argument against Tkachev's conception of the "seizure of power." In later years he used
the same argument against Lenin.

51. Tkachev, *Izbr. soch.,* vol. 3, pp. 88–98.

tion can be more easily carried out in a country because, although it has no proletariat, it has no bourgeoisie either, only proves that he has still to learn the ABC of socialism."[52]

Among Russian revolutionaries of the 1870's attitudes to Tkachev —initially hostile—began to change under the impact of the two unsuccessful "go to the people" movements. Seeing the growing popularity of his ideas, Tkachev tried to bring out his *Tocsin* in St. Petersburg. The move was unsuccessful: the police discovered the printing plant, and the journal ceased to appear.

Shortly afterwards Tkachev moved to Paris, where he collaborated with the French "Blanquists" on their journal *Ni Dieu, ni Maître*. In 1882 he began to show symptoms of mental illness and was taken to a psychiatric hospital, where he died a few years later.

NIKOLAI MIKHAILOVSKY

Mikhailovsky's Theory of Progress

Unlike Lavrov or Tkachev, NIKOLAI MIKHAILOVSKY (1842–1904) was not a revolutionary, although he was in touch with revolutionary leaders and occasionally collaborated with them.[53] He owed his moral and intellectual authority almost entirely to his serious journalism, first for the *Annals of the Fatherland* and later (after 1892) for the journal *Russian Wealth (Russkoe Bogatstvo)*. Mikhailovsky was a prolific publicist, but his most serious theoretical contribution was in the field of sociology. The first outline of his sociological conception of history, to which he remained in all essentials faithful until the end of his life, was contained in the article "What Is Progress?," published soon after Lavrov's *Historical Letters*.

Mikhailovsky began his article with a critical assessment of Herbert Spencer's theory of progress, which he accused of overlooking a fact of fundamental importance, namely that social progress does not necessarily imply the progress of the individual human being. Following Spencer, Mikhailovsky based his argument on the definition known as "Baer's law" according to which progress in the organic world is a process of transition from simplicity (homogeneity) to complexity (heterogeneity). His conclusions, however, differed from those of Spencer: "Baer's law" suggested to him that there was an irreconcilable antagonism between Spencer's "organic

---

52. K. Marx and F. Engels, *Selected Works* (London, 1950), vol. 2, pp. 46–47.
53. See J. H. Billington, *Mikhailovsky and Russian Populism* (Oxford, 1958). As to Mikhailovsky's collaboration with revolutionaries, see above, pp. 234–35.

evolution of society" and the ideal of many-sided individual human development. Organic social development presupposes social differentiation based on the division of labor, and therefore deprives individuals of their all-around versatility and wholeness, turning them into specialized organs of an allegedly superior organic whole. The heterogeneity and complexity of society are thus in inverse proportion to the heterogeneity and complexity of its individual members. Primitive society is a homogeneous substance, but each of its members, taken separately, is a heterogeneous being and "combines within himself all the powers and capacities that can develop, given the cultural level and the local physical conditions of the times."[54] In tribal society man lives a primitive but full life, developing all his potentialities and an integral personality[55] (*tselostnaia lichnost'*). The division of labor and social differentiation destroy this equilibrium and turn men into specialized monofunctional organs of the social organism. The growth of this organism is incompatible with the growth of individuals, because the differentiation of the whole organism necessarily depends on the "simplification" of its separate organs, i.e. the loss of independence caused by one-sided specialization. Just as the human body develops (differentiates itself) at the expense of its organs, so the social organism develops at the expense of its human members. The concept "social organism" is, however, an abstraction: only man is a real organism, only his pleasures and sufferings are real, and therefore only his welfare should be the yardstick of progress. From this point of view, Mikhailovsky concluded, Spencer's formula of progress turns out to be a formula of regress. The reason is simple: "individual progress and social evolution (on the model of organic evolution) are mutually exclusive, just as the evolution of organs and the evolution of the whole organism are mutually exclusive."[56]

Mikhailovsky underpinned his argument with a philosophical interpretation of history that related the history and intellectual evolution of mankind to changes in the organization of labor or cooperation. In its general outline his scheme closely resembles that put forward by Lavrov in his *Historical Letters*; it is given a further dimension, however, because in Mikhailovsky's conception

54. Mikhailovsky, *Pol. sob. soch.*, vol. 1, p. 32 (*Russian Philosophy*, vol. 2, p. 177).

55. In Mikhailovsky's terminology the "integral" personality was the opposite of the "integrated" personality, that is a personality that had undergone a process of adjustment (integration) to the social whole. In short, he used "integrality" when he meant "all-aroundness," and "integration" when he meant specialization.

56. Mikhailovsky, *Pol. sob. soch*, vol. 1, p. 41 (*Russian Philosophy*, vol. 2, p. 180).

the "phases of intellectual development" are linked to the problem of the division of labor and its destructive effect on the human personality.

Mikhailovsky called the first important epoch in his historical scheme the "objectively anthropocentric period." Man at this time saw himself as the objective and absolute center of nature and explained all natural phenomena by referring them to himself—hence the animistic and anthropomorphic character of his religious representations. At the beginning of this period social cooperation was almost unknown. Later, when the instinct of self-preservation forced people to form groups, two types of cooperation appeared: the simple and the complex. The prototype of the first was the "free group of hunters," whereas the prototype of the second was the patriarchal family, which established the division into "men's work" and "women's work" and the subordinate role of women. Simple cooperation did not require specialization of functions and consequent social differentiation; individuals could preserve their heterogeneity (or all-around versatility) while the group remained homogeneous. In complex cooperation the reverse held true: "In the first case [simple cooperation] we have a homogeneous society whose members are differentiated, equal, free, and independent; in the second, a differentiated society whose members are unequal, unfree, one-sidedly specialized, and hierarchically subordinated to one another."[57] Simple cooperation made possible the progressive evolution of man, both physical and spiritual; complex cooperation set in motion *social* progress, the obverse of which was individual regress. The division of labor in the family, for example, increased the differences between men and women, thus depriving both sexes of a part of their human wholeness.

In the objectively anthropocentric period simple cooperation prevailed. Its final displacement by complex cooperation, with its twin evils of division of labor and social differentiation, marked the beginning of a new epoch—the "eccentric period." Mikhailovsky chose this singular name in order to emphasize the distorted vision of the world he thought characteristic of men who had been damaged by specialization: by "eccentricity" he meant a lack of center, reflecting damaged wholeness. The fragmentation of the human personality resulting from the division of labor led to a fragmented vision of the world: reality disintegrated into a number of autonomous spheres, each claiming to exist "in itself and for itself." Anthropocentricity, although nominally preserved in the religious

57. Mikhailovsky, *Pol. sob. soch.*, vol. 1, pp. 82–83.

sphere, gave way to polycentricity; natural and social phenomena began to appear to man as external and "objective" forces alien to him.

The source of this "eccentricity," in Mikhailovsky's view, was the increasing complication of human relationships. In simple co-operation everyone worked for a clearly recognizable goal, and this encouraged a feeling of solidarity and mutual understanding among the members of the group. In conditions of complex cooperation, the common aim became more and more elusive, and finally split into a multitude of separate, autonomous aims; theory became divorced from practice, and science, art, and economy no longer served man but were "ends in themselves"; men ceased to understand each other, although they were "bound together as tightly as possible."[58] This encouraged the emergence of isolated and antagonistic groups and the loss of all sense of social solidarity. An analogous process took place in the sphere of knowledge, which on the one hand broke up into narrow fields of specialization, and on the other became a metaphysical science, that is an abstract theory perceived in isolation from man and dehumanized in its allegedly "absolute" and "objective" quality. Functions that had once belonged to the all-around, whole individual were divorced from man, and ended up by living their own life and becoming indifferent, if not hostile, to each other. There is, of course, a striking resemblance between these ideas and the young Marx's comments on the alienation of man arising from the alienation of the various spheres of human activity.[59]

Mikhailovsky did not deny the great achievements of the eccentric period in the domain of art, science, and industry; but he thought that too high a price had been paid for them, and that in any case not all of them were necessarily a consequence of the division of labor. Even the modern age, he argued, had retained some enclaves of "undivided" labor; because complex cooperation had not entirely ousted simple cooperation, with its corresponding social bonds depending on community of aims and solidarity, men were still able to protect their individuality against the forces of alienation threatening its destruction. The survival of simple co-operation was, for Mikhailovsky, proof of the possibility of a human

58. *Ibid.*, p. 91.
59. Marx wrote: "The nature of alienation implies that each sphere applies a different and contradictory norm, that morality does not apply the same norm as political economy, etc., because each of them is a particular alienation of man; each is concentrated upon a specific area of alienated activity and is itself alienated from the other" (Marx, *Early Writings*, p. 173).

renaissance that would inaugurate a new epoch in history—the long-awaited epoch of universal regeneration. This new epoch Mikhail-ovsky called the "subjectively anthropocentric period": at this time man will know that objectively he is not the center of the universe, but he will recognize his "subjective" right and indeed duty to regard himself as such and to judge everything from the point of view of his own vital and indivisible human individuality.

A recapitulation of these ideas was contained in Mikhailovsky's famous "formula of progress," which reads as follows:

> Progress is the gradual approach to the integral individual, to the fullest possible and the most diversified division of labor among man's organs and the least possible division of labor among men. Everything that impedes this advance is immoral, unjust, pernicious, and unreasonable. Everything that diminishes the heterogeneity of society and thereby increases the heterogeneity of its members is moral, just, reasonable, and beneficial.[60]

From the sociological point of view this definition is very interesting indeed. It expresses the very essence of the backward-looking Populist utopia, with its idealization of the self-sufficient primitive peasant economy. Mikhailovsky frequently reaffirmed that the interests of the integral individual coincided with the interests of "undivided" nonspecialized labor, or, in other words, with the interests of the Russian peasantry. The Russian peasant, like primitive man, lived a life that was poor but full; he was economically self-sufficient; and he could therefore be called an example of an all-around and independent personality. He satisfied all his needs by his own efforts, making use of all his capacities, so that he was farmer and fisherman, shepherd and artist in one person. The peasant community was egalitarian and homogeneous, but its members had differentiated and many-sided personalities. The low level of complex cooperation enabled them to preserve their independence, whereas simple cooperation united them in mutual sympathy and understanding. This moral unity was expressed in the common ownership of the land and the self-government of the Russian *mir*.

Mikhailovsky was quite aware that the existing peasant commune had very little in common with his ideal vision of it; he put this down, however, to destructive influences from outside and the low level of simple cooperation. This particular explanation depended on a distinction Mikhailovsky had made between types and levels (or stages) of social development. From the point of view of the

60. Mikhailovsky, *Pol. sob. soch*, vol. 1, p. 150 (*Russian Philosophy*, vol. 2, p. 187).

level of development, the peasant commune could not match a factory; but at the same time it represented a higher *type* of development. The same distinction held good for peasant Russia and capitalist Europe: Western man's individuality was more highly developed, but nevertheless inferior in kind to the "integral" personality of the Russian peasant. It appears from this argument that for Mikhailovsky the "personality principle" was not something to be introduced into the village commune from outside, as Herzen had suggested; he made it clear that in defending "folk principles" he was also defending a higher type of individuality. Indeed, the very notion of individuality changed its content and came to stand for "wholeness" rather than the personal characteristics distinguishing one individual from another. It followed from this that the individuality of great scholars or thinkers—the individuality of "one-sided specialists"—represented a lower type of development: "The self of a Hegel," wrote Mikhailovsky, "is strictly speaking but a meager fraction of the human self."

It is interesting to note that although Mikhailovsky thought of the "personality principle" as a cornerstone of his world view, this line of argument brought him very close to Tkachev, who violently rejected that principle as the quintessence of bourgeois values. Mikhailovsky, of course, would never have accepted Tkachev's idea of the forced "leveling of individualities"; but nevertheless both men upheld the ideal of a homogeneous society and tried to give theoretical expression to a certain primitive peasant egalitarianism.

It is understandable that the author of the *Historical Letters* should have had many serious misgivings about Mikhailovsky's theory of progress. In a long article entitled "N. K. Mikhailovsky's Formula of Progress (1870),"[61] Lavrov set out his main objections. Abolishing the division of labor, he pointed out, would obstruct technological and scientific advance, and absolute social "homogeneity" would prevent the emergence of "critically thinking individuals," who were to be the carriers of new ideas. The implementation of Mikhailovsky's "formula of progress" would result in a stagnating, nonprogressive society; indeed, if this view of progress was accepted, it would be tantamount to proclaiming that history had always been a retrogressive process.

Lavrov's arguments did not convince Mikhailovsky. On the contrary, in his later articles Mikhailovsky's criticism of the accepted view of progress became even more radical, and the backward reference of his social ideal was given even stronger emphasis. In

---

61. Lavrov, *Formula progressa N. K. Mikhailovskogo*, pp. 12ff.

"What Is Progress?" he had shown certain reservations about accepting Rousseau's criticism of civilization, and had tried to convince his readers that he believed the "golden age" of mankind was still to come. A few years later, however, he stated explicitly in one of his articles ("On Schiller and on Many Other Things," 1876) that Rousseau and Schiller had been right in claiming that the "golden age" was already behind us.[62] A symptom of this change of perspective was the importance Mikhailovsky now attached to the idealization of the Middle Ages in Western European working class ideologies and the growing interest in archaic forms of social life shown by both socialist and conservative scholars. In "What Is Progress?" the retrospective ideal had been primitive tribal society; the Middle Ages, as an epoch of rigid social divisions, was seen as the culmination of the "eccentric" period. In fact it was a peculiar feature of Mikhailovsky's "formula of progress" that it could be turned against both feudalism and capitalism or, to be precise, against certain aspects common to both. The ideal of social homogeneity could be used as a weapon simultaneously against the division of society into separate, hermetically sealed estates and against the "complex cooperation" of capitalist society. Bourgeois progress had its positive side as a process corroding feudal privilege, but was to be rejected as a process depriving small independent producers of their economic self-sufficiency. Even in 1869 Mikhailovsky had largely concentrated on criticizing the new capitalist structure of society idealized by Spencer, although he thought of it as a mere continuation of the "eccentric" tendencies of feudalism, which had seemed to him not worth "looking back to" (with the exception of such enclaves of equality and "simple cooperation" as the military communes of the Cossacks). In the 1870's, the rapid expansion of Russian capitalism made Mikhailovsky more sensitive still to the specific and (from his point of view) negative features of the emerging bourgeois order; at the same time, too, that expansion showed in a new light some aspects of medieval society to which he had not previously paid much attention. In particular he was struck by the similarity between the peasant commune and the medieval craft guilds. Though he did not deny that the guilds and contemporary Russian communes had restricted individual potential, he appeared to be convinced that such restrictions were less harmful than the effects of capitalism. Using terminology borrowed from Marx, one might say that for Mikhailovsky the commune and guild were supe-

62. See especially Mikhailovsky's article on Schiller (Mikhailovsky, *Pol. sob. soch.* vol. 3).

rior to capitalist social structures because they represented a type of development in which human relations had not become reified; or, as he put it himself, in them "capital was not united with capital but men were united with men, individuals with individuals."[63] In the Middle Ages individuals suffered much less from the consequences of social development than under contemporary capitalism. This fact, Mikhailovsky claimed, was becoming recognized both by European workers, who "were reconstructing some purely medieval institutions" (i.e. the trade unions, in Mikhailovsky's view a reconstruction of medieval guilds), and by a growing number of scholars, who were "looking backward toward the Middle Ages and even to the more remote past."[64] Therefore there were no good reasons for maintaining that capitalism had liberated the individual or that bourgeois political economy displayed such excessive concern for his freedom or well-being that they were likely to give rise to "individualism and atomism." Individualism—in the sense of the setting of a paramount value on the human individual—was the only proper philosophical attitude to adopt, but it had absolutely nothing in common with *laissez-faire* economics. The liberal economists had their own phantom (Stirner's *Spuk*) to which they mercilessly sacrificed the freedom and welfare of concrete human beings. This new phantom was the "system of maximum production." This system was not even capable of making the rich happy because it set in motion a frantic race of ambitions and needs without offering any real hopes of satisfying them. True individualism, Mikhailovsky concluded, must look to the past, to the Middle Ages and the archaic golden age.

There is little doubt that of the various authors whose books had a formative influence on these theories, the most important was Karl Marx.[65] In volume one of *Capital* Mikhailovsky could read a dramatic account of how "great masses of men were suddenly and forcibly torn from their means of subsistence" and hurled as free and "unattached" proletarians on the labor market; by divorcing the producer from his means of production, capitalism deprived him (to use Mikhailovsky's terminology) of his economic self-suffi-

63. *Ibid.*, vol. 1, pp. 457–63.

64. *Ibid.*, p. 432. Mikhailovsky mentioned in this context such scholars as G. L. Maurer, E. Nasse, L. Brentano, Sir H. S. Maine, and E. L. Laveleye. He also wrote about Marx, saying: "Both Marx and the representatives of Kathedersozialismus display a great tolerance in their attitude toward some medieval forms of social life, such a tolerance as would, until recently, have been absolutely impossible" (*ibid.*).

65. See Mikhailovsky's articles "On the Publication of the Russian Edition of K. Marx's Book" and "Karl Marx Arraigned Before Mr. Zhukovsky."

ciency and wholeness and turned him into a specialized organ of the social organism (capitalist market mechanisms). In Marx's dialectical scheme, capitalism sets out to annihilate "medieval forms of production" (the abolition of self-earned private property, that is, the expropriation of the laborer); socialism, in turn, being the negation of the negation, will expropriate the expropriators, restoring the means of production to the producers. Like other Populists, Mikhailovsky deduced from this that in order to avoid the costs of primitive accumulation, Russia must do everything possible to bypass capitalism. Moreover, taken in conjunction with his own views, his reading of *Capital* confirmed him in the belief that socialism and "medieval forms of production"—especially the common ownership of the land preserved in the Russian peasant commune—were only different "levels" of the same type. It therefore seemed clear that the shortest way to the achievement of socialism in Russia was through developing the labor and property relations that already existed, although in a crude form, in the Russian villages and in the *artels* of the Russian artisans. Mikhailovsky's final conclusion sounds paradoxical: "The workers' question in Europe is a revolutionary question because its solution depends on restoring the means of production to the producers, that is on the expropriation of the present proprietors. In Russia the workers' question is a conservative question because its solution depends merely on keeping the means of production in the hands of the producers, that is in protecting the present proprietors against expropriation."[66]

It is clear from this argument that Mikhailovsky misinterpreted Marx by adopting only such aspects of his theories as fitted easily into the general framework of his own Populist views. Nevertheless, Marx's impact on Mikhailovsky went much deeper than this. As early as 1869, in his article on "Darwin's Theory and the Social Sciences," Mikhailovsky referred to Marx's views on the division of labor; indeed, it is not difficult to find in *Capital* many passages that Mikhailovsky could have quoted in support of his own ideas.

In chapter 14 of *Capital* (Division of Labor and Manufacture), Marx wrote:

The one-sidedness and the deficiencies of the detail laborer become perfections when he is part of the collective laborer. The habit of doing only one thing converts him into a never failing instrument, while his connexion with the whole mechanism compels him to work with the regularity of the parts of a machine. . . . In manufacture, in order to make the collective laborer and, through him, capital, rich in social pro-

66. Mikhailovsky, *Pol. sob. soch.*, vol, 1, p. 703.

ductivity power, each laborer must be made poor in individual productive powers. . . . Some crippling of body and mind is inseparable even from the division of labor in society as a whole.

In conclusion, Marx quoted with approval from D. Urquhart's *Familiar Words*: "To subdivide a man is to execute him if he deserves the sentence, to assassinate him if he does not. . . . The subdivision of labor is the assassination of a people."[67]

For Mikhailovsky, these ideas were something more than just confirmation of his own point of view; it seems more than probable that they were the real starting point for his own conceptions. No doubt it was only after reading Marx that he found references to the problem of the division of labor and its destructive effect on individual wholeness in earlier writers such as Rousseau, Ferguson, and Schiller. The fundamental premise on which this theory of progress was based—that the progress of society is incompatible with the progress of individuals—also presumably derived from Marx's view that the perfection of the "collective laborer" was achieved at the cost of the individual laborer.

In his conclusions Mikhailovsky of course differed completely from Marx. For the latter, the division of labor culminating in modern capitalism represented a tremendous step forward, enabling the laborer "to strip off the fetters of his individuality" and to "develop the capacities of his species." Mikhailovsky thought the reverse was true. Finding in Marx corroboration of Chernyshevsky's view equating "national wealth" with the poverty of the people, he proclaimed that the welfare of the people—that is the welfare of the individual laborer—must be regarded as the only yardstick of progress. Having learned from Marx about the high price of capitalist development he refused to pay this price and placed all his hopes in the alleged possibility of restoring archaic forms of social life and adapting them to new conditions. He thus became more and more attached to his backward-looking utopianism, which, by analogy with Lenin's category of "economic romanticism," might be called "sociological romanticism."

The "Struggle for Individuality"

In the mid-1870's Mikhailovsky evolved a more comprehensive sociological theory, which he called "the struggle for individuality" (a series of articles with this title appeared in 1875–76). An interesting aspect of this theory is the extent to which it reflects in-

67. K. Marx, *Capital* (Eng.-lang. ed.; M, 1954), pp. 349, 361, 363.

consistencies in the author's thought, stemming from his preoccupation with ideas he was trying to oppose. Despite his criticism of
biological "organicism" in social theory, Mikhailovsky yielded to
it in his own theoretical constructions. Though he rejected the
"method of analogy," his own theory of "the struggle for individuality" was based on biological analogies and treated society as an
organism, or at any rate as a growth threatening to turn into some
kind of superorganism whose human members would be reduced
to the role of submissive "organs." Although he accused the social
Darwinists of being apologists for bourgeois society, Mikhailovsky
himself remained within the confines of naturalism and evolutionism. The only difference was that he challenged the "organicists' "
complacent trust in the survival of the fittest with the pessimistic
theory that "natural evolution"—both in the organic world and in
human society—was accomplished at the cost of a constant lowering
of quality (in terms of "types" of development) and was therefore
a retrograde process from the point of view of the individual of
the species. The only hope, therefore, was not to "adjust oneself"
to the "natural course of events," but to join other determined individuals in the struggle to adapt society to their own aims.

Mikhailovsky's theory was founded on the proposition that there
"are different stages of individuality that struggle against each other
and try to dominate each other." This proposition was derived from
Haeckel's classification of biological organisms and his thesis that
the perfection of the whole is in direct proportion to the imperfec-
tion of its parts (and its converse). This implies that the relationship
between the whole and its parts is always antagonistic: the organ
insists on subduing the "individuality" of the cells and, at the same
time, defends itself against submission to the higher "individuality"
of the organism; the individual organism, in its turn, wages a struggle for its individuality against the higher "individuality" of the
colony. Man represents one of the stages of individuality (the sixth
stage in Haeckel's classification) and has above him a whole hierarchy of suprahuman "individualities" (factories as units of "complex cooperation," estates, classes, nations, states, etc.), all of them
also trying to dominate each other. From the point of view of the
individual, all these *social* individualities can only develop at the
cost of man's freedom and wholeness. Therefore, Mikhailovsky
concluded, "society is man's chief, closest and worst enemy, an
enemy against whom he must always be on guard."[68]

68. Mikhailovsky, *Pol. sob. soch.*, vol. 1, p. 474. Mikhailovsky's words should not
be interpreted as a declaration of extreme anarchism. He was not an etatist, but his

It must be remembered, of course, that this warning referred only to a society developing organically according to the laws of "natural evolution"—in other words to capitalist society, which according to Mikhailovsky represented the fullest victory of the social organism over the individual man. In accordance with his "formula of progress," Mikhailovsky assumed that there was a choice open to men; they could struggle against the imposition of capitalism by creating a nonorganic society based on "simple cooperation." A society of this type would not overshadow its component parts, and its welfare would coincide largely with the welfare of its individual members. Based on a minimum of "socialization" (in the sense of imposing impersonal and supra-individual social mechanisms on its members) and, at the same time, on a maximum degree of conscious human solidarity and community of interest, such a society was Mikhailovsky's ideal of true socialism. This point must be stressed, because the theory of the "struggle for individuality" leaves the impression that his ideal was rather the self-sufficiency of a lonely monad. The retrospective aspects of this ideal were connected with Mikhailovsky's romantic view of archaic social bonds, which in contrast to newer, organic ties were simple, direct, and intelligible, and which united men through a community of feelings and aims without increasing their mutual dependence. At the same time he was too much the conscious intellectual to idealize an unreflective acceptance of tradition or the merging of the individual consciousness in the collective. What he dreamed of was a community based on *conscious consent and the free and rational choice of common aims*—which meant that he was unconsciously reverting to the model of individuality that had been formed due to "bourgeois" progress, as a result of the dissolution of archaic bonds. Though he felt that all he wanted was to raise to a higher level the type of cooperation and community life represented by the archaic peasant commune, his model turned out to be a hybrid combining idealization of the precapitalist rural economy with a "bourgeois democratic" conception of individual freedom. Mikhailovsky's theories in fact exemplify both the backward- and the forward-looking faces of the Populist Janus, and they show clearly that the Populist world view owed its unity not so much to its homogeneity as to the peculiar tension existing between two sets of contradictory values.

---

chief enemy was capitalism, the most dangerous form of "complex cooperation." Like many other Populists, he even thought that state intervention could be utilized to prevent capitalist development, in the interests of human individuality.

Mikhailovsky's theory of "the struggle for individuality" had a number of subdivisions that explained, more or less ingeniously, different aspects of biological and social evolution. One of them, presented in the article "The Heroes and the Mob" (1882) dealt with problems of social psychology and the irrational behavior of crowds, and anticipated to some extent Tarde's theory of imitation. Another subtheory was concerned with "pathological magic" and explained different psychic phenomena (stigmata, mediumism, and hypnotism) as expressions of the revolt of the organs of the human body against forced submission—the result of the breakdown of the personality under the disintegrating influence of the capitalist division of labor.[69]

The most interesting of these secondary applications of the "struggle for individuality" was Mikhailovsky's theory of love,[70] which bears a striking and unexpected similarity to the theories of such romantic philosophers as Franz von Baader, who saw love as an urge to regain the lost unity of primitive androgyny. Love, argued Mikhailovsky, is a striving for reintegration through self-fulfillment in another being. The fact that this urge exists shows that there must be a sense of lost "totality" or "wholeness," and proves the superiority of hermaphroditism as a type of personality. To illustrate this idea, Mikhailovsky quoted an ancient myth told by Aristophanes in Plato's *Symposium*. Once the world was inhabited by a race of hermaphrodites, giants in stature and infinitely superior physically and intellectually to the men of today. Vaingloriously they attempted to invade Olympus, and their punishment was to be severed into two halves by the gods. These two halves, however, clung to each other and refused to be parted, so that many died of hunger. Seeing this, Zeus had pity on them and gave each half the shape of a separate human being—man or woman. Love was born of their longing for their lost unity.

The oddest aspect of Mikhailovsky's theory was that through the notion of "self-sufficiency," which the hermaphrodites had in common with the primitive peasantry, he linked this romantic longing for a lost unity to his idealization of the peasant commune. It is true, Mikhailovsky conceded, that human beings had never been hermaphrodites; but nevertheless the distinction between the two sexes had been much less marked in the past, and among the peasants it was still less marked than among the upper classes. Emphasis on the division into two different sexes, and the consequent empha-

69. See his article "Patologicheskaia magiia" (1887).
70. Mikhailovsky, *Pol. sob. soch.*, vol. 1, pp. 493–579.

sis on the importance of love, had become stronger with the progress of civilization. As might be expected, Mikhailovsky thought the explanation for this lay in the advance of the division of labor: people who were more "divided" had a greater need of love, which they hoped would help them to regain their primitive wholeness.

The Social Content of Mikhailovsky's Sociological Theory

It is a matter of dispute whether Mikhailovsky's ideas represented an important contribution to the development of sociological theory. Yet as a historical document revealing the specific nature as well as the internal contradictions and predicaments of Populist thought, his work is of the greatest interest.

Objectively, his idealization of "undivided" labor expressed the interests of the peasantry as a precapitalist social formation, the point of view of the small producer whose livelihood was threatened by industrialization. But the nature of his "peasant" program leaves no doubt that it was formulated by a member of the intelligentsia. Unlike Tolstoy, Mikhailovsky never attempted to identify his own point of view with that of the patriarchal peasantry; he was and remained an intellectual, a product of Westernization, and it was only natural for him to try and adapt his peasant utopianism to the traditions of the Russian "enlighteners" and to the view of the value of individuality generally accepted by the progressive intelligentsia. When he spoke in his own name, he called himself a "layman"—by which he meant not a narrow specialist in a particular branch of learning but a man of wide intellectual interests and all-around ability.[71] The "layman" who consciously refused to yield to pressures for the division of labor in the intellectual domain was the counterpart of the peasant in the domain of physical labor. The two were therefore natural allies in their common struggle against the "complex cooperation" of capitalism, which forced the individual to become a mere cog in a superior social mechanism.

Despite this alleged community of interests, Mikhailovsky conceded that the gulf between peasant and layman was not at all easy to bridge. He even foresaw the possibility of a conflict between the two arising out of the obscurantism of the peasantry, and therefore he was always careful to distinguish between the "interests" and the "opinions" of the people.[72] At a time when these "opinions"

71. In his series of articles "Notes of a Layman" (1875–77).

72. An entirely different point of view was put forward by Y. Yuzov (Y. I. Kablits). In his *Osnovy narodnichestva* (1882) he treats "people" and "intelligentsia" as two poles of an antithesis; his defense of the archaic traditions of the peasantry and his attacks on the intelligentsia were almost obscurantist.

were often quoted by notorious reactionaries, fond of holding up the peasantry's loyalty to the tsar as a model to the disloyal radical intelligentsia, Mikhailovsky had a tragically clear view of what such a conflict might entail: "I am a layman," he wrote. "Upon my desk stands a bust of Belinsky which is very dear to me, and also a chest with books by which I have spent many nights. If Russian life with all its ordinary practices breaks into my room, destroys my bust of Belinsky, and burns my books, I will not submit to the people from the village; I will fight. . . . And even if I should be overcome with the greatest feelings of humility and self-abnegation, I should still say at least: 'Forgive them God of Verity and Justice; they know not what they do.' For all that, I should still protest."[73]

Here is another quotation in similar vein:

The voice of the village only too often conflicts with its interests, so that what must be done—after we have sincerely and honestly identified our aims with the interests of the people—is to preserve in the village only that which is truly compatible with those interests. What I have in mind is an exchange of values with the people, an honest equal exchange, without cheating or reservations. Oh, that I might be submerged in that uncouth featureless crowd and dissolve irrevocably, yet preserving that spark of truth and idealism which I succeeded in acquiring at the cost of the people! Oh, if only all of you readers were to take the same decision, especially those whose light burns more brightly than mine and without smoking. What a great illumination there would be, and what a great historical occasion it would celebrate! Unparalleled in the annals of the past.[74]

These quotations from the *Notes of a Layman* throw light on the peculiar contradiction in Mikhailovsky's thought. Unlike Tkachev, he tried to reconcile the egalitarian ideal of social homogeneity with values that—in his own words—had been "acquired at the cost of the people," that is, as a result of the process of social differentiation he had attacked in his sociological theory. By conceding that the "spark of truth and idealism" had been acquired at the cost of the people, he was in fact returning to Lavrov's theory of "critically thinking individuals." This was tantamount to admitting that the Westernized elite in Russia represented certain values which—as Herzen had claimed—should be introduced from outside into the archaic world of the peasant commune. By the same token, Mikhailovsky partially and involuntarily rehabilited certain ideals as-

73. Mikhailovsky, *Pol. sob. soch.*, vol. 3, p. 692 (quoted in the translation by J. H. Billington in his *Mikhailovsky and Russian Populism*, p. 95).

74. Mikhailovsky, *Pol. sob. soch.*, vol. 3, p. 707.

sociated with Western bourgeois progress. This is what Lenin meant when he wrote: "When Mr. Mikhailovsky begins his 'sociology' with the 'individual' who protests against Russian capitalism as an accidental and temporary deviation from the right path, he defeats his own purpose because he does not realize that it was capitalism alone that created the conditions which made possible this protest of the individual."[75]

There is, of course, a certain polemical oversimplification in this statement, which must not be taken too literally: there is no direct causal relationship between Mikhailovsky's ideals of individuality and the rise of Russian capitalism; but it cannot be denied that the ideas of the "layman" could only appear as a result of the processes of modernization, processes begun in Europe by capitalism and brought to Russia as part of the Westernization to which the nineteenth-century Russian intelligentsia owed its existence.

The values and ideas created by these processes showed a marked tendency to become autonomous and to transcend the framework of bourgeois society, which often proved unable to realize them. This accounts for the fact that the Russian Populists were able to take them over and fit them into their negative critique of capitalism. But it proved difficult—in fact impossible—to adjust these ideals to the archaic institutions and world view of the peasants whom the Populists wished to defend against capitalist exploitation. This fundamental contradiction is a feature of almost all variants of Populism. In Mikhailovsky's utopianism the archaic peasant element predominated, but it, too, was seen through the eyes of an intellectual. The peasant element was stronger than in the views of Lavrov, the spokesman of the "critically thinking" intelligentsia, but to ignore the other element in Mikhailovsky's thought would be to give a distorted view of his role. One might say that his world view represented an interesting synthesis of an anticapitalist and backward-looking utopianism with the bourgeois-democratic Westernizing ideals of Belinsky—a synthesis that expresses very well the Populists' largely unsuccessful attempts to achieve a synthesis between the archaic world of the Russian peasantry and the ideological heritage of the Russian intelligentsia.

75. Lenin, *Collected Works*, vol. 1, p. 415.

CHAPTER 13

ANARCHISM

Besides Populism, another characteristic product of radical and socialist thought in Russia in the second half of the nineteenth century was anarchism. Both trends overlapped in a number of ways: the outstanding theorist and leader of international anarchism, Mikhail Bakunin, was also one of the men who inspired Populism; and Petr Kropotkin was a member of the Populist revolutionary movement in his youth.[1] Populism, however, developed on its home ground alone and was concerned with specifically Russian problems, whereas the Russian theorists of anarchism were active in the international workers' movement. For the anarchists, the most important problem was the abolition of the state; whereas for the Populists, the chief enemy was capitalism, and their main theoretical interest was in proving that Russia need not necessarily become capitalist. Therefore, though the two trends could appear together, they were not bound to do so. Even in the 1870's, when Bakunin's influence in the Russian revolutionary movement was at its height, there was a Populist grouping (G. Z. Eliseev, followed by V. Vorontsov and the "Legal" Populists) that thought capitalism could be fought by means of increased state interference in the social and economic sector, a postulate that was quite incompatible with anarchist tenets.

MIKHAIL BAKUNIN
Biographical Note

As we saw in Chapter 7, the first philosophical period in Bakunin's life came to a close with his famous article "The Reaction in

1. See E. Carr, *Michael Bakunin* (New York, 1961); B. Hepner, *Bakounine et le panslavisme révolutionnaire* (Paris, 1950); E. Pyziur, *The Doctrine of Anarchism of Michael A. Bakunin* (Milwaukee, Wisc., 1955); E. Lampert, *Studies in Rebellion* (London, 1957); P. Avrich, *The Russian Anarchists* (Princeton, N.J., 1967); and A. Lehning, *Michel Bakounine et ses relations avec Sergei Nečaev, 1870–1872* (Leiden, 1971). The most comprehensive and best monograph of Bakunin is the four-volume work by the Soviet historian Y. M. Steklov, *M. A. Bakunin, ego zhizn' i deiatel'nost'* (2d ed.; M, 1926–27). On Kropotkin see J. Joll, *The Anarchists* (Boston, 1965); G. Woodcock and I. Avakumović, *The Anarchist Prince* (London, 1950); and M. A. Miller, *Kropotkin* (Chicago, 1976).

Germany," which argued the need for the total revolutionary destruction of the old order. The new period that now opened can be seen largely as a preparatory stage for future political action during which Bakunin established contact with many of Europe's leading revolutionary leaders. In Switzerland he met the German utopian Communist Wilhelm Weitling (in 1843), and a little later he became well known in radical and socialist circles and among politicals émigrés in France. Here Bakunin met two thinkers who were to have an important influence on his social philosophy—Proudhon and Marx. He was also on good terms with Polish émigrés, especially with the historian Joachim Lelewel, who interested him in his theory of Slavic community self-government. He was acquainted with Mickiewicz, but was not convinced by the latter's messianic views on the role of the Slavs put forward in his lectures at the Collège de France. In 1847, at a meeting to commemorate the Polish uprising of 1831, Bakunin made a moving speech in which he declared that Russia could never be free so long as Poland had not regained her independence. This speech led to his expulsion from France at the instigation of the Russian ambassador. He went to Brussels, but soon afterwards was enabled to return by the outbreak of the revolution of 1848.

During the "Springtime of Peoples" Bakunin initially raised the banner of a "revolutionary Pan-Slavism," that is, of a free and democratic federation of all Slavic nations. He was anxious to be close to the pulse of Russian affairs and believed that the national independence movements among the Slavic nations would act as a fuse to detonate a revolution in Russia. At first he intended to go to Poznań, where he wanted to persuade the Poles to give up their "unnatural" anti-Russian alliance with German liberals and turn the uprising in Poznania into an all-Slavic revolution. As he did not have the necessary financial means, he asked the Provisional Government of the French Republic for a loan; this was granted, largely because the French feared his presence in Paris. Caussidière, the Prefect of Paris during the revolution, summed up this attitude very neatly when he said of Bakunin: "On the first day of a revolution he is a treasure; on the second he ought to be shot."

Bakunin's plans for Poznania were frustrated by the police in Berlin. He was arrested and only released after giving guarantees that he would not go to Poznan. Instead he went first to Wroclaw (Breslau) and then to Prague, where he took part in the Slavic Congress (June 2–12, 1848). At the congress he spoke as a member of the Polish section on the grounds that Polish independence was the common aim of both Russians and Poles. Together with the Poles, he stood out against the legalistic Austro-Slavic program of the Czech liberals and did his best to persuade delegates to adopt a more revolutionary stance. When the congress was interrupted by the outbreak of an armed uprising in Prague, Bakunin himself helped to man the barricades.

Bakunin's Slavic activities and his articles on this issue (e.g. "A Russian Patriot's Proclamation to All Slavs," 1848) were attacked by Marx and Engels. Their criticism was not always just, since it was based on the assumption that the Czechs and other small Slavic nations—unlike the Poles—lacked conditions for independent development, and that their independence movements were basically reactionary. The conflict was exacerbated by the fact that the *Neue Rheinische Zeitung*, edited by Marx, published an unconfirmed report (in July 1848) that Bakunin was a Russian agent. Shortly afterwards it became obvious that this was a calumny, presumably spread deliberately by the tsarist government. The paper published an apology, but Bakunin continued to harbor a grudge against Marx and suspected that he had not acted entirely in good faith. Bakunin's attitude toward Marx and Engels was also influenced by his instinctive dislike of Germans, which was greatly intensified in 1848 by the abject timidity of most German democrats and, especially, by the Frankfurt Parliament's nationalistic response to the just demands of the Slavs. (For the sake of historical truth it should be added that Marx's and Engels's attitudes toward the Frankfurt Parliament was no less critical than Bakunin's).

After the suppression of the Prague uprising, Bakunin went into hiding in Leipzig; he turned up later (in May 1849) as the most energetic leader of the revolution in Dresden. When this was put down, he was arrested and condemned to death, though this sentence was later commuted to life imprisonment. He was then handed over to the Austrian government, and after spending a year in a Prague prison and in the fortress at Olomouc (where he was chained to the wall) he was again condemned to death. The sentence was not carried out, however, as the tsarist authorities now demanded his extradition as a dangerous political conspirator.

On arrival in St. Petersburg, Bakunin was imprisoned in the famous Peter and Paul Fortress. As in the trial of the Decembrists, Nicholas I now played the part of the paternal sovereign anxious to know what inner motives had led one of his subjects to adopt such evil ways. This was how Bakunin came to write his famous *Confessions*, giving a detailed account of his activities after leaving

Russia. This document, which was not published until 1921, is very strange indeed. Bakunin began by expressing his respect for Nicholas I as the only sovereign who had not lost confidence in his imperial calling, and referred to himself as a "repentant sinner"; at the same time his tone was far from humble and he refused to give any testimony that might incriminate anyone other than himself. He painted a gloomy picture of social evils not only in Western Europe (which met with the emperor's approval), but also in Russia which, he declared, was set apart from other countries by the pervasive rule of fear and deception. He confessed that he might have been mistaken in his endeavors so far, but did not offer to give up his impetuous designs. What is more, he even attempted to convert his "father confessor," suggesting that he assume the mantle of liberator of the downtrodden Slavic nations.

In 1854 Bakunin was transferred to the Schlüsselburg Fortress, and three years later the new emperor, Alexander II, allowed him to settle in Siberia. Thanks to the influence of his uncle, the governor-general of Eastern Siberia, Count Nikolai Muraviev-Amursky, Bakunin was permitted to live in Irkutsk and to enter government service. He married a Polish woman (Antonina Kwiatkowska) and soon regained his earlier revolutionary fervor. In 1861 he escaped by way of Japan and the United States, and joined his old friends Herzen and Ogarev in London. Right away he became involved in two important developments: the "thaw" in Russia following the emancipation edict, and the patriotic demonstrations in Poland. In connection with the situation in Russia he published a pamphlet entitled *The People's Cause: Romanov, Pugachev, or Pestel?* (1862), in which he suggested that the crisis might be resolved by convening a Land Assembly and transforming the "Petersburg imperial ruler" into a "people's tsar." When the January uprising broke out in Poland, he gave active backing to Teofil Lapinski's hopeless attempt to organize a surprise raid in order to provide support for the insurgents. After the suppression of the uprising he transferred his hopes to Italy—a country with a tradition of conspiratorial political societies and with especially tense unresolved social conflicts. He now became more radical in his outlook: the cause of national independence and political liberties began to pale by comparison with the paramount issue of social revolution, which in Western Europe was to be carried out by the working class, and in Russia by the peasantry.

In 1868 Bakunin became interested in the international League for Peace and Freedom, which he tried to turn into an instrument of his own ideas and plans. With this in view he wrote the lengthy but unfinished essay "Federalism, Socialism, Anti-theologism," which was the first mature expression of his anarchism. Having lost patience with the League's deep-rooted bourgeois liberalism, he founded his own international organization, called Alliance of Socialist Democracy, and began a campaign to have it affiliated—as a separate autonomous body—with the First International. When this maneuver was rejected, the Alliance was disbanded and its members joined the International's various sections. This was, however, a purely tactical measure, for Bakunin's supporters only joined the International in order to polemicize with the dominant faction represented by Marx and the General Council. Bakunin accused Marx of dictatorial centralism, of "etatism," and in fact of betraying the revolution by concentrating on legal struggle for reforms and political rights. He regarded Marx as a spokesman of the skilled workers in the bourgeois countries, who in his view were themselves deeply imbued with bourgeois tendencies; he himself claimed to represent the "proletariat of misery," the laboring masses of the poor and backward countries. In his polemics with Marx Bakunin often played unscrupulously on the anti-German sentiments of the Italian and French workers, even at times sounding an anti-Semitic note. Something that exacerbated relations right at the outset was the Nechaev affair, in which Bakunin had involved the International without authorization, compromising it in the eyes of world public opinion. The General Council, for its part, responded with a determined and bitter struggle against the Bakunin line. The final outcome was the resolution passed at the Hague Congress (September 1872) expelling Bakunin for dissenting activities and personal irregularities. The latter accusation was not entirely just, as many supporters of Marx were later to admit. Bakunin had taken an advance payment for translating Marx's *Capital*, and after failing to produce the work was said to have blackmailed the publisher when he asked for a return of his money.

The General Council had to pay dearly for its victory: in effect the split was to put an end to the first International. Weakened by the removal of Bakunin's supporters, who opened their own anarchist organization, the International moved its headquarters to New York and shortly ceased to function. The last congress took place in Philadelphia in 1876. Bakunin died on July 1 of the same year, and the anarchist International closed down a year later.

Bakunin's last years were spent in a fever of revolutionary activity. In 1871 he took part in an uprising in Lyon, in 1873 in the

Spanish revolution instigated by his followers, and in 1874 in a rebellion in Bologna. All these enterprises ended in failure, and the aging Bakunin almost lost his life on the barricades—the death he apparently most desired. During these years he also found time to write his most important theoretical works: *The German Empire of the Knout and Social Revolution* (1870–71), and *State and Anarchy* (1873).

Bakunin's Philosophical Views

During his anarchist years Bakunin thought of himself as a consistent materialist, atheist, and positivist. As the greatest thinkers of his time he admired Feuerbach, Comte, Proudhon, and Marx. From Feuerbach he took over the notion of religious alienation—the assumption that man, the creator of God, became the slave of his own creature and that "as heaven became richer, earth became poorer." Comte he praised for transcending the theological and metaphysical stages of thought with the help of "positive science," and for conceiving of philosophy as a systematization of the data of the individual sciences. In his analysis of the differences between positivism and materialism, Bakunin called Comte a thinker who, in contrast to Hegel, had "materialized the spirit by showing that the sole basis of psychic phenomena is matter."[2] Proudhon he admired not only as a great theorist of anarchism, but also as a philosopher who had attempted to transcend historical idealism. The most important contribution in this sphere had admittedly been made by Marx, whom Bakunin admired as a thinker even when he was most at loggerheads with him over political issues. By building his argument on an "abstract idea of law," Bakunin wrote, Proudhon had remained committed to idealism and metaphysics; Marx, by contrast, had proved scientifically that the economic structure of society preceded and determined its legal and political structure.[3] Bakunin considered Marx to be the greatest economist of his day and called *Capital* a "magnificent" work. Nonetheless, he accused its author of making a fetish of his own discovery—that is, of the dependence of ideals on "economic facts"—thus encouraging a fatalistic interpretation of history.

Bakunin, like Marx and Engels, thought that the basic problem of philosophy was the dispute between materialists and idealists. In accepting materialism he was prompted not only by theoretical

2. M. Bakunin, *Izbrannye sochineniia*, preface by James Guillaue (Petrograd-Moscow, 1919–22), vol. 3, pp. 149, 154.
3. *Ibid.*, vol. 1, pp. 246–47.

considerations but also—and even primarily—by moral principles. "By making things that are human divine," he declared, "idealists invariably pave the way for the victory of brutal materialism. . . . All those who defend idealism are inevitably drawn into the camp of the oppressors and exploiters of the masses."[4] In practical day-to-day affairs, he argued, it is materialism that is the real idealism; this is because every development contains within itself the negation of an attitude or starting point, so that if the starting point is material, then the negation must be ideal. In this way materialism leads to true idealism, postulates the complete and entire liberation of society, and holds aloft "the red standard of economic equality and social justice."[5] Bakunin illustrated his argument by pointing to the contrasting examples of Italy, which he considered to be a country with a materialistic civilization, and Germany, the home of the most lofty idealism. In Italy, he wrote, it was possible to breathe freely, whereas the name of Germany was "synonymous with brutal and triumphant servility."[6] In compensating for the shortcomings of real life by a spiritual flight into the sphere of metaphysical ideas, the Germans had become the worst kind of philistines, servile henchmen and obedient executors of the most antihumanitarian orders of the government: "One might say that the more noble-minded the ideal universe of a German is, the more repulsive and shabby are his life and his actions in the sphere of concrete reality."[7]

Man is himself a product of nature, Bakunin argued, and therefore the starting point of his development is the animal stage. The first step toward his emancipation is thought—the act of abstraction —the awakening of reason to which man owes his ability to arrive at a conscious self-definition, to control his instinctive reflexes, to perceive the interdependencies of the objects surrounding him, and to transform his environment in accordance with his needs.[8] Initially, however, man thinks in images; he therefore hypostatizes his own abstractions and, while overcoming his animality, becomes a slave to the products of his own imagination. The supreme and most dangerous of these personified abstractions is God. The creation of the Deity was a historical necessity but at the same time a terrible error and misfortune. The idea of God is the most emphatic negation of human freedom. Every religion—and especially Christianity —implies the "impoverishment, subjugation, and annihilation of humanity in favor of divinity";[9] every religion is cruel, sanctifies

4. *Ibid.*, vol. 2, pp. 179, 184.
5. *Ibid.*, p. 184.
6. *Ibid.*, p. 181.
7. *Ibid.*, vol. 1, p. 231.
8. *Ibid.*, vol. 3, pp. 170–71.
9. *Ibid.*, vol. 2, p. 159.

the principle of sacrificing life to abstractions, and continually demands blood. Hence the annihilation of God is a necessary precondition of human freedom. Reversing Voltaire's well-known aphorism, Bakunin wrote: "If there were really a God, one would have to make sure he ceased to exist."[10]

It is clear, therefore, that Bakunin called for a rejection of God not only in the name of science but also (and above all) in the name of freedom. This fitted in with his overall conviction that in order to achieve total emancipation it was not enough to rely on thought —rebellion was equally important. Man had become human through an act of insubordination and cognition; therefore his model should be Satan, "the eternal rebel, first freethinker and first fighter for the emancipation of the universe."[11] The whole of human history was a triad in which stage one, animality, was followed by stage two, thought, and stage three, revolt. In a synchronic interpretation of society these three stages had their counterparts in the three spheres of economics, science, and freedom.

For Bakunin (as for Feuerbach), the prototype of all forms of idealism were religion and theology. That was why he insisted that the victory of materialism and positivism over idealistic philosophical systems was synonymous with the victory of freedom. A materialist or positivist approach in science (for Bakunin there was little difference between the two) meant working out a view of the world "following the natural path, from the bottom upward," and not, as in idealism, "from the top down, from the center to the periphery." The fact that nature was subject to causality was not incompatible with freedom, because freedom was the opposite of external constraint, not of internal necessity. The laws to which man as a product of nature must submit were the laws of his own being, against which it would be absurd to revolt. Freedom should be opposed not to determinism but to coercion and different forms of alienation, as represented by religion and the state. There was nothing humiliating in dependence on the laws of nature; this could not be called slavery, for "there is no slavery without a master, a lawgiver who is external to the being to whom the commands are given."[12]

Though Bakunin stressed the importance of science as a force liberating men from theology and all external dictates, he criticized it for its tendency to reduce to a regular pattern the infinite diver-

10. *Ibid.*, p. 163.
11. *Ibid.*, p. 145.
12. *Ibid.*, p. 164.

sity of life. He rebelled against scientific abstractions in the name of the particular, of the individual flavor that could not be expressed in abstract concepts or explained by theories. This anti-intellectual strand in Bakunin's world view provided a link between the anarchist philosophy of his maturity and the romanticism of his youth; at the same time it was an interesting anticipation of Bergsonian ideas and the idealistic "philosophy of life"[13] a startling association considering that Bakunin thought of himself as a materialist and follower of positivism). The essence of life, he declared, is spontaneity, unforced creativity that does not yield to rationalization. Science is always "unchanging, impersonal, general, and abstract," and abstractions, as history teaches, easily become transformed into vampires feeding on human blood.[14] Science is indispensable to man, but to give science the power to govern men—even though it were "positive science," without any trace of idealism—would prove fatal. Men of learning, like theologians, can neither understand nor sympathize with individual and living creatures; they would always be ready to accommodate life to theory, to experiment on the body of society—something that must be prevented at all costs.[15]

The cutting edge of these arguments was directed against Marxism. Bakunin regarded Marx as a typical doctrinaire thinker and felt that the very term "scientific socialism" revealed a tendency to give science authority over life, to make the "untaught" masses subservient to the "learned" leaders of the Social Democratic party.[16]

Bakunin's Social Philosophy

Because of its emphasis on the importance of the collective, Bakunin's anarchism differed from the individualist anarchism of Proudhon and was at the opposite pole from the antisocial and amoral anarchism of Marx Stirner. Unlike Stirner, Bakunin did not rebel against society or glorify egoism; on the contrary, he made it clear that to rebel against society was as senseless as to rebel against the laws of nature. Dependence on laws governing social behavior does not restrict the autonomy of the individual, because social norms—unlike political legislation—have not been imposed by an alien will but represent an inner necessity. Where there are no

13. See H. Temkinowa, *Bakunin i antynomie wolności* [*Bakunin and the Antinomies of Freedom*] (Warsaw, 1964), pp. 95–96.
14. Bakunin, *Izbr. soch.*, vol. 2, pp. 192–96.
15. *Ibid.*, p. 193.
16. *Ibid.*, vol. 1, p. 295.

external dictates, a sense of freedom and fulfillment are only possible within society, for they arise from the spontaneous fusion of the individual will with the will of the collective.

As these arguments show, Bakunin's anarchism was founded on a view of state and society as diametrical opposites; society is man's natural element, providing a form of internalized control, whereas the state is an alien, antisocial force that must be destroyed in order to liberate the social instinct deeply embedded in the human personality (Bakunin glossed over the fact that in revolutionary practice it would hardly be possible to differentiate between the two spheres). Society is a product of nature, whereas the "social contract," with its postulate of a superior presocial state and its view of society as a mechanical and entirely artificial aggregate of individuals, is a harmful metaphysical theory that in practice (regardless of the liberal intentions of those who hold it) sanctions the absolute authority of the state.[17] The entire political-legislative sphere is, in fact, an artificial product of the stage of thought in human evolution, and politics is closely related to theology: both assume that man is evil by nature and must be restrained and subjected to enforced discipline. Every state is essentially a temporal Church, and every Church nothing but a divine state.[18] Using more modern terminology, we might say that Bakunin thought of the state as an alienated social force that expands by tearing apart "vital" and "natural" social bonds. It is worth adding that he recognized certain parallels between his own conception and Konstantin Aksakov's view of the state as an "external truth," "the principle of evil, of external constraint."[19] This partial identity of views is interesting because it reveals that anarchism, too, had a tendency to look backward—a tendency expressed most clearly in its idealization of the nonrationalized, prepolitical level of social life.

In attacking all forms of political organization—monarchies as well as republics—Bakunin also appealed to a universalist ideal. The state, he wrote, is "the most flagrant, the most cynical, and the most complete contradiction of everything human";[20] because it divides people from each other, sets the citizens of one country against the citizens of another, and arrogates to itself absolute sovereignty, it nullifies the universal bonds of human solidarity. The

17. *Ibid.*, vol. 3, pp. 184–85.
18. *Ibid.*, p. 195.
19. See V. J. Bogucharsky, *Aktivnoe narodnichestvo semidesiatykh godov* (M, 1912), pp. 20–21.
20. Bakunin, *Izbr. soch.*, vol. 3, p. 190.

patriotism cultivated by governments is essentially a means of justifying all crimes as long as they are committed at the behest of the
authorities. The most perfect embodiment of the *esprit d'état* is
the German officer, "a civilized beast, a lackey by conviction and
an executioner by vocation"; a man who combines "education with
boorishness, boorishness with valor, orderliness with bestiality, and
bestiality with a curious honesty"; someone who is always ready in
an instant "to slaughter tens, hundreds, thousands of human beings
at the merest nod on the part of his superior officers."[21]

These arguments of Bakunin's were directed not only against the
bourgeois state but also against what he called "state socialism"—
a trend represented in his view by Marx and Lassalle (Bakunin ignored the essential differences between the two). Socialism and freedom, he insisted, must be inseparable; "freedom without socialism
means privilege and injustice," but "socialism without freedom
means slavery."[22] It was because freedom could not be reconciled
with political organization that it was necessary to strive to abolish
states or at least to transform them by a thoroughgoing decentralization that would grant every constituent part the chance of voluntary secession. Social organization ought to proceed "from the bottom up" in keeping with the true needs and natural tendencies of
society's different parts. In this fashion "individuals and associations, communes and districts, provinces and nations, would unite
on the principle of a free federation to form—humanity."[23]

A characteristic aspect of Bakunin's social vision was his demand
for the "abolition of science as a moral entity existing outside the
social life of the community and represented by a body of titled
scholars."[24] Science ought to be the property of all, and this goal
could be attained by equal universal education for everyone. Once
it belonged to the community and had lost its own separate organization, science would lower its aspirations for a time but in return
would become a part of real life, would be better able to serve the
needs of real life, and would cease to produce an arrogant and socially destructive aristocracy of the intellect.

On the issue of private property Bakunin was far less radical than
Tkachev: the latter's egalitarian communism did not suit Bakunin's
ideal of freedom and dislike of uniformity. Nevertheless, he was
utterly opposed to the right of inheritance. The sole heir of all dead

21. *Ibid.*, vol. 1, pp. 158–61.
22. *Ibid.*, vol. 3, p. 147.
23. *Ibid.*, pp. 192–93.
24. *Ibid.*, vol. 2, p. 201.

men ought to be "a public fund devoted to the upbringing and education of all children of both sexes and providing for their maintenance until they reach maturity."[25]

When describing his collectivist ideal, Bakunin occasionally referred to the "ancient social instincts of the Russian people," whose institutional expression was the village commune. His attitude to the commune was not entirely uncritical. He discussed the issue in some detail in an essay published as Appendix A to *State and Anarchy*. In the essay he listed the three main positive features of "the ideal of the Russian people." These were (1) the conviction that the whole of the land ought to belong to the people, (2) the attachment to the communal ownership of land, and (3) the principle of self-government and consequent hostility to officials and state institutions. There were, however, three negative features as well, namely (1) patriarchalism, (2) the engulfing of the individual by the *mir*, and (3) faith in the tsar.[26] For these reasons Bakunin did not believe in the commune as a revolutionary force, although he held the archaic collectivism of the peasantry in high esteem. At the same time he was convinced that the revolution could only be carried out by means of the people and in the name of popular ideals, and he had a deep-rooted faith in the vitality of the great tradition of the peasant revolts of Stenka Razin and Pugachev. He was therefore bound to believe that within the people itself slumbered a revolutionary force capable at any moment of challenging the patriarchal conservatism of the commune, and impelling the masses to revolt against the artificial civilization of the state.

Bakunin pointed to the long history of robber bands in Russia as proof of the existence of such a revolutionary force. "Brigandage," he wrote, "is an important historical phenomenon in Russia"; the first rebels, the first revolutionists in Russia, Pugachev and Stenka Razin, "were brigands."[27] This idealization of peasant banditry—the most archaic form of social protest—was one of the most characteristic aspects of Bakuninism. The English Marxist historian E. J. Hobsbawm has called Bakunin a classic example of a markedly archaic and romantic revolutionist.[28] In the nineteenth century Bakunin's variety of anarchism, which struck roots to a remarkable

---

25. *Ibid.*, vol. 3, p. 146.

26. Like Belinsky, Bakunin considered the peasantry's religious devotion to be superficial and therefore did not list it as one of the aspects of the ideal.

27. Quoted from *Bakunin on Anarchy*, ed., trans., and with an Introduction by Sam Dolgoff (New York, 1972), p. 347.

28. See E. J. Hobsbawm, *Primitive Rebels. Studies in Archaic Forms of Social Movement in the 19th and 20th Centuries* (Manchester, 1963), p. 165.

extent in Italy and Spain (especially in Andalusia), was the political movement that best reflected the spontaneous revolutionary aspirations of backward peasant populations.[29]

Bakunin's ideas exerted an important influence on the Populism of the 1870's and were mentioned in that context in the previous chapter. Of the two factions that took part in the 1873–74 "Go to the People" movement, the Bakuninites were in the majority, representing the "romantic" side of the movement; they appealed to the *emotions* and *instincts* of the peasants, whereas the Lavrovites (the other faction) wished to *teach* the peasants, to mold their consciousness. The Bakuninites were also rightly known as "rebels," believing with Bakunin that the Russian peasants were always ready to rise in rebellion; they accordingly went to the villages—particularly in the Ukraine and Volga regions—hoping to resuscitate the traditions of the Cossack peasant uprisings. The followers of Lavrov (the "propagandists") went to the villages with the peaceful propaganda of socialist ideas, hoping to enlighten the peasants and prepare them for a future revolution that would be a conscious enterprise rather than a spontaneous revolt. Both factions thought highly of the peasant commune, but the Lavrovites were much less inclined to idealize its archaic features; what they prized was not so much existing social relations as the socialist potentialities of commune self-government. Both factions rejected the struggle for "political freedom" as "bourgeois" and "deceptive," but whereas the Lavrovites were sympathetic to the German Social Democratic Party, the Bakuninites regarded it as a party that was betraying the ideals of revolutionary socialism.

PETR KROPOTKIN

Biographical Note

The other leading figure in nineteenth-century anarchism was Prince PETR KROPOTKIN (1842–1921), a member of an ancient noble family that claimed to trace its ancestry back to Rurik, the legendary founder of the first Russian state. After completing his education at the *Corps de Pages* in St. Petersburg (where future high government officials were trained), he astonished his relations and teachers by chosing the modest post of officer in a Siberian Cossack regiment in the Amur district of Transbaikalia. During his years in Siberia (1862–67) he carried out research into local ethnography, geology, and geography (for his work he received a gold medal and

29. *Ibid.*, pp. 82–83.

was appointed secretary of the Imperial Russian Geographical Society). The bloody suppression of a revolt among Polish exiles in Transbaikalia led him to decide to give up army service—which he felt could not be reconciled with his convictions—and to devote himself to scientific work at the University of St. Petersburg. In 1872, on a visit to Switzerland, he joined the Bakuninite wing of the International Workingmen's Association, gave up his promising career at the university, and threw himself wholeheartedly into revolutionary activities. He was one of the founders of the Populist Chaikovsky Circle, for whom he drafted a program entitled "Should We Undertake to Consider the Ideal System of the Future?" (1873). At the time of the "Go to the People" movement, he very successfully carried out revolutionary propaganda among the workers of St. Petersburg. In 1874 he was arrested and imprisoned in the Peter and Paul Fortress; two years later he planned a daring escape, which friends outside (with whom he communicated by means of a special code) helped him to put into effect. His escape infuriated tsarist officialdom, but in spite of an intensive police search he managed to flee abroad. He settled in Switzerland and was soon recognized as one of the chief theorists and leaders of international anarchism. In 1879 he founded the famous anarchist journal Le Révolté. After being expelled from Switzerland in 1881, he moved to France, where he was arrested two years later and sentenced to five years imprisonment. He was amnestied in 1886, after a successful campaign for his release, and settled in London, where he wrote his more important works. After the February Revolution of 1917 he returned to Russia, but was not active in politics; he settled in Dmitrovo, near Moscow, and pursued his studies. Although he had important reservations about the October Revolution, in 1920 he issued an appeal to the workers of Western Europe to oppose all attempts by their governments to overthrow the young Soviet republic.

Kropotkin's best-known book is the celebrated *Memoirs of a Revolutionist*, written in English for the *Atlantic Monthly* (1898–99), in which he gives a vivid account of his life, including his celebrated escape. His theoretical views are contained in *The Conquest of Bread* (written in French, 1892);[30] *Anarchism: Its Philosophy and Ideal* (in French, 1896);[31] *Mutual Aid, a Factor of Evolution* (in English, 1904); *The State, Its Historic Role* (in French, 1906);[32]

---

30. English translation published in New York in 1913, reissued in 1968.

31. English translations published in London in 1897 and in San Francisco in 1898.

32. English translation published in London in 1903, reissued in 1943.

and *Ethics,* written in Russian and published posthumously in 1922. Kropotkin is also the author of a valuable history of the French Revolution *(La Grande Révolution,* 1917).

Kropotkin's Philosophy of History

Kropotkin's classic work *Mutual Aid, a Factor of Evolution* was an attack on the unrestrained competition of capitalist society and its defense by the social Darwinists. As a natural scientist, Kropotkin thought of himself as a Darwinist also, but he felt that the facts discovered by Darwin had been given a one-sided interpretation: though he was ready to concede that the struggle for survival and the "self-affirmation of the individual through competition" were important factors in evolution, he drew attention to another, equally important factor whose validity, he maintained, Darwin had accepted (though apologists for capitalism passed over it in silence). This factor was cooperation between members of the same species. Examples of cooperation or mutual aid were common in the animal world, Kropotkin argued. There were highly organized animal communities, such as anthills, where competition was unknown. As they progressed up the ladder of evolution, animal societies formed more highly organized and more "conscious" social groups that allowed individual members greater independence without depriving them of the benefits of social organization (Kropotkin cited beaver colonies as an example).[33]

Primitive human communities were also based on mutual aid, Kropotkin contended. He dismissed as absurd the idea that during an allegedly presocial state primitive man had been engaged in a constant struggle against others of his species. Unrestrained individualism, he insisted, was the product of modern times and would have been incomprehensible to so-called "savages." Tribal or clan communities lived by the principle of mutual solidarity, sharing food supplies and putting on public view all the trophies any individual member had acquired during the course of the year. This principle was only applied within the clan, and regrettably the "dual morality" that divided people into "us" and "them" had still not been abolished.

The emergence of separate families disrupted the clan and ushered in a new and higher stage of evolution, which Kropotkin called "barbarism." The basic social unit and organization through which mutual aid was realized at this time was the rural commune—now no longer a clan based on blood bonds but a neighborhood unit.

33. *Mutual Aid, a Factor of Evolution* (Boston, 1955), chap. 2.

The populations of all countries had passed through the stage of rural communes (Kropotkin illustrated his argument with examples taken from the works of the English historian Sir Henry Maine); the communes had shown great vitality and had not disappeared by themselves, whatever apologists for bourgeois individualism might say to the contrary. In England rural communes had partially survived until the eighteenth century, and in France they had only been destroyed by the legislation of Turgot and the French Revolution.

In the Middle Ages urban communities had reached a particularly advanced stage of mutual aid. Kropotkin thought that the great age of the medieval free cities (including the Russian city-states of Novgorod and Pskov) represented the highest peak in the history of mankind. Material civilization developed rapidly then and brought immediate benefits to the urban populace (in this the age differed from that of the Industrial Revolution); neither before nor after were manual workers so well off. Medieval towns were informal associations of streets, parishes, and craft or trade guilds. Kropotkin thought particularly highly of the guilds as organizations that had perfected, on a higher level, the cooperative principle of the older rural communes. By restricting competition and establishing an efficient system of mutual aid for their members, the medieval guilds guaranteed stability and prosperity; work was a pleasure and the distinction between craftsman and artist was almost negligible. The magnificent medieval cathedrals were testimony to the high level of both the craftsmanship and the artistry of the age.

On reading these reflections, two other nineteenth-century thinkers immediately spring to mind: the Englishmen John Ruskin and William Morris. Ruskin, a writer who turned from art criticism to criticism of social evils, also admired the medieval cathedrals and condemned industrial civilization in the name of an ideal of beauty. Morris, a poet whose cult of the Middle Ages led him to try and revive medieval craft techniques in printing and wallpaper design, was—like Kropotkin—active in the socialist movement. Kropotkin himself was aware of the similarity in their views and called Morris the only Englishman who understood the Middle Ages and gave them their due.[34]

In the sixteenth century the civilization of the free cities was destroyed. Although Kropotkin was aware that growing social antagonisms within the towns were partly responsible for their decline, he thought that outside factors were more to blame. The cities were

34. *The State, Its Historic Role* (London, 1943), p. 19.

invaded by "new barbarians"—kings, prelates, and lawyers (representatives of the Roman tradition)—who joined forces in order to impose their rule and establish a single center of government. This led—for the first time in the history of Christian civilization—to the establishment of the state in the true meaning of the word, that is (according to Kropotkin's definition), to "the concentration of the leadership of local life in one centre, or in other words territorial concentration," and to "the concentration of many or even all functions of the life of society in the hands of a few."[35] The prototype and consciously imitated model of the new state was ancient Rome; its basic aim was to tear apart all immediate human bonds in order to become the sole force linking men and to prevent the emergence of "states within the state." The old federalist spirit—the spirit of unforced initiative and voluntary agreements—withered away and was replaced by the spirit of discipline, of a "pyramidal" (hierarchical) organization of government.[36]

The bourgeois revolutions against absolute monarchies did not change the overall trend in social evolution—on the contrary, they helped to establish this trend more firmly by attacking what was left of the corporate spirit of the Middle Ages. The French Revolution was a late offspring of the Roman juridical tradition (in a republican interpretation), and it refused to accept the survival of enclaves of common law and gave the last, mortal blow to the rural communes. In the postrevolutionary period the "etatist" spirit penetrated deeply into even those social and political movements that questioned the existing system and were opposed to the class government of the bourgeoisie. The contemporary radical, Kropotkin declared, "is a centralizer, a state partisan, a Jacobin to the core, and the socialist walks in his footsteps."[37]

One would suppose that this diagnosis could only lead to pessimistic conclusions. Kropotkin, however, was an incurable optimist with a deep-rooted belief in man's innate goodness, the spirit of cooperation, and a future based on the avoidance of force in human relations. He was convinced that, despite many defeats, the natural bent for cooperation had not died out in the masses but was only buried deep in their unconscious.[38] Revolutionaries whose object was to bring about a radical transformation of the world should, therefore, base their efforts on this natural instinct. It was a danger-

35. *Ibid.*, p. 10.
36. *Ibid.*, pp. 28–29.
37. *Ibid.*, p. 41.
38. *Mutual Aid, a Factor of Evolution*, p. 223.

ous illusion to suppose that the state—which throughout its history had prevented men from becoming united, suppressed freedom, and paralyzed local initiative—could now suddenly change into its opposite. A choice would have to be made between two conflicting traditions: one Roman and authoritarian, the other popular and free.[39]

Kropotkin's opposition of two traditions and two types of human relationships can be compared to the two contrasting types of social bonds—"community" and "society"—posited by T. Tönnies, who was mentioned earlier in this book in connection with the Slavophiles.[40] Tönnies, like Kropotkin, contrasted organic communal bonds based on mutual cooperation (*Gemeinschaft*) with bonds based on the assumption that society is an aggregate of conflicting individuals whose relations must be regulated by a strong external state apparatus (*Gesellschaft*). Like Kropotkin, he regarded the rural commune and medieval cities as examples of the former, organic type of bond, and Roman civilization and capitalism (based on competition, synonymous with conflict) as classic examples of the latter type of bond. This comparison cannot, of course, be taken too far: Kropotkin, for instance, did not emphasize the role of tradition or religion in the formation of communal bonds, or the importance of rationalism in establishing political-legal bonds—those aspects of Tönnies's sociological theory that are paralleled most closely in the Slavophile conceptions. Nevertheless, the comparison with Tönnies throws an interesting light on the sociological content of Kropotkin's philosophy of history, explaining in particular his characteristic tendency to idealize archaic forms of social cohesion. This tendency was something he had in common with the Slavophiles, although Slavophilism was a gentry ideology, whereas Kropotkin's anarchism—like Russian Populism—was a nostalgic expression of the longing for a lost ideal community of immediate producers, craftsmen, and peasants.

Kropotkin's Vision of the Future

In contrast to Bakunin, who was more interested in criticism of existing social relations and the actual act of revolution, Kropotkin might be called a systematizer of anarchism. In his book *The Conquest of Bread*, for instance, he set out in great detail his vision of an anarchist utopia. Another difference in emphasis is that Kropotkin's anarchism was not only collectivist but also commu-

39. *The State, Its Historic Role*, pp. 41–44.
40. See above, pp. 108–9.

nist in character. The immediate aim of the social revolution, he declared, should be to transform economic relations in keeping with the principle "to each according to his needs." The principle "to each according to his work," he thought, did not ensure social justice and was incompatible with personal freedom: there were many different types of work that were obviously not comparable, and therefore settling the value of any particular task would entail bargaining or, in other words, constant conflict. This, in turn, would make it necessary to set up some kind of authority above the community to act as mediator and ensure social harmony. In practice, therefore, "work credits" would not differ from money.

Kropotkin was convinced that the enormous production potential of modern technology would make it easy to implement the communist principle of paying "each according to his needs." The scheme he proposed was set out in considerable detail. If technology were harnessed to the common sense and resourcefulness found among the common people, he suggested, the results would exceed all expectations: the workday could be reduced to four or five hours, and output would show a fourfold increase in industry as well as in agriculture. Members of communist communities would be obliged to work a certain number of hours and in return would be able to satisfy their basic needs for food, accommodation, education, etc. without restriction; those who wanted more than this would be able to produce luxury goods in their spare time. Kropotkin was optimistic about the future of his scheme and suggested that it was already being applied in capitalist countries where public libraries made their books available to all borrowers, and where season tickets could be used for unlimited travel over certain distances.

One of the problems Kropotkin had to consider was what should be done with people who were too lazy to work. No one is lazy by nature, he argued, and if exceptions occur they too deserve to have their basic needs satisfied, since every human being is entitled to stay alive. Nevertheless, the community would have to treat such individuals differently from its other members and deal with them as if they were sick or social misfits. The inborn human dislike of being isolated would be enough to induce such people to join in the common tasks (unless they really were sick). On the other hand, any persons who consciously rejected the basic principles of communism would be permitted to quit the community and look for something that suited them better. Possibly they would choose like-minded companions and establish a new community founded on different principles.[41] There would be very few such people, Kropotkin assumed, so that their noncommunist enclaves would not represent a threat to the principles of social cooperation accepted by the great majority.

Kropotkin was an opponent of the division of labor, as were Tolstoy and Mikhailovsky, although he avoided extremes in his views on the subject; he realized that certain types of work required specialization, and in any case he assumed that in his ideal society thousands of different specialist associations would cater to different tastes. What he was absolutely firm about, however, was that the division between physical and mental work must be abolished. People who wanted to write and publish books, for instance, ought to join together to form associations, establish printing presses, train as compositors, and print their own works. No doubt some books would be slimmer, Kropotkin commented, but in size rather than substance.[42]

The injurious division into mental and physical labor was a subject Kropotkin had touched on even earlier when, as a member of the Chaikovsky Circle, he had drafted a blueprint for the ideal social system of the future. In it he had insisted that even scholars of genius ought not to be exempt from carrying out various unpleasant manual tasks: "A Darwin employed in clearing away refuse only strikes people as preposterous because they cannot get rid of notions borrowed from present-day society."[43] Not only the privilege of birth but also the privilege of education would have to be abolished as one of the sources of social inequality.

Rather than call for a leveling "down," however, as Tkachev had done, Kropotkin's optimism and dislike of force led him to put the emphasis on leveling "up," which he thought would become possible thanks to widespread mechanization and more efficient organization. In particular this would benefit women, who would at last stop being slaves to domestic work. He forecast the widespread introduction of machines for washing dishes, cleaning shoes, and

41. *The Conquest of Bread* (New York and London, 1968), p. 207.

42. *Ibid.*, p. 139.

43. See P. A. Kropotkin, "Dolzhny-li my zaniat'sia rassmotreniem ideala budushchego obshchestvennogo stroia?" (reprinted in *Revoliutsionnoe narodnichestvo 70kh godov XIX veka*, ed. B. S. Itenberg [Moscow, 1964], vol. 1). In the name of social equality young Kroptotkin called for "the closing of all universities, academies, and scientific institutes and the establishment of school-workshops that will very quickly undertake the necessary lectures and will soon attain and even surpass the standards of present-day universities."

doing laundry, as well as central heating and home delivery of food products or even complete meals by special vans. Such labor-saving devices, he pointed out, were already being introduced under capitalism, especially in the United States, which was ahead of the rest of the world in this respect.

Another sphere that would benefit from the abolition of the division of labor was the human environment. Art would fuse with industry just as it had once been an integral part of craftsmanship. "Art in order to develop," Kropotkin argued, "must be bound up with industry by a thousand intermediate degrees, blended, so to say, as Ruskin and the great socialist poet Morris have proved so often and so well. Everything that surrounds man, in the street, in the interior and exterior of public monuments, must be of pure artistic form."[44] In a society where all men had achieved a certain degree of affluence and leisure, where all worked to satisfy their own wants, it would not be difficult to achieve such a standard of beauty.

Kropotkin's reflections on the subject of revolution are interesting, though completely utopian. Unlike Bakunin, who made use in his activities of conspiratorial methods borrowed from Carbonari secret societies, Kropotkin utterly rejected this tradition; he was himself so strictly ethical and had such a horror of violence that he would have found it impossible to collaborate with an adventurer like Nechaev, who was convinced that the end sanctified the means. Once the revolution had been successful, Kropotkin believed, its gains would not be challenged. Factories, shops, and houses would be taken over by the armed populace, who would make a fair redistribution of social wealth, and further violence would quickly become unnecessary. Curiously enough, he assumed than an anarchist revolution might be successful on a relatively small territory, for instance Paris and two neighboring departments (Seine and Seine-et-Oise). In *The Conquest of Bread* he explained his plan for making such autonomy possible. All that was needed was for half the adult population of Paris and its environs to devote 58 five-hour days a year to working on the land (in the Seine and Seine-et-Oise departments); efficient modern agricultural techniques would enable them to become self-sufficient and independent of the rest of the country.[45] Apparently Kropotkin thought it possible that the rest of France would be content to apply economic sanctions to its revolutionary capital and would not dare to take

44. See *The Conquest of Bread*, p. 152.
45. *Ibid.*, p. 298.

recourse to armed intervention. It is difficult to avoid the impression that despite his passionate attacks on the bourgeois state, Kropotkin had rather too much confidence in the democratic achievements of Western Europe. This was part of his deep conviction that the evolutionary cycle unfavorable to the instinct of "mutual aid" had completed its course, and that modern states were already about to "abdicate" in favor of free social initiatives.[46]

In the history of anarchism—a movement whose ultrarevolutionary and ultraleftist wing has often indulged in irresponsible political extremism, glorification of violence, and primitive anti-intellectualism—Kropotkin holds a very special place. He was without doubt one of the most principled and attractive personalities in the movement—the naiveté of many of his views was an essential aspect of his innate goodness and boundless faith in humanity. In theory as well as in daily practice he was a revolutionary, but many of his ideas were closer to pacifist or even Christian anarchism (Tolstoy's brand of anarchism, for instance). His theories were also very influential in the cooperative movement, which advocated the peaceful transformation of society through the establishment of cooperatives and associations founded on the principle of mutual aid. Among his disciples was the outstanding Polish theorist of "stateless Socialism," Edward Abramowski.

46. *Ibid.*, p. 188.

CHAPTER 14

IDEOLOGIES OF REACTION
AFTER THE REFORMS

The term "reactionary" is normally used in a number of different meanings. Within the context of a history of ideas, a distinction should be made between ideologies that are reactionary in content, and those that are reactionary in function (in a situational sense). In the former instance "reactionary" is a descriptive term used to convey the fact that a given ideology is backward-looking and idealizes (directly or indirectly) an earlier stage of social evolution. Such a retrospection was characteristic of Populism; and it was this that Lenin had in mind when he distinguished between reaction "in its historico-philosophical sense" (which he called "the error of theoreticians who take models for their theories from obsolete forms of society") and reaction "in the ordinary sense of the term" (that is, political support for extreme right-wing movements).[1]

Used in a functional sense, the term "reactionary" describes not the content of a given ideology but the way it functions in a specific set of circumstances. In this sense, for instance, it is possible (whether it is true is another question) to speak of the reactionary nature of Russian liberalism: those who do so are concerned not with the content of Russian liberal thought but with its function, since by opposing the revolutionary movement it objectively helped to shore up the tsarist system. It is evident, therefore, that reactionary content need not coincide with reactionary function. Liberal reformist ideologies advocating capitalist development in Russia could, in certain circumstances, stand in the way of progress and thus function in a reactionary way; the revolutionary Populism of the 1870's, by contrast, was (from the functional point of view) the most radical and therefore most progressive social movement of its day, despite its undoubtedly backward-looking ideology. The term "reactionary" in a functional sense describes not a "historico-philosophical" so much as a primarily political category, and it is thus largely

1. See V. I. Lenin, *Collected Works* (Eng.-lang. ed.; M, 1960–66), vol. 2, p. 217.

interchangeable with the more commonly used term "right-wing."

Many authors also differentiate between conscious (subjective) and unconscious (objective) reaction. This distinction, which implies that it is possible for a conflict to arise between the subjective motivation of an ideologist and the objective content or function of the ideas he advocates, can also be useful as an analytical aid in interpretation.

The present chapter is concerned with thinkers to whom the term "reactionary" can be applied without any additional explanations or reservations, thinkers who were reactionary both objectively and subjectively, from the point of view of the function as well as the content of their ideas. They actively opposed not only revolution or social radicalism, but even the partial reforms introduced by Alexander II. The emergence of such reactionary ideologies was an important symptom of the polarization brought about by the changes in the intellectual climate of the 1860's and the headway made by the revolutionary movement.

NIKOLAI DANILEVSKY

The most dynamic, and in some respects the most up-to-date, version of Russian reaction in the 1870's was Pan-Slavism—a movement whose aim was to force the tsarist government to adopt a more aggressive and chauvinistic foreign policy, especially toward Turkey, in order to create a powerful federation of Slavic nations under Russian leadership. The most active politician in the Pan-Slavic movement was Ivan Aksakov (mentioned in Chapter 6); he was not its leading theorist, however, since pietism toward Slavophile doctrine prevented him from undertaking its revision and reinterpretation. The first and probably only systematic exposition of Pan-Slavism was in Nikolai Danilevsky's *Russia and Europe*, published in 1869 and reissued several times in subsequent years.[2]

NIKOLAI DANILEVSKY (1822–85), a natural scientist and former member of the Petrashevsky Circle, had never been associated with classical Slavophilism. As the theorist of Pan-Slavism he made use of Slavophile ideas, but by means of conscious selection and revision he was able to fit them into an entirely different ideological structure.

2. The most comprehensive study of Russian Pan-Slavism is Frank Fadner, *Seventy Years of Pan-Slavism in Russia: Karamzin to Danilevskii* (Washington, D.C., 1962). See also M. Boro-Petrovich, *The Emergence of Russian Panslavism* (New York, 1958). On Danilevsky see a recent monograph by R. E. McMaster, *Danilevsky: A Russian Totalitarian Philosopher* (Cambridge, Mass., 1967).

In the first place Danilevsky had to jettison the Slavophile standpoint on statehood, since a doctrine that regarded the state as a "necessary evil" or "external truth" obviously conflicted with a program calling for the creation of a powerful economic and military federation led by Russia. In his assessment of Peter the Great, too, Danilevsky laid rather more stress on the political and military successes that helped to create a powerful empire than on the undignified "aping" of Europe accompanying the reforms. The greatest changes were to be found in the interpretation of Russia's historical mission: for the Slavophiles the goal had been the defense of certain universal ideals ("true Christianity," traditional social bonds); for Danilevsky the goal that justified all the cruelties of Russian history was the creation of a powerful state organism whose expansion would be subject only to the natural laws of evolution. Europe, he wrote indignantly, refused to recognize Russia's mission and assigned her merely a modest role in "civilizing" Asia. No great nation would be content with such a role. Fortunately her destiny was manifestly quite different: the Russian people, like the other Slavs, bore within it the germ of a new type of civilization that had nothing in common with the Germano-Romanic civilization of Europe. This new civilization would only flower after the conquest of Constantinople and the establishment of that city as the capital of a Slavic empire liberated and united by Russia. The "concept of Slavdom" ought therefore to be, after God, the supreme ideal of every Slav, an ideal standing "higher than freedom, higher than science, higher than education, higher than all worldly goods, for none of these is attainable unless this ideal is realized."[3]

The mistake the Slavophiles had made, according to Danilevsky, was to attribute an absolute and therefore universal value to "Russian" or "Slavic" principles. In effect they had fallen into the same error as the Westernizers, who had identified European civilization with a universal culture. There could be no such thing as "universal values" shared by the whole of mankind, Danilevsky declared; humanity expressed itself solely in specific "historico-cultural" types that were simply different and that could not be compared; to attempt to evaluate these types from the point of view of their allegedly universal significance was just as absurd as to ask which concrete plant form—palm or cypress, oak or rose—better expressed "the concept of plant." Since there could be no such thing as a universal

3. N. Ia. Danilevsky, *Rossiia i Evropa, Vzgliad na kul'turnye i politicheskie otnosheniia slavianskogo mira k germano-romanskomu* (4th ed.; St. Petersburg, 1889), p. 113.

mission, the Slavs could not have been selected to fulfill such a mission; nor could they, as a collective body, represent "true Christian principles" in their actions, since such principles were only valid in relation to individuals. The demand for the application of Christian principles to politics, the "mysticism and sentimentalism" of the period of the Holy Alliance, did not take into account the fact that only individuals were immortal and that self-sacrifice, the supreme "yardstick of Christian morality," could be demanded of them alone. The laws governing the relations of states and nations could only be based on self-interest—"An eye for an eye, a tooth for a tooth." In accordance with this "Benthamite principle of utilitarianism," Danilevsky demanded the rejection of the surviving hold of legitimism on Russian foreign policy and preached an openly cynical attitude toward international alliances.

Such a programmatic political immoralism was bound to be most convenient for Russian great-power chauvinism. The term "immoral" is perhaps not entirely appropriate in this context: Danilevsky did not ignore moral criteria but only selected a different concept—that of realizing the "Slavic historico-cultural type"—as the supreme moral frame of reference for Russia and all other Slav nations. From this "Slavic" point of view it was easy for him to pronounce judgment on the "Jesuitical gentry state of Poland," that "Judas of Slavdom," which he compared to a hideous tarantula greedily devouring its eastern neighbor, unaware that its own body was being eaten by its western neighbors.[4] It was from this standpoint, too, that he condemned Tsarist policy for its "softness" toward Europe and accused the government of overlooking the interests of Russia and her Slavic sister nations by currying favor with the West. Even toward the Poles, Danilevsky thought, the tsarist government had shown an excess of chivalry by agreeing to incorporate Congress Poland into Russia instead of leaving her to non-Slavic Austria and Prussia.

In home policy Danilevsky believed in a "social monarchy" that would stand above classes and safeguard social harmony by subordinating particular interests to the general good. At the outset it seemed to him that this ideal would be well served by the reforms of Alexander II, but later he came to change his mind, especially where the juridical reforms were concerned. In the early editions of his *Russia and Europe* he had defended these reforms against the charge that they were "aping" Europe, citing Khomiakov's assertion that the jury system was an indigenous Slavic institution. In

4. *Ibid.*, p. 33.

the third posthumous edition, however, Nikolai Strakhov included marginal notes made by Danilevsky himself (probably in 1880–81). Presumably motivated by his dissatisfaction with the proceedings and verdicts of the great political trials of the 1870's, Danilevsky confessed that he had been wrong: "Everything I wrote here is nonsense," he commented. "The reforms had only just been introduced and we wanted to believe—and therefore did believe—that they would assume a sensible character; in actual fact they turned into a caricature of foreign ideas. If we had been more sober in our appraisal we would and should have foreseen this."[5]

Danilevsky owes his place in Russian intellectual history not only to his political doctrine but also to his theory of historico-cultural types," which cannot be regarded simply as a theoretical underpinning for Pan-Slavism.

Danilevsky's precursor here was Apollon Grigoriev, who had argued (see Chapter 11) that particular nations or groups of related nations are unique self-contained organisms, governed by laws specific to themselves and independent of the allegedly universal laws of human evolution.[6] Grigoriev developed this notion from the later views of Schelling and set it against the universalistic scheme of Hegel's philosophy of history. His polemic with Hegel's "historical view" had its counterpart in Danilevsky's polemic with Darwinism, in which the classification of species made by the French zoologist Baron Cuvier assumed the significance Schelling's ideas had had for Grigoriev. Although Danilevsky replaced Grigoriev's romantic philosophy of history with a naturalistic one, in both instances evolutionary categories were supplanted by a morphological point of view. Aestheticism, or rather somewhat special aesthetic criteria deriving beauty from the multiformity and distinctiveness of "types of organization,"[7] also figured largely in Danilevsky's doctrine. Cuvier's contribution, in his view, was that he differentiated between the "evolutionary stage" (or level) of organisms and their "types": "These types are not evolutionary stages on the ladder of gradual perfectibility (stages that are, as it were, placed in a hierarchical order of subordination), but entirely different plans— plans without any common denominator—in which each entity evolves in a specific and distinct fashion toward the multiformity and perfection within its reach."[8]

5. *Ibid.*, p. 300.
6. See above, p. 218.
7. Danilevsky, *Rossiia i Evropa*, pp. xxx–xxxi.
8. *Ibid.*, p. 87.

When translated into historical terms, this meant the elimination of the concept of unidirectional and universal progress. In place of an abstract "universal humanity" (*obshchechelovechestvo*, conceived as a common yardstick of everything human), Danilevsky proposed the notion of "all-humanity" (*vsechelovechestvo*), by which he meant a rich variety of cultural and national differences that could not be reduced to a common denominator or arranged in an evolutionary sequence. Anticipating the later theories of Spengler[9] and Arnold Toynbee, Danilevsky divided mankind into "historico-cultural types" comparable to different styles in architecture and paintings; progress was something that could not only take place within the type, and categories of organic growth such as youth, maturity, and old age were applicable only to these various types and not to humanity as a whole. In view of the heterogeneity and variety of historical phenomena, there was no point in attempting to formulate theories that claimed to embrace the whole of history; these were invariably based on the characteristic "false perspective" of Europocentrism—the unconscious identification of the history of Europe with the history of mankind.

This differentiation between "evolutionary types" and "evolutionary levels or stages" within the various types met with the enthusiastic approval of Mikhailovsky.[10] The Populist thinker's interpretation of historical types differed somewhat from Danilevsky's, since he was primarily interested in types of economic development rather than specifically national characteristics. However, the concern they both showed for distinguishing between evolutionary types and evolutionary stages or levels was not fortuitous: both Danilevsky and Mikhailovsky wished to justify their insistence on Russia's development by "native" principles and therefore had to reject all universalistic evolutionary schemes or conceptions of unidirectional development.

Danilevsky distinguished ten types of civilization in the past: (1) Egyptian, (2) Chinese, (3) Assyrian-Babylonian-Phoenician or Ancient Semitic, (4) Hindu, (5) Iranian, (6) Hebrew, (7) Ancient Greek, (8) Roman, (9) Neo-Semitic or Arabian, and (10) Romano-Germanic or European. These civilizations were "incommensurable" as far as their "principles" were concerned, but they could

9. On the question of the possible influence of Danilevsky's ideas on Spengler, see P. Sorokin, *Modern Historical and Social Philosophies* (New York, 1963), pp. 50, 69, 73–82.

10. N. K. Mikhailovsky, *Polnoe sobranie sochinenii* (4th ed.; St. Petersburg, 1906–14), vol. 3, pp. 867–68 ("Notes of a Layman").

be compared from a formal point of view. There were "mono-ele-mental" types, for instance, that could lay claim to achievements in one cultural sphere alone, and "multi-elemental" types that could boast of achievements in many spheres; some types were completely "self-contained," whereas others were capable of assimilating "cul-tural material" (but not principles) created by types contemporary with them or preceding them. Cultural activity, in the broadest sense of the word, evolved in four principal spheres: (1) the religious sphere, (2) the cultural sphere (in the narrower meaning of science, the arts, and technology), (3) the political sphere, and (4) the socio-economic sphere. Hebrew civilization was a mono-elemental re-ligious type, ancient Greece a cultural (primarily artistic) type, and Rome a political type; in contrast to the Chinese and Hindu civiliza-tions, each of these types was capable of assimilating the achieve-ments of other cultures. European civilization was a "dual" one composed of both the political and the cultural elements, and was capable of far-reaching and creative assimilation.

Unlike the Slavophiles, Danilevsky was not hostile to the Ro-mano-Germanic principle. Of his "historico-cultural types," the European type was one of the most outstanding, perhaps the finest produced so far; at the same time, however, he reaffirmed the Slavo-phile diagnosis of European decay. In his scheme European history had three periods of peak achievement. The first was the thirteenth century, which saw the flowering of an aristocratic and theocratic culture. The second was the seventeenth century, after the intellec-tual liberation of the Renaissance and the liberation of conscience of the Reformation; this period represented the creative apogee of European history (it was also the age to which all European con-servatives looked back with the greatest nostalgia—with the excep-tion of the Ultramontane Catholics, who wanted to go back even further). Liberation from feudalism at the end of the eighteenth century ushered in the third and last period of achievement—the technical and industrial age. During this period (in 1848) new forces had emerged that desired the total liberation and total de-struction of the old European civilization. The Paris Commune, Danilevsky wrote in a note to a later edition of his book, was an-other and more terrifying embodiment of these forces: "It was the beginning of the end."[11]

The eclipse of Europe did not, however, concern Russia or the Slavic nations. Whatever arguments the Russian Westernizers might put forward to the contrary, Russia emphatically did not belong to

11. Danilevsky, *Rossia i Evropa*, pp. 253–54.

Europe; the best proof of this was that Europe itself did not consider Russia "one of us," and turned its back on her in abhorrence. Positive evidence of Russia's originality was the solution to the peasant question, which entailed the distribution of the land to the peasants but also the preservation of the village commune as a bulwark against the proletariat that was ruining Europe. By turning her back on Europe and shutting herself off from her, by conquering Constantinople and liberating and uniting her fellow Slavs, Russia would create a new, eleventh cultural type. Danilevsky suggested that this would be the first "tetra-elemental" type, as he claimed for the Slavs the ability to be active in all four spheres of culture, especially in the religious sphere (Orthodoxy) and the socioeconomic sphere (the agrarian solution). Thanks to the Slavs' extraordinary capacity for understanding other cultures and assimilating their achievements, the Slavic type was likely to be closest to the ideal of "all-humanity." Until this new type was fully formed, however, it would be better to concentrate on individuality and distinctiveness than on the ideal of all-humanity, which was fully attainable by God alone. Particularly in relations with Europe Danilevsky recommended "exclusivity and patriotic fanaticism" as essential counterweights to Western influences. In order to straighten the bent tree, the utmost force must be used to pull it to the other side.[12]

In the everyday political context of those years, Danilevsky's theories amounted to an appeal to launch an out-and-out campaign not only against the revolutionary movement but also against the moderate liberal opposition. Like all convinced reactionaries in Russia at that time, Danilevsky regarded liberalism and all radical movements as symptoms of a disease with which tainted Europe had infected the healthy organism of Mother Russia.

KONSTANTIN POBEDONOSTSEV

Unlike Danilevsky, KONSTANTIN POBEDONOSTSEV (1827–1907) was neither an original nor an interesting thinker. If he has a place in Russian intellectual history, it is mainly as a typical and influential representative of reactionary thought during the crisis of Russian absolutism. His name will always be associated with the oppressive, all-encompassing triumph of reaction in Russia during the reign of Alexander III. The poet Alexandr Blok describes this depressing age in his poem "Revenge":

12. *Ibid.*, pp. 109, 468.

In those mute and distant years
A dull gloom filled all hearts.
Pobedonostsev had unfurled
His owlish wings over Russia.
There was neither day nor night,
Only the shadow of giant wings.

Pobedonostsev was a jurist, author of a three-volume textbook on civil law and many works on the history of Russian jurisprudence. He abandoned a successful university career in order to enter politics, and in quick succession became senator (1868), member of the Council of State (1872), and Director General of the Holy Synod (1880–1905). In this post he encouraged anti-Semitism, persecuted Old Believers and Sectarians, and pursued a policy of Russification that systematically restricted the religious rights of national minorities. He owed his impact on the internal policies of the tsarist government not only to his official position, but also to his close influence on the imperial family, which had engaged him as tutor in the 1860's. He was responsible for the upbringing of the last two tsars, Alexander III and Nicholas II, and their obstinate and shortsighted policies were no doubt partly a result of his efforts.

Pobedonostsev expounded his social philosophy in a collection of articles entitled *Moscow Miscellany* (*Moskovskii Sbornik*, 1896). In them he criticized Western European civilization for its rationalism and belief in man's innate goodness. He himself put his faith in inertia, which he thought of as a mysterious force cementing society. This force was epitomized in the lives of the illiterate peasantry, who were faithful to old traditions and deeply attached to church ritual although they could not understand the prayers they were reciting. Following the French sociologist Frédéric Le Playe (whose *La Constitution essentielle de l'humanité* he had translated into Russian), Pobedonostsev also emphasized the conservative and stabilizing function of the family. He saw national evolution as an organic process determined by such factors outside the conscious control of individuals as land, the collective unconscious of the masses, and their history. Every nation, he wrote, is the prisoner of its own history, and every one evolves according to laws specific to itself, so that imitating other nations is always unnatural and injurious. In Russia absolutism was a truly national institution, and therefore all attempts to liberalize the system—including the juridical reforms introduced during the reign of Alexander II[13]—were

13. Pobedonostsev had a very poor opinion of Alexander II: he accused him of weakening the state and maintained that this was connected with the immoral life

likely to have fatal consequences. Pobedonostsev was particularly severe in his attacks on the parliamentary system, although he conceded that it had a place in the Anglo-Saxon countries, where it was a product of organic historical development. In all other countries, he insisted, parliamentary government led to universal corruption, the tyranny of the masses, and uncontrolled "party-mindedness," i.e. the abandonment of the general good to the mercy of the brutal struggle of particular interests.

These views show many points of similarity with the romantic conservatism of the first half of the century. This is not fortuitous; Pobedonostsev's ideas on jurisprudence were formed by a theorist of the German "historical school," F. C. Savigny, and among Pobedonostsev's favorite writers we find the "feudal socialist" and romantic conservative Thomas Carlyle. The Russian's personality, however, was far from romantic: he was a dry, pedantic bureaucrat and regarded all romantic enthusiasm or excessive show of feeling with extreme suspicion. Despite his largely friendly relations with Ivan Aksakov[14] and the high esteem in which he held Slavophilism, he was little influenced by it; the bureaucratic conservatism of the reign of Nicholas was much closer to his heart. In contrast to the Slavophiles, Pobedonostsev did not believe in the fellowship of *sobornost'*, since he could not have reconciled such a belief with his deep conviction that man's weak and indeed wicked nature required strong discipline imposed from without. Believing as he did that Russia's "native principle" was the inviolability of absolutism, he firmly dismissed any demands for convening a Land Assembly and praised the Petrine reforms largely because they had consolidated autocracy. His view of the peasant commune was influenced by purely practical considerations: he regarded it initially as a conservative institution that helped to stabilize the state, but in the late 1880's he came to the conclusion that it was in the interests of absolutism to abolish the common ownership of land and create a class of wealthy farmers (here he anticipated the central idea of Stolypin's agrarian reforms).[15] It is also significant that Pobedonostsev was not an opponent of industrialization—he thought it would

---

he led. See R. F. Byrnes, *Pobedonostsev, His Life and Thought* (Bloomington, Ind., 1968), pp. 143–44. He also attacked the juridical reforms and declared they had been the responsibility of the emperor and the liberals, although he had in fact taken an active part in their preparation (Byrnes, *Pobedonostsev*, pp. 54–59).

14. The relationship was not entirely free of conflict, for Aksakov—faithful to the traditions of Slavophilism—defended freedom of speech and conscience.

15. Byrnes, *Pobedonostsev*, p. 301.

be possible to modernize the economy without introducing basic changes in the social structure or the political system.

His pessimistic view of human nature and deep distrust of strong emotions and spontaneous social movements inclined Pobedonostsev to treat the aggressive nationalism of the Pan-Slavists with considerable reserve. On the eve of the war with Turkey in 1877 he did, it is true, succumb to the general Pan-Slavic mood, but he soon regained his sober restraint and returned to his conception of a passive and defensive foreign policy. His American biographer R. F. Byrnes, in fact, has called him a typical isolationist.[16] The Director General of the Holy Synod had no faith in Russia's "all-Slavic" mission. It would be more apt to say, perhaps, that he was entirely lacking in any faith in the future. Orthodox, autocratic Russia was, for him, a "separate world"; but it was a world threatened from without and within, defending itself desperately against disaster, which sooner or later was bound to overtake it.

KONSTANTIN LEONTIEV

A far more colorful and complex personality was KONSTANTIN LEONTIEV (1831–91). His outlook was formed in the course of the ten years (1863–74) he spent in the Russian consular service in various parts of the Ottoman empire, during which period he frequently stayed with the community of Greek Orthodox monks on Mount Athos. After resigning from the diplomatic service (over disagreements with Russian policy toward Turkey), he worked in Russia as a censor; but he again handed in his resignation after a few years and settled in the Optina Cloister, famous for its holy elders. Toward the end of his life he took monastic vows.

A contemptuous dislike of "bourgeois plebeianism," of the "man in the street" and his philistine ideals of "universal prosperity" and "rational middle-class happiness"—this was the emotional mainspring of Leontiev's entire work. After his death he was often referred to as the "Russian Nietzsche."[17] An exceptionally important aspect of his aversion to bourgeois values was his aestheticism: even as a very young man Leontiev had disliked the railway—that archsymbol of bourgeois civilization—and had condemned European dress as "unbearably commonplace" and devoid of the picturesque.

16. *Ibid.*, pp. 119–20.
17. See N. A. Berdiaev, *Konstantin Leontiev. Ocherki iz istorii russkoi religioznoi mysli* (Paris, 1926), pp. 37–39. There is an English translation of this book (by S. Reavey), *K. N. Leontiev* (London, 1940).

Man, he wrote, ought to model himself on nature, which "adores variety and luxurious forms." Beauty revealed itself in clear-cut distinction, peculiarity, individuality, specific coloring; it depended on differentiation and therefore on inequality. By attacking extreme social differences, liberal humanism and individualism were in effect an anti-aesthetic force "destroying the individuality of persons, provinces, and nations."[18] In the same way "sentimentalism" or "eudaemonism" prevented the emergence of powerful and splendid personalities who were only formed by misfortunes and injustices. The victory of such liberal and egalitarian ideals as universal prosperity and the universal acceptance of middle-class values would make history meaningless. "One would have to blush for mankind if this shabby ideal of universal utility, of shallow commonplace work and inglorious prosiness were to triumph for centuries."[19]

The same thoughts are developed in more detail in Leontiev's major work, *Byzantinism and Slavdom* (1875). This puts forward an original interpretation of the evolution of societies anticipating Spengler's theory of the transition from "culture to civilization."[20] It also shares certain features with the conceptions of Ortega y Gasset and other anti-egalitarian critics of mass culture.

All development, Leontiev argues, passes through three fundamental stages that are common not only to biological evolution but also to the evolution of artistic styles or whole social organisms. The starting point is a period of simplicity in which a primitive homogeneity prevails both in the whole and in its component parts. The transition to the second stage is a process of growing complexity in which both the whole and its parts become individualized, but at the same time are welded together more strongly by the "despotic unity of form"; this second stage culminates in "flourishing complexity," i.e. maximum differentiation within the framework of a specific individualized morphological unity. From this moment evolution passes into disintegration and, through secondary simplification, leads to a leveling fusion of the component elements and therefore to a new monochromatic simplicity. This third stage—that of a "leveling fusion and simplicity"—heralds the approaching death of the organism.

In applying this scheme to the philosophy of history, Leontiev made use of Danilevsky's "types," which he substituted for "ab-

---

18. K. N. Leontiev, *Sobranie sochinenii* (St. Petersburg, 1912), vol. 5, p. 147.
19. *Ibid.*, p. 426.
20. See P. Sorokin, *Contemporary Sociological Theories* (New York and London, n.d.), pp. 25–26, note 49.

stract humanity" as the protagonist in the process of evolution and disintegration. The history of Western Europe naturally supplied him with a classic example of cultural decay that was both a lesson and a warning for Russia. The culmination of European progress, according to Leontiev, was the period between the Renaissance and the eighteenth century; this was followed by a period of "decay" that heralded the third stage, the disintegration of the differentiated morphological unity. During this stage everything became laxer and shallower. While industry expanded and prosperity increased, culture disintegrated, because cultural individuality (its unrepeatable uniqueness) is possible only under an integrating "despotism of form"; by this standard, China or Turkey was more highly cultured than Belgium or Switzerland.

The main symptom of Europe's decay was the "liberal-egalitarian process," which, Leontiev declared "is the antithesis of the process of development. In the process of development the inner ideal firmly holds the social fabric in its organizing and despotic grip, and restrains its divergent and centrifugal tendencies. Progress, on the other hand, in its struggle against despotism—the despotism of estates, guilds, monasteries, and even fortunes—is nothing other than a process of disintegration, . . . a process that levels the morphological contours and destroys specific features organically (i.e. despotically) related to the given social organism."[21]

From this theory special conclusions could be drawn about the role of statesmen. Prior to the period of "flourishing complexity," Leontiev suggested, right is on the side of the progressives who lead the nation from the stage of primitive simplicity toward differentiation and proliferation of forms. During the stage of disintegration, however, right is on the side of the conservatives, who try to hold back the process of atomization. This was the situation not only in Europe but also in Russia, where the "liberal-egalitarian process" had made headway after the death of Nicholas I. "We must freeze Russia to save her from rotting" was the sinister aphorism Leontiev coined in justification of Pobedonostsev's ultrareactionary program.

Leontiev agreed with Danilevsky that Russia, though exposed to the "pestilent breath" of Europe, did not belong to the European "type," but he had different ideas about the specific nature of "Russianness." In his view Russia was not a purely Slavic country; the originality of her culture was determined by its Asiatic elements as well. Slavdom was "amorphous, spontaneous, unorganized," where-

21. Leontiev, Sob. soch., vol. 5, pp. 198–99.

as Russia was above all heir to the Byzantine civilization that Danilevsky had overlooked in his theory of "historico-cultural" types. The conquest of Constantinople therefore would enable Russia to create a new cultural type that would be not Slavic but neo-Byzantine. Byzantinism, as embodied in Orthodoxy and autocracy, was the "organizing principle" in Russian history; "Slavism" as such did not exist, for without Byzantinism the Slavs were merely so much ethnographic material, vulnerable to the disintegrating influence emanating from Europe. If the southern Slavs had retained their originality, Leontiev concluded, it was only thanks to Turkey, which had "frozen" their culture and fenced them off from liberal Europe.

To understand Leontiev better, we must remember that during his years in the Near East he had fallen in love with the Turks and had, at the same time, come to hold the Slavs in thorough aversion. In particular he disliked the Bulgarians, in whom he claimed to see symptoms of a premature old age—the uninterrupted transition from the first to the third evolutionary stage, or the transformation of swineherds into middle-class liberals.

Leontiev's harsh judgment of the Slavs was in part determined by his wider attitude to nineteenth-century nationalism; the separate essay he devoted to this subject has the revealing title *National Policy as an Instrument of World Revolution*. In it he put forward the view that nations were a creative force only when they represented a specific culture: "naked" or purely "tribal" nationalism was a corrosive force destroying both culture and the state, a leveling process that was, in the last resort, cosmopolitan; in fact, nationalism was only a mask for liberal and egalitarian tendencies, a specific metamorphosis of the universal process of disintegration.

Leontiev illustrated this thesis by pointing to the example of Greece and Italy, which, he maintained, had rapidly begun to lose their "native" character after gaining independence. Nationalist movements among the Slavs were tending in the same direction: nationalist passions had caused the Bulgarians to quarrel with Orthodoxy as represented by the Greek Metropolitan and to adopt a European constitution. On the Slavic question Leontiev tended to agree with Nicholas I rather than Pogodin and the Pan-Slavists. In *Byzantinism and Slavdom* he argued that it was not the Slavs as such that were deserving of affection and support but merely their "originality"; in practice this meant that support should be given not to the Slav nationalists but to the standard-bearers of Byzantinism—the Greek "phanariots." This conclusion conflicted with the

"Slavic" policies of the government of Alexander II and put a stop to Leontiev's diplomatic career.

From having been Danilevsky's enthusiastic admirer and in a sense his disciple, Leontiev thus came to repudiate Pan-Slavism, Danilevsky's brainchild. "From now on," he wrote, "we should regard Pan-Slavism as something very dangerous if not downright disastrous."[22] The "younger brothers"—the Slavs—had been infected by the spirit of egalitarian liberalism, and were in fact the worst enemies of the distinctive Orthodox-Byzantine culture. It was not by chance, Leontiev thought, that Pan-Slavism had gained ground in Russia together with liberal ideas—that is, during the period of the "great reforms" that had blurred the distinction between Russia and Europe in her decline. This comment should not be taken to imply that Leontiev was no longer interested in the conquest of Constantinople; his real opposition was to the emphasis on the "liberation" of the other Slavic nations. Austria and Turkey, he felt, should long continue to rule over their Slavic subjects, for it was only the absence of political independence that induced the latter to cultivate their cultural distinctiveness. In fact, the Turkish and Austrian yokes should only be thrown off when Russia was mature enough for her mission and, after conquering Constantinople, able to direct the future of Slavdom.

That Constantinople would ultimately be conquered was not in doubt for Leontiev, but he was far from sure whether this in itself was enough to allow Russia to create a new and original civilization. Russia could hardly be called a young country, he wrote with regret; the policy of Alexander III was one of "salutary reaction," but it was impossible to tell whether this would "heal" Russian society, which since the 1860's had been profoundly affected by corrosive processes. Although the conquest of countries with an original Orthodox-Byzantine culture would strengthen Russian Byzantinism, Leontiev deplored the fact that in the process of gaining independence these countries would fall prey to the plague of egalitarian liberalism. Toward the end of his life, in the early 1890's, he finally lost his faith in Russia's ability to create a distinctive new cultural type. The future, he prophesied, belonged to socialism; possibly a Russian tsar would stand at the head of the socialist movement and would organize and discipline it just as the Emperor Constantine had "organized" Christianity; or perhaps, he wrote in another apoc-

22. Leontiev, *Natsional'naia politika kak orudie vsemirnoi revoliutsii* (M, 1889), p. 54.

alyptic prediction, a democratic and secular Russia would become the home of the Antichrist.[23]

In his catastrophic vision of the future Leontiev found only one thing to console him: the hated liberals, he was convinced, would never triumph; the new rulers who would emerge from the crisis of European and Russian civilization would be neither "liberal" nor "mild." If further imitation of the ailing West were to bring about a revolution in Russia, he wrote in 1880, this revolution would ultimately set up "a regime whose strictness will surpass anything we have seen so far."[24] European and Russian socialists, he wrote elsewhere, would not put up monuments to the liberals:

They are right to despise them. . . . However hostile these people [the revolutionary socialists] are to the actual conservatives and the forms and methods of their activity, nevertheless all the essential aspects of conservative doctrine will prove useful to them. They will require terror, they will require discipline; traditions of humility, the habit of obedience, will be of use to them; nations who (let us suppose) have managed successfully to reconstruct their economic life, but have nevertheless failed to find satisfaction in life on earth, will blaze up with renewed enthusiasm for mystical doctrines.[25]

In his ideas Leontiev recapitulated, to a considerable extent, reactionary doctrines formulated at the beginning of the nineteenth century, in particular the ideas of the German conservative romantics and the theocratic conceptions of deMaistre. Conservative romanticism in fact was the common provenance linking Leontiev and the Slavophiles.[26] Leontiev himself conceded this relationship, but at the same time condemned Slavophilism as an inconsistent doctrine with elements that he considered unacceptable.[27] As he put it:

Slavophilism seemed to me to be too close to egalitarian liberalism to serve as a protective fence against the contemporary West. This is one thing; another aspect of this doctrine that aroused my mistrust was a certain one-sided moralism. At the same time this doctrine seemed to me

23. See Berdiaev, *Konstantin Leontiev*, pp. 212, 217.

24. Leontiev, *Sob. soch.*, vol. 7, p. 205.

25. *Ibid.*, p. 217.

26. That is why Miliukov considered Leontiev a product of the decline of Slavophilism, whereas Trubetskoi called him a "disillusioned Slavophile." See P. N. Miliukov, *Iz istorii russkoi intelligentsii* (St. Petersburg, 1902), and S. N. Trubetskoi, "Razocharovannyi slavianofil'," *Vestnik Evropy*, 1892, no. 10.

27. Ivan Aksakov denied the resemblance and dismissed Leontiev's ideas as a "lascivious cult of the truncheon."

unsatisfactory in relation to the State and unaesthetic. On the issue of statehood Katkov was far more satisfactory. . . . As far as aesthetics are concerned, both in history and in the outward manifestations of reality, I felt much closer to Herzen than to the Slavophiles.[28]

This was a reference to Herzen's critique of the Western European bourgeoisie, in which aesthetic revulsion had played an important role. Undoubtedly, however, Leontiev's aestheticism was closer to that of Grigoriev and Danilevsky, and their rejection of universalist criteria. In Leontiev we see the intimate connection between this type of aestheticism and the rejection of morality as a guiding principle; immoral acts and traits can in fact be "beautiful," because variety, color, vigor can be enhanced by the element of evil.

It is obvious that the Slavophile vision of ancient Russia—with its harmony, homogeneous traditions, and alleged absence of clearly demarcated social divisions—could not be reconciled with Leontiev's aesthetic ideal. Far closer to his vision of "flourishing complexity" was the West as criticized by the Slavophiles, with its government "based on force," its harsh social divisions, its splendid knighthood, and its Church ambitious for hegemony over the secular government. As might be expected, Leontiev admired "ancient" Europe and ascribed Slavophile criticism of feudalism and the Western aristocracy to the influence of the new "liberal-egalitarian" Europe.[29] This naturally affected his interpretation of the central problems of Russian history and led him to regard the cleavage between the nobility and the common people, which had so disturbed the Slavophiles, as a positive symptom.

Before Peter our society and *mores* showed greater homogeneity, a greater similarity of the component parts; Peter's reign initiated a more specific, more clear-cut social stratification and gave rise to that diversity without which life cannot attain its full prime and there can be no creativity. It is a well-known fact that Peter further consolidated serfdom. . . . In the above sense Peter's despotism was progressive and aristocratic. Catherine's liberalism was definitely of a similar stamp. She led Russia to an age of prosperity and creativity. She increased inequality— that was her main contribution. She guarded serfdom (the integrity of the *mir*, the communal ownership of the land) and introduced it even in Little Russia, and on the other hand relieved the nobility by diminishing their sense of being "servitors" and thereby strengthening such aristocratic traits as family pride and individuality; from the time of Cath-

28. Leontiev, *Sob. soch.*, vol. 6, p. 335.
29. *Ibid.*, pp. 431–32.

erine the nobility became somewhat more independent of the state, but dominated and ruled over other classes just as before. As an estate it became still more distinct, clear-cut, and individualized, and entered the age when it gave birth to Derzhavin, Karamzin, Zhukovsky, Batiushkov, Pushkin, Gogol, and others.[30]

On the political plane, too, Leontiev's attitude toward the aristocracy, class divisions, and the class privileges of the nobility differed from that of the Slavophiles. A supporter of the reactionary measures by which the government of Alexander III attempted to restore "differentiation," Leontiev could not forgive the Slavophiles their collaboration in the liberal reforms of the 1860's. The anti-aristocratic pronouncements of the epigones of Slavophilism (Iu. Samarin and Ivan Aksakov), their constant reiteration that the Russian nobility was descended from "servitors" of the state and ought therefore to show moderation in its claims, were indignantly dismissed by him as an open concession to egalitarianism. How consistent he was is shown by the fact that he rejected even the Slavophile-inspired "democratic" policy of Russification. The aristocratic traditions of the German barons and Polish gentry ought to be carefully protected by the tsarist government, he wrote—especially at a time when nihilism and other symptoms of decay were spreading among the Russian masses. To persecute the Polish gentry and Catholicism, and to support the Latvians and Estonians at the expense of the Livonian and Courland barons, was to aid the disintegrating force of egalitarianism and hasten the fatal process of homogenization. Oddest of all, Leontiev even sympathized with the Polish uprising of 1863 as a "reactionary" movement and expressed regret that after its defeat the victors were largely responsible for speeding up the process of democratization.[31]

It is interesting to note Leontiev's attitude toward the land reforms in Russia. In his comments he emphasized the twofold implications of the program—what he called its liberal-individualistic (European) aspect, and its communal-conservative (Russian) aspect.[32] By confusing these two aspects and failing to differentiate between the "beneficial effects of being chained to the soil" (i.e. the preservation and legal codification of the commune) and the "risky

30. *Ibid.*, vol. 5, pp. 133–34.
31. *Ibid.*, vol. 6, pp. 170–71. It is interesting to note that a very similar opinion about the Polish uprising of 1863 was held by Proudhon—of course with the opposite value judgment. The argument that the uprising was allegedly a reactionary movement of the Catholic nobility was also used and abused in the government-sponsored anti-Polish campaign in the Russian press.
32. *Ibid.*, vol. 7, p. 322.

liberation of the peasants from the rule of the nobility," the Slavophiles and even Danilevsky and Katkov had, according to Leontiev, fallen into the "liberal trap."

Last but not least, Leontiev's conception of religion and therefore his interpretation of Orthodoxy[33] differed radically from that of the Slavophiles. The "Russian Nietzsche" had a deep-seated aversion to any kind of moralizing and evangelical Christianity and all attempts to "humanize religion"; he was equally repelled by religious sentimentalism and by doctrines of love that overlooked fear (*timor Domini*), obedience, and authority. In his view, Khomiakov's "ecclesiastical democratism" and the Slavophile ideal of "free unity" were typical examples of a "rose-colored" Christianity that was utterly alien to the authentic "black" Christianity of the Orthodox monks on Mount Athos and in the Optina Cloister. For Leontiev, "ascetic and dogmatic Orthodoxy" was mainly distinguished by its "Byzantine pessimism," its lack of faith in the possibility of harmony and universal brotherhood. In this respect, he suggested, Schopenhauer and Hartmann were perhaps closer to Christianity than the liberal-socialist prophets of universal justice and welfare.[34] All great religions were "doctrines of pessimism sanctioning suffering, wrongs, and the injustices of life on earth."[35] It was with an almost sadistic satisfaction that he recalled the New Testament's failure to promise universal brotherhood and also its prediction that a time would come when love would weaken and the kingdom of the Antichrist be established.

As this account of his ideas shows, Leontiev was one of those rare thinkers who do not hesitate to take their ideas to their logical conclusion. In contrast to the epigones of Slavophilism, he cannot be called an ideologist of the "Prussian" or any other road to capitalism: he was an integral reactionary; the last uncompromising defender of Russian, Western European, or even Ottoman feudalism; and the most extreme representative of the romantic conservatism of the aristocracy in its decline—so extreme that he was indeed isolated in his extremism.

33. Leontiev, "Moia literaturnaia sud'ba," in *Literaturnoe nasledstvo*, vol. 22–24 (M, 1935), p. 441.
34. Leontiev, *Sob. soch.*, vol. 7, pp. 232–43.
35. *Ibid.*, p. 230.

CHAPTER 15

TWO PROPHETIC WRITERS

Russian literature, perhaps more than any other in the nineteenth century, was given to philosophical reflection on the meaning of human existence and was imbued with a deep sense of moral responsibility for the fate of its own nation and mankind as a whole. In nineteenth-century Russia, as indeed in Poland, great writers came to treat literature as a moral mission, a tool in the struggle to change the world.

The most characteristic writers in this respect are those two great literary prophets Dostoevsky and Tolstoy. Both men experienced a spiritual crisis that marked a turning point in their lives and led them to become aggressive critics of modern civilization. Both assailed the conscience of their readers with violent pictures of corruption and at the same time pointed the way to moral and religious rebirth. Both expressed with profound insight the utter despair about God and the meaning of existence, and as an antidote put forward faith in Christ. In both men the return to religion was linked to the terrifying experience of approaching death. Finally, both writers were deeply influenced by their contact with the Russian peasants—the simple folk who seemed to them to represent a superior, truly Christian understanding.

For all these apparently far-reaching similarities, it would be difficult to name two novelists who were less alike. Any comparative analysis of their work—and this kind of confrontation has long been a critical tradition—immediately brings to light numerous deep-seated differences.

This chapter does not attempt to analyze the entire body of work of both Dostoevsky and Tolstoy from the point of view of its philosophical content,[1] for that would require a blend of ideological

1. The literature on both writers is enormous. From the point of view of their philosophical, religious, and political views the following works in English are of special importance: K. V. Mochulsky, *Dostoevsky: His Life and Work* (Princeton, N.J., 1967); N. A. Berdiaev, *Dostoevsky*, trans. Donald Attwatter (New York, 1957); A. B. Gibbon. *The Religion of Dostoevsky* (London, 1973); J. Carrol, *Break-out from the*

analysis and detailed literary criticism that would be beyond the scope of the present book. In the following pages we shall therefore confine ourselves to giving an account of the views that these writers came to hold in maturity, or that they were confirmed in after experiencing an ideological crisis—views that they advocated not only in their novels but also in various other writings.

FYODOR DOSTOEVSKY

The "Crystal Palace" and the "Dark Cellar"

In contrast to the aristocratic Tolstoy, FYODOR DOSTOEVSKY (1821–81) was born into an "accidental family"[2] that was constantly haunted by the fear of losing the modest social position it had gained by enormous effort. His talent was nurtured not in a "gentry nest" but against the hectic background of a great city—amid humiliations, unappeased ambitions, the daily struggle for existence, and tragic social conflicts. The favorite characters of the young Dostoevsky were the "wronged and humiliated," the drab and humdrum folk (see especially his literary debut, *Poor Folk* [1846]), the romantic dreamers living in their own self-contained world of delusions (*White Nights* [1848]), or men devoured by unhealthy ambition and schizophrenic hallucinations (see especially *The Double* [1846]). The setting of almost all of his novels is St. Petersburg, seen through the eyes of someone who has only just been torn away from patriarchal immediacy and senses the city as a strange, fantastic, and alien world.[3] That is why Dostoevsky's St. Petersburg is so much like Gogol's: a city of mists and white nights, a ghost town

---

Crystal Palace: the Anarcho-Psychological Critique. Stirner, Nietzsche, Dostoevsky (London, 1974); V. Rozanov, *Dostoevsky and the Legend of the Grand Inquisitor* (a classic study translated from the 3d Russian ed. of 1906 by E. Roberts) (Ithaca, N.Y., 1972); I. Berlin, *The Hedgehog and the Fox: An Essay on Tolstoy's View of History* (London, 1967). The fundamental work on Tolstoy's religious views is N. Weisbein, *L'Evolution religieuse de Tolstoi* (Paris, 1960). The best comprehensive monograph on Tolstoy is still B. M. Eikhenbaum, *Lev Tolstoi* (3 vols.; L, 1928–31). See also the works quoted below in the notes and two important books by Soviet scholars recently translated into English: M. M. Bakhtin, *Problems of Dostoevsky's Poetics*, trans. R. W. Rotsel (Ann Arbor, Mich., 1973); and L. P. Grossman, *Dostoevsky: a Biography*, trans. Mary Mackler (Indianapolis, Ind., 1975). Comparative analyses of Dostoevsky's and Tolstoy's views are given in F. A. Stepun, *Dostojewski und Tolstoj, Christentum und soziale Revolution* (Munich, 1961), and M. Doerne, *Tolstoj und Dostojewskij, 2 Christliche Utopien* (Göttingen, 1969).

2. See the reflections on the hereditary nobility and "accidental" families in the last chapter of *The Adolescent*.

3. See V. Y. Kirpotin, *Molodoi Dostoevsky* (M, 1947), pp. 341–42.

whose pulse beats to a faster tempo, a symbol of the forces that had swept in from the West and destroyed the peaceful life of "Holy Russia."

As was mentioned earlier, the young Dostoevsky had belonged to the Petrashevsky Circle and was one of the members condemned to death by firing squad. The moments he spent waiting in Semenovsky Square before the last-minute reprieve were a terrifying experience he was never able to forget. It is true that he had no reason to feel guilty, but there is no doubt that the shock of this experience played its part in inducing him to read with great attention every word of the New Testament—the only book he was allowed to have with him during his four years of penal servitude in Siberia.

After his period of hard labor in Omsk was over, Dostoevsky had to do another five years of penal military service in Semipalatinsk. When he was released from the army in 1859, he returned to his writing with ideas very different from those that had been current among the Petrashevtsy. In 1860 he and his elder brother Mikhail began publication of a literary journal, *Time* (*Vremia*), on which their chief collaborators were Apollon Grigoriev and Nikolai Strakhov. In this journal Dostoevsky called for "a return to the soil," opposition to the ideas of the radical intelligentsia, and a return to the "purely national" and at the same time truly Christian values of the Russian people.

How did this metamorphosis come about? In his *Notes from the House of the Dead* (1862), a fictionalized account of his experiences of hard labor, Dostoevsky strongly emphasizes the crucial influence of his contacts with the criminals who were his daily companions. These men of simple origins, who accepted their fate with resignation, seemed to him authentic representatives of the common people; they were men who, though criminals, still had not abandoned the strong and simple beliefs of the Russian peasantry. It was then that he became acutely aware, he tells us, of the difference—the profound gulf even—dividing the Russian people from the Westernized intelligentsia, and realized that the values of the common people were infinitely preferable.

Other factors of course also played their part in this intellectual evolution, which was a complex process, difficult to present in all its aspects (Dostoevsky admitted that he himself would have found difficulty in doing so).[4] But we should note that the decisive turning point came during his years of penal servitude in Siberia, and that

4. See V. Y. Kirpotin, *F. M. Dostoevsky* (M, 1960), p. 448.

it was at this time that the characteristic antithesis between intelligentsia and common people, or European and Russian values, became part of his world view.

In 1862 Dostoevsky went abroad for the first time. The masterly essay cycle *Winter Notes on Summer Impressions* (1863) is a description of his travels in Western Europe. London, where an exhibition of world industry was being held in the Crystal Palace in Hyde Park, made the deepest impression on him. He was surprised and shocked by the might of capitalist civilization, the extreme rationalization of life, the "colossal regimentation" which was not only external but also "internal, spiritual, emanating from the soul." At the exhibition he was torn between admiration and fear; in his confusion he felt that he was witness to some kind of victory, triumph, that something "final" had been enacted . . . "some scene from the Bible, something about Babylon, some kind of prophesy from the Apocalypse." Paxton's Crystal Palace, that huge structure of glass and metal, became for him a symbol of the power of capitalist progress, although it was a pagan power, the "might of Baal" feeding on human sacrifices.[5]

In these essays Dostoevsky showed an unusually acute insight into the fact that it was the divisive force of bourgeois individualism that provided the motive power of Western civilization. Individualism had created a powerful reified material force, but at the same time it had isolated human beings, had brought them into conflict with nature and their fellow men. Partly under the inspiration of Herzen, whom he met in London, Dostoevsky emphasized that bourgeois freedom was a purely negative quality, that it was essentially freedom for the "man who has a million," that by "eradicating all inequalities" the power of money, which was the obverse of victorious bourgeois individualism, diminished the personality.[6] These ideas, which were first put forward in *Winter Notes on Summer Impressions*, were later taken up again in the novel *The Adolescent* (1875).

Against the rational egoism of European capitalism Dostoevsky set the ideal of the authentic fraternal community preserved in Orthodoxy and Russian folk traditions. In a community of this kind the individual does not oppose the collective but submits to it totally without setting conditions or calculating the advantages involved; the collective, for its part, does not demand so great a sacrifice but grants the individual freedom and safety, guaranteed by

5. *Winter Notes on Summer Impressions*, trans. Richard Lee Renfield (New York, 1955), p. 90.
6. *Ibid.*, pp. 104–5.

fraternal love. A community of this kind must "happen of itself";[7] it cannot be invented or made. Although Dostoevsky probably arrived at these ideas independently of the Slavophiles, they bear a striking similarity to Slavophile notions, including Khomiakov's conception of the "free unity" of *sobornost'*.

A year after the *Winter Notes* Dostoevsky published his novel *Notes from the Underground* (1864), which portrays a man who has rejected all social bonds and is an embodiment of protest against any subordination of "what is most precious and most important to us, namely our personality and our individuality." The narrator is "a man of the nineteenth century divorced from the people's principles"; he sets his own Ego against the objective world and revolts against being nothing but a cog in the social mechanism, or "the keys of a piano on which alien laws of nature are playing any tune they like." He interprets freedom as license and insists that to accept logic and common sense as guilding principles is "not life but the beginning of death." Dostoevsky's hero challenges the entire moral order: "Is the world to go to wrack and ruin or am I to have my cup of tea? Well, so far as I'm concerned, blow the world so long as I can have my cup of tea."[8]

The interpretation of *Notes from the Underground* is complicated by the fact that the narrator at times voices the author's own thoughts. In the description of the rationalized society of the future we again find the "crystal palace" of the *Winter Notes*:

Then . . . new economic relations will be established, relations all ready for use and calculated with mathematical exactitude, so that all sorts of problems will vanish in a twinkling simply because ready-made solutions will be provided for all of them. It is then that the crystal palace will be built. . . . But man is stupid, phenomenally stupid; I mean, he may not be really stupid, but on the other hand he is so ungrateful that you won't find anything like him in the whole wide world. I would not be at all surprised, for instance, if suddenly and without the slightest possible reason a gentleman of ignoble or rather reactionary and sardonic countenance were to arise amid all that coming reign of universal common sense and, gripping his sides firmly with his hands, were to say to us all, "Well, gentlemen, what about giving all this common sense a great kick and letting it shiver in the dust before our feet simply to send all these logarithms to the devil so that we can again live according to our silly will?"[9]

7. *Ibid.*, p. 112.
8. *Notes from the Underground*, trans. David Magarshak, in *The Best Stories of Dostoevsky* (New York, 1955), pp. 134, 136.
9. *Ibid.*, p. 130.

The partial confusion between author and narrator has given rise to a number of erroneous interpretations; even today books are published stating that Dostoevsky "reaffirms the absolute value and integrity of the single, separate individual," [10] Nothing is further from the truth—it is clear that Dostoevsky approves not of the "underground man's" individualism but only of his attack on the rationalization of social bonds common to both Western capitalism and socialism (for Dostoevsky the representative of Western socialist ideas in Russia was Chernyshevsky, whose reputation was then at its height). In his *Notes from the Underground* Dostoevsky wanted to express the almost Freudian idea that in the "dark cellars" of the human consciousness irrational demonic forces lie dormant that tend to be sublimated in a society held together by non-rational spiritual bonds, but that are likely to rise in revolt against a civilization based only on "rational egoism." Since men are not rational beings, they cannot be at home in a rationalized society; however, in a society deprived of authentic bonds of solidarity the irrational, anarchistic protest of the "underground man" is quite justified. In his original text Dostoevsky used this argument to prove the "need for faith in Christ," but to his indignation the censor crossed out the passage concerned. Nevertheless, the author's intention is quite clear; the narrator himself comments thus on his own position:

> All right, do it. Show me something more attractive. Give me another ideal. Show me something better and I will follow you. . . . Well perhaps I'm afraid of this palace just because it is made of crystal and is forever indestructible and just because I shall not be able to stick my tongue out at it. . . . I know as well as twice-two that it is not the dark cellar that is better, but something else, something else altogether, something I long for but cannot find! To hell with the dark cellar.[11]

It is worth noting that Dostoevsky's attitude to the irrationalistic ultra-individualism of the "underground man" is exactly analogous to Khomiakov's attitude toward the irrationalistic individualism of Max Stirner. The latter's work *The Ego and His Own*, Khomiakov wrote, was a *valid* protest against a rationalistic civilization: "It is the outcry of a soul that may perhaps be immoral, but only because it has been deprived of all moral support; a soul that reaffirms ceaselessly though unconsciously its longing to be able to subordinate itself to a principle it would wish to realize and believe in, and that

10. R. L. Jackson, *Dostoevsky's Underground Man in Russian Literature* (The Hague, 1958), p. 14.
11. *Notes from the Underground*, pp. 141, 143.

rejects with indignation and aversion the daily practices of the Western 'systematizers,' who have no faith themselves but demand faith in others, who create arbitrary bonds and expect others to accept them meekly."[12]

The Devious Paths of the Man-God

The clash between individualistic "license" and the "Christian truth" receives more profound treatment in Dostoevsky's great novels of the 1860's and 1870's. By this time he had come to the conclusion that both Western capitalism and socialist ideas were a consequence of man's falling away from God. European civilization had rejected the way of Christ, the God-Man, and had instead chosen the idolization of man, the way of the Man-God. This idea, which runs through *The Possessed* (1871–72), *The Brothers Karamazov* (1879–80), and *The Diary of a Writer* (1873–81), was probably suggested to Dostoevsky by Feuerbach, to whose writings he was introduced in his youth as a member of the Petrashevsky Circle. "The divine being is nothing else than the human being," Feuerbach wrote. "All the attributes of the divine nature are, therefore, attributes of the human nature . . . Man is the real God."[13]

Feuerbach's anthropotheism was criticized by Max Stirner, who argued that the philosopher had not really stopped being a "theologian": the liberation proclaimed by him was essentially a substitution of a "God within us" (or "Man" as the abstract essence of humanity) for a "God outside us." The religion of "Man" was therefore only a new way of enslaving the individual by subjugating him to the tyranny of the "universal." The way to true freedom of the individual was barred by the God-Man; it was not enough, therefore, to kill God—it was also necessary to kill "Man."[14] In order to liberate himself the individual must commit a crime,[15] must recognize himself as the supreme value and shed his miserable "holy ter-

12. A. S. Khomiakov, *Polnoe sobranie sochinenii* (M, 1914), vol. 1, p. 150.

13. L. Feuerbach, *The Essence of Christianity*, trans. George Eliot, introduced by Karl Barth (New York, 1957), pp. 14, 230.

14. Max Stirner, *Der Einzige und sein Eigentum* [*The Ego and His Own*] (Berlin, 1926), p. 182.

15. "The autonomous Ego," Stirner wrote (*ibid.*, p. 236), "cannot refrain from committing crimes, for crime is the essence of its existence . . . . Crime represents the significance and dignity of Man." Compare this with Raskolnikov's words "all great men or even men a little out of the common, that is capable of giving some new word, must from their very nature be criminals" (*Crime and Punishment*, trans. Constance Garnett [New York, 1956], p. 235). A detailed analysis of Raskolnikov's ideas and the corresponding ideas of Stirner is contained in my essay "Dostoevsky and the Idea of Freedom," in A. Walicki, *Osobowość a historia, Studia z dziejów literatury i myśli rosyjskiej* (Warsaw, 1959).

ror" of sinning against moral laws imposed in the name of an abstract humanity.

In *Crime and Punishment* (1866) Raskolnikov argues along exactly the same lines. Ostensibly he kills his victim in order to steal her money and save his mother and sister from disgrace; in fact his crime is an experiment in pure murder, an attempt to find out if he is "a louse like everyone else" or a free man, a Napoleon with the right to transgress against moral principles and hold men's lives in his hand. He wants to find out if he has the *right* to kill: "I began to question myself whether I had the right to gain power. Whether I can step over [moral] barriers or not. Whether I dare stoop to pick up [power] or not. Whether I am a trembling creature or whether I have the *right....*"[16]

The theory by which he justifies his act is the Russian equivalent of the philosophy of Stirner, who wrote: "My authority to commit murder derives from within myself; I have the right to kill if I do not forbid it myself, if I am not bound by the view that murder is an 'injustice,' something 'impure.'"[17]

Raskolnikov's experiment ends in failure. He cannot ignore his humanity or overstep the barrier that would allow him to leave behind both Good and Evil: "I killed the principle, but I didn't overstep. I stopped on this side...."[18] He is oppressed by nightmares, cannot face other people, and is forced to confess his guilt to those he had once thought of as lice. In Dostoevsky's intention the story of Raskolnikov's experiment shows the fallacy of the argument that everything is permissible, that ethical norms can be ignored; in the last resort God exists as the necessary guarantor of moral law.

The second variant of absolute self-assertive license—the suicide experiment—is described in *The Possessed*. For Kirilov suicide is the only means of affirming his own freedom in a world devoid of God.

If there's no God [Kirilov reasons] then I'm God. If God exists, then the will is his and I can do nothing. If he doesn't exist then the will is mine and I must exercise my own will, my free will. . . . I can't imagine that there's not one person on our whole planet, who, having put an end to God and believing in his own free will, will dare to exercise that will on the most important point. . . . I have an obligation to shoot myself because the supreme gesture of the free will is to kill oneself.[19]

16. *Crime and Punishment*, p. 377.
17. Stirner, *Der Einzige und sein Eigentum*, p. 221.
18. *Crime and Punishment*, p. 248.
19. *The Possessed*, trans. Andrew R. MacAndrew (New York, 1962), p. 635.

By killing himself Kirilov wants to kill his fear of death and thus to free mankind from God, to show that man himself is God; it seems to him that "this alone will redeem all men and allow them to be physically reborn in the next generation."[20] In fact he merely achieves his own annihilation, and his death (by his own consent) is exploited by petty persons for their own shabby ends. Thus ends the second great experiment in the exercise of individualistic freedom.

In the sphere of social relations the final outcome of absolute license, Dostoevsky argues, can only be despotism. Freedom without God gives rise to a "lascivious" and "sadistic" lust for power and is thus transformed into its opposite. "I started out with the idea of unrestricted freedom," says Shigalev in *The Possessed*, "and I have arrived at unrestricted despotism. I must add, however, that any solution of the social problem other than mine is impossible."[21] "Shigalev's system" is a gloomy vision of a society based on absolute obedience and absolute depersonalization. He offers as a final solution the division of mankind into two uneven categories. "One-tenth will be granted individual freedom and full rights over the remaining nine-tenths, who will lose their individuality and become something like a herd of cattle. . . . They will attain a state of primeval innocence, something akin to the original paradise on earth, although of course they will have to work." The insistence on absolute equality does not even allow for inequality of talent: "They cut out Cicero's tongue, gouge out Copernicus's eyes; they throw stones at Shakespeare—that's Shigalev's system for you! The slaves must be equal; without tyranny there has never yet been freedom or equality, but in the herd there is equality and that's what Shigalev teaches."[22]

A modified and nobler version of Shigalev's system is presented in the "Legend of the Grand Inquisitor" in book five of *The Brothers Karamazov*. This is preceded by the rebellion of Ivan Karamazov —a rebellion against alleged divine or historical justice, a refusal to accept a harmony for which too high a price must be paid. Ivan rejects not God but the world he has created—because it is a world of injustice, because divine Providence does nothing to prevent the suffering of innocent children, and because no future "harmony"

20. This idea can be found in the work of Ludwig Feuerbach. In his *Lectures on the Essence of Religion* (trans. Ralph Manheim [New York, 1967], p. 274) he wrote about "the future immortal man, differentiated from man as he exists at present in the body and flesh."

21. *The Possessed*, pp. 384–85.

22. *Ibid.*, p. 399.

can make up for the tears of a tormented child.[23] His revolt suggests that men ought to take their fate into their own hands, reject the revealed truths of the Gospels, and build the Kingdom of God on earth—but without God. This, of course, was Dostoevsky's explanation of the origins of revolutionary socialism.

The "Legend of the Grand Inquisitor" was intended to be a parable of the just kingdom the socialists were trying to establish on earth. The Grand Inquisitor exchanges freedom for bread, and takes away freedom in order to bestow happiness on his "pitiful children." However, an indispensable condition of this happiness is total and herdlike depersonalization. Knowing that men are weak, the Inquisitor lifts from them the burden of freedom, conscience, and personal responsibility; he replaces freedom by authority, and consenting, free unity by a unity based on compulsion. The Church transformed into State unites "all in one unanimous and harmonious ant heap." When Christ descends to earth in order to be among his people once more, the Inquisitor tries to have him arrested and burned as a heretic. Christ listens in silence to his long monologue and then kisses him on the mouth as a sign of his forgiveness; the Inquisitor lets him go but begs him never to return to disturb the tranquil happiness men have achieved without him.

The "dialectic of individualism" by which individualistic freedom is transformed into universal unfreedom was explained by Dostoevsky's philosophy of history, which has obvious similarities with the Slavophile critque of Western Europe. Like the Slavophiles, Dostoevsky pointed to the classical heritage as a source of the evil that had distorted the Christian faith in the West. It was from pagan Rome that Catholicism adopted the idea of the man-God (the emperor, the Apollo of Belvedere) and the concept of unity based on compulsion.[24] The individual's protest against the Catholic "unifying idea" led to social atomization and put power into the hands of the bourgeoisie, whose philosophy was egoism ("every man for himself and for himself alone") and the law of the jungle. A new negation—the protest against individualism and anarchy—gave birth to socialism, which Dostoevsky called a secularized form of the Catholic "unity through compulsion."

23. Ivan Karamazov's rebellion recalls Belinsky's revolt against Hegel—even to the extent of identity of phrasing. It is quite likely that Dostoevsky made use of fragments of Belinsky' letters to Botkin. which were published in 1876 in A. N. Pypin's life of Belinsky. See A. Walicki, *Osobowość a historia*, pp. 405–9; the same observation was made by V. Y. Kirpotin, *Dostoevsky i Belinsky* (M, 1960), pp. 228–39.

24. *The Diary of a Writer*, trans. Boris Brasol (New York, 1954), p. 1,005. Similar thoughts are expressed by Ivan Karamazov.

The notion that there was an organic relationship between Catholicism and socialism, emphasized in the "Legend of the Grand Inquisitor," was one of Dostoevsky's favorite and almost obsessive theories. It first occurs in *The Idiot*, in Prince Myshkin's well-known monologue:

For socialism too is an offspring of Catholicism and the essential Catholic idea. It too, like its brother atheism, springs from despair in opposition to Catholicism as a moral presence, to replace the lost moral power of religion, to quench the spiritual thirst of parched humanity, and to save it not through Christ but also through violence! This too is freedom through violence, this too is union through blood and the sword![25]

Dostoevsky developed this notion in *The Diary of a Writer*, where he wrote: "The present-day French socialism itself . . . is nothing but the truest and most direct continuation of the Catholic idea, its fullest, most final realization, its fatal consequence which has been evolved through centuries."[26]

This analogy seems less curious if we remember that the Saint-Simonians in France held similar views on the connection between Catholicism and socialism (although for them this was a matter of approval) and imagined the future "organic period" as a "new theocracy" based on the Catholic principles of hierarchy and authority. In any case Dostoevsky's ideas on the evolution of Western civilization were not new in Russia. The view of Catholicism as the heir to ancient Rome derives from Slavophile theory; the formula "unity through compulsion" recalls Khomiakov's "unity without freedom," and the description of bourgeois social atomization can be compared to his "freedom without unity." The interpretation of the essence of socialism as a search for the lost "unifying principle," and the desire to impose this principle arbitrarily on an atomized society, also have their counterparts in Slavophile thought. Another variation of this theme is to be found in some comments on Western civilization made by Grigoriev apropos of a letter by George Sand. This letter, Grigoriev wrote,

is a terrible exposure of an existence in which such notions as love and fraternity must be *invented*, in which the *universal* can only gain the submission of the particular, the individual, by compulsion and despotism . . . an exposure of an existence that, in a word, reveals two unavoidable extremes: the despotic absorption of personality by "papism," whether Roman papism or (basically it is all the same) Fourierist and Saint-Simonian popery; and the immoderate protest of the individual, a

25. *The Idiot*, trans. Henry and Olga Carlisle (New York, 1969), pp. 561–62.
26. *Diary of a Writer*, p. 563.

protest expressed in the doctrine of Max Stirner as a consistent deification of the individual.[27]

In the 1870's Dostoevsky became closely associated with extreme
right-wing circles. In 1872 he was asked to take over the editorship
of the conservative periodical *Citizen* (*Grazhdanin*), and he soon
became a close friend of Pobedonostsev. He would visit him every
Saturday for long conversations and even asked his advice when he
was writing *The Brothers Karamazov*. It is worth stressing, therefore, that *The Brothers Karamazov* (in contrast to *The Possessed*)
cannot be seen simply as an attack on revolutionary socialism; Ivan
Karamazov's rebellion is shown by Dostoevsky with profound understanding, although the author himself was anxious to refute the
motives that he portrayed with such insight. This can be explained
partly by the fact that *The Possessed* was written under the influence of the Nechaev trial, whereas *The Brothers Karamazov* was
written under the influence of the heroic struggle of the Populist
terrorists, whose personal nobility and purity of motive Dostoevsky
did not question. The essential difference, however, is that Ivan
Karamazov's struggle no doubt reflects a conflict Dostoevsky had
once experienced himself. As a former member of the Petrashevsky
Circle he too must have felt the temptations of militant atheism;
his cry of "Hosanna," as he himself put it, came "through a great
flame of doubt."[28]

Pobedonostsev was somewhat alarmed after reading the chapter
on Ivan Karamazov's rebellion and the "Legend of the Grand Inquisitor"; he wondered, not without cause, whether Dostoevsky
would be able to give equally good arguments to the other side.
The "counterpoise" Pobedonostsev required was the Orthodox
monk, Father Zoshima, who turned out to be a pale and rather lifeless figure. Alyosha Karamazov's angelic goodness is also far from
convincing. As for the "Legend," it is a highly ambiguous piece of
writing from an ideological point of view; there could be no guarantee that its readers would see the threat to freedom and individuality as coming solely from Catholicism and socialism and not, for
instance, from the Orthodox autocracy in whose services the Director General of the Holy Synod labored so faithfully.

National Messianism and the Idea of "All-Humanity"

To the Roman Catholic ideal of the church as state, Dostoevsky
opposed the Orthodox ideal of the state as church. As Lunacharsky

27. A. Grigoriev, *Sochineniia* (St. Petersburg, 1876), pp. 175–76.
28. Dostoevsky, *Polnoe sobranie sochinenii* (St. Petersburg, 1883), vol. 1, p. 375.

aptly pointed out, Dostoevsky needed this utopian concept partly because it enabled him not to "sever completely his inner connection with the socialist truth while cursing materialistic socialism."[29] It is significant that Dostoevsky did not even repudiate the label "socialism": in the last number of *The Diary of a Writer* he used Herzen's term "Russian socialism" to describe the ideals he attributed to the Russian people—"the ideals of the state as church, of universal brotherhood, and the free unity of mankind."

The leitmotif of Dostoevsky's Orthodox utopia—and indeed of the Slavophile utopia—was the idea of a return to the people, to the "native soil." The messianic note, the emphasis on the "universally human mission of the Russian people," was much stronger in Dostoevsky than in classical Slavophilism. Unlike Danilevsky, who emphatically rejected the very idea of a universal mission, Dostoevsky believed that the conquest of Constantinople and the unification by Russia of all the Slavic peoples would herald a new epoch in world history—an epoch in which Orthodox Russia would pronounce "a new word" that would bring about the rebirth and salvation of mankind. It must be made clear, however, that this universalism did not mean approval for the ideal of "abstract humanity" rejected by the proponents of "a return to the soil." For Dostoevsky the "all-human man" (*vshechelovek*) was to be the antithesis of the "man in general" (*obshchechelovek*). By "all-humanity" he meant heterogeneity and an all-around, fulfilled personality —the opposite of the abstract ideal of an abstract Humanity, which he accused of reducing human complexity to a shabby common denominator or, more likely, of simply being a disguise for the desire to force everyone into the same mold.

In Dostoevsky's novels messianism appears in two versions. One of them is expressed by Shatov in *The Possessed*:

A people forms the body of its god. A nation is a nation only so long as it has its particular god and excludes as irreconcilable all other gods; so long as it believes that with the help of its gods it will conquer and destroy all other gods. . . . But there is one truth and therefore only one people can possess it and, with it, the only true god, though other people may have their own particular gods and even great ones. Now the only god-bearing nation is the Russian nation.[30]

For Dostoevsky, nation was synonymous with common people. Again and again in his novels and journalism we find scathing criti-

29. *F. M. Dostoevsky russkoi kritike* (M, 1956), p. 442.
30. *The Possessed*, p. 238.

cism of the uprooted intelligentsia, whose atheism was, he suggested, a function of their divorce from the "soil." "You are godless," Shatov says to Stavrogin, "because you're the son of the idle rich, the last of the idle rich. You've lost the ability to distinguish between good and evil because you've lost touch with the people of your own country. . . . Listen Stavrogin, find God through labor. That is the essence of everything. Find God or you'll vanish without a trace like a rotten fungus. Find God through labor." "What sort of labor?" Stavrogin asks. "The work of a laborer, a peasant," is Shatov's reply.[31]

The extreme doctrine advanced by Dostoevsky through his mouthpiece Shatov is both nationalistic and anti-intellectual. As mentioned earlier, however, *The Possessed* was written under the immediate impact of the Nechaev trial and is therefore a very one-sided reflection of its author's world view. A somewhat different messianism—one that instead of rejecting "alien gods" emphasizes Russia's mission in reconciling Europe and Russia, the intelligentsia and the people; one that in fact propounds a universal synthesis—is to be found in the articles Dostoevsky wrote for the periodical *Time* even in the early 1860's. This version of messianism was later developed in *The Diary of a Writer*.

"Oh, do you know, gentlemen," he wrote in 1877, "how dear this very Europe, this 'land of sacred miracles,' how dear it is to us, Slavophile dreamers—according to you—haters of Europe! Do you know how dear these 'miracles' are to us; how we love and revere with a stronger than brotherly feeling, those great nations that inhabit her, everything great and beautiful which they have created."[32]

Westernization had widened Russia's horizons, Dostoevsky acknowledged, and this must be appreciated by all. The intelligentsia, too, had a valuable contribution to make:

We must bow before the people's truth and recognize it as such, we must bow like prodigal chidren who, for two hundred years, have been absent from home, but who nevertheless have returned Russians. . . . [H]owever, we must bow on one condition only, and this—*sine qua non*: that the people accept from us those numerous things which we have brought with us. . . . This is our need to serve humanity, although it might be to the detriment of our own dearest and most essential interests, our reconciliation with the civilization of Europe, the understanding and justification of their ideals, even though they did not even harmonize with ours.[33]

31. *Ibid.*, p. 242.
32. *Diary of a Writer*, p. 782.
33. *Ibid.*, p. 204.

Dostoevsky, therefore (like Chaadaev before him), regarded divorce from the soil and "homeless wandering" not just as a misfortune, but also as a chance to create a new type of a "universal man" free from the burden of the past and from national prejudices —a man who would "bear the world's sufferings." He agreed with Herzen that "the thinking Russian is the most independent man in the world." The cultivated elite in Russia, says Vershilov in *The Adolescent*, has "produced perhaps a thousand representatives (give or take a few) who are freer than any European, men whose fatherland is all mankind. No one can be freer and happier than a Russian wanderer belonging to the 'chosen thousand'; I really mean that; it's not just a joke. Besides, I would never have exchanged that mental anguish for any other kind of happiness."[34]

Nevertheless, Dostoevsky called on the "chosen thousand" to give up their wanderings and return home. Only a "return to the soil" and submission to "the people's truth" would enable them to find true peace and would heal their split personality. A symbolic expression of this is the scene in *The Adolescent* when Vershilov breaks the ancient icon of the old pilgrim Makar. Here we have the smashing of the folk (Orthodox Christian) heritage, the inner dualism (the icon breaks into two equal parts), and the hint of the return to the people through Sonia, a woman of the people. The marriage of Sonia and Vershilov is a symbol of future reconciliation between the lost intelligentsia and the people who, in spite of temptation (Sonia's seduction by Vershilov), have kept faith with their moral ideas and have preserved in their religion the pure, undefiled image of Christ.

A lengthier treatment of the same theme, summing up two decades of reflection, is to be found in Dostoevsky's famous "Address on Pushkin" made at the unveiling of the Pushkin Monument in Moscow (June 8, 1880). In this speech Dostoevsky enlarged on Apollon Grigoriev's favorite image of Pushkin as a synthetic expression of the Russian spirit, a "prophetic" apparition who had shown the Russian nation its mission and its future.

In the character of Aleko, the hero of the poem "Gypsies," and in Evgeny Onegin, Dostoevsky suggested, Pushkin had been the first to portray "the unhappy wanderer in his native land, the traditional Russian sufferer detached from the people. . . ." For Dostoevsky the term "wanderer" was an apt description of the entire Russian intelligentsia—both the "superfluous men" of the forties and the Populists of the seventies. "The homeless vagrants," he continued,

34. *The Adolescent*, trans. Andrew R. MacAndrew (New York, 1971), p. 490.

"are wandering still, and it seems it will be long before they disappear"; at present they were seeking refuge in socialism, which did not exist in Aleko's time, and through it hoped to attain universal happiness, for "a Russian sufferer to find peace needs universal happiness—exactly this: nothing less will satisfy him—of course, as long as the proposition is confined to theory."[35]

Before the wanderer can find peace, however, he must conquer his own pride and humble himself before "the people's truth." "Humble thyself, proud man, and above all, break thy pride," was the "Russian solution" Dostoevsky claimed to have found in Pushkin's poetry. Aleko failed to follow this advice and was therefore asked to leave by the gypsies; Onegin despised Tatiana—a modest girl close to the "soil"—and by the time he learned to humble himself it was too late. Throughout Pushkin's work, Dostoevsky declared, there were constant confrontations between the "Russian wanderers" and "the people's truth" represented by "positively beautiful" heroes—men of the soil expressing the spiritual essence of the Russian nation. The purpose of these confrontations was to convince the reader of the need for a "return to the soil" and a fusion with the people.

Pushkin himself was proof that such a return was possible without a rejection of universal ideals. Dostoevsky drew attention to the poet's "universal susceptibility," his talent for identifying himself with a Spaniard (Don Juan), an Arab ("Imitations of the Koran"), an Englishman ("A Feast During the Plague"), or an ancient Roman ("Egyptian Nights") while still remaining a national poet. This ability Pushkin owed to the "universality" of the Russian spirit: "to become a genuine and complete Russian means . . . to become brother of all men, an all-human man."

In his speech Dostoevsky also spoke about the division into Slavophiles and Westernizers, which he regretted as a great, though historically inevitable, misunderstanding. The impulse behind Peter's reform had been not mere utilitarianism but the desire to extend the frontiers of nationality to include a genuine "all-humanity." Dreams of serving humanity had even been the impulse behind the political policies of the Russian state: "For what else has Russia been doing in her policies, during these two centuries, but serving Europe much more than herself? I do not believe that this took place because of the mere want of aptitude on the part of our statesmen."[36]

35. *The Diary of a Writer*, p. 968.
36. Here Dostoevsky was polemicizing with Danilevsky, who (in *Russia and Europe*)

"Oh, the peoples of Europe," Dostoevsky exclaimed in a euphoric vein, "have no idea how dear they are to us! And later—in this I believe—we, well, not we but the Russians of the future, to the last man, will comprehend that to become a genuine Russian means to seek finally to reconcile all European controversies, to show the solution of European anguish in our all-human and all-unifying Russian soil, to embrace in it with brotherly love all our brothers, and finally, perhaps, to utter the ultimate word of great, universal harmony, of the fraternal accord of all nations abiding by the law of Christ's Gospel!"[37]

Before delivering his "Address," Dostoevsky was seriously worried that it might be received coldly by his audience. His fears proved groundless. The speech was an unprecedented success: carried away by enthusiasm, the crowd called out "our holy man, our prophet," and members of the audience pressed around Dostoevsky to kiss his hands. Even Turgenev, who had been caricatured in *The Possessed*, came up to embrace him. The solemn moment of universal reconciliation between Slavophiles and Westernizers, conservatives and revolutionaries, seemed already at hand. "When at the end I proclaimed the idea of universal reconciliation," Dostoevsky wrote to his wife, "the audience fell into a frenzy; I can hardly tell you what a tumult, what a roar of approval broke out when I finished; people who did not know each other burst into tears, sobbed, fell into each others' arms, and swore that they would become better, that they would no longer hate but love each other."[38]

The enthusiasm aroused by the "Address" turned out to be short-lived; men who had embraced each other under its immediate impact decided, after some reflection, that the differences dividing them had not diminished in the slightest. Only Ivan Aksakov continued to regard the "Address" with lasting and uncritical enthusiasm.

One member of the enthusiastic audience was the Populist writer Gleb Uspensky; in his report for the *Notes of the Fatherland* he wrote that the address had had a "staggering impact" that was fully deserved, despite talk about "some kind of *humility*," to which the audience paid no attention. After the full text had appeared, Uspensky felt compelled to correct his report, to warn his readers that the impression made by the "Address" failed to reflect "its real content"

---

had ridiculed Russian statesmen for trying to curry favor with Europe to the detriment of their country's interest.

37. Dostoevsky, *Pol. sob. soch.*, vol. 10, p. 458.
38. Dostoevsky, *Pis'ma*, ed. A. S. Dolinin (M, 1959), vol. 4, p. 144.

and that its success was largely based on an erroneous interpretation.

Criticism from the conservative side came from Leontiev. He called Dostoevsky a heretic who wanted to replace the teaching of the church by a "rose-colored Christianity." The Gospel, he pointed out, did not promise universal brotherhood, concord, or harmony, and the realization of such ideals would be the greatest misfortune for the church.

From his own point of view Leontiev was quite right in his criticism. An attentive reading of *The Brothers Karamazov* and the "Address on Pushkin" leaves no doubt that Dostoevsky's essential concern was not with salvation in heaven but with salvation on earth. His emphasis on a world without injustice or violence, and on universal brotherhood, reflected a longing for "harmony" that was an echo of his youthful ideas and showed the gulf that divided him from such reactionary patrons as Pobedonostsev.[39] The term "harmony" itself, it should be remembered, was one of the entries in the *Pocket Dictionary* compiled by the Petrashevtsy.

LEV TOLSTOY

The Phases of Moral Crisis

At the end of the 1870's, Count LEV TOLSTOY (1828–1910) was at the height of his literary fame: *War and Peace* had appeared in 1869 and *Anna Karenina* in 1877. Now, when his creative genius was at its peak, he experienced a moral crisis that marked a turning point in his life. After a period of depression and thoughts of suicide, he became more and more obsessed by the idea that he must turn his back completely on the system of values accepted by the comfortable elite to which he belonged.

In the years 1878–79 Tolstoy wrote his famous *Confession*; he followed this with the *Critique of Dogmatic Theology* and the tracts *What I Believe* (1884), *What Are We to Do?* (1886), *On Life* (1887), and *The Kingdom of God Is Within You* (1893). In 1881 he sent an appeal to Alexander III asking him to commute the death sentences passed on the revolutionaries who had assassinated his father. In the same year he went on a pilgrimage to the Optina Cloister, where discussions with Father Ambrose, one of the famous elders there, confirmed him in his distrust of official Orthodoxy. Another experience that helped to change his outlook was the work he did for the Moscow census a year later, when he saw at first hand the conditions of the urban poor. For the sake of his family he did not hand over

39. See M. Gus, *Idei i obrazy F. M. Dostoevskogo* (M, 1962), pp. 492–95.

his estate to the peasants as he wished to do, but he cut down his personal expenditures, gave up his former aristocratic life-style, and undertook regular physical labor. Gradually he gathered around him a group of disciples, the most important being Vladimir Chertkov. Together they founded "The Intermediary" (*Posrednik*), a publishing company that was to bring literature to the people. Through this company Tolstoy published several of his own works (e.g. *What Do Men Live By?*, *God Sees the Truth but Waits*). The venture was very successful and helped to popularize his ideas, especially among the religious sectarians. After a disastrous harvest in 1891, Tolstoy tried to rouse public opinion with a series of articles on hunger in the countryside and personally organized aid for the starving peasants. When the Dukhobor sect was being persecuted by the government a few years later, he spoke up in their defense and together with Chertkov helped to arrange their emigration to Canada. There was worldwide indignation when Tolstoy's criticism of official Orthodoxy led the Holy Synod to excommunicate him in 1901.

This is the accepted account of how Tolstoyan doctrine came into being and continued to function in popular tracts and philosophical-cum-religious pamphlets (which, in view of the censorship, were largely published abroad). Many researchers have pointed out, however, that elements of Tolstoy's later philosophy can be found in works written before the "turning point."[40] In adolescence Tolstoy had been fascinated by Rousseau's criticism of civilization; when he was fifteen he wore a medallion with Rousseau's portrait around his neck.[41] In the story *Three Deaths*, written in 1858, we already find the characteristic Tolstoyan contrast between the fear of death felt by the "upper classes" and the peaceful resignation of a simple man of the people as he faces his end. Articles published in 1862 in the periodical *Yasnaya Polana* (when he was running a school for the village children on his estate) contain the earliest outline of the social philosophy he later elaborated in the 1880's. Condemnation of individualism (embodied for Tolstoy—as for Dostoevsky—in Napoleon) runs as a continuous motif through *War and Peace*. In the novel this individualism is contrasted again and again with the instinctive "truth" of the common people. Even Tolstoy's pessimism was not something that only emerged with his ideological

40. See A. Semczuk, *Lev Tolstoy* (Warsaw, 1963), pp. 221ff.
41. See N. N. Gusev, *Letopis' zhizni i tvorchestva L. N. Tolstogo* (M, 1958), p. 30. In 1901 Tolstoy told a certain professor in Paris that he had read "the whole of Rousseau, all 22 volumes, including the *Dictionary of Music*."

crisis. From a letter we know that he was reading Schopenhauer in 1869; the works of this "greatest genius among men," he wrote to his friend Fet, filled him with "unceasing rapture" and a pleasure never known before.[42]

The importance of the crisis of the 1870's should not be underestimated, however, though in his *Confession* Tolstoy undoubtedly exaggerated the suddenness and violence of the changes in his outlook. His vivid tale of a repentant sinner was a piece of artistic license obviously intended to shock readers into abandoning their own evil ways. Nevertheless, the sincerity and authentic fervor of the *Confession* speak for themselves: before he wrote it, Tolstoy suffered from a severe bout of depression that in 1876 led him to contemplate suicide. During his recovery he turned to religion and finally broke with the generally accepted world view of his own milieu. In sum, one may say that whereas this crisis was only a stage in the gradual evolution of Tolstoy's ideas, it did mark a real turning point in his life.

In his *Confession* Tolstoy wrote that he had been baptized and brought up in the Orthodox faith, but had soon abandoned it, like most members of his class. He had killed men in the war; fought duels; squandered money extorted from the peasants on eating, drinking, and gambling; and indulged in debauchery. Although there was hardly a crime he had not committed, he was generally accepted as a moral man.

What, then, took the place of his lost faith? Like most educated men of his day, Tolstoy wrote, he believed in progress; but when he saw a man being guillotined in Paris, he understood that no theory could justify the taking of human life. He longed for fame, but in his heart of hearts he did not believe that there was anything of substantial value to be gained by becoming the most famous writer in the world. When his beloved brother died, how was he to explain and justify his death? There was no adequate answer. The inevitability of death made life a total absurdity, a cruel and stupid joke. The human condition could be compared to the lot of the traveler in an oriental fable. Pursued by a wild beast, he climbs down into a well, only to see at the bottom the gaping jaws of a dragon. Unable to go either up or down, the poor man clings to a bush growing in a crevice. As his strength begins to fail he sees two mice, one white and one black (symbolizing night and day), gnawing at the branch he is hanging from. Knowing that he must inevitably fall, the traveler still makes a supreme effort and licks the drops of

42. *Ibid.*, p. 363.

sweet sap oozing from the leaves. "This is no fairy tale," Tolstoy comments, "but a genuine, indisputable, and universally comprehensible truth."[43]

If they had the courage to face the truth, men must surely realize that, from the point of view of the individual clinging to the idea of personal survival, human existence must be summed up in the words "vanity of vanities, all is vanity." This was a truth known to all the wise men in history—Socrates, Solomon, and the Buddha. The newest philosophy, represented by Schopenhauer, had also come to the conclusion that "happy is he who has never been born, death is better than life." The best solution to the terrible dilemma was suicide, and that was the way out chosen by strong and energetic men. Other palliatives were Epicureanism, unconsciousness, or—for men who were wise but weak (like Solomon or Schopenhauer)—the acceptance of life as it was, in full awareness of the fact that it was senseless and evil. This was the way out he himself had chosen, Tolstoy writes in the *Confession*: he knew that life was a stupid joke played on humanity, but nevertheless he went on living, washing, getting dressed, eating dinners, conversing, and even writing books.

At this point there is a sudden change in the argument, analogous to the switch made by Kant who, after demonstrating that theoretical reason leads to irreconcilable antinomies, opposes theoretical reason with practical reason, which resolves these contradictions.[44] Reason denies life, Tolstoy writes, but is itself the child of life. Life is all; the individual's reason denies that it has meaning, but at the same time millions of human beings live their lives without doubting that their existence is meaningful.

"How can this be?" Tolstoy asks. "Are we two—Schopenhauer and I—the only two men wise enough to have insight into the meaning of life?"[45] Would you not say we were infatuated by pride in our own reason? According to the rational understanding of learned men life may be meaningless, but the vast masses find meaning in life on the basis of irrational understanding or faith. Faith is not revelation, or the supernatural, or a concern solely with man's relationship to God—it is just this suprarational insight into the meaning of human existence thanks to which man does not annihilate himself.

43. L. N. Tolstoy, *Polnoe sobranie sochinenii* (M-L, 1928–58), vol. 23, p. 14.
44. Later Tolstoy himself noticed the analogy; he read Kant's *Critique of Practical Reason* (in 1887) with "joyous delight" (see Gusev, *Letopis'*, p. 679).
45. Tolstoy, *Pol. sob. soch.*, vol. 23, p. 30.

Having come to this conclusion, Tolstoy relates in the *Confession*, he set out to look for spiritual help from men of religious belief. At first he turned to men of his own circle, but he soon understood that their faith was not genuine but only one of their Epicurean pleasures. He therefore "turned his eyes to the huge masses of simple, ignorant, and poor people"—pilgrims, monks and peasants, orthodox Christians as well as Old Believers and sectarians. In their company he could see that they accepted sickness and misfortune with quiet resignation, and death without terror or despair. He came to love them and to understand that the meaning life had for them was the true one, so that he too accepted this meaning. He regained his faith in God and understood the universal wisdom handed on by tradition, which proclaims that the world is governed by a superior will, and that he who would understand its meaning must bow before this will.

A further stage in Tolstoy's evolution began when he noticed the difference between the faith of the theologians and that of the common people. At first, under Khomiakov's influence, he took part in all church ceremonies, even those whose meaning he failed to understand; he abased his intellect and submitted to tradition, for only thus, he believed, would he "become united in love" with past generations, with the whole of humanity. Soon, however, he could not fail to notice that theological dogmas served to divide people rather than to unite them, that they countenanced persecution and were exploited for particularist and secular ends.

After examining official theology, Tolstoy came to the conclusion that it was not interested in the meaning of life; obscure dogmas concealed no deeper meaning, but were merely a means of diverting people's attention from the clear and simple truths of religious faith because these truths, which the common people understood instinctively, were often inconvenient to their rulers. Taking reason as his guide, therefore, Tolstoy set out to make a critique of theology. What he demanded of belief was that there should be no incomprehensible, suprarational truths apart from those whose acceptance arose out of the nature of reason itself, as a faculty realizing its own limitations.[46] He submitted the teachings of the church to rational examination in order to eliminate from them everything that was inconsistent with reason and had been imposed upon it artificially.

In this way reason—by-passed in order to allow the writer to embrace faith conceived as an irrational but life-enhancing insight—

46. *Ibid.*, p. 57.

now had its rights fully restored. Later still, Tolstoy came to the conclusion that there must be absolutely no dissonance between reason and religion if the latter was not to be a pseudo-faith.[47]

At first sight this argument appears to be self-contradictory: first reason capitulates before faith, and then it is set up as the arbiter in matters of faith; first all rational argument is condemned as life-denying (the way from Cartesian doubt to Schopenhauerian pessimism), and then, at the other extreme, we have an out-and-out rationalistic, "commonsense" criticism of the mysteries of faith.[48] In fact there is no inconsistency—only a state of tension between two poles of thought forming an interdependent dialectical whole. In order to follow Tolstoy's argument we have to realize that he was writing about two different kinds of reason: the life-denying reason that is forced to submit to faith is the *individual reason* of man as a being subject to spatiotemporal limitations; reason in harmony with faith, on the other hand, is *universal reason*. It is a peculiar feature of Tolstoy's philosophy that the supra-individual universal reason extolled by him has certain features in common with the critical Enlightenment intellect—that is, the brand of rationalism the religious critics of the Enlightenment (e.g. Lamennais) condemned as stemming from *individual* reason, incompatible with universal reason.

Another unusual aspect of Tolstoy's thought is that he arrived at the idea of the futility of individual reason partly through his reading of Schopenhauer. He thus differed both from the Slavophiles, who drew their inspiration from the German romantics, and from Chaadaev, who was influenced by the French traditionalists. Under Schopenhauer's influence, Tolstoy became convinced of the essential difference between true reality and the illusory world of phenomena. Schopenhauer argued that all suffering, fear of death, and the sense of the absurdity of life flow from the imprisonment of the will—the metaphysical substance of the universe—within the body of the individual. The way to salvation, therefore, is to repudiate the self, to shed the burden of spatiotemporal individuality. "Salvation," Schopenhauer wrote, "is something utterly alien to our personality; in order to achieve it, it is necessary to deny and annihilate this personality."[49] This is the guiding idea of Schopenhauer's ethics, which points the way to salvation through metaphysical im-

47. See Tolstoy, *Chto takoe religiia i v chem sushchnost' eyo?* (1902).
48. Of French Enlightenment authors, Tolstoy appreciated not only Rousseau but also Voltaire.
49. A. Schopenhauer, *Sämmtliche Werke* (Leipzig, 1922), vol. 2, p. 482 (*Die Welt als Wille und Vorstellung*).

personalism. To love one's fellow man means to forget one's own individuality, to abolish the barriers between the self and the other: "for him who actively loves his neighbor, the veil of Maya becomes transparent, the mirage of the *principium individuationis* disappears."[50] Another way to salvation is through art, which has an intuitive understanding of all that is eternal, unchanging, and impersonal. Total liberation, however, is to be found only in the "euthanasia of the will," the state of perfect indifference, the abandonment to Nirvana. This moral ideal can be achieved through ascetic resignation as exemplified by the Christian saint or the Indian holy man.

It will be seen from this that Schopenhauer's role in Tolstoy's spiritual crisis and its resolution was of considerable importance. He did not, it is true, take over Schopenhauer's philosophy in its entirety (in particular he did not accept the conception of the will as the metaphysical essence of the universe): moreover, what he did take over he often modified or combined with other ideas completely alien to the German philosopher. Indeed, Tolstoy's new outlook led him, as we shall see, to a radical questioning of the entire culture and way of life of the upper classes—something that had no counterpart in Schopenhauer's philosophy or outlook on life. Nevertheless, it was to Schopenhauer that Tolstoy owed the formulation of the leading idea of his philosophy of life—the notion that there is an essential difference between true life and spatiotemporal existence. It was Schopenhauer, too, who confirmed him in his conviction that the time- and space-bound individual cannot escape discovering that his life has to be seen as totally absurd, and who showed him that the way to salvation lies, consequently, in overcoming "the principle of individuation." Finally, Schopenhauer was partly responsible for turning Tolstoy's attention toward Buddhism and the other great religions of the East, and for showing him how they were related to Christianity.

Tolstoy's Philosophy of Life

The best exposition of Tolstoy's metaphysics is to be found in his treatise *On Life* (1887).

"The true life of man," he wrote, "is the aspiration toward goodness, which is achieved by submitting one's individuality to the law of reason. Neither reason nor the degree of submission to reason is determined by time or space. True life has its course outside time

50. *Ibid.*, pp. 440–41.

and space."[51] Only life like this—life that recognizes no difference between one minute and fifty thousand years—can be said truly to exist.

It is time and space that lie at the roots of the "principle of individuation." It follows from this that to renounce the individual welfare is not an act of exceptional merit but a necessary law of life. In order to live a true life—not a life of animal instincts—it is necessary to be reborn and become a "reasonable consciousness," to transcend individuality by identifying one's own welfare with the welfare of others. Whoever achieves this finds that death no longer holds any terror and perceives the world as a reasonable whole, subject to a single law. Individual life is not true life—the Hindu yogi who spends years standing on one leg in order to achieve Nirvana is more truly alive than the brutish inhabitants of the so-called civilized countries.[52] What is normally called life is actually only a game with death (on this point the "latest pessimists," Schopenhauer and Hartmann, are in agreement with the Buddhists, Tolstoy declared). True life is not the world of phenomena but an invisible and impersonal "reasonable consciousness," a universal force not bounded by time or space. Individuality is evil, an illusion that cuts man off from true life, imprisons him in the world of phenomena and condemns him to suffering and death. The way to transcend individuality is through love—love not as an emotional impulse, but as total submission to the tranquil clarity of the "reasonable consciousness" that enjoins men to renounce their individual welfare.[53]

Though Tolstoy demanded the renunciation of "individual welfare" and not personality as such, he was also concerned to make the point that true personality should not be identified with the "brutish" nature of the spatiotemporal world. Personality as a sense of identity has, in fact, nothing to do with individuality: our bodies are constantly altering, and individual consciousness is a series of changing psychological states, whereas a sense of identity is something permanent and unchanging. On the basis of this argument, Tolstoy attempted, in his treatise *On Life*, to prove that "man's true self" is not subject to the power of death. These ideas were not, however, fully developed and seem to stem from certain hesitations rather than a principled standpoint. The chief content

51. L. N. Tolstoy, *Polnoe sobranie sochinenii* (St. Petersburg, 1913; ed. P. I. Biriukov), vol. 17, p. 248.

52. *Ibid.*, p. 261.

53. *Ibid.*, p. 270.

of the Tolstoyan philosophy of life was undoubtedly metaphysical impersonalism—entirely consistent, apart from the above-mentioned reservations, and extreme in its ethical implications.

In its overall postulates Tolstoy's ethics, with its exhortations to love of one's fellow man and ascetic resignation, does not differ from Schopenhauer's. The similarity also extends to the view of the illusory nature of the world of space and time put forward to justify these postulates. In his practical conclusions, however, Tolstoy differs widely from his model. In Schopenhauer's system the overcoming of the "principle of individuation" represents the climax of the unfolding of individuality. His "renunciation of the world" does not lead to an idealization of the consciousness at the pre-individuation stage, or a cult of simplicity or Rousseauesque condemnation of civilization. Above all, in his politics Schopenhauer was a conservative liberal who firmly defended the rights of the individual;[54] Tolstoy's metaphysical impersonalism, on the other hand, led him to condemn individualism and to call for humility in the face of the "people's truth," for total immersion in the "masses" and nonviolent resistance to evil. The character who best exemplifies this "people's truth" is Karataev in *War and Peace*—a simple peasant who is only a small part of the anonymous crowd and feels he has no separate existence. Pierre Bezhukhov longs to experience Karataev's "truth." "To be a soldier, simply a soldier," he muses before going to sleep. "To enter with all one's being into this general life, to adopt the qualities that made them what they are. But how to throw off everything superfluous, demonic, this burden of the pseudoman?"

What is original in Tolstoyan philosophy is that the dream of throwing off the burden of the "principle of individuation" is more than just an aspect of the crisis of individualism that, after reaching its climax, passes into its dialectical opposite. Following Schopenhauer, Tolstoy looked for confirmation of his theories in the religions of the East, but his most important inspiraton came from his observations of the Russian peasants—from his sympathetic understanding of their way of life, made easier by the patriarchal links that in his case still bound master and man. Tolstoy's family belonged to the ancient Russian aristocracy, which was part of a cultural formation rooted in non-Westernized semi-Asiatic Russia but which through its elite actively participated in European intel-

54. In Turgenev's world view, too, we find a combination of metaphysical impersonalism with a liberal defense of the rights of the individual. See A. Walicki, "Turgenev and Schopenhauer," *Oxford Slavonic Papers*, 10 (1962).

lectual life. No doubt this specific situation enabled him to assimilate sophisticated European culture and to experience its crisis "from within," while at the same time confronting it with his profound understanding of the culture and social consciousness of the Russian peasantry, who were still at the pre-individuation stage. The result of this confrontation is what Soviet scholars (following Lenin) have called a "shift to the position of the patriarchal peasantry." Tolstoy's ideology became a reflection of the "Asiatic" elements in the social consciousness of the Russian peasantry. Tolstoy's ideas, Lenin wrote, should therefore be treated "not as something individual, not as a caprice or a fad, but as the ideology of the conditions of life under which millions and millions actually found themselves for a certain period of time"; as an ideology of "an Oriental, an Asiatic order."[55]

Tolstoy's Views on Religion

As a religious thinker Tolstoy represented an extreme rationalistic and ethical evangelism—a brand of Christian heterodoxy whose most characteristic representatives in the Slavic countries were the Bohemian Brethren (it was no coincidence that he had always admired Petr Chelčicky) and the Polish Brethren. At the opposite pole was the tendency represented in Russia by the religious and philosophical ideas of Vladimir Soloviev. Both men proclaimed the need for a Christian renaissance and the religious regeneration of mankind, but their conception of religion in general, and of Christianity in particular, was so utterly different that all attempts to arrive at a mutual understanding were doomed to failure. Tolstoy was irritated by Soloviev's mysticism, and Soloviev could not stomach Tolstoy's moralizing. The two men were almost physically incapable of breathing the same air, writes Soloviev's biographer.[56]

For Tolstoy the essence of Christianity was contained in Christ's ethical teachings; Jesus himself, he thought, was only a man, though the greatest among such great moralists and teachers of mankind as Confucius, Lao-tzu, Buddha, and Socrates. Christ's teachings were not mystical or mysterious, but simple, clear, and easily understood by all; their quintessence was to be found in the Sermon on the Mount.[57] From this Tolstoy took five commandments in which

55. V. I. Lenin, *Collected Works* (Eng.-lang. ed.; M, 1960–66), vol. 17, pp. 51–52.
56. See K. Mochulsky, *Vladimir Soloviev, Zhizn i uchenie* (Paris, 1951), p. 248.
57. The Sermon on the Mount is the favorite text of all who profess an evangelical and ethical Christian heterodoxy. See L. Kołakowski, *Świadomość religijna i więz-*

he attempted to sum up Christ's message: "thou shalt not be angry, thou shalt not commit adultery, thou shalt not swear or judge thy neighbors, thou shalt not resist evil by evil, and thou shalt have no enemies."[58] To Tolstoy the fourth commandment was the most important. The words of the Gospel—"Ye have heard it said an eye for an eye and a tooth for a tooth; and I say unto you, resist not evil" (Matt. 5: 38–39)—were a key that opened all to him.[59] When his theory of passive resistance was attacked as a mere idle day-dream, he answered that what was really a daydream—or rather a nightmare, like the ravings of a madman—was a world created in defiance of Christ's teachings and founded on violence. Christ's teaching, he wrote, is not eccentric but reasonable and practical; its meaning can best be expressed in the sentence: "Christ enjoins men to refrain from stupid actions."[60] The teachings of the Gospels demand neither martyrdom nor superhuman sacrifice, for they proclaim the ideal of a life in harmony with human nature, ensuring health and a tranquil death. It is "worldly teaching" that asks men to make sacrifices and calls on them to live in overcrowded cities, to hate and kill each other, to be so concerned with safeguarding their existence that they have no time for life itself. "Worldly teaching" turns life into hell, whereas Christ shows us how to establish the Kingdom of Heaven on earth—a kingdom of eternal peace in which swords will be beaten into plowshares and all men will be brothers.

As part of his tendency to reduce religion to a system of ethics, Tolstoy undertook a critical reappraisal of Christian dogma and ceremonial in the light of moralistic and rationalistic criteria. Dog-

---

kościelna [*Religious Consciousness and the Bond of the Church*] (Warsaw, 1965), p. 289.

Kołakowski's book throws an interesting light on the contrast between Tolstoy's and Soloviev's religious consciousness. "Since the earliest days, Christworship has developed as part of a conflict of divergent trends, gravitating to either of two extremes: at the one pole are those who are only interested in Christ's teaching and mission on earth and who deny or play down his divinity (the Socinians, Nestorians, Arians, etc.), whereas at the other pole we have those who pay less heed to Christ's life on earth and even regard it merely as a symbol . . . , but stress his divinity, even going so far as to identify the Son with the Father . . . (the Monophysites, etc.). This gravitation to one of two ideal models can be easily traced within the complicated diversity of various Christian doctrines: there is Christ the moral teacher, the Man, the model to be followed; and Christ the God, the mystical bridegroom of the soul, the Logos, the Divine Light, the emanation of the Absolute. These are two extreme versions of Christianity, both equally unacceptable to the Roman Catholic [and Orthodox—A. W.] Church." (*Ibid.*, p. 288.)

58. See the tract *What Do I Believe?* in Tolstoy, *Pol. sob. soch.* (1913 ed.), vol. 23.
59. *Ibid.*, p. 311.
60. *Ibid.*, p. 423.

mas that he rejected included the Holy Trinity, Revelation, the Immaculate Conception, and the Resurrection; this was not just because he thought them inconsistent with logic, but above all because they did not seem to him to contain the slightest hints of any "reasonable" rule of conduct. Toward the end of his life he undertook to combine all four Gospels in one continuous narrative, and in the course of this work he eliminated from the New Testament its entire cosmology and ontology, as well as all descriptions of miracles; to all intents and purposes he also eliminated the teaching on the word (John I) by stripping it of its mystical and ontological meaning and interpreting the *logos* as "ethical comprehension of life." In his eagerness to eliminate anything smacking of the supranatural he even rejected the teaching on Grace and the Holy Ghost, which he called an immoral doctrine that "struck at the roots of everything that is best in human nature."[61]

It remains to be asked whether a religion stripped of so many vital elements can still be called Christianity. A careful examination of Tolstoy's ideas would suggest that it cannot. In his tract *What Is Religion and How Is It to Be Defined?* (1902), Tolstoy argued that true religion embraces the basic principles common to all the great faiths, the beliefs that they all share and thanks to which humanity has not become extinct. In this eternal and universal religion, Christianity does not occupy a privileged place, although Tolstoy did regard Jesus as mankind's greatest teacher, someone whose teachings were divine, even if he himself was not. In this last sense—and in this sense only—can we talk of Tolstoyan philosophy as being Christian. At the same time Tolstoy called the institutionalized Christianity of the official church the most degenerate of the world's religions. Every religion, he argued, consists of two parts: its ethical doctrine, and the metaphysical doctrine elaborated to justify that ethical doctrine. A religion can be said to degenerate when it substitutes the external symbols of a cult for its ethical principles. All religions suffered from this type of degeneration, but Christianity most of all. The first signs of a split between "metaphysics" and "ethics" were the Epistles of St. Paul, which proclaimed a metaphysical and cabalistic theory alien to the teachings of Christ himself. The last stage in the degeneration of Christianity came with its adoption as the official creed under Constantine the Great. The emperor came to a singular agreement with his high priests by virtue of which he was able to live as he liked and indulge in murder, arson, pillage, and debauchery, while at the same time continu-

61. *Ibid.*, p. 230 (*Issledovanie dogmaticheskogo bogosloviia*).

ing to call himself a Christian and being assured of his place in heaven.[62] From now on Christianity was a religion that did not demand any kind of moral conduct of its followers and gave its stamp of approval to the immorality of the established order.

In his impassioned condemnation of the hypocrisy and falsehood of official Christianity, Tolstoy quite overlooked Christ's injunction to refrain from anger. Lenin called his criticism an expression of "the sentiments of the primitive peasant democratic masses among whom centuries of serfdom, of official tyranny and robbery, and of Church Jesuitism, deception and chicanery had piled up mountains of anger and hatred."[63]

In the last resort Tolstoy's criticism of religion can be seen as a total rejection of the Church as an institution and an attack on the very foundations of all "positive religions." The idea that "certain special men are necessary as mediators between man and God," as well as the belief in miracles or in the "magical power of certain formulas repeated through the centuries or noted down in books," was for Tolstoy only evidence of the degeneration of religion. The true universal faith of which he was to be the prophet was to be a religion without a priesthood, without dogmas, without sacraments, without liturgy—in fact without any trace of the supranatural.

What was to be the place of God in this religion? Tolstoy's views undoubtedly had little in common with traditional theism. It is true that in his popular tracts he compared man's relationship with God to the relationship of a son to his father, or a farmhand to his master, but these comparisons must not be taken literally as evidence of an anthropomorphic conception of the Godhead. There would seem to be better grounds for classifying Tolstoy's philosophy of God as a specific version of theological immanentism. It is difficult to arrive at a more precise definition, since Tolstoy himself did not attempt anything of this nature. He was content to state "God exists as the principle [origin] of all things; a particle of this divine principle exists in man, and it may be diminished or increased according to one's way of life."[64] Tolstoy's reluctance to define the essence of God was not only a result of his concentration on ethical issues. Of equal importance is the fact that he was convinced of the futility of such a definition. Thus, despite the extreme rationalism of his *critique* of dogmatic theology, the author of the *Confession* cannot

---

62. *Ibid.*, p. 480 (*Tserkov' i gosudarstvo*).
63. Lenin, *Collected Works*, vol. 16, p. 324.
64. Tolstoy, *Pol. sob. soch.* (1913 ed.), vol. 15, p. 317 (*Chto takoe religiia i v chem sushchnost eyo?*).

be classed among the representatives of religious rationalism. "God and the soul," he wrote, "are as well known to me as infinity—not through definition, but in quite a different way. Definitions only help to destroy this knowledge."[65] Like Kant (whom he quoted), Tolstoy categorically rejected a "rational theology"; he was, it is true, a rationalistic critic of positive religion, but, like Kant, he was convinced of the impotence of theoretical reason as an instrument for proving the existence of God or analyzing the essence of His being.

Tolstoy's Criticism of Civilization and Social Ideals

As a social ideology Tolstoyan philosophy is unusual in that it combines radical criticism of the existing social system and the spiritual state of the privileged classes with an equally radical rejection of revolutionary doctrines and all attempts to resist evil by force.

Tolstoy's criticism is entirely anti-historical; Lenin commented that "he reasons in the abstract, he recognizes only the standpoint of the 'eternal' principles of morality, the eternal truth of religion."[66] This was a conscious and deliberate choice: he rejected the "historial view"—belief in historical necessity and rationality—because he considered it to be distorted by amoral relativism and blind optimism. This attitude naturally went hand in hand with a total rejection of the faith in progress so popular among his contemporaries. The idea of progress, according to Tolstoy, was acceptable if interpreted as an eternal law of individual perfectibility, but when "transferred to the sphere of history it becomes sterile and empty prattle serving to justify all kinds of nonsenses." Moreover, the concept of historical progress only applied to countries within the sphere of influence of European civilization or, to be more precise, to a small proportion of the inhabitants of these countries. The common people had only been harmed by "progress"; everywhere the masses "had a lively hatred of progress and tried to counteract it by all possible means."[67]

It must be stressed that the article containing these thoughts was published in 1862 (in the educational periodical *Iasnaia Poliana*), that is, nearly twenty years before Tolstoy's ideological "crisis." The idealization of a natural economy based on relations before the di-

65. Tolstoy, *Pol. sob. soch* (1928–58 ed.), vol. 23, p. 132.
66. Lenin, *Collected Works*, vol. 17, p. 50.
67. Tolstoy, *Pol. sob. soch.* (1928–58 ed.), vol. 8, pp. 334–35.

vision of labor, which is so typical of his philosophy, also goes back to the period before the turning point of the late 1870's. The last word on the subject is to be found in the tract *What Are We to Do?*, published in 1886. In it Tolstoy took up Mikhailovsky's favorite theme—the criticism of organicist theories of society (especially those of Comte and Spencer) and their advocacy of the division of labor. Theories comparing society to an organism, Tolstoy wrote, are a piece of fiction invented for the benefit of the privileged, and the division of labor is a "shameless excuse for idlers." It is interesting to note that, like Mikhailovsky, he thought the division of labor also harmed the privileged minority who had used "deceit and force" to avoid physical labor, because varied and changing work was essential for health and happiness: "It is in the nature of a bird to fly, peck, and calculate, and only when he can perform all these actions is he satisfied and happy, only then is he a bird. The same holds true of man: only then is he satisfied, only then does he feel himself to be a man, when he walks, busies himself, lifts, carries, uses his fingers, eyes, ears, tongue, and head."[68] Tolstoy proposed that the division of labor according to individual capacities be replaced by the division of the working day (the "harness" principle), so that each day every individual would in turn work at all occupations serving to satisfy his material and spiritual needs. The similarity between this ideal and Mikhailovsky's formula of progress will be readily perceived.[69]

When Tolstoy inveighed against progress and the division of labor, he was of course thinking of a capitalist economy, and his idealization of "undivided" labor was clearly part of his romantic view of the natural peasant economy. It is interesting to note that unlike such critics as Rousseau and Schiller, Tolstoy regarded the division of labor not as a dialectical contradiction of progress but simply as a "tool for the oppression of the working majority by the idle minority."[70] This is, of course, an obvious sociological oversimplification: its strength lies in the forcefulness of its attack, and in the "nihilistic" boldness of its negation rather than in the subtlety of its philosophical analysis.

In his wholesale condemnation of civilization and culture Tolstoy

68. *Ibid.*, vol. 25, p. 390 (*Tak chto zhe nam delat'?*).
69. See above, pp. 336ff. Mikhailovsky himself recognized the analogies between his ideas and those of Tolstoy (especially his educational articles) and discussed them in his essay "Desnitsa i shuitsa L'va Tolstogo" (1875). In the post-"crisis" period the parallels are even more obvious.
70. Cf. V. F. Asmus, "Mirovozzrenie Tolstogo," in *Literaturnoe nasledstvo*, vol. 69 (M, 1961), book I, pp. 43–51. Asmus's study is, in my estimation, the best and most representative Soviet work on Tolstoy's view of the world.

did not fail to include science. The role of contemporary science, he wrote, is to satisfy the artificial needs of the rich and to bolster their power over the people. Science must be called totally immoral, for it has lost sight of the only truly important issue—understanding the nature of man's vocation and the essence of virtue. The study of this problem requires neither division of labor nor any kind of specialization, and the science that applies itself to solving it is indistinguishable from religion interpreted as a system of ethics. Its high priests are such great moralists and religious leaders as Confucius, Socrates, Marcus Aurelius, Jesus Christ, and Muhammad. Mankind needs no other science than this.

As might be expected, the embodiment for Tolstoy of everything that was evil in sophisticated civilization was the institution of the state. One significant aspect of the radical change in his world view was his adoption of a thoroughgoing Christian anarchism. As a system of oppression that set people against one another the institution of the state clearly transgressed against the Sermon on the Mount. Therefore it was blasphemy for Christianity to allow itself to be closely associated with the state; this would prove its undoing, for like "burning ice" the concept of a "Christian state" was a contradiction in terms.[71] In his zeal, Tolstoy now dismissed even such civic and military virtues as valor and patriotism, which he had praised in *Sevastopol Sketches, War and Peace,* and other works written before the "turning point." Patriotism, he wrote in his tract *Christianity and Love of the Fatherland* (1894), is always an instrument of oppression: the patriotism of the rulers is only selfish concern for their own welfare, whereas the patriotism of the ruled implies the renunciation of human dignity, reason, and conscience, i.e. a mere slavish submission to those who are at the helm of power. The patriotism of subject nations is particularly dangerous, because their greater bitterness usually leads to greater violence.[72]

Tolstoy's criticism ultimately led him to a total negation of the established order. The ideal he put forward in its place was a way of life that would abolish all force and all forms of social inequality. This was to be achieved through passive resistance—through condemnation of the existing system and the refusal to have any share in it. Tolstoy dismissed as illusory the liberals' hopes of achieving piecemeal improvements by entering the government or other forms of collaboration; at the same time he opposed revolution

71. Tolstoy, *Pol. sob. soch* (1928–58 ed.), vol. 23, p. 479.
72. In practice Tolstoy did not follow his own advice literally and accepted the justice of national independence movements. See his Caucasian novel *Hadji Murat,* and the story *What For?* (1906), about the tragic fate of a Polish insurgent of 1863.

on the grounds that it was not only un-Christian but also ineffective, since it led to an increase in the use of force and not to its elimination.

The Russo-Japanese War and the Revolution of 1905 aroused the aged writer to energetic activity. He protested against the war in the article "Bethink Yourselves" and condemned the massacre of the unarmed crowd that marched on the Winter Palace on Bloody Sunday; in his articles "A Great Sin" and "The Century's End" he defended the peasants' right to increase their holdings and called for the nationalization of the land; he attacked the government's repressive policies but also called on the revolutionaries to give up their struggle (*An Appeal to All Russians—Government, Revolutionaries and People*, 1906). He certainly did not welcome the October Manifesto or the convocation of the First Duma, which he regarded as purely "etatist" measures and therefore powerless against evil, but he never ceased to speak up on behalf of the persecuted. In 1908 he wrote a burningly sincere manifesto—"I Cannot Be Silent"—protesting the bloody methods of repression used by the reactionary Stolypin government against the revolutionaries.

In his articles on Tolstoy, Lenin gave a perceptive summing-up of his philosophy. As a thinker, he wrote, Tolstoy is great because his ideology is a reflection of the "great human ocean [of Russian peasantry], agitated to its very depths, with all its weaknesses and all its strong features." [73]

At the same time he stressed that Tolstoyan doctrine was "certainly utopian and in content reactionary in the most precise and profound sense of the word." [74] As the exponent of the feelings and aspirations of the patriarchal peasantry, Tolstoy looked backward rather than forward; he wanted to reestablish an archaic and preindustrial way of life and openly proclaimed that "the ideal of our times is behind us." All these were aspects of his "reactionary" side. On the other hand—and Lenin was fully aware of this—Tolstoy's "reactionary and utopian" ideas struck a powerful blow against the very foundations of the Russian state and social system, which were reactionary in a more commonly accepted meaning of the word. With some reason, therefore, many Russian émigrés in later years accused Tolstoy of having helped the revolutionaries by undermin-

73. Lenin, *Collected Works*, vol. 16, p. 353.
74. *Ibid.*, vol. 17, p. 52.
75. In his will Tolstoy made his royalties over to his disciples instead of to his family.

ing the belief of many of the opponents of revolution in the justice of their cause.

There is also an archaic and utopian flavor about Tolstoy's last tragic act of protest against a corrupt world—the circumstances he chose to accompany his death. Disagreements with his wife on the disposal of his estate[75] led him to attempt once more to realize his old dream of "giving up the world" and turning his back on the "luxury by which I have always been surrounded." On October 28 (November 10), 1910, he fled home at night with one of his disciples, Dr. D. P. Makovitsky, and with the approval of his daughter Alexandra, in order to find a place where he might finish his life in solitude and silence. He was not allowed to succeed: all over the world the public was kept informed by their newspapers of every stage of his journey. A cold that turned into pneumonia forced him to make a prolonged stop at the tiny railway station of Astapovo, where he died on November 7 (20).

The news of Tolstoy's death echoed throughout the world. But although he was mourned by governments and parliaments, the appeals of the great moralist and the impression made by his death were powerless to prevent the outbreak of the First World War.

The Role of Art

Reflections on the nature of art formed an integral part of Tolstoyan thought and found their fullest expression in the essay *What Is Art?* (1898). Many years earlier, in his educational articles written for the periodical *Iasnaia Poliana*, Tolstoy had called the art of the privileged classes the "empty entertainment of idlers" and had dismissed the entire cultural achievement of the "wealthy classes" (including the works of Pushkin and Beethoven, his own favorites) as "vain and meaningless" by comparison with art speaking with the voice of the people.

What Is Art? is an emphatic reaffirmation of these ideas. In the opening pages of the essay Tolstoy exhaustively analyzes the aesthetic credo of his day, which claimed that the aim of art is beauty, or, in other words, aesthetic pleasure divorced from moral values. To believe in "art for art's sake," he argues, is as totally absurd as to maintain that the aim of eating is to delight the palate. But while rejecting aestheticism, Tolstoy also rejects the ascetic revulsion against art to be found in Plato, the early Christians, orthodox Muslims, and Buddhists. Art has a place in his scheme of things: it is one of the tools helping to "unite people in a community of feeling" and therefore is an essential "aspect of social life." However, not only paintings, statues, symphonies, sonnets, and novels are worthy of the name of art: "The entire span of life is furnished by works of art of all kinds, from lullabies, jests, teasing games, adornment of the home, and household goods, to church services and processions."[76]

The nature of art is best expressed by folk art, which is closely bound up with religion and the daily rhythm of labor, with human existence as an integral whole in which there can be no isolated or autonomous spheres.

The function of art is to express feelings by means of external symbols and to "infect" other people with these feelings. The value of a work of art therefore depends on the conviction and moral worth of the feelings it is trying to express. The chief task of true art is to unite human beings; the art of the "wealthy classes," by contrast, is exclusive and attempts only to convey the feelings of a thin privileged layer. These cannot be called truly human emotions, since they deepen the divisions between men instead of overcoming them.

Tolstoy distinguished three groups of such "divisive" feelings in art: the first fanned feelings of nationalism and chauvinism, pride, social or caste exclusivity, and contempt for weaker natures; the second pandered to the excessive sensuality typical of men leading idle and aimless lives (in literature these were expressed in works of pervasive eroticism and a naturalistic cult of man as an animal); the last catered to feelings of surfeit and world-weary pessimism, all of which were alien to the common people. The growing popularity of works of art expressing these emotions was only a form of progressive degeneration, Tolstoy declared. The art of the elite was becoming more and more divorced from the people, more and more exclusive; its subject matter was becoming more restricted, until finally, when artists felt they had nothing more to say, it would disappear altogether. That was why artists chased after originality and novelty at all costs, though all they achieved was a formal sophistication typical of all art in its decline. This formalism made for even greater exclusivity, so that finally art became entirely incomprehensible to more than just a narrow circle of connoisseurs.

The last stage in this process of intellectual and artistic degeneration was the "decadent" art of the French Symbolists—Baudelaire, Verlaine, and Mallarmé—and the music of Wagner. Tolstoy pointed out, however, that the source of present degeneracy must be sought

76. Tolstoy, *Pol. sob. soch.* (1928-58 ed.), vol. 30, pp. 66-67.

in the past, and that the difference between contemporary "decadents" and artists of the previous generation was only a quantitative one. The turning point in the history of Western European art had been the Renaissance—the period when the upper classes lost their religious belief and ceased to be guided by the same feelings that guided the common people. Thereafter the art of the elite split off from the art of the nation as a whole, and instead of one art there were two: the "high" art of the masters and the "low" art of the masses. In Russia, the Petrine Reforms brought about a similar turning point. Tolstoy followed his argument to its logical conclusion and included among the representatives of "high" art who were alien to the common people not only Raphael, Michelangelo, and Shakespeare but also his own former favorite, Pushkin.

In contrast to the "immoral" art of the ruling classes, Tolstoy's ideal "art of the future" was to be truly free from internal as well as external constraints—no longer locked within the restrictive sphere of selfish and immoral feelings, and no longer dependent on "the moneybags and his riches." "The art of the future," he wrote, "will drive the moneylenders out of the temple." It will be an art for all, just as the *Iliad* and the *Odyssey*, Bible stories and psalms, and the art of the Middle Ages belonged to everyone. Artistic creation will cease to be the domain of the professional and will be undertaken by all working people of talent. This will bring about a great flowering and invigoration of art, for the feelings of working people are infinitely richer and of greater value than the feelings of the rich.

Of art that wanted to live up to his standards Tolstoy demanded sincerity, easily understood and morally praiseworthy content, and clear, simple, and pithy form. Plekhanov has rightly pointed out that these were the qualities Chernyshevsky called for in his dissertation on the *Aesthetic Relations Between Art and Reality*.[77] It is not surprising, therefore, that Tolstoy's brochure was welcomed enthusiastically by Vladimir Stasov, the leading heir to the Chernyshevsky tradition in artistic criticism and at the same time Tolstoy's chief adviser on aesthetics and the history of art.[78] There are even certain points in common between Tolstoy and Pisarev—Tolstoy's attack on the art of the "upper classes" was equally "nihilistic" and coincided on many points with Pisarev's crusade against "aesthetics."

77. See G. V. Plekhanov, "Eshche o Tolstom," in *L. N. Tolstoy v russkoi kritike* (M, 1952), p. 438.
78. See L. N. Lomunov, *Tolstoy v bor'be protiv dekadentskogo iskusstva*, pp. 80–81, in *L. N. Tolstoy, Sbornik statei in materialov* (M, 1951).

These similarities stem partly from the fact that Tolstoy, like the radical democrats of the sixties, set out to propagate a realistic and "socially committed" art. Another explanation is the partial affinity between Tolstoy's world view and that of the "enlighteners." As was pointed out earlier, his "reason" had much in common with eighteenth-century rationalism, especially with its unswerving devotion to the "search for ultimate sources" and its anti-historical rejection of authority and tradition. In this respect, therefore, it may be said that Tolstoy was related to the "enlighteners" of the sixties, although his religious insistence on the renunciation of self-interest and on nonviolent resistance to evil clearly ran counter to their "rational egoism."

DOSTOEVSKY AND TOLSTOY: A COMPARISON

Let us try to sum up. There is no doubt that what distinguishes Dostoevsky and Tolstoy from other nineteenth-century writers is their passionate moralistic fervor. The label "moralist," however, is not an adequate description. Some of the greatest moralists—the Stoics and Skeptics, for instance—did not believe in the possibility of radical change and deliberately refrained from giving way to moral indignation. Dostoevsky and Tolstoy, on the other hand, reacted vigorously against "all disturbance or perversion of the civic or moral order" and called for a total religious and moral rebirth.[79] Their concern with ultimate human destiny bears all the hallmarks of authentic prophetic zeal.

Each of these two great Russian writers, however, was a prophet in his own way. Dostoevsky attempted to gain insight into the mystical meaning of history through the concept of God-manhood, whereas Tolstoy rejected history altogether in the name of the eternal truths of the Christian Gospel. For Dostoevsky, Russian history offered the way to salvation through Christ; the ideal of reintegration with the people, of a "return to the soil," was his specific version of reconciliation with history, with the historical traditions of Orthodoxy and the national traditions of the common people. For Tolstoy, on the other hand, true life was not bound by time: truth and the common people were outside history, and the historical process only gave rise to evil, which must be destroyed before the kingdom of the moral Absolute could be established on earth. Both writers desired 'harmony" on earth, but whereas Dostoevsky dreamed of State becoming transformed into Church and con-

79. See J. Wach, *Sociology of Religion* (London, 1947), p. 355.

demned rationalism in the name of *mystical* and evangelical ideals, Tolstoy denied the need for any kind of institutionalized religion and stood for a *rationalistic* evangelical heterodoxy. Tolstoy's metaphysical impersonalism and his consequent rejection of individual immortality was alien to the author of *The Brothers Karamazov*; Dostoevsky was equally hostile to Tolstoy's egalitarianism, which he thought of as a leveling that would extinguish both individuality and freedom. As a prophet Dostoevsky was closer to the national messianism of the Old Testament (Shatov's version of messianism). If there is any Old Testament element in Tolstoyan philosophy, it is only because the author's uninhibited and blunt railings against evil call to mind the zeal of the great Hebrew prophets.[80]

The differences between the two writers become even clearer when we examine them from the point of view of the links each of them had with specific trends in Russian thought. Dostoevsky was a romantic nationalist, a continuator of the Slavophile tradition, whereas Tolstoy—that uncompromising critic of all versions of nationalism and even patriotism—was more at home with rationalistic and Enlightenment modes of thought. In his social and political outlook Tolstoy was closer to the Populists and anarchists, although he reinterpreted their message in an antirevolutionary and evangelical spirit. These differences had their practical political consequences: Dostoevsky, condemned in his youth to hard labor in Siberia, in later life moved in reactionary circles, was friendly with Pobedonostsev, and had dreams of annexing Constantinople. Tolstoy, the aristocratic landowner, rejected his own class and for more than thirty years inveighed without cease against the moral evil of all state institutions and against exploitation and the use of force.

It would of course be doing Dostoevsky an injustice to identify him with the reactionary ideologists of the 1870's. In fact, many Populist leaders considered him (of course mistakenly) to be their ideological ally;[81] it was not by chance, Lunacharsky wrote, that Pobedonostsev and other "highly placed patrons never trusted him entirely and always expected him to provide an unpleasant surprise."[82] The nervous, uprooted intellectual who was able to portray the moral and spiritual conflict of the Karamazov brothers with such superb intuition was in fact closer to the radical intelligentsia of his day than Tolstoy, the prophet of the eternal truth of the Gos-

80. *Ibid.*
81. A good deal of evidence on this was collected by A. S. Dolinin. See *F. M. Dostoevsky, Materialy i issledovaniia* (L, 1935), pp. 52–53.
82. *F. M. Dostoevsky v russkoi kritike*, p. 452.

pels, who was half-aristocrat, half-peasant, and all patriarch. Tolstoy's religious and ethical doctrines are a static system of finished truths, whereas all that is most valuable in Dostoevsky's thought forms a dialectical complexity. It would be wrong to reduce Dostoevsky's world view to nothing more than Orthodox utopianism and a matter of reactionary political leanings. Even today some of his ideas have an astonishing freshness, whereas in Tolstoy we sense a genuinely and not just superficially archaic mode of thought—a mode of thought that is forceful but at the same time anachronistic, that shocks by the boldness of its perceptive oversimplifications but also irritates by its "nihilistic" single-mindedness and Manichaean dualism.

Dostoevsky's ideas influenced thinkers of many different ideological complexions, whether conservative or progressive, religious or secular. His fame reached its height in the twentieth century. Together with Vladimir Soloviev (with whom he became friendly toward the end of his life and on whom he exerted considerable influence), he was responsible for the resurgence of interest in religion (the so-called "religious renaissance") among many educated Russians in the early years of our century. Almost all Russian idealist philosophers and religious thinkers without exception whose ideas were formed at the beginning of the century and who continued their work abroad after the Russian Revolution—men as different as Berdiaev, Bulgakov, Frank, Merezhkovsky, Shestov, Lossky, and Hessen—were fascinated by Dostoevsky at one stage of their lives and absorbed his ideas into their world view. Among Western European thinkers it was the secular existentialists (especially Sartre and Camus) who showed most interest in his work. What attracted them was not his "Orthodoxy" but his dialectical view of individualism, his conception of the problem of "revolt" and the burden of freedom—in a word, the ideas he analyzed through the medium of his "self-assertive" heroes.

As a moralist and religious thinker Tolstoy enjoyed worldwide authority during his lifetime. His home in Yasnaya Polana was visited by pilgrims of all nations, and hundreds of letters flowed in from supporters and opponents throughout the world. His ideas—especially his pacifist teachings—enjoyed enormous publicity. Nevertheless, Tolstoyan philosophy and religious thought were not destined to be very influential doctrines. The force of his ideas depended entirely on his own charismatic personality; after his death his ideas were quickly forgotten, with one important exception—in Mahatma Gandhi Tolstoy did find at least one truly great continuator of his teaching.

CHAPTER 16

VARIANTS OF POSITIVISM

Unlike Polish positivism, which expressed the realistic aspirations of the younger generation (after the failure of the 1863 uprising) for social change through careful "organic" work, Russian positivism never became an influential ideology. Positivist ideas of course had a considerable impact on the general intellectual climate of the day, and some Russian positivists were not without talent, but none of them can be said to have played a really prominent role in the history of Russian ideas.

The first echoes of positivist ideas came to Russia as early as the latter half of the 1840's. Some of Comte's theories (especially his conception of three phases of human development—the theological, metaphysical, and positive stages) found supporters in Russia among men connected with the Petrashevtsy, especially Valerian Maikov and the economist Vladimir Milutin (1826–55). Belinsky's attitude, on the other hand, was one of considerable reserve; he considered Comte to be an interesting thinker, noteworthy as a "reaction to theological intervention in science," but thought that he lacked genius and that it was ridiculous to suppose he might be "the founder of a new philosophy." Comte, he wrote, attempted to demolish metaphysics not only as a science concerned with "transcendental absurdities," but also as a science dealing with the nature of the human mind; this showed that the domain of philosophy was alien to his nature and that only mathematics and the natural sciences were within his grasp.[1]

The "enlighteners" of the sixties, too, found it difficult to accept Comte without reservation, especially because of their materialism and social radicalism. Comte's philosophy, however, exerted a certain influence on Pisarev, who used positivist arguments in his polemics against the vitalists' notion of a mysterious principle of life. He was even more impressed by Comte's philosophy of history, to

1. See V. Belinsky, *Izbrannye filosofskie sochineniia* (M, 1948), vol. 2, pp. 326–29.

which he devoted a lengthy article ("The Historical Ideas of Auguste Comte," 1865). For Pisarev, Comte's notion of the three phases of human development provided excellent confirmation of his two favorite theories: the dependence of historical progress on the evolution of knowledge, and the liberating mission of the natural sciences.

The attitude of the Populist thinkers to Comte was even more complicated. They were undoubtedly influenced by positivism, but to call them positivists is absolutely unwarranted.[2] Lavrov and Mikhailovsky wrote their works at a time when positivism in the social sciences was largely represented by the evolutionist theories of Herbert Spencer. Both Russian thinkers utterly rejected positivist evolutionism as an extreme version of "objectivism," to which they opposed their own "subjective sociology"; they were repelled also by positivistic scientism, especially by its programmatic elimination of value judgments. At the same time, however, in their opposition to "objectivism" they found an ally in Comte himself, who recognized the validity of both the "objective" and the "subjective" methods. In his polemics with Spencer, therefore, Mikhailovsky was able to claim the support of Comte, whom he called a precursor of the "subjective-anthropocentric" age in the history of mankind. This in itself reveals clearly the essential difference between Mikhailovsky's ideas and the positivism of his day. In the second half of the nineteenth century only a small group of sectarian, "orthodox" Comteans (e.g. P. Laffitte and J. F. Robinet) still defended Comte's "subjective method"; Littré, the chief representative of the main school of post-Comtian positivism in France, rejected the "subjective method" together with the "religion of Humanity" and other romantic elements in Comte's system.

Lavrov, who was less inclined to "sociological romanticism," defined his attitude to positivism in the essay "The Problems of Positivism and Their Solution" (1868). There he discussed different variants of positivist thought (Comte, Littré, Mill, Spencer, and Lewes) and warned that they could not be underestimated. Paraphrasing Hegel's comment on philosophy, he defined positivism as "our age captured in a syllogism."[3] A lasting contribution made by positivism, Lavrov wrote, was that it had formulated the tasks facing the human intellect, namely that the relations between all

2. They are classified as positivists in B. Jakovenko, *Dejiny ruske filosofie* (Prague, 1929), and N. O. Lossky, *History of Russian Philosophy* (London, 1952), V. V. Zenkovsky, in his *A History of Russian Philosophy* (trans. George L. Kline [2 vols., London, 1953]), treats them as "half-positivists."

3. P. L. Lavrov, *Filosofiia i sotsiologiia* (M, 1965), vol. 1, p. 584.

phenomena should be investigated by strictly scientific methods without reference to the metaphysical "thing-in-itself," and that the knowledge gained in this way should be used to interpret not only the nonhuman world but also society and history. Like Mikhailovsky, Lavrov emphasized the importance of the "subjective method" and attempted to show, by quoting Comte himself, that it was not incompatible with the basic premises of positivism. His conclusion, however, was that positivism was incapable of solving the problem it had itself posed because it lacked a unifying philosophical principle. This principle was man as a feeling and thinking being—a symbol of the true unity of mind and body. The historical role of positivism was only to pose problems—their solution would be tackled by an anthropological philosophy whose germs could be found in the ideas of Feuerbach, Proudhon, and Mill.

Lavrov's "anthropologism" formed a bridge between Chernyshevsky's "anthropological principle" and the "subjective anthropocentricity" of Populist sociology. Though it was capable of assimilating many elements of positivism, it was quite clearly a separate doctrine.

DOGMATIC POSITIVISM: GRIGORY WYROUBOFF

The first consistent adherent of Comtian positivism in Russia was GRIGORY WYROUBOFF (1843–1913), who as a philosopher, however, was active mainly in France.

Wyrouboff was still a pupil at the Alexander Lycée in St. Petersburg when he was introduced to Comte's teaching by one of the masters at the school, a Frenchman named Pommier, who was a disciple of Comte and a friend of Littré. After studying medicine and natural sciences at the University of St. Petersburg, Wyrouboff went to Paris and contacted Comte's widow and his circle of disciples. He became intimate with Littré and joined him as one of the cofounders of the chief organ of French positivism, *La Philosophie Positive*. In 1903, after the death of P. Laffitte, he was appointed to the chair of history of science at the Collège de France. Although he settled permanently in France, Wyrouboff retained his interest in Russia and Russian culture—he was in touch with Bakunin, Herzen, and Lavrov, and after Herzen's death undertook the first complete edition of his works.[4] During the Russo-Turkish War of 1877–78, Wyrouboff came to the Caucasus as a Red Cross

4. See his reminiscences in "Revolutsionnye vospominaniia," *Vestnik Evropy* (1913), no. 1.

delegate and undertook the organization of field hospitals, for which he was decorated with the Order of St. Vladimir. All his philosophical and scientific works, however, were written in French (he specialized in chemistry and crystallography).

Wyrouboff's philosophical standpoint is expressed most clearly in his article "Le certain et le probable, l'absolu et le relatif," published in the first volume of *La Philosophie Positive*. Its basic proposition is that scientific knowledge can lay claim to absolute truth and that the opposition between the absolute and the relative is in itself relative. Anything real that can be translated into the language of scientific laws can be called absolute. Positivism rejects only theological and metaphysical absolutes, not the absolute as such; if it failed to recognize any absolute, it would not be an integral view of the world. Truth does not exist outside science, outside the sphere of human understanding; every truth is the result of experience verified by confrontation with previously established scientific laws. Both the absolute and the relative belong to the sphere of the comprehensible. Absolute truths are verifiable and incontrovertible statements, whereas relative truths are uncertain, controversial, and of low probability. As scientific knowledge accumulates, more and more relative truths will be transformed into absolute truths.[5]

The role of philosophy, Wyrouboff stated, is to make generalizations on the basis of the facts accumulated by particular sciences. What is striking in this argument is not only the dismissal of the classic philosophical concern with ontological problems (especially apparent in the attacks on the "metaphysics" of the materialists),[6] but also the rejection of epistemology, which Wyrouboff equated with psychology. For epistemology he proposed to substitute the methodology of the individual sciences; faith in science, he wrote, is the "fundamental axiom" that silences all doubt. He regarded the Cartesian method of philosophical doubt as an empty intellectual pastime and firmly rejected Mill's criticism that Comte had been wrong to neglect logic and psychology. The problem of the criterion of truth, he insisted, was not a philosophical problem but belonged to the sphere of the natural sciences, which had long since established such a criterion; philosophy should therefore accept the scientific formula that the yardstick of truth was "the recurrence

5. G. Wyrouboff, "Le Certain et le probable, l'absolu et le relatif," *La Philosophie Positive*, vol. 1 (1867), pp. 171, 176–81.

6. See G. Wyrouboff, "La Philosophie materialiste et la philosophie positive," *La Philosophie Positive*, vol. 22 (1879).

of a given phenomenon in identical conditions, expressed in a formula known as a law."[7]

It is understandable that Wyrouboff was deeply hostile to any signs of a renewal of interest in Kant. The German philosopher seemed to him to be the absolute antithesis of Comte; the founder of "positive philosophy" was concerned with the real world, whereas Kant, by concentrating on the investigation of the thinking subject, had rejected the chance to understand the objective laws governing reality. Neo-Kantianism, in Wyroboff's view, was an attempt to revive metaphysics—and was all the more dangerous because it was not aware of its own "metaphysical nature."[8]

In contrast to Kant's critical philosophy, Wyrouboff's positivism was a thoroughly dogmatic system. One of its chief tenets was that every true philosophy must be based on a certain "fundamental axiom" that cannot be subjected to critical reflection.[9] On certain issues Wyrouboff differed from Comte, possibly without realizing it (for instance, he did not share his master's phenomenalism); nevertheless, he insisted that Comtian positivism was the only authentic variant of positivist philosophy and the only entirely complete philosophical system of its day. "As a philosophy," he declared, "positivism is totally complete, nothing can be added or taken away. Comte certainly made many mistakes, but as an astronomer, chemist, or biologist, not as a philosopher."[10] His disciples, therefore, had only to apply his guidelines, particularly in disciplines to which the master had paid little attention.[11]

CRITICAL POSITIVISM: VLADIMIR LESEVICH

Quite another type of positivism was represented by VLADIMIR LESEVICH (1837–1905). In view of its epistemological bias and attempt to utilize the principles of Kantian critical philosophy, it might be called "critical positivism."

7. Wyrouboff, "Le Certain et le probable," p. 181.

8. See G. Wyrouboff, "Remarques sur la philosophie critique en Allemagne," *La Philosophie Positive*, vol. 22 (1879).

9. See Wyrouboff, "Le Certain et le probable," pp. 174–75.

10. Wrouboff, "Remarques," p. 394.

11. Despite this declaration, Wyrouboff rejected Comte's political philosophy. He defended the sovereignty of the common people, for instance, which Comte dismissed as a metaphysical dogma, and advocated decentralization of the authorities, quoting Proudhon on this issue. See G. Wyrouboff, "La Politique qualitative et la politique quantitative," *La Philosophie Positive*, vol. 8 (1872).

Littré also made a political revision of Comtianism, but Wyrouboff (probably under Herzen's influence) went further in this respect, although in other respects he was more reluctant to make any innovations.

Lesevich devoted his chief works to critical reflection on the origins and development of "scientific philosophy."[12] Although he declared that Comtian positivism represented a turning point in the history of philosophy, he found it lacking in a number of respects. Comte had underestimated Kant, for instance, and had failed to recognize that he, too, was a precursor of positivism; in fact, Comte had altogether underestimated the importance of epistemology and refused to incorporate it as a separate section into his philosophy. The same was true of his attitude toward logic, which, despite Mill's criticism, he refused to recognize as an independent discipline that ought to have a place in his classification of the sciences. On the other hand, Comtian philosophy showed at least the germs of a critical epistemology—otherwise his system would have been nothing more than an encyclopedia of the sciences. Comte's followers, however, wasted this valuable asset, busied themselves with summing up scientific facts, and chose to regard Comte's classification of the sciences as the most important aspect of positivism. Emil Littré, in Lesevich's view, knew nothing of the history of philosophy outside France and was totally ignorant of epistemology.

Lesevich reserved his most stringent criticism for Wyrouboff, whom he accused of an exaggerated "scientism"—a naive belief that all problems could be solved by science—that led him to "dephilosophize" and trivialize positivist philosophy. By reducing the distinction between absolute and relative knowledge to a difference of degree, Wyrouboff had rejected the relevance of epistemological theory.[13] This was a great error, because positivism ought to concentrate on the theory of knowledge if it wanted to lay claim to being a philosophy. To get out of this impasse, positivists ought to return to authentic Comtian ideas, Lesevich suggested, and then sharpen their critical faculties by a study of Locke, Hume, and the English empirical tradition. To begin with, however, they ought to overcome their prejudice against Kant and reform positivism in the spirit of neo-Kantian epistemological criticism. Lesevich also warmly recommended the works of such German thinkers as C. Göring, E. Laas, F. A. Lange, and A. Riehl, who were urging a rapprochement between neo-Kantians and positivists. At the same time he stressed that there was a clear line of demarcation between the two systems and that positivists could not accept the possibility

12. V. V. Lesevich, *Opyt kriticheskogo issledovaniya osnovonachal positivnoi filosofi* (St. Petersburg, 1878), and *Chto takoe nauchnaia filosofiia?* (St. Petersburg, 1891).

13. Lesevich, *Opyt*, pp. 185–86.

of *a priori* knowledge: they must learn from the neo-Kantians while remaining firmly rooted in realism. Positivism could not restrict itself to epistemological reflections, but must assimilate Kantian criticism in order to become "a critical philosophy of reality" and thus attain its highest stage of development.[14]

Lesevich expounded these ideas in the 1870's. A decade or so later his ideas underwent a certain evolution and shifted from Kantianism toward the empiriocriticism of the Austrian physicist and philosopher Ernest Mach. In his book *What Is a Scientific Philosophy?* Lesevich devoted separate chapters to the ideas of Mach, Avenarius, and especially Petzoldt, who, he stressed, had finally solved the question of the relations of philosophy to science. Philosophy, Lesevich now contended, was ceasing to be a separate science; even epistemology would soon cease to exist as a distinct specialized sphere of philosophical inquiry. The role of philosophy now was to create a system of universal knowledge based on the positive sciences, but one that scrutinized the data of those sciences on the highest level of abstraction, evaluating them from an integral point of view and uncovering their interconnections. A "scientific philosophy" of this kind would replace all previous "unscientific" philosophical trends.[15]

On the issue of "scientific philosophy," therefore, Lesevich's standpoint ultimately did not differ from the classical positivist position, which defined the role of philosophy as the generalization of the particular sciences. But although he no longer granted a separate place to the theory of knowledge—the last bastion of philosophy in the traditional meaning of the word—he never underestimated the importance of epistemological reflection. Throughout his entire career, in fact, Lesevich represented the so-called "second positivism," which put the emphasis on epistemological criticism.[16] The victory of the "scientific philosophy" he advocated with untiring energy was to make science "philosophical" instead of just making philosophy "scientific."

Lesevich was convinced that "scientific philosophy" could be of tremendous social significance: it would help to overcome routine and traditionalism, make clear the need for changes in different fields, and encourage scientists to concentrate their efforts on solving problems in the public interest. In his political sympathies he

14. *Ibid.*, pp. 161–63.
15. Lesevich, *Chto takoe*, pp. 248–51.
16. Cf. L. Kolakowski, *The Alienation of Reason: A History of Positivist Thought,* trans. Norbert Guterman (Garden City, N.Y., 1968).

was close to the Populists. (He was banished to Siberia in 1879 for his connections with the Populist revolutionaries, and after his return lived under police surveillance in Poltava and Tver; he was not allowed to return to St. Petersburg until 1888.) He thought highly of Lavrov and Mikhailovsky, referred to them as "the most competent judges of positivism," and agreed with their criticism of prevailing trends in positivist philosophy.[17] The influence of Lavrov and Mikhailovsky is apparent in Lesevich's defense of the "subjective method." The positivists, he argued, had dismissed the "subjective method" because "positive science" was weak on epistemological theory. The abstract sciences—that is, sciences investigating the general laws of a given sphere of phenomena—only made use of "objective" empirical methods, but the concrete (or applied) sciences were directed toward activity, and therefore had to solve problems of value-implementation. Lesevich was able to find numerous arguments in support of this line of reasoning in the works of the neo-Kantians.

Lesevich's efforts to bring about a rapprochement between positivism and neo-Kantianism found very little response in Russia. This was due in part to the mediocre professional level of the Russian neo-Kantians, but above all to the fact that in Russia the function of neo-Kantianism was not so much to undertake a critique of metaphysical systems as to pave the way for a revival of metaphysical idealism. The chief representative of Russian neo-Kantianism, ALEKSANDR VVEDENSKY (1856–1925), a professor at the University of St. Petersburg, was a convinced opponent of positivism. His philosophy, which he called "logicism," was based on a consistently idealistic and anti-empirical interpretation of Kantian philosophy. In Vvedensky's version, Kantianism was a kind of "middle way" philosophy that made it possible to avoid the harmful and outdated claims of metaphysical maximalism without falling into the trap of positivist "scientism," which he accused of undermining the meaning of life and leading to a dangerous moral nihilism. In order to counteract these dangers, Vvedensky defended the ideas of the personal existence of God, free will, and the immortality of the soul, stressing at the same time that these could be perceived not by the intellect but only by "conscious faith."[18] Realizing the dangerous ethical implications of subjective idealism, he insisted that one of the "postulates of practical reason" was belief in the "sub-

17. See Lesevich, *Opyt*, pp. 241–45.
18. See A. I. Vvedensky, *Filosoficheskie ocherki* (St. Petersburg, 1901), pp. 89, 108, 205–12.

jective" existence of other people. Like Lesevich, Vvedensky stressed the importance of epistemology, but his standpoint was far removed from positivism and he had no sympathy for the idea of a "scientific philosophy" as conceived by Lesevich.

POSITIVISM AND PSYCHOLOGY

In the positivists' discussions on epistemology, psychology had a prominent place. This is understandable if we remember that frequently no distinction was made at that time between epistemology and psychology. For Wyrouboff the increased interest in epistemology was a symptom of confusion between philosophy and psychology; Kavelin argued that the theories of Locke and Kant actually belonged to the sphere of psychology, and that concentration on epistemological issues was evidence of the key importance of psychology in modern philosophy. Even Lesevich, who made a clear distinction between epistemology and psychology (and engaged in polemics on this issue with Sechenov), was convinced that epistemology was largely based on psychological data.[19]

The positivist attack on metaphysics was undertaken in the sphere of psychology by a professor at Moscow University, MATVEY TROITSKY (1835–99), who represented the English school of positivism. Troitsky's chief work[20] was a vehement attack on the philosophical bias of German psychology, written from the point of view of English empirical, associationist psychology. Vladimir Soloviev relates that Troitsky always began his annual course of lectures on psychology with a short account of German idealism, ending with the pronouncement: "Well, gentlemen, you can see for yourselves! What is it? Wood shavings, wood shavings! Well then, into the stove with them!"[21]

A man of far wider mental horizons was the historian KONSTANTIN KAVELIN (see Chapter 8). Although he was close to positivism and supported the positivists' arguments against metaphysics, he was distressed by the prevailing cult of scientific facts, which made serious philosophical discussion "almost as ridiculous as wearing a powdered wig."[22] Kavelin thought that the positivists were wrong to dismiss metaphysics or explain metaphysical problems in terms

19. See Wyrouboff, "Remarques," p. 392; K. D. Kavelin, *Sobranie sochinenii* (St. Petersburg, 1899), vol. 2, pp. 364–71, 375, 578; Lesevich, *Opyt*, pp. 124–25.

20. M. M. Troitsky, *Nemetskaia psikhologiia v tekushchem stoletii* (M, 1867).

21. V. S. Soloviev, *Sobranie sochinenii* (St. Petersburg, 1903), vol. 8, p. 417.

22. Remarks made in 1874. See K. D. Kavelin, *sob. soch.*, vol. 3, p. 271.

of material processes; instead they ought to pluck out the real psychological kernel buried in the metaphysical systems (albeit in disguise) and examine it on its own terms—that is, they should acknowledge psychological processes to have their own autonomous existence on a par with material existence.[23] The fact that positivism had still not complied with this postulate inclined Kavelin to the view that it was not yet a scientific philosophy but only a transitional stage in the evolution of the human mind.[24]

When criticizing the positivists' refusal to admit the reality of mental phenomena, Kavelin used arguments borrowed from agnosticism. The supporters of "scientific realism," he pointed out, ought to remember that science itself is a "psychological fact that has no existence outside our minds."[25] We can only comprehend signs, symbols of reality, and not reality "in itself."[26]

In his main work, The Tasks of Psychology (1872), Kavelin argued that materialism and idealism are essentially belated heirs of scholasticism that do not remember their own origins and regard the two sides of Christian dualism as absolutes.[27] This dualism cannot be overcome by explaining mental phenomena in terms of material phenomena or vice versa. Mental phenomena are irreducible, though this should not be taken to imply that they are independent of man's physical constitution. In his theory of the relation between mind and body, Kavelin defended a standpoint halfway between psychophysical parallelism and interactionism. Everywhere there are examples, he pointed out, of two parallel series of phenomena whose interconnection is not in doubt, although it has not been fully investigated. The integrality of human nature will not be violated if we accept the hypothesis that in man there are two organisms deriving from a common stem and therefore intimately connected; each of these organisms influences the other while still retaining its separateness.[28]

In psychology Kavelin distinguished two main trends: empirical psychology, deriving from Locke, and idealist psychology, deriving from Kant. The former concentrated on that part of the psyche directed toward the material world and conditioned by it; the latter

23. Ibid., pp. 319–20.
24. Ibid., pp. 346–47. Kavelin stressed that the positivists were themselves beginning to transcend their previous one-sidedness. He thought he saw evidence of this in Problems of Life and Mind by George Henry Lewes (Sob. soch., vol. 3, p. 338).
25. Kavelin, Sob. soch., vol. 3, p. 341.   26. Ibid., p. 337.
27. Ibid., pp. 420, 438.   28. Ibid., pp. 485, 837–38.

was only interested in those psychic phenomena in which the mind expressed its autonomy and activity.[29] English psychology represented the trend initiated by Locke, German psychology that initiated by Kant. It will be readily apparent that Kavelin himself considered both trends to be one-sided and postulated their reconciliation as mutually complementary systems.

This was part of Kavelin's attempt to undertake a cautious rehabilitation of German idealism, which he interpreted as a disguised form of psychological investigation concentrating on the active side of the human psyche. The speculative constructs of German idealism become comprehensible, Kavelin argued, if they are translated into the language of psychology; one only has to realize that the logical formulas on which they rest in fact describe the moment when the soul splits into two halves and sees itself reflected in its otherness. The realistic-empirical trend that only recognizes the receptive side of the psyche has made no contribution in this field and therefore has no right to dismiss German idealism as valueless.[30]

Kavelin's standpoint, understandably enough, did not satisfy either the materialists or the consistent idealists and spiritualists. The Tasks of Psychology was attacked on two fronts: the eminent physiologist I. M. Sechenov criticized the treatment of psychic processes as autonomous phenomena, while the Slavophile Yury Samarin accused Kavelin of exaggerating the soul's dependence on the body and external environment, which, he stressed, conflicted with the dogma of immortality.

In his introduction to the book Kavelin explained that there was a clear connection between his interest in psychology and the Hegelian liberalism of his youth. Both in The Tasks of Psychology and in his Brief Survey of Juridical Relations in Ancient Russia (1847) his main concern was the defense of the strong autonomous personality.[31] In the 1840's he had discussed the evolution of personality in the light of Russia's past and future; in The Tasks of Psychology he discussed it from the point of view of its universal, or at least European, relevance. The second half of the nineteenth century, he argued, was seeing the diminution of individuality—the emergence of the impersonal masses and the loneliness of the crowd.[32] Although more stress was placed on sociality than ever before, in reality men felt increasingly alienated from each other. Statesmen and civic

29. Ibid., pp. 507–8.
30. Ibid., pp. 509–11.
31. Ibid., p. 375. See above, pp. 148–50.
32. Ibid., p. 613.

leaders saw individual human beings as so many statistical data, figures in a budget, or symbols in an equation. Scientists and "philosophical realists" treated people like things, objects of the external world subject to the inexorable laws of causality.[33] Only psychology attempted to counteract this process: it spoke up on behalf of the personality and restored it to its central position in the universe by showing that allegedly objective social processes were in fact the work of individuals, and that science itself had no existence outside the human mind.[34]

Kavelin's other important book, *The Tasks of Ethics* (1885), also dealt with the problem of personality. In it he attacked the utilitarian and eudaemonistic approach to ethics, with its emphasis on happiness, and argued that prerequisites of a strong moral personality were faith in supra-individual ideals and the constant effort to achieve perfection. Happiness itself could not be regarded as the ultimate purpose of human existence, although the most powerful source of happiness was the effort involved in reaching a goal (the ideal). Chasing after happiness and advantage contributed to external, material progress; but at the same time it deprived life of any deeper sense, took away men's faith and hope, and in doing the latter ultimately destroyed men's happiness.[35]

As these arguments make clear, the common practice of classifying Kavelin as a positivist is not entirely justified. There would seem to be better grounds for calling him a "semipositivist";[36] it is true that he defended positivism against Soloviev's attacks,[37] but he himself opposed the exaggerated cult of scientific facts and tried to bring about a rapprochement between positivist philosophy and idealism —this indeed was the main aim of his philosophical work.

NIKOLAI GROT (1852–99), son of the philologist J. K. Grot, was a more militant and consistent positivist (though only in the first phase of his intellectual development). His interest in philosophy and psychology was stimulated by Kavelin, who was a frequent visitor in his home and invited the young Grot to take part in "peripatetic conservations" on philosophical themes. At the university Grot studied under Troitsky; he was also influenced by Sechenov's work on the physiology of the nervous system. In 1886 he was ap-

33. *Ibid.*, pp. 629–32.
34. *Ibid.*, pp. 638–46.
35. *Ibid.*, pp. 981, 1009–17.
36. See Zenkovsky, *History of Russian Philosophy*, vol. 1, pp. 345–48.
37. See his article "Apriornaia filosofiia ili polozhitel'naia nauka?," in Kavelin, *Sob. soch.*, vol. 3, p. 285.

pointed professor at Moscow University; shortly afterwards he became president of the Moscow Psychological Society,[38] and in 1889, he founded the periodical *Problems of Philosophy and Psychology* (*Voprosy Filosofii i Psikhologii*).[39] By virtue of his official functions, he became one of the leading figures in academic philosophical circles in Russia.

In his first works—his master's thesis on the psychology of sense perception, and his doctorate on the psychological interpretation of problems of logic[40]—Grot displayed a consistently associationist standpoint.[41] Following Spencer, he defined psychic processes as one of the means used by the organism to adjust to the external environment. In order to explain these processes he formulated a theory of "psychic circulation," which postulated a cycle of automatic reactions analogous to the circulation of elementary substances in the body. In his interpretation of mental processes (based on Spencer's biological principles and on his own theory of "psychic circulation"), he reduced the rules of inference to six types of association; the first three were purely mechanical (simple association, dissociation, and the dissassociation of the psychic elements), the other three organic (integration, disintegration, and differentiation). This scheme was linked to a defense of "naive realism" in epistemology and a fascinated interest in the possibility of applying a strictly deterministic evolutionism to psychic processes. In sociology Grot rejected the "subjective method" but at the same time— somewhat inconsistently—treated human happiness as the goal of historical progress. His attempt to make the philosophy of psychology more "scientific" led him to call for the elimination of metaphysical concepts such as that of the "soul" (he suggested it should be replaced by the term *sensorium*); philosophy that was "unscientific" he dismissed as a subjective creative art, like poetry. One of his theories was that philosophical systems were products satisfying

38. Thanks to Grot, the society (which was founded in 1885 by Troitsky) became an important center of intellectual life. The other body to which professional philosophers in Russia could belong was the St. Petersburg Philosophic Society, whose leading personality was A. Vvedensky.

39. If we do not count the ephemeral periodicals edited by A. Kozlov, this was the first—certainly the first regular—professional periodical devoted to philosophy in Russia.

40. *Psikhologiia chuvstvovanii v eyo istorii i glavnykh osnovach* (St. Petersburg, 1879–80); *K voprosu o teorii logiki* (Leipzig, 1882).

41. The following account of Grot's views is based on P. P. Sokolov, "Filosofskie vzglady i nauchnaya deyatelnost N. Y. Grota," in *N. Y. Grot v ocherkakh, vospominaniiakh i pis'makh* (St. Petersburg, 1911).

the subjective requirements of the mind; different systems were of equal psychological value and followed each other according to specific laws of psychic development.

Grot's faith in the validity of his theories did not stand the test of time. As early as the mid-1880's, after studying the works of Giordano Bruno and Plato, Kant, and Schopenhauer, he turned away from positivism and openly declared his conversion to metaphysics. His new philosophy, which he called "monodualism," was to be a synthesis of monism and dualism, that is a resolution of ontological antinomies: the idea of God was to be the principle reconciling spirit and matter, and the idea of the soul the principle reconciling matter and force. In psychology Grot rejected mechanism and associationism as mere "theoretical superstitions." A single novel by Dostoevsky, he declared, had more to say about psychology than the entire body of Spencer's theories.[42]

Grot's metaphysics did not represent a return to the speculative constructs of German idealism; in keeping with the spirit of the age, it was an inductive metaphysics that attempted to base itself on the data of inner experience and that was therefore closely (and deliberately) linked to psychology. Toward the end of his life Grot even attempted to reconcile his new system with positivism. This was owing to his interest in the energetics of Wilhelm Ostwald, which encouraged him in his belief that a scientific explanation of metaphysical problems was within the realm of probability. Arguing that the concept of psychic energy is just as valid as the concept of physical energy, Grot attempted to prove the validity of immortality on the basis of energetics. He returned to the formulas of evolutionism, but by interpreting nature as the pedestal of the spirit, and biological evolution as an instrument in the realization of reason and freedom, he gave those formulas a new spiritualist content.[43]

POSITIVISM AND SOCIOLOGY

The field in which Russian positivism made its most valuable—and indeed international—contribution was sociology. The chief representatives of positivist sociology, however—EUGENE DE ROBERTY (1843–1915) and MAKSIM KOVALEVSKY (1851–1916)—belonged to entirely different schools of thought, in positivism as well as in sociology.

De Roberty, a friend of Wyrouboff and a contributor to *La Phi-*

42. *Ibid.*, p. 118.   43. *Ibid.*, pp. 120–28.

losophie Positive, represented the French, Comtian tradition; he therefore regarded sociology, the latest and highest science in Comte's classification, from the point of view of philosophy. His own *Sociology* (published in Russia in 1880) was aptly called by him a "philosophy of sociology."[44] As the book's full title makes clear, the subject matter includes reflections on the fundamental role and methodological features of sociology, and on sociology's place in relation to other sciences, especially biology and psychology.

In accounts of the history of sociology de Roberty is treated as one of the first and most outstanding representatives of sociologism, a point of view which maintains that regular social processes discovered in sociological research are nonreducible and cannot be explained by reference to other disciplines, such as biology, psychology, or economics.[45] Social phenomena, de Roberty declared, are symptoms of a specific property of organized matter;[46] as such they are not comparable to any wider class of better-known phenomena, and must therefore be tackled by a new fundamental or abstract science (in the Comtian meaning of the word). The constant appearance (even among positivists) of "unitary theories"—that is, reductionist theories ignoring the qualitative differences between different groups of phenomena—was, in de Roberty's view, part of the renewed metaphysical preoccupation with finding an all-explanatory "thing-in-itself."[47]

De Roberty's sociologism was directed mainly against the Spencerian view of social processes as analogous to biological ones, though it was also directed against the "psychologism" of J. S. Mill. De Roberty thought that Spencer, and indeed the entire English evolutionist school, suffered from the same weakness as the materialists—namely a kind of metaphysical "monism," the tendency to formulate all-embracing hypotheses that tried to reduce the complexity and diversity of the living world to one common denominator. Psychologism, on the other hand, whose most extreme manifestation was neo-Kantianism, was guilty of drawing attention away from the external world of things and concentrating excessively on subjective phenomena. Both trends were guilty of "reductionism," because neither understood the qualitative dis-

44. E. de Roberty, *Sotsiologiia. Osnovnaia zadacha eyo i metodologicheskie osobennosti, mesto v riadu nauk, razdelenie i sviaz's biologiei i psikhologiei* (St. Petersburg, 1880).

45. See P. Sorokin, *Contemporary Sociological Theories* (New York and London, n.d.), pp. 438–63.

46. Roberty, *Sotsiologiia*, p. 77.   47. *Ibid.*, p. 199.

tinctiveness of sociology. However, de Roberty was inclined to regard "biologism" as a weightier theory than psychologism. Like Comte, he accepted biology as a fundamental discipline immediately preceding sociology in the hierarchy of the sciences; it might not be able to explain sociological phenomena, but it nevertheless provided the foundations without which sociology would lack substantiality. De Roberty also followed Comte in regarding psychology as nothing more than a branch of research into certain concrete phenomena belonging partly to the sphere of biology and partly to that of sociology. An isolated individual cannot be a reasoning or thinking being (on this issue he often cited de Bonald); men are essentially a product of social development, and therefore psychology ought to be based on sociology, and not vice versa.[48]

Although in his intellectual evolution de Roberty gradually moved away from Comte, he continued to regard him and Saint-Simon rather than Hume and Kant as the founders of the authentic positivist tradition. He called his own new conception (which he expounded in books published in French)[49] "hyperpositivism" or "neopositivism." This neopositivism had nothing in common with the later neopositivism (logical positivism) of the Vienna Circle, which continued the traditions of epistemological positivism. De Roberty, on the other hand, was a determined opponent of what he called the "gnoseological obsession" of contemporary philosophy, which he claimed to trace even in the work of Comte himself.[50] In his view gnoseological problems would be solved not by a philosophical theory of knowledge, but by sociology.

A characteristic motif in de Roberty's thought was his determined opposition to philosophical agnosticism, which he called a survival of the belief in a metaphysical "nature of things." Against Montesquieu's theory of laws as necessary relationships deriving from the nature of things he put forward the proposition that the "nature of things" is derived from necessary relationships or laws. Since no other "nature of things" exists, and since relationships between things are capable of being understood, the problem of the uncertainty of knowledge, or agnosticism, is no longer meaningful. In the same way the dualism of *phenomenon* and *noumenon* is eliminated and the "unknowable" turns out to be merely something

48. *Ibid.*, pp. 299–301.

49. Roberty's other chief works include *Politiko-ekonomicheskie etiudy* (St. Petersburg, 1869); *Proshedsheye filosofii* (M, 1886); *L'Inconnaissable* (Paris, 1889); *L'Agnosticisme* (Paris, 1892); *Nouveau programme de sociologie* (Paris, 1904); *Sociologie d'action* (Paris, 1908); *Les Concepts de la raison et les lois de l'univers* (Paris, 1912).

50. *Nouveau programme*, pp. 187–88.

"not yet known." This argument was linked to a rejection of the classical definition of truth, which in de Roberty's view implied the existence of a metaphysical "thing-in-itself." Truth, he suggested, is only the mutual congruity of ideas and concepts, and the only guarantee and yardstick of this congruity is collective experience; therefore truth is the inevitable result—the most categorical and operative expression—of collective experience.[51] The difference between objective and subjective is essentially the difference between individual experience that has been entirely formed and dominated by collective experience, and individual experience that has been subjected to collective experience only to a minor extent (for except at the animal level there can be no experience that is not at least partly social).[52] Every branch of knowledge starts from subjectivism and gradually becomes more and more objective as it becomes formed within the matrix of social experience.

De Roberty based his conception of the social roots of knowledge on a hypothesis interpreting sociality as a specific and supreme form of energy—"supra-organic energy"—arising out of the interaction of many minds. Thanks to this interaction, there is a transition from mental phenomena such as impressions, imagination, emotions, and impulses (the subjective and particular—which are together referred to in French as *conscience* or individual consciousness) to abstract ideation, which gives rise to *connaissance* or supra-individual consciousness; in other words, a biological, receptive process becomes transformed into a social, conceptual process.[53] Being constantly renewed and multiplied, social experience produces the phenomenon known by the name of various abstract ideas (time, space, causality, purpose, necessity) or—synthetically—by the name of "reason." Basically, reason is the same thing as sociality—that is, supra-organic energy. Therefore theories of knowledge and consciousness ought to be the concern of sociologists rather than philosophers or psychologists, whereas sociology itself should become part of energetics—the general science of all forms of energy.[54]

It seems reasonable to suppose that a sociological theory of knowledge linked to energetics would postulate the primacy of social action over cognition. De Roberty, however, was definitely opposed to such a conception. His theory of the four factors (or moduses) in

51. *Les Concepts de la raison*, pp. 30–31.
52. *Nouveau programme*, pp. 193–94.
53. *Les Concepts de la raison*, pp. 11–14.
54. Here Roberty based himself on Ostwald's energeticism, although he postulated that the three types of energy (physical, chemical, and organic) should be supplemented by "supra-organic" energy. (*Ibid.*, pp. 117–19.)

society ascribes a decisive role to scientific cognition and reveals his essentially idealistic intellectualism.[55] These four factors are (1) detailed scientific knowledge (the analytical and hypothetical modus), (2) philosophy and religion (the synthetic and apodictic modus), (3) art (the syncretic and symbolical modus), and (4) social action (the practical or teleological modus). De Roberty described his theory as a corrective to Comte's conception of the three phases of development, in which religious and philosophical knowledge (the theological and metaphysical stages) preceded scientific knowledge. (De Roberty held that in fact the reverse was true). Basically, however, he was arguing against activist sociological theories (including Marxism) that claim that social praxis engenders intellectual development. Among men living in organized societies based on reason, de Roberty insisted, action is always preceded by thought; the end product of thought may be action, but accepting the primacy of the practical point of view within the thinking consciousness does not mean accepting the thesis concerning the primacy of practical activity over consciousness. De Roberty thought that his own sociological theory resolved the false antinomy between "rationalism" and "activism" by proposing an activism that was logical and rational. It showed that there were two kinds of pragmatism: one that might be called extra- or prescientific (the pragmatism of the animal world); and another that was based on science, this latter being proper to man.[56]

In his criticism of "activism," de Roberty emphasized its connection with the cult of the common man; those who glorify practice, he declared, also want to glorify the *demos* regardless of the fact that in social practice a decisive role is played by knowledge and rational leadership.[57] In his own social ideal de Roberty tried to reconcile elitism (government by an intellectual elite) with egalitarianism (maximum educational opportunities). He argued that progress was the function of two laws: (1) the law of social advance, by which some men outstrip others (this explains the intellectual heterogeneity of the collective and the emergence of ruling elites); and (2) the law of the increasing diffusion of knowledge, which safeguards democratic rights.[58]

De Roberty's ideas found little acceptance in Russia, among either philosophers or sociologists. Lesevich regarded him as being

55. *Nouveau programme*, pp. 65–81.
56. *Les Concepts de la raison*, p. 160.
57. *Nouveau programme*, p. 211.
58. *Les Concepts de la raison*, p. 24.

on a par with Wyrouboff—that is, a thinker who gave positivism a bad name by his lack of understanding of epistemological problems. Lavrov accused him of being too abstract and indifferent to the burning problems of the day. It can be argued, however, that de Roberty deserves a more favorable hearing. His philosophical sociology—or rather sociologizing philosophy—represents an interesting attempt at bridging the gap between Comtian positivism and other philosophical systems of the late nineteenth and early twentieth centuries. Despite his confessed dislike of "gnoseological obsessions," de Roberty did not refuse to tackle fundamental epistemological problems. In many respects his conception of the social roots of knowledge recalls Emile Durkheim's sociological philosophy.

Like de Roberty, the other leading Russian sociologist at this time, Maksim Kovalevsky, also spent many years abroad. He studied in Berlin, Paris (where he became friendly with Wyrouboff), and London (where he was introduced to Marx and Engels). After completing his studies he taught at Moscow University, but he was deprived of his chair in 1887 for political "unorthodoxy." He left Russia and did not return until 1905, when he founded the moderate liberal Party of Democratic Reform. During his years abroad he represented Russia at numerous international sociological congresses; in 1901 (together with de Roberty) he founded the Russian High School of Social Sciences in Paris, where Lenin later taught. In 1895 he was elected vice-president and in 1907 president of the International Institute of Sociology.

In his academic work, Kovalevsky represented a completely different type of sociology from de Roberty.[59] The latter was interested mainly in the philosophical implications of his theories and did not attempt to apply them in concrete sociological research (this must be considered a shortcoming, especially when we compare de Roberty to Durkheim). Kovalevsky, on the other hand, devoted himself to investigating the concrete historical evolution of society and did not even publish a systematic exposition of his own sociological theories. Like de Roberty, he was accused of lack

59. His chief works include *Obshchinnoe zemlevladenie* (M, 1879); *Zakon i obychai na Kavkaze* (2 vols.; M, 1890); *Tableau des origines et de l'évolution de la famille et de la propriété* (4 vols.; M, 1895–99); *Ekonomicheskii rost Evropy do vozniknoveniia kapitalisticheskogo khoziaistva* (3 vols.; M, 1898–1903); *Ot priamogo narodopravstva k predstavitel'nomu i ot patriarkhal'noi monarkhii k parlamentarizmu* (3 vols.; M, 1906); *Sotsiologiia* (2 vols.; St. Petersburg, 1910). His ideas are discussed in Alexander Vucinich, *Social Thought in Tsarist Russia: The Quest for a General Science of Society, 1861–1917* (Chicago, 1976).

of interest in specifically Russian problems; but in his case the criticism was hardly justified.[60] By attempting to show the historical inevitability of "production for exchange" and representative government, his books made a contribution to the leading ideological controversies of his day and provided ammunition for the supporters of the thesis that Russia could not bypass the capitalist phase. Kovalevsky's work on the peasant commune influenced the young Plekhanov and was instrumental in making him abandon Populism for Marxism.

Kovalevsky referred to himself as a "supporter of the philosophy of Comte and a disciple of Marx."[61] He valued his friendly association with Marx and Engels and made use of their research into European economic history; Engels, for his part, thought highly of Kovalevsky's work on the evolution of the family and private property, and used some of this material in his own books. It is scarcely possible, however, to talk of the influence of Marxism on Kovalevsky's views; for him the founder of scientific sociology was Comte, Marxism being only a special variant of positivist evolutionism.

Kovalevsky himself was a typical social evolutionist, convinced of the uniformity and universal applicability of the basic laws of social development. Sociology, he wrote, is "the science dealing with the organization and evolution of societies." This was a modification of Comte's classic formula defining sociology as the science of the "order and progress of society," because, Kovalevsky argued, not every social organization deserves to be called "orderly," and evolution is not always synonymous with progress. Nevertheless, he was convinced that the overall movement of evolution was progressive and that progress was one of the inexorable laws of history. He defined progress as the strengthening of the bonds of human solidarity—the constant expansion of the "environment of peaceful coexistence" (*zamirennaia sreda*) from tribal unity through patriotism to cosmopolitanism, the solidarity of the whole human race. This general formula of progress took different forms, depending on its application to different spheres of social life. Comte's law of the three phases of development sufficed, in Kovalevsky's view, to express the nature of progress in the intellectual sphere. Political progress he defined as the expansion of individual autonomy and popular self-government, its culmination being parliamentary government; progress of this kind was relatively indepen-

60. See B. G. Safronov, *M. M. Kovalevsky kak sotsiolog* (M, 1960), pp. 19–24.
61. See A. P. Kazakov, *Teoriia progressa v russkoi sotsiologii kontsa XIX veka* (L, 1969), p. 100.

dent of the outward forms of statehood and could be reconciled with a monarchical system. In the economic sphere, progress consisted in the constant expansion of economic relations; Kovalevsky believed that the growth of international trade would bring about the economic integration of the whole world, eliminate the causes of war, and ultimately lead to a world federation of democratic states.

These views show clearly that what Kovalevsky stressed in his theory of social evolution was not struggle, but factors making for integration and thus favoring the growth of solidarity and peaceful coexistence. In this he differed not only from Marx but also from Spencer and the social Darwinists. On the other hand, he shows some affinity with the "academic" socialists (Kathedersozialisten) in Germany, whose influence is apparent in his work, and he was also clearly influenced by such Russian opponents of social Darwinism as Kropotkin, Lavrov, and Mikhailovsky.

It is the generally accepted view that Kovalevsky was a representative of the demographic school that believed the main driving force behind progress to be population growth. This is not entirely correct: Kovalevsky did indeed attach great importance to the demographic factor, but only in the economic sphere. In general he was opposed to all attempts to explain social change by a single cause and preferred to account for evolution by the "simultaneous and parallel action and counteraction of many factors."[62] Such a standpoint, he maintained, sprang from the very nature of positivism—that is, from an understanding of the mutual interdependence of all spheres in society.

In his political outlook Kovalevsky was a moderate liberal who believed in transforming tsarism into a constitutional monarchy. These views by no means conflicted with sympathy for "academic" socialism. On economic issues he sharply disagreed with the classical theories of economic liberalism, since he regarded free competition as a form of struggle likely to stand in the way of progress. Socialism to him was a way of organizing the forces of production so as to eliminate class conflicts;[63] revolution, on the other hand, seemed to him a pathological phenomenon. These ideas influenced his interpretation of contemporary issues: he drew attention to Marxs' struggle against revolutionary voluntarism,[64] laid stress on the Marxist contribution to a definition of the objective laws of social progress, argued that a Social Democratic party need not be repub-

---

62. M. M. Kovalevsky, *Sovremennye sotsiologi* (St. Petersburg, 1905), p. xiv.
63. See Safronov, *Kovalevsky*, pp. 84–85.
64. *Ibid.*, p. 86.

lican, thought highly of the German Social Democrat Eduard Bernstein, and praised Plekhanov for his consistent support of an alliance between the proletariat and the liberal sections of the bourgeoisie. Even the communist slogan "workers of the world unite" was, in his view, merely a call for the establishment of legal working class associations.[65]

Another important representative of positivist sociology in Russia was NIKOLAI KAREEV (1850–1931). Unlike de Roberty and Kovalevsky, Kareev attempted to combine positivism with the Populist sociology of Lavrov and Mikhailovsky. In his theoretical works he laid special stress on the importance of the evaluational element (or "subjective" factor) in all attempts at making an orderly presentation of historical data, and attacked theories ascribing a decisive historical role to supra-individual and impersonal forces.[66] One of the failings of which he accused Marxism was its tendency to fatalism and the one-sided depersonalization of history.[67] Comte, on the other hand, he thought guilty of exaggerating the significance of intellectual evolution—to the detriment of economic history.

Kareev's theories were only an eclectic attempt at reconciling positivism with "subjective sociology" and certain elements of Marxism. As in the case of Kovalevsky, Kareev's most important contribution was in the sociological interpretation of history, where he kept to concrete facts. This includes, for instance, his monograph on *The Peasants and the Agrarian Issue in France in the Last Quarter of the Eighteenth Century* (1879), which Marx called an excellent book.[68]

65. See Kazakov, *Teoriia progressa*, p. 126.

66. See especially the following works: *Osnovnye voprosy filosofii istorii* (M, 1883); *Sushchnost' istoricheskogo protsessa i rol' lichnosti v istorii* (St. Petersburg, 1890); *Istoriko-filosofskie i sotsiologicheskie etiudy* (St. Petersburg, 1895).

67. See N. I. Kareev, *Starye i novye etiudy ob ekonomicheskom materializme* (St. Petersburg, 1896).

68. See the letter from Marx to Kovalevsky in April 1879; *Perepiska K. Marxa i F. Engelsa s russkimi politicheskimi deiateliami* (M, 1951), pp. 232–33.

CHAPTER 17

VLADIMIR SOLOVIEV
AND METAPHYSICAL IDEALISM

Despite the unfavorable intellectual climate, the last quarter of the nineteenth century saw a revival of idealist philosophy in Russia. The positivists' concerted attack on all forms of "metaphysics" was met by strong resistance. Metaphysical idealism did not, it is true, regain the position it had held in Russian intellectual life at the time of Chaadaev, of the heated polemics on Hegel, and of classical Slavophilism. It developed apart from the leading trends in social thought, as it were, but on the other hand it now became systematized. This was, of course, part of the general trend toward greater autonomy and professionalism in philosophy.

The thinkers discussed in this chapter represent various trends and were often critical of each other. Basically, all they had in common was their defense of metaphysical idealism and their uncompromising opposition to materialism and positivism. The most outstanding and colorful personality among them was undoubtedly Vladimir Soloviev. His originality and influence sprang from his ability to reconcile the ambitious attempt to create a philosophical system with the Russian intellectual tradition of reluctance to investigate "purely theoretical" problems. Although his system was a product of the process whereby philosophy was becoming an autonomous sphere taken over by professional philosophers, it also expressed the ambition to oppose this process in the name of the ideal of "integrality," which postulated that theoretical philosophy should be organically linked to religion and social practice.

SOLOVIEV'S RELIGIOUS PHILOSOPHY

Soloviev's Life

VLADIMIR SOLOVIEV (1853–1900) was the son of Sergei Soloviev, a leading Westernizing historian and a professor at Moscow University. One of his grandfathers had been an Orthodox priest, and

Vladimir was brought up by his mother in an atmosphere of strict piety. His friend L. M. Lopatin relates that when he was fourteen Vladimir experienced a crisis of faith that turned him into a "total materialist . . . a typical nihilist of the sixties."[1] He now professed a somewhat chiliastic atheism linked to a burning faith in the total transformation of the world—a faith, it should be added, that never left him. When he was seventeen he enrolled in the history and philosophy faculty of Moscow University, although under the influence of Pisarev's article "Our University Studies" he soon transferred to the science faculty instead. He continued to read philosophical works, however (Spinoza, Schopenhauer, Kant, the later Schelling, Fichte, and Hegel); and as a result of his reading and his own reflections and experiences, he gradually regained faith in God and in the profound philosophical significance of Christianity. In 1872, at the age of nineteen, he was once again a convinced Christian. He gave up his scientific studies and devoted himself entirely to philosophy under the guidance of the philosopher and theologian P. D. Yurkevich. He also attended lectures at the Moscow Theological Academy.

Soloviev's master's thesis, *The Crisis in Western Philosophy: Against the Positivists*, was published in 1874, and shortly afterwards he began lecturing at St. Petersburg University. In the following year, however, he applied for permission to visit England in order to make use of the facilities of the British Museum library. In London he devoted himself to studying the history of mysticism, especially the Neoplatonic tradition and German mysticism and theosophy (Jacob Boehme, Franz Baader). A sudden impulse led him to undertake a journey to Egypt, which very nearly had a tragic outcome. Dressed in the clothes he normally wore in London, he set out one day on a walk through the desert in search of a tribe that was believed to have kept alive ancient cabalistic traditions. Seeing his long black coat and tall black hat, nomadic Bedouins took him for an evil spirit, and he barely escaped with his life.

The real reason for Soloviev's journey to Egypt was a mystical vision he called *Sophia*—a personification of the passive aspect of God, of "eternal womanhood"—which appeared to him three times. The first appearance was in his childhood, when he was suffering from unrequited love for a little girl of nine; the second was in the British Museum, when he was told to go to Egypt; and the third was in the desert, after the adventure with the Bedouins. Twenty

1. L. M. Lopatin, "Filosofskoe mirovozzrenie V. S. Solovieva," in *Filosofskie kharakteristiki i rechi* (M, 1911), p. 123.

years later Soloviev, who also wrote poetry, described the three visions in his lighthearted autobiographical poem "Three Meetings."

After his return to Russia (in the summer of 1876), Soloviev established close relations with Slavophile and Pan-Slavic circles (chiefly Ivan Aksakov) and also with Dostoevsky, on whom he made a very deep impression (there are good grounds for supposing that the novelist modeled Alosha Karamazov on Soloviev and also borrowed from him certain characteristics used in the portrait of Ivan Karamazov).[2] In 1878 Soloviev gave a series of extremely successful lectures on Godmanhood in St. Petersburg. Two years later he submitted his doctoral thesis, entitled *A Critique of Abstract Principles* (1880), and after receiving the title of "Dozent" resumed his lectures at the university and at higher courses for women. His academic career, however, was short-lived. After the assassination of Alexander II he gave a public lecture in which he condemned the revolutionaries but also appealed to the new emperor to spare their lives. As a result he was forbidden to lecture in public and shortly afterwards was forced to resign from the university.

As Soloviev approached intellectual maturity he began to move away from the epigones of Slavophilism. The final break came in 1883, when he stopped publishing in Ivan Aksakov's *Rus'* and instead—to the indignation of his right-wing friends—became a contributor to the liberal and Westernizing *European Messenger* (*Vestnik Evropy*). This marked the close of the first phase in his intellectual evolution and the beginning of the second, which Prince Evgeny Trubetskoi (author of a two-volume work on Soloviev's philosophy) has called his "utopian period."[3]

The utopia to which Soloviev aspired was the unification of all the Christian churches, to be followed by the establishment of a theocratic Kingdom of Heaven on earth. It was on behalf of this ideal that he attacked all forms of nationalism, rejected the Slavophile idealization of Orthodox Christianity, and condemned the persecution of national and religious minorities (his articles on this subject published in the *European Messenger* were later collected in two volumes under the title *The National Problem in Russia*).

2. See K. Mochulsky, *Vladimir Soloviev. Zhizn i uchenie* (Paris, 1951), p. 80.

3. See E. N. Trubetskoi, *Mirosozertsanie V. S. Solovieva* (M, 1913), vol. 1, pp. 87–88. Trubetskoi divides Soloviev's intellectual evolution into three periods: (1) preparatory period, to 1882; (2) the "utopian" period, 1882–ca. 1894 (in his biography Mochulsky suggests that this period ended in the early 1890's); and (3) the "positive" period, that is the years when Soloviev no longer believed in the possibility of realizing his utopian vision and concentrated on working out the theoretical foundations of his metaphysics and ethics. D. Stremoukhoff, in his *V. Soloviev et son oeuvre messianique* (Strasbourg, 1935), distinguished a final apocalyptic phase in Soloviev's evolution.

He also shared with the liberals a belief in bourgeois progress, which aroused the particular ire of his ultrareactionary admirer Konstantin Leontiev. However, the vision of the future that Soloviev expounded in books published abroad in order to evade the censor (*The History and Future of Theocracy*, 1887; *L'Idée russe*, 1881; and *La Russie et l'Eglise Universelle*, 1889) was far from liberal: mankind's crowning fate on earth was to be spiritual unification under the pope and political unification under the Russian emperor. Soloviev attempted to gain the Croatian bishop Josip Strossmeyar for his cause, and through him Pope Leo XIII. Strossmeyar, engrossed in dreams of universal Slavic unity, greatly admired Soloviev; Pope Leo, too, agreed that the Russian philosopher's ideal was a beautiful one, but thought that only a miracle could make it come true.[4]

At the beginning of the 1890's Soloviev himself began to lose faith in the possibility of establishing his ideal kingdom. He now entered the third phase of his intellectual evolution, during which he returned to his earlier interest in pure philosophy. Toward the end of his life his views underwent a further change; he finally lost his optimistic belief in the future and became increasingly prey to eschatological premonitions of disaster.

Soloviev had a subtle but complex personality that was not without a certain enigmatic quality. His sensitive features gave him a rather otherworldly look, so that simple people often took him for a priest and knelt down in front of him. At the same time he was not without a sense of humor and in his poems often poked gentle fun at himself. His nature was childlike and trusting, and he tended to see everything in spiritual terms, as a "reflection of the invisible world"; but although he preached acceptance of "worldliness" through its "transfusion by godliness," he could not come to terms with his prosaic everyday life. He fell in love easily, and his mysticism was undoubtedly a sublimation of erotic feelings, though it cannot be dismissed as mere displaced eroticism. He led an untidy life, often sleeping during the day and working at night, and showing little concern for the future. It was well known that he found it impossible to send away beggars, and was likely to hand over all the money he had on him or even to give away his boots. Once he was found shivering in the cold because he had given away all his warm clothes. Like Tolstoy, he was a visionary, but his visions were not the wrathful thunderings of a patriarchal prophet but the sensitive dreams of an eccentric romantic poet.

4. See Mochulsky, *Soloviev*, p. 185.

The Philosophy of Reintegration

In Soloviev's early works the influence of the philosophical romanticism of the older Slavophiles is clearly apparent.[5] In particular Soloviev based himself on the ideas of Kireevsky, especially his conception of the "integral wholeness" that was to counteract the destructive effects of rationalism.

In his master's thesis Soloviev defined the crisis of Western European philosophy as a crisis of rationalism—of all abstract and purely theoretical knowledge. In the development of the human spirit, he argued, philosophy expresses the stage of individualistic reflection, and as such forms an intermediate link between primitive religious unity and the future restoration of spiritual unity through a universal synthesis of science, philosophy, and religion. The pluralism of philosophical systems was a product of the dissolution of primitive unity, the result of alienation and the self-affirmation of the individual Ego. Western philosophy was born of the conflict of individual reason and faith: its successive stages were the rationalization of faith (scholasticism), the total rejection of faith, and finally the total negation of all immediate knowledge—a conception that threw doubt on the substantiality of the external world and identified being with thought (Hegel). Within this Slavophile framework, Soloviev advanced several notions of his own concerning nodal points in the dialectic of European thought and devoted considerable attention to a number of systems, including those of Schopenhauer and Eduard von Hartmann. The section devoted to Hegel and post-Hegelian philosophy is of particular interest: in it Slavophile criticism of Hegelianism blends with Dostoevsky's warnings on the destructive effects of the deification of man (the Man-God).[6]

For Soloviev the ideas of Hartmann provided the most extreme example of the crisis of Western philosophy, although paradoxically they also foreshadowed the day when philosophy would fuse with religion, thus bringing about the restoration of spiritual unity. Hartmann's "philosophy of the unconscious" appeared to Soloviev to be a rehabilitation of the metaphysics rejected by the positivists, a return to the religious concept of "universal unity." Ascribing to Hartmann his own ideas, Soloviev proclaimed that the annihilation

5. A detailed comparison of Soloviev's views with Slavophile philosophy will be found in A. Walicki, *The Slavophile Controversy*, Chap. 15. For the relationship between Soloviev, Dostoevsky, and Russian Slavophilism, see N. Zernov, *Three Russian Prophets: Khomyakov, Dostoevsky, Solovyov* (London, 1944).

6. See above, pp. 103, 315–20.

of the egoistic self-affirmation of warring individuals would be followed not by the Buddhist Nirvana but by the *apokatastasis ton panton*, the "kingdom of spirits bound together by the universality of the absolute spirit." Soloviev considered this notion to be the end product of the entire evolution of Western philosophy (i.e. philosophy in general), amounting to a rediscovery of ancient truths preserved in the traditions of Eastern Christianity.

The first work in which Soloviev outlined a system of his own was *Philosophical Principles of Integral Knowledge* (1877). The title itself clearly harks back to the notion of *tselnost'*, or "wholeness," which was the kernel of Kireevsky's philosophical work. In addition, however, Soloviev introduced a number of ideas not found in Slavophile doctrine—for instance the Comtian notion that mankind, "a real, though collective organism," is the collective subject of history.[7]

Every evolutionary process, Soloviev argued, passes through three phases: a phase of primitive undifferentiated unity; a phase of differentiation during which the individual parts become separated; and a new phase of reintegration in which unity is restored, but as a "free unity" that instead of nullifying differentiation welds the separate elements together by an organic inner bond. In the evolution of mankind (to which this scheme also applies), the first phase—that of substantial monism—was represented by the Eastern world (including nineteenth-century Islam), and the second phase by Western European civilization. Both phases were necessary stages in the development cycle but in themselves were of unequal value; any kind of monism, Soloviev suggested, is superior to atomism, so that "the Moslem East was superior to Western civilization."

During the period of primitive unity the three spheres of human activity—the spheres of creativity, knowledge, and social practice—were entirely subordinated to religion. In the sphere of creativity, technology (the first or material grade) was fused with art (the second or formal grade) and mysticism (the highest or absolute grade) in an undifferentiated and mystical creativity—in other words, in what Soloviev called a *theurgy*. In the sphere of knowledge, positive science (the material grade) was fused with abstract philosophy (the formal grade) and theology (the absolute grade) in an undifferentiated whole that might be called *theosophy*. In the realm of social practice, the economic society of producers or *zemstvo* (the material grade) was fused with the state (the formal grade) and the church

7. V. S. Soloviev, *Sobranie sochinenii* (St. Petersburg, n.d.), vol. 1, p. 232.

(the absolute grade), forming a homogeneous and *theocratic* whole. In the second evolutionary phase (represented by Western Europe), the different grades within each sphere strove for autonomy and for mastery over one another. In the resulting struggle matter conquered spirit: the final outcome of Western civilization was economic socialism (the true scion of capitalism, as Soloviev called it) in the social sphere, positivism in the sphere of knowledge, and utilitarian realism in the sphere of creativity. This was not, however, the final stage in the evolution of mankind; according to the universally valid law of development, the first two phases must be followed by a third—the phase of free unity—in which the separate spheres or "grades" of human creativity, knowledge, and social practice would once more be united, though they would still retain their distinctive flavor. In the three spheres of life this renewed unity would express itself as a *free theurgy*, a *free theosopy*, and a *free theocracy*. "In this way," Soloviev concluded, "all spheres and grades of human existence will become united in this third and final phase into an organic whole whose organs and members are based on trichotomy. The normal harmonious activity of all organs will give birth to a new general sphere—the sphere of *integral life*. At the beginning* its bearer among mankind can only be the Russian nation." [8]

To digress for a moment: it is interesting to examine the more detailed justification of the historical destiny of the Russian nation to be found in Soloviev's public lecture on "The Three Forces" given in the same year (1877, the year of the Russo-Turkish War "for the liberation of the Slavs"). In this lecture, Soloviev suggested that the actual bearers of the "three forces that have governed the evolution of mankind from the dawn of history" were "three historical worlds," or rather three distinct cultures, the Moslem East, Western civilization, and Slavdom. The first represented a fossilized and despotic unity in which all spheres of life were subordinated to religion, thus turning man into the lifeless instrument of an "inhuman God." The second set the "godless man" against the "inhuman God"; its last word was "universal egoism and anarchy, atomization in life, atomization in science, atomization in art." These forces never occurred (and never could occur) in their pure form—they should rather be seen as specific trends whose total and final realization would mean the annihilation of mankind. To prevent this was the mission of the third force, which was capable of

8. *Ibid.*, p. 262.

achieving a synthesis of "unity" and "multiplicity," of making God "human" and turning man toward God, of reconciling East and West. This force could only draw its strength from divine revelation, and its exponent could only be a nation able to mediate between the divine and the human. Such a mediator must be entirely devoid of exclusivity or one-sidedness; he must have unshaken faith in the divine, the ability to transcend his own particular interests, a contempt for the things of this world, and the ability not to fritter away his energy in many separate spheres of activity. These features, Soloviev concluded, "are certainly typical of the tribal character of the Slavs and especially of the national character of the Russian people."[9]

Let us now return to the *Philosophical Principles of Integral Knowledge*. After his introductory exposition, Soloviev proceeded to examine the idea of a "free theosophy" (or in other words "integral knowledge") in greater detail. He distinguished three types of philosophy—naturalism (empiricism), rationalism, and mysticism. Empiricism and rationalism, he suggested, take different paths to arrive at the same result—the denial of the substantial reality of both the external world and the knower himself. The absurdity of such a conclusion illustrates the bankruptcy of all "scholastic" or purely theoretical philosophy. A superior type of cognition is mysticism, which draws on supernatural sources of knowledge and looks for "vital and integral" truths that involve not only the intellect but also "the will to goodness" and the "sense of beauty." Mysticism itself, however, cannot be equated with "true philosophy," since the latter postulates the inner, organic synthesis of all types of philosophical thought, analogous to the synthesis of science, philosophy, and theology in the superior free theosophical unity. Summing up his reflections on the sources, methods, and aims of integral knowledge, Soloviev wrote:

Free theosophy is knowledge whose subject is true being in its objective manifestations, whose goal is man's inner integration with true being, and whose material are the facts of human experience in all its forms—above all mystical experience, followed by inner or psychic experience, and finally external or physical experience. Its basic form is intellectual insight or the intuitive perception of ideas, systematized with

9. *Ibid.*, p. 224. Here there are clear echoes of Dostoevsky's messianism, especially his conception of the "all-human" mission of the Russian nation. The connection between Soloviev's ideas and those of Dostoevsky has been analyzed by Serge Hessen in his "Der Kampf der Utopie und der Autonomie des Guten in der Weltanschauung Dostoewskis und W. Solowjows," *Die Pädagogische Hochschule* (Baden, 1929), no. 4.

the help of purely logical or abstract thought; its active source, or causative principle, is inspiration, that is the influence of higher ideal beings upon the human spirit.[10]

Soloviev intended also to elaborate the three main elements of his free theosophy—organic logic, organic metaphysics, and organic ethics—but the *Philosophical Principles of Integral Knowledge* breaks off at the section on organic logic. By logic Soloviev meant the science of the first principle or *Urprinzip*, or, more accurately, the *logos* or first principle in its second phase of self-differentiation, corresponding to the second member of the Holy Trinity. Soloviev called this method "positive dialectics" and insisted that it differed fundamentally from Hegel's rationalist dialectics. "Positive dialectics" allows every item to be defined through its trichotomous relation to the absolute first principle: (1) in its substantial unity with the first principle, i.e. in pure potentiality or positive nothingness (in God the Father); (2) in self-differentiation, i.e. in the act of self-realization (in the *logos*, or the Son); and (3) in free or mediated unity with the first principle (in the Holy Spirit). Differentiation among the separate logical categories (Soloviev intended to introduce 27 such categories) is only possible in the *logos* and is therefore relative, since the *logos* is by its very nature a relation. The three ways in which the first principle is related to everything else as well as to itself can be called the concealed *logos*, the revealed *logos*, and the embodied or concrete *logos* (Christ). These notions provide a connecting link, as it were, between Soloviev's "logic" and the theme of "Godmanhood."

The work in which Soloviev summed up and systematized his ideas in the spheres of epistemology, ethics, and social philosophy was his doctoral dissertation, the *Critique of Abstract Principles* (1880). In this work he reverted to the conception of a "free theosophy" and "free theocracy," although he now substituted the term "All-Unity" for "integral wholeness." What Soloviev called "abstract principles" were various aspects of All-Unity, which, by separating from the whole and establishing their autonomy, lost their true character, conflicted with each other, and plunged humanity into a state of disunity and chaos. In this crisis it fell to philosophy to attempt to restore spiritual unity in the sphere of knowledge as well as in society. In support of this program of reintegration Soloviev denied the autonomy of "theoretical philosophy" ("abstract knowledge") and the autonomy of ethics ("ab-

10. Soloviev, *Sobr. soch.*, vol. 1, p. 294.

stract moralism"). In other sections of the thesis he again made use of Slavophile ideas: the view that faith lies at the root of all knowledge was derived from Khomiakov's epistemology; and the ideal of a "free community" (*svobodnaia obshchinnost'*) founded on love and precluding "external authority" is again a clearly recognizable version of Slavophile *sobornost'*.

Godmanhood and "Sophia"

For Soloviev epistemological and ethical questions were secondary to the philosophy of religion, which was closely bound up with anthropology, cosmology, and the philosophy of history. At the root of his philosophy of religion lay the concept of "Godmanhood"— or the mysterious idea of "God made Man"—which he saw as the true meaning of Christianity. The religion of Goodmanhood (which, Soloviev insisted, must be distinguished from the official theology of the Christian churches) was the highest form of religious consciousness, because faith in God is most valuable when God can unite with man without overwhelming or engulfing him. Godmanhood contains the truths of both East and West and indeed the truth of all religions, not excluding the atheists' faith in Humanity.

The idea of Godmanhood enabled Soloviev to overcome the dualism of traditional Christian theology between the divine and the temporal without falling into pantheism. The concept of "God made Man" does not assume either dualistic belief in the transcendence of God, or pantheistic belief in His immanence as an all-pervading principle. Nevertheless, God is both transcendent and immanent, and the mediating principle that allows the world to become transfused by the Divine spirit—the link between God and created matter—is Man.[11] The ultimate purpose of the universe is the synthesis of the temporal and the divine—universal reintegration in a living All-Unity. The whole of nature tended toward Man, and humanity harbored the God-Man within its womb. The incarnation of God in Jesus Christ was the central event not only of the history of mankind but of the entire cosmic process.

The concept of Godmanhood in Soloviev's work is closely tied to

11. There is a striking affinity between these ideas and those of the Polish romantic philosophers (especially A. Cieszkowski, B. Trentowski, and Z. Krasiński) who tried to reconcile theism with pantheism, and transcendence with immanence, in order that "the world might not be godless, or God worldless" (Cieszkowski). The resemblance was noted by Berdiaev, who suggested that in some respects Cieszkowski was superior to Soloviev. See N. A. Berdiaev, *Russkaya idea. Osnovnye problemy russkoi mysli XIX i nachala XX veka* (Paris, 1946), pp. 213–15.

the idea of *Sophia*, or Divine Wisdom, of whom it was written that "The Lord created me at the beginning of his works, . . . at the beginning, long before earth itself." (Proverbs 8: 22–23.) Soloviev, who identified *Sophia* with the mysterious being who appeared to him in his mystical visions, read all he could about her in the enormous body of mystical and theosophical literature in which she figures. He studied the Jewish mystical writings of the *Cabala* (in which *Sophia* takes the form of a woman); the works of Jakob Boehme, where she is identified with "eternal virginity"; and the writings of Swedenborg, Saint-Martin, and Baader. He believed that *Sophia* was especially close to the mystical traditions of Eastern Christianity, because she was portrayed on an old ikon in Novgorod Cathedral. In later years he attempted to prove that *Sophia* was identical with the concept of *Le Grand Etre*—the "ideal being" in the philosophy of Comte.[12]

The concept of *Sophia* is not entirely explicit in Soloviev's philosophy, especially since it underwent various modifications in his different works. In developing his theories, Soloviev made use of ideas taken from Plato and the neoplatonists, Leibniz (the monadistic conception of ideas), and Schelling. Broadly speaking, *Sophia* represents the World Soul, ideal Humanity, and "eternal womanhood." In every organism, Soloviev argued, there are two types of unity—creative unity and created unity. In Christ (as the second substance of the Godhead) the active, creative unity is the Word or *logos*, and the created unity is *Sophia*. Representing the essential "oneness" of divine archetypal ideas (which Soloviev thought of as living forces), she is the World Soul and at the same time ideal Humanity, whose role it is to mediate between God and the world. As the "word made flesh" or divine matter, she epitomizes the passive receptive principle and is therefore feminine.

The World Soul has its own will, and it was this fact that made possible the Fall, the beginning of the cosmic drama. Having conceived the desire to separate from God and affirm her existence outside God, *Sophia* lost her freedom, central position, and power over creation. The outcome of her falling away from God was the spatiotemporal world of objects, in which unity disintegrated and life came to be at the mercy of death. Before the ideal of All-Unity can be realized this world must once again become united with God—the World Soul must fuse with the *logos*. The process of reintegration is a slow one: the urge toward All-Unity first mani-

12. See Soloviev's 1898 lecture on "The Idea of Humanity in Auguste Comte" (in Soloviev, *Sob. soch.*, vol. 8).

fests itself in nature as a blind force (the law of gravity, the combination of elements in chemical processes, etc.), then as the principle of organization (organic life), and finally (after the appearance of the human race) as conscious and free activity. The successive phases of the process of creation (cosmogony) have their counterpart in the phases of the theogony, that is in men's ideas about God. A moment that was a turning point (although the entire previous history of the world and of mankind had led up to it) was the coming of Christianity, when God became Man in the historical Jesus Christ, this being a perfect theophany after a series of incomplete preparatory theophanies. After this the urge toward All-Unity proved stronger than the forces of death and disintegration. Nevertheless, the ideal of the perfect man embodied in Jesus—that is, the ideal of the Godman—can only be realized in the ideal society, the Kingdom of God on earth. This will mark the closing stage of the history of mankind on earth; the natural world will be redeemed for the second time, will become "transfused by the Divine," and will be liberated from the power of death and united with God in free All-Unity.

In this theory the instrument of final reintegration was to be mankind united with God through Christ, that is the Christian Church. Christianity, however, suffered from internal divisions. In the West the Church had fallen prey to the temptations of temporal power (Catholicism) or the sin of intellectual pride (Protestantism); in the East Orthodoxy had preserved the pure truth of Christ, but had not tried to incorporate it in the external historical world of culture. Western civilization had developed the human principle, whereas the East had remained faithful to the divine principle. The realization of Godmanhood in human society—the essential precondition of the total transformation of the world—therefore required the reconciliation of East and West and the unification of the Christian churches.

Soloviev's Theocratic Utopia and Theory of Love: The Influence of Fedorov

Soloviev imagined that the Kingdom of God on earth would be realized as a "free theocracy." Since God is the supreme authority, he argued, government by men is always usurpation and tyranny. On the other hand, God does not exercise his power directly—he is represented on earth by his high priest, by the emperor and by prophets. The structure of legitimate authority is triune, corresponding to the three substances of the Holy Trinity: the triunity of the papal, imperial, and prophetic elements is the temporal reflection of the triunity of God the Father, the Son, and the Holy Ghost. The Kingdom of God will be established on earth when humanity becomes united under the authority of one high priest and one emperor, and when genuine prophets—"the free breath of the Divine Spirit"—appear constantly among the common people to mediate between the temporal and spiritual authorities. After becoming united and submitting to God, the human race will fulfill its mission in the universe—it will fuse the created with the divine world, reintegrate fallen nature, and overpower the forces of chaos and death.

As was mentioned earlier, Soloviev's choice for high priest of a united mankind had fallen on the pope. Like Chaadaev before him, Soloviev had come to the conclusion that in the quarrel with Byzantium Rome had been in the right. Having seceded from universal unity, the Orthodox Church had allowed Christianity to become subservient to national particularism. The Catholic Church had also made mistakes, but it was an active historical force committed to building the Kingdom of God, whereas in Orthodoxy the current of authentic Christianity was only represented in the contemplative life of the monasteries. Soloviev was confirmed in his critical view of Orthodoxy as a religion subservient to the secular authorities by Pobedonostsev's persecution of religious and national minorities and by the Church's role in their Russification. In his article "Saint Vladimir et l'Etat chrétien" (1888) he even suggested that in Russia the ideal of a universal church was expressed not by official Orthodoxy but by the persecuted Old Believers.

Soloviev was a man of strange contradictions: though he condemned all forms of nationalism, he believed that Russia had a messianic role to play in the political unification of mankind under the tsar. The Russian empire was to become the "third Rome," reconciling the first two.[13] The success of this mission depended, in Soloviev's view, on the internal transformation of Russian society and in particular on the solution of the Jewish and Polish questions. Although he made these reservations, it is surprising how much he clung to an idealized picture of Russian autocracy and how greatly his judgment was affected by views current in the reactionary circles he opposed. Russian absolutism was

13. The idea that Moscow might be a "third Rome" was first formulated at the end of the fifteenth century by the monk Philotheus, who declared that after the fall of Bzyantium (the second Rome) Russia had been chosen by God to be the third and last Rome.

to bring about the revival and redemption of Europe by confronting the godless forces of the Western world; it is true that Soloviev did not state precisely what he had in mind, but there is no doubt that his faith in an official government mission of this kind was incompatible with his stated ideal of total freedom of conscience.

Soloviev's opinions on the Polish question[14] were also naive and basically reactionary. He was convinced that Polish hostility to Russia was rooted in purely spiritual causes, and that on the material side the association with Russia had been to Poland's advantage. Since he identified "Polishness" with Catholicism and the leading position of the gentry (a widely held view popularized by the Slavophiles and Populists), he naturally thought Russia's reconciliation with Rome would remove the main cause of Polish hostility, especially if Poland were asked to play the important role of mediator in this reconciliation. At the same time the gentry's social aspirations would be satisfied if they were invited to fill the place of the independent and active upper class that Russia herself lacked. The moral satisfaction of the Poles would automatically cause the disappearance of Russian "nihilism," which Soloviev called "a mere mask for the Polish question."

It is to Soloviev's credit that he was capable of acknowledging his mistakes. He became increasingly disillusioned with the "Christianity" of conservative circles, where he was regarded with growing mistrust, and—in connection with the severe famine of 1891—he even began to have doubts about the positive role of the autocratic state. In his lecture "On the Decline of the Medieval World View" (given in 1891, the year of the famine), he suggested that nonbelievers had done more for the progress of mankind than Christians. (After this lecture Leontiev denounced him as a scoundrel and tool of the Antichrist.) In the following year Soloviev told E. Trubetskoy that he would be willing to join nonbelievers in the struggle against the Christians of his day.[15] No doubt this was said in a moment of exasperation, but this exasperation expressed the authentic bitterness of a disappointed idealist.

Although Soloviev had become disillusioned as far as Russia's national mission and his cesaropapist utopia were concerned, this did not mean that all utopian motifs were automatically eliminated from his world view. On the contrary, during the early 1890's he gave much thought to a utopian vision with a specifically erotic

14. See Trubetskoi, *Mirosozertsanie*, vol. 1, pp. 499–502, 523.
15. See Mochulsky, *Soloviev*, p. 195.

flavor. The fruits of his reflections were five articles published under the title *The Meaning of Love* (1892–94).

A strand of eroticism, closely bound up with the ideal of "eternal womanhood," runs through Soloviev's entire philosophy. His vision of All-Unity was based on the idea of a *syzygetic* union between the part and the whole, a kind of loving cooperation in which the urge toward reintegration and wholeness would overcome the disintegrating centrifugal force of egoism.[16] This "pan-eroticism" in Soloviev's world view was, however, accompanied by a dislike of physical relationships, which he regarded as a symptom of the Fall: he made a distinction between "sexual" love (by which he meant an ideal love linking the two sexes) and mere physical intercourse. He also rejected the view that the goal of love was procreation—i.e. the continuation of the species—and argued that in nature there was no direct correspondence between fertility and the strength of sexual love. Love between men and women was to him one of the supreme values, and he refused to accept the Schopenhauerian view that it was a mirage used by nature to dazzle lovers into sacrificing themselves for the sake of future generations. The essence of love, Soloviev insisted, is the urge toward reintegration—toward realizing the ideal of the "genuine human being," who represents the indivisible free unity of the male and female elements. Total man is made in the image of his Creator, and the most profound meaning of sexual love is that it allows man to be "transfused by God" and torn from the grasp of death. The physical act of love, on the other hand, helps to maintain the power of death because it leads to an "evil infinity"—to the absurd proliferation of generations, each being only a means to the next. Physical relationships therefore degrades love and negate its true meaning. The powerful force that, as a result of *Sophia*'s Fall, had been turned outward toward procreation ought to be directed inward and become an instrument of universal reintegration.

These ideas recall the German Romantics' fascination with the concept of androgyny. Soloviev was especially close to Baader, who wrote that "love is a means by which a man and a woman can find inner fulfillment (in soul and spirit) and thus realize the idea of the integral human being, that is the image of man's original divinity."[17] The common source of both Soloviev's and Baader's conception was of course the Platonic myth of the first beings, who

16. Soloviev, *Sob. soch.*, vol. 6, p. 416.
17. See E. Susini, *Franz von Baader et le romantisme mystique* (Paris, 1942), vol. 3, pp. 569–72.

were punished for their presumptuousness by being cut into two halves.

It must be stressed, however, that Soloviev also drew his inspiration from another, purely Russian source: the conceptions of NIKO-LAI FEDOROV (1828–1903), illegitimate son of Prince Pavel Gagarin, librarian at the Rumiantsev Museum in Moscow (now the Lenin Library), and author of the *Philosophy of Common Action* (published posthumously). Fedorov was an eccentric little known during his lifetime, and the importance accorded to him by some Russian émigré historians appears to be somewhat exaggerated.[18] It should be noted, however, that both Dostoevsky and Tolstoy were greatly impressed by his theories and that Soloviev attempted to develop them further in his philosophy. Soloviev became acquainted with Fedorov's ideas in 1878 and at once thought them "not far from the truth." Subsequent personal acquaintance deepened this impression. At the beginning of the 1880's Soloviev acknowledged Fedorov as his teacher and called his conceptions "the first step forward made by the human spirit on the road to Christ."[19]

Fedorov's world view was a strange blend of religious and mystical motifs with common-sense utilitarianism, of radical criticism of capitalism and industrialization with a cult of technology and the natural sciences. He had an almost magical belief in man's ability to master the forces of nature and to use them to find a solution to "ultimate issues." Although he advocated the purposeful and planned transformation of reality, he subordinated this "projective" attitude toward life to a utopian fantasy of "collective action" in which all effort would be concentrated on resurrecting the dead and conquering death itself. This led him to regard progress as fundamentally immoral, since he could not accept the "death of the fathers"—the dismissal of past generations as mere stepping-stones to the happiness of future ones. These ideas must have impressed Dostoevsky, who through Ivan Karamazov criticized all historiosophical theodicies attempting to vindicate the ultimate justice of divine providence. Against the "will to birth"—the proliferation of generations of mortal men—Fedorov set the "will to resurrection"—the conquest of death and the substitution of fraternal and filial for physical love. He thought this goal could be

18. See the chapters devoted to Fedorov in Zenkovsky's and Lossky's histories of Russian philosophy. For fragments from Fedorov's writings, see J. Edie et al., *Russian Philosophy* (Chicago, 1965), vol. 3, pp. 16–54.

19. Mochulsky, *Soloviev*, pp. 153–54.

reached through mastery over nature and through the establishment of a social system founded on communal ownership and the
exclusion of all factors dividing men and introducing elements of
struggle into their mutual relations.

Soloviev took over from Fedorov his criticism of the "will to
birth" as well as the idea that victory over death was the only moral
solution to the drama of history. He also accepted that redemption
must be a collective act and that the only way to achieve immortality
was for mankind to become united in a Kingdom of God on earth.
It is obvious, however, that he must have been repelled by Fedorov's naturalism and his seeming cult of science, and could have had
little sympathy for the ancestor worship and egalitarian communism
connected with it. Soloviev's condemnation of procreation, moreover, was linked to a specific pan-eroticism, just as his conception
of a universal resurrection was part of the Neoplatonic and romantic ideal of cosmic reintegration and Godmanhood. In a word,
Soloviev took over certain ideas from Fedorov, but assimilated them
into an infinitely more complex philosophical world view that undoubtedly had more in common with the ideas of Novalis and
Baader than with the conceptions developed in the *Philosophy of
Common Action*.

Autonomization of Ethics and Epistemology;
Apocalyptic Forebodings

Disillusionment with his theocratic utopianism led Soloviev to
change his mind about the growing secularization of culture and
various intellectual trends connected with it. He began to speak
with approbation of Lesevich (to whom he had previously denied
any philosophical qualifications whatsoever),[20] discovered the contribution made by Comte to the Christian consciousness, proposed
including the founder of positivism among the Christian saints,[21]
and even expressed his agreement with the main theses of Chernyshevsky's dissertation on *The Aesthetic Relation Between Art
and Reality*.

This gradual change in his outlook meant that Soloviev became
less critical of the growing emancipation of the spheres of knowledge, artistic creation, and social practice from the leading strings
of religion. While preparing a new edition of his *Critique of Abstract Principles* he came to the conclusion that his ideas on ethics

20. *Ibid.*, p. 191.
21. Soloviev, *Sob. soch.*, vol. 8, pp. 244–45.

had changed to such an extent that he ought to revise them completely. This is how he came to write his major study in ethics, *A Justification of the Good* (1897).

The most important innovation in this work is the acceptance of the independence of ethics not only from religion but also from metaphysics. There is some disagreement over how far this extends: some students of Soloviev's philosophy assume that he was tending toward the total autonomy of ethics,[22] whereas others suggest that this autonomy is in fact only apparent, since it assumes as a necessary precondition the existence of God and the immortality of the soul.[23] Nearest to the truth appears to be the view that in his *Justification of the Good* Soloviev was concerned to emphasize the *relative* autonomy of the ethical sphere—its independence from metaphysical knowledge about God and the dogmas of positive religion.[24]

In Part I of his work ("The Good in Human Nature") Soloviev attempted to give his ethics empirical foundations by deriving it from feelings of shame, compassion, and religious adoration (*blagogovenie*). Shame (whose prototype is sexual shame) expresses man's attitude to what is below him; a sense of shame reminds him that he is a spiritual being intended for higher purposes than the world of physical matter. A further development of shame is conscience, whose role is to restore wholeness in the inner life of the individual. Compassion is a social feeling expressing man's attitude to his equals, i.e. his fellow men; its role is to transform society into an integral organism, to bring to pass "the truth of coessentiality" or the real solidarity of all beings. Finally, religious adoration (*pietas, reverentia*) expresses man's attitude to what is superior to him; its role is to restore the wholeness of human nature by uniting it with the absolute center of the universe. The fact that feelings of shame, compassion, and religious adoration were universal feelings was for Soloviev convincing proof that it was possible to set up a universally valid and autonomous system of ethics (i.e. one not dependent on metaphysics or positive religion). At the same time, Soloviev followed Kant in insisting that ethics cannot be founded on psychological data. Universality and necessity are imparted to ethics by reason. It is only possible to speak of ethics when reason deduces the inner ethical content from natural data and confirms it

22. See Mochulsky, *Soloviev*, p. 229.
23. See Trubetskoi, *Mirososzertsanie*, vol. 2, p. 80.
24. See Hessen, "Der Kampf der Utopie."

as a *categorical imperative* independent of its psychological foundations.[25]

In Part II of *A Justification of the Good* ("The Good from God"), Soloviev developed the proposition that good is rooted in the Absolute. In the last part ("The Good in the History of Mankind") he examined the problem of morality in international political and economic relations. He advocated that ethical considerations should play a greater role in politics and criticized national egoism, but he also opposed cosmopolitanism, arguing that respect for nationality cannot be separated from respect for a person. He called economic activity the "spiritualization of nature" and insisted that it should not be considered as a mere struggle for existence. The essential role of the state, in his view, was to defend the weak (an "organized compassion") and therefore to make itself responsible for placing economic relations on a sounder ethical basis. On this issue he engaged in polemics with Chicherin, who defended *laissez-faire* economics, and also with Tolstoy, for whom the state as such was only "organized robbery."

That Soloviev was increasingly inclined to allow philosophy as such, as well as the various philosophical disciplines, a measure of autonomy was shown even more clearly in three epistemological articles published under the title *Theoretical Philosophy* (1897–99). These open with the author's declaration that it is the first duty of a theoretical philosopher to relinquish all interests apart from purely philosophical ones, and to forget about every other will except the will to find out the truth.[26]

His reflections on epistemological issues led Soloviev to reject the "spiritualist dogmatism" that assumes the substantiality of the knower. The Cartesian "I think," he argued, does not necessarily imply that "I am"; all that is immediately accessible are states of consciousness, apart from which the knowing subject is only an empty form.[27] Polemicizing with his friend L. M. Lopatin, and with his own earlier views expressed in the *Lectures of Godmanhood*, Soloviev argued that the human mind is not a substance but only a "hypostasis." The only substance in the true meaning of the word is the Absolute. Only after death is man finally substantiated in eternal ideality; substantiality, therefore, is the ultimate destiny and not an innate property of the human soul.

25. Soloviev, *Sob. soch.*, vol. 7, pp. 130, 169, 173.
26. *Ibid.*, vol. 8, p. 157.
27. *Ibid.*, pp. 165–72.

It is also interesting to examine Soloviev's discussion of the "three types of credibility" on which speculative philosophy may rely. These are, first, subjective states of consciousness, or the psychic material of cognition; second, logical reasoning as such (divorced from content); and third, purposeful cognition (*zamysel*), or the "vital act of decision" that directs the consciousness toward the absolute truth and transforms immediate sense impressions into the material of the complex process of active cognition.[28] The concept of "purposeful cognition" to some extent recalls the phenomenological notion of "intention" and the "intentional act." It is difficult to decide how far this correspondence extends, for Soloviev's premature death prevented him from developing his epistemological theories.

In the last year of his life Soloviev's views appeared to undergo another change. His optimistic faith in liberal progress and his confidence that even secularization was essentially part of the ultimate process of salvation through Jesus began to give way to a mood of pessimism. An expression of this was the philosophical dialogue *Three Conversations* (1899–1900), and especially the *Tale of the Antichrist* appended to the dialogue.

Leaving out less important details, the *Tale of the Antichrist* can be summarized as follows. In the twentieth century Europe is invaded by a yellow-skinned race. Subsequently the nations of Europe throw off the Mongolian yoke and in the face of the common danger set up a powerful federation of democratic states. In the twenty-first century an unusual man appears—he is 33 years old; is a spiritualist, ascetic, and philanthropist; believes in God (although he loves only himself); and desires the happiness of mankind. Under his leadership the nations of the world become united in one universal state; the longed-for age of eternal peace is at hand and social reforms put an end to poverty. The great benefactor of mankind governs in a Christian spirt and courts the favors of the Christians (of whom only an insignificant minority are left). He even convenes an Ecumenical Council in order to unite the Christian Churches. In actual fact, however, he does not believe in Jesus and puts himself in His place. Among the Christians attending the Council only a handful (the followers of Pope Peter II, of the Elder John representing the Orthodox Church, and of the Protestants' leader Professor Ernest Pauli) recognize the benefactor of mankind as the Antichrist. After bringing about his false unification of the Christians, the Antichrist proclaims himself to be God incarnate; the true Christians recog-

28. *Ibid.*, pp. 203, 209, 219–21.

nize the Pope as their leader and depart into the desert in order to wait for the appearance of Christ. In the meantime there has been an uprising of the Jews, who originally believed that the Antichrist was the expected Messiah but turned in anger on the usurper when they realized their mistake. The Emperor-Antichrist marches with his army against the rebels, but thanks to supernatural intervention he perishes in a lake of fire. Jews and Christians make their way to Jerusalem, where they see Jesus descending to earth. All the dead are resurrected to reign with Christ for the millennium.

Soloviev himself (and many of his followers and students of his work) regarded the *Tale of the Antichrist* as a work of outstanding importance.[29] This is certainly saying too much; if we compare the *Tale* with the "Legend of the Grand Inquisitor," similar in certain respects, Dostoevsky's vision must be acknowledged as far more impressive. The *Tale* does make it clear, however, that Soloviev's world view had undergone certain radical changes; it also shows his paradoxical nature in an unexpected light. Its originality consists in its portrayal of the Antichrist as a great philanthropist who puts into effect progressive humanitarian ideals and even attempts to give these ideals a Christian form. This, of course, is how Konstantin Leontiev, the consistent critic of "liberal and egalitarian progress" and "rose-colored Christianity," imagined the kingdom of the Antichrist. The ultimate aim of Soloviev's Antichrist appears to be almost a parody of the ideal of a "free theocracy." Are we to understand that toward the end of his life Soloviev came to agree with Leontiev, and perhaps even to feel that his own life's work had prepared the way not for the Kingdom of God on earth but for the kingdom of the Antichrist? The lack of additional evidence makes it impossible to give a final answer to this question, but there are certainly good grounds for asking it.

Soloviev's Aesthetics

Soloviev commented on aesthetic problems on numerous occasions throughout his life—both in strictly philosophical works and in literary criticism—but his views in this field did not reflect his intellectual evolution or undergo any essential changes. Their most systematic exposition is to be found in his *Beauty in Nature* (1889) and *The Overall Meaning of Art* (1890).

As a motto for his essay on beauty in nature Soloviev chose Dostoevsky's words "Beauty will save the world." Natural beauty, he declared, is a manifestation of the concrete operation of the Abso-

29. See Mochulsky, *Soloviev*, p. 248.

lute in the material world; by "transilluminating" and spiritualiz-
ing matter, beauty helps to raise up the fallen World Soul and to
introduce an element of the divine into reality.

The role of artistic beauty is analogous: art is an instrument of
universal reintegration; creating a work of art means communing
with a higher world and is therefore related to mysticism. The role
of art is to become a theurgic force capable of transforming and
"transilluminating" the human world.

Beauty is something objective and cannot be separated from
Truth or the Good; everything beautiful ought to help to perfect
reality. Soloviev rejected theories of art for art's sake, even quoting
Chernyshevsky in support of the view that such theories were a
symptom of "aesthetic separatism."[30] As part of his attempt to
harness Beauty in the service of Truth and the Good he stressed
the value of socially committed realistic art. This justification of
the "relative truth" of realism by reference to a mystical theory
of art based on Platonic and Schellingian motifs is one of the most
curious features of Soloviev's aesthetics.

Realism, however, was to Soloviev only a precursor of the truly
religious art of the future. As a harbinger of this art of the future
he pointed to Dostoevsky, whom he praised as a writer-prophet,
an artist who "created life" and regarded his art as an instrument
in the realization of the Kingdom of God on earth.

For Soloviev the prophetic element in Dostoevsky's work was a
magnificent expression of the essential profundity of art. Willingly
or not, every great artist is to some extent a prophet. This is because
a work of art (according to Soloviev's definition), is a representation
of a given object that shows it from the point of view of its ultimate
end, i.e. in the light of the future world.[31]

Soloviev's Continuators

It was only after his death that Soloviev's ideas became really
influential. It is no exaggeration to say that an entire generation of
Russian idealist philosophers and religious thinkers was schooled
in his philosophy. Thanks to his many eminent disciples (largely
working outside Russia after the Revolution) he gained the posthumous reputation of being Russia's greatest philosopher. Even
today this is a widely held view among historians of philosophy of
an idealistic orientation.

The reception of Soloviev's ideas is a complex issue, but two

30. Soloviev, Sob. soch., vol. 6, pp. 424–31.
31. Ibid., p. 78.

aspects can clearly be distinguished: on the one hand, his work contributed enormously to spreading and consolidating the influence of religious idealist philosophy (this may be seen very clearly in the intellectual evolution of the former Legal Marxists—Bulgakov, Berdiaev, and Frank); on the other hand, by stimulating interest in religion, his ideas helped to make clear the need for a far-reaching modernization of the religious consciousness and introduced a number of obviously heterodox motifs into Russian religious thought.

S. L. Frank (1877–1950), L. P. Karsavin (1882–1952), and the philosopher-theologians S. N. Bulgakov (1871–1944) and P. A. Florensky (1882–ca. 1948) based themselves entirely on Soloviev's metaphysical conception of All-Unity and the closely related conception of *Sophia*. The intuitivist N. O. Lossky (1870–1965) attempted to combine the notion of All-Unity and *Sophia* with a monadistic pluralism taken over from A. Kozlov. By contrast, Prince S. N. Trubetskoi (brother of E. N. Trubetskoi, author of the monograph on Soloviev) made use of Soloviev's ideas in his polemics against "epistemological individualism" in which he argued that the individual consciousness is rooted in a supra-individual collective consciousness identified by him with *Sophia*. Soloviev's influence is also apparent in the "new religious consciousness" of the critic and novelist D. S. Merezhkovsky (1865–1941), and in the well-known Christian existentialist N. A. Berdiaev (1874–1948), who largely concentrated on the messianic and eschatological motifs in his thought. All the above-mentioned philosophers also shared Soloviev's convinced antirationalism, his tendency to blur the boundaries between philosophy and religion, and his tendency toward mysticism.

The work of Serge Hessen (1887–1950), a philosopher and pedagogue who settled in Poland in 1935, represents a more rationalistic continuation of Soloviev's thought. Hessen, too, took over the idea of All-Unity, but he undertook a critical reexamination of the utopian motifs in Soloviev's philosophy, defending the autonomy of philosophy and of all the remaining relative spheres of culture against the "alleged Absolute."[32]

Soloviev's seminal influence can also be traced in the work of the Russian Symbolist poets V. Ivanov, Andrei Bely, and above all Alexandr Blok, whose early *Poems of the Beautiful Lady* were devoted to the ideal of "eternal womanhood." In his critical works Blok also made use of Soloviev's aesthetic theories, especially the

32. Hessen, "Der Kampf der Utopie."

"theurgic" conception of art as a force for transforming the world, and the notion that aesthetic contemplation is related to mystical experience. But the Symbolist poets were also interested in Soloviev as a religious thinker and philosopher of culture. In 1920 (in his article "Vladimir Soloviev and Our Times") Blok called him a "carrier and harbinger of the future"—a harbinger of the "third force" that would one day reconcile the world, just as Christianity had once reconciled the ancient world in its decline with the German barbarians.

ALEKSEI KOZLOV AND PAN-PSYCHISM

Another important representative of metaphysical idealism in Russia was ALEKSEI KOZLOV (1831–1901).[33] Like Soloviev he rejected idealism in the narrow sense of the word, i.e. the monistic view of the world as pure thought; he called this interpretation of idealism a typical philosophy of an era of transition, a kind of compromise between spiritualism and materialism or between theism and atheism.[34] Unlike Soloviev, however, he was not concerned to restore the links between philosophy and religion, or to make a philosophical interpretation of Christian truths; on the whole he confined himself to strictly philosophical problems and attempted to work out the ontological and epistemological foundations of spiritualism. This is what his biographer, S. A. Askoldov, had in mind when he stated that the ideas of Kozlov and Soloviev are "one and the same problem, approached from different ends, as it were."[35]

Kozlov only began to study philosophy seriously when he was nearly 40, after coming across a book on Schopenhauer by J. Frauenstädt. A few years later he published a work on the philosophy of Hartmann, and in 1875 he was appointed to the chair of philosophy at the University of St. Vladimir in Kiev. In 1878 he published a book about Dühring in which he polemicized with the positivist conception of "scientific philosophy." In 1885 he began publication of the *Philosophical Quarterly* (*Filosofskii Triokhmesachnik*), the first philosophical journal in Russia, but he soon had to give it up as a result of a stroke that left his right side paralyzed for six months. His biographer suggests that by forcing him to concentrate on his inner self for so long, this illness allowed him to experience

33. Kozlov was the illegitimate son of I. A. Pushkin, a distant relative of Alexandr Pushkin.

34. See S. A. Askoldov, *Alexey Alexandrovich Kozlov* (M, 1912), pp. 212–13. Askoldov was Kozlov's illegitimate son.

35. *Ibid.*, p. 217.

the substantiality of the Ego and thus contributed toward the ultimate shape of his metaphysics.

In 1888 Kozlov again started to publish occasional issues of a new journal, *My Own Word* (*Svoe Slovo*), in which he expounded his mature philosophical ideas (he was the sole contributor to the journal, which appeared at irregular intervals). Of the articles published in this journal, the most important is the philosophical dialogue "Conversations with a Petersburgian Socrates." In this the Russian Socrates represents the author's views while his chief opponent is the positivist Shugaer. Other "contributors" included the brothers Ivan and Alyosha Karamazov; no doubt this was Kozlov's way of suggesting that his philosophy offered an answer to the problems posed by Dostoevsky.

The point of departure for philosophical speculation, Kozlov argued, can be neither the notion of "pure being" (as in Hegelian logic) nor Hume's description of the mind as a "bundle of sense impressions." An analysis of the consciousness shows that it can be divided into primary consciousness (the sum of simple immediate sense experiences) and derivative, or complex, consciousness (the totality of all mental acts). Within the primary consciousness it is possible to distinguish between (1) awareness of the content of experiences, (2) awareness of one's acts, and (3) awareness of the "I-hood," of one's own identity as an individual spiritual substance. It is within and by means of the I-hood that a synthesis takes place of awareness of experiences with awareness of one's acts, allowing a transition to the complex consciousness. The I-hood is therefore a prerequisite of reason and consciousness, and there can be no justification or ignoring it as a category of being, as both empiricism and idealistic monism do. The knowing subject is a substance and not an empty vessel; discounting all concrete attributes of being does not empty if of content, but leads to the concept of the I as a simple, irreducible spiritual monad.

Kozlov treated the spatio-temporal world as the sum of states of consciousness. He differed from Kant in not allowing space and time to be categories of *a priori* knowledge, but he was even more opposed to the empiricists' mechanistic associationism. Basically he saw the world as a system in which an infinite plurality of spiritual substances interact with one another. What we call material objects, he suggested, are really symbols of substance with which we happen to be interacting. Time and space are also symbols: space is a symbol of the interconnection of substances, whereas time symbolizes the fact that substances, though themselves unchanging, are variable and mobile in their nonessential attributes. The network of mutual relationships linking substances is nontemporal, but owing to the narrow grasp of our consciousness we cannot encompass that network as a whole; hence we move over it from point to point, thus arriving at the notions of "before," "now," and "after." The world evolves, but in a logical rather than a temporal sequence. Every moment of being is determined by all other points of the sequence within which the substance is developing, not excluding those which from a temporal point of view appear to be in the future.

The name Kozlov gave to his philosophy was "Pan-psychism." He also used the term "pluralistic monism"; the point of this self-contradictory label was to show that the principle of pluralism (the infinite plurality of separate spiritual substances) does not nullify the unity of the world, since all substances are linked to the central substance, or God.

The main source of Kozlov's philosophy was of course the monadism of Leibniz and the views of his nineteenth-century continuators, especially Rudolf Lotze and Gustav Teichmüller, professor at the University of Dorpat (now Tartu, in Estonia) from 1871 to 1888. Kozlov also followed Leibniz in his conception of immortality based on a certain version of the idea of reincarnation.

Kozlov's leading disciple was N. O. Lossky, who, as was mentioned earlier, attempted to combine a spiritual monadism with Soloviev's metaphysics of All-Unity. Kozlov's ideas were also developed by his son, S. A. Askoldov (1871–1945), one of Lossky's colleagues at the university. Lossky and Askoldov were active in the twentieth century, and therefore their work does not fall within the scope of this book.

Another philosopher who continued Kozlov's ideas was a student of Teichmüller, E. A. Bobrov (1867–1933). The philosopher and psychologist L. M. Lopatin (1855–1920), a friend of Soloviev, was also close to Kozlov (and was a far more original thinker than Bobrov). In his two-volume work entitled *Positive Tasks of Philosophy* (1886–91), Lopatin, who was a professor at Moscow University, also returned to the monadism of Leibniz and attempted to combine a dynamically conceived spiritualistic pluralism with a "rational theism" in which God was interpreted as the "monad of monads." This metaphysical idealism, which its author called "dynamic spiritualism" or a "system of concrete dynamism," supplied the foundations of an ethical personalism emphasizing the activity and creative force of the human psyche.

BORIS CHICHERIN AND THE HEGELIANS OF THE
SECOND HALF OF THE NINETEENTH CENTURY

BORIS CHICHERIN (1828–1903) was discussed in an earlier chapter in connection with the evolution of Russian Westernism.[36] An outstanding historian and jurist, and a student of Granovsky and Redkin,[37] Chicherin thought of himself as a Hegelian from his earliest years and remained loyal to Hegelian philosophy to the end. In political outlook he was a liberal conservative—a convinced opponent of all radical or revolutionary movements, but at the same time a consistent Westernizer who urged the need to defend and indeed extend the liberal reforms of the 1860's. In 1868 he resigned his chair at Moscow University in protest against the authorities' violation of academic independence. In 1882 he was elected mayor of Moscow, but he soon fell afoul of the government and had to resign (Alexander III and his reactionary advisers were outraged when Chicherin declared that the rights of the zemstvos should be extended and that the work of local self-government institutions should be "crowned" by the establishment of a national representative body). Despite his great talent and enormous erudition (shown in his History of Political Doctrines [5 vols.; 1869–1902]), Chicherin was never a popular figure. He was keenly aware of his intellectual isolation; recalling the days of his youth, he often referred to the second half of the nineteenth century as an age of general cultural decline.

Chicherin only took up philosophy in the 1870's largely in order to inveigh against the prevailing positivist trends. A systematic exposition of his ideas is to be found in his Science and Religion (1879). Some years later he published his Positive Philosophy and the Unity of Science (1872), in which he took issue with the theories of Comte (whom he nevertheless valued more highly than Mill or Spencer). Chicherin's attack on positivism was from a Hegelian position: for him Hegelian philosophy was "absolute rationalism"[38] and he therefore emphatically rejected Soloviev's mystical brand of idealism, which he criticized in his Mysticism in Science (1880). He conceded that Soloviev's understanding was superior to the "limited ignorance of the positivists,"[39] but at the same time he argued that his theories were inconsistent with logic as well as facts and

36. See above, pp. 150–51.
37. The Russian Hegelian Petr Redkin (1808–91) lectured on the philosophy of law at Moscow University during the 1840's.
38. See D. I. Tschiževskij, Gegiel w Rossii (Paris, 1939), p. 291.
39. See B. N. Chicherin, Mistitsizm v nauke (M, 1880), p. 2.

encroached on the domain of religious revelation, thereby bringing discredit on philosophy and providing ammunition to its positivist critics. In the *Foundations of Logic and Metaphysics* (1894), Chicherin suggested that the present age was about to move beyond positivism and witness a revival of metaphysics, but that nevertheless metaphysics itself ought to become a "positive science."[40]

Chicherin regarded dialectics as the "supreme philosophical science" and thought that the motive power of all development was the "internal contradiction of principles." He also argued that the beginning and end of dialectical development was the Absolute. Indeed, the efforts of human reason to rise from the relative to the Absolute—and even the existence of the very concept of the Absolute—were for him conclusive arguments against positivism. When criticizing empiricism and materialism, he pointed out that there could be no science without the notion of "regular processes"— a notion that assumed the existence of a universal Reason, since a regular pattern could hardly be derived from experience alone. For the ontological aspect of dialectics he used the traditional term "metaphysics," and in his polemics with the positivists he declared emphatically that the whole universe was governed by the laws of metaphysics (read "dialectics") and that only metaphysics could bring desirable unity to science.[41]

Chicherin's Hegelianism was far from orthodox, however. On the one hand, he criticized "absolute rationalism" as a one-sided system and proclaimed that it was time for rationalism and realism (positivism being one of the trends within realism) to become united in "universalism." On the other hand, he went further than Hegel in the direction of reconciling philosophy and religion by identifying universal Reason with a personal God, and by insisting that religion, as an example of "concrete unity," was superior to philosophy. This was connected with a departure from Hegel's "theological evolutionism," that is his notion of the Absolute as developing itself and rising to self-consciousness by means of Man. In his *Reminiscences* Chicherin accounted for this by a religious experience that had given him a sense of the transcendence of the Absolute. "I realized," he wrote, "that if the spirit is the ultimate form of the Absolute, it is also the initial form—an inexhaustible all-powerful force, the source of all existence."[42] In this way he stopped halfway between the Hegelian view of the immanence of the cosmic principle and

40. B. N. Chicherin, *Osnovaniia logiki i metafiziki* (M, 1894), p. 2.
41. B. N. Chicherin, *Polozhitel'naia filosofiia i edinstvo nauki* (M, 1892), p. 318.
42. B. N. Chicherin, *Vospominaniia* (M, 1929), pp. 2, 148.

the traditional theistic concept of a transcendent Creator of the world. Attempting to interpret the dogma of the Trinity in philosophical terms, he argued that the Absolute is both immanent and transcendent;[43] as Strength, Reason (the Word), and Spirit it possesses personality; the only impersonal "moment" of the Absolute is matter (the element antithetical to Reason), but this too acquires rational consciousness in man.

Chicherin distinguished four stages of the Absolute: (1) creative force giving rise to antithetical (2) reason and (3) matter, which are finally reconciled in (4) the unity of the spirit. On this issue, too, he departed from the orthodox Hegelian view. Hegel, he thought, had been mistaken in beginning his logic from the concept of pure unspecified being; the process of reasoning must take its departure from "something specific," the concrete unity of the universal and the particular.[44] Moreover, not three stages (as in Hegel) but four can be distinguished in the dialectical process: primary unity, giving rise to the opposites of abstract universality and abstract particularity (the second and third stages), followed by their ultimate unity on a higher plane (the fourth stage, after which the process is repeated). Tracing this scheme in all phenomena under investigation was for Chicherin the chief aim and touchstone of knowledge. He was convinced that his modification of the Hegelian dialectic was a discovery of outstanding importance, bringing the dialectic of development into line with the Aristotelian theory of four types of causes through the application of the concepts of analysis and synthesis—the two fundamental processes of reasoning. The stage of primary unity (creative force in the Absolute) corresponded to Aristotle's active cause; abstract universality and abstract particularity (Reason and matter in the Absolute) corresponded to his formal and material causes; and the new and higher unity (the Spirit) corresponded to the final cause.

Let us now see how Chicherin applied this scheme to the philosophy of history, which he identified with the philosophy of the history of philosophy because he was convinced that since ideas form the motive power of history, the history of philosophy is a key to our understanding of history, and not the other way around.[45]

Mankind, Chicherin argued, evolves from primary unity through division into two opposites to final unity. Each of these three great evolutionary phases is divided into a synthetic (religious) period and

43. B. N. Chicherin, *Nauka i religiia* (M, 1909), pp. 95–98.
44. *Ibid.*, pp. 61–62.
45. *Ibid.*, pp. 129, 243.

an analytical (philosophical) period that form the transition to the next synthesis. Each of these periods in turn represents one or more cycles that encompass the evolution of the four basic stages of thought and being, i.e. the stages of primary unity (the active cause), the two opposites (the formal and material causes), and ultimate unity (the final cause). Within the framework of a cycle, progress can be subjective—from primary to ultimate unity through the contradiction of matter and form—and objective—from the formal to the material cause through the contradiction of the active and the final cause.

Mankind, according to Chicherin, had already passed through two important evolutionary phases—the phase of primary unity and the phase of division. The synthetic period of the first phase saw the emergence of natural religion, whereas the analytical period (forming the transition to the second phase) saw the development of Greek philosophy from universalism by way of realism to rationalism. With the decline of the ancient world came the transition to the second phase—the phase of division—within which medieval Christendom saw the development of modern philosophy from rationalism through realism to universalism (in reverse order from the development of ancient philosophy). At present mankind was passing through the stage of realism, this being expressed in the twofold preponderance of the particular over the universal: in materialistic realism (i.e. materialism and positivism) and in spiritualistic realism (i.e. in spiritualistic monadism). Confident that an understanding of the laws of dialectic made it possible to forecast the future accurately, Chicherin declared that a stage of philosophical universalism, which would pave the way for an all-embracing religious synthesis, was close at hand. Thus mankind would return to the Creator from whom it had issued. The primary religious synthesis was the revelation of Strength (the Father); the second Christian synthesis (the synthesis of the phase of division) was the revelation of the Word (the Son); and the third, future synthesis (the synthesis of the phase of ultimate unity) would be the revelation of the Spirit (the third person of the Trinity).[46]

It is interesting to note that this philosophy of history bears a striking resemblance to the ideas of the Polish Hegelian August Cieszkowski (mentioned above in connection with Herzen), who also divided history into three great epochs that he described as ages of primary unity, division, and ultimate unity mediated by development, and that he named the epochs of the Father, the Son, and the

46. *Ibid.*, pp. 444–51.

Holy Spirit. There was one essential difference, however: in his book *Our Father*, the Polish messianic philosopher thought of himself as an instrument of the Holy Spirit called upon to reveal the principles of the ultimate religious synthesis; Chicherin, by contrast, kept religion and philosophy strictly apart, and considered his own philosophy to be merely a transition to the final universalist stage of the second analytical period in the intellectual history of mankind.

Chicherin's most interesting theoretical contributions are undoubtedly his philosophical reflections on law (which he regarded as intimately related to economics) and on the state. Although these themes occur in almost all his works, they are treated separately in two books: *Property and Law* (2 vols.; 1882–83), and the *Philosophy of Law* (1900).

Like Hegel, Chicherin regarded the state as the highest form of human cooperation. Where he differed from Hegel—and came closer to Kant—was in treating man not instrumentally but as an end in himself. He was even inclined to call his own position "individualism," because he placed the individual's freedom and autonomy above the state and all forms of social association.[47]

In Chicherin's system the state represents a higher unity of three social associations—the family, or natural association; the society of citizens, or juridical association; and the church, or moral association.[48] The higher unity of the state does not, however, affect the relative autonomy of the social associations subordinated to it. Every sphere has a clearly defined scope and is governed by its own laws. This separation of the elements within the state was for Chicherin the most important guarantee of liberty, and he therefore condemned any tendency of one particular sphere (including the highest) to "swallow up" the others or violate their autonomy. In the Middle Ages the state had been subordinated to private persons and consequently had been exploited by monarchs and feudal lords for their own ends; progress in modern times consisted essentially in the emancipation of the state from this dependence, and the demarcation of clear boundaries between the private and public

47. Tschiževskij, *Gegiel w Rossii*, pp. 296–97.

48. For an analysis of Chicherin's political philosophy see L. Schapiro, *Rationalism and Nationalism in Russian Nineteenth-Century Political Thought* (New Haven, Conn., 1967), pp. 89–101. An interesting attack on Schapiro's interpretation is to be found in Aileen Kelly, "What Is Real Is Rational: The Political Philosophy of B. N. Chicherin," *Cahiers du monde russe et sovietique*, 18, no. 3 (Jul.–Sep. 1977), pp. 195–222. The main thesis of this article is that Chicherin was in fact not a moderate liberal but a staunch conservative.

spheres. A reaction to this was the dangerous tendency of the state to interfere in the private sphere, to engulf all other spheres of life, and in particular to infringe on the economic freedom of citizens by the introduction of social and economic legislation. Socialism was the most extreme, but by no means isolated, expression of this destructive trend.

Chicherin did not share the leading liberal economists' faith in the automatic nature of progress. He was not a naive advocate of the virtues of unrestrained competition and conceded that valid moral objections could be put forward against free-market capitalism. On the other hand, he stressed that it was not the business of the state to interfere on behalf of moral postulates. The solution to social problems should come about as part of the improvement of individual moral standards; the rich had a *moral duty* to help the poor, but the poor were not *legally entitled* to demand such help.

These arguments, which today strike us as strangely anachronistic, are an indication of the limitations of Chicherin's thought. It is true that he rejected the extreme optimism of the *laissez-faire* view, but he could not go beyond its dogmas. A comparison with his contemporary, the English Hegelian Thomas Hill Green—whose revision of classical liberalism took into account and justified the need for state intervention—must be to Chicherin's disadvantage.

In fairness to Chicherin, however, it should be stressed that one aspect of his arguments in favor of economic liberalism is still to some extent relevant today. What he did was to draw attention to the danger implicit in a confusion of juridical law and moral law. Juridical law, Chicherin argued, is not "minimum morality" (Soloviev's definition), but an entirely separate sphere that should not be confused with morality. Juridical law defines the limits of liberty, whereas moral law defines the dictates of moral duty. The law, backed up by coercive powers, decides what is permitted and what is not permitted, but cannot be an instrument of morality. The legal definition of the limits of liberty does not destroy the individual's autonomy but—on the contrary—demarcates a certain sphere where the individual is not subject to the interference of state or society. A legal definition of moral duty, on the other hand, is incompatible with freedom of conscience and therefore morality. The only result of such an attempt could be "the worst imaginable tyranny."[49]

These arguments were directed not only against the socialists,

49. Chicherin, *Mistitsizm v nauke*, p. 60.

whom Chicherin accused of contempt for the law arising out of their ethical maximalism, but in equal measure against Soloviev's theocratic utopianism. We may suppose that Chicherin also had in mind the Slavophiles' ideal community, and their criticism of the law as an "external truth." Konstantin Aksakov's unanimous community to which every individual was to submit without any legal guarantees would undeniably mean the total obliteration of individual freedom and moral autonomy.

If we may digress for a moment, it is worth recalling the critical attempt to develop Chicherin's ideas made in our century by Serge Hessen (mentioned earlier), who propounded something he called "juridical socialism." His aim was in fact to link Chicherin's conception of juridical law as a force defending the autonomy of the individual to Soloviev's conception of law as "minimum morality." "Juridical socialism" was to reconcile the socialist postulate of morality in social relations with respect for the law, whose role was to protect the individual's "extra-social nucleus" against both excessive state interference and the pressure of social conformity.[50]

Hegelians in Russia in the second half of the nineteenth century also included NIKOLAI DEBOLSKY (1842–1918), professor at the St. Petersburg Theological Academy and author of an excellent translation of Hegel's *Logic*, and PAVEL BAKUNIN (1820–1900), brother of the anarchist Mikhail Bakunin. Both these thinkers, however, departed so radically from orthodox Hegelianism that it would be more correct to call them neo-Hegelians rather than Hegelians in the strict sense of the word.

Debolsky, a mathematician by training, made an attempt to reconcile Hegelian rationalism with traditional Christian theism. In his chief work, *The Philosophy of Phenomenalistic Formalism* (2 vols.; 1892–95),[51] he tried to make a clear distinction between the infinite reason of the Absolute and its individualization—finite human reason. The fundamental mistake of Hegelian philosophy, according to Debolsky, was that it identified human reason with Absolute Reason; Hegel also erred in equating logic with ontology— in reality his logic was not a "system of being" but only a "system of possible ideas about being." Furthermore, Hegel paid too little at-

50. See A. Walicki, "Introduction" to S. Hessen, *Studia z filozofii kultury* [*Studies in the Philosophy of Culture*] (Warsaw, 1968), pp. 35–40.
51. *Filosofiia fenomenal'nogo formalizma*. Of Debolsky's other works, mention should be made of his *Filosofiia budushchego. Soobrazheniia o eyo nachale, predmete metode i sisteme* (1882). In the introduction to this work, Debolsky outlines the evolution of his philosophical ideas.

tention to the relative validity and autonomy of empirical reasoning and formal logic. It was in fact Debolsky's interest in reviving formal logic that led him to try and bring Hegelian dialectics closer to pre-Kantian rationalism.[52]

Debolsky defined his own philosophical position as formalistic meta-empiricism, which he opposed both to empiricism and to mystical conceptions of immediate nondiscursive cognition. Every experience, he argued, should be analyzed into its empirical and meta-empirical, phenomenalistic and metaphysical aspects. Meta-empirical cognition enables the human mind to acquire knowledge about Absolute Reason, but the mind cannot come to know the reality of the Absolute because only its formal aspect is accessible to cognition. It is not possible to grasp the meaning of the absolute First Principle through reasoning, or through mystical contemplation, because the Absolute only reveals itself to man in the formal aspects of the world of phenomena. Finite individual human reason cannot penetrate to the inner essence of the Absolute, but its formalism is a reflection of the formalism of Absolute Reason.

Pavel Bakunin represented an entirely different school of philosophy. His two books—*A Belated Voice from the Forties* (1881) and *Foundations of Faith and Knowledge* (1886)—are the religious reflections of a romantic against a Hegelian background,[53] a belated echo of the discussions held in the Stankevich Circle in the late 1830's. Bakunin's pantheistic vision of a world animated by the "breath of the Absolute" is combined with theist and personalist motifs, a defense of the immortality of the soul, and a romantic cult of womanhood. Hegelian dialectics makes its appearance in the concept of a "universal dispute"—the reciprocal negation of particular entities struggling with each other and attempting to devour each other. This "dispute," according to Bakunin, only dies down in the presence of Beauty. Man's mission is to transcend his sinful self-affirmation in his own "particularity." Thanks to the bonds linking it to the Absolute, the human mind is capable of grasping the world as a whole and of transcending its own subjectivity through its understanding of reality as a higher rational unity of opposites.

Bakunin formulated his ideas in conscious opposition to positivism, which he accused of overturning the "mystical ladder" reach-

---

52. Tschiževskij, *Gegiel w Rossii*, p. 303.
53. See V. V. Zenkovsky, *A History of Russian Philosophy*, trans. George L. Kline (2 vols.; London, 1953), vol. 2, p. 629.

ing from earth to heaven.[54] As a belated romantic he was an isolated thinker and found few readers, although his *Foundations of Faith and Knowledge* was enthusiastically praised by Tolstoy.[55]

Another variant of a broadly conceived Hegelianism was the philosophical theories of the dramatist Alexandr Sukhovo-Kobylin (1817–1903). His philosophical writings remained unpublished, and it is only recently that a short account has been published of his three-volume manuscript dealing with the nature of the universe (*Ucheniie Vsemira*) and the philosophy of the spirit.[56]

In contrast to Chicherin, who was a strong opponent of Darwinian evolutionism, Sukhovo-Kobylin appears to have thought of his own philosophy as a specific synthesis of Hegelian and Darwinian ideas. In fact, he considered Darwinian theory to be part of the Hegelian teaching on the dialectical development of the Absolute Idea. In his historiosophical conceptions he combined Hegelianism with social Darwinism, and stressed the importance in society of the struggle for survival, natural selection, and the rights of the stronger. He foretold the victory of reason in the coming final epoch, interpreting it as the victory of a higher race directed by an aristocracy of the spirit.

As Sukhovo-Kobylin's philosophical writings are not available in print, it is difficult to analyze or assess them adequately. Nevertheless, in view of the prevailing opposition to positivism and naturalism among the Russian Hegelians, this attempt to incorporate positivistic naturalism into a system based on metaphysical idealism is worth mentioning as an interesting exception.

The late Russian Hegelians had no heirs; it is true that the Constitutional Democrats borrowed certain ideas from Chicherin, but they were interested only in his philosophy of law and the state, not in his reform of dialectics or metaphysical conceptions. There was a tremendous revival of interest in Hegel under the impact of Marxism (here Plekhanov's contribution was of peculiar importance), but this was, of course, an entirely different, materialistic trend in the reception of Hegelianism.

54. See Tschiževskij, *Gegiel w Rossii*, p. 315.
55. *Ibid.*, p. 311.
56. See *Istoriia filosofii v SSSR*, ed. V. E. Evgrafov (M, 1968), vol. 3, pp. 321–23. The chapter on Sukhovo-Kobylin was written by I. A. Korkhova.

CHAPTER 18

FROM POPULISM TO MARXISM

INTRODUCTION

In the chapter on Populism in the 1870's mention was made of the Populist reception of Marxism. Marx's description of the cruelties accompanying primitive accumulation and the Industrial Revolution horrified the Populists and confirmed them in their belief that the price to be paid for capitalist progress was too high and that all efforts should be directed toward enabling Russia to bypass capitalism. At the same time the Populists of the first half of the 1870's did not notice any contradictions between Marxist theory (which they frequently quoted) and "subjective sociology," or the notion of Russia's distinctive development according to "native" principles. They thought of Marx chiefly as an economist, a critic of capitalism and the man responsible for the theory of surplus value, which they greatly admired for its exposure of the mechanism of capitalist exploitation. Even the Bakuninite wing, which followed Bakunin himself in accusing Marx of political opportunism, was inclined to accept Marxism as an economic theory. One of that wing's most representative members, Jakob Stefanovich, wrote: "Marxism as a theory—not as membership in the Western Socialist Party and espousal of its practical policy—does not exclude Populism."[1]

Engels's polemic with Tkachev (1875)[2] drew attention to the fact that Marxism was also a theory of social development which postulated that an indispensable condition of socialism was the high-level development of productive forces attained under capitalism. The evolution of every economic formation, Marx wrote in the Preface to the first German edition of *Capital*, is a process of natural history,

---

1. See *Gruppa "Osvobozhdenie truda"* (M-L. 1926), no. 4, p. 196. For more information about this early stage of the Populist reception of Marxism, see A. L. Reuel, *Russkaia ekonomicheskaia mysl' 60–70-kh gg. XIX veka i marksizm* (M, 1956), and V. F. Pustarnakov, *'Kapital' Marksa i filosofskaia mysl' v Rossii* (M, 1974). Cf. also A. Walicki, *The Controversy Over Capitalism*, pp. 132–39.
2. See Chapter 12, pp. 251–52.

objective and independent of the human will: a society "can neither clear by bold leaps nor remove by legal enactments the successive phases of its normal development." The laws of social development operate with "iron necessity," and backward countries must pass through the same phases that the advanced countries have already completed: "The country that is more developed industrially only shows, to the less developed, the image of its own future."[3]

The Populists found this a proposition hard to accept. The case was put most dramatically by Mikhailovsky in his article "Karl Marx Arraigned Before Mr. Zhukovsky" (1877). For the Western European socialist, Mikhailovsky wrote, Marx's theory of social development provides a scientific explanation of the past and arguments for the inevitability of socialism; its acceptance, therefore, does not involve a moral dilemma, a cleavage between ideal and reality. Yet a Russian socialist who came to accept the correctness of Marxian theory would be in a different position: for him the description of capitalist development would be an image of Russia's immediate future, and Marxian historical determinism would force him to become reconciled to the tragic aspects of capitalist progress, with all its painful consequences for the masses. As a socialist he would have to accept the need for capitalist development, and therefore the ruin of his own ideal. Faced with the choice of either participating in the progress implemented by the "knights of accumulation" or struggling for the realization of his ideals (knowing that "iron necessity" had doomed this struggle to failure), he would no doubt reject both choices and become merely a passive onlooker—a dispassionate observer of social processes.[4]

Marx himself disputed this point of view in a letter to the editor of *Notes of the Fatherland* (*Otechestvennye Zapiski*), the journal in which Mikhailovsky's article had been published. Though in the end Marx did not in fact submit the letter, he stated that the process of accumulation described in *Capital* only concerned Western Europe during the period of transition from feudalism to capitalism, and could not be mechanically extended to other parts of the world; processes that might be strikingly similar but that took place in different historical circumstances could have entirely different outcomes. Every separate sequence of historical-economic development must be investigated on its own merits and compared with others; one can never arrive at scientific explanation of a concrete historical

3. K. Marx, *Capital* (Eng.-lang. ed.; M, 1954), p. 9.
4. N. K. Mikhailovsky, *Polnoe sobranie sochinenii* (4th ed.; St. Petersburg, 1909), vol. 4, pp. 167–73.

development "By the universal passport of a general historico-philosophical theory, the supreme virtue of which consists in being superhistorical."[5]

This letter was only published in 1886.[6] By this time Russian Marxists (especially Plekhanov) had worked out their own theories, in which the thesis of the inevitability of the "capitalist phase" was given special emphasis. The fact that Marx himself had doubts on the matter was passed over in silence by Plekhanov, and its significance was belittled. In the 1890's, when industrialization in Russia was beginning to make obvious headway, Engels ascribed these doubts to tactical considerations: Marx, he thought, had been reluctant to dampen the ardor of the Russian revolutionaries, whose courage was kept alive by faith in the future socialist possibilities of the peasant commune.[7]

Engels's explanation is contradicted by the three drafts of a letter Marx wrote to Vera Zasulich in 1881, which make it clear that he both believed Russia might bypass the capitalist phase and considered the issue to be of great theoretical significance.[8] A detailed analysis of Marx's views on the future of the underdeveloped countries does not, however, fall within the scope of this book. For the purpose of this study it need only be said that Marx gave this problem very brief consideration and that his comments, though extraordinarily penetrating, were not generally known; his best-known works, on the other hand, contained formulations suggesting that capitalism was an inevitable natural stage through which every country must pass.

Marxist views began to make headway among the Russian revolutionaries as the latter became increasingly disillusioned with the methods of struggle formerly used and were no longer able to overlook the obvious progress capitalism was making in agriculture. The break with Populism was neither easy nor painless, and the radical polarization of attitudes was often preceded by attempts to reconcile Marxism with the old dream of bypassing the capitalist stage.

5. K. Marx and F. Engels, *Correspondence, 1846–1895* (London, 1936), p. 354.

6. In 1884 Engels gave Marx's letter to the "Emancipation of Labor" group. Plekhanov's group refrained from publishing the letter, but it appeared two years later on the pages of the Populist *Messenger of the "People's Will"* (no. 5, Geneva, 1886) and was later reprinted in a legal journal in Russia (*Juridical Messenger*, no. 10, 1888). The Populist publicists (Mikhailovsky, Vorontsov, and Krivenko) interpreted it as proof that Marx himself had not shared the view of his Russian followers and immediately took advantage of it in their polemics with the Russian Marxists.

7. Cf. *Perepiska K. Marksa i F. Engelsa s russkimi politicheskimi deiatel'iami* (M, 1951), p. 296.

8. See above, pp. 199–200.

BETWEEN POPULISM AND MARXISM

Of particular interest in this context is the ideological evolution of GEORGY PLEKHANOV (1856–1918),[9] who was associated in his youth with the orthodox Populist revolutionary movement (orthodox in the sense of advocating activities solely "among the people" and "through the people"). In his article "The Law of Society's Economic Development and the Tasks of Socialism in Russia," published in the journal *Land and Freedom* (*Zemlia i Volia*) in January 1879, Plekhanov attempted to interpret Marxian theory in such a way as to bring it into line with the program of the "Land and Freedom" organization.

The article opened with an attack on the followers of Tkachev and their theory of the "seizure of power"—a highly significant fact in the light of Plekhanov's future political evolution. Even then, while still a spokesman for the orthodox Populists, Plekhanov (who was to remain uncompromisingly hostile to all forms of "Blanquism" for the rest of his life) turned to Marxism for arguments against what he thought of as the political adventurism of his opponents. The times have passed, he wrote, when people thought that in order to establish a better social system it was enough to "form a conspiracy, seize power, and shower one's subjects with a number of benevolent decrees." Views of this type were an expression of the *theological* phase in sociology; at present, however, sociological understanding had entered the *positive* phase, represented in socialist theory by Marx and Engels (Rodbertus and Dühring were also mentioned). The author of *Capital*, Plekhanov continued, had shown that a country's social system was determined by economic development, and that society was governed by laws that could not be changed at will. This did not mean that one must agree with liberal publicists who used these arguments to suggest that there was no point in struggling for socialism in backward Russia. The laws of economic development were not by any means the same everywhere; "history was not a monotonous or mechanical process"; and Karl Marx did not belong to the "category of persons who would be glad to stretch mankind on the Procrustean bed of 'universal laws.' "

At this point Plekhanov—probably without realizing it—repeated Tkachev's chief argument that socialism was possible in Russia only because capitalism had not yet made headway there. Marx

9. The most important monograph on Plekhanov in English is S. H. Baron, *Plekhanov: The Father of Russian Marxism* (Stanford, Calif., 1963).

tells us, he declared, that when a society "has got upon the right track of the natural laws of its movement" it can "neither skip the natural phases of its development nor remove them by legal enactment"; Russia, however, Plekhanov insisted, had not yet entered upon this disastrous track. Western Europe was forced to develop along capitalist lines because the village commune there had disintegrated in the struggle with feudalism; in Russia, though, the village commune had been preserved relatively intact. In Europe the objective basis of socialism was the "socialization of labor," introduced by capitalism; in Russia it was the communal possession of the land. The socialization of labor, on the other hand, (i.e. the communal cultivation of the land) would come about in agriculture with the advance of technology and the introduction of agricultural machinery. The Russian people were capable of undertaking the spontaneous organization of all aspects of social life according to socialist principles, and were only prevented from doing so by the interference and demoralizing influence of the state (at this point the views of Plekhanov and Tkachev begin to diverge, since the latter, as we know, had no faith in popular "spontaneity"). Even if the government succeeded in destroying the institution of the village commune, Plekhanov concluded, the collectivist ideals and traditions of the masses would take some time to change. The program of the "Land and Freedom" organization therefore rested on firm foundations and did not need to be amended.

Unfortunately for Plekhanov's case, his argument rests on a mistranslation (and misinterpretation) of the phrase quoted from Marx. The correct and unabridged version reads as follows:

... Even when a society has got upon the right track for the discovery of the natural laws of its movement—and it is the ultimate aim of this work to lay bare the economic law of motion of modern society—it can neither clear by bold leaps nor remove by legal enactments the obstacles offered by the successive phases of its normal development.[10]

It is obvious that "to get upon the right track *for the discovery* of the natural laws" is not the same thing as "to get upon the right track of the natural laws," which Plekhanov interpreted as "coming within the sphere of influence of" these laws. What Marx intended to say in *Capital* is that even a scientific understanding of the laws of economic development cannot change the natural sequence of a society's development. Plekhanov's conclusion that the laws of capitalist development did not apply in Russia because she had not

10. Marx, *Capital*, p. 10.

yet come within the orbit of capitalism was therefore based on a misunderstanding.

If we take Plekhanov's line of reasoning to its logical conclusion and ask what he thought would happen if Russia did finally enter the orbit of capitalism, we can only give a pessimistic answer. Tkachev would have said that it was all a matter of the relative strength of the two conflicting forces—the spontaneous capitalist tendency and the disciplined revolutionary vanguard. For Plekhanov, who disapproved of political conspiracies and of the very idea of opposing natural laws of development, the problem was a much more difficult one. Recognizing capitalism as a natural tendency meant turning his back on Populism. By a peculiar historical paradox, Plekhanov's break with the classical Populist thesis about bypassing capitalism resulted from his orthodox position in the Populist movement, i.e. from his opposition to "Blanquism," which he attempted to continue in the "Black Reparation" organization after the split among members of "Land and Freedom." One might even say that Plekhanov became a Social Democrat because he wanted to remain true to the old "Land and Freedom" program, which proclaimed that "Revolutions are made by the masses and prepared by history."

Plekhanov's way to Marxism was not, however, the only one. In the 1880's there existed in Russia—in St. Petersburg, Kiev, Nizhnii Novgorod, and Kazan and other towns on the Volga—a large number of revolutionary societies whose members gradually evolved toward Marxism, very often continuing to combine Marxian economic theories with a cult of the heroic traditions of the "People's Will."[11]

An interesting and significant example of such a transitional personality was Lenin's older brother, ALEKSANDR ULIANOV (1866–87), who should not be overlooked even in a brief review of the Populist reception of Marxism. Ulianov was of course only a Populist in the broadest sense of the word. He considered himself to be a continuator of the traditions of the "People's Will," but in his *Program of the Terrorist Faction of the "People's Will" Party*[12] he dropped the accepted name "socialist Populists" and simply referred to his followers as socialists. There was nothing backward-looking about his views; the main revolutionary force mentioned in his *Program*

11. Cf. S. V. Utechin, "The 'Preparatory' Trend in the Russian Revolutionary Movement in the 1880's," *Soviet Affairs* (London), 1962, no. 3. See also Y. A. Polevoy, *Zarozhdenie marksizma v Rossii* (M, 1959).

12. Reprinted in N. K. Karataev, ed., *Narodnicheskaia ekonomicheskaia literatura* (M, 1958), pp. 631–36.

was the urban working class, not the peasantry, and socialism was explained as the "inevitable result of capitalist production and the capitalist class structure." This does not mean, he wrote, that there might not be "another, more direct transition to socialism if special favorable conditions exist in the traditions of the people and the character of the intelligentsia and government." The law of the transition from capitalism to socialism "expresses the historical necessity governing each country's progress to socialism if this process is left to develop spontaneously, without any conscious intervention on the part of a particular social group."[13]

The peculiar nature of Ulianov's attempt to combine Populism with Marxism is better understood if we remember that he had translated an early paper by Marx entitled "A Contribution Toward the Critique of the Hegelian Philosophy of Law" (this was published in Switzerland with an interesting preface by Lavrov). Criticism of religion, the main content of Marx's paper, was of secondary importance for Ulianov; he was chiefly interested in Marx's view that it was possible to compress a country's historical development by passing through some phases of this process on the ideological plane. The young Marx had suggested that Germany's political development was ahead of its historical development, because Germany had experienced in *thought* everything that France had lived through in reality. Ulianov quite rightly saw in this an important argument for the thesis that countries that were historically backward (but ideologically developed) could skip or telescope some phases of their "natural" development. B. Koltsov, a member of the St. Petersburg group of the resuscitated "People's Will," commented on this as follows: "We often talked about this paper by Marx, and Ulianov always argued that the idea that Germany had experienced in thought everything other countries had experienced in practice did not contradict the later views of Marx and could also be applied to Russia. . . . Later I happened to hear from other Russian Social Democrats that they too had interpreted Marxism in this way at one time."[14]

The further ideological development of Ulianov was cut short by his death—he was executed for his leading role in an attempt on the life of Alexander III (the so-called "affair of the first of March 1887"). "His brother's fate without a doubt influenced Vladimir Ilyich profoundly," wrote Lenin's wife, N. Krupskaya. The future leader of the Bolshevik Revolution was also deeply affected by the

13. *Ibid.*, p. 631.
14. Quoted in Polevoy, *Zarozhdenie marksizma v Rossii*, p. 315.

cowardice of local liberals in Simbirsk, who cooled toward the family after his brother's arrest. According to Krupskaya, "this youthful experience undoubtedly left its imprint on Lenin's attitude towards the liberals."[15] It is interesting to note that suspicion and dislike of liberals from the very beginning sharply distinguished Lenin from Plekhanov.

PLEKHANOV AND THE "RATIONAL REALITY"

As was noted previously, in the late 1870's Plekhanov was primarily concerned to establish whether (and to what extent) capitalism could be considered a "natural" tendency in the Russian economy. It was with some agitation, therefore, that he studied the statistics collected by Orlov on the development of capitalist relations in the Russian countryside.

His observation of the headway made by capitalism in Russia was not, however, the only reason why Plekhanov rejected the Populist conception of bypassing capitalism. The break was determined in equal measure by the lessons learned in the course of Populist revolutionary agitation—i.e. that socialist propaganda was more likely to appeal to the urban working class than to peasants living in the village commune, and that the first task of Russian socialists must be to overthrow the tsarist system. Members of the "People's Will" were the first to draw these conclusions—which of course meant giving up the characteristic Populist disregard for political struggle—but they were divided on the goals to be achieved. Some wanted to seize power (the Tikhomirov faction), whereas others (led by Zhelabov) wanted to introduce a constitution that would safeguard democratic freedoms. Plekhanov, who was one of the last to cling to "apolitical" Populism, rejected Tikhomirov's program as "Blanquist" but criticized Zhelabov's program for coming close to abandoning socialism. He thought that a solution to this dilemma had been found by the German Social Democratic party, which was engaging in legal political activities without giving up its socialist character.

The significance of Plekhanov's conversion to social democracy will become even clearer if we recall the opinion current among Russian revolutionaries about the German Social Democrats. L. Deutsch, cofounder with Plekhanov of the "Emancipation of Labor" group, defined this as follows: "In the entire civilized world the term 'social democracy' was then associated with a certain peace-

15. N. K. Krupskaya, *Memories of Lenin* (London, 1930), pp. 4–5.

ful and parliamentary party and its activities, which were characterized by an almost total avoidance of determined, revolutionary
methods of struggle."[16] For that very reason Deutsch and Vera
Zasulich did not wish to adopt the name. Plekhanov, for his part,
liked it just because it implied moderation; he hoped to work out a
political program that would also be acceptable to the liberals, one
that while "not scaring anyone with an as yet distant red spectre"
would attract "all except the declared enemies of democracy."[17]
In the end a compromise was agreed upon: Plekhanov's followers
set up a Marxist organization with the neutral name of "Emancipation of Labor" (1883) but at the same time took pains to stress
their sympathy for the German Social Democrats.

For Plekhanov social democracy represented a chance to salvage
what he called the "practical" aspect of classical Populism. In the
Preface to his first Marxist pamphlet, *Socialism and Political Struggle*, he wrote: "The endeavor to work *among the people* and for
the people, the conviction that the emancipation of the workers
should be accomplished by the workers themselves—this practical
tendency of the old Populism is something I shall always hold
dear."[18]

The program outlined in *Socialism and Political Struggle* (1883)
and in the book *Our Differences* (1885) consisted, to put it briefly, of
an emphatic commitment to political struggle and a resolute rejection of "Blanquism." The dictatorship of a revolutionary class
(i.e. the proletariat), Plekhanov wrote in an article criticizing "Blanquist" tendencies among members of the "People's Will," has nothing in common with the dictatorship of a group of revolutionaries;
"No executive, administrative, or any other committee is entitled
to represent the working class in *history*."[19] The great mission of
the working class, he continued, is to complete the Westernization
of Russia begun by Peter the Great; a seizure of power by revolutionary socialists would only hinder this, would indeed be a disaster
that in the end could only be a great step backwards. Authentic
socialism can only be established when economic development and
proletarian class consciousness have attained a certain high level.
Political authorities trying to organize from above socialist production in a backward country would be forced "to resort to the ideals

16. Quoted in V. Vaganian, *G. V. Plekhanov. Opyt kharakteristiki sotsial'nopolit-
cheskikh vozrenii* (M, 1924), pp. 94–95.
17. G. V. Plekhanov, *Sochineniia* (2d ed.; M-Petrograd, 1920–27), vol. 2, p. 83.
18. *Ibid.*, p. 27.
19. *Ibid.*, p. 166.

of a patriarchal and authoritarian communism; the only change would be that the Peruvian 'sons of the Sun' and their officials would be replaced by a socialist caste."[20] There is no doubt, Plekhanov added, "that under such tutelage the people not only would fail to be educated for socialism but would either lose all its capacity for further progress or retain this capacity at the cost of the reemergence of the same economic inequality that the revolutionary government had set out to abolish."[21]

The logical conclusion of this argument was that Russians must choose the "long and difficult capitalist way."[22] A sufficiently long time must elapse between the political revolution (i.e. the overthrow of tsarism) and the future socialist revolution to enable the capitalist forces of production to become fully established and the Russian proletariat to receive political training in a law-abiding parliamentary state. The interval might well be shorter than in the West, because in Russia (owing to Western influence) the socialist movement became organized very early, while capitalism was still in its infancy. Thanks to their early adoption of Marxism, Russian socialists could accelerate the development of proletarian class-consciousness among the Russian workers. On the other hand, the capitalist stage should not be too brief—it was possible to shorten a "natural" process, but every attempt to shorten it too much or to replace it by an "artificial" process entailed the danger of an undesirable "chemical change."[23]

It is interesting to note that Plekhanov never abandoned the views outlined above: he was not exaggerating when he wrote a quarter of a century later that on tactical issues his standpoint had not changed in any important particular, and that in the controversies between the Bolsheviks and the Mensheviks he remained firmly committed to the ideas worked out by the "Emancipation of Labor" group.[24] To the end of his life he fought against two opposing tendencies that he considered to be fraught with the greatest danger for the Russian working-class movement: one was the trade-union mentality of the workers, which was later to be taken to extremes in the "economism" of the right-wing Social Democrats (in Plekhanov's eyes this was yet another version of the old "apolitical"

20. *Ibid.*, vol. 3, p. 81.
21. *Ibid.*
22. *Ibid.*, p. 325.
23. G. V. Plekhanov, *Izbrannye filosofskie proizvedeniia* (M, 1956–58), vol. 4, p. 140. Plekhanov quoted Chernyshevsky's argument that though it is possible to shorten the process of drying cigars, the cigars thus treated lose their flavor.
24. Plekhanov, *Sochineniia*, vol. 19, p. 283.

Populism); the other was "Blanquism," which exaggerated the "subjective factor" in history and showed a dangerous tendency to "skip" natural phases of development. In later years Plekhanov accused the Bolsheviks of being heirs to this latter tendency.

In the Populists' revolutionary wing Plekhanov's program was thought to amount in practice to a betrayal of socialism. The mood among the survivors of the "People's Will" was summed up in the article "What Should We Expect from Revolution"[25] by Lev Tikhomirov, the party's leading theoretician, who was to become later a staunch supporter of tsarism. It must be a strange sort of socialist indeed, Tikhomirov argued, who proclaims the inevitability and progressive nature of capitalism, although he knows it involves the suffering of millions, and who accepts this suffering for the sake of some distant goal. To be consistent, socialists of this kind should turn themselves into capitalists, because only capitalists are really able to push forward the development of capitalism. Plekhanov's theory, he insisted, was psychologically unacceptable to a true revolutionary; its real source was the Russian habit of gaping at the West and following the example of Western countries, although their development had been completely different from Russia's.

Plekhanov himself was, of course, aware of the tragic dilemma in which he found himself as a socialist arguing for the capitalist development of his country. This was one of the main reasons for his passionate attacks on "subjectivism" and his emphasis on the conscious acceptance of necessity. It would hardly be an exaggeration to say that "necessity" is the central category in Plekhanov's model of Marxism. In his writings we can discern two lines of reasoning based on different theoretical assumptions: sometimes he argued that capitalist development along European lines was the most desirable alternative (implying that there were other, less desirable alternatives, as for instance a "Peruvian" authoritarian communism); at other times he flatly rejected any possibility of choice, claiming that his political program was based on an understanding of the "objective laws of development," that the validity of its prognosis could be demonstrated with "mathematical exactness," and that its goals would be realized as surely as tomorrow's sunrise. In his early Marxist works—*Socialism and Political Struggle* and *Our Differences*—the first line of argument was more in evidence, whereas later the second type prevailed (especially in his philosophical works *A Contribution to the Development of the Monistic Conception of*

25. *Vestnik Narodnoi Voli* (Geneva), 1884, no. 2.

History [1894] and *On the Role of the Individual in History* [1898]).
Against Populist "subjective sociology" Plekhanov set his rigid
"objectivism," eliminating and indeed ridiculing all attempts even
to think in terms of "what should be." Scientific socialists, he insisted, are striving for socialism not because it is desirable, but because it is the next stage in the "magnificent and irresistible forward-
march of History"; "Social Democracy swims with the tide of
History," and the causes of historical development "have nothing to
do with human will or consciousness."[26]

This shift of emphasis—from what is desirable to what is inevitable—is not difficult to explain. At the roots of Plekhanov's conversion to Marxism there was an act of choice determined by his system of values, a system according to which "natural" processes were
considered superior to "artificial" ones. In order to overcome the
objections of the revolutionary socialists, Plekhanov tried, naturally
enough, to persuade both himself and them that his choice was
the only scientific one and that, strictly speaking, he was merely following the path mapped out by history itself, one that no amount of
"subjective" protest could change. In view of his conviction that
capitalism necessarily involved the suffering of the masses, he had
to put a strong emphasis on the inevitability of the process; absolute
necessity (and a necessity, moreover, that could be accepted as "rational") was, after all, the only justification for the acceptance of
human suffering.

It is clear, therefore, that Plekhanov's "necessitarianism" cannot
be entirely explained by reference to the prevailing spirit of scientific determinism and positivistic evolutionism characteristic of
his age. The "necessity" to which he appealed could not be a simple
matter of objective facts—adjusting oneself to mere facts would be
sheer opportunism. Therefore it had to be conceived as an *ontological* necessity inherent in the structure of the universe. We may say
that Plekhanov needed a theodicy and found it in the Hegelian idea
of a necessary and rational unfolding of history.

Especially illuminating, from this point of view, are Plekhanov's
articles on Belinsky, which help to indicate Plekhanov's place in
Russian intellectual history. The most important of the articles—
"Belinsky and the 'Rational Reality' "—was written in 1897 and
was in a sense an answer to Mikhailovsky, who in a polemic with
Struve had drawn a comparison between the "objectivism" of the
Russian Marxists and Belinsky's views during his phase of "recon-
ciliation with reality." In both cases, Mikhailovsky asserted, the

26. Plekhanov, *Izbrannye*, vol. 1, p. 392, vol. 4, pp. 86, 113–14.

conflict between "personality" and historical reality was resolved in favor of the latter; in both cases the individual was subordinated to an allegedly rational and beneficial necessity. Belinsky, however, realized his mistake, revolted against the "rational reality," and refused to go on accepting the alleged inevitability of human suffering.

Plekhanov did not deny that there were points of similarity between Belinsky and the Russian Marxists—on the contrary, he himself laid great stress on them. Unlike Mikhailovsky, however, he was fascinated not by Belinsky's revolt against reality but by his previous reconciliation. In his interpretation the period of "reconciliation with reality" was the most fruitful in Belinsky's entire intellectual development.[27] He called Belinsky a precursor of Russian Marxism who had shown the inadequacy of an "abstract ideal" and had realized the need to justify revolutionary negation as part of the regular development of the historical process.

Plekhanov distinguished three stages in Belinsky's intellectual evolution—before, during, and after "reconciliation." In the first phase Belinsky had "sacrificed reality to an ideal," and in the second the "ideal to reality": in the third phase, on the other hand, he had endeavored to reconcile the two, to transform the abstract ideal into a concrete one through the concept of *becoming*, that is by emphasizing the dynamic aspect of society. This scheme, in Plekhanov's interpretation, reflected the three chief stages in the evolution of European thought.

The first phase—the stage of the "abstract ideal"—was embodied in Enlightenment rationalism, which used the subjective yardstick of individual human reason to evaluate social realities. The "subjective sociology" of the Russian Populists, Plekhanov argued, was a relic of this abstract, ahistorical rationalism. When it came up against reality, however, Enlightenment reason was defeated—the events following the French Revolution made it clear that social processes were governed by objective laws that were independent of the human will and that thwarted human plans. An expression of the new phase in the evolution of consciousness was anti-Enlightenment German idealist philosophy: its idea of a universal Reason of History, as opposed to individual reason, could be seen as a metaphor drawing attention to the objective pattern, the immanent necessity and "inner logic," of the historical process. This too was a specific version of the "reconciliation with reality," based

27. *Ibid.*, vol. 4, pp. 542, 271.

on the assumption that what is real must be rational since history is governed by necessary and rational laws. In Hegel's conservative philosophy "reconciliation" appeared to be a justification of the Prussian state; but this conclusion was contradicted by Hegel's own dialectic, which demonstrated that every aspect of reality is governed by the law whereby all forms of existence that have outlived their usefulness have to be negated and transformed into their opposites. Hegel's *dialectic*, therefore, provided the tool for transcending the Hegelian *system* and set the human intellect a new problem to solve: namely how to discover the objective laws of historical development and create an ideology that would both be in harmony with those laws and encompass the revolutionary negation of empirical reality without succumbing to utopianism. This problem was solved by Marx: having discovered the laws governing economic development, he transformed socialism from a utopian system into a science and thus prepared the ground for overcoming the tragic conflict between ideal and reality.

The significance that Belinsky's "reconciliation with reality" had for Plekhanov is understandable in the light of this scheme. In a variety of works written on different subjects and at different times, Plekhanov cited it as an example of fearless intellectual honesty, of profound understanding of the impotence of "abstract ideals" and the absurdity of "subjectivism." In his "reconciliation" phase Belinsky was a "sociological genius" who instinctively understood that the Hegelian doctrine of the rationality of everything real provided the only possible foundation for the social sciences. It was not his general attitude toward reality that was in error, but only his excessively static understanding of it, his identification of the dynamic Reason of reality (i.e. the progressive tendencies inherent in it) with the existing "empirical" reality. Mikhailovsky had been wrong, Plekhanov insisted, to suggest that Belinsky made up for his previous error by his revolt against the authority of Hegel; on the contrary, this was a "theoretical original sin," a lowering of rigorous intellectual standards that could only be justified as an outburst of suppressed passions.[28] In returning to his previous utopianism, Belinsky forgot his own argument that the "philosophy of reconciliation" was based on the sound postulate that all phases of social development have their own validity—an idea that only needed to be coupled with the development of the "concept of negation."[29]

28. *Ibid.*, vol. 1, p. 458.
29. Plekhanov was thinking of the following paragraph from Belinsky's letter to

Plekhanov took pains to emphasize that during the period of "reconciliation" Belinsky had not adopted reactionary views, that this rejection of "abstract ideals" sprang from his recognition of necessity and should be seen as an act of self-denial, not conformity. Intelligent readers of Plekhanov's article were inevitably drawn to the conclusion that there was a close analogy between Belinsky's rejection of "abstract heroism" and Plekhanov's own rejection of the "abstract" Populist ideal of a direct transition to socialism. The Marxism adopted by Plekhanov and his comrades could also be called a specific variant of "reconciliation with reality" (the reality of Russian capitalism) in the name of historical necessity; it had of course been purged of Belinsky's error and represented the acceptance of dynamic reality as a process of becoming, coupled with the "idea of negation." It is interesting to note that in his unfinished *History of Russian Social Thought* Plekhanov himself had intended to draw this parallel between Belinsky's "reconciliation with reality" and Russian Marxism.[30]

For Plekhanov the "rational reality"—that is, reality as a dynamic process unfolding according to the rational laws of historical progress—was the development of capitalist relations in Russia. On this issue, too, he quoted Belinsky, whose comment that "the process of internal civic development will begin in Russia only when our gentry has become transformed into a bourgeoisie"[31] he called a perceptive guess about "Russia's future fate as a civilized country."[32]

Though Plekhanov presented Belinsky as virtually a precursor of Russian Marxism (or, more accurately, of his particular version of Marxism), he did not think there was any contradiction between this and the "subjective" sociologists' claim to Belinsky as their own ideological predecessor. Belinsky, Plekhanov admitted, had not entirely succeeded in overcoming his "utopianism"; in his "negation" of Russian reality he had frequently abandoned the dialectical view in favor of the subjectivist attitudes of Enlightenment rationalism (*prosvetitel'stvo*). The Russian Marxists based them-

---

Botkin (Dec. 10, 1840): "Of course the idea I tried to develop in the article dealing with Glinka's book on the Battle of Borodino (that is the idea that whatever is real is rational) is founded on correct premises, but I should also have developed the idea of negation as a historical law . . . without which the annals of mankind would be merely a stagnant and putrid swamp." V. C. Belinsky, *Polnoe sobranie sochinenii* (M, 1953–59), vol. 11, p. 576.

30. Plekhanov, *Sochineniia*, vol. 20, p. xxviii.
31. See above, p. 146.
32. Plekhanov, *Izbrannye*, vol. 4, p. 521.

selves on Belinsky's strong side, whereas "subjective sociology" harked back to his weak side, to the "theoretical original sin" shown in his moral revolt against Hegelianism. In later years Plekhanov tried to demonstrate that the Bolsheviks' "subjectivist" tactics also sprang from this "original sin." It is significant that at the very end of his life—after the October Revolution, which he considered to be a voluntaristic violation of the laws of history—he continued to draw attention to Belinsky's struggle against utopianism and felt impelled to warn the victorious Bolshevik party against the dangers of an "abstract ideal."[33] Equally characteristic was his desire to be buried in St. Petersburg next to the grave of Belinsky.

Plekhanov's interpretation of Belinsky's ideological development throws light on Plekhanov's own tragedy. This will become even clearer if we pause to examine what exactly he meant by the notion of "historical necessity." For Plekhanov the most important thinkers were Hegel and Spinoza; he even held Spinoza (interpreted from a materialist point of view) in higher esteem than Hegel and went so far as to state that "during the *materialist* period of their development Marx and Engels never abandoned Spinoza's standpoint."[34] What he admired in the systems of Spinoza and Hegel was their monism and strict determinism—determinism conceived as an ontological necessity inherent in the rational structure of the universe. Plekhanov's necessity, therefore, was essentially the rational necessity of Spinoza made dynamic and historical by Hegel and reinterpreted scientifically by Marx. The principle of determinism (causality), widely accepted in the natural sciences, was extended by Plekhanov to the social sciences and raised to the rank of a "rational" necessity—of greater significance, therefore, than an ordinary empirical necessity or regular pattern that could be empirically deduced. Plekhanov was able to portray Belinsky's tragic conflict between ideal and reality with such dramatic insight because his favorite

33. In 1918 Plekhanov still argued for the need to pass through the capitalist phase: "One of the creators of scientific socialism, F. Engels, once expressed a brilliant thought: without ancient slavery modern socialism would have been impossible. Let us reflect on this thought: it amounts to a relative justification of slavery, a justification within a certain historical epoch. Is this not a shameful betrayal of an ideal? Please ease your mind—there is no betrayal at all. It is only the rejection of a utopian idea born in the vague sphere of abstraction and divorced from the concrete conditions of *hic et nunc*. Engels was right to reject such an ideal, not wrong. An abstract ideal has too long hindered the development of the human mind. And it was not without reason that our Belinsky deplored the period in which he found himself under its harmful influence." Plekhanov, *God na rodine* (Paris, 1921), vol. 2, p. 260.

34. Plekhanov, *Izbrannye*, vol. 2, p. 360.

hero, too, had conceived necessity as an ontological principle: if his "reconciliation with reality" had been submission merely to empirical reality rather than to Historical Reason, it would have been nothing more than an act of despair or conformity, interesting at most from the psychological point of view.

The conception of "necessity" cannot, of course, be separated from the conception of "freedom." In his book *On the Role of the Individual in History* Plekhanov declared with pride that Marx's Russian followers had overcome the dualism of ideal and reality, had attained the higher level of monism, and viewed themselves as conscious instruments of historical necessity. Their freedom had its roots in necessity: "Strictly speaking, it is a freedom that identifies itself with necessity, necessity that has transformed itself into freedom."[35]

It is also revealing to examine what social processes were held by Plekhanov to be "necessary" or "regular." To begin with, he clearly felt these qualities to be associated with spontaneous and "organic" development—only a process "that has its own intrinsic cause, that starts from within and not from some alien 'without'" fitted in with his conception of historical necessity. If we add that he condemned as starting from "without"—or as a subjectivist violation of history— every attempt on the part of a body of revolutionaries (or the government) to resist the "inner logic" of economic development, it becomes clear that what he meant by the inevitable development trend was very often simply the specific pattern of development associated with laissez-faire capitalism. This was of course a form of "economic materialism," aptly defined by Gramsci as a blend of bourgeois liberal political economy with an appropriately castrated and simplified Marxism.[36] Moreover, despite his alleged objectivity, Plekhanov's conception of what was "regular" and "necessary" inevitably involved a normative view of the ideal development process. From the proposition that the "course of ideas" was determined by the "course of events" he would often draw the conclusion that men were in duty bound *not* to attempt to interfere from without in events with the object of changing their course in accordance with their own ideals. It is readily apparent that this was a prescriptive argument, a deviation from facts to value-judgments.

An additional element here was Plekhanov's "Europocentrism," an essential component of his Westernism. On this particular issue

35. *Ibid.*, p. 308.
36. See A. Gramsci, *The Modern Prince and Other Writings* (London, 1957), pp. 153–61.

he broke most decisively with his own past and accepted with pride the reproach of "Westernism" leveled by the Populists against the Russian Marxists. His hostility to "Asiatic despotism"[37] (whose mainstay, as he saw it, was the peasant commune), coupled with his view of regular processes of development as inviolate laws of universal Historical Reason, meant that his conception of "historical necessity" was something extraordinarily abstract—seen in isolation from the "historical and geographical conditions of development," as Belinsky once wrote about his own "abstract ideal." It is ironical (and part of his tragedy) that the recognition of historical necessity, which he thought would save him from "utopianism," turned out to be the very essence of his own utopianism. When, after the first successes of the Russian Revolution, Plekhanov accused the Bolsheviks of ignoring the "concrete conditions of time and place," it was because he had his own abstract ideal that laid down the most rational way to achieve a socialist Russia; this was the ideal of a Russian Westernizer who wished for his country a "normal" European type of development, following a rational sequence of "phases" and always perfectly in harmony with the intrinsic tendencies of economic and cultural growth. In the end the ideal of a socialism to be built in Russia *after* the final completion of the process of Westernization on the firm foundations of a highly developed capitalist democracy proved to be no less "abstract" than the ideals of the Russian Populists.

PLEKHANOV'S LITERARY CRITICISM AND AESTHETICS

Plekhanov's writings on art and literature should be regarded as an integral part of his work as a whole. It is true that many of these pieces were written only in the early twentieth century, but the views they express were largely formed much earlier. The motivation underlying such aesthetic studies as the *Letters Without Address* (1899–1900), *French Dramatic Literature and Eighteenth-Century French Painting from the Standpoint of Sociology* (1905), and *Art and Society* (1912–13) was the desire to show through the example of art the value of historical materialism as an interpretative tool. In these works Plekhanov chiefly disputes not so much idealistic aesthetics as attempts to explain art from the standpoint of naturalistic materialism (above all Darwinian evolutionism) or

37. Cf. the excellent analysis of this aspect of Plekhanov's views in Baron, *Plekhanov*, pp. 295–307.

positivistic psychologism. A common denominator of both these points of view, according to Plekhanov, was the attempt to explain art by invoking an ahistorical concept of "human nature" or variations on this theme (i.e. Taine's notion of "race"). Plekhanov conceded that there were certain "general laws of human psychology," certain inborn tendencies such as the instinct of imitation or contradiction (Darwin's "principle of antithesis"); but he argued that the manner in which they manifested themselves, or even whether they appeared at all—in other words the transition from potentiality to reality—was determined by differing historical circumstances.

Plekhanov derived this argument directly from the theory of evolution; in his view, the difference between Darwinian evolutionism and historical materialism could be reduced to the proposition that in historical development it is not the natural environment that plays the decisive role (although it must be taken into consideration) but *social* conditions, determined by the level of the forces of production. Plekhanov found numerous arguments in favor of this thesis in ethnological and sociological literature on the life of primitive tribes. He pointed out, for instance, that in ornamentation animal motifs give way to plant motifs when tribes cease to be hunters and become cultivators, and that musical rhythm depends on the rhythm of work, and therefore also on the development of the productive forces. He also laid great stress on the fact that useful activity—i.e. work—is older than play and that man's recognition of objects for their use value precedes any aesthetic point of view.

It was a peculiar paradox of Plekhanov's aesthetic theories (of his philosophy, too) that though he insisted on the superiority of historical to naturalistic materialism, his sociological interpretation of beauty made use of many of the categories of naturalism: it was not for nothing that he declared that his investigations of social phenomena would utilize principles applied by Darwin in the realm of biology.[38] By explaining the history of art in terms of the operation of external conditions on man's psycho-physical nature, Plekhanov's sociology conceived man not as the creator of his own nature and history, but merely as a product, a passive medium of objective processes subject to the strict determinism of "natural necessity."

Apart from the clear evidence of positivistic naturalism, Plekhanov's aesthetics also reveal the influence of Hegel, which was

38. Plekhanov, *Sochineniia*, vol. 14, p. 10.

mostly absorbed at second hand through Belinsky. Hegel regarded art as a separate form of the Absolute Spirit; Plekhanov saw art as a separate, irreducible form of social ideology. The sphere of beauty, he wrote, is not the intellect but instinct; a true artist, as Belinsky was right to stress, thinks in images. By implying that art has its own specific rules and develops according to laws that are not straightforward reflections of the laws of society, this argument ran counter to the positivists' reductionism. It also implied that writers ought to avoid the excessive rationalization of the creative process, as well as the substitution of the language of political journalism for the language proper to art. This was a criterion that Plekhanov applied rigorously, regardless of his personal attitude toward the ideology advocated in a given work of art: he criticized the Populist writer N. Naumov for using literature as a vehicle for Populist propaganda, just as he later criticized Maxim Gorky for subordinating art to Marxist propaganda in his novel *Mother*.

As part of his emphasis on "objectivity," Plekhanov also felt that critics ought to be moderate in expressing their own political preferences. Since all social and aesthetic ideals are historically and sociologically justified, a normative approach in aesthetics is clearly unscientific. If aesthetics intends to be taken seriously as a scientific discipline, it must stop preaching to artists what art should be and what ideals art should proclaim, and must instead try to explain what art is and why it takes a particular form in a particular age. In literary and art criticism strict scientific canons are of course less binding and prescriptive views more in place. Even a critic, however, Plekhanov thought, ought not to judge a work of art by the subjective yardstick of his own abstract ideal. In particular a critic ought not to ask the artist to support a particular political line by his art, since this must detract from the work's authenticity and its aesthetic and intellectual impact. The function of art is to reflect the consciousness of the community, and if it wants to do this well it cannot pay heed to the critics' views on what it should be like.

Plekhanov outlined his views on the critic's role in his theory of "two acts of materialist literary criticism." The "first act" is to trace and investigate the "sociological equivalent" of the work of art under review, to transpose the ideas of the work analyzed from the language of artistic imagery into the language of sociology. The "second act" is the artistic analysis of the work, which means establishing how adequately its form expresses the content.[39]

Although this theory did not advise critics to judge a work of art

39. *Ibid.*, vol. 14, pp. 183–89.

from the standpoint of their own aesthetic and social ideals, a closer investigation suggests that here, too, Plekhanov's "objectivism" was not consistent—either in theory or in practice. The most glaring departure from his theoretical objection to a normative aesthetics was Plekhanov's acceptance of what he called "Belinsky's aesthetic code." This code, which it should be noted was not so much taken over from Belinsky as ascribed to him by Plekhanov, laid down five requirements for a work of art; it must (1) represent life as it is with the help of images, not syllogisms; (2) portray the truth without embellishments or distortions; (3) express a concrete idea that encompasses the whole subject in its unity; (4) have a form appropriate to its content; and (5) show unity of form, that is, the harmonious coordination of all its parts.[40] It is obvious that these five requirements were essentially a reiteration of the aesthetic principles of nineteenth-century realism, and that raising them to the status of a universal norm not only was incompatible with Plekhanov's declared opposition to evaluational aesthetics, but also sinned against historicism.

If we examine Plekhanov's contribution as a critic more closely, it is striking that he was far readier to accept historical relativity in his evaluation of past achievements than in his assessment of more recent trends. This showed itself most clearly in his radical condemnation of the modernist movement, especially Symbolism, which he judged by the standards of realism.

This inconsistency sprang from the internal contradictions of Plekhanov's standpoint. On the one hand it was based on the assumption that everything that existed was historically justified and inevitable, but on the other it also postulated that a scientific understanding of the laws of development made it possible to determine which trends were progressive; therefore anything that contradicted this diagnosis by its existence could be condemned. In his attitude toward contemporary intellectual and artistic movements (those he did not approve of as well as those he had not foreseen), Plekhanov behaved less like an objective scholar interested in discovering their social genesis than like someone delivering a final judgment from the heights of his superior scientific understanding of "what should be." This, of course, was another expression of the same dogmatic certainty that led him to condemn the Bolshevik Revolution as a violation of the scientifically established laws of historical development.

His insistence on the absolute value of nineteenth-century real-

40. *Ibid.*, vol. 23, pp. 156–57.

ism and his inability to foresee or accept other trends in modern art show that Plekhanov's historical materialism suffered from the same limitation as Hegel's historical idealism; it was able to explain the necessity of what *had* been, but it failed as a compass for the future. It would be doing Plekhanov an injustice, however, to conclude on this note. Today his aesthetics is certainly outmoded, but it is important to remember that he was a pioneer in Marxist art criticism. Of considerable interest are his attempts to create a Marxist interpretation of social psychology as a sphere that would explain those features of works of art that cannot be directly related to the development of the forces of production. His study *French Dramatic Literature and Eighteenth-Century French Painting from the Standpoint of Sociology*, in which these ideas were developed in most detail, still has many fruitful insights to offer to the contemporary reader.

LEGAL POPULISM

At the beginning of the 1880's the need for political methods of struggle was accepted by all sections within the Russian revolutionary movement. This does not mean that the old Populist principle of the primacy of "social" over "political" aims had been entirely abandoned. Revolutionary Populism had become politically oriented, but it was not so in the social reformist trend that had long existed within the movement and for which the 1880's and 1890's were a period of intense activity. Russian scholars have been accustomed to call this trend "liberal Populism," although this label is not particularly suitable from either the political or the economic point of view. The term "legal" or nonrevolutionary Populism would appear to be more appropriate. Representatives of this trend were "apolitical" in a much more literal sense than the revolutionaries; they did not advocate a liberal parliamentary system and were uniformly hostile to economic liberalism. In fact they were "liberals" only in the very broad and specifically Russian sense of opposing revolution and hoping for social reforms from above. Even in the early 1870's a characteristic representative of this trend, G. Z. Eliseev, declared that Russians ought to be grateful for not having a parliamentary government; thanks to this the state was still in a position to introduce reforms benefiting the masses, and to defend them against kulaks, "commune-baiters," and a voracious plutocracy.[41]

41. See Chapter 12 above, note 8.

At the beginning the boundaries between legal and revolutionary Populism were ill-defined. Mikhailovsky, for instance, was basically a legal Populist, although he sympathized and collaborated with the revolutionaries and in his theoretical works formulated the general ideals of the movement to which both revolutionary and non-revolutionary Populists could subscribe. The Populist economist VASILY BERVI-FLEROVSKY (1829–1918), author of *The Position of the Working Class in Russia* (1869), was closely associated with revolutionary circles but appealed to the good will of the authorities and was not convinced of the need for a "political revolution" in Russia. He even appealed to the landowners, offering them advice on how to fraternize with and work for the benefit of the people without relinquishing their social position.[42] These appeals stemmed from his conviction that bypassing capitalism lay in the interests of the Russian nation as a whole and was, indeed, the only way to avoid a national disaster.

In the 1880's, after the revolutionaries had clearly abandoned their indifference to political forms, legal Populism became a distinctly separate movement with its own ideology. The common denominator linking the often very different members of this movement was the postulate of noncapitalist industrialization to be initiated and directed by the state, which would safeguard the interests of the small producers. The leading and most characteristic representative of this trend was V. P. VORONTSOV (1847–1918), who signed his work with the initials V. V.[43] His book *The Fate of Capitalism in Russia* (1882) was the first ambitious attempt to analyze the specific features of Russian capitalism; at the same time, it was an original statement of the theoretical assumptions of economic development along noncapitalist lines.

The Populist thinkers of the 1870's had been deeply imbued with the pessimistic conviction that time was working against them, that the allegedly "objective" course of events—the automatic nature of economic development—was pushing their country along the capitalist path. Mikhailovsky, for instance, called into question not the existence of that "objective" course as such, but only its inevitability; he opposed it in the name of his "subjective" moral postulates, but admitted that the chances of a successful realization

42. V. Bervi-Flerovsky, *Izbrannye ekonomicheskie proizvedeniia* (M, 9158), vol. 1, pp. 612–13.

43. An interesting discussion of Vorontsov's economic views and of "Legal Populists" versus "legal Marxists" is to be found in A. P. Mendel, *Dilemmas of Progress in Tsarist Russia. Legal Marxism and Legal Populism* (Cambridge, Mass., 1961).

of these postulates were diminishing year by year. Vorontsov's book was to provide arguments in favor of the more optimistic view that circumstances in Russia were not altogether favorable to the bourgeoisie. This optimism, however, was only partial: Vorontsov argued that capitalism could not be the dominant form of production in Russia, but he did not rule it out as a future form of exploitation of the masses.

Vorontsov based his belief in the ultimate failure of industrialization along capitalist lines on his analysis of the conditions in which Russian capitalism had to function:

> The peculiar historical circumstance affecting our large-scale industry is that it must expand at a time when other countries have already attained a high level of development. Two things follow from this: first, our industry can make use of all the forms created in the West and does not have to crawl at a snail's pace from stage to stage; second, it must compete with the more experienced, highly industrialized countries, and competition with such rivals might utterly extinguish the weak sparks of our scarcely awakening capitalism.

In his general conclusion Vorontsov added to this the idea that Russia's backwardness could be regarded as a kind of historical privilege:

> The countries which are latecomers to the avenue of history have a great privilege in comparison with their foregoers, a privilege consisting in the fact that the accumulated historical experience of other countries enables them to work out a relatively true image of their next step and to strive for what the others have already achieved not instinctively but consciously, not groping in the dark but knowing what should be avoided on the way.[44]

The idea that backwardness could be a kind of privilege had been put forward earlier by Herzen (inspired by Chaadaev) and also by Chernyshevsky, who expressed it in the aphorism "History is like a grandmother; she is particularly fond of the youngest grandchildren."[45] In their manifesto *To the Younger Generation* (1861), one of the earliest documents of revolutionary Populism, the authors (Shelgunov and Mikhailov) expressed the same thought: "We are latecomers as a nation and this is our salvation." Vorontsov thus had a certain tradition behind him. What distinguished him from

---

44. V. V. Vorontsov, *Sud'by kapitalizma v Rossii* (St. Petersburg, 1882), pp. 13–14. Essential fragments are reprinted in Karataev, ed., *Narodnicheskaia ekonomicheskaia literatura*.

45. N. S. Chernyshevsky, *Izbrannye filosofskie sochineniia* (L, 1950–51), vol. 2 ("Philosophical Prejudices against the Communal Ownership of the Land").

his predecessors (with the partial exception of Chernyshevsky) was the shift of emphasis to the purely economic aspect of the problem— the idea that the "privilege of backwardness" could be used not only to build a juster social system, but also to accelerate the process of industrialization.

The disadvantages of competing with more developed countries were seen by Vorontsov as another obstacle in the way of the *capitalist* development of Russia. Capitalist enterprises in Russia, he argued, had no external markets, and their home market was shrinking owing to the falling purchasing power of the population caused by capitalist expropriation. On the basis of a ready-made modern technology, large-scale capitalist enterprise in Russia could develop intensively even in the absence of markets by increasing productivity, but it could not develop *extensively*—i.e. give employment to the growing number of workers. It could create small islands of modern production that would be able to satisfy the wants of the upper classes, but it could not become the dominant mode of production; it could exploit the masses and bring ruin to many independent small producers, but it would be unable to give them employment and thus train them in superior "socialized" methods of production. In Western Europe, capitalism was historically necessary and progressive as a form of the "socialization of labor"; in Russia, and in backward countries in general, it could only be a form of exploitation, "an abortive effort," the "bastard child of history." Having identified industrialization as such with *capitalist* industrialization, the Russian government made every effort to support native capitalism by artificial injections and generous subsidies, by "treating it with kid gloves"; the result of all these efforts was more like "playing at capitalism"—a parody of the real thing. Russian capitalists themselves felt the need to explain their lack of success, and they found in the village commune an appropriate scapegoat.

Russian agriculture, too, was cited by Vorontsov as proof of the failure of Russian capitalism. He even claimed that with the exception of England all European countries were retreating from capitalist methods of agricultural production. (To understand this strange statement, one must realize that for Vorontsov capitalism in agriculture consisted in the expropriation of the smallholders and not in highly developed commodity production for a capitalist market, even on a small scale.) Vorontsov ascribed the drop in agricultural yields and the continuing disintegration of the peasant commune to the government's absurd fiscal policies, which even included flogging the peasants in order to force them to sell their livestock and seed corn—in other words to destroy their forces of production. Despite this, the peasants were fighting to preserve their independence and were even succeeding, though at the cost of maximum restriction of their own consumption; the owners of large estates, moreover, were tempted by high rents to lease their land rather than to cultivate it with hired labor and were thus playing their part in handing agriculture over to the peasants.

What Vorontsov proposed as an alternative to capitalism was industrialization initiated and managed by the state. He suggested that the government should nationalize large-scale industry and arrange for the gradual transfer of smaller enterprises to workers' *artels*, which could be controlled indirectly; artisans and home-workers should be encouraged to organize themselves into cooperatives, which would receive state aid in the purchase of raw materials and the marketing of their products. Similar help should be extended to the peasant communes. It would be wrong to conclude from this that Vorontsov wanted to preserve rural crafts in perpetuity—all he wanted was to ensure a smooth and painless transition to "socialized forms of production." He was only partially a disciple of Mikhailovsky—he did not espouse the ideal of nondivided, non-socialized labor, and indeed often quoted Marx, from whom he learned to regard socialized production as a historical necessity and an indispensable condition of economic development. Economic development, in his view, passed through three stages: (1) preindustrial "popular" production, (2) socialization of labor as part of the process of industrialization, and (3) socialized "popular" production (in view of the censorship Vorontsov had to avoid the word "socialism"). Noncapitalist industrialization under the auspices of the state appeared to represent the most efficient way of reaching this final, highest stage of economic development. Therefore Vorontsov thought he was entitled to conclude that Russia might still teach the West something valuable: "Let us hope that it will be Russia's role to serve them [Western workers] as an example in their attempts to reorganize the social system; let us hope that it will be Russia's destiny to bring about equality and fraternity, though she is not destined to fight for liberty."[46]

This hope that tsarist Russia might move toward socialism without first settling the question of political freedom sprang from Vorontsov's belief that the state required industrialization but could not achieve it by capitalist methods: "Following the capitalist

46. V. V(orontsov), *Sud'by kapitalizma*, p. 124.

path," he wrote, "we shall never create an advanced large-scale industry"; this was because "the later the process of industrialization
is commenced, the more difficult it is to carry it out along capitalist
lines."[47] The state was the only institution able to invest capital not
for the sake of profit but for the public benefit; only planned industrialization directed by the government could ensure Russia's
economic independence and prevent her exploitation by the more
developed capitalist countries; only state-sponsored economic development would enable Russia to compete with her Western rivals
—to oust Britain from the Asian markets and take America's place
in corn exports.

Similar conclusions were drawn by N. DANIELSON (pen name Nikolai-on), the Russian translator of Marx's *Capital*, who in his long
years of correspondence with Marx and Engels (starting in 1868)
provided them with first-hand information about economic developments in Russia. Danielson was a Populist who, not without justification, considered himself to be a Marxist. His main work—
*Outline of Our Social Economy After the Enfranchisement of the
Peasants* (1893)—was written at the suggestion of Marx himself.
Danielson made every effort to emphasize the differences between
himself and the economic publicists who "defended the people's
cause from a narrow peasant point of view."[48] He deliberately
avoided quoting Vorontsov (although in fact he had borrowed a
good deal from him), and lost no opportunity to refer to the authority of Marx and Engels, even quoting from his private correspondence with them. Nevertheless, there can be no possible doubt
that Danielson belonged to the legal Populists. On basic issues he
was in agreement with Vorontsov, the only difference between them
being one of emphasis. Danielson, for instance, did not insist that
the capitalist industrialization of Russia was impossible; like Vorontsov, however, he made much of the argument about the lack of
foreign markets and drew attention to the catastrophic situation in
agriculture as part of his campaign to persuade the government
that capitalist development was contrary to the true interests of the
Russian state. Like Vorontsov, he was a spokesman for the small
producers and defended cottage industry and the village commune
in the belief that they provided an adequate base for future socialized production. In a word, he shared Vorontsov's conviction that

47. *Ibid.*, p. 15.
48. Quoted in *Istoriia russkoi ekonomicheskoi mysli*, ed. A. Y. Pashkov and N. A.
Tsagolov (M, 1960), vol. 2, part 2, p. 329.

state-sponsored industrialization would make it possible to combine increased productivity with increased mass consumption.

The problem facing us could have been summed up in the following terms: What should we do to bring our industry up to the level of Western industry, in order to prevent Russia from becoming a vassal of more advanced countries, and at the same time raise the living standards of the people as a whole? What we did, instead, was to identify large-scale modern industry with its capitalist form, thus reducing the problem to the following dilemma: To what should we sacrifice our cottage industries—to our own capitalist industry or to English industry? When the issue was presented in this way—and this is how it was presented—our cottage industries were doomed and we began to propagate our own capitalist industry.[49]

What Danielson's readers did not know was that these doubts, which he tried to present as a false dilemma, were in fact shared by Engels. On September 22, 1892, Engels wrote to Danielson: " . . . the real issue for you seems to me this: that the Russians had to decide whether their own *grande industrie* was to destroy their domestic manufacture, or whether the import of English goods was to accomplish this. With protection, the Russians effected it, without protection, the English."[50] By calling this a false dilemma, Danielson was in fact carrying on a concealed polemic with Engels. This was not an isolated instance of such disagreement, although considering himself to be a Marxist Danielson was by no means inclined to give up his own, long-established views of his country's economic development. He did everything possible to convince Engels of the correctness of his ideas, but when he failed to do so, he continued to stick resolutely to his point of view. Whenever it suited him, he would appeal to the authority of Marx and Engels, but when he disagreed with them he did not mention them by name in order not to lose his reputation as an orthodox Marxist.

Under the influence of Marxism, Danielson endeavored to stress his disapproval of "economic romanticism." That was why he rejected projects entailing organized government help for village craftsmen and home-workers put forward by Vorontsov, Krivenko, and other Populist writers. Work must become "socialized," he insisted; "patriarchal production" must be transformed into proper large-

49. Nikolai-on (Danielson), *Ocherki nashego poreformennogo obshchestvennogo khoziaistva* (St. Petersburg, 1893), pp. 390–91. The relevant sections of the book are reprinted in Karataev, ed., *Narodnicheskaia ekonomicheskaia literatura*.

50. K. Marx and F. Engels, *Correspondence, 1846–1895*, pp. 499–500.

scale industry, and this is only possible through the structural transformation of the entire economic system. In fact Danielson himself was not free of the tendency to romanticize survivals of precapitalist "patriarchal production." Fundamentally both he and Vorontsov were agreed on their general aim, which was a program of industrialization that would prevent the "expropriation of the small producers" and falling standards of living. The main difference between them was that whereas Vorontsov advocated cheap credit for artisans, lower taxes, and free advice for the peasants as ways of combating capitalism, Danielson was much more skeptical about such half measures and therefore emphasized the need for a global transformation of the system by the state.

Lastly, it must not be forgotten that both these Populist writers believed it was possible to implement their economic programs without any prior political reforms. This characteristic aspect of legal Populism aroused the indignation of the Russian Marxists. In a letter to Engels Plekhanov wrote: "Let us suppose that the peasant commune really is the sheet anchor that will save us. Who then will carry out the reforms postulated by Nikolai-on? The tsarist government? Better the plague than reforms undertaken by such reformers! Socialism introduced by Russian gendarmes—what a monstrous vision!" [51]

It would not be fair to finish on this note. From the perspective of our own times we see in the theories of Vorontsov and Danielson not only a legitimate attempt to defend the peasants, whom so many socialists of that time too readily proclaimed to be doomed, but also the first attempt to pose and find solutions to problems that still face some of the Third World countries today. They may have underestimated the potentialities of capitalist development in Russia, and may have been too optimistic about the chances of reconciling noncapitalist industrialization with a steady increase in mass consumption; there is little doubt, either, that they misinterpreted facts and often gave a tendentious interpretation of statistical data, thus presenting a false picture of trends in the Russian economy. On the other hand, they were the first to realize that economic backwardness creates its own specific problems, and that underdeveloped countries not only should not but cannot model their development on that of the advanced countries of Western Europe. Vorontsov might have been wrong when he argued that Russian capitalist industry would never be able to win foreign markets, but the problem itself—as he stated it—of the influence of international condi-

51. *Perepiska K. Marksa i F. Engelsa s russkimi politicheskimi deiatel'iami*, p. 334.

tions on the industrialization of backward countries was certainly not a pseudoproblem. His hope that the tsarist government might carry out the noncapitalist industrialization of Russia in the interests of the people was no doubt illusory, but it sprang from a correct grasp of the relationship between economic backwardness and the role of the state in initiating economic development.

LEGAL MARXISM

The controversy over capitalism reached its climax in the 1890's, when Marxism had become an influential trend in Russia and was widely accepted in the workers' movement. It was then, when the policies of the minister of finance, Count Witte, were rapidly transforming the country, that the debate between Populists and Marxists focused the attention of the Russian intelligentsia on the problems of capitalist industrialization. An important role was played in this debate by the trend known as "legal Marxism." Lenin called this "an altogether curious phenomenon" that would have seemed impossible in the 1880's or early 1890's.

In a country ruled by an autocracy, with a completely enslaved press, in a period of desperate political reaction in which even the tiniest outgrowth of political discontent and protest is persecuted, the theory of revolutionary Marxism suddenly forces its way into the *censored* literature and, though expounded in Aesopian language, is understood by all the "interested." The government has accustomed itself to regarding only the theory of the [revolutionary] Narodnaya Volya [People's Will] as dangerous, without, as is usual, observing its internal evolution, and rejoicing at *any* criticism levelled against it. Quite a considerable time elapsed (by our Russian standards) before the government realised what had happened and the unwieldy army of censors and gendarmes discovered the new enemy and flung itself upon him. Meanwhile, Marxist books were published one after another, Marxist journals and newspapers were founded, nearly everyone became a Marxist, Marxists were flattered, Marxists were courted, and the book publishers rejoiced at the extraordinary, ready sale of Marxist literature.[52]

Here Lenin is of course writing about "legal" Marxism in the widest meaning of the word, i.e. the whole of Marxist writing that was legally published. The expansion of Marxist literature was due (as Lenin emphasized) to "an alliance between people of extreme and of very moderate views"—that is, an alliance of the revolutionary Marxists with the "legal" Marxists *sensu stricto*, or supporters of

52. V. I. Lenin, *Collected Works* (Eng.-lang. ed.; M, 1960–66), vol. 5, p. 361.

legal methods of struggle who saw in Marxism a theory stressing
the necessity of capitalist industrialization and political liberty. The
leading representative of this current was PETR STRUVE (1870–1944).
After the publication of Struve's *Critical Remarks on the Economic
Development of Russia* (1894), Legal Marxism became an influential trend with its own periodicals and representatives among university professors (A. Skvortsov, A. Chuprov, M. Tugan-Baranov-
sky, and others). Indeed, for the average Russian intellectual (if he
was not directly connected with the revolutionary movement),
Marxism in Russia began not with Plekhanov but with Struve.[53]

A forerunner of Struve was N. Ziber, a professor at the university
of Kiev and author of the study *David Ricardo and Karl Marx*,
which was well thought of by Marx himself.[54] The book as a whole
was not published until 1885, but parts of it—a dissertation on
Ricardo's theory of value (1871), and a series of articles entitled
"The Economic Theory of Marx"—had appeared in the 1870's
and had contributed greatly to the popularization of Marxism
among members of "Land and Freedom." It is worth noting that
Ziber's writings exerted a considerable influence on the young
Plekhanov, who quoted from them in his article "The Law of the
Economic Development of Society and the Tasks of Socialism in
Russia." Soviet scholars have tended to see Ziber in a much more
favorable light than Struve, and have emphasized his pioneering
role in propagating Marxism in Russia. In the other hand, if we are
considering the general typology of different variants of Russian
Marxism, it cannot be denied that it was Ziber who also initiated
the liberal-economic interpretation of Marxism later taken up by
the Legal Marxists. For Ziber, Marx was first and foremost a disciple
and continuator of Ricardo. "*Capital*," he wrote, "is nothing but a
continuation and a development of the same principles on which
the doctrine of Smith and Ricardo is founded."[55]

Ziber's main emphasis was on the evolutionary inevitability of
capitalism. Social formations, he wrote, are not a matter of choice
but the inevitable result of natural development; men's conscious
interference cannot achieve more than a midwife who may shorten
the birth pangs. The necessity of passing through the capitalist
phase is implied by the universal law of economic development; it
is possible to counteract some socially harmful effects of indus-

53. The most detailed study of Struve's thought (before 1905) is R. Pipes, *Struve, Liberal on the Left, 1870–1905* (Cambridge, Mass., 1970).
54. See the afterword to the second German edition of *Capital*.
55. N. I. Ziber, *Izbrannye ekonomicheskie proizvedeniia* (M, 1959), vol. 1, p. 556.

trialization by factory legislation on the English model, but "the attempt to liquidate capitalism before it is ready to liquidate itself is tantamount to trying to lift oneself up by one's own hair."[56] Economic development is evolutionary and its natural phases cannot be skipped or artificially shortened: the institutional structure of the state always adjusts itself automatically to the economic base.

Ziber's faith in automatic progress was so strong that he believed socialism would take over without a revolution as soon as it became economically justified. The inauguration of the new system, he thought, ought to be decided on by an international congress of the highly industrialized states.

A man of Ziber's views was bound to be implacably hostile to Populism. He was convinced that the peasant commune was doomed to extinction and that the development of the economy required the expropriation and proletarianization of a major part of the Russian peasantry. "Nothing will come of the Russian peasant if he is not put through the industrial boiler," was one of his sayings. It was axiomatic to him that the scattered output of small, independent producers must be replaced by large-scale capitalist production. No wonder Akselrod commented in a letter to Plekhanov that Ziber's theory led Russian socialists to a depressing conclusion: "The fate of the peasantry must be left to the spontaneous process of history, and we ourselves must become liberals or simply sit down and fold our hands."[57]

On this particular question, Struve, interestingly enough, held a different view: it was not socialists who should become liberals, he thought, but liberals who (if they wanted to be effective) should, at least for a time, turn themselves into Social Democrats. Surely this is a revealing comment on the political weakness of the liberal movement in Russia.

In his *Critical Notes* Struve attacked Populist doctrine and defended the progressive nature of capitalist industrialization. The will of individuals and their subjective ideals counted for nothing, he insisted as part of his polemic against "subjective sociology." The correct attitude to capitalism, therefore, was not "ideological" but objective, the stance of a scientist who demonstrates the inevitability of a given process. "Let us conclude that we lack culture and take lessons from capitalism," was the book's appropriate conclusion.

Naturally enough, this phase provoked an outburst of indignation in Populist circles. In order to understand this, we must take into

56. *Ibid.*, vol. 2, p. 673.
57. *Perepiska G. V. Plekhanova i P. B. Akselroda* (M, 1925), vol. 2, p. 197.

account the fact that both Plekhanov and the German Social Democrats had made serious mistakes in their treatment of the peasants
as "a homogeneous reactionary mass," and that the program of the
German Social Democrats adopted in Erfurt in 1891 spoke of the
ruin of small independent enterprises (including farms) as a "natural necessity" of economic development. All these factors added
up to a situation in which every Marxist was suspected by Populist
writers of advocating the expropriation of the peasants or even of
representing the interests of the bourgeoisie. In the polemics between Marxists and Populists, one of the most active participants
was Mikhailovsky, who attacked not only Struve and the Legal
Marxists but Marxism as such, accusing it of fatalism and doctrinaire inflexibility, coupled with dialectical sophistry, dogmatic conceit, and high-handed indifference to the fate of living human
beings.

The phrase about "taking lessons from capitalism" was felt to be
particularly unfortunate. However, only the young Lenin felt
obliged to disown it and to point out clearly the difference between
Struve's views and revolutionary Marxism. Among most other
Marxists of the time his *Critical Notes* gained Struve a great reputation, and his revisionist views were overlooked for the sake of his
contribution to the struggle against Populism. At the first congress
of Russian Social Democrats in Minsk in 1898, it was Struve who
was invited to write the party's *Manifesto*. This program, which
was adopted by the congress, shows the common platform on which
both legal and revolutionary Marxists found it possible to agree;
there is no mention in it of the seizure of power or the hegemony of
the proletariat, and the task facing the working class is defined as
taking the place of the "weak and cowardly" bourgeoisie in the
struggle for political liberties. Struve himself later admitted that
for him personally the issue of political rights had been far more
important than the ultimate goal of socialism. He "passionately
loved freedom," whereas socialism as such never inspired any emotions in him, to say nothing of passion: "It was simply by the way of
reasoning that I became an adept of socialism, having come to the
conclusion that it was a historically inevitable result of the objective
process of economic development."[58]

It is significant that even in his early *Critical Notes* Struve anticipated some of the central ideas of Bernstein's "revisionism." He

58. P. B. Struve, "My Contacts and Conflicts with Lenin," *Slavonic Review*, vol.
12 (April 1934), p. 577.

rejected the theory of the ultimate collapse of capitalism (the *Zusammenbruchstheorie*) and of the impoverishment of the working class (*Verelendungstheorie*), and although he acknowledged Marxism as "the only scientific theory" of social development, he suggested that its philosophical foundations were as yet inadequate and ought to be supplemented by Kantian criticism. No wonder that at the end of the 1890's he was ready to take an active part in the German revisionist movement. His paper on the Marxian theory of social development (*Die Marxische Theorie der sozialen Entwicklung*, 1899)[59] was in some respects much more radical in its criticism of Marx than Bernstein's theses. Struve accused Marx of being a "utopianist" (the same charge he had previously leveled at the Populists in the name of Marx), described social revolution as an essentially evolutionary process, and insisted that socialism was not a "negation" of capitalism but rather the inevitable outcome of the natural development of capitalism itself.

The fact that the revision of Marxism was undertaken even earlier in Russia than in Germany should not surprise us. When Plekhanov wrote "It is a peculiar feature of our recent history that even the Westernization of our bourgeoisie was accomplished under the banner of Marxism,"[60] he meant what Struve had in mind when he said that Legal Marxism was essentially a "justification of capitalism," and that its part in the development of Russian thought could be compared to the role of economic liberalism in the West. Indeed, Legal Marxism was the first procapitalist ideology that appealed to the Russian intelligentsia. It won wide popularity largely because it was not openly bourgeois and seemed to stem from the socialist tradition. On the other hand, it is hardly surprising that a theory so deeply committed to capitalism had to undertake an appropriate revision of Marxism from the very beginning.

In about the year 1900 the majority of the former Legal Marxists finally broke their associations with the Russian Social Democratic movement and joined the liberal leaders of the *Zemstvo* assemblies, forming an alliance that was to become the nucleus of the future Constitutional Democratic Party. Struve himself became the leader of the right wing of this liberal caucus. Those Populist leaders who from the beginning had regarded the Legal Marxists as advocates of the bourgeoisie (Mikhailovsky was one of them) now appeared to be vindicated. It was typical of Plekhanov, however, that he did

59. In *Archiv für soziale Gesetzgebung und Statistik*, vol. 14 (Berlin, 1899).
60. Plekhanov, *Sochineniia*, vol. 24, p. 281.

not feel impelled to break off his political alliance with Struve; in keeping with his earlier program, he continued to believe that cooperation with the progressive sections of the bourgeoisie was the only way to complete the Westernization of Russia.

For Struve Legal Marxism was only a short-lived period of transition. In subsequent years his intellectual evolution was to lead him from Marxism (supplemented by Kantianism) to neo-idealism (he was co-author of an important collection of articles under the challenging title *Problems of Idealism*, 1902). In 1909 he took part in the famous symposium published under the title *Vekhi (Signposts)*, which called for a radical break with the revolutionary and materialist traditions of the Russian intelligentsia and for a return to Russian religious thought, especially to the ideas of the Slavophiles, Dostoevsky, and Soloviev.

A similar intellectual evolution (from Legal Marxism to *Vekhi*) marked the careers of Nikolai Berdiaev, Sergei Bulgakov, and Semyon Frank—thinkers who after the Revolution of 1905 became the leading representatives of the movement known as the Russian religious renaissance.

LENIN'S EARLY WRITINGS

Unlike Plekhanov, who remained a man of the nineteenth century although he lived until 1918, Lenin—both as a political theorist and as a political leader—was a twentieth-century figure in the full meaning of the word. However, in view of his significant contribution to the controversy over capitalism, which was a continuation of the discussions on the future development of Russia that had been raging for the previous half century, he should not be omitted from a history of nineteenth-century Russian social thought.

Like his older brother Aleksandr (and in contrast to Plekhanov), the young Vladimir Ulianov was emotionally committed to the traditions of the "People's Will" organization. There is no doubt that he was one of the leaders of the Russian workers' movement who, in their early youth, "enthusiastically worshipped the terrorist heroes. It required a struggle to abandon the captivating impressions of those heroic traditions, and the struggle was accompanied by the breaking off of personal relations with people who were determined to remain loyal to the Narodnaia Volia and for whom the young Social Democrats had profound respect."[61] In her recollections of

61. Lenin, *Collected Works*, vol. 5, pp. 517–18.

her husband, Nadezdha Krupskaya quotes this closing passage from Lenin's pamphlet *What Is to Be Done?*, with the comment: "This paragraph is a piece of the biography of Vladimir Ilyich." [62]

Lenin began his career as a revolutionary in a Marxist students' circle in Kazan, one of the circles organized in the Volga region in the 1880's by the young revolutionary Marxist NIKOLAI FEDOSEEV (1871–98). Members of these circles did not think of themselves as opponents of Populism and indeed wished to continue the still-living traditions of the movement's revolutionary wing. Fedoseev was of course utterly opposed to the Legal Marxists' "justification of capitalism" or the expropriation of the peasants; in fact he insisted that one of the main aims of the revolutionary struggle was to return to the peasants the land that had been taken away from them by the agrarian reform of 1861. He therefore felt personally insulted by Mikhailovsky's attacks on Russian Marxists and in November 1893—at the beginning of Mikhailovsky's campaign—wrote him a long letter stating his case. [63] He insisted that he could not understand Mikhailovsky's allegations, since both Populists and Marxists spoke up on behalf of the exploited masses, tried to defend the peasants, and, if possible, tried to transform the rural proletariat into independent peasant proprietors. He conceded that "where there's smoke there's fire" and that he himself had heard of some Orenburg Marxists who were supposed to have said that helping the starving peasants meant "hindering the establishment of capitalism." A man like Mikhailovsky, however, should not have identified Russian Marxism with the nonsense spouted by some provincial students.

Fedoseev's next letter was the size of a lengthy article. Its tone was largely conciliatory and its aim was to convince Mikhailovsky that the true Russian Marxists had nothing in common with such bourgeois economists as Skvortsov and Chuprov (this was before the publication of Struve's *Critical Notes*) who concealed their true nature under cover of Marxist phraseology. Fedoseev even conceded that he had been wrong in feeling himself personally insulted by Mikhailovsky's views and should have adopted a different tone in his earlier letter.

The suicide of Fedoseev a few years later was to provide a tragic epilogue to this correspondence. Deported to forced labor in 1898, he became deeply depressed when he found that some of his fellow exiles accused him—as a Marxist—of representing the interests of

62. Krupskaya, *Memories of Lenin*, p. 43.
63. N. Fedoseev, *Stat'i i pis'ma* (M, 1958), pp. 96ff.

the bourgeoisie; this depression was the main reason he took his life.[64]

The alliance between Populists and Marxists desired by Fedoseev was impossible to achieve. To some extent this was because Populism in the 1890's was almost exclusively represented by its legal wing, among whom only Mikhailovsky had some authority in revolutionary circles; Vorontsov, Danielson, and Yuzhakov had been widely discredited because of their conciliatory attitude toward autocracy. On the one hand, then, the Legal Marxists (like Struve) provoked the Populists into accusing all Marxists of being "agents of the bourgeoisie," whereas on the other hand the Populists were compromised by people like Vorontsov who, because of their attitude to political rights, had been nicknamed "police" Populists by the Marxists. This situation contributed greatly to the polarization of ideological positions and forced the young Lenin to cut himself off from the Populist "friends of the people."

The sharp polemical tone of Lenin's criticism should not, however, obscure the fact that his attitude toward Populism differed not only from that of Struve but also from that of Plekhanov. These differences come out clearly in a work of his entitled "The Economic Content of Populism and Its Criticism in Mr. Struve's Book" (1894–95). In the opening paragraphs we find the statement that "Marxism has nothing in common with Hegelianism, faith in the necessity of each country having to pass through the phase of capitalism and much other nonsense."[65] (In later years Lenin accepted that there was a close connection between Marxism and Hegelianism but thought it was to be found in the concept of the struggle of opposites, and not in the notion of the imperious "rational necessity" stressed by Plekhanov.) Lenin also ridiculed Mikhailovsky's formulation that people exercise an influence on the objective "course of things"; the "course of things," he wrote, consists of nothing else but actions and "influences" of people, "and so this is again an empty phrase."[66] Although these words were directed against Mikhailovsky, they could also be applied to Plekhanov and Struve; all three believed in an "objective course of events" existing independently of people, the only difference being that Mikhailovsky called for a heroic struggle against it, whereas Plekhanov and Struve dismissed this as "subjectivism."

In the characteristic Russian dispute over the role of the "subjec-

64. See B. Volin's introduction to Fedoseev, *Stat'i i pis'ma*, pp. 24–28.
65. Lenin, *Collected Works*, vol. 1, p. 338.
66. *Ibid.*, p. 399.

tive" and "objective" factors in history, Lenin thus rejected not only the subjectivism of the Populist but also the "objectivism" that in those years seemed to be an intrinsic part of historical materialism. "When demonstrating the necessity for a given series of facts," Lenin shrewdly remarked apropos of Struve, "the objectivist always runs the risk of becoming an apologist for these facts; ... a materialist discloses the class contradictions and in so doing defines his standpoint." Objectivism, he argued, gives a survey of the process as a whole, but not of those particular antagonistic classes whose struggle goes to make up the process; materialism, on the other hand, obliges one in any assessment of events to stand up simply and openly for the standpoint of a definite social class.[67] In short, Lenin treated history not as a reified process whose driving force is an impersonal necessity, but as a battleground, a scene with human actors whose participation implies conscious or unconscious identification with a specific class and therefore the conscious or unconscious choice of certain values. In the light of this conception, the antithesis between the "objective course of events" (stressed by Plekhanov and the Legal Marxists) and the conscious will of the individual (stressed by the Populists) lost its meaning—any objective course could not be conceived otherwise than in terms of the actions of human beings, and the conscious will of individuals could not be divorced from its social determinants.

Equally original and unexpected was Lenin's position in the controversy over capitalism. Vorontsov had insisted that capitalism could never make any real headway in Russia; Lenin countered this with the startling thesis that capitalism had not only gained a foothold in Russia, but was already "definitely established."[68] This argument, first expressed in the polemic with Struve and developed in detail in the work *The Development of Capitalism in Russia* (written between 1896 and 1899), was directed against the Populists, but also ran counter to the views generally accepted among Russian Marxists of the day, who conceded that capitalism in Russia had entered its initial stage, but who took pains to stress that it could not become "definitely and irrevocably established" until after the political defeat of the tsarist system.

It is an interesting point whether it is possible to claim that capitalism was indeed definitely established in Russia in the last decade of the nineteenth century. Did Lenin believe that it was possible for capitalist economic relations to become firmly and irrevocably

67. *Ibid.*, p. 401.
68. *Ibid.*, p. 495.

established during the early stages of a country's industrialization, before the government had been taken over by the bourgeoisie? Some Western European and American scholars, for instance, have suggested that he deliberately exaggerated the degree of development of the productive forces in order to justify more revolutionary political tactics.[69] The answer to this question, of course, depends entirely on our understanding of the basic premises on which Lenin based his analysis. The important point is not that he underestimated Russian backwardness, but that in his diagnosis of the state of economic development he placed the emphasis on the question of the prevailing relations of production and the nature of the fundamental class contradictions. By the total and irrevocable establishment of capitalism he meant the establishment of commodity production based on the exploitation of hired labor. Lenin's thesis, therefore, was not concerned with the extent of capitalist development, but with the nature and intensity of the fundamental class antagonisms; moreover, unlike the legal Populists, he laid particular stress on the class divisions within the peasantry. It seems justified to say that, unlike the other Russian Marxists, he saw the heart of Marxism in the theory of class struggle rather than in the theory of stages of economic development. Accordingly, "passing through the capitalist age" meant for him above all "passing through the experience of the capitalist class struggle" and not necessarily the highest possible development of capitalist production.

Following this line of thought, we come to another essential difference between Lenin and the "objective" interpretation of Marxism. In 1923, in his article "On Our Revolution," he ridiculed those who thought that "a textbook written on Kautskian lines" could foresee "all the forms of development of subsequent world history," and set against their deterministic dogmatism the maxim of Napoleon: "On s'engage et puis . . . on voit" ("First engage in a serious battle and then see what happens").[70] A careful reading of Lenin's early works shows that from the beginning he refused to see Marxism as a closed system of ready-made truths. He was led to reject the deterministic version of Marxism not only by his activism but also by his empirical distrust of *a priori* evolutionary schemes. When he wrote of the firm rejection of "belief in triads, in abstract dogmas and schemes that do not have to be proved by

69. Cf. R. Pipes, "The Origins of Bolshevism," in *Revolutionary Russia* (Cambridge, Mass., 1968), p. 40.
70. Lenin, *Collected Works*, vol. 33, p. 480.

facts,"[71] he was not just making a verbal declaration. In his interpretation (as in Marx's), the thesis that socioeconomic formations do not collapse until they have exhausted their development potential was a formula that described the classic model of development rather than an abstract universalistic scheme that was bound to be confirmed in every case, regardless of the objective circumstances of a given country.[72] The *Development of Capitalism in Russia* is an example of Lenin's acute observation of all facets of the Russian economy. Its detailed documentation of the peculiarities of Russian capitalism—peculiarities stemming from the "simultaneous existence of the most advanced forms of industry and semi-medieval forms of agriculture"[73]—provides a concrete answer to the questions of how it was possible for the October Revolution to succeed twenty years later and to what it owed its specific features.

It is also interesting to note that in his polemics with the Populists, Lenin differed from Plekhanov in his interpretation of the thesis that capitalism is a necessary prerequisite of socialism. Where Plekhanov stressed the importance of the expansion of the capitalist forces of production and the role of bourgeois democracy as a political training ground, Lenin stressed the lessons to be learned in the school of capitalist economic relations and the class struggle. His writings make it clear that he thought it was possible to learn these lessons even in the autocratic system of tsarist Russia. A necessary premise of a socialist movement was the destruction of "the old cramped conditions of human life," of the patriarchal stagnation that gave rise to mental obtuseness and prevented the immediate producers from taking their fate into their own hands.[74] To a large extent these barriers had already been overthrown by Russian capitalism. As Lenin put it:

In Russia this process has been fully manifested in the post-Reform era, when the ancient forms of labour very rapidly collapsed and prime place was assumed by the purchase and sale of labour power, which tore the peasant from the patriarchal, semi-feudal family, from the stupefying conditions of village life and replaced the semi-feudal forms of appropriation of surplus-value by purely capitalist forms. This economic process has been reflected in the social sphere by a "general heightening of the sense of individuality," by the middle-class intellectuals squeezing

71. *Ibid.*, vol. 1, p. 394.
72. Lenin referred to Marx's letter to the editors of *Notes of the Fatherland*. Marx's letter to Vera Zasulich of March 8, 1881, unambiguously confirming the possibility of a noncapitalist development of Russia, was published only in 1924.
73. Lenin, *Collected Works*, vol. 3, p. 594n.
74. *Ibid.*, vol. 1, p. 414.

the landlord class out of "society," by heated literary war against sense-less medieval restrictions on the individual and so on. The Narodniks will probably not deny that it was post-reform Russia which produced this heightened sense of individuality, of personal dignity.[75]

Lenin was an important figure in the controversy between Populists and Marxists not only because he was the author of a fundamental work on the development of capitalism in Russia, but also because he showed the greatest insight into the social content of Populist ideology. He called Populism an ideology of small producers (especially the peasants as smallholders and artisans) who were vitally interested in removing the last relics of feudal exploitation even though they were already being ruined by the expansion of capitalism. That was why (in the phrase quoted earlier in this book) he described the Populist Janus as "looking with one face to the past and the other to the future."[76]

The forward-looking face of Populism was its antifeudal aspect and its emphasis on democracy; the backward-looking face was its socialism. Lenin frequently stressed that the Populists' socialist theories were petty-bourgeois (in the Marxist meaning of the term), utopian, and permeated by reactionary "economic romanticism"—a reference to their idealization of the precapitalist and early-capitalist rural economy.[77] Marxists should draw two conclusions from this: first, the need to make clear their rejection of Populist socialism, and second, the desirability of an alliance with Populism as a bourgeois democratic ideology opposed not to capitalism as such but to its undemocratic variant supported by the liberals and large landowners. That is why in his essay "The Economic Content of Populism and Its Criticism in Mr. Struve's Book" Lenin reproached Struve (whom he considered an ally at that time) with emphasizing only the differences dividing Populism and Marxism and overlooking the basic community of aims of two ideologies, both representing the small producers. He totally rejected Struve's attempts to extol large-scale capitalist industry on the grounds that it rationalized production; what is more, comparing Struve's views with those of the Populists (even their legal wing) on the need for cheap credits and other help for small producers, Lenin resolutely took the Populist side:[78] "The Populists," he wrote, "in this respect understand and represent the interests of the small producers far more correctly, and the Marxists, while rejecting all the reactionary features of their

75. *Ibid.*
76. *Ibid.*, vol. 2, p. 507.
77. Lenin, "A Characterization of Economic Romanticism," in *ibid.*
78. *Ibid.*, vol. 1, p. 504.

program, must not only accept their general democratic points, but carry them through more exactly, profoundly, and further."

Lenin's attitude to both liberals and Populists met with Plekhanov's disapproval. In 1895, during their first meeting, Plekhanov told Lenin (who in fact made an excellent impression on him): "You turn your back on the liberals, while we turn round to face them." [79] This difference of viewpoint concealed a serious divergence on the choice of tactics and even on the interpretation of Marxism, although neither side at that time was fully aware of this. Plekhanov was in favor of an alliance with the liberal bourgeoisie, who, as representatives of capitalist progress, were continuing the process of Westernization. Lenin, for his part, thought a Marxist should have no illusions about the nature of liberalism. For Plekhanov the most backward class—the chief prop of "Asiatic" despotism—was the Russian peasantry; Lenin also stressed that the peasants were backward and "Asiatic" but he nevertheless regarded them as the main force in the approaching bourgeois-democratic revolution. Plekhanov saw Populism mainly as an ideology of the intelligentsia laying stress on "subjectivism" and an "abstract ideal"; Lenin, on the other hand, paid less attention to Populist theory, which he dismissed as an expression of a false consciousness, and thought that the essential "economic content" of Populism was not its anticapitalist declarations but its defense of the concrete interests of the small producers in the struggle for the most democratic variant of capitalist development (the peasant model). That was why he felt closer to the Populists than to the liberals, although the liberal standpoint on Russian capitalism was far closer to Marxism than the Populist viewpoint.

Lenin's original position in the debates of the 1890's clearly foreshadows his later political biography—his emphasis on the importance of the agrarian question, his refusal to treat the peasants as a "reactionary" mass (an attitude characteristic of the Mensheviks and the Second International as a whole), and, finally, his political tactics, which were based on an alliance not with the liberal bourgeoisie (as postulated by Plekhanov) but with the democratic sections of the petty bourgeoisie and peasantry.[80] He himself was aware

79. *Perepiska G. V. Plekhanova i P. B. Akselroda*, vol. 1, p. 271.

80. At the end of 1909 Lenin wrote as follows: "While fighting Populism as a wrong doctrine of socialism, the Mensheviks, in a doctrinaire fashion, overlooked the historically real and progressive historical content of Populism as a theory of the mass petty-bourgeois struggle of democratic capitalism against liberal-landlord capitalism, of "American" capitalism against "Prussian" capitalism. Hence their monstrous, idiotic, renegade idea that the peasant movement is reactionary, that a Kadet is more progressive than a Trudovik." (*Collected Works*, vol. 16, pp. 119–20.)

of this continuity and in 1912 remarked that the beginnings of Bolshevism were associated with the attempt to extract from the Populists' utopianism its "valuable democratic kernel."[81]

Looking back with the hindsight of history we can add that Lenin's debt to the Populists was even greater than this. After all, he
realized the Populist dream of a direct transition from the overthrow of the tsarist autocracy to the building of socialism. How this
was achieved, and at what cost, is, however, a subject for another
book.

81. *Ibid.*, vol. 23, p. 359.

INDEX OF NAMES

449